THE QUAKER WORLD

The Quaker World is an outstanding, comprehensive and lively introduction to this complex Christian denomination. Exploring the global reach of the Quaker community, the book begins with a discussion of the living community, as it is now, in all its diversity and complexity.

The book covers well-known areas of Quaker development, such as the formation of Liberal Quakerism in North America, alongside topics which have received much less scholarly attention in the past, such as the history of Quakers in Bolivia and the spread of Quakerism in Western Kenya. It includes over sixty chapters by a distinguished international and interdisciplinary team of contributors and is organised into three clear parts:

- Global Quakerism
- Spirituality
- Embodiment.

Within these sections, key themes are examined, including global Quaker activity, significant Quaker movements, biographies of key religious figures, important organisations, pacifism, politics, the abolition of slavery, education, industry, human rights, racism, refugees, gender, disability, sexuality and environmentalism.

The Quaker World provides an authoritative and accessible source of information on all topics important to Quaker Studies. As such, it is essential reading for students studying world religions, Christianity and comparative religion, and it will also be of interest to those in related fields such as sociology, political science, anthropology and ethics.

C. Wess Daniels is the William R. Rogers Director of Friends Center and Quaker Studies at Guilford College, United States. He is the author of *Resisting Empire: The Book of Revelation* (2019) and *A Convergent Model of Renewal: Remixing the Quaker Tradition in Participatory Culture* (2015).

Rhiannon Grant is Deputy Programme Leader in the Centre for Research in Quaker Studies at Woodbrooke and Honorary Senior Lecturer in Modern Quaker Thought at the University of Birmingham, United Kingdom. Her most recent books are *Theology From Listening: Finding the Core of Liberal Quaker Theological Thought* (2020) and *Hearing the Light: The Core of Quaker Theology* (2021).

ROUTLEDGE WORLDS SERIES

The Routledge Worlds are magisterial surveys of key historical epochs, edited and written by world-renowned experts. Giving unprecedented breadth and depth of coverage, they are the works against which all future books on their subjects will be judged and are essential reading for anyone with a serious interest in the subject.

THE BUDDHIST WORLD
John Powers

THE HINDU WORLD
Sushil Mittal, Gene Thursby

THE ISLAMIC WORLD
Andrew Rippin

THE OCCULT WORLD
Christopher Partridge

THE GNOSTIC WORLD
Garry Trompf, Jay Johnston, and Gunner Mikkelsen

THE WORLD OF THE BAHÁ'Í FAITH
Robert H. Stockman

FORTHCOMING:

THE BIBLICAL WORLD, SECOND EDITION
John Barton

THE EARLY CHRISTIAN WORLD, SECOND EDITION
Philip F. Esler

For a full list of titles in this series, please visit https://www.routledge.com/Routledge-Worlds/book-series/WORLDS

THE QUAKER WORLD

Edited by C. Wess Daniels and Rhiannon Grant

Routledge
Taylor & Francis Group

LONDON AND NEW YORK

Cover image: mammuth / Getty Images

First published 2023
by Routledge
2 Park Square, Milton Park, Abingdon, Oxon OX14 4RN

and by Routledge
605 Third Avenue, New York, NY 10158

Routledge is an imprint of the Taylor & Francis Group, an informa business

© 2023 selection and editorial matter, C. Wess Daniels and Rhiannon Grant; individual chapters, the contributors

The right of C. Wess Daniels and Rhiannon Grant to be identified as the authors of the editorial material, and of the authors for their individual chapters, has been asserted in accordance with sections 77 and 78 of the Copyright, Designs and Patents Act 1988.

British Library Cataloguing-in-Publication Data
A catalogue record for this book is available from the British Library

ISBN: 978-0-367-14251-3 (hbk)
ISBN: 978-1-032-35293-0 (pbk)
ISBN: 978-0-429-03092-5 (ebk)

DOI: 10.4324/9780429030925

Typeset in Bembo
by Apex CoVantage, LLC

To Quaker Studies students and scholars of the future

CONTENTS

Contents

Contents

Contents

Contents

ACKNOWLEDGEMENTS

Wess: I would like to acknowledge all of my students at Guilford College: those in the Quaker Leadership Scholars Program, all the Quaker Studies minors, and those who take REL110 – An Introduction to Quakerism with me each year. You are the main inspiration behind this book. The questions and interest you bring to class and the Quaker tradition pushes me to imagine a renewed Quaker tradition that will be here for you into the future. I want to thank Rhiannon for all her hard work, patience and good humor throughout this process. You were an incredible colleague to partner with on this project and I'm grateful to know you better through all of this. Finally, I want to honor my family – my wife, Emily, and our three children, Lily, Mae and Clem – with the work I do. You continue to support my efforts despite the challenges we have faced in recent years. Thank you for your love and patience.

Rhiannon: I would like to thank everyone at Woodbrooke, and especially Ben Pink Dandelion and Betty Hagglund for their support during the time of this project. Many thanks also to Wess for his persistence, vision and capacity to send hundreds of emails. I am intensely grateful for the support of my family, especially Piangfan Angela Naksukpaiboon, whom I both met and married between the initial proposal of the project and the final publication of this book.

Wess and Rhiannon would like to thank Ben Pink Dandelion and Stephen Angell for guiding us at the beginning of this process, talking us through how to tackle such a huge project, and making themselves available throughout to offer any help we needed. Marge and Carl Abbott and Carole Spencer were also early conversation partners as we dreamed up *The Quaker World*. We also want to recognize the hard-working and patient contributors to this volume, who have responded to emails and endured long silences, who have struggled to access childcare and archives and other resources during the pandemic but kept working, and who bring all their expertise and multiple perspectives to make this book unique. Thank you to Avery Edwards and Jim Glenn, two Guilford College students and Friends Center Fellows who helped us organize and collect needed documents for the book's completion. Thank you to all of you who did not write but helped connect us to writers, who lifted up other voices, and who continue to share your Quaker witness all around the world. May you find parts of your story reflected back here as well. Finally, we recognize the great work of the editors at

Routledge, who were patient and generous as we undertook such a large book project during such a challenging time in the world.

Our hope is that this book lifts up voices and perspectives both historical and present that are not always heard in these volumes and that it mirrors a renewed, global Quaker faith that will continue on well into the future.

NOTES ON CONTRIBUTORS

Hans Eirik Aarek is a retired assistant professor of philosophy and theory of science at the University of Stavanger, Norway. He has also been a teacher at the Norwegian Library and Information Science School and has engaged in library research. Since 2000, his research and publication focus has been on Norwegian and European Quaker history. He has written chapters on Quaker subjects in Norwegian and international periodicals and books. In 2022–23 he will finish his thesis on the Norwegian Quaker Society as a heterotopic denomination. He has long experience in Quaker organisational work both in Norway and internationally.

Damon B. Akins grew up in Oklahoma and traveled west to California, where he attended UCLA and taught high school in the (east) San Fernando Valley. He later returned to Oklahoma to earn a PhD in Native American/California history at the University of Oklahoma. He is currently a professor of history at Guilford College in Greensboro, North Carolina, where he teaches on Native America, California and the American West. He is the co-author with William J. Bauer Jr. of *We Are the Land: A History of Native California* (University of California Press, 2021).

Christopher Allison is a scholar of American religious history and is interested in material and visual culture. He is Collegiate Assistant Professor in the Humanities at the University of Chicago and affiliate faculty in the history and art history departments.

Matt Alton is an independent scholar and poet based in Brighton, UK. He is a member of Brighton Local Quaker Meeting and has served locally and nationally to work on the inclusion and engagement of young adults in British Quakerism.

Richard J. Barnes is a graduate of University of Chicago and is completing a master's degree at the University of Hawai'i at Manoa, where he studies Japanese history. He is a graduate fellow of the East-West Center.

Brian T. Blackmore teaches about Quakerism, world religions, and religion, gender and sexuality at Westtown School in West Chester, Pennsylvania. He is a doctoral candidate at

Temple University and sits on the Steering Committee of the Gay Men and Religion Unit of the American Academy of Religion.

Matt Boswell is the pastor of Camas Friends Church in Camas, Washington. He has an MDiv from George Fox Evangelical Seminary, Portland, Oregon, and a PhD in Christian spirituality from the Graduate Theological Union, Berkeley, California. His first book, *The Way to Love: Reimagining Christian Spiritual Growth as the Hopeful Path of Virtue*, was published in September 2018 by Cascade Books. He is married to Joann and is the father of Clara (6), Renee (4) and Teddy (2).

Stephen D. Brooks has been a member of The Religious Society of Friends (Quakers) in the UK since 2007. He is currently employed at the University of Brighton and is a fourth-year PhD student in Quaker studies at the University of Birmingham. He also deejays on the community internet station Radio Lewes and bothers a guitar in the folk-pop band The Dead Sea Scouts.

Jennifer M. Buck is an assistant professor of practical theology at Azusa Pacific University. She holds a PhD in philosophy of religion and theology from Claremont Graduate University and an MDiv from Fuller Theology Seminary. She is the author of *Reframing the House: Constructive Feminist Global Ecclesiology for the Western Evangelical Church* (Pickwick, 2016) and of multiple forthcoming books: *Distinct: Quaker Holiness in Everyday Life* (Barclay Press), *Bad and Boujee: Towards a Trap Feminist Theology*, and a book on fashion and theology.

Maia Carter Hallward is a professor of Middle East politics at Kennesaw State University and editor of the *Journal of Peacebuilding and Development*. She holds a PhD in international relations with an emphasis on peace and conflict resolution from American University's School of International Service. She is the author or co-author of seven books, including *NGOs and Human Rights: Comparing Faith-Based and Secular Approaches* (University of Georgia Press, 2021) and *Struggling for a Just Peace: Israeli and Palestinian Activism in the Second Intifada* (University of Florida Press, 2011), as well as over two dozen peer reviewed articles. A lifelong Quaker, she taught at the Ramallah Friends School from 1998 to 2000.

Ronis Chapman, Secretary of AWPS for seven years, connects with the Quaker world from her home office in Canberra, Australia.

Emma Condori Mamani is a member of the Santidad (Holiness) Friends Yearly Meeting. She was one of the editors and writers of the book *Spirit Rising: Young Quaker Voices*. In the last eight years, she has been traveling among Friends in the United States, Mexico, Kenya-Africa, and Central America. Currently she works as a director at the Friends International Bilingual Center.

Mary Crauderueff, MLS, is Curator of Quaker Collections at Haverford College. She assists researchers, fosters relationships with donors and arranges collections to ensure preservation and accessibility. She strives to build community and teach skills to empower all researchers in their work. She has served on several Quaker boards, including a term as president of the Friends Historical Association, 2019–2021. In 2020, she was the first visiting Quaker archivist for the Africa Quaker Archives in Kaimosi, Kenya. She was awarded a Clarence and Lilly Pickett Endowment for Quaker Leadership grant for an oral history project titled "Quaker Works:

Journeys of Quakers Leading Friends Organizations" in 2015. She enjoys hiking in the woods with friends, taking pictures of and drinking coffee, and finding ways to fight white supremacy, transphobia and patriarchy.

Penelope Cummins grew up in South Africa, where she worked as a journalist during the height of apartheid. Since then she has been a civil servant and an academic both in South African and in Britain. She has a doctorate in Quaker studies from the University of Birmingham.

Pink Dandelion directs the work of the Centre for Research in Quaker Studies at Woodbrooke and is Professor of Quaker Studies at the University of Birmingham. He has written and edited numerous books on the history, theology and sociology of Quakerism, and he edited *Quaker Studies* from 1995 to 2021.

C. Wess Daniels is the William R. Rogers Director of Friends Center and Quaker Studies at Guilford College. He lives in Greensboro, North Carolina, which is part of the Haw River watershed. He and his wife Emily have three children and a rescue dog. He is the author of *Resisting Empire: The Book of Revelation* (2019) and *A Convergent Model of Renewal: Remixing The Quaker Tradition in Participatory Culture* (2015) and is a contributor in the recent *We Cry Justice: Reading the Bible with the Poor*, edited by Liz Theoharis (2021). He is interested in teaching liberation theology and working towards the revitalization of faith traditions that embody love and justice in the world.

Michael Dutch is a professor of business at Guilford College in North Carolina. As a faculty member at a Quaker college, he became intrigued by the seeming paradox of Quakers as industrial leaders. This subject became the focus of a fellowship project. The influence of religious beliefs on business practice aligns with his broader interest in organizational culture.

Richard Kent Evans is Visiting Assistant Professor of Religion at Haverford College. He is the author of *MOVE: An American Religion* (Oxford University Press, 2020).

Chuck Fager has been a writer, reporter, historical researcher, peace and racial justice activist, and Quaker for more than 50 years. As the Cadbury Scholar at Pendle Hill in 2013–14, he produced two volumes that were the first detailed, intensively researched history of the seminal Progressive Friends movement (1840–1940), the long-forgotten seedbed of the contemporary liberal and humanist branches of American Quakerism. He retired in 2012 and now lives and writes in Durham, North Carolina.

Carlos Figueroa is an associate professor in the politics department of the School of Humanities and Sciences, Ithaca College. He has a dual PhD in political science and historical studies from The New School for Social Research. He researches and writes on race, religion, citizenship, class politics, the politics of American Quakerism, and US–Puerto Rico affairs. He has written for the University of Virginia Press and the University Press of Kansas, as well as the *Journal of Public Affairs Education, Journal of Race and Policy, Political Science Quarterly, Annales: Ethics in Economic Life, Fair Observer* and *Common Dreams*, among others. His first book, *Quakers, Race, and Empire: Political Ecumenism and U.S. Insular Policy in the Early Twentieth Century* (under review, University Press of Kansas), shows how and why progressive-era Quakers intervened in US insular policy discourses over the organizing and governance of acquired territories (Puerto

Rico and the Philippines), and the struggles for self-determination and citizenship within the context of an expanding American empire from 1898 to 1917. He also is working on a second book, *Bayard Rustin: The Pragmatic Quaker, 1912–1987*, which examines how and why Rustin's Quaker faith informed his political thought, organizing and activism in the context of dealing with the various social injustices and inequalities facing working and poor people and other marginalized groups in the United States and abroad during his 50 years in public life.

Andrew Fincham is a socio-economic historian interested in the relationship between ethical values and commercial success. His doctorate used social network analysis to establish the role of the Quakers' discipline in their early commercial success. His recent publications address corporate governance, social responsibility, the "Wigan Diggers," and business management history.

Deb Fuller is a graduate of the University of Leicester Department of Museum Studies and a longtime member of Alexandria Friends Meeting at Woodlawn. She has been active in the museum community in the Washington, DC, area for over 25 years. She has written and presented about the history of early American sheep breeding, textiles in ancient Rome and the craftivist activity of yarn bombing. In 2016, she was asked to consult on the Quaker clothing portion of the exhibit An Agreeable Tyrant: Fashion After the Revolution at the Daughters of the American Revolution Museum. Her main interests are the history of knitting and Quaker clothing.

Rhiannon Grant is Deputy Programme Leader in the Centre for Research in Quaker Studies at Woodbrooke and Honorary Senior Lecturer in Modern Quaker Thought at the University of Birmingham. She has published two volumes in the Brill series Research Perspectives in Quaker Studies: *British Quakers and Religious Language* (2018) and *Theology from Listening: Finding the Core of Liberal Quaker Theological Thought* (2020). She also writes fiction, poetry and accessible volumes on Quakerism in the Quaker Quicks series from Christian Alternative, mostly recently *Hearing the Light* (2021).

Krishauna Hines-Gaither is Vice President for Equity, Diversity and Justice at Mount Saint Mary's University in Los Angeles, California. She formerly served as the vice president for diversity, equity and inclusion at Guilford College. While at Guilford, she co-chaired the Curry-Coffin Commission on Slavery, Race and Recognition. She has published on African descendants of Latin America, Francophone communities and the United States. She is the author of *The Antiracist World Language Classroom* (Routledge, 2022). She is the owner of Hines-Gaither Consulting, LLC, and is a blogger at Cupofdiversity.com.

Virginia Jealous is a Friend who travels and works widely in the Asia–West Pacific Section region. She is based in Western Australia.

Hugh Jones is a retired publishing lawyer and lives in Brighton. He has recently completed his MA in Quakerism in the modern world at Lancaster University. He is now building on his dissertation into 50 years of key Quaker introductory texts by undertaking a PhD at Birmingham University with the working title "An Analysis of the Role and Significance of the Annual Swarthmore Lectures."

Jon R. Kershner holds a PhD in theology from the University of Birmingham, UK. He is Visiting Assistant Professor of Religion at Pacific Lutheran University and Honorary Researcher at Lancaster University. His recent books include *John Woolman and the Government of Christ: A Colonial Quaker's Vision for the British Atlantic World* (Oxford University Press, 2018) and *"To Renew the Covenant": Religious Themes in Eighteenth-Century Quaker Abolitionism* (Brill, 2018). He has written numerous articles and chapters on John Woolman. He lives near Seattle, Washington, where he enjoys hiking, working on household projects, and reading with his family.

Abigail Lawrence is a lifelong Quaker and North Carolina native. She is 17 years old and is dually enrolled at New Garden Friends School and Guilford College. In her spare time, she enjoys playing classical violin and Celtic fiddle, reading and painting.

Chris Lord is a British Quaker and schoolteacher (classics). He is working on a PhD at the University of Birmingham via Woodbrooke. His thesis began with the connections between Quaker silent worship, Wittgenstein's philosophy of language, and the fact that non-human animals (more or less) are not language users. His other activities include working with local environmental groups, cycling in London and experimental cooking.

Barbara Schell Luetke is a convinced, unprogrammed Friend who also attends services at Madison Temple Church of God in Christ, an African American Pentecostal congregation. She is 69 years old, white and middle class. She has written one book and several articles about seventeenth-century "adult young Friends" and began writing *The Kendal Sparrow* after a pilgrimage to "1652 Country" in 2015. In 2019, using money awarded by the Lyman Fund and an Eva Koch scholarship, she traveled to Ireland and worked in England. She is well published in the field of Deaf education, having written seven books and over 100 research articles.

Oscar Lugusa Malande is a member of the Religious Society of Friends (Quakers) in Vihiga Yearly Meeting, Kenya, and has served as both a pastor and chaplain for 12 years. He taught and served as registrar and assistant academic dean at Friends Theological College Kaimosi for three years. He holds a master of arts degree from Earlham School of Religion in Richmond, Indiana, and currently teaches at Friends Theological College Kaimosi. He has contributed to writing on "Quakers in Africa" in *The Cambridge Companion to Quaker Studies*, edited by Pink Dandelion and Stephen Angell (Cambridge University Press, 2018).

Stuart Masters is a member of the Learning and Research Team at Woodbrooke Quaker Study Centre in Birmingham, UK. His book, *The Rule of Christ: Themes in the Theology of James Nayler*, was published in 2021. His research and teaching focuses on Quaker spirituality and theology, eco-theology and the relationship between Quakerism and other Christian traditions. He is the West Midlands Regional Representative for the Anabaptist Mennonite Network, the Quaker representative on the Churches Together in Britain and Ireland Interfaith Theology Advisory Group, and a member of the Advisory Council for *Quaker Religious Thought*.

Isaac Barnes May is a graduate of Earlham College and Harvard Divinity School. He is a doctoral candidate in religious studies at the University of Virginia. His work has been published in *Quaker Studies, Quaker History* and other journals.

Robin Mohr has served as Executive Secretary of the Friends World Committee for Consultation Section of the Americas since 2011. Until taking this position, she was a member of San Francisco Monthly Meeting in Pacific Yearly Meeting. She and her husband, Christopher, are now members of Green Street Monthly Meeting in Philadelphia Yearly Meeting, and they have two children in high school and college. She holds a bachelor of science in foreign service from Georgetown University. She frequently writes for Quaker magazines, books and her own blog, "What Canst Thou Say?"

Mackenzie Morgan is a Quaker and amateur dress historian. Her research focuses on early modern England and Italy. She has traveled in ministry among Friends across the United States since 2017, with special attention to Friends outside of Friends General Conference. She facilitates conversations online about outreach, communication and use of social media by Quakers. She lives near Washington, DC, and is a member of Adelphi Friends Meeting.

David Niyonzima holds master of arts degree in counselling and a doctoral degree in leadership and global perspectives from George Fox University. His leadership experience as the general secretary and general superintendent of the Burundi Yearly Meeting exposed him to sharable insights on global Quakerism. He is married to Felicity, and they have four grown children and two grandsons. He lives in Bujumbura, Burundi, where he is currently the Vice Chancellor of the International Leadership University–Burundi. He is co-author with Lon Fendall of *Unlocking Horns: Forgiveness and Reconciliation in Burundi* (Barclay Press, 2001) and many other essays on peacebuilding.

Andrew Pisano is an assistant professor of English at the University of South Carolina Union (USCU). His research interests include early American religious writing, colonial-era networks of nonwhite writers, the eighteenth-century transatlantic literary world and American gothic writing. He teaches courses in rhetoric and composition and American literature. In addition, he currently runs the ongoing USCU film series, which asks audiences to consider critical questions pertaining to race, class, gender and forms of expression.

David Pocta is a Christian spirituality scholar with 26 years of ministry experience in the United States and Africa. His research interests include the spiritual journey, secularity and Christian mysticism. The working title for his PhD dissertation is "Lost at Sea: Why So Few Wandering Christians Find Their Way Home."

Kristianna Polder studied American history at the University of California, Santa Cruz. After pursuing a master of divinity and a master of arts in intercultural studies, she moved to Scotland to complete her doctorate, with a specialization in Quaker history, at the University of Aberdeen. She currently teaches courses in British civilisation and history at the Université Sorbonne Nouvelle–Paris III as well as *anglais juridique* at Université Paris II Panthéon–Assas. She is the author of *Matrimony in the True Church: The Seventeenth-Century Quaker Marriage Approbation Discipline.*

Timothy Rainey II received his PhD from the Department of Religion at Emory University, where he concentrated in American religious cultures. His research focuses on religion, race and economy in the Black Atlantic world, and he gives particular attention to the ways corporations interacted with Black faith communities in the nineteenth and twentieth centuries. He holds a BA in religious studies from Morehouse College and an MDiv from Princeton Theological Seminary.

Diane Randall was the fourth general secretary of the Friends Committee on National Legislation. A lifelong advocate for peace and social justice, she is a fierce proponent for citizen engagement that advances policies and practices to create a better society for all.

Christy Randazzo is a convinced Friend and a member of Haddonfield Friends Meeting in Haddonfield, New Jersey. Currently an independent scholar, Randazzo is a theologian and activist whose work has been engaged in bridging the divide between the contemplative nature of theological writing with the active, lived theology of congregational life. They have done ministry across multiple religious communities in diverse settings, including six years of youth and young adult ministry in the Episcopal Church, chaplaincy and religious education in Friends education, social ministries amongst unhoused populations, and peacemaking in situations of ethno-religious conflict. They have earned several degrees in theology, including an MA in general theology from St. Mary's Seminary and University, an MPhil in reconciliation theology from Trinity College Dublin, and most recently a PhD in Quaker theology from the University of Birmingham.

Judith Roads retired as senior lecturer at Middlesex University, London, in 2007, coordinating and lecturing on linguistics to international students. Following the completion of an interdisciplinary PhD in historical linguistics and Quaker studies at the University of Birmingham in 2015, she published articles on aspects of Quakerism and historical pragmatics. She is an associate tutor at Woodbrooke Quaker Study Centre.

Carole Dale Spencer is Adjunct Professor of Spiritual Formation at Portland Seminary at George Fox University. She holds a PhD in theology from the University of Birmingham, UK. Her publications include *Holiness: The Soul of Quakerism: An Historical Analysis of the Theology of Holiness in the Quaker Tradition*. She has authored many articles on Quaker religious thought, Quaker history and Quaker studies, as well as chapters in edited collections on Quaker history and theology.

Sychellus Wabomba Njibwakale is a PhD student (All But Dissertation) with an emphasis in New Testament in the Biblical Studies Department at Carolina University, Winston-Salem, North Carolina. His research interest is in examining the sociology of Jesus Christ and how this impacted the early church, as well as its implication today in relation to evangelism and social justice.

Robert J. Wafula grew up in Kenya. He serves as Principal of Friends Theological College (FTC), Kaimosi, Kenya, and is a pastor, Christian leader, scholar of religion, a social scientist and educator. He is an alumnus of FTC, St. Paul's University, Kenya, Earlham School of Religion and Ohio University. He earned his PhD from Ohio University in cultural studies in education, and he holds master of arts degrees in religious studies and international affairs. He has published in the fields of cultural studies, development studies, Quakerism, comparative religions and new religious movements. He has taught comparative religions, anthropology, cultural diversity, sociology and comparative literature at Columbus State College and at Central Ohio Technical College.

Ashley M. Wilcox is the author of *The Women's Lectionary* (Westminster John Knox Press, 2021) and is the founder of Church of Mary Magdalene. She is a graduate of Candler School of Theology and Willamette University of Law. Her writing has been published in *Friends Journal, Western Friend*, Quaker anthologies and on www.ashleymwilcox.com.

Lloyd Lee Wilson has been a recorded minister in North Carolina Yearly Meeting (Conservative) for over 30 years. For about 12 years, he was a member of Virginia Beach Friends

Meeting; while there, he served with Helen Louise Wilson on the meeting of ministers, elders and overseers. Among his writings is a 2009 master's thesis for the Earlham School of Religion titled *"The Remnant of Like Faith": The First Fifty Years of North Carolina Yearly Meeting (Conservative)*. Despite their common last names, he has no known family relationship to Helen Louise Wilson.

Benjamin J. Wood has taught theology and religious studies at the University of Leeds, the University of Manchester, the University of Chester and Leeds Trinity University. His research explores the intersection of Christian ethics and secular/liberal politics. He is a member of Britain Yearly Meeting and previously was a member of the Quaker Committee for Christian and Interfaith Relations.

Greg Woods is a Quaker minister and scholar living in Minneapolis, Minnesota, with his wife and daughter. He participated in workcamps as a teenager and a young adult, and later he served as the coordinator of Washington Quaker Workcamps in Washington, DC. He is a graduate of Earlham College and Princeton Theological Seminary.

Ann Wrightson was born into a Christian family rooted in Anglican, Welsh Presbyterian and non-denominational mission church traditions, and she has been a member of Britain Yearly Meeting for most of her adult life. Her academic training was in philosophy, with a strong focus on logic and philosophy of language, which led naturally to a career in information technology. She is Head of Information Architecture at the Aneurin Bevan University Health Board in South Wales and is a member of North Wales Area Meeting of Britain Yearly Meeting.

Rebecca Wynter is Postdoctoral Research Fellow (Diversity and Inclusion) in the School of Psychology, and Lecturer in History at the Centre for Research in Quaker Studies (University of Birmingham and Woodbrooke, Birmingham). She is on the Executive Committee and is Roy Porter Prize Chair for the Society for the Social History of Medicine. She is editor of *Quaker Studies* and has published on the histories of psychiatry, mental health, neurology, and ambulance and First World War medicine. Her latest book, co-edited with Pink Dandelion, is *A Quaker Conscientious Objector: The Prison Letters of Wilfrid Littleboy, 1917–1919* (Handheld Press, 2020).

Stewart David Yarlett completed his PhD in theology and religious studies (Quaker studies) at the University of Birmingham in 2020. His thesis is titled *The Accommodation of Diversity: Liberal Quakerism and Nontheism*. He received his MA from Durham University in religion and international relations in 2012 and his BA from Durham in theology and religious studies in 2011. He is an associate supervisor at the Woodbrooke Centre for Quaker Studies and an honorary research fellow at Lancaster University, where he tutors on the Quakerism, Peace and Justice module. Along with modern Liberal Quakerism, his broader research interests relate to dynamics, boundaries and questions of authenticity between religious and non-religious cultural forms. This includes an interest in the concept of political religions, fiction-based religions and the role of academic reflexivity in both the study and practice of religion. He is campaign lead for Faiths United Youth Network's Listen Up! campaign, which looks at current affairs and human rights issues that are of interest to the interfaith community, and he hosts the Interfaith Maverick Podcast.

INTRODUCTION

C. Wess Daniels and Rhiannon Grant

Quakers around the world are a vibrant, complex, and continually developing community. Known as a peace church, Quakers do not always agree with one another; known for their use of silence, Quakers also have strong traditions of speech and song; familiar figures in some parts of British and American history, Quakers are also present today in every inhabited continent. In order to explore this living tradition as such, this volume begins with chapters showing the global reach of the Quaker community. Where previous similar volumes have begun with the historical foundations of the Quaker movement, we have begun with the living community, as it is now, in all its diversity and complexity. Looking at a wide area or a specific country, we cover the well-known areas of Quaker development – the formation of Liberal Quakerism in North American and the progress of Quakerism in Europe, for example – alongside topics which have received much less scholarly attention in the past, such as the history of Quakers in Bolivia and the spread of Quakerism in western Kenya.

We have welcomed authors currently outside academia as well as those who are established or early-career scholars. Chapters in this book draw on a wide range of disciplines, including history, theology, philosophy, social sciences, and linguistics, and on multiple ways of knowing, including archival research, interviews, earlier academic work, personal experience, and theological reasoning. The work on some chapters was interrupted by the coronavirus pandemic, and some authors were not able to travel as they had planned, use library resources, or work together in person as they would have wished, or other demands on their time took over. Knowing this, we have chosen to retain some chapters which show signs of these problems rather than to exclude those topics and authors.

This book cannot be the final word on any of the topics included. Each chapter is intended as an introduction to an aspect of the Quaker world. We have explained technical terminology throughout. Although some authors have focussed more on issues internal to the Quaker community, every chapter should be accessible to readers previously unfamiliar with Quakers.

In choosing topics, we have tried to include some which are highly specific (case studies or biographies of individuals) alongside those which work at a high level of generality (covering a whole century, complex practice, or area of Quaker Studies). This diversity of focus enables us to cover a wider range of types of topic, to provide detail in topics of particular importance, and to give a fuller impression of the richness of the Quaker world. We hope that this volume will be a stimulus to further research in all the areas covered and those we have not been able

DOI: 10.4324/9780429030925-1

to include. For example, we are aware that this volume excludes some groups of Quakers, such as convergent Friends, and does not address directly some of the tensions which arise from the material presented here. We have a chapter on William Penn, who was an enslaver, and a chapter which uses Penn's theology and political theory as a source. These issues exist alongside one another in the real world as in this book, and Quaker communities and Quaker Studies scholars have more work to do to understand how to move forward in truth and justice.

The book is structured in three parts. Part I, Global Quakerism, begins with chapters covering the geographical spread of Quakers today, showcasing Quaker diversity and examining the international structures which bring Quakers together as a community. It also provides introductions to some key periods of Quaker history. Part II, Spirituality, moves from examples of Quaker spirituality as expressed in individual Quaker lives to broader considerations of aspects of Quaker theology, theological development, and the teaching of Quaker theology. Finally, Part III on Embodiment explores the ways in which Quaker ideals have been put into practice with varying levels of success. Using examples from all periods of Quaker history, as well as present-day experience, this part of the book covers pacifism, campaigning, attitudes to abolition, marriage, and many other issues. Throughout the book, one of our approaches is to offer biography which is or can be read as theology. Case studies and especially the biographies of individual Quakers – some famous and others previously neglected – provide examples of lived experiences which serve as thinking ground for exploring the relationships of Quaker spirituality, religious practice, ethics, and action.

Although this volume serves as an introduction to many aspects of the Quaker world and provides a survey of the diversity of the Quaker community, it should be read alongside a range of other sources. Overviews of Quaker history, practice, and development are provided in a number of places, notably *The Cambridge Companion to Quakerism* (eds. Stephen Angell and Pink Dandelion, 2018) and *The Oxford Handbook of Quaker Studies* (eds. Stephen Angell and Pink Dandelion, 2013). Each chapter in this book provides references to further sources on the particular topics covered, but readers seeking material on the Quaker tradition as a whole might want to try the following. More introductory material can be found in *Quakerism: The Basics* (Margery Post Abbott and Carl Abbott, 2021) and in the Quaker Quicks series (published by Christian Alternative). More scholarly material can be found in the Research Perspectives in Quaker Studies series (published by Brill) and the open-access journal *Quaker Studies* (published by Liverpool University Press).

We acknowledge the complexity of history which has contributed to the creation of this volume and the community it is about. Authors in this book include members of communities which have historically been colonised and those who are colonisers, some living on colonised land and others in the nations from which colonising missions originated. As white editors living in the United Kingdom and United States, we acknowledge our place in ongoing structures of white privilege and economic inequality. We hope that the work of building greater equality in the scholarly community is advanced in some small ways by the editorial decisions we have made and that it will continue.

PART I

Global Quakerism

1

QUAKERS IN AFRICA

History of the Quaker Movement in Africa

Robert J. Wafula

Introduction: Pre-colonial Africa

Before the domination of European colonial powers on the African continent, the African peoples lived in communities based on ethnic chiefdoms. The concept of money and its exchange for cattle or land was foreign.[1] Land and cattle were major foundations of the clan economy. They were owned by individuals but regarded as property of the community under laws that were regulated by the clan. People led a life of egalitarianism. European colonial powers took a grip on Africa in the mid-1800s, but in reality, European explorations in sub-Saharan Africa began in the fifteenth century with the Age of Discovery led by Henry the Navigator.[2]

North American Quakers arrived in East Africa at the dawn of the 1900s under the British colony. Levinus Painter points out in his book *The Hill of Vision* that the primary objective of their coming was somewhat different from that of the colonists – to share the Gospel of Jesus Christ with the African communities. They came into premier ministry with true and sacrificial love in their hearts but with little knowledge of the African people's culture.[3] However, some missionaries and colonists said they were bringing Christianity and/or civilization to the African societies while they also had economic motives in mind.

Early Foundations

The history of the Quaker movement in Africa began with three young North American men from the Midwest who were enrolled for theological studies at Cleveland Bible Institute in Cleveland, Ohio, in 1898–1900. Arthur Benton Chilson, Willis R. Hotchkiss, and Edgar T. Hole are household names among East African Quakers. Painter terms the adventure of the three missionaries to Kenya as having been a "co-operative enterprise from the very beginning."[4] Quakers in the Midwest denied themselves basic needs to financially support the three young missionaries who were led across the Atlantic Ocean to the unknown cultures of Africa.[5]

On his return to North America in 1895 after having been in Africa for four years, Hotchkiss presented a proposal to the faculty and students at Cleveland Bible Institute and challenged Friends to pray and think about establishing a Friends mission in Kenya. The institute was by then headed by Walter and Emma B. Malone.[6] Hotchkiss and his companion, Peter Scott, are credited with the foundations of the Africa Inland Mission (AIM) in Kenya.[7]

DOI: 10.4324/9780429030925-3

Hotchkiss' promotion of the idea of a Friends mission in Africa became indefatigable with the publication of his book *Sketches of the Dark Continent*; to me, the title itself plays into the existing stereotypes about Africa. However, the release of this book to the public coincided with and stirred the hearts and minds of Friends of nine American yearly meetings gathered in Cleveland. As a result, the gathering came out with an agenda to organize the Friends Africa Industrial Mission (FAIM), which was later completed and registered under the laws of the state of Ohio on February 2, 1901.[8]

The resplendent narrative from Hotchkiss' book about Africa stole the heart of Arthur Chilson, who had previously nursed the idea of going to Africa as a missionary. Born in LeGrand, Iowa, on June 16, 1872, Chilson shared the entrancing idea with his colleague Edgar Hole from Salem, Ohio.[9] United in mind and spirit, the three young men began to map out plans to take Quakerism to Africa. To what extent the title of Hotchkiss' book had an effect on their minds remains but a guess.

The trio was commissioned for the mission by the FAIM chaired by Emma Malone, followed by deputation among North American yearly meetings. They gave addresses and stirred up missionary interests for Africa. Finally, reality came home. Friends and well-wishers gathered in Cleveland Friends Meeting House on a Sunday for a farewell fellowship. Chilson gave a moving speech in the form of a sermon with a text from Psalm 91. Some of what he said that day can be remembered but one remark stands out: "In the plan of God, nothing happens. God's plans move smoothly and according to order." Chilson was confident that their plans were not man-made, but that they were ordered by the Lord, the "one who never failed nor been late in fulfilling His [God's] plans." He knew well in his heart that "God would keep them, guide them, uphold them, sustain them, and let nothing come or happen to them that was not for the good of God's glory."[10]

On April 23, 1902, Walter and Emma Malone joined New York and Brooklyn Friends at the pier in New York to wish the three young prospective missionaries God's blessings on the apex of their calling for Africa. Leaving their young wives and infants behind, Hole and Hotchkiss, with Chilson their companion (still unmarried then), boarded the steamship *St. Paul* on the shores in New York bound for London, en route for Mombasa, a coastal port town of Kenya founded by Persia in 975. Hole's wife Adelaide and their infant, Leona May, together with Hotchkiss' wife, would follow their husbands to Africa a year later in July 1903. They were accompanied by Dr. Elisha Blackburn, who pioneered the Friends' medical services.[11]

While on board, Chilson wrote in his diary, "I bless God for His multiplied blessings and the honor He has bestowed upon me in appointing me a representative of His message of hope to the hopeless ones of Africa."[12] Chilson may have been right in his own ambivalence to insinuate Africa as so perceived, especially based on the negative, condescending, and snide remarks about Africa as a backward, hopeless, and dark continent. I would give him the benefit of the doubt because in his generation, children in the Western world grew up with a perception ingrained in their minds that nothing good can come out of Africa. "It seems almost too good to be true," Chilson continues in his diary, "that at last, after many years of waiting, I am on my way to help start an industrial mission in Africa."[13] Chilson is describing his skills accurately here. Painter would come to testify of Chilson's practical mechanical abilities and Hole's business expertise 64 years later in *The Hill of Vision*.

On April 30, 1902, a day prior to docking in London, Chilson wrote again in his diary, "We only have one life, only one. How sacred then that life ought to be. My soul longs for Africa tonight . . . I do not believe I have anything to regret."[14] The vessel arrived in London on May 1, and on May 3 the trio attended Ireland Yearly Meeting of Friends. The Irish and British Friends provided additional funds and supplies, plus a metal house named Devonshire House that was later shipped to Kenya. Devonshire House was also the name of the London building where Quaker work was conducted during the time. The trio received counsel and encouragement from British Friends who had already established a mission on the island of Pemba, off the east coast of Kenya,

in 1896. The British Friends would later become a great asset after the American missionaries settled at Kaimosi. There was frequent communication between Kaimosi Mission station and British Friends in Pemba. While in London, the trio paid a courtesy call on Bishop William Taylor,
bishop of the Church of England in Africa. After learning that they were headed to East Africa,
he advised them to locate near Lake Victoria where there was great need for mission work. Taylor
prayed with them and gave them the anointing as they left with their spirits lifted high.[15]

Arrival on the African Soil

On June 16, 1902, the trio sailed across the Mediterranean Sea aboard the steamship *Bundersrath*,
entered the Suez Canal and finally docked in Mombasa on June 24.[16] They had finally arrived
in the land with different people of different resources they had been hearing and dreaming to
reach. Many Quaker missionaries who came to Africa since then would take the same route,
whereas others chose to go around the southern tip of Africa.

Travel inland by caravan is a known old mode of travel. Biblical references such as Genesis
37:25[17] point to this mode. However, there was a difference between the African caravans and
the caravans of the Holy Land. The latter engaged animal labor whereas the African caravans
used human labor – in most cases coerced human labor. But I have not seen evidence in my
research pointing to the three Quaker missionaries as having coerced the African porters in their
caravan from Kisumu to Kaimosi. I do not even think they had such thoughts of coercing the
African porters into this endeavor.

Having used this means already, Hotchkiss would therefore become resourceful to his companions in the imminent trek inland. He gives a vivid description of the African caravans in his
book *Then and Now in Kenya Colony: Forty Adventurous Years in East Africa* (1936):

> Could it be that these dandified fellows in their clean white robes, like glorified night-
> gowns, and jaunty fezzes, they were going to carry our loads all those weary miles into
> the blue? They looked altogether too fine for this sort of thing.

Hotchkiss goes further to say that African caravans were paid advances before they could embark
on a voyage.[18] However, Irene E. Hoskins in her book *Friends in Africa* has a different perspective on the African caravans. She calls them "unrequited, unremembered heroes . . . who have
borne the Whiteman's burdens through malarious swamps and over desert sands till the caravan
routes might almost be traced by a trail of bones they have left."[19] To me, this polite condition
was mere slavery of a different kind.

Just as they received good counsel from Bishop Taylor while in London, the trio similarly
made another courtesy call on a Mr. Jackson, sub-commissioner of Mumias District, for advice
and direction. "I feel like I am getting near home now," Chilson wrote in his diary, "for Africa
is more home than any place on earth, for my life work is here, be it long or short. I believe
I know my master better tonight than I ever have before."[20]

The inland journey for the trio from Mombasa did not require human caravan yet. The trip
was made relatively easy owing to the recently constructed railroad from Mombasa to Kampala,
Uganda, which was nearing completion. On July 4, 1902, they boarded a goods train, as pas-
senger trains were yet to be introduced to Port Florence, Kisumu, via Nairobi. Without specific
plans, Chilson, Edgar, and Hotchkiss may have felt completely misplaced in a strange land. But
they were men of extraordinary hope who relied on the Divine leading in every step of their way.
They knew the God who drew them from the comfort of their lives would make their course
clear. Painter vividly describes the three missionaries as men from a relatively humble beginning.

Rural life in Kenya would prove difficult but not a complete shocker to them.[21] They may have translated their experiences in rural America into terms that would suit them in rural Kenya.

Arrival at Port Florence, Kisumu

The three American missionaries came with deep concern for the people. They would soon become aware of the spiritual potential of the African people. On arrival at Port Florence, Kisumu, they were well received by railway officials and Mr. C. W. Hobbley, district commissioner of North Kavirondo District of Kenya Colony. Being erudite in the languages of local communities in his district, Hobbley gave the three missionaries a few Luragoli language basics, which became the basis for their language study and decision-making to direct their missionary base among the Luhya community.

However, besides the warm reception at Port Florence, the trio was also met with some disappointments. Their camping outfit that was shipped to Kisumu a week prior to their travel from Mombasa had not arrived. This is where Hobbley came in handy. After allowing them accommodation in sort of a hotel for a few days before their cargo arrived, Hobbley invited them on jaunt to Mumias. It was a journey they gladly accepted on July 11, and on Thursday, July 17 they paid a courtesy call on the 65-year-old Chief Mumia Nabongo. On their return to Port Florence, they found their cargo had arrived but was missing two poles for one of their two tents. A certain Mr. Heywood lent them his. They were overwhelmed with the hospitality they received.

There was no open way for a vehicle or wagon caravan except a winding path through the dark, hilly wooded land to Kaimosi. On July 18 they assembled 27 strong African porters accompanied by another young African man they found while in Mombasa, who became their acolyte in language translation. The team began trekking eastward and northward, pitching tents at various locations in the jungle. Up the hills and down the valleys, they were drenched in rain as they waded through mud swamps. Scorched by the tropical sun, stung by brush nettles, and pricked by thistles as they crossed the thick wild Nandi country, eventually the legs of the three American missionaries could not carry them any longer. They were literally carried shoulder-high by the African porters, especially when crossing streams.

Arrival at the Destined Mission Site, Kaimosi

After trekking for 22 days, the trio in the company of a battalion of African porters finally pitched tent on Sunday, August 9 at a place beside the river Galgol. On learning that there were three White men with a group of African men camping in his location, the local chief came to see them with his headmen. After listening to the missionaries' intentions, he granted them permission to stay, make the place their home, and teach his people. However, the Tiriki chief may also have hoped that the missionary camp would function as a buffer zone between the Tiriki (Luhya) and Nandi ethnic groups that had experienced fierce conflicts over cattle-rustling for some time. The missionaries were convinced by the site. Exasperated by Hotchkiss' bout of malaria and Hole's attack of fever, the missionaries stopped looking any further.

With Chilson now taking lead, he climbed a tree and peered through the verdant slopes sprawling down and up the hill at an altitude of 5300 feet above sea level. While up in the tree, Chilson exclaimed, "This is it," as he hurried down and led the caravan across the Galgol River and settled at a gradual slope that would later become an epicenter of the Kaimosi Friends Mission activities. There was a tract of unoccupied land with splendid, heavy timber and a river running through with good falls and rapids.[22]

Special practical reasons informed the Quaker missionaries' choice of Kaimosi as a possible location of their mission. The potential water power from the Galgol River falls would become a valuable asset for their envisioned industrial program. The hardwood forest provided assurance for adequate supplies of lumber for the proposed sawmill. The terrain and rolling uplands would be a suitable location for infrastructure and agriculture. The altitude, located only a few miles from the equator, assured a moderate climate and good rainfall for the crops. As time went by, social life would prove that they selected a location with friendly and receptive people.[23]

Eventually, Hobbley granted the Quakers permission to occupy the land on a temporary basis, but later he officially granted approximately 850 acres for a fee of US$0.68 per acre. Later, an additional 150 acres was given to the Quakers on leasehold basis. In total, Friends obtained approximately 1000 acres for Christian missionary use. The land became the property of FAIM. In 1912, the property was transferred to the American Friends Board of Missions. When African Friends became a yearly meeting under the name East Africa Yearly Meeting (EAYM) and assumed control of the mission, the property changed hands again now to EAYM and was put under the management of the board of trustees. This transfer took place in a special ceremony in February 1964.[24]

The first business meeting on the mission station took place on September 14, 1902. Missionaries continued living in tents for a few months after settling in Kaimosi. They began erecting temporary and permanent structures, which included living quarters for employees, learning spaces for children and adult education, a grass-thatched chapel for worship, and a temporary clinic. In three months, 35 men were hired, 15 of them from Uganda for payment in food rations and 2 rupees (US$0.60) per month. The concept of money was still foreign to the African people. They cleared the land and planted subsistence crops such wheat, millet, potatoes, and vegetables. They purchased two oxen, two milk cows with calves, 14 sheep, four goats and 60 chickens.[25] Division of duties fell into place, as Chilson devoted much of his time to developing an industrial department and Hole engaged in supervising and teaching the African employees and their families on the station. Hotchkiss' return to the United States after six months of their settlement on the mission ushered in an influx of Quaker missionaries of varied expertise and educational backgrounds.

The primary objectives of FAIM were clearly outlined in the report sent to the North American Friends Board of Industrial Mission in early 1903. First, it was to evangelize the African communities; the industrial feature was added later to sustain continuous influence. Second, FAIM was to teach the African peoples habits of industry, agriculture, education, and medicine. This approach would lead to a self-supporting, self-propagating, and self-sustaining Christian church. Some 118 years later, the industrial Christian approach would turn out to be a revolutionary idea. The three missionaries followed the pattern that had been developed hundreds of years prior to their coming to Africa. They scored high on this one. The medical ministry on the mission station was made possible with the arrival of Dr. Elisha Blackburn, a trained medical doctor, and his wife, Virginia, with knowledge in nursing, on July 5, 1903.[26]

To make evangelical work successful and witness of the Gospel realistic, the missionaries needed more language interpreters. This need took them to Kaptum, government offices a few miles after Kapsabet town. Their visit captured the interest of Daudi Lung'aho, father to Thomas Ganira Lung'aho, who later became the first general secretary of EAYM in 1964. Daudi had been employed on a White settler's farm to tend to horses. On hearing about the mission of the Quaker missionaries, "My heart was drawn to the kind of work," Thomas testified in a biography of his father.[27] Daudi trekked about 30 miles down to Kaimosi, where he stayed and worked with missionaries for many years. He married Maria Maraga while on the mission station. Ten years later, after he buried his wife, Daudi Lung'aho passed away on November 21, 1967, at age 85. Daudi Lung'aho, Maria Maraga, Akhonya, Kueyu, and Mango among others go down in history as having been the first African converts, as well as full-time employees in mission homes of the Friends Mission.[28]

Other Mission Stations and Outreach

The arrival of Emory and Deborah Reece to the Kaimosi Mission Station in July 1904 made literary work more manageable. The couple had served a term as missionaries in southern Africa. They had a working knowledge of one Bantu dialect, which gave them a head start on the study of the Luragoli language that would equip them to translate the Bible from English to Luragoli. This was made possible with the help of Joel Litu, a local resident of Vihiga area. Litu was recommended to the missionaries by Yohana Amugune, one of the pioneer Christian teachers trained at Kaimosi. Literate and erudite in both Luragoli and Kiswahili, Litu became Emory's acolyte in literary works at the new Vihiga Friends Mission Station. Litu would later become the first presiding clerk of EAYM of Friends in 1946. Chembuim Matolas from the British Friends Mission in Pemba arrived to serve as a teacher. He was later joined by his brother Bartholamayo.[29]

In 1906, Hole and Chembuim relocated to Lirhanda to set up the third mission station. They were later joined by Yohana Lumwagi, who served as pastor of a local church and administer to ten outpost schools by 1922. These young people – Lumwagi, Andrea Agufana, Petro Wanyama, Maria Ngaira, Joseph Ngaira, and Maria Maraga – became great assets in the development of the Christian church in the eastern part of Africa. The arrival of the printing press in 1914 revolutionized the literary enterprise in Kaimosi Friends Mission. Songbooks, pamphlets, and literature to schools and churches were printed and supplied across the East African community. Just as the hospital became a referral facility for the East African communities, the printing press became a center for literature production in the region, including government offices.[30]

The first Christian Endeavor Rally, which would later became Young Friends Program, was held in Lirhanda on a Sunday in December 1912. In the meantime, 50 miles north of Kaimosi, a new mission station was in the making by the initiative African Friends. This was among the Kitosh people, now known as Bukusu, in the present Bungoma County. With the government's permission, the fourth mission station was officially launched at Lugulu. Dr. Andrew and Mrs. Estock from Oregon Yearly Meeting were put in charge. Drs. Estock and Blackburn dug out a well, constructed a temporary chapel, and set mission work in full gear.[31]

The arrival of Jefferson and Hellen Farr Ford on the Lugulu Mission Station in December 1915 set in motion infrastructural development in the region. Before they landed in Kaimosi in 1914, the Fords had spent years of mission work in Jamaica.[32] After 17 years of dedicated service, Hellen Farr Ford was taken ill and succumbed in 1931. She was interred in the serene mission cemetery, now being maintained by Friends Theological College. Ford returned from the United States after his furlough in 1933 with Hellen Kersey Ford, his new bride. Everett Kellum married them in a colorful wedding ceremony inside the Kaimosi Chapel. The Fords spent most of their time in mission at Lugulu until their retirement in December 1948.[33]

Ford's indefatigable determination developed an indelible mission work in what is now Bungoma, Kakamega, and Trans Nzoia Counties. Among other accomplishments, Ford will be remembered particularly for his translation of the Old Testament and for having started the Bible Training Institute in 1942, which was later transferred to Kaimosi in 1950, which was renamed Friends Theological College in 1994. The author of this chapter is a graduate of this college (class of 1985) and is now serving as principal since October 2014.[34]

Petro Wanyama knew about Lugulu mission station at age 13. He married Esther Namaemba at Lugulu on September 5, 1919. Besides working as school inspector on White settlers' farms, Petro would be fully involved in mission work at Lugulu all his life. After repeatedly hearing Ford's voice singing and/or preaching, Rasoa Mutuha joined the worship at Lugulu in August 1919. She was among the first group of converts to be registered as associate members of the church. In 1922, Rasoa became the first African woman to be appointed preacher and teacher in the Quaker domain of the northern area. She was among the first three women to graduate from Friends Bible Institute, Lugulu, in 1946. The other two were Raeli Wangwe and Elizabeth Munyole.[35]

Joseph and Maria Mwaitsi Ngaira came to Kaimosi in 1906 and began housekeeping and gardening for the Chilson family. They became instrumental in leading Chilson for the foundation of Malava Friends Mission station in 1914. It is because of their willing hands and hearts that the Friends Church has a strong influence in the present Kabras community of Kakamega County.[36]

Toward a Self-Supporting, Self-Propagating, and Self-Sustaining Church

The period from 1920 to 1963 was an era for development in areas beyond Kaimosi. Schools, churches, and related development enterprises were put in place, mostly under the leadership of African Quakers. On September 19, 1921, Lirhanda Girls Boarding Secondary School was opened followed by Vihiga Boys School in February 1922 and Kaimosi Technical Training School on October 10, 1923, under the leadership of Fred Hoyt. The boys' school in Vihiga was later moved to Kaimosi, only to be moved again further north in 1956 to be officially opened in the following year under the name Kamusinga. Kamusinga Boys School was commissioned on July 8, 1957, by Sir Evelyn Baring, governor of Kenya Crown Colony.[37] Many prominent political and religious leaders in Kenya are alumni of Kamusinga Boys School. To this day, this school has maintained high academic record in national examinations.

Between the years 1926 and 1946, the Quakers had established five stations: Kaimosi, Vihiga, Lirhanda, Lugulu, and Malava. The hospital at Kaimosi had been completed and was fully operational; brick chapels had been built at Kaimosi and Lirhanda; and new schools had been set up. African leaders increasingly took responsibilities in all these institutions. A report of 1935 presented a record of 269 local congregations with weekly attendance of over 19,000 Friends. There were 298 schools in operation with a total enrollment of 15,534 children. The need for training of personnel had been organized, where teachers also served as pastors in Friends churches. A Friends church had been established in Eldoret among the White settlers, with 150 congregants who worshiped in open fields under trees and the canopy of the blue sky. As of 2020, this region has two yearly meetings, Lugari and Soy, with overflowing congregations, permanent church buildings, numerous Friends schools, and full-time trained pastors.[38]

The Birth of EAYM

Three requests were made to the Five Years Meeting (now Friends United Meeting [FUM]) from African Friends requesting for autonomy. The first request was filed in December 1931 but never made it to the agenda. The second request was made to the Missions Board in Richmond, Indiana, but no action was taken. In early 1945, the Africa Mission Board sent a third request, and with enthusiasm the Five Years Meeting passed a minute to establish a new yearly meeting among African Friends the following year.[39] Four American Friends were approved to participate in the inaugural ceremony, but only two made it: Merle Davis, executive secretary of the Mission Board, and Levinus K. Painter.[40]

Congregated in the T-shaped Lugulu Friends Church on bright Sunday of November 17, 1946, African Friends witnessed and welcomed the birth of EAYM of Friends. Attended by an estimate of 10,000 people, the most historic colorful ceremony was presided over by Petro Wanyama, local monthly meeting clerk. Jefferson Ford was the preacher of the day. The ceremony extended to the following day in which Painter, who represented the Five Years Meeting, read the authorization and made the pronouncement. The following Friends with outstanding records were installed as leaders of the new yearly meeting:

Presiding clerk:	Joel Litu – Vihiga Monthly Meeting
Assistant presiding clerk:	Yohana Lumwagi – Lirhanda Monthly Meeting
Recording clerk:	Benjamin Shidzugane – Malava Monthly Meeting
Assistant recording clerk:	Thomas Ganira – Lirhanda Monthly Meeting
Treasurer:	Petro Wanyama – Lugulu Monthly Meeting
Assistant treasurer:	Jacob Osolika
Superintendent:	Paul Barnet, Kaimosi Friends Mission
Assistant superintendent:	Joel Litu[41]

The culmination of the 44 years of the American Friends mission work in East Africa came to fulfillment and put the African Friends Church on its journey to the future. Members of various boards and committees were also selected and installed. The entire Friends mission and all programs in East Africa were turned over to the African administration in 1964, with Thomas Ganira Lung'aho as the general secretary.[42]

Outreach to New Missions

Autonomy should open the way for more growth. The Friends Church in East Africa began to expand to other territories beyond Luhya land. On his own initiative, Isaka Kiribwa, a native of Kaimosi, took the mission to the Masai land in 1952. Masai is a community in East Africa that has been obdurate to outside influence to this day, but Isaka was welcomed and allowed to share the Gospel of Christ among them. A new mission was founded at Poroko,[43] now being managed by Highland Yearly Meeting of Friends. In June 1958 EAYM launched a new Friends Church in the heart of the capital city, Kampala, Uganda. However, Quakerism had a foothold in Uganda as early as 1945 by Kenyan Friends who migrated to settle or work in Uganda. They settled mainly in four areas: Kigumba in Western Uganda; Nangóma, about 20 miles from the shores of Lake Victoria; Sibuse; and Nabiswa in Eastern Uganda at the slopes of Mt. Elgon.[44]

During the mid-1950s, when Kenyans were fighting for independence, the British colonial government in Kenya declared a state of emergency.[45] EAYM established a Friends Centre camp at Ofafa in Nairobi in 1955. The initial purpose for this center was to feed and rehabilitate the freed detainees from detention camp. A similar center was put up in Mwea, Central Province of Kenya. This center was named *Mucu Waurata*, which means "Friends Village" in the Kikuyu language.[46] It was meant to be an extension of the Friends Centre in Nairobi. Supported by the British Friends, African Friends raised money for the construction of these centers.

When Jomo Kenyatta, the first president of Kenya, was incarcerated in Maralal in what is now Samburu County, a section of Friends leaders sought permission from the British government to go visit him on June 2, 1961. These included Allan Bradley, headmaster, Friends School, Kamusinga Boys; Walter Martin, warden, Friends Centre, Ofafa, and Friends Service Council representative; Samweli Mwinamo, elder; Thomas Lung'aho, administrative secretary, EAYM; Fred Reeve, secretary to Friends Africa Mission; and Hezekiah Ngoya, treasurer, EAYM. Friends regard this visit as having been important in a variety of ways. First, it points to the significant role the Friends Church in East Africa played in the pursuit of peace and freedom for the African people. Second, it demonstrated the friendship that existed between Kenyatta and the Religious Society of Friends. In retrospect, in November 1931, Kenyatta enrolled in the Woodbrooke Quaker Study Center in Birmingham, England, where he attained a certificate in English writing in the spring of 1932.[47] Seven months later, after the Quaker leaders' visit, Kenyatta was released from detention in August 1961, and this paved the way toward Kenya's independence.[48]

Kenyatta's friendship with Quakers further came to be demonstrated at his acceptance of an invitation to dedicate a new building at Kaimosi Friends Mission Hospital on Sunday, April 25, 1965, a year after being sworn in as president of the Republic of Kenya. He presented a check of Ksh. 21,000 ($3080) as government contribution toward hospital development. Fifty-two years later his son, Uhuru Kenyatta, returned to Kaimosi Friends Mission Hospital; on Sunday June 25, 2017, he commissioned the facility under the new management and ownership of the National Council of Churches of Kenya (NCCK). I was honored to share the stage as master of ceremonies with Dr. Nelson Makanda, the NCCK's deputy general secretary.

After Kenya became independent on December 12, 1963, Kenyans moved into White settlement schemes vacated by White farmers. On January 6, 1964, Friends officially opened Lugari Farmers Training Center. In June 1970 Friends launched a technical center and orphanage at Kalokol in Turkana. This was done at the request of the Kenya government and the Christian Council of Kenya. This was meant to provide Turkana people who live in arid lands to have an option of a technical education.[49] Friends still maintain and have immensely expanded mission work in Turkana under the support of FUM.

In the New Dispensation, 1973–2020

As it is globally perceived, East Africa has the highest number of Friends in the world. However, this assumption could be true as it sounds, but for actual numbers, there has not been a credible research to prove this claim. The last time I checked, there were 22 yearly meetings operating in Kenya, one in Uganda, and one in Tanzania. The following is a list of yearly meetings, mother meetings and the year they were launched.

Bware Yearly Meeting – launched from Vihiga Yearly Meeting on June 26, 1994
Central Yearly Meeting – from EAYM, Kaimosi
Chavakali Yearly Meeting – from Vihiga Yearly Meeting, November 5, 1997
Chebuyusi Yearly Meeting – from Kakamega Yearly Meeting, 2012
Chevaywa Yearly Meeting – from Malava Yearly Meeting, 2019 (yet to be officially registered by the government)
East Africa Yearly Meeting, Kaimosi – mother to all yearly meetings since 1902
East Africa Yearly Meeting, North – intersects two counties, Trans Nzoia and Bungoma, registered on June 5, 1988
Elgon East Yearly Meeting – from Elgon Religious Society of Friends, August 1993
Elgon Religious Society of Friends – carved from East Africa Yearly Meeting, Kaimosi, April 19, 1973
Highland Yearly Meeting – from Bware Yearly Meeting, November 11, 2012
Kakamega Yearly Meeting – from EAYM, Kaimosi, September 20, 1993
Kamusinga Yearly Meeting – carved from Elgon Religious Society of Friends, August 11, 2014
Lugari Yearly Meeting – from EAYM, Kaimosi, July 26, 1992
Malava Yearly Meeting – from EAYM, Kaimosi, September 13, 1992
Nairobi Yearly Meeting – from East Africa Yearly Meeting, Kaimosi, 1987
Soy Yearly Meeting – from Lugari Yearly Meeting, April 7, 2013
Tongaren Yearly Meeting – from Elgon East Yearly Meeting, August 2005
Tuloi Yearly Meeting – from EAYM, Kaimosi, 2001

Uganda Yearly Meeting – from EAYM, Kaimosi launched first monthly meeting in Kampala in June 1958

Vihiga Yearly Meeting – carved from EAYM, Established in 1981 under the name East Africa Yearly Meeting, South.

Vokoli Yearly Meeting – from Vihiga Yearly Meeting, May 5, 1996

West Yearly Meeting – carved from Elgon Religious Society of Friends, October 9, 2016[50]

This list is important because it demonstrates the Quaker movement's growth from its inception in 1902 as one yearly meeting.

Conclusion: New Mission in the Sunset of Arthur B. Chilson

While attending a meeting in Lawrence, Kansas, during his furlough in the United States in 1932, Arthur Chilson received a request from Kansas Yearly Meeting to launch a new mission work in yet another untouched field of Africa. With support from Oregon Yearly Meeting and endorsed by leaders of Unevangelized Africa Mission (UAM) based in Congo, Chilson and his wife, Edna, along with their two children, Ester and Rachel, felt God's seal on this vision. They consented to the request and embarked on plans for the new mission.[51]

They received a new commissioning and in October 1932 and set sail via England, stopped in Belgium for paperwork, and docked in Mombasa on December 15, 1933. They purchased a vehicle in Nairobi, and in the first week of January 1934 they drove through Masai land, Serenget, Mwanza in Tanzania, and across to Bukoba in Uganda. They arrived at Musema, Urundi (Burundi), the district of Belgian Congo. They settled in Kibimba where they set up a Friends Mission Station, out of which Quakerism spread to Rwanda and the Democratic Republic of Congo (DRC). After 37 years of dedicated service to the Friends Mission in Africa, Arthur B. Chilson passed away on January 14, 1939. His grave lies quiet in Kibimba, Burundi. Bryon L. Osborne, editor of *Evangelical Friends*, wrote: "If greatness is measured in terms of consecration, vision, courage, humility and love for God and man [humanity], then Arthur Chilson deserves to be called great.[52]

Notes

1 Painter, pp. 12–14.
2 Martin and O'Meara, pp. 49–70.
3 Painter, p. 9.
4 Painter, p. 20.
5 Chilson, pp. 9–10.
6 Cleveland Bible Training Institute was later renamed Malone College (and again to Malone University) after it was moved to Canton, Ohio.
7 Painter, p. 20.
8 Painter, p. 20.
9 Chilson, p. 1.
10 Chilson, p. 10.
11 Chilson, p. 11
12 Chilson, p. 11.
13 Chilson, p. 11.
14 Chilson, pp. 12–13.
15 Painter, p. 21.
16 Chilson, pp. 14–17.
17 "As they sat down to eat their meal, they looked up and saw a caravan of Ishmaelites coming from Gilead. Their camels were loaded with spices, balm and myrrh, they were on their way to take them down to Egypt" (Genesis 37:25, NIV).

18 Hotchkiss, p. 24.
19 Hoskins, p. 13.
20 Chilson, p. 18.
21 Painter, p. 21.
22 Herbert and Beatrice Kimball, eds., *Go Into All the World: A Centennial Celebration of Friends in East Africa* (Friends United Press, Richmond, IN, 2002).
23 Painter, p. 22.
24 Painter, p. 23.
25 Painter, p. 24.
26 Ganira, p. 6.
27 Thomas Ganira, *Daudi Lung'aho: An African Missionary,* p. 6 (East Africa Yearly Meeting of Friends, Evangel Press, n.d.).
28 Painter, p. 29.
29 Painter, p. 33
30 Painter, p. 34.
31 Ford, p. 30.
32 Ford and Anderson, p. 30.
33 Kimball, p. 26
34 Kimball, p. 25.
35 Kimball, p. 25.
36 Painter, p. 38.
37 Painter, p. 50.
38 Painter, p. 68.
39 Painter, p. 68.
40 Painter, p. 68.
41 Kimball, p. 38.
42 Kimball, p. 58.
43 Kimball, p. 41.
44 Kimball, Herbert and Beatrice, eds.
45 B. Robert Edgerton, *Mau Mau: An African Crucible* (First Ballantine Books, New York, 1991).
46 Kimball, p. 43.
47 W. O. Maloba, *Kenyatta and Britain: An Account of Political Transformation, 1929–1963* (Palgrave Macmillan, London, 2018).
48 Painter, p. 138
49 Kimball, p. 74.
50 Kimball, p. 78.
51 Chilson, pp. 175–178.
52 Chilson, p. 261.

Bibliography

Adede, Rose. *Joel Litu: Pioneer African Quaker* (Pamphlet 243, Pendle Hill, 1982).

Chilson, Edna. *Ambassador of the King* (E. H. Chilson, Wichita, KS, 1943), p. 10.

Edgerton, B. Robert. *Mau Mau: An African Crucible* (First Ballantine Books, New York, 1991).

Ford, Hellen Kersey and Esther Anderson. *The Steps of a Good Man Are Ordered by the Lord: A Biography of Jefferson W. Ford 1879–1949* (Africa Inland Mission, Pear Rivers, NY, 1976).

Hoskins, Irene E. *Friends in Africa* (American Friends Board of Missions, Richmond, IN, no date).

Hotchkiss, Willis. *Then and Now in Kenya Colony* (Fleming H. Rewell Company, New York, 1936).

Kimball, Herbert and Beatrice (Eds). *Go Ye into the All the World: A Centennial Celebration of Friends in East Africa* (Friends United Press, Richmond, IN, 2002).

Lung'aho Thomas Ganira. *Daudi Lung'aho: An African Missionary* (East Africa Yearly Meeting of Friends, Evangel Press, date unknown).

Maloba, W. O. *Kenyatta and Britain: An Account of Political Transformation, 1929–1963.* (Palgrave Macmillan, London, 2018).

Martin, M. Phyllis and Patrick O'Meara (Eds). 1995. *Africa*, 3rd Edition (Indiana University Press, Blooming and Indianapolis, 1985).

Painter, K. Levinus. *The Hill of Vision* (The English Press, Nairobi, Kenya, 1966).

2

TRANSMISSION OF QUAKER MISSIONARY IDEAS AS DEVELOPMENT OF CHRISTIANITY IN WESTERN KENYA FROM 1902 TO 1970

Sychellus Wabomba Njibwakale

Introduction

According to Busia (1967, p. 189), sociologists and anthropologists have demonstrated that *homo africanus homo religiosus radicaliter* (the African is a radically religious person, religious at the core of his or her being). In other words, Africans' communal activities and their social institutions are inextricably bound up with religion and the spirit world. This does not mean that Africans are sacralists; rather, Africans seem unable to express their life and its mysteries without some reference to the supernatural. Christians, for instance missionaries of a certain type, have tended to talk as if Christianity is the best thing that an African can receive. As much as we appreciate that Christianity has a credible record in Africa, especially through the good work done by missionaries through social services, Africans have also other opinions on this. There were some negative aspects that Africans noticed with the incoming of Christian religion, which induces pride and attitudes of superiority and as such is destructive of social structures. In any case, Africans had their own religion before the advent of Christianity.

The missionary church has itself to blame for any criticism of its work because, while we may concede that mission is about the transformation of people's life and community, it is true that the missionary practice made Christianity foreign and its missionaries' bearers of an alien culture to Africa. Busia (1967, pp. 86–89) writes that those who have been responsible for the propagation of the Christian gospel in other lands and cultures have not shown sufficient awareness of the need for an encounter between the Christian religion and the cosmology of the people outside European cultures and traditions. It is this which made Christianity either alien or superficial or both. Busia (1972, pp. 239–246) continues to clarify that the concept of African Christianity does not mean that there is a version of Christianity that is African any more than that there is European Christianity. Christ as the Truth and the Way belongs to all ages and all climes. From this note, one is reminded that God's world and God's church are much bigger and broader than our own little turfs. God's *oikos*, or household, includes more than our tribes and our friends. On the other hand, we must develop cultures that are hospitable and inclusive.

DOI: 10.4324/9780429030925-4

In Revelation 7:9–10 (KJV), John provides an eloquent image:

> After this I beheld, and, lo, a great multitude, which no man could number, of all nations, and kindreds, and people, and tongues, stood before the throne, and before the Lamb, clothed with white robes, and palms in their hands; And cried with a loud voice, saying, Salvation to our God which sitteth upon the throne, and unto the Lamb.

The African must also be there in God's household, alongside all the people from other nations. All that has been said above is about the growth of Christianity. Something worth noting is that Africa presents to the world with religious pluralism. In most of the African nations, in addition to several Christian denominations, there are other religions; especially African Traditional Religions, Buddhism and Islam are existing and worshipping freely.

With this in mind, this chapter presents the transmission of the Quaker missionary ideas and how these ideas impacted the people and their lives in western Kenya. The Quaker missionaries came from the western mission (of the left strain of Protestantism). The chapter will explore how the Quaker missionary ideas were received and understood, and later on extensively developed against the background of African lifestyle and African sense of genuine religiosity. The approach, however, will be historical, phenomenological and structuralist.

Origin and Development

As a starting point, the Quaker Mission had such a great success in Kenya that up to today, Kenya has in percentage, a half of the world Quakers, or churches affiliated with them, than other Quakers from other regions in the world. Thunberg (1998, pp. 157–186) writes that Quakerism is particularly interesting through its religio-phenomenological structure as a challenge and a resource for evangelism. Lingering question include: What does this particular form of Christianity offer through its interpretation of Christian faith or insight? What does it have to assimilate from outside to become effective in transmitting its missionary ideas, especially in an African setting? The answer to these questions opens the door to investigate the beginning of the group called Quakers. However, this topic will be spared for another article.

Psychological Characteristics

First of all, Fox experienced "the inner Light" as a regaining in Christ of Adam's state of innocence. Christ appears directly to man. Rasmussen (1995, p. 3) explains that the seed is sown by God inside the individual and can be activated only by the Holy Spirit. The Spirit who spoke to the apostles now speaks again to the chosen. What we should notice here structurally, in regard to the development in Kenya, is (1) the importance of repentance, (2) purity as a characteristic of the re-established status and (3) the reception of the Spirit.

What happened in Philadelphia through the so-called Hicksite Separation of 1927–1928 is also worth noting. As Rasmussen (1995, p. 9) explains, Elias Hick, a farmer and preacher, reacted against a "beginning institutionalization" and "orthodoxisation" and underlined the original concept of "the inner light": the true Cross was not the historical cross of Christ but "the Light of Christ in the soul calling for the crucifixion of self-will."

During the latter part of the nineteenth century, American Quakers were caught by a general evangelical revival. This led, for instance, to a new outburst of emotional religiosity: sighs, confessions, prayer cries, joyful recognition of forgiveness and a renewed fellowship. In some places a "mourners' bench" was erected in front of the meeting house. In general, however, the revival was dominated by holiness Methodism, which demanded a definite date of conversion (basically against the original Quaker idea of "the inner light"; Rasmussen, 1995, pp. 13–17).

In Kenya, the effect of this revival is observable. Arthur Chilson, who arrived in Kenya as a missionary in 1914, had a personal experience of conversion and sanctification and had in a metaphorical sense put all his sinfulness "on the altar" (cf. Evangelical revivalist piety in general, an influence of Methodism and the idea of a spiritual mourners' bench). This message Chilson transmitted to his missionary service, despite losing part of its character of personal experience as he preached about baptism with the Holy Spirit (Rasmussen, 1995, pp. 42, 59).

Basing on the revivalist tradition, but against the original Quaker vision, Chilson strongly underlined the immediate forthcoming of Jesus Christ (an element which was taken up by the Holy Spirit churches in the beginning). In September 1924, at a prayer conference in Lugulu, northwestern Kenya, Chilson preached a sermon which resulted in the experience of the visit of the Holy Spirit among the people present, interpreted as a baptism with the Spirit (Rasmussen, 1995). This is obviously a Pentecostal element, which also united the new independent churches with the Pentecostal missions in Kenya for some time. The Pentecostal phenomenon was characterized and strengthened through speaking in tongues (e.g., in Kaimosi in 1927). This Pentecostal mission was influential with in Quakerism but in different degrees in different regions.

Quaker Mission Arrives in Kenya

Wafula (2001), in his article titled *Crossroads of Western Quakerism in Africa*, aptly argues:

> The history of the foundation of the Quaker movement in East Africa is straightforward and easy to understand. At least it seems so, basing oneself on face value research. But, with its combination of a variety of theological ideals, it is a complex one. One cannot comprehend African Quakerism unless one studies how Western Quaker theological ideas have changed and shaped the African people's lifestyle. Even though it is a carryover religious practice engraved in Western culture, Quakerism has become a part of our modern social life. I use "our" because as an African, I happen to be a descendant product of Western theological metamorphosis.

In the wake of the nineteenth century, the railroad was sufficiently completed in 1902 so that the first Quaker missionaries could take advantage of its facilities. Painter (1966, p. 18) notes that the railroad became the lifeline by which many new influences came to western Kenya. The same railroad over which the missionaries traveled provided transportation for scores of European settlers during the next few years. The settlers were attracted by the rich soil and good climate of the Rift Valley. Many immigrants, including the Indians who had come as laborers on the railroad were settling down to form associations for settlers. Levinus observes that the motives of both the settlers and the Indians were personal and selfish, with no thought of the Africans or their welfare. Only missionaries had come with a deep spiritual and unselfish concern for the African people (Painter, 1966, p. 61).

The beginning of the Quaker movement in Kenya can be appreciated somewhat better in the light of the historical, cultural and political background of the time. The American Quakers arrived in Kenya as foreigners in a British Crown colony. Wafula (2001) states that the missionaries were led by Arthur Benton Chilson (born June 16, 1872, in LeGrand, Iowa), who conceived the idea of exporting Quakerism to East Africa. Chilson (1943, p. 9) states that he met Willis R. Hotchkiss while a student at Cleveland Friends Bible Institute. Hotchkiss had recently returned from Africa along with Edgar T. Hole, who also had felt a call to Africa. With encouragement from Hotchkiss, Chilson's vision to go to Africa was stirred up. The Institute was then under the able management of Walter and Emma B. Malone (it was later moved to Canton, Ohio, where it is now named Malone University after its founders). Wafula (2001) explains that Chilson shared the conceived idea with his colleague Hole, who was also enrolled at the Institute. The former had also nursed the idea of being a missionary abroad.

The three young students were of one mind and united in the Spirit. The Malones had total confidence in these young men and encouraged them to go ahead with the plan, and they would support them in any way possible. Emma Malone was a member of the newly formed mission board for the work in Africa. The board formed to oversee the plans for the three young men was later called the Friends Africa Industrial Mission (FAIM). From the mission statement of the FAIM of September 20, 1901, its primary purpose is evangelization. Kimball (2002) writes that the industrial feature is introduced into the work for the purpose of exerting a continuous Christian influence on the natives employed in the hope of obtaining the following results: to teach them the habit of industry and ultimately to establish a self-supporting Christian church.

Ministry Work at Kaimosi

Now the long journey was over, but the real task lay ahead. When the missionaries arrived at Kaimosi, there were hardly any Africans living there. It was a land of nobody between Tiriki and Nandi. But when the mission station was set up, the British settlers' attempt to pacify the Nandi soon brought the inter-ethnic fighting to an end. As a result, many Tiriki moved into the area and settled around Kaimosi (Chilson, 1943, pp. 17ff., 52ff.). Kaimosi was and still is the headquarters for Quakers in Kenya. The three missionaries arrived Kaimosi on August 9, 1902. The following day, Arthur Chilson wrote in his journal that it was a hard tramp through a wild country, but the question of a good camping place was becoming more and more serious every moment, with one man sick and another far from well.

Kaimosi was found to have productive soil, springs of fresh abundant water and river falls. The forest had good indigenous trees for timber. The elevation is 5300 feet above sea level, thus making it a healthful climate especially for the Western expatriates. The temperatures ranged from 48 to 98 degrees Fahrenheit.

Wafula (2001) writes:

A people who lived in this area were described to have been the neediest on earth, yet they never complained or went on begging. They wore no clothes and lived in huts with their cattle but were healthy and not ashamed. They had no written language yet were rich in oral tradition. These people were very religious in all aspects of life. They had a knowledge of God, the ultimate reality in their own understanding.

With the assistance from the local leaders (chiefs), about 858 acres of land were purchased from the British government (Kenya was still a British colony). Much of this land was forested. Later a leasehold of 40 acres of timberland was acquired.

The arrival of the Quakers in western Kenya in 1902 among the Luhya people marked the first missionary interactions with them. There had been no other missionary agency in the region. As already stated, the FAIM was the first missionary society to reach the Luhya land. But after the completion of the railway line, other missionary societies followed. Immediately after the FAIM followed the South African Compounds and Interior Mission (later called the Church of God); then came the Church Missionary Society (CMS) and the Roman Catholic Mill Hill Fathers. All these groups began their mission work in 1905. Amatsimbi (2015, pp. 53–100) notes that in 1924, the Pentecostal East African Mission (PEAM) established a station at Nyang'ori, about 20 kilometers from the FAM station at Kaimosi, and began wooing Friends converts.

Rasmussen (1995, p. 45) observes:

> As pioneers in a new and, to them, unknown country, the Friends missionaries had to make their own experiments to find out how best to carry through their evangelizing mission. With very little knowledge of the people, they had come to, and with no other missionaries' experiences in the same area to build on, they had to try to find their own ways of reaching the people.

The industrial and construction work at Kaimosi created a contact point between the missionaries and the local Luhya people. Many young people who had nothing to do were attracted by the missionary arrival, and they flocked to the center to work for the missionaries. Some of the well-known names to pick the jobs included Akhonya and Lung'aho, both from Isukha area. Others were Amugune from North Maragoli and Maraga from Tiriki. Painter (1966, p. 32) explains that Maraga, a woman, later married Lung'aho.

The communication between the missionaries and the Luhyas who could not speak and understand English was done through a teacher from Pemba called Kwetu. Kwetu knew English and translated English into Swahili, the language that Lung'aho and Akhonya understood. Akhonya and Lung'aho could then translate the Kiswahili into Kiisukha. Communication improved when the missionaries learnt enough Kiswahili to communicate with Africans who understood the language. Chilson (1943, p. 44) says, Arthur Chilson spoke the first message in Kiswahili in February 1903. The arrival of Emory Rees in 1904 improved the language when Emory realized the significance of missionaries using the local language. Afterward, the language was reduced to written form. The written tracts to Friends schools could be translated into the vernacular. After some years, Rees and his wife relocated to Maragoli. The language they had learnt helped them to translate the Bible into Luragoli, and the Luragoli language became the dominant language among Friends African Mission for years.

When the missionary message spread into the people, the indigenous people found it relevant to their day-to-day life. The relevance of the missionary's message proved powerful to the traditional elders and the ancestors in solving problems for their people. Many of the indigenous people turned to Christianity to improve their lives. The connection between the hardships that people encountered and their willingness to become Christians is described by Benjamin Wegesa's biography of Abraham Sangura. Chief Murunga a Wanga, who ruled North Bukusu for many years, had taken Abraham Sangura, a Bukusu from Bugembe in 1920, to do forced labor in his farms. Benjamin Wegesa (mid-1950s, n.p.) writes of Sangura:

> He wanted to help abolish this slavery which he himself was suffering. There was no freedom in Kenya then. People were ruled by force, and they obeyed from fear. Because of these conditions that haunted the lives of African men and women, Abraham made up his mind to become a Christian, if he could get the chance. He wanted to help his people understand the value of the human soul. He wanted the African courts to learn what justice in human lives.

From the above description, Christianity is viewed as a religion that is capable of freeing those who are suffering and restoring justice to its followers. This change is to happen in people's lives at personal and social levels. Old people who had been kept under slavery toward freedom recounts how they started learning about Christianity and accepting the good news of the gospel in the early 1920s. The missionaries realized that African Christians stands a better chance to influence other Africans to Christianity than the white missionaries. One couple that was hailed for the good work was Joseph Ngaira and Maria Mwaitsi. This couple accompanied the Chilson family from Kaimosi to Malava in 1915. Dr. Bond praises the couple, saying "they have gotten a vision of Jesus and can far outreach us in helping these black people to Christ" (FUM, 1921).

Africans Take Over Church Leadership

The enemy to the mission churches of Friends African Mission included, in the former North Kavirondo District, as was referred to in the 1940s and 1950s, was the rise of Dini ya Msambwa led by Elijah Masinde wa Nameme. Elijah, a member of the Friends Church, was expelled from the church for his polygamous life Ford (1941) states that the activities of Dini ya Msambwa did not result in a lasting loss of large number of members, as the Holy Spirit revival had. The number of memberships for the Friends Church grew tremendously after from 7000 in 1939 to 17,000 in 1949 (Wines, 1949; Omulokoli, 1981, p. 330). Such growth in numbers prompted the discussion of establishing a yearly meeting in Kenya.

After several years of deliberating on when to establish a yearly meeting in Kenya, a decision was reached by the American Friends Board of Foreign Missions. The Mission Board presented its application to the Five Years Meeting in the October 1945 Conference session. The application was accepted, and the Five Years Meeting recommended that the Board of Missions send representatives from America to attend a session in Kenya and carry a minute from the Five Years Meeting giving authority to the new yearly meeting (FUM, 1945). After that, on November 18, 1946, the East Africa Yearly Meeting of Friends was officially established, with Joel Litu from Maragoli as its first Presiding Clerk, Benjamin Ngaira from Idakho as Recording Clerk, and Petro Wanyama from Tachoni as Treasurer (Ford, 1946; Painter, 1966 p. 68; Adede, 1982, p. 20). Since most of Friends from Kenya had migrated to Uganda, the name of the yearly meeting was settled at East Africa Yearly Meeting was preferred than Kenya Yearly Meeting. By 1946, Kenya was still a British colony, as such, the church could not hold property. At this time, the American Friends only transferred the responsibility for the religious work. After independence in 1963, the American Quakers transferred administration and property to the Kenyan Quaker leaders.

Despite the successes witnessed by the opening of the yearly meeting, there were problems that arose as a result. One of them was when the Friends Bible Institute was moved from Lugulu to Kaimosi in 1949 after the exit of Jefferson Ford. The reason for moving the Bible Institute was based on the idea that since most missionaries are in Kaimosi, it would be easier to have part-time teachers to help in the work of the Bible school. Wines (1949) writes, "it is our policy to make the Bible Institute an indigenous part of the Yearly Meeting, as far as possible, and not an institution thrust upon it by America." He continues: "in carrying out this policy we asked the various Monthly Meetings to help financially with the preparation for the opening of the Bible Institute. The response has been very good except for the Monthly Meetings in the north." That is where the problem lay.

Another problem between the northern and the southern parts of the Friends Church, and between Africans and missionaries, was the issue of location of good schools. Hoyt (1971, p. 31) states that "since the 1920s, the only two such schools, one for boys and one for girls, had both been at Kaimosi." The Bukusu Quakers from the northern region demanded that one such school be relocated to their region. The unrest caused by Elijah Masinde and his Dini ya

Msambwa made the government to support the move of the school to the northern region of Bukusu Friends. Because of pressure from the government, the American Friends Board of Missions gave in to the government demand and moved the Boys' School from Kaimosi to Kamusinga in the north, the current Friends School Kamusinga. They also agreed to hire an English headmaster plus a few English teachers so that the new school would compete well with others in the country's education system. The new school opened doors in January 1957, with Bradley as the first headmaster (Bradley, 1967, pp. 39 ff., 51ff., 79ff.).

By and large, the contribution of these missionaries is what makes western Kenya thrive academically and economically than most areas in the country today. The only area that has not succeeded since the missionary started is healthcare. So far, throughout the Quaker regions, Lugulu mission hospital is the only one standing strong. The western region and the country at large applaud the contributions made by early Quaker missionaries between 1902 to 1970.

References

Adede, R. (1982). *Joel Litu: Pioneer African Quaker*. Wallingford, PA: Pendle Hill.

AFBM. (2012). *Foreign Mission Work of American Friends: A Brief History of Their Work from the Beginning to the Year 1912*. Whitestrand: HardPress.

Amatsimbi, H.M. (2015). "The Friends Church and Economic Transformation Among the Luhya of Western Kenyan 1902–1988." PhD thesis, pp. 53–100.

Bradly, A. (1967). *One Man's Education: An Autobiographical Scrapbook*. York City: Session of York.

Busia, K.A. (1967). *Africa in Search of Democracy*. London: Routledge & Kegan Paul.

Busia, K.A. (1972). "The Commitment of the Laity in the Growth of the Church and the Integral Development of Africa." *Laity Today*, special number, 1972, 239–46.

Chilson, E.H. (1943). *Ambassador of the King*. Wichita, KS: E.H. Chilson.

Ford, J.W. (1941). "FUM Annual Report of the Evangelistic Department."

Ford, J.W. (1946). "FUM: Report of the Evangelistic Department."

FUM. (1921). "Letter from A.A. and Mira C. Bond to Friends."

FUM. (1945). "Minutes of the Executive Committee Meeting of the AFBM."

Hotchkiss, W.R. (1937). *Then and Now in Kenya Colony*. New York: Fleming H. Revell.

Hoyt, A.H. (1971). *We Were Pioneers*. Wichita, KS: Fleming H. Revell.

Kimball, H. & B. (2002). *Go Into All the World: A Centennial Celebration of Friends in East Africa*. Richmond, IN: Friends United Press.

Omulokoli, W. A. O. (1981). "The Historical Development of the Anglican Church among Abaluhya 1905–1955." Unpublished PhD dissertation, University of Aberdeen.

Painter, L.K. (1966). *The Hill of Vision*. Kaimosi: East Africa Yearly Meeting of Friends.

Rasmussen, A. M. B. (1995). *A History of the Quaker Movement in Africa*. London: British Academic.

Thunberg, L. (1998). "Quaker Mission and the Holy Spirit Churches in Western Kenya." *Swedish Missiological Themes*, 86, 2, 157–186.

Wafula, R.J. (2001). "Crossroads of Western Quakerism in Africa." *Quaker Theology* Issue # 5, Richmond, IN.

Wegesa, B. (mid-1950s). *A Life of Abraham Sangura, East African Friend*. Richmond, IN: AFBM.

Wines, L.E. (1949). "FUM: Evangelistic Report."

3

A BRIEF HISTORY OF QUAKERS IN SOUTH AFRICA

Penelope Cummins

In any discussion of Quaker history in Southern Africa, one needs to be aware of the wider social and economic context in which Friends were living. Since 1652, when the Dutch East India Company established a refreshment station at the Cape for its ships, South Africa has always been an enormously exploitative society, with gross inequalities of opportunity for its inhabitants. The first slaves were brought to the Cape in 1653.[1] Indentured labourers were brought from India to work in the cane fields of Natal in the 1860s; and by the 1890s the colonial government was drafting labour and civil legislation to limit the Indians' rights.[2] After the Union of South Africa in 1910, the Natives Land Act of 1913 reserved 87% of the landmass of South Africa for white ownership; the African population, more than 70% of the total, was confined to Native Reserves and allowed only for purposes of employment to live in urban areas.[3] South Africa became a country of migrant labour and differential, race-based, access to education, housing, health services, entertainment and jobs. After the Nationalist government won the 1948 elections, an intensive policy of apartheid (separateness) prevailed, supported by forced removals and repressive policing. Many of these patterns of inequality persist more than a quarter century after the end of apartheid.[4] The first free elections were held in 1994, when the African National Congress (ANC), led by Nelson Mandela, came to power.

The first record we have of Quakers in Southern Africa is in two letters written from the Cape in 1728 by employees of the Dutch East India Company to a British Friend, Benjamin Holme. In one letter, John George Holtz described the difficulties Friends had finding time and opportunity to meet.[5] The group of Friends and attenders included Abram (Ibrahim) de Haan, the son of the raja of Tambora, who had been exiled by the Dutch East India Company to the Cape from Indonesia in 1701.[6]

Later in the eighteenth century, Quaker whalers from Nantucket regularly fished off the Cape between July and September each year; by 1795 the visiting fleet included between twenty and thirty ships in a season.[7] The whalers set up stations at Cape Town, Saldanha and Walvis Bay (now in Namibia) and presumably held meetings for worship at each of these places. Their Cape Town Meeting was recognised as an Allowed Meeting of Hudson Monthly Meeting of New York Quarterly Meeting,[8] and the whalers established a meeting house which had closed by 1807.[9]

During the Napoleonic Wars the British took over the Cape, which was formally designated a British colony in 1814. With a view to extending the inhabited area of the colony and

DOI: 10.4324/9780429030925-5

providing a buffer along its eastern border, the government offered free land to about 4000 British migrants. One of these 1820 settlers was a carpenter and Wesleyan lay minister, Richard Gush. Mainly through his reading, Gush became a convinced Friend. Soon after his death in 1858, the Yorkshire Friends Tracts Association published a pamphlet describing Gush's unusually pacific relationships with the Xhosa people, in whose territory the 1820 settlers found themselves, and incidents such as an occasion when he sent away an armed group with food and good will.[10]

An English Quaker botanist, James Backhouse, and his companion George Washington Walker spent just over two years investigating the indigenous flora and also 'travelling in the ministry' in South Africa on their way home from Australia from 1838 to 1840.[11] They covered more than 6000 miles, and visited the scattered Quakers, including Gush. They also spent time with missionaries, such as Robert Moffatt in Kuruman,[12] and visited prisons including the penal settlement on Robben Island. In addition to their meetings for worship with Friends, they held public revivalist or temperance meetings for large crowds. In 1840, using funds provided by English Friends, Backhouse established a school for poor children in Cape Town, which stayed open until 1879.

In that year, a small delegation of British Quakers, under the leadership of Isaac Sharp, visited Friends in South Africa. The visitors were critical of British imperialism in southern Africa and established cordial relations with Afrikaans ministers of the Dutch Reform Church. These experiences helped to inform London Yearly Meeting's criticism of British policies during the Boer War (1899–1902).

By 1900 there were about 150 Quakers scattered throughout South Africa, many of them living in rural areas, remote from other Friends. This was an early peak of the Quaker population in South Africa, which has never yet reached even 200 members and attenders. The distribution of Friends has however become less scattered, with fewer Friends in rural areas; Quakers today are mainly clustered in Cape Town, Johannesburg, Pretoria and Port Elizabeth.[13] Cape Town Meeting became a Monthly Meeting of London Yearly Meeting in 1906. South Africa General Meeting became a Quarterly Meeting of London Yearly Meeting in 1918.

From the 1870s a small group of Quakers gathered at Cradock in the Eastern Cape; these were mostly family and friends of James Butler,[14] who had moved to South Africa for his health in the 1870s. Butler founded and edited a newspaper, the *Midland News*, 'partly with a view to promoting better feelings between the Boer and British races'.[15] He was one of the Friends who, with advice from London Yearly Meeting, successfully lobbied the South African Parliament to ensure that a limited conscience clause was included in the Defence Act of 1912, providing for exemption from compulsory military service for religious reasons.

In the early part of the twentieth century, most South African Quakers were very accepting of the racial disparities in the country, and it is hardly surprising that each of the three black South Africans who joined the Religious Society of Friends while studying in London decided to retain their membership of English rather than South African Meetings.[16]

A prominent Johannesburg mining accountant and philanthropist, Howard Pim, a Quaker who arrived from Ireland in the 1890s, might be described as having been for most of his life a 'benevolent segregationalist',[17] advocating for limited education for Africans and supporting the creation of the Native Reserves. But by the late 1920s he asserted that 'segregation was quite impossible, "except under conditions of slavery"'.[18]

South African Friends were not actually blind to the racial inequalities in the country. In 1921 a General Meeting concluded: 'The great need in South Africa today is for men and women who would consecrate the whole energy of brain and heart to the solving of the race problems on the Christian basis of human solidarity'.[19] And in 1931 the General Meeting declared that 'we cannot admit that difference of race can set limits upon our friendships'.[20]

But in 1928, when plans for a Quaker school were being mooted, it was envisaged as an entirely white affair, in keeping with the culture of the country at the time. A black Friend, Davidson Jabavu, wrote to a local Quaker in exasperation: 'It seems to me an untenable position for the Society of Friends to say that at a Friends school they cannot allow children of their own members to attend, because they are coloured'.[21]

In 1946, South Africa General Meeting became an independent Yearly Meeting. After the Nationalist government came to power in 1948, Quaker opposition to white supremacist policies grew. In 1956, Quakers in Natal Province issued a statement rejecting the concept of apartheid:

> We believe that South Africa is not for one people alone, or for any one more particularly, but that every section of the population has come to this land under the hand of God. . . . We believe that as Christians it is laid upon us to do all in our power to draw together the separated peoples of South Africa to the end that we may become one nation.[22]

Despite their small size, by the 1950s various Monthly Meetings in South Africa supported their own social responsibility projects, often with financial support from Quakers abroad and from other donors.[23] The Quaker Service Committee of the Transvaal Monthly Meeting helped African families meet the bills for the uniforms, books and fees necessary for children to attend state schools; Quaker bodies offering small-scale poverty relief existed in Natal, Cape Town and the Eastern Cape, and similar work continues today. In the 1980s Quakers provided financial support for initiatives such as Steve Biko's Black Communities Programmes[24] and for Winnie Mandela's home industries groups for women.[25]

Many Quaker women were members of the Black Sash, a civil rights organisation which from 1955 to 1994 campaigned for human rights in South Africa, monitored events and ran advice offices (some of which still operate). For instance, May Murray-Parker and Anna Pierce of Cape Western Monthly Meeting were early members. Bunty Biggs, a clerk of Natal Monthly Meeting, was active in the Sash monitoring of the removal of whole communities from 'black spots' in Natal to the 'Homelands' in the 1960s. Friends who were members of the Black Sash campaigned against forced removals, imprisonment without trial, and discriminatory legislation, and in favour of children's rights. They engaged in demonstrations, monitored police action and the destruction of shanty dwellings, and chauffeured the visiting families of political prisoners to the Robben Island ferry port and to Pollsmore prison.[26]

While Quakers everywhere do move around, there have been many moments in South African history when Friends have left the country for political reasons, for instance during the State of Emergency in 1960 following the Sharpville massacre, and in the period of repression in the 1960s after South Africa became a republic and left the commonwealth. One such Friend was Shelagh Willett, who moved to Botswana in 1967 and in the 1970s established a place of refuge, Kagisong, for refugees from South Africa and other African countries; in 2002 she also founded a refuge for victims of domestic violence.[27]

Robynne Rogers Healey discusses the widely different views of South African Friends and the American Friends Service Council (AFSC) about the possible role of Quakers in apartheid South Africa in the 1970s. At a meeting held in Botswana in 1977, South African Friends resisted what they perceived as the 'American cultural imperialism' of AFSC,[28] which advocated working closely with members of resistance organisations, while the AFSC staff perceived the local Quakers as fairly conservative, middle-class beneficiaries of the apartheid system. If any-thing, events around this meeting helped the South Africans to enunciate their commitment to fostering peace directly rather than to supporting violence intended to promote the greater good. Healey refers to Olive Gibson, a past clerk of the Yearly Meeting and key staff member of Quaker Service in the Transvaal, who declared that a commitment to non-violence even in a context of injustice was surely not, as the AFSC staff appeared to suggest, a dilemma; and that it was vitally important to support people engaged in peaceful work towards reconciliation – which, she affirmed, could only be defined as the achievement of justice.[29]

It was this kind of insight, and friends' attachment to the historic Quaker peace testimony, which attracted some of the new members to the Society in South Africa in the 1970s and 1980s. South Africa was engaged in war both outside and within its borders, and it was a period of universal national conscription for young white men. The National Defence Act of 1957 only allowed non-combatant status to conscientious objectors,[30] which was not an acceptable option to some conscripts, including Richard Steele and Jeremy Routledge, who were both imprisoned for their absolutist stance and spent time in solitary confinement.[31] Jeremy later married another political activist, who had also experienced prison and more than a year of solitary confinement. Nozizwe Madlala-Routledge became a member of Parliament in 1994, and in 1999 was appointed as probably the first Quaker, pacifist, deputy minister of defence in the world,[32] having insisted that she would not accept any responsibility for weapons or war. She subsequently became deputy minister for health and deputy speaker. She has since helped to found an NGO combatting sex trafficking and exploitation. In 2021, she was announced as the forthcoming director of the Quaker United Nations Office in Geneva (https://www.quak ersintheworld.org/quakers-in-action/190/Nozizwe-Madlala-Routledge. Accessed 12 Febru-ary 2022). She instead addressed herself to the welfare of veterans and military families and to policies for the management of HIV/AIDS within the Defence Force, which at that time was a taboo issue.

Quaker peacebuilding during the apartheid era was undertaken at local and national levels, notably in the negotiations quietly brokered by Hendrik van der Merwe between the Nation-alist government and the African National Congress. Van der Merwe, an Afrikaans-speaking South African, had become drawn to Friends while studying in the United States; the AFSC and other American Quaker groups helped to fund the Centre for Intergroup Studies,[33] which he led at the University of Cape Town from 1968 to 1992.[34]

Towards the end of the apartheid years, various Friends were engaged either as Quaker rep-resentatives or in their personal capacity in a range of organisations critical of apartheid and its effects, such as the Community for Reconciliation, the South African Council of Churches, the Free the Children campaign, the Detainees Parents Support Group, the Treatment Action Campaign and the End Conscription Campaign, each of which was dealing with current injus-tices while also trying to provide for an alternative, more constructive future. In the 1980s, Cape Town Quakers helped to organise a weapons amnesty in the Western Cape; and some Friends continue to support Gun Free South Africa, a nongovernmental organisation (NGO) com-mitted to reducing gun violence. Friends are also associated with the Phoenix Project, which fosters restorative justice among prisoners in KwaZulu-Natal.

The establishment of the Quaker Peace Centre in Cape Town in 1987 arose from reconcilia-tion and monitoring work undertaken in the 1980s by a Quaker peace worker and other mem-bers of the Western Cape Monthly Meeting, especially among the regularly displaced squatter communities on the Cape Flats.[35] The work of the Centre included community development and conflict management; and it ran an innovative peace education programme for teachers, helping to mitigate violence in schools. The Peace Centre was primarily funded from abroad, by British and other Friends and also by donors such as German churches. Many international donors withdrew after the fall of apartheid, and formal British Quaker support ceased in 2016. With each reduction in donor funding, the Centre had to reduce its activities. In 2018 the Cape Western Monthly Meeting relinquished responsibility for the Peace Centre, which dropped 'Quaker' from its name, though Friends still constitute most of its board members. It was also decided to focus the activities of the Centre among communities most affected by violence, particularly in Khayelitsha, one of the poorest townships in the metropolitan area, and to maximise the role of volunteers in the absence of the core of paid staff, which could no longer be afforded.[36]

In the years since the first free elections in 1994, the economic and social structure of South Africa has changed very little from that constructed under apartheid. Friends have spoken out repeatedly about justice, equity and government fraud[37] and have been associated with the Alternatives to Violence programme, anti-bullying projects in schools and other peacebuilding activities. For almost twenty years they have campaigned for a basic income grant. Although Cape Western Monthly Meeting has relinquished its responsibility for managing the Peace Centre, the Yearly Meeting itself has not disengaged from the concerns which prompted the work of that project. At the Yearly Meeting sessions in 2022, Friends began to explore a proposal for developing a new peace education programme in the region called Investing in Peacebuilding.[38]

South Africa remains one of the most violent countries in the world, with one of the highest rates of gun crime, murder, rape and domestic violence,[39] and there is a great need for people especially in the most disadvantaged communities to have strategies at their disposal to minimise this violence. The Yearly Meeting envisions training 10,000 young people in Lesotho, South Africa and Zimbabwe in responsible, loving and nonviolent parenting; relaunching its Alternative to Violence peace education programme in KwaZulu-Natal and extending it throughout southern Africa; and establishing a postgraduate programme in peacebuilding at the National University of Lesotho.[40]

Friends in South Africa are part of Central and Southern Africa Yearly Meeting, which meets only every second year. It extends from the Cape to Malawi, Namibia, Zimbabwe, Zambia, Botswana, Lesotho, Eswatini and Madagascar. The entire Yearly Meeting has fewer than a thousand members spread over many thousands of miles, but the work of the Yearly Meeting, and the lives of many of its individual members, have had far greater effect than the small numbers might indicate.[41]

Notes

1 By 1798 slaves from Africa, Indonesia, Madagascar and elsewhere outnumbered the employees of the Dutch East India Company and the rest of the free population from abroad (James Armstrong, 'The Slaves, 1652–1745' in Richard Elphick & Hermann Gilliomee (eds.) *The Shaping of South African Society 1652–1840*, London and Cape Town: Longman, 1979, p. 75, Quoted by Betty Tonsing, *The Quakers in South Africa; a Social Witness*, Lewiston, Queenston, Lampeter: Edwin Mellen Press, 2002, p. 37).

2 A young lawyer, Mohandas Gandhi, came to South Africa in 1893 at the behest of the Indian community to advocate for their rights. He stayed until 1915, during which time he formulated his strategy of satyagraha (devotion to the truth/non-violent direct action) in the course of Indian and other workers' protests against government policies.

3 In 1923, Quaker botanist Will Fox (later a clerk of the Yearly Meeting) undertook a study of land use in the Transkei on behalf of the Chamber of Mines. He found conclusively, only a decade after the 1913 Land Act, that settled agriculture at the necessary density of population had already degraded the land to the point of soil erosion, and that extreme poverty and malnutrition were inevitably prevalent. (Francis William Fox & Douglas Back, *A Preliminary Survey of the Agricultural and Nutritional Problems of the Ciskei and Transkeian Territories with Special Reference to Their Bearing on the Recruiting of Labourers for the Gold Mining Industry*. Historical Papers Research Archive, University of the Witwatersrand, Johannesburg, South Africa, 1923).

4 The World Bank shows that South Africa today still has the biggest Gini coefficient in the world (i.e., the largest income gap between its poorest and wealthiest inhabitants). World Population Review, https://worldpopulationreview.com/country-rankings/gini-coefficient-by-country. Accessed 12 February 2022.

5 Holtz' letter is quoted by Hope Hay Hewison, *Hedge of Wild Almonds: South Africa, the 'Pro-Boers' & the Quaker Conscience*, London: James Curry, 1989, p. 9. Other people who attended Meetings included another member of the company staff, Philip Schols and 'a black man Philip Brutton and his son Pan Hertog and Flores Brand these are freemen who dwell in the town'. It is not clear from the context whether in using the term 'freemen' Holtz is referring to manumitted slaves, or to 'vrije burgers', ex-employees of the Dutch East India Company who remained at the Cape as settlers.

6 The second letter, from a Friend who signed himself 'Casimir', thanked Holme for books received and asked whether British Friends might help finance the printing at the Cape of some Bibles embellished by annotations by the French mystic, Madame de Guyon, which Casimir himself had translated into High Dutch.

7 Alan R. Booth, 'American Whalers in South African Waters' *South African Journal of Economics*, vol. 32:4, December 1964, pp. 278–282, https://onlinelibrary.wiley.com/doi/abs/10.1111/j.1813-6982.1964.tb02962.x

8 Robert Leach & Peter Gow, *Quaker Nantucket*, Nantucket, MA: Mill Hill Press, 1997.

9 Hewison, *Hedge of Wild Almonds*, p. 9.

10 Thomas Brady, *Life of Richard Gush – an African Emigrant*, York: York Friends' Tract Association, 1860.

11 James Backhouse, *Narrative of a Visit to the Mauritius and South Africa*, London and York: Hamilton, Adams & Co; John L. Linney, 1844.

12 Father-in-law of the explorer David Livingston.

13 Southern Africa Yearly Meeting website https://www.quakers.co.za/how-to-find-us. Accessed 12 February 2022.

14 Butler's sister Mary worked as a dispenser in the health centre in the 'native township' near Cradock and wrote in the *Midland News* about living conditions in the township. Another Cradock Friend, William Walpole Lidbetter, a cabinet maker and photographer, bequeathed to the 'native people of Craddock' funding for a community hall.

15 Butler papers, quoted by Tonsing, *The Quakers in South Africa*, p. 64.

16 John Tengo Jabavu (1859–1921) edited the first isiXhosa newspaper, *Isigidimi samaXhosa*, (the Xhosa Messenger) and later founded *Imvo Zabantsundu* (Black Opinion). He also founded Imbumba, a political movement which was a precursor to the ANC, currently the ruling party in South Africa. His son, Davidson Don Tengo Jabavu (1885–1959) was one of the first black university professors in South Africa, at Fort Hare. He was also active in the Temperance movement and one of the founders of the South African Institute for Race Relations in 1929. He was president of the All Africa Convention, an umbrella body for organisations opposed to segregation legislation in the 1930s. Innes Gumede was a doctor who qualified in Britain in 1930 and later worked in KwaZulu-Natal.

17 Saul Dubow, *Racial Segregation and the Origins of Apartheid 1919–1936,* London: Macmillan, 1989, p. 45, quoted by Tonsing, *The Quakers in South Africa*, p. 83.

18 Ibid.

19 Central & Southern Africa Yearly Meeting, *Living Adventurously, the Central & Southern Africa Book of Discipline,* Johannesburg: C&SAYM, 2009, p. 54.

20 General Meeting of the Society of Friends in South Africa: Memorandum on Inter-Racial Problems in South Africa, Cape Town, South Africa, 1931.

21 Letter from Don Davidson Jabavu to Olive Warner, 9 July 1928, quoted by Tonsing, *The Quakers in South Africa*, p. 105. Tonsing also quotes, on p. 107, from another letter, in which he explains that 'I prefer to keep quiet so that the proposed school may materialize or fail on its own merits and not as due to my opposition, lest I be cursed for ever having joined the Friends as a Society (for I did not know they became different people in South Africa)'. (Letter from Don Davidson Jabavu in September 1928 to Edward Garnett).

22 South African Institute for Race Relations, *A Survey of Race Relations in South Africa 1956–1957*, Johannesburg: SAIRR, 1958, Statement by Natal Quakers, 1956.

23 George Ellis, *The Quakers, a Brief Introduction*, 1980, http://www.math.uct.ac.za/sites/default/files/image_tool/images/32/Staff/Emeritus_Professors/Prof_George_Ellis/Overview/The%20Quakers.pdf

24 Bantu Stephen Biko (1946–1977) was an anti-apartheid activist, founder of the Black Consciousness movement and a community development organiser. He set up self-help, education and health

initiatives, particularly in Ginsberg township outside King Williamstown. He was 'banned' (effectively under house arrest) from 1973 and was murdered in police custody in 1977.

25 Nomzamo Winifred Madikizela-Mandela (1936–2018) was the second wife of President Nelson Mandela. She was banished to the town of Brandfort in the Orange Free State from 1977 to 1985, where she helped to set up a creche, a clinic and home industry initiatives for women.

26 Mary Burton, *The Black Sash; Women for Justice and Peace*, Johannesburg: Jacana, 2015.

27 Central & Southern Africa Yearly Meeting, 'Testimony, Shelagh M Willett', *C&SA YM 2016 Public Minutes 4.1*, https://www.quakers.co.za/wp-content/uploads/2016/06/YM-2016-Minutes-Public-FINAL-0602.pdf. Accessed 12 February 2022.

28 Robynne Rogers Healey, 'Conflict between Friends: Southern African Quakers' Critique of AFSC's Approach to End Apartheid', in Ross, David R., and Michael T. Snarr (eds.) *Quakers, Politics and Economics*; Quakers and the Disciplines, vol. 5, Longmeadow, MA, Philadelphia, PA, Windsor, CT: Friends Association for Higher Education, 2018, pp. 235–260, p. 236.

29 Ibid., p. 241.

30 In 1912 London Yearly Meeting had become alert to the government's plan to introduce national conscription in the colonies as a precursor to conscription in England. With advice from London Yearly Meeting, South African Quakers were able to insert a modicum of protection for faith-based conscientious objectors into the 1912 Defence Act.

31 In his letter to the commanding officer of the Witwatersrand Command Headquarters, Richard Steele explained: 'As a Christian, I strive to live a life which is pleasing to Jesus Christ. I have come to the conclusion that . . . military service is incompatible with my Christian convictions. I see war as being the most overt form of violence. I believe that violence is the antithesis of love and love is at the very centre of the Christian way of life. I want to be a peacemaker here in South Africa. I want to be used by God in the process of reconciliation between the peoples of our land so that we may live together in true peace – a peace undergirded by justice and righteousness. The principles of Christ-like love and non-violence are absolutely central to my Christianity and to myself'. Quoted in Central & Southern Africa Yearly Meeting, *Living Adventurously, the Central & Southern Africa Book of Discipline,* Johannesburg: C&SAYM, 2009, p. 82.

32 Hendrik W. Van der Merwe, *The James Backhouse Lecture 2001: Reconciling Opposites; Reflections on Peacemaking in South Africa,* Australia Yearly Meeting of the Religious Society of Friends (Quakers), 2001.

33 Latterly titled the Centre for Conflict Resolution.

34 From 1982, Hendrik and his wife Maritjie hosted Winnie Mandela when she went to Cape Town to visit her husband Nelson, later the first president of post-apartheid South Africa, who had been imprisoned for life in 1962 for his part in the liberation struggle.

35 John Harding, 'Help for Quaker Service in the Cape', *The Friend* 17 April 1987.

36 Cape Town Peace Centre, https://www.peacecentre.org.za/. Accessed 12 February 2022.

37 See, e.g., Central & Southern Africa, *Statement on the Failed Insurrection and Civil Unrest in South Africa*, August 2021; see also *Quaker News* (2014–present), all at https://www.quakers.co.za/publications/. Accessed 12 February 2022.

38 Central & Southern Africa Yearly Meeting, *Epistle of the Quaker Community in Southern Africa Yearly Meeting 2021*, https://www.quakers.co.za/epistle-of-the-quaker-community-in-southern-africa-yearly-meeting-2021. Accessed 12 February 2022.

39 World Population Review, *Crime Rate by Country*, https://worldpopulationreview.com/country-rankings/crime-rate-by-country.

40 Ibid.

41 In the words of Samuel Snipes, a visitor from Friends World Committee for Consultation to South Africa in the 1970s: 'I have never known so much accomplished by so few Quakers'. Samuel M. Snipes, *Report of Samuel M. Snipes on Trip to Southern African Yearly Meeting on Behalf of Friends World Committee: August–September 1979*, p. 1. File K.2.2, Quaker Collection. University of Cape Town. Manuscripts and Archives, Cape Town. Quoted by Healey, 'Conflict between Friends, p. 237. There were only about a hundred Quakers in South Africa at that time.

References

Backhouse, *Narrative of a Visit to the Mauritius and South Africa*. London and York: Hamilton, Adams & Co; John L. Linney, 1844

Booth, Alan R, 'American Whalers in South African Waters' *South African Journal of Economics*, vol. 32:4, December 1964, pp. 278–282 https://onlinelibrary.wiley.com/doi/abs/10.1111/j.1813-6982.1964.tb02962.x

Brady, Thomas, *Life of Richard Gush – an African Emigrant*. York: York Friends' Tract Association, 1860

Burton, Mary, *The Black Sash; Women for Justice and Peace*. Johannesburg: Jacana, 2015

Cape Town Peace Centre. https://www.peacecentre.org.za/. Accessed 12 February 2022

Central & Southern Africa Yearly Meeting, *Living Adventurously, the Central & Southern Africa Book of Discipline*. Johannesburg: C&SAYM, 2009

Central & Southern Africa Yearly Meeting, 'Testimony, Shelagh M Willett' *C&SA YM 2016 Public Minutes 4.1*. https://www.quakers.co.za/wp-content/uploads/2016/06/YM-2016-Minutes-Public-FINAL-0602.pdf. Accessed 12 February 2022

Central & Southern Africa Yearly Meeting, *Epistle of the Quaker Community in Southern Africa Yearly Meeting 2021*. https://www.quakers.co.za/epistle-of-the-quaker-community-in-southern-africa-yearly-meeting-2021. Accessed 12 February 2022

Central & Southern Africa, *Statement on the Failed Insurrection and Civil Unrest in South Africa*, August 2021. https://www.quakers.co.za/publications/. Accessed 12 February 2022

Dubow, Saul, *Racial Segregation and the Origins of Apartheid 1919–1936*. London: Macmillan, 1989

Ellis, George, *The Quakers, a Brief Introduction*, 1980. http://www.math.uct.ac.za/sites/default/files/image_tool/images/32/Staff/Emeritus_Professors/Prof_George_Ellis/Overview/The%20Quakers.pdf

Fox, Francis William & Douglas Back, *A Preliminary Survey of the Agricultural and Nutritional Problems of the Ciskei and Transkeian Territories with Special Reference to Their Bearing on the Recruiting of Labourers for the Gold Mining Industry*. 1923. Historical Papers Research Archive, University of the Witwatersrand, Johannesburg, South Africa

Harding, John, 'Help for Quaker Service in the Cape' *The Friend*, 17 April 1987

Healey, Robynne Rogers, 'Conflict between Friends: Southern African Quakers' Critique of AFSC's Approach to End Apartheid' *in* Ross, David R., and Michael T. Snarr (eds.) *Quakers, Politics and Economics*; Quakers and the Disciplines, vol. 5, Longmeadow, MA, Philadelphia, PA, Windsor, CT: Friends Association for Higher Education, 2018, pp. 235–260

Hewison, Hope Hay, *Hedge of Wild Almonds; South Africa, the 'Pro-Boers' and the Quaker Conscience*. London, James Curry, 1989

Madlala-Routledge, Nozizwe, 'Richard Gush Lecture 2006' *Speaking Truth to Power – Peace Is a Struggle*. Heronbridge, Gauteng, 2006

Richards, Rhys & Thierry Du Pasquier, 'Bay Whaling off Southern Africa, c. 1785–1805' *South African Journal of Marine Science*, vol. 8:1, 1989, pp. 231–250. https://doi.org/10.2989/02577618909504564

Snipes, S. M., 'Report of Samuel M. Snipes on Trip to Southern African Yearly Meeting on Behalf of Friends World Committee – August–September 1979' File K.2.2, Quaker Collection. University of Cape Town Manuscripts and Archives, Cape Town. P, Quoted by Healey, *Conflict between Friends*, 2018, p. 237

South African Quaker News. http://www.quakers.co.za/wp-content/uploads 2016-2022

Tonsing, Betty K., *The Quakers in South Africa*, Lewiston, Queenston, Lampeter: Edwin Mellen Press, 2002

Van der Merwe, Hendrik W., *The James Backhouse Lecture 2001: Reconciling Opposites; Reflections on Peacemaking in South Africa*, Australia Yearly Meeting of the Religious Society of Friends (Quakers), 2001

World Population Review, *Crime Rate by Country*. https://worldpopulationreview.com/country-rankings/crime-rate-by-country

World Population Review, *South Africa Gini Coefficient*. https://worldpopulationreview.com/country-rankings/gini-coefficient-by-country. Accessed 12 February 2022

4

QUAKERS IN BOLIVIA

The Beginning of Bolivian Friends

Emma Condori Mamani

Introduction

The Bolivian Quaker community arose in 1919. Friends missionaries from the United States evangelized and preached to Bolivians who mainly belonged to the indigenous Aymara community of the Bolivian highlands The pioneer missionaries who arrived in Bolivia that year were Emma Morrow and Mattie (Matilde) Blount, both graduates of the Union Bible Seminary in Indiana; and William (Guillermo) Abel from California, a graduate of Hunting Park Training School for Christian Workers (now Azusa Pacific University). The missionaries had to cope with some challenges in Bolivia, including the traditional Aymara religion, the dominance of the Roman Catholic church, and the language barrier (many Bolivians spoke only Aymara). In spite of the troubles in Bolivia, the missionaries witnessed how God touched the souls of Bolivians who testified about their encounter with God experientially, just as George Fox did in the seventeenth century. For instance, in her letter, missionary Emma E. Canaday said there is "a need for missionaries in three different centers. There are more people than trees and so many are in spiritual darkness. . . . One of them could neither read nor write but she had an 'Open Heaven' at the end of the road" (Central Yearly Meeting of the Friends Church, 1952:34). As a result of this mission work and spiritual awakening among Bolivians, Friends in Bolivia became an important Quaker community within the Religious Society of Friends.

When Friends missionaries started their work during the growth of the Bolivian Protestant church, they encountered Bolivians living in extreme poverty. Several Protestant movements were already working in Bolivia before 1919, and at that time, the Roman Catholic Church obligated Aymara people to tithe in honor of one of the Catholic saints; this further increased their poverty. Many Bolivian subsistence farmers did not own property because of the Bolivian feudal system (Stansell, 2009:210). Despite the fact that Friends missionaries spoke Spanish but not Aymara, they found ways to communicate. Ron Stansell says that missionary Jack L. Willcuts "threw himself into preaching through interpreters who translated from English to Spanish and to Aymara during his first months as a missionary in Bolivia" (Stansell, 2009:211). Not only the homemade clothes of the Aymaras were fascinating for the missionaries: so was their behavior and attitude moulded by colonialist life. A missionary wrote, "There's Pedro, steady and mild. He looks as though he were grinning all the time, even when he isn't!" (Cammack,

DOI: 10.4324/9780429030925-6

1966:11). Colonial oppression made Bolivian people serious and timid. Thus, Bolivian people's suffering increased the missionaries' commitment to their ministry.

Protestant Christianity meant hope for Bolivians living an oppressed life. Missionary Esther Smith, a member of California Friends Yearly Meeting, visited Bolivia in 1929 and observed that Aymaras were "mistreated, withdrawn, and cut off from the mainstream of Bolivian society" (Stansell, 2009:208). Bolivians wanted to hear more about the Gospel, so missionaries offered the word of God eagerly. For example, missionary Jack L. Willcuts gave sermons on "'Christ the Truth,' 'Christ the Liberator,' and 'Christ the Good Shepherd'" (Stansell, 2009:211). Friends missionaries often narrated to their families and Friends in the United States how Aymaras testified that the Lord was their Savior and the Holy Spirit searched their souls. But "many still need the gospel" (Central Yearly Meeting of the Friends Church, 1951:34). Furthermore, Friends missionaries not only taught but also helped to build schools, and some missionaries assisted Bolivians as doctors. Thus, Aymara believers understood Christianity as a way of life when they saw the missionaries' work for education and healthcare.

These missionaries spread the Gospel in Bolivia in spite of many struggles. Missionary Phyllis Cammack wrote, "The people are underprivileged and eager, receptive to the gospel message. The seed is planted and frosty watered. It sprouts and grows, but not without the frost of persecution and trouble" (Cammack, 1966:13). The Bolivian Friends community was growing even though "during much of the 1930s, Bolivia was at war with Paraguay and new converts were either pressed into the military or went into hiding" (Stansell, 2009:208). In addition, political instability and Catholic persecution seemed endless in the country. But in 1938 one of the main Friends Church buildings, Max Paredes Church of Iglesia National Evangélica Los Amigos (INELA) Yearly Meeting, was dedicated and opened in the city of La Paz. Thus, the INELA Yearly Meeting, Santidad Amigos Yearly Meeting, and Amigos Central Yearly Meeting have grown strongly and widely since the 1920s both in rural and urban areas.

Iglesia Evangélica Misión Boliviana de "Santidad Amigos" Yearly Meeting was started with churches in rural areas in 1919. The missionaries who established this yearly meeting came from Union Bible Seminary in Westfield, Indiana, which was run by Westfield Monthly Meeting, but there were splits between 1924 and 1926 among Gurneyite Meetings. On January 31, 1924, Union Monthly Meetings of Friends was founded, which became part of the Central Yearly Meeting of Friends on September 17, 1926 (Central Yearly Meeting of the Friends Church, 1976:11). So, the seminary came under the care of this yearly meeting.

This seminary, where students were trained to be ministers and missionaries, is now called Union Bible College and Academy. Bible teacher William Smith (1872–1964) managed the seminary until he died. He studied at the Quaker school Cleveland Bible Institute (now Malone University), where one day he was sanctified after praying on his knees. "He testified to the fact that the Holy Ghost had come into his life, and he ever after pointed back to that occasion as the time when he was sanctified" (Smith, 1982:28). Smith shared his belief about sanctification at the seminary and encouraged seminary students to daily Bible study and pray. Therefore, the students sought to walk in a sanctified life and devote their lives to the service of the Lord, especially in the mission field.

Emma Morrow (1885–1973) studied and worked at the Union Bible Seminary. She "expressed a call to be a missionary in South America" at the seminary in August 1918 in a meeting worship (Union Bible College, 2011:58). She had been an elementary school teacher there since 1911. For Morrow, the mission field in Bolivia was new; she "had no knowledge of the language[s], . . . and was about to begin a work among antagonistic Roman Catholics" (Central Yearly Meeting of the Friends Church, 1976:66). She trusted in God, though. At the beginning, there was not a room for her on the ship to South America, but she kept praying about her delayed trip. In February 1919 the senior seminarian Mattie Blount "told of her call to go with Emma Morrow to South America" as a missionary (Union Bible College, 2011:58). As soon as Mattie finished her schooling and the funds were raised, they left Westfield for New Orleans by train on April 13, 1919, and then sailed from New Orleans to South America. Once there, they traveled by train to Lake Titicaca and then crossed from Peru to Bolivia by boat. Then they took a train from the lake to La Paz. Finally, "they arrived [at noon] in the city La Paz, Bolivia on May 14th" (Central Yearly Meeting of the Friends Church, 1976:66). Morrow was 34 years old that year. In 1921 she and the missionary Walter Langston married. She served God in the mission field for 40 years. The Aymara people welcomed her as their sister for those years. They loved and respected her because she ate simple traditional meals with them and took care of them in spite of the culture, where a woman was hardly recognized as a leader. During this time, she went to the United States only once for a treatment for goiter. In 1959, her husband died. In 1962, when she was 77 years old, she returned from her mission field to the United States. She died at age 88 in Kokomo, Indiana.

Blount and Morrow carried on the mission field work in La Paz. Dorcas Seawell, the daughter of missionaries Alva and Mabel Hinshaw, says that Emma and Mattie started holding outdoor worship on the streets together with two independent US Friends missionaries: Florence Smith, a Friends missionary from Kansas Yearly Meeting, and William Abel, a Native American Friend who attended a Friends school in California. Seawell stated, "They had an average of one hundred people listening every night. Some were regular attenders" (Seawell, 199–?:25). Morrow and Blount had been working by themselves for six months when they welcomed Friends missionary Alva O. Hinshaw and his family at the train station in La Paz.

Alva O. Hinshaw (1888–1953) grew up as a Christian child in Kansas. He married Sarah Mabel Eisenhour on June 4, 1910, and in 1914 they moved with their two children to Westfield, where he would study at Union Bible Seminary because of his deep spiritual encounter with God. Seawell says that her father was baptized with the Holy Spirit. That day he "yielded one area after another of his life to God's control and promised the Lord he would preach the gospel" (Seawell, 199–?:27). In 1916 he finished his studies but stayed at the seminary because he was helping with the press work. There he heard about Bolivia from professor of missions Ellen Briles. She mentioned that "South America was called 'the Neglected Continent'" (Seawell, 199–?:34). The Hinshaw family got support from the school community at the seminary for the trip to Bolivia. In October 1919, Alva and Mabel, along with their four children, Basil, Alice, Dorcas, and baby Esther, boarded a ship for Panama from New Orleans. From Panama they traveled to Peru. The family suffered from altitude sickness as they crossed Lake Titicaca at 12,500 feet above sea level. Finally, they arrived in La Paz at 10:00 PM after a five-week trip.

Friends missionaries felt led to establish a mission station in the northern part of Bolivia. "Having heard that there was no [mission] work in Sorata [Friends missioners] set out for that city which is located in a beautiful valley" (Central Yearly Meeting of the Friends Church, 1976:67). It used to be a one-day trip to get to Sorata. During their second trip there, they bought a hotel with 20 rooms, which would provide them enough room for bedrooms, classrooms, a worship room and a printing press shop. They moved to Sorata in November 1920. They traveled by car from La Paz to the town of Achacachi, and from there they rode mules to Sorata, which is located on the slopes of Bolivia's highest snow-capped mountains. When they opened the worship room's door, local farmers and miners came. Seawell says, "After that the missionaries sang for several nights in a rather informal service. Soon there were as many as 40 people coming in, while others listened on the outside. Some sat on trunks and boxes but there were not enough seats for everyone" (Central Yearly Meeting of the Friends Church, 1976:50).

The missionaries took turns giving sermons because they had two worship services on Sundays and two more services during the week.

In 1921 Walter E. Langston arrived at the new mission station in Sorata. Langston (1875–1959) was born near Dublin, Indiana, and owned a farm in Idaho. He experienced being born again in one of the revival worship gatherings. After this experience, he felt compelled to go to Nazarene Bible School and later to Union Bible Seminary. Once he got to Bolivia, he preached with the help of an interpreter, as he was learning Spanish. On November 14, 1921, he and Miss Emma Morrow got married. Bolivians highlighted their married life, saying "they respected each other, and lived like saints. Their lives were an example to follow for the brethren."[1] The Langstons did not have any children, so they worked a lot at the mission field.

Soon the missionaries planted Friends churches in and around Sorata. But the local Catholic priest was against them, so people threw straw mixed with mud on the missionaries. Seawell wrote, "As the congregation in Sorata increased, opposition grew" (Seawell, 199–?:65). Nevertheless, more missionaries arrived in Sorata and Achacachi: Emma Canaday, Esther Hunt, Imogene Hendrickson, Lola Thornburg, Mary Morrow, James Fulton and his wife Grace, Eunice Riley, James Price, and Joseph Enyart. This yearly meeting was established on May 7, 1970, and Emma Canaday was its first general executive (and now president). She led the first yearly meeting gathering in Achacachi during December 6–8, 1971. Achacachi is the headquarters of this yearly meeting, where the representatives of the eight sub-yearly meetings of Santidad Amigos (Holiness Friends) Yearly Meeting gather each December.

The beginning of the INELA Yearly Meeting was in 1919. The independent missionary William Abel from the United States and Juan Ayllon, who was Bolivian, started this yearly meeting. The mission station for this yearly meeting was mainly located in La Paz. Today the INELA-Bolivia Yearly Meeting is a prominent Protestant church.

The missionary Abel was born on the San Pascual Indian Reservation in California. At Ramona Friends Church in California he was saved, saying, "I take Christ as my personal Savior" (Hibbs, 1976:4). He felt led to be a missionary and received training for this purpose at Huntington Park Bible Training School (now Azusa Pacific University). Abel had been a missionary to the Philippines for 11 years before he "finally chose Bolivia as a neglected field for colportage itinerating" (for being taking part of missions fields) and traveled to Bolivia in 1919 (Hibbs, 1976:5). For some months Abel preached and played hymns on his guitar on the streets of La Paz. On one such occasion, he met Juan Ayllon, a young Aymara. Juan helped him with the meetings for worship, but after a few weeks Abel got smallpox and succumbed to the disease when he was 47 years old. He handed the work of the Lord to Juan Ayllon.

Juan Ayllon was born in 1900. He felt that Bolivian people needed the Gospel. The missionary Ralph Chapman wrote, "From early childhood [Ayllon] enjoyed helping in open air street meetings. Upon his conversion, under the ministry of William Abel, Juan Ayllon saw the need for preparation in a Bible School" (Hibbs, 1976:3). On November 25, 1920, he left Bolivia in order to study at the Bible Training School (now Berea Bible School) in Chiquimula, Guatemala. His journey by ship from Peru took more time than he planned, but finally he arrived in Chiquimula, Guatemala, on March 9, 1921.

Ayllon returned to Bolivia in 1924 to continue the mission work that was started by Abel. When he graduated from Bible Training School, he married Tomasa Valle, who was from Honduras and attending that school. The young couple held a worship service in a rented small room in La Paz. Also they "went out on the streets preaching and giving out tracts . . . . More people accepted the Lord" (Haines, 2011:118). They had not only converts in the city but also rural areas. They were supported by the Guatemalan Friends for this mission work at the beginning.

The mission field in Bolivia became part of the Oregon Yearly Meeting (now Northwest Yearly Meeting), founded in 1893 on the Pacific coast by William Hobson and some Orthodox and Gurneyite Friends. The missionary Ruth Esther Smith, who was the superintendent of the Friends mission in Guatemala, visited Bolivia in 1929. She felt that mission work in Bolivia needed more support, so in 1930 she sent a letter to Oregon Yearly Meeting requesting them to take over the Friends mission in Bolivia. Ron Stansell says, "The letter was accepted at Yearly Meeting in 1930 and it was approved that Oregon Friends adopt Bolivia as a field for ministry" (Stansell, 2009:207). Thus, this yearly meeting sent missionaries to Bolivia for many years.

Friends at this yearly meeting felt called to do missionary service in several countries. For example, in 1930 they appointed Carroll and Doris Tamplin as their first missionaries to La Paz, Bolivia. The Tamplins had already served as missionaries for four years in Guatemala. They arrived in La Paz on February 27, 1931, and met Juan Ayllon and the new converts there. The missionaries gave sermons in Spanish and had someone interpret their sermons into Aymara until 1944. At that time the missionaries learned basic Aymara by living and working among the Aymara people. Preaching and giving out Christian literature on the streets were done often. Carrol Tamplin wrote, "We have believers in at least 12 cities and villages" (Chapman, 1980:6). Thus, many Aymara people converted to Quakerism as the first Bolivian mission staff (the Tamplins, the Howard and Julia Pearson family, Helen Cammack, and Estel Gulley) worked for the Lord.

Missionary Helen Cammack arrived in Bolivia in 1932 and helped to establish Friends schools for Bolivians. She had taught elementary school in the United States before she went to Bolivia. She wrote a curriculum for Bolivian Friends Schools. Friends missionaries did not offer elementary schools as an evangelistic outreach, but they wanted to educate children who were attending their Friends churches because there were no public schools available. Jack Willcuts wrote about this school approach: "We have never started schools apart from the church being planted previously" (Wagner, 1970:106). Hence, Cammack's work in education helped a lot for Bolivian Quakers before she died in La Paz in 1944.

In the early INELA church, missionaries from Oregon Yearly Meeting provided education to Bolivians and encouraged strong leadership among Bolivian Friends. After 1963 Bolivian Friends were running the Friends schools. According to C. Peter Wagner, Friends missionaries developed the largest Aymara church and the third-largest Bolivian denomination, as a result of focusing on a monocultural church (Wagner, 1970:98). Thus, the INELA-Bolivia Yearly Meeting was well established due to the devoted work of missionaries in preaching the Gospel and to the education opportunities given to Bolivians.

The third Quaker community founded in 1919 by other friends missionaries from Union Bible Seminary is Amigos Central Yearly Meeting. This seminary sent missionaries who had a deep understanding about people living in an oppressed country. At that time, most Bolivians were not allowed to attend schools and had little access to health care and food. This knowledge helped missionaries to obey God's calling to go to Bolivia, and they worked for many years at this yearly meeting.

Union Bible Seminary was established on January 7, 1861, in Westfield, Indiana. In 1911, Friends at this seminary approved a school to train students to be ministers and missionaries. That year, William M. Smith, who was a young Bible and prophecy teacher, accepted to be the principal of this school. In September of 1911, the school offered a two-year course. Every day there was prayer at the end of class. It was written, "The first prayer meeting at the Friends Church in Westfield after the Seminary opened was almost carried off by the students" (Wagner, 1970:51). Students received training under the school's philosophy that says, "We need a ministry that is converted, sanctified, called, anointed, educated in the Bible, who love

God supremely and souls passionately, and who have the love of the world taken out" (Wagner, 1970:52). The seminary raised funds for mission work through its periodical called *The Friends Minister* (later *The Gospel Minister*). Dorcas Seawell wrote about how the seminary gave a lot of support to the first missionaries to Bolivia in 1919 (Seawell, 199–?:35). Thus, the seminary students had strong support for their ministry at the spiritual and economic levels.

More missionaries traveled to work in Bolivia. In May 1926, Walter R. Rhoades joined a 1923 graduate Perry F. Rich for the trip to support the missionary Alva O. Hinshaw in Riberalta, in the department (state) of Beni, Bolivia. Later, on June 4, 1929, Mattie Blount and Mary Barnard arrived in Bolivia. They and the missionary Rhoa Warrick went to Coroico in order to start a new mission station. Mary recounts her two-day journey to Coroico by *autocarril* (an auto that runs on rails) and mule, and how people there welcomed them because the locals "never had anyone come to live among them before" as a missioner (Enyart, 1978:21). Later, Arthur Enyart and his brother Paul C. Enyart, along with 1930 graduate William S. Barnard, traveled to Coroico on December 17, 1930. Paul and Mary Barnard were married in Bolivia, and they stayed at the mission station in Coroico for a long time in their first missionary term. In 1941, this couple returned to Bolivia with their five children and served an eight-year term.

Amigos Central Yearly Meeting was the result of the mission work done in the mission stations of Coroico, Irupana, Coripata, Chulumani, and La Paz. Many missionaries' children returned to Bolivia as missionaries. It is written, "And still another generation follows – Grace Merrill, daughter of William Barnard, and Paul Enyart Jr., son of Mary (Barnard) Enyart are serving in the mission [in the late 1960s and early 1970s]" (Enyart, 1978:77). Friends churches planted in Riberalta, Coroico, Irupana, Coripata, Chulumani and La Paz formed the Amigos Central Yearly Meeting. In the 1980s, Bolivian Friends had already been leading their church work, Bible schools and seminaries.

Conclusion

Bolivia, a huge Quaker community, was seen as a hopeful mission field by the early Friends missionaries in 1919. Bolivians received with gratitude the Gospel preached by many missionaries because Bolivia was a country where people were oppressed. These missionaries, who were grounded in the love and faith of God, offered the good news about Jesus Christ, who could redeem them in their body and soul. Once the first three yearly meetings were established, the work in the Lord's field kept growing among Bolivians. In the 1990s, Quakers gathered for yearly meeting sessions in the thousands; they ran the most successful Friends schools, as well as Bible schools. The Bolivian Friends church growth has been due to Bolivians' encounters with God experientially, and they serve God faithfully by spreading the word of God. Therefore, the mission work done by the Friends missionaries bore fruit in Bolivia for the glory of the Lord.

Note

1 Historia de la IEMIBSA (translated text) (La Paz, Bolivia: Imprenta Vargas, 2014:77).

References

Phyllis Cammack, *Missionary Moments* (Newberg, OR: The Barclay Press, 1966)
Central Yearly Meeting of the Friends Church, *Minutes of Central Yearly Meeting of the Friends Church*, 1951
Central Yearly Meeting of the Friends Church, *Minutes of Central Yearly Meeting of the Friends Church*, 1952
Central Yearly Meeting of the Friends Church, *History of Central Yearly Meeting of the Friends Church* (Westfield, IN: The Meeting, 1976)

Ralph Chapman, *Bolivian Friends: From Mission to Yearly Meeting* (Newberg, OR, 1980)

Mary H. Enyart, *Sow in Tears . . . Reap in Joy* (Shoals, IN: Old Paths Tract Society, Inc., 1978)

Marie Haines, *Lion-Hearted Quakers* (Newberg, OR: Oregon Yearly Meeting Press, 2011)

Iverna Hibbs, *From One to Multiplication, Oregon Yearly Meeting in Bolivia 1919–1962* (Newberg, OR: Williams Printing, 1976)

Dorcas Seawell, *This One Thing I Do* (Shoals, IN: Old Paths Tract Society, Inc., 199–?)

Simeon O. Smith, *Biography of William Martin Smith: And History of Union Bible Seminary, Inc.* (Westfield, IN: Union Bible Seminary, 1982)

Ron Stansell, *Missions by the Spirit* (Newberg, OR: Barclay Press, 2009)

Union Bible College and Academy, *A Heritage to Remember and A Heritage to Keep* (Westfield, IN: Jostens Printing & Publishing, 2011)

C. Peter Wagner, *The Protestant Movement in Bolivia* (South Pasadena, CA: The William Carey Library, 1970)

5

EUROPEAN QUAKERS

Hans Eirik Aarek

History of European Friends

Quakerism originated in England in the middle of the seventeenth century. In 1647, George Fox had his life-changing experience that Jesus Christ could speak to him in his condition. In 1652, he had a vision on Pendle Hill in Westmoreland, England, and spoke to a gathering of 1000 seekers at Firbank Fell. This year is regarded as the beginning of the Quaker movement. This happened in the middle of great political uproar in Britain: the civil war from 1642, the Cromwell rule from 1649 and the Restoration in 1660.

During these years, Quakers in Britain developed their spiritual basis, organisational structure and practice. The collection of *Queries and Advices*, giving a condensed statement of Quaker belief and practice, was first circulated in 1656. The Declaration of the Peace Testimony to Charles II was published in 1661. The Valiant Sixty, 60 men and women eager to spread the Quaker message, travelled across Britain and abroad in the 1650s and 1660s. Even if some adjustment to the wider society took place after the first revolutionary years, suffering, imprisonment and persecution occurred until the Toleration Act of 1689. Even so, the first Yearly Meeting (YM) was held in 1668, and Robert Barclay's *Apology*, published in 1676, gave a systematic theological exposition of the Quaker faith.

Quakerism was soon exported to countries outside the British Isles. The most important growth took place in North America from 1656 and made the United States an important arena for Quaker life and expression, of which the establishment of Pennsylvania in 1681 was a clear statement. The period 1647–1827 was the transatlantic and trans-European period, with one single Quaker theological culture in which London YM was the centre. (From 1995 the name was changed to Britain YM.) The American schisms from 1827 meant an end to unified Quakerism and were challenging to Quakers on both sides of the Atlantic (Dandelion 2007, pp. 11–79).

On June 22, 1897, American Quaker Rufus Jones and English Friend John Wilhelm Rowntree climbed Mount Schilthorn (elev. 2970 m) in Mürren, Switzerland, and observed the morning star over Mont Blanc. This was the first meeting of the two architects of liberal modern Quakerism, and a deep Friendship and strong determination to cooperate to reform Quakerism grew forth on this tour. They wondered if the morning star symbolised a blessing of their concern: "And I will give him the Morningstar" (Revelation 2:28; Jones 1921, p. 997). The Quakerism they promoted came to be the main form of Quakerism in modern Europe.

DOI: 10.4324/9780429030925-7

Relation to Continental and Nordic Europe

Quaker missionaries travelled on the European continent from the very beginning, including Scandinavia and Mediterranean countries, trying to approach the Pope and even reach Jerusalem. The aim was to spread the good tidings to the whole world. Some of the expeditions met resistance and had severe consequences including imprisonment, torture and death. Destinations closer to the UK were also visited. The Netherlands had extensive contact with British Friends. In 1677, George Fox, William Penn and Robert Barclay travelled to Europe and took part in founding a European YM in Amsterdam, gathering groups of Friends from Holland and northern Germany (Murphy 2019, pp. 122–123; Otto 1972, p. 112). This YM faded out about 1710, after years of persecution and emigration to America. The YMs with the longest unbroken history in continental Europe are found in Norway, established in 1818, and Denmark, dating back to 1875 (Aarek & Ryberg 2018, pp. 216–217).

From 1725 to 1825, Quietism, a religious movement originating in Europe in the seventeenth century, became dominant in the Quaker world. The Quietist period may be looked upon as a period of recession, but also allowed the development of spiritual sensibility and identity, characterised by strict internal control and a Society that isolated itself from the surrounding world (Jones 1921, pp. 32–103; Dandelion 2007, pp. 58–60).

The splits among Quakers that originated in America from 1827 had no great consequence in London YM, which managed to contain nearly all the differences and remain one YM. However, great changes appeared from the 1850s with the blossoming of Evangelical Quakerism. Old habits of dress and language disappeared. An ecumenical attitude developed and led to cooperation with other churches on social issues as peace, slavery and drink. Mission overseas in India, China and Africa took place, and Quakers eagerly took part in the great World Mission Conference in Edinburgh in 1910 (Stanley 2009).

This may have provided space for the next revolutionary change initiated by the Manchester Conference, 1895, which led to modern, liberal, unprogrammed Quakerism where the Meeting for Worship based in silence is fundamental. One of the main conclusions of the Conference was the need for education. This led to a concern for arranging adult schools and the establishment of Woodbrooke College in 1903. These changes were to have a significant impact on European Quakerism outside the British Isles. The All Friends Conference in 1920 was the beginning of internationalisation of Quakerism and a renewal of the peace testimony. The inter-war period also brought renewal and a strong growth of continental European Quakerism and at the same time brought new organisational structures (Kennedy 2001, pp. 404–414).

London YM as 'Mother Church' and Authority Structure in Quaker Europe

London YM was the first and oldest Quaker Society and by far the largest in membership. Britain YM still has strength both in regard to history, tradition, resources (both spiritual and financial) and membership.

For many years, London YM had control and power in relation to other Quaker groups. In the last part of the nineteenth century, Norway YM was expected to send a report to Continental Committee in London every year. Friends travelling in the ministry were 'released', supported and freed of other commitments in order to serve, and certified for mission by London YM. This was another aspect of the supervision of Quaker groups in Europe. When Quaker meetings grew forth in the inter-war period, new meetings were recognised by London YM, first as an Allowed Meeting, then as a Monthly Meeting under London YM and finally to become an independent YM. After the Second World War, British control was somewhat relaxed and gradually replaced by consultation, first by other European YMs and later the Europe and Middle East Section of the Friends World Committee for Consultation (EMES-FWCC; see the paragraph on 'FWCC' that follows).

The spiritual influence through basic literature was great. A bulk of classic Quaker books and pamphlets were translated into European languages. Through the years, London and later Britain YM's books of *Discipline, Faith and Practice* have been important resources and in recent years inspired several YMs to produce their own books of discipline that, in addition to traditional Quaker insights, would reflect their local faith and practice.

Woodbrooke College Serving Quakers Outside Britain

Developments in British Quaker culture and events greatly influenced what happened in mainland Europe. One of the most significant examples is Woodbrooke College. Already from its first years, Woodbrooke had students from continental and Nordic countries, who became important in spreading Quaker thought and modern, liberal Quakerism in their home countries. This applies in particular to the Netherlands and Norway. The *Vereniging Woodbrookers Barchem* was created in 1909–11 to provide adult education (Lignac 2007). In Norway, the YM was led into modern, liberal Quakerism with a strong interest in enlightenment or education of the public.

Through the years, a number of continental European Friends have attended courses at Woodbrooke. Today, a curriculum of shorter and more varied subjects makes it easier to attend. In addition, some courses are tailored for continental Friends, and the ambulant service 'Woodbrooke on the Road' may visit meetings in mainland Europe.

From 2007, Woodbrooke and the Europe and Middle East Section (EMES) have sponsored 'The Quaker in Europe', an online study project in several languages. The use of internet and webinar courses has grown, especially during the Covid-19 pandemic. In cooperation with the University of Birmingham, Woodbrooke offers-post graduate studies with MA and PhD tuition. In this way, Woodbrooke College is an indispensable centre for learning and inspiration for both British and continental European Quakers of all ages, Woodbrooke being another international actor besides and in cooperation with EMES.

International Cooperation Between Quaker Groups

After the First World War, British and American Quakers wanted to take part in the rebuilding and reconciliation work in Europe. Friends Service Council (FSC) and American Friends Service Committee (AFSC) had field workers placed in several European locations. British Quaker Carl Heath (1869–1950), a visionary and newcomer among Friends, was the architect and driving force in this work and built up a network of international Quaker activities which still serves as a model. While he started this work in Europe, he was secretary of FSC. His great idea was to establish Quaker Embassies or Centres in Europe for outreach and reconciliation work. The aim was that 'the centres should be growing points for the spirit' (Kennedy 2001, p. 418). After initial resistance, he had a breakthrough for his idea at London YM in 1918. The first centre was established in Paris in 1919. Other centres appeared in Berlin, Frankfurt, Nuremberg, Vienna, Geneva, Warsaw and Moscow, operating for various periods of time in the 1920s and 1930s (*Quaker Embassies* 1934, pp. 6–17).

As part of the work of these embassies, a series of conferences were held. The first in Elsinore in Denmark in August 1931, later the same year in Paris; in Amsterdam in 1933; and in Geneva and Prague in 1934. Considerable international activity took place during the years before the World Conference in 1937, especially among young European Friends. Youth Conferences were held in Brussels in 1928 and in Denmark in 1934. The many conferences were forerunners of the Friends World Committee for Consultation in 1937 (*Quaker Embassies* 1934, 17–19). This work was instrumental in building Quaker groups and constituting YMs in countries which had a history going back to the first century of Quakerism.

Over the years, London YM had been involved in the development of meetings in continental Europe. The establishment of the Quaker Centre in Berlin in 1920 was followed by the establishment of German YM in 1925 (Otto 1972, pp. 176–206). The founding of France YM in 1933 was preceded by a Quaker Centre in Paris in 1919, and the Quaker group in Geneva in 1920 was the forerunner of Switzerland YM in 1944. In addition to the YMs mentioned above, Netherlands YM was established in 1931 and Sweden YM in 1935 (Hollsing 2009, p. 38). Belgium and Luxembourg YM was established in 1976, and Finland YM changed from a Monthly Meeting under Sweden YM into a separate YM in 1992 (FWCC 2019).

FWCC

The work of Carl Heath, the Quaker Embassies and their networks and conferences made Friends aware of the need for more permanent structures for international cooperation. At the World Conference in Philadelphia in 1937, which has later been counted as 'The Second' after the All Friends Conference in 1920, a proposal to establish an international organisation to promote contact, cooperation and consultation was considered and adopted. In 1938, the Friends World Committee for Consultation (FWCC) held its first committee gathering at the eighth European Quaker Congress in Vallekilde in Denmark, and the foundations of two Sections (the American and the European) were laid. The ninth European Conference and second FWCC Committee Meeting took place in Geneva in August 1939.

The original name of the European Section was ENES (European and Near East Section), and was changed to EMES in 1992. FWCC expanded to include the Africa Section in 1971 and the Asia and West Pacific Section in 1985, while the North American Section from 1938 was expanded to include the whole of the Americas in the 1970s. The vision of FWCC was 'to Keep Friends connected and in touch with each other across the diverse spectrum of the Society' (FWCC 2019, p. 3). FWCC would soon take on considerable tasks.

After the Second World War, European YM in FWCC-ENES together with Friends Service Council and American Friends Committee again played an important role in reconstruction and reconciliation in Europe. In 1948, FWCC was recognised as an international nongovernmental organisation with General Consultative Status at the UN, and the Quaker Centres in Geneva and New York became known as Quaker United Nations Offices and central agents in international Quaker work together with the centres in Paris, Moscow and Vienna. In 1979, QCEA (Quaker Council for European Affairs) was founded in Brussels to work for peace and human rights in the European Union and the Council of Europe; it cooperates with EMES (FWCC 2019, pp. 65–66).

Modern European Quakerism – Current Situation

Today, Quaker groups are found in 25 of the 51 independent states in Europe and five in the Middle East. They are organised as Worship Groups, Monthly Meetings and Yearly Meetings, and the total number of members is about 25,000. The largest YMs are found on the British Isles: in Britain about 21,500 and in Ireland about 1500. Reports from EMES show that there are considerable fluctuations, especially in regard to the small groups. In 2019, ten Yearly Meetings, two Monthly Meetings, and 18 Worship Groups or Quaker contacts are recognised by EMES (FWCC 2019).

However, Quaker Europe is greater than the members of EMES. In recent years, Evangelical Quakers with pastors and programmed services have been established in six European countries. The largest group is found in Hungary with more than 4000 members; other groups are found in Albania, Croatia, Romania, Serbia and Ukraine. According to FWCC statistics, about 9% of Quakers in the world live in Europe and the Middle East (FWCC and EMES Annual Reports: http://fwcc.world/about-fwcc, https://fwccemes.org/journals-reports/).

Continental and Nordic Europe is a conglomerate of different languages, ethnic groups and nationalities, different religious confessions and political systems, which is also reflected in the various Quaker Meetings and groups whose characteristics often mirror national characteristics. The degree of difference is also influenced by the size of the group. Most of them are members of EMES or have a connection to EMES.

This poses a special challenge for European Quakers and is a central assignment for Quaker work and service. Europe's history, previously characterised by wars and conflicts – some closely connected to religion and religious schisms – has also been fertile soil for new political and religious thinking and movements. Much Quaker work has been to apply the Quaker Peace Testimony to current problems.

EMES: Cooperation, Intervisitation and Regional Conferences

EMES has fulfilled a more practical role for the manifold Quakers on the European continent than for the more homogeneous British Quakers. Much of the EMES work in Europe has been, and still is, about creating arenas and platforms for mutual cooperation and sharing of information.

In 1964, the ENES Annual Meeting in Berlin took an important step towards further European Quaker cooperation when they agreed to establish a European Section Service Council (ESSC) in support of FWCC-ENES' common involvement in the Kabylie project and coordination of later European service projects. In recent years, EMES has arranged annual Peace and Service Consultations for mutual information about work undertaken by the various YMs and their Peace and Service Committees. European Friends and YMs take on an array of practical humanitarian work, both locally and internationally (EMES 2019, p. 9).

Building external and internal relations has always been an important arena. This often takes the form of intervisitation among individual Friends as well as between sections of FWCC, and is of special significance to Young Friends. Individual Quaker representatives find that they carry more weight in ecumenical settings and in conferences on peace and environmental issues when they take part as representatives of the whole of FWCC-EMES.

European Quaker plurality has led to a general and growing interest in regional conferences and other meetings based on a common language or geographical proximity. The focus of these gatherings is fellowship and sharing rather than decision-making. One example of such regional conferences is Border Meetings, which are held on a regular basis bringing together Friends from Switzerland, Germany and France, and also between Friends from Austria and Hungary. New worship groups are coming into being on the Iberian Peninsula, and local Friends plan similar regional gatherings. EMES has supported these initiatives, while the groups are encouraged to become increasingly self-sustaining. One advantage of regional conferences is that travelling distances are reduced, resulting in savings of both time and money.

Changes in the 1990s

The most significant changes in the work of EMES were caused by the fall of the Berlin Wall in 1989 and the introduction of the Internet in the 1990s. These had a decisive impact on the life of Quaker groups in Europe. Small groups of Quakers have emerged in several of the former communist countries in Eastern Europe. The Internet has made it possible to provide knowledge of a variety of Quaker traditions.

The impression of EMES workers visiting eastern Europe in the 1990s was that the new religious and political freedom opened many new possibilities, but lack of knowledge and experience of democratic thinking and practice created some problems. The problems also reflected a lack of understanding of Quaker egalitarianism, founded on the theology of the 'priesthood of all believers', as well as the importance of faith as a basis for action (Aarek & Ryberg 2018, pp. 217–236).

In Poland, the Internet has enabled the formation of different meetings with varying faith profiles, some liberal, some conservative. The emergence of small Quaker groups in Eastern Europe has given rise to a new situation and a special concern, and has added an extra challenge to EMES workers in providing appropriate support, guidance and pastoral care (Aarek & Ryberg 2018, pp. 217–236). On the other hand, witnessing the enthusiasm and vitality of new small meetings, using their limited resources to keep meetings running, and eager to share with other seeking persons is an inspiration to established, traditional YMs.

Central European Gatherings started as a meeting place in the 1990s for both liberal and Evangelical Friends in Eastern and Central Europe and have grown to be an annual self-supporting event. During recent years they have developed in a more formal way, moving in the direction of a Monthly Meeting (EMES 2019, p. 17; FWCC 2019, p. 62).

Friends in Eastern Europe have initiated a variety of regional gatherings. In 2011, EMES sponsored a Russian-speaking gathering, and All Poland gatherings were arranged, starting in 2013 (Aarek & Ryberg 2018, p. 227).

In Russia the situation is special. Friends' House Moscow is an international charity organisation supporting Quakers in Russia. In Moscow there is also a Monthly Meeting connected to EMES. Given the political climate, it is important to distinguish between giving information and proselytising.

Even if Quakers in the Middle East, Palestine and Lebanon YM suffer from travel restrictions which make it difficult to arrange gatherings, Ramallah Friends and their Meeting House have an important function in receiving guests and informing them about the situation and their Quaker witness.

Generally speaking, gatherings and conferences are important for creating a living Quaker fellowship across borders. To attend larger gatherings of various kinds is important, especially for isolated Friends and small groups. To meet and share worship and take part in and experience the various expressions of Quaker witness is felt as inspirational learning for both seasoned Friends and newcomers. Travelling is a valuable part of the Quaker tradition of spiritual journeys that may involve deeply moving experiences or life-changing events that may result in instructive narratives of the Quaker way.

Technology

The Covid-19 pandemic led to a flowering of creative solutions. When people cannot meet physically, they have established new platforms for Quaker activities in the form of meetings for worship and for business, and study groups on the Internet, streamed meetings in which some people meet physically and other Friends take part from their computers. Woodbrooke College has presented a number of webinars instead of courses requiring physical presence. This will influence Quaker interaction in the future, also in a 'green' perspective of less travelling.

Children and Young Friends

European Quaker groups acknowledge the importance of integrating children and young people in their activities. This can be a challenge in small groups. In the larger YM gatherings, it is easier and more common to find a meaningful programme for young people and children. YMs also arrange all-age-gatherings.

European and Middle East Young Friends (EMEYF), was established in 1984 and is an autonomous organisation within EMES for Friends 18–35 years of age. EMEYF is a dispersed community making an exciting experimental group, testing Quaker faith, traditions and practices as well as creating good fellowship. EMES also arranges family gatherings (FWCC 2019, pp. 64–65).

Traditional arrangements for younger Friends were the Quaker Youth Pilgrimages started in the 1950s, supported by FWCC but now in a process of evaluation, and the Geneva Summer School, which started in 1954. Britain YM's youth gatherings also provide an opportunity for European Junior Friends to meet.

Special Features of Continental European Quakerism

Most of the Quaker Meetings in Europe are small. This makes the group dependent on the contribution of every member; consequently, more members are involved in committees and other work. This serves to strengthen fellowship and inclusion, as well as a feeling of responsibility towards the group. On the other hand, it gives room for individual initiatives and concerns that sometimes need serious discernment in order to be 'owned' by the whole group. Few of the offices are paid; most of the work is done on a voluntary basis.

Quakers in Europe and the Middle East used to belong within the liberal unprogrammed tradition, and this tradition is still is dominating. Most European YMs have had a solid history of about a century or more of building their identity as Liberal Quakers. However, most national groups have developed their own culture, influenced by special concerns and projects in their particular national religious context. Thus, continental European liberal Quakerism is different from the modern liberal Quakerism in Britain and the United States in the way that it is defined in relation to the dominating national and regional churches and personal experiences, as well as of dogmatic or evangelical, local, traditional Christianity, but it is also influenced by liberal revolutionary Christianity, often promoted by theologians inside the larger Churches.

Liberal unprogrammed Friends represent about 11% of Quakers in the world. In Europe, unprogrammed Friends outside Britain count for fewer than 1500 (Aarek & Ryberg 2018, table 12.1; https//en.wikipedia.org/wiki/Quakers Unprogrammed worship). Still, they feel strong because they are part of a tradition that goes back to the first century of Quakerism.

Summary

Quakerism has long roots in continental Europe, but activity has varied. Groups emerged and disappeared, partly due to political conditions and emigration. In the first centuries, international cooperation was accidental and limited to translation of Quaker publications into non-English languages and visits from British and American missionaries. From the beginning of the twentieth century, Liberal Quakerism was the new paradigm, strongly rooted in Woodbrooke College in England with students from many countries, who helped create a renewed interest in Quakerism in Europe.

The All Friends Conference in 1920 signified a new direction in Europe introducing stronger cooperation and communication and a dedication to work for peace and service. Refugee and relief work were carried out by AFSC and FSC. Carl Heath's work on Quaker Embassies or Centres and a series of conferences, was instrumental in creating functional Quaker networks throughout Europe. New YMs grew forth in Germany, France, Netherlands, Switzerland and Sweden, adding to the old YMs in Norway and Denmark. In 1937, Friends World Committee for Consultation was founded and a European and Near/Middle East Section established in 1938.

After the Second World War, extensive reconciliation and reconstruction took place. A number of conferences were arranged, some of them creating bonds between East and West Europe. A big change happened in 1989 with the fall of the Berlin Wall and the opening up of former communist countries, resulting in the emergence of new, small unprogrammed Quaker groups as well as Evangelical Friends churches in these countries, followed up by EMES as a new area of commitment. Today this work is still important with support from YMs and small groups in the rest of Europe.

The vision of a renewal of Quakerism on the top of Schilthorn in the Alps came true in Europe, as YMs and other Quaker groups embraced a modern, liberal Quakerism led by London YM and with influence from Woodbrooke. Quakers in Europe still have a strong foothold in the liberal, unprogrammed tradition.

Bibliography

Aarek, Hans Eirik, and Ryberg, Julia H. "Quakers in Europe and the Middle East", 216–236. In: Angell, S. W. and Dandelion, P. (eds.) *The Cambridge Companion to Quakerism*. Cambridge: Cambridge University Press, 2018.

Dandelion, Pink. *An Introduction to Quakerism*. Cambridge: Cambridge University Press, 2007.

EMES. *Annual Report 2019*. Cambridge: Europe & Middle East Section, 2019.

FWCC. *Friends around the World. 2019 International Handbook and Directory*. London: Friends World Committee for Consultation, 2019.

Hollsing, Ingmar. *Stillhet och handling. Det svenska kväkersamfundets historia*. Skellefteå: Artos, 2009.

Jones, Rufus M. *The Later Periods of Quakerism*. In two volumes. London: Macmillan and Co., 1921.

Kennedy, Thomas. *British Quakerism 1860–1920. The Transformation of a Religious Community*. Oxford: Oxford University Press, 2001.

Lignac, D. *Verdieping & Beweging. 100 jaar Woodbrookers*. s.l.: Vereniging Woodbrookers Barchem, 2007.

Murphy, Andrew R. *William Penn. A Life*. Oxford: Oxford University Press. 2019.

Otto, Heinrich. *Werden und Wesen des Quäkertums und seine Entwicklung in Deutschland*. Wien: Sensen-Verlag, 1972.

Quaker Embassies. *A Survey of Friends' Service in Europe since 1919*. London: Friends Service Council, 1934.

Stanley, Brian. *The World Missionary Conference, Edinburg 1910*. Cambridge: William B. Eerdmans Publishing Company, 2009.

6

FRIENDS WORLD COMMITTEE FOR CONSULTATION, SECTION OF THE AMERICAS

Robin Mohr

Twenty-First Century: Experiments and Integration

In the twenty-first century, Friends World Committee for Consultation (FWCC) trains yearly meeting representatives to be better communicators, better listeners, and to develop the stamina to stay in difficult conversations without running away or escalating the conflict, in order to understand and communicate with people from different backgrounds, for the traditional religious purposes of peacemaking and evangelism. Section of the Americas (SoA) programs focus on developing these skills around diversity of language and theology, but these skills are transferable to other issues that divide people.

Structure

In the SoA, the Executive Committee serves as the board of directors, while the Finance Committee and Nominating Committee are separate entities.[1] The committees that plan and conduct the programmatic work are called Program Groups. The number and purpose of the Program Groups varies over time. The SoA groups its constituent yearly meetings into nine geographic regions, each including all the yearly meetings in the territory. Each region is assigned a volunteer to serve as regional coordinator to orient new representatives and foster ongoing communication between representatives of neighboring yearly meetings across the branches of Friends.

The Section Meetings are the largest conferences for the SoA, held every two years. Representatives are expected to participate in the bilingual business sessions held with full consecutive interpretation. All Friends are welcome to attend, including the worship, workshops, and small group activities.

The level of paid staff has varied over the years. In 2021, the full-time staff comprised an executive secretary, operations manager, and advancement manager in the United States plus a contracted coordinator of Latin American programs who works from Guatemala, and a collection of consultants and contractors around the Section.

In 2014, Gayle Matson, of North Pacific Yearly Meeting, and Noah Merrill, of New England Yearly Meeting, as members of the Executive Committee, and the author as executive secretary, led the Section through a series of strategic planning exercises. The resulting document, "Weaving the Tapestry 2015–2020,"[2] identified three priority issues for the SoA. The first was

DOI: 10.4324/9780429030925-8

addressing the growing polarization of society, in theology, in economics, and in politics. The second was improving the communication of the purpose and accomplishments of the Friends World Committee, telling the compelling story of FWCC. The third was to seek new funding streams for the support of the organization, its staff and programs, and to ensure that the first two were accomplished. In 2015, after the Section Meeting in Mexico City, the programmatic focus of the Section was reorganized along these lines.

Integration

In the twenty-first century, FWCC has returned to volunteer committees as working bodies rather than depending primarily on staff service. Advances in technology and bilingual skills made this a forward motion rather than a regression. The development of electronic conferencing technology, at first telephone based and later web based, enabled committees to meet virtually with increasing frequency and growing satisfaction in the experience. FWCC committees began meeting by telephone conference call around the turn of the century, as the technology became available in the United States.[3] Starting in 2012, the Executive Committee experimented with a series of web-based video conferencing applications. Around the same time, the Executive Committee minuted its commitment to the full integration of the committees of the Section, beginning with itself, as an intention to achieve greater inclusion and wider acceptance among yearly meetings throughout the Section.[4] In 2013, the first Latin American member of the Executive Committee was Kenya Casanova Sales, a bilingual Friend from Cuba Yearly Meeting. She had previously served on the FWCC Central Executive Committee.[5] The Section of the Americas also stopped meeting for business in even-numbered years, which had been held with no or minimal representation of Latin American yearly meetings.[6] SoA is the only international Quaker organization that conducts its business bilingually.

In 2013, the first monolingual Spanish speaker on the Finance Committee necessitated the translation of all financial reports and policies for the first time.[7] In 2015, the first non-English-speaking committee clerk was Velinda Landaverde, El Salvador Yearly Meeting, for the Convocations Program Group.[8] In 2016, the first non-English-speaking member of the Section Executive Committee was Timoteo Choque Vargas from the National Evangelical Friends Church (INELA) Bolivia.[9] In 2019, half the members of Finance Committee were primarily Spanish speakers, including the clerk, Rodolfo Hernandez from Guatemala Holiness Friends.[10]

Visitation

FWCC had organized speakers to travel across yearly meeting lines since its inception, as part of the long-standing tradition of Friends. The FWCC Traveling Ministry Corps launched in 2017.[11] This was the first attempt by FWCC to create a cohesive body of Friends across language, theology, and age who were equipped and financed to travel in the ministry. Four Friends from the United States and five from Bolivia were chosen for the first cohort. However, only three of the Bolivians were able to attend the training at the 2017 Section Meeting because of the US government visa restrictions. To avoid this difficulty, in 2018 the training was held in two locations: in Bolivia with Spanish-speaking Friends from Mexico, El Salvador, Guatemala, and Cuba in addition to Bolivians; and in Pennsylvania with English-speaking Friends, all from the United States. In 2019, a smaller bilingual cohort was trained at the Section Meeting in Missouri, and in 2020, separate trainings were again held in the United States and Peru, and an online training that incorporated the Friends from Cuba and Central America into the international program during the Covid-19 pandemic restrictions. Between 2017 and 2019, the

Traveling Ministry Corps traveled alone or in pairs to local meetings and other gatherings of Friends across national boundaries, or geographic or theological divides. In 2020, they began offering large group conferences online in Spanish and small group gatherings in English as a result of the pandemic travel restrictions.

The transition to this widespread and more frequent program of visitation began in 2010. The Salt and Light gatherings asked public Friends from across the Section and other Sections to introduce the theme of the 2012 World Gathering, "Being Salt and Light: Friends Living the Kingdom of God in a Broken World," to local Friends. After the 2012 conference in Kenya, another series, called "Let the Living Water Flow: Friends Serving God's Purposes" brought the experience of the World Gathering back to local Friends.[12]

The change to biannual Section Meetings went into effect after 2013. In 2014, four Section Consultations, held in El Salvador, Bolivia, California and North Carolina, focused on cross-cultural communication, environmental issues, and leadership development, all issues that had been identified as urgent Quaker concerns in an FWCC survey of Friends in 2013.

1980s–2010: Expanding and Contracting

The period between 1980 and 2010 saw a series of expansions and contractions of the work (and the staff) of the SoA.

Visitation to yearly meeting sessions was an important program. Many representatives found that attendance at another yearly meeting's sessions was a profound opportunity to learn to understand both another form of Quaker practice but also their own faith and practice. Julie Peyton, then a representative of the evangelical Northwest Yearly Meeting of Friends Church, wrote about this in her 2010 Wider Quaker Fellowship pamphlet:

> I learned that Friends in FWCC want to hear about me, yes, but they also want to know about my Yearly Meeting. This has been a profound challenge, because it has forced me to engage my own people, outside my safe local meeting, and join them more fully. I have come to love and trust my own Yearly Meeting in a way that I wouldn't have thought possible just a couple years ago. . . . I carry their concern with me when I come to these meetings. This is hard, deepening work. This is the work of peace-making. This is the work that FWCC has and is preparing me to do.[13]

World Gatherings of Young Friends (WGYF) were held in 1985 in Greensboro, North Carolina, and 2005 in Lancaster, UK, and Kaimosi, Kenya.[14] These were not formally organized by FWCC, but they were supported by the Section offices and the World Office. Friends who attended either gathering have often found further opportunities for connections and leadership development with FWCC.

The 2006 Section Meeting was held in Chiquimula, Guatemala. A significant number of WGYF'05 participants attended the 2006 Section Meeting, partly to see each other again and partly for the opportunity to get to know other Friends in the Americas who had a similar interest in broadening their Quaker experience.

The tripartite FWCC World Conference in 1991 included one site in the Americas (Tela, Honduras) in addition to sites in the Netherlands and Kenya.

In the early 1980s, Gordon Brown, as executive secretary, engaged new people and new sources of funding and programs. Many of these programs persisted into the 21st century; however, financial support was not sustained. In 2000, the section staff consisted of ten people, including field secretaries in Mexico and Western and Midwestern offices. From the 1960s until the early 2000s, field secretaries were an important support for representatives around the Section.[15]

Several large bequests and a major fundraising campaign in the early 2000s sustained the work for a few more years, but between 2007 and 2009, volunteers on the Financially Responsible Program Implementation Committee (FRPIC) reorganized the work and reduced the staff.[16] By 2014, there were only two full-time staff, with contracted bookkeeping services and other professionals contracted as needed.

1960s–1970s: Justice and Equality

In the 1960s and 1970s, the SoA saw a series of consultations that resulted in Friends exploring both theological issues and economic justice issues.

The 1967 World Conference in Greensboro, North Carolina, gave voice to a concern for more just sharing of the world's resources.[17] At first, it was called the 1% Fund, and it recommended that Friends in "first world" countries dedicate 1% of their income to "third world" countries. In the SoA, this came to be known as Right Sharing of World Resources, which was a fundraising and redistribution program that settled on a microfinance model, primarily in Africa and India.[18] Another parallel program was called International Quaker Aid from 1965–1999 that primarily raised funds from North American Quakers and made grants to yearly meetings and Quaker projects in Africa, Northern Ireland, and Central and South America. This was popular on both sides for many years, but increasing awareness of the imbalance of power and the lack of appropriate monitoring led to conflict. In 1999, IQA was laid down and RSWR was spun off into a separate organization that is still thriving 20 years later.[19]

In 1970, a conference on "The Future of Friends" in St. Louis, Missouri, brought together many Friends from the Evangelical, Orthodox, Hicksite and the newly formed yearly meetings. The plenary address by Everett Cattell, then president of Malone College, led to a series called the Faith and Life conferences, on ethics, eschatology, and other religious topics.[20] These brought Friends from different branches together to discuss Friends' positions on these theological issues.

In 1977, the All American Friends Conference in Wichita, Kansas, saw the first significant participation of Latin American friends in FWCC events. The gathering of a round table discussion group during the conference led to the formation of the Comité Organizador de Amigos Latinoamericanos (COAL). COAL includes representatives of affiliated yearly meetings from Mexico, Cuba, Guatemala, El Salvador, Costa Rica, Peru, and Bolivia. Through regular meetings held in conjunction with the biannual Section meetings, and two volunteer regional coordinators, COAL continues to connect and coordinate the voices, perspectives and participation of Spanish-speaking Friends in the SoA.[21] Even as Latin American Friends have become more integrated into the governance of the Section as a whole, they continue to value the opportunity to work directly with each other.

Beginning in the early 1980s, a group of volunteer interpreters began to organize language services at the annual Section meetings of representatives. Over the next 40 years, the interpreters team, including both native Spanish and English speakers, advocated effectively and continuously for greater integration of the section's work, ensured greater inclusion of language equality, and called attention to biases and racism in the Section's programs and events. In 2019, this work was formally acknowledged at the Section meeting. Minute FWA 19–23 reads:

> "The Friends World Committee for Consultation Section of the Americas gratefully acknowledges the profound impact of the Interpreters Team on the Section, its business

meetings and its committees. Their dedication to full inclusion of all Friends in the deliberations of the Section and the planning of our work has changed everything we do: how and where we plan events, how we make decisions, call Friends to service, write our documents and develop our vision for the future. We thank God for these brothers and sisters, their many hours of volunteer work, their enthusiasm and eldering, and for the high quality of the translation and interpretation services over more than 30 years. Without their work, we would not be the vibrant spiritual community we have become, and that, with their help, we will continue to become in the future."[22]

1940s–1960s: Supporting Post-War Spread of Quakerism in the United States

After World War II, the SoA was instrumental in supporting over 100 new meetings and yearly meetings that formed in areas previously unsettled by Friends, particularly in college towns. Lake Erie Yearly Meeting, Southern Appalachian Yearly Meeting and Association, Southeastern Yearly Meeting, and later Piedmont Yearly Meeting and Association were all nurtured by FWCC.[23]

In this same period, the Wider Quaker Fellowship grew from the original invitation from Rufus Jones in 1935 that preceded the formation of FWCC.[24] The story of the Wider Quaker Fellowship deserves its own book. In the 1940s and 1950s, it brought together interested persons who were not formally members of the Religious Society of Friends for a variety of reasons through study groups and a corresponding secretary. It became a program of FWCC when the American Friends Fellowship Council merged with the American Section of FWCC in 1954[25] until the program was laid down in 2015.[26]

1920–1940s: Inspiration Becomes Reality

In the aftermath of the First World War, the 1920 peace conference in London, and the 1929 American Friends Conference in Oskaloosa, Iowa, helped Friends to see that there was work for Friends to do to heal the wounds of the divisions of the 1800s. In the years between the First and Second World Wars, the growing awareness of the need for a standing body to sustain communication even in times of war and economic depression led to the Second World Conference in Pennsylvania in 1937.[27]

The 1937 World Conference of Friends was held on the campuses of Swarthmore and Haverford Colleges in Pennsylvania. This joint location was not only a convenient use of dormitories and other conference facilities within the Quaker family. It was a symbol of the collaboration of the Hicksite and Orthodox branches of Friends, which had stood apart for nearly 75 years. The Fifth Commission of the conference on "International Cooperation of Friends" was charged with exploring the possibility of founding a standing organization between conferences to facilitate the communication between distant and estranged bodies of Friends.[28]

The role of Anna and Passmore Elkinton was highly significant in the years before and after the Second World Gathering of Friends. As a marriage between the two Philadelphia Yearly Meetings, they embodied the reunification movement of young Friends in North America. Both worked extensively, separately and together, to build the network that would become the Friends World Committee.[29]

The American Section was one of the two founding elements of the World Committee. The first volunteer chairman (a position now called clerk) was Alvin T. Coate from Western Yearly

Meeting. The first paid staff, a position still called executive secretary, was Leslie Shaffer, starting in 1938, and for the better part of a decade.[30]

Other Quaker Organizations in the Americas

The Five Years Meeting, now Friends United Meeting (FUM), and the Friends General Conference, were formed before FWCC. The Association of Evangelical Friends, now the Evangelical Friends Church International, was not formally established until later but has roots in the divisions of the 1920s.[31] These three umbrella organizations in North America consist of mostly similar meetings within each organization, divided by style of worship and theology. The three remaining conservative yearly meetings are not united in a specific organization but are all affiliated with FWCC and do have some commonalities and a commitment to mutual communication and encouragement. The unaffiliated yearly meetings are very few at this point in the twenty-first century. In North America, there are three. Central Yearly Meeting was formed in the early 1900s as a group of monthly meetings in Indiana; it took up the holiness movement and withdrew from the Western and Indiana Yearly Meetings.[32] North Pacific Yearly Meeting was formed by a geographic division of Pacific Yearly Meeting in 1972[33] and is a primarily liberal and unprogrammed group, fiercely committed to their independence, even though they are otherwise indistinguishable from other FGC affiliated yearly meetings. Sierra-Cascades Yearly Meeting of Friends was formed in 2018 after a split in Northwest Yearly Meeting. In Central America, the yearly meetings in Guatemala, Honduras and El Salvador are primarily affiliated with EFCI, growing from missionary efforts from California Yearly Meeting, now known as Evangelical Friends Church Southwest.[34] Friends in Cuba, Belize and Ciudad Victoria in Mexico were founded by Friends affiliated with FUM.[35] In South America, the yearly meetings in Peru and Bolivia grew from two streams of missionaries, from Central Yearly Meeting and Oregon Yearly Meeting (now Northwest Yearly Meeting of Friends Church).[36] Since 2010, a growing cooperation fostered by FWCC has strengthened communications among the six recognized yearly meetings in Bolivia.

Conclusion

In the Americas, FWCC is a small organization with an expansive mission. The twentieth century may come to be known as the golden age of in-person conferences.[37] Previously, long-distance travel was too onerous; in this century they are increasingly seen as environmentally unsound, like many aspects of the twentieth century. The Covid-19 pandemic saw a massive adoption of online meeting technology by Friends, as well as the rest of the world. The SoA was already using these tools but saw more widespread acceptance and adoption across all the branches of Friends and in all the countries of the Americas. As of this writing, the long-term transition is still uncertain. How will Friends test the tools that best serve our unity with God's will? Will the increasing use of technology bring Friends closer together, or will it lead to new inequality and divisions?

In the long run, Quakers are, if nothing else, human beings, angelic and fallible. While it may be true that the world needs what Quakers, at their best, have to offer, the divisions among Friends make each branch on its own brittle and sieve-like. FWCC brings Friends from different groups together in circumstances conducive to dialogue and engagement. The complete mixture is more robust, supple and dynamic in responding to God's call and the needs of the world.

Notes

1 FWCC bylaws, revised 2019.
2 FWCC, *Weaving the Tapestry*, 2014.
3 FWCC Executive Committee minute FWX99–44 in March 1999 contains the first reference to conference calls, as if it were already a regular format for committee work. The first Executive Committee meeting held by conference call was in December 2003.
4 FWCC Executive Committee Minute FWX12–69.
5 Trustees for the FWCC World Office. This international body operates entirely in English.
6 FWCC Executive Committee Minute FWX12–68.
7 FWCC Finance Committee Minute FWF13–41.
8 FWCC Section Meeting Minutes 2015.
9 FWCC Nominating Committee report, March 29, 2016.
10 FWCC Nominating Committee report, February 28, 2018, and Section Meeting Minute FWA19–20.
11 https://fwccamericas.org/visitation/traveling-ministry.shtml.
12 http://fwccamericas.org/_wp/wp-content/uploads/2018/02/LivingWaterStudyBooklet2013.pdf.
13 Peyton, Julie. "A Personal Journey: Why I Deeply Love FWCC," *Wider Quaker Fellowship Pamphlet*, FWCC publishers, Philadelphia, PA, 2010. https://fwccamericas.org/pub/Peyton2010.pdf
14 Angell, pp. 467–468.
15 Mohr, Robin. Unpublished correspondence with Anna Baker, Susan Lee Barton, and Johan Maurer, former FWCC staff, 2020.
16 FWCC Executive Committee Minute FWX08–31, May 2008.
17 Hadley, pp. 155–157. Roland Kreager, "On Good Soil and Increasing Yield," *Friends Journal*. October 2007.
18 https://rswr.org/about-us.
19 FWCC Section Meeting Minutes FWA99–6 and FWA99–13; Hadley, pp. 168–169.
20 Williams, p. 290; Abbott, p. 42.
21 Williams, p. 291; Hadley p. 154.
22 https://fwccamericas.org/_wp/wp-content/uploads/2019/06/2019-03-Section-Minutes-Doniphan-bilingu-06.14.pdf.
23 Hadley, p. 89.
24 Hain Poorman, Vicki. "Whither the Wider Quaker Fellowship?" *Friends Journal*, October 2007, https://www.friendsjournal.org/2007141/.
25 Hadley, pp. 137–138.
26 FWCC Section Meeting Minute FWA15–21.
27 Hadley, pp. 8–10.
28 Elkinton, Steve. "A Portrait of Two Founders," *Friends Journal*, October 2007, https://www.friendsjournal.org/2007125/.
29 Elkinton.
30 Hadley, p. 19.
31 Abbott, pp. xvii–xviii.
32 Williams, p. 216.
33 https://npym.org/viewHistory.php.
34 Abbott, pp. 43–46.
35 Abbott, pp. 40–41.
36 Abbott, pp. 267–268.
37 Williams, pp. 297–299.

Bibliography

1980–2020 Minutes, FWCC Section of the Americas. www.fwccamericas.org; www.rswr.org

Abbott, Margery Post, Mary Ellen Chijioke, Pink Dandelion, and John William Oliver, Jr. *Historical Dictionary of the Friends (Quakers)*. Lanham, MD: The Scarecrow Press, 2003.

Angell, Stephen and Pink Dandelion. *The Oxford Handbook of Quaker Studies*. Oxford: Oxford University Press, 2013.

Elkinton, Steven. "A Portrait of Two Founders," *Friends Journal*, 2007. https://www.friendsjournal.org/2007125/

Hadley, Herbert M. *Quakers World Wide: A History of Friends World Committee for Consultation*. London: Friends World Committee for Consultation, 1991.

Hain Poorman, Vicki. "Whither the Wider Quaker Fellowship?" *Friends Journal*, October 2007. https://www.friendsjournal.org/2007141/

Kreager, Roland. "On Good Soil and Increasing Yield," *Friends Journal*, October 2007. https://www.friendsjournal.org/2007142/

Mohr, Robin. Unpublished correspondence with Anna Baker, Susan Lee Barton, and Johan Maurer, 2020.

Peyton, Julie. "A Personal Journey: Why I Deeply Love FWCC" *Wider Quaker Fellowship Pamphlet*, FWCC Publishers, Philadelphia, PA. 2010. https://fwccamericas.org/pub/Peyton2010.pdf

Williams, Walter. *The Rich Heritage of Quakerism*, 1962, Eerdmans, 1987 edition, Barclay Press, Newberg, OR. Paul Anderson (epilogue).

7

TOGETHER APART

An Overview of the Asia–West Pacific Section (AWPS)

Ronis Chapman and Virginia Jealous

It's late April 2020. A group of Friends is meeting for worship. It's one of those truly gathered meetings, where we are together in intention and Spirit is with us. Today, though, we are not sitting together in a circle in a meeting house around the customary low table holding copies of *Advices and Queries*, a Bible and, perhaps, a vase of flowers. Today, as we do every week, we are sitting in our homes or offices, in front of a screen, worshipping online. We may be in India or Japan or Singapore or Hong Kong or the Philippines or Australia or Aotearoa/New Zealand – or elsewhere. We are worshipping together, apart. Welcome to the community of Asia–West Pacific Section of Friends in the 21st century.

Where on Earth Are We?

Our geographical span is huge. It stretches roughly from Mongolia in the north to Tasmania in the south: about 11,000 km (7000 miles). From Pakistan in the west to Fiji in the east is about 13,000 km (8000 miles). Groups of Friends worship in 16 of the region's countries; individual Friends worship in others.

Where Friends Worship in AWPS in 2020

Aotearoa/New Zealand; Australia; Bangladesh; Bhutan; Cambodia; Hong Kong SAR; India; Indonesia; Japan; Myanmar; Nepal; Philippines; Singapore; South Korea; Taiwan; Thailand.

The Asia–West Pacific Section is multicultural and multilingual, with governments that range across the political spectrum and offer varying degrees of religious and other freedoms. More than 20 official languages are used in the region, as are several thousand indigenous

Editors' note: The writing style in this chapter was chosen to authentically represent as wide a range of voices as possible from the Asia–West Pacific Section of the Friends World Committee for Consultation. Due to this stylistic choice, which is in line with our aim for this book, we recognize some quotations may appear to lack contextual information or narrative.

DOI: 10.4324/9780429030925-9

languages and dialects. Our economies and environments are equally varied, along with the skills and experience we bring to Friends and the places and ways in which we meet to worship.

Where We Worship: A Snapshot

Bohol, Philippines

I worship with two other Quakers in the residence of one of us. It's a 25-year-old house mostly made of cement with galvanized iron roofing. There are several trees and plants in its surroundings. It's a 36 m^2 house built on a 280 m^2 lot, with glass jalousie windows secured by iron grills, wooden door, and fenced with cement and iron grills, too. Just right for a tropical climate, it's very simple. But since it is located on a hill, it is usually peaceful, except that the houses around it are clustered to each other closely because this is part of a socialized housing project. When there are visitors, we usually choose to worship elsewhere at an office or at a garden resort that serves organic food.

Marj Angalot

Denmark, Western Australia

'The Sanctuary' is a community meeting place beside the river. It's shaped like a hexagon, is made of mud bricks, and has an earth roof with native plants growing on top. There are glass doors, and light reflects onto the walls and floor tiles. In the angle of one wall there is a wood stove for winter fires. It blends into the landscape and is very peaceful.

We are a core group of four. Once or twice a month we join with Friends from Albany, 50 km away, when we worship and share lunch together.

Virginia Jealous

Canberra, Australian Capital Territory

Just five minutes on my bike gets me to Canberra Friends Meeting House. My children grew up in this meeting so there are many memories for me attached to this place. The meeting room is a hexagon (now I know this is the same as Denmark WA) and although it is in an inner city suburb, is surrounded by trees and a garden recently built by local Friends. Canberra is blessed with native birds and I love listening to them during worship time.

Thirty or 40 Quakers gather each Sunday morning – sometimes more. Canberra is the capital of Australia and we often have visitors that remind us of the worldwide family of Friends and the web of friendship that connects us.

Ronis Chapman

Bhopal, India

We gather together for worship every Sunday in a newly constructed meeting house. The old building was sold to Friends in Bhopal in 1939 by the then Nawab (King of Bhopal) at very nominal cost. Even before purchase we have been worshipping in that building since long. It is located in Pari Bazar – means 'fairy's market'. Before independence, this place was well secured, because only ladies (and on a fixed day, women from the Nawab family) used to come to this place for

55

purchases. Now it is not so. Some old historical buildings are still around our meeting; one of them is Golghar – means 'round house'.

About 100 people can participate in the meeting but 25 to 40 people gather for worship every Sunday. Mostly we have programmed worship meetings but on the first Sunday of the month we hold open worship meeting where who so ever is moved by the spirit leads the meeting by singing, praying or sharing his/her witness. We have one monthly meeting at Raisen. We visit Raisen once in a year where lunch is provided by Raisen MM. We celebrate Christmas and Easter joyfully and always have lunch together.

Ronald Titus

Palmerston North, Aotearoa/New Zealand

My home place of worship is a meeting house set on a small piece of land with a small space of lawn, fruit trees, and two lovely birches. It is built from concrete blocks, simple, not lined on the inside but with big windows so that the trees outside can be seen as the breeze blows through them. The sun shines onto a plain wooden floor, bringing warmth, and instils calmness to the small group who worship together, mostly in silence.

Patricia Macgregor

Hong Kong SAR

A forest of buildings, tall and dense. Think 'urban'. A place of peace, a pre-school, with soft mats, and order. People: from near and far. Language: English, but Chinese too. Visitors: welcomed, and we'll be friends with you. A meeting: growing, healing, bonding, seeking more truth on our journey together and journeys individually. Communicating: not just Sundays, but all days – with WhatsApp. A future: how to be Quaker in China, how to seek more of being Quaker in China. Change: the speed of change, the effects of change on society.

John Leighton

Making and Sustaining Friendly Connections in AWPS

Changing technology has been, literally, a Godsend for our diverse and dispersed region. It has offered an alternative to one of our greatest conundrums: how to maintain geographically distant relationships given our concerns around travel, carbon emissions and the climate crisis.

We have been holding business meetings and offering a regional meeting for worship online since 2016. During the coronavirus pandemic and global lockdown of 2020, this served us well, as small and isolated groups and individuals were able to learn from our wider experience. We modified our use of technology (and its challenges) and maintained connections in ways and with effects that we hadn't considered. We expect to take what we have learned about e-connecting into the future.

The voices quoted throughout speak for many Friends in AWPS who have shared their experiences of gathering online versus meeting face-to-face, and of what being part of a world community of Quakers means to us. We spoke as informal friends rather than as corporate Friends: these comments are individual reflections.

Good Vibrations: The Differences Between Connecting Online and Connecting Face-to-Face

In practical terms, online meeting costs less in time and money, and less in effort for those who might be unable to get to physical meeting:

> 'More people have been connecting with our worship group. . . . people who used to live here can now join us on Sunday as we meet on zoom'; 'online is easier than making your way to a meeting place, especially in a big city'; 'it includes others who might not be able to get to actual meeting'; 'for me living alone in Delhi, it means that I can access Friends and meetings like the AWPS worship. . . . to me worship on line is spiritually a nourishing place. With people around you digitally we create a silent space that works well for me. . . . I'm fortunate to be having three types of online worship.'
>
> *(Myanmar, Singapore, Aotearoa/NZ, India)*

In spiritual terms, knowing one another in 'the things which are eternal' (A&Q18) can be more difficult online:

> In face-to-face gatherings we have opportunity to know each other closely, there is more time for discussion and more worship time; these are some of the gains from seeing each other in person. And when we gather in person it's not just a physical gathering but there is an emotional binding and we listen and hear each other in a different way. While it's good to meet online, something is missing.
>
> *(India and others)*

Silence can include the noises of life:

> When we started worshipping on line we thought about muting our microphones. But one Friend now lives in New Zealand on a farm and we could hear her sheep in the background. We all decided we liked the sheep and so leave our mikes on so we can hear the signs of life in the background during our worship time.
>
> *(Myanmar)*

Technology matters:

> 'Technical matters can be difficult. Many members, especially the older people, don't know how to use devices so it's not possible for them to meet online'; 'It's all about connection and adaptability, and reaffirming when we meet in person the precious links that we maintain remotely.'
>
> *(India, Cambodia)*

Friends in the World: Belonging to the Extended Family of Quakers

The global voice of Quakers, Friends World Committee for Consultation (FWCC), encourages fellowship and understanding.

As a member of FWCC, the AWPS committee brings Friends in the region together to build community and to work on global issues. How well do we do this in our online and face-to-face connections around the region?

Historically, AWPS has been good at building community and (mostly) less focussed at working on global issues. More recently our common, though often culturally different, contemporary experiences (e.g., the climate crisis and social justice) engage us all. Technology allows us to share our skills, experience and knowledge via webinars and online courses, and it can better enable us to work together.

Quaker Schools in AWPS

The first Friends School in our section opened in 1875 in Sohagpur, Madhya Pradesh, India. There are now a total four Friends schools in Madhya Pradesh, including Sohagpur, Itarsi, and Bundelkhand. These early schools were founded by British and American Friends and supported until Indian Independence in 1947. While resources are few, the schools continue to be supported by faithful Indian Friends.

Friends School Tokyo, Japan, opened in 1887 with support from the Women's Board of Mission of Philadelphia Yearly Meeting. This girls' high school is founded on the belief there is that of God in every person; today it has 800 students. Links are maintained with the wider Quaker world through a Friends-in-Residence programme.

Friends School Hobart, Australia, also opened in 1887. It remains highly regarded and continues as the only Quaker school in Australia. Japanese is taught at the school, and strong links are maintained with Friends School Tokyo. The school is based on a spirit of inclusion, service to others, and being a welcoming community

The operation of each school is influenced by Quaker values and practices, and each welcomes students of any faith or none.

Building Community

Here many people still prefer living in joint families with grandparents, parents and children. A big family gives you a feeling of confidence. One can get advantage of experience and precious advices. Belonging to the world community of Friends gives the same feeling. You never feel alone or helpless.

(India)

'AWPS makes me feel like a friend'; 'AWPS makes me feel at home with a family of diverse culture/background/context but with the same values and common connection'.

(India, Philippines)

Traditionally Japanese Friends had a much stronger connection to U.S. Quakers. But maintaining broader connections with the massive numbers of Americans or remote Europe would be very trying, so AWPS is probably an ideal venue for us. We can interact with Quakers from small meetings in other Asian countries who have similar perspectives, but at the same time there are Friends from larger Yearly Meetings in Australia and Aotearoa/NZ who tie back into the broader mainstream of English-speaking Quakerism.

(Japan)

Being part of FWCC is important because it means I'm not alone. We're connected in what can be the deepest but most coincidental of ways. For example I went from Cambodia with a Friend from Korea to visit a potential Friend in Myanmar who had been enquiring about membership – and that enquirer had come across Quakers in a Bible study course in the Philippines!

(Cambodia)

Culturally we often feel hesitation when talking with strangers, but as Quakers we feel comfortable with our Quaker visitors. They are very open-minded and we can talk freely about significant things with Friends. We have Friends who we can share with, and know their thinkings, views, lives, work, ways of worship. This helps us to reevaluate ourselves and to grow spiritually. We must not take this for granted; like any relationship it needs work and commitment to stay connected.

(India)

It strikes me that my horizons have been greatly broadened and I have been enriched by a number of FWCC contacts. I served as a 'visitor' (by Skype) for someone seeking international membership. This introduced me to Singapore Quakers in addition to the pleasure of getting to know the person seeking membership. I'm a member of Canberra Meeting, which has had a number of Quaker Day annual events, including Skyping with Friends from Singapore, Philippines, Cambodia, Japan and India. Our Meeting held a study group (also by Skype) with our companion meeting in Hong Kong. We studied a Pendle Hill pamphlet and shared our thoughts.

(Australia)

Working on Global Issues

Cross-cultural exchange can be both rich and difficult. . . . when we spend time getting to know each other we begin to understand the different challenges we all face, and how we might best help each other. For example there's a Friend we know from Hong Kong who we are supporting at the moment. . . . For me, other ways of being connected to the global community include reading – of FWCC newsletters and emails; of epistles; Backhouse lectures and so on. A pamphlet about racism in the US spoke strongly to us in NZ, despite our different context. I also participate in online seminars. The testimony to equality webinar linked us with Woodbrooke teachers, and such links with worldwide Quakers really enriches our community.

(Aotearoa/NZ)

How AWPS Works With Other Organisations in the Region: An Example

In 2013 an earthquake and Super Typhoon Haiyan caused extreme damage in the Philippines. Concerned Friends from around the world sent money via AWPS to support Quakers and others in their recovery. This concern has led to a long-term clean drinking water initiative in rural communities on the island of Bohol. A collaboration has been established between local Quakers, the local Catholic church, community organisations, several Rotary groups, and the small development agency Abundant Water to design a sustainable health and hygiene project.

At a webinar hosted by AWPS in 2019, Friends from Aotearoa/NZ, Australia, India and Japan learned about developing a coherent message about climate crisis that speaks to the wide spectrum of global Quaker traditions. Susanna Mattingly, FWCC's Sustainability Officer, spoke about the benefits of recognising that 'while Friends come from different theological positions, we face a shared concern of caring for the earth. Finding a way to articulate this together is offering a model for all Friends to find common ground' (article in the *Australian Friend*, by Michael Searle).

Asia–West Pacific Section and Quaker United Nations Office (QUNO)

Asia–West Pacific Section has worked with QUNO since 1985. We provide:

- a presence at QUNO governance meetings of one representative from AWPS for each QUNO office, helping maintaining a global shape to the work of QUNO
- a source of additional information to the QUNO team about our geography and its human landscape
- a source of additional perspectives to the QUNO team, as we are geographically and culturally different and distant from the two QUNO offices and the vast number of people with whom QUNO works
- a tangible link between Friends within AWPS and the work that is being done globally by Friends in the Quaker name
- a channel of visibility for those who may wish to connect in more detail with QUNO work, including the possibility of providing funds

Our involvement with QUNO also offers us a means of connecting with the other FWCC sections, offering us a broader view of the world of Friends and Quaker work that we all share. The work of QUNO is supported, respected and valued throughout AWPS.

Coming Together in Person: An AWPS Family Reunion

From the Epistle of the September 2018 AWPS Gathering in Hong Kong, when 35 Friends from AWPS gathered on Cheung Chau Island:

'We came together as a community, mindful of the great diversity of the Section and keen to explore what it means to be a Quaker in this part of the world (the theme of the gathering). We heard warm messages from Quakers across the region and beyond as these absent Friends expressed goodwill for the upcoming days of discussion and fellowship. . . . We arrived as a disparate group and very quickly developed a kindred spirit and felt the love deep down and all around.'

We hadn't anticipated that we would also be joined in Hong Kong by some wild weather. One of us wrote in her journal: 'I am experiencing my first typhoon as I write, Typhoon Mangkhut. Sometimes it sounds like a freight engine, but it doesn't stop. I have a new appreciation for the expression "sustained winds". Water is blowing sideways and the trees are whipping around, not just when a gust comes through, but all the time.'

Indeed it went on and on and on. Relentless. Happily, our sense of being gathered in the Spirit also went on and on. We had an unexpected extra 24 hours together when we prayed and sang and talked. Fellowship and friendships were strengthened by these powerful physical and spiritual elements, laying deeper foundations for our continuing work 'together apart'.

Asking Hard Questions; Questioning Our Answers

We continually ask ourselves questions about our purpose.

As you read, please hold these questions in your heart – as we do.

The Asia–West Pacific Section is so vast and has so many different cultures and languages; can we really be a community?

Is the barrier of language artificial? Do we let our language differences get in the way of building friendships and partnerships?

There are so many different forms of Quaker worship across our section. Does this mean that it is impossible to unite as Friends? How can we get better at respecting and celebrating our differences?

Quakers have always embraced equality. But equality means different things in different cultures. How can we be part of the one religious community but see equality differently?

Climate change is affecting us all. Is this an issue on which we can come together? There are already many groups working on climate change. Is there a Quaker contribution that we have to make together in the Asia–West Pacific Region?

Covid-19 has shown us how connected our world is. As Friends, what is our common bond?

How can we use our shared Quaker faith to overcome our differences and work together on building a more just world?

8

NITOBE INAZŌ AND QUAKER INFLUENCES ON JAPANESE COLONIAL THOUGHT

Isaac Barnes May and Richard J. Barnes

Nitobe Inazō (1862–1933) was a Japanese Quaker, chiefly remembered for his strong advocacy for pacifism and diplomacy in international affairs and his support for women's education. He was the first under-secretary-general of the League of Nations and the author of the work *Bushido: The Soul of Japan*, which is still often read as an introduction to Japanese culture. Because of these accomplishments, his portrait was featured on the 5000-yen banknote from 1984 to 2007. Yet Nitobe also retains a far more controversial legacy. As both a scholar and an administrator, Nitobe was one of the architects of early Japanese colonial policy. His work laid the foundations of a theory that, in the hands of his academic successors, would be used to legitimate Japanese imperial expansion and the creation of the so-called Greater East Asian Co-Prosperity Sphere.[1] Scholars have been attentive to the two halves of this intellectual activity, yet "Nitobe the Quaker Diplomat" becomes somewhat removed from "Nitobe the Imperialist and Colonial Theorist" in these readings of history. As So Jung Um observed in his assessment of the field of Japanese colonial policy studies, however, "[this] categorical dichotomy between 'internationalist' and 'imperialist' may fail to effectively capture the position of Nitobe and other colonial policy scholars" (So Jung Um, 2017:24).

Within Quaker religious and academic circles, references to Nitobe's imperialist teachings and writings are often given only a cursory mention as a deviation from his pacifism and religious background or otherwise ignored entirely (Stargardt, 2012; Meager, 2011). In fact, Nitobe's work and thought were both internally consistent and conceptually united by his Quaker faith. Indeed, Quakerism served to provide a kind of glue that let Nitobe fuse his devoted internationalism and his paternalistic colonialism, one which saw imperial expansion as fully benefiting subaltern populations as much as those originating from the metropole. Drawing upon an imagined history of American Quakers' relationship with Native Americans, Nitobe envisioned a reality where Japanese expansion could be both nonviolent and benevolent in nature.

Nitobe's Impact on Colonial Theory

The Japanese colonial empire is typically depicted as having emerged with the annexation of Taiwan in 1895 and Korea in 1910.[2] As such, when Nitobe established the field of Colonial Policy Studies at Kyoto Imperial University in 1904, he did so just as Japan began to be recognized

DOI: 10.4324/9780429030925-10

on the world stage as a prominent colonizing power (Oshiro, 1985:149–152). The waning years of the Edo Period (1603–1868) had already marked the expansion of the early modern Japanese polity into historically non-Japanese lands such as Hokkaido and Okinawa, though this is often presented as a rationalization of pre-modern borders.[3] The ideological justifications for such expansion evolved significantly throughout the modern period, however, transforming from a settler-colonialism driven by concerns of economics and security into an imperial system that nominally supported Pan-Asian liberation. Nitobe's work was immersed in these changing conceptions of colonialism.

Colonialism was at first understood in Japan as being a mechanism that allowed migration and population increase in peripheral areas for the nation's economic benefit, with the translation used being *takuchishokumin* or "to open up lands and increase people on them" (Xu Lu, 2019:15). This can be seen in the 1869 Iwakura Proposal, following the Meiji Restoration, which argued that the foremost needs of the new government were not only in developing a nationwide tax system and normalizing relations with European powers but also in remaking the northern island of Hokkaido "into a little Japan" (Kōmon, ed., 1968:703–704). For the Meiji leadership, the colonization of Hokkaido held the promise of being immensely profitable once the island's resources were properly tapped. This was matched by an ideological impetus among the elite for establishing firm boundaries for the nation-state. The young Nitobe attended school in colonial Hokkaido at the newly founded Sapporo Agricultural College to become an agricultural administrator. As a member of its faculty during the 1893 World's Columbian Exhibition, he later extolled the college's activities in the wider colonial project, noting: "To [Hokkaido], then, the northern frontier of the Empire and a land endowed with magnificent natural resources, as yet untouched by human hand, the new Imperial Government wisely began to extend its fostering care" (Nitobe, 1893:1). During this period, colonization differed little in its stated rationale from other modernizing projects of the Meiji government, being positioned as economically strengthening the Japanese state.

This began to change with the military expansion of the state into highly populated foreign territories, with colonization no longer articulated as solely an economic endeavor. Nitobe was invited by the colonial administration of Taiwan to head the management of its sugar plantations in the face of sustained economic losses, serving as a technical advisor for the colony from 1901 to 1903 to numerous accolades and public notice (Oshiro, 1985:150–152). However, when presenting the justifications for Japanese rule over Taiwan to an English-speaking audience in 1912, rather than focusing solely on the economic impacts for the nation, he would point toward Japanese colonial policy as being essential in eliminating banditry and disseminating law, as well as promoting the health, education and industry of the colonial population (Nitobe, 1912a:359–361). In contrast to the Ainu population of Hokkaido, which had largely been ignored in the ideological consensus surrounding the colonial project there, the welfare of the indigenous populations of Taiwan, and later Korea, Manchuria and the wider empire, soon became central to rhetorical justifications for Japanese colonialism (Howell, 2004). Nitobe and his students would increasingly argue for an alternative translation of colonization, that of "planting people" for the moral purpose of increasing civilization in harmony with nature (Lu, 2019:161). In the 1910s, while teaching at Tokyo Imperial University, Nitobe was known for writing the phrase "Colonization is the Spread of Civilization" on the blackboard each day before he began his lessons (Dudden, 2005:60).

Within this construction, conflict between the colonizers and the colonized was portrayed as an unfortunate if not uncommon outcome. Nitobe argued that if colonized populations let others make efficient and productive use of their land and territory, then each group could benefit from what would be a mutual exchange (Dudden, 2005:134; Um, 2017:60). In direct response to the "white man's burden" animating European and American colonial policy at the time, Nitobe advocated Japanese colonialism as a moral mission to protect and uplift the peoples of Asia. However, that is not to suggest that Nitobe viewed this relationship as one of equals. Writing about Koreans in 1906, Nitobe regarded them as pastoral people "who predated history," with it being Japan's task to drag them into the contemporary world (Nitobe, 1960–1982:327–328). After Japan annexed Korea in 1910, Nitobe made his thoughts on the colonial process clear: "Firmness in government is something which they did not have before, and that is what we offer to them" (Nitobe, 1912a:361).

Nitobe and Quaker Colonialism

Nitobe's idealistic views on colonial policy were an outgrowth of his liberal religious sensibilities. After embracing Christianity during his time at the Sapporo Agricultural College, as part of a group of students who converted who became known as the "Sapporo Band," Nitobe became familiar with Quakerism while studying at Johns Hopkins University and ultimately became a convinced Friend. Colonial policy as Nitobe taught it to his students was supposed to be a humanitarian enterprise for all concerned. He argued that each nation was endowed by God with different abilities, and these national characteristics made them suited to different enterprises, ranging from music to handicrafts and agriculture, with some nations being best suited for maintaining the welfare of others (Um, 2017:60). Nitobe's studies in the United States convinced him that American expansion had exactly this kind of benevolent character. In a 1904 essay, he declared:

> Whenever American influences have found their way, be it among the savage Indians or the Negroes; be it in the semi-barbarous Hawaiian Islands, or in the Philippines, or in the Far Eastern seats of alien and ancient civilizations, they have mainly been mainly educational, and these educational influences have even existed, not unconsciously as a necessary consequences of a policy uneducational in its motive but consciously and steadily.
>
> *(Nitobe, 1909a:68)*

As a highly educated and well-read man, Nitobe must have been aware that these "educational" efforts were backed with considerable military force and that they had been accompanied by atrocities committed against civilian populations, yet he maintained that these actions were a moral good. Because the welfare of colonized populations was theoretically a central consideration in his thought, Nitobe drew much of his model of the idealized relationship between colonized populations and colonizers from Quakers' self-understanding of their relationship with Native Americans.

In the late nineteenth century, American Quakers prided themselves that the Religious Society of Friends had nurtured a uniquely close relationship with Native Americans, and Yearly Meetings had committees devoted to "Indian Affairs." Under the Grant administration, Quakers had been one of the groups recruited to take part in the so-called Peace Policy, where religious denominations were allowed by the federal government to appoint the Indian Agents to designated tribes. Through the use of schools and missions work, Quakers understood themselves to be participating in efforts to both Christianize and "Americanize" native peoples. (Sim, 2008) They saw William Penn's treaty with the Lenape as showing the beginning of an amicable and trusting relationship between themselves and native populations. The depiction of Penn's treaty as a moment of peaceful cooperation between Quakers and Native Americans was embedded in the written and visual culture of Quakerism and was ubiquitous in the artwork of Quaker Edward Hicks.

American Quakers' perception of their relationship with Native Americans was considerably rosier than the reality. In Pennsylvania, even when Penn was alive, relations had never been conflict free. Late nineteenth-century Quaker involvement in the Grant Peace Policy was also premised in part on the threat that the US Army would intervene if the tribes Quakers served did not cooperate. In one case, an Orthodox Quaker Indian agent, Lawrie Tatum, called for and received military intervention (Graber, 2014). Nineteenth-century schooling of Native Americans was coercive in nature and inseparable from the attempted destruction of indigenous cultures. Colonial expansion was always accompanied by the use of force, whatever the ostensibly humane policy espoused. Nitobe, however, ignored the inconvenient reality and began to conceive of the development of Hokkaido, and Japanese colonial efforts more generally, as a moral and religious project rather than purely an economic endeavor, and consciously sought to emulate the Quaker experience in colonial Pennsylvania and the American West. From his time studying in the United States, Nitobe brought back a sizable collection of books on Quakerism and, drawing on these resources, he began to write about Quakerism for a Japanese audience. George Masaaki Oshiro, one of Nitobe's biographers, contends that Nitobe's views on this topic were particularly influenced by reading an article on Quaker history in the November 1882 issue of *Harper's* magazine (Oshiro, 1985:61–63).

Written and illustrated by American Quaker Howard Pyle, who would gain fame the following year for his *Merry Adventures of Robin Hood*, the article, "The Early Quakers in England and Philadelphia," presented an account of Quakerism from its beginnings under George Fox until the arrival of William Penn in the Pennsylvania colony. Pyle described Quakerism as the animating force that had led contented English farmers to choose to brave an Atlantic voyage and settle a new continent. Pyle's work was a piece of mythmaking; it included illustrations of Penn and Fox, of the same kind that would grace his later works on King Arthur and Robin Hood, and it depicted the English settlers as devoted Friends who had tamed a wilderness. Native Americans were conspicuously absent from his narrative, except insofar as they had provided some of the place names for contemporary Pennsylvania.

Not only was Quakerism compatible with material gain, but according to Pyle's account, it seemed to generate it:

> Through [the Pennsylvania colonists'] industry, temperance, and economy their summer came at last, bringing with its increase in power and wealth, until the fruits of that season are such as we of the present day behold. Where they found a measureless wilderness of forest, we behold a country teeming with population, ripe in wealth, and strong in beneficent government which they founded.
>
> *(Pyle, 1882:828)*

Pyle's description of how religion and virtue had brought worldly success to colonists must have seemed particularly appealing to Nitobe, who sought a recipe for Japan to modernize. If the industrious Japanese colonizers stood in for the Pennsylvania settlers, then the colonized peoples they were interacting with could thusly be analogized to Native Americans. In a 1912 lecture on the racial characteristics of the Japanese people at the University of Illinois at Champaign-Urbana, Nitobe suggested the Ainu were "pushed out of Japan much as the American Indians were pushed out of [the United States] until finally only a handful are left in northern Japan" (Nitobe, 1912b). This was not a source of distress to Nitobe but an inevitable facet of the progress of civilization.

If Nitobe was seeking more recent examples than Penn for this kind of ostensibly benevolent colonialism, he did not have to look outside his family by marriage. During an 1886 visit to Philadelphia while studying abroad, Nitobe met Mary Patterson Elkinton at a gathering at the home of Philadelphia Orthodox Quaker leader Wistar Morris, and the couple would marry in 1891. Mary Nitobe's uncle, Joseph Elkinton, was well known among Friends for his missionary efforts among the Seneca in New York. Alongside other missionaries, he taught European-style agriculture and various skilled trades as an attempt to persuade the Native American population to abandon their culture and traditions. While working with the tribe, he had earned the ire of its tradition-minded leaders, who had threatened him for meddling in local politics and urging the tribe to embrace democratic governance. Elkinton established Tunesassa Indian School, and as an instructor there he developed a reputation as a stern disciplinarian to his young Seneca charges (Lappas, 2019:160; Heather and Nielsen, 2015:317–318; Kelsey, 1917:98–102). Between Penn and his relatives, Nitobe's religious associations were hardly a hindrance to his involvement in the Japanese colonial enterprise; if anything, they seemed to justify the idea that colonialism could be done morally.

While he was in Hokkaido teaching at Sapporo Agricultural College, Nitobe tried to disseminate this version of Quakerism to Japanese audiences. Nitobe worked with the editor of a local paper, *The North Gate Daily*, to allow the editor to publish a series of newspaper articles on the life of William Penn. In 1894, he would collect and publish these, along with a few chapters of his own writings, as a book. Not content with only a single book being available on William Penn in Japanese, Nitobe would work to publish two more. He translated the writings of American Quaker Thomas Cope on William Penn and George Fox. He also supervised the translation of Lucy Robert's *A Short Biography of William Penn* by a local teacher at the Friends Girls school, Sasai Shū, and another (uncredited) collaborator, which was later published under the name *Tales of the Beautiful Country*. Nitobe tried to distribute this book widely, taking a financial loss to give it away. He even left copies in hotels, a strategy strikingly like that later employed by the Gideons to distribute Bibles (Oshiro, 1985:61–63). Extolling Penn was intertwined with the colonial project that Nitobe was advocating; Quakerism was bound up with his faith in civilizational progress.

Quaker Nationalism

Nitobe's Quakerism was linked to his outward avowal of pacifism and internationalism, but ultimately it did not inhibit his support for Japanese militarism. He saw Japan as justified in the Russo-Japanese War in 1905, believing that Japan had a special mission to civilize its neighbors unimpeded. In 1932, Nitobe toured the United States, seeking to convince American audiences of the wisdom of the Japanese invasion of Manchuria, which he claimed was a humanitarian undertaking for the "salvation of China" (Dudden, 2005:141; Burkman, 2008:146–149). Prominent American Quakers in the early twentieth century had balanced their own nationalism with their religious identities; in the most visible example, as president, Herbert Hoover had very publicly been commander in chief of the US armed forces. As such, Nitobe was doing nothing new in professing hostility to the idea of war while admitting it could be regrettably necessary. The largest effect of Nitobe's Quakerism in this regard was probably that it helped him convince himself that using force to pursue Japan's national interest was a selfless act, undertaken for all of humanity.

A number of Nitobe's followers would become influential in public life and were close to the levers of state power. Journalists Sterling and Peggy Seagrave have described "a network of Quakers and near-Quakers" in the 1930s and 1940s who connected the top levels of Japanese society, including Nitobe, the imperial family, and American Friends.[4] Nitobe prized international cooperation and tried to foster stronger ties between the United States and Japan. He understood both portions of his career, as a liberal internationalist and colonial theorist, as being unified and consistent with his Quaker faith. Yet the colonial policies he espoused contributed to the geopolitical circumstances that led to the Second World War. While it is possible to overstate Nitobe's influence, he trained a generation of experts in Japanese colonial policy who would effect change at every level of the empire. Though his more liberal sensibilities should be acknowledged, contemporary Quakers or other admirers who see Nitobe as inspiration for the present should perhaps heed his wisdom: "Seldom is your hero as perfect as you believe him to be" (Nitobe, 1909b:238).

Notes

1 Peter Duus identifies the intellectual roots of this ideology in the colonial discourses of race and modernization, with Nitobe being an influential teacher to several of the founding members of the pro-Pan-Asianism *Shōwa Kenkyūkai*, including Gotō Ryūnosuke and Rōyama Masamichi. See Peter Duus, "The Greater East Asian Co-Prosperity Sphere," *Journal of Northeast Asian History* 5, no. 1 (June 2008): 143–154.
2 For an overview of this school of thought, see Ramon Myers and Mark Peattie, eds., *The Japanese Colonial Empire, 1895–1945* (Princeton, NJ: Princeton University Press, 1984).
3 This orthodox position has come under increasing scrutiny over the past three decades; see Brett Walker, *The Conquest of Ainu Lands: Ecology and Culture in Japanese Expansion, 1590–1800* (Berkeley: University of California Press, 2001) and Michele M. Mason, *Dominant Narratives of Colonial Hokkaido and Imperial Japan: Envisioning the Periphery and the Modern Nation-State* (New York: Palgrave Macmillan, 2012).
4 Sterling Seagrave and Peggy Seagrave, *The Yamato Dynasty: The Secret History of Japan's Imperial Family* (New York: Broadway Books, 2001), 11, 245, 343n205–206. Many of Seagrave's specific charges about the role of Quakerism in connecting American Friends and the Japanese government require more investigation from scholars. Particularly provocative is their claim that the choice of the United States not to charge Hirohito with war crimes was strongly influenced by advice given to Brigadier General Bonner Fellers, who was raised a Quaker and had attended Quaker-run Earlham College, by one of Nitobe Inazō's proteges, Michi Kawai.

References

Thomas W. Burkman, *Japan and the League of Nations: Empire and World Order, 1914–1938* (Honolulu, HI: University of Hawaii Press, 2008)

Alexis Dudden, *Japan's Colonization of Korea: Discourse and Power* (Honolulu, HI: University of Hawaii Press, 2005)

Peter Duus, "The Greater East Asian Co-Prosperity Sphere," *Journal of Northeast Asian History* 5, no. 1 (June 2008)

Jennifer Graber, "'If a War It May Be Called': The Peace Policy with American Indians," *Religion and American Culture* 24, no. 1 (ed 2014): 36–69

Barbara Heather and Marianne O. Nielsen, "(Dis)Armed Friendship: Impacts of Colonial Ideology on Early Quaker Attitudes toward American Indians," *Culture and Religion* 16, no. 3 (July 3, 2015): 317–318

David Howell, "Making 'Useful Citizens' of Ainu Subjects in Early Twentieth-Century Japan", *Journal of Asian Studies* 63, no. 1 (2004): 5–7

Iwakura kojikki: chukan, ed. Tada Kōmon (Tokyo, Japan: Hara Shobō, 1968)

Rayner Wickersham Kelsey, *Friends and the Indians, 1655–1917* (Philadelphia, PA: Associated Executive Committee of Friends on Indian Affairs, 1917), 98–102

Thomas J. Lappas, "Tunesassa Echoes and the Temperance Struggle: A Family Tradition at Tunesassa Quaker Indian School, Allegany Indian Reservation across Generations," in *Quakers and Native Americans*, ed. Ignacio Gallup-Diaz and Geoffrey Plank (Leiden, The Netherlands: Brill, 2019)

Sidney Xu Lu, *The Making of Japanese Settler Colonialism: Malthusianism and Trans-Pacific Migration, 1868–1961* (New York: Cambridge University Press, 2019)

S. Meager, "The Life of Japanese Quaker Inazo Nitobe – Samuel M. Snipes," *Friends Journal* (blog), July 1, 2011, https://www.friendsjournal.org/life-japanese-quaker-inazo-nitobe-1862-1933/

Ramon Myers and Mark Peattie, eds., *The Japanese Colonial Empire, 1895–1945* (Princeton, New Jersey: Princeton University Press, 1984)

Inazō Nitobe, *The Imperial Agricultural College of Sapporo, Japan* (Sapporo, Japan: Imperial College of Agriculture, 1893)

Inazō Nitobe, "Americanism in the East," in *Thoughts and Essays* (Tokyo, Japan: Teibi Publishing Company, 1909a)

Inazō Nitobe, "Cum Grano Salis," in *Thoughts and Essays* (Tokyo, Japan: Teibi Publishing Company, 1909b)

Inazō Nitobe. "Japan as a Colonizer," *The Journal of Race Development* 2, no. 4 (April 1912a): 359–361

"Dr. Inazo Nitobe Asserts Japanese Are Mixed Race." *Daily Illini*. April 12, 1912b. Illinois Digital Newspaper Collections. https://idnc.library.illinois.edu/?a=d&d=DIL19120412.2.2&e=en-20-1-img-txIN

Inazō Nitobe, "Primitive Life and Presiding Death in Korea," in *Nitobe Inazō Zenshū*, Vol. 12 (Tokyo, Japan: Kyōbunkan, 1960–1982), 327–328

George Masaaki Oshiro. *Internationalist in Prewar Japan: Nitobe Inazō, 1862–1933* (Dissertation University of British Columbia, 1985)

Howard Pyle, "The Early Quakers in England and Pennsylvania," *Harper's New Monthly Magazine*, November 1882, 828

David Sim, "The Peace Policy of Ulysses S. Grant," *American Nineteenth Century History* 9, no. 3 (September 1, 2008): 241–268

Julian Stargardt, "Nitobe, Inazo Ota," in *Historical Dictionary of the Friends (Quakers)*, ed. Margery Post Abbott et al. (Lanham, MD: Scarecrow Press, 2012)

So Jung Um, *Japanese Colonial Policy Studies, 1909–1945: Nitobe Inazō, Yanaihara Tadao, and Tōbata Seiichi* (PhD Dissertation University of Michigan, 2017)

9

PROGRESSIVE FRIENDS

Shaping the Liberal Quaker Past and Present

Chuck Fager

The Progressive Friends were an American Quaker reform movement that appeared in the 1840s. They took form in the aftermath of the major division of US Quakers called the Great Separation of 1827.

Beginning in Philadelphia, the 1827 separation divided Friends into two opposed groups: the more numerous became known as Hicksites, after the well-known Quaker preacher Elias Hicks, who was their inspiration but did not want to be their leader. Hicks called for a reform of Quaker structures and beliefs, to recover what he considered the original authenticity of Quakerism.

Hicks's opponents came to be called Orthodox Quakers (or Friends), because they represented the Quaker establishment, organizationally and theologically. Both aspects were important, and disputed (Cf. Ingle, *Quakers in Conflict*).

Theologically, the Orthodox were being influenced by the rising evangelical outlook, especially among Protestant middle- and upper-class church people. It emphasized the emerging biblical literalism, the blood atonement of Jesus, and a drive for enforced uniformity of belief in the Quaker community.

Organizationally, the Orthodox Friends clustered at or near the top of what was then a sharply defined, hierarchical form of Quaker church governance. The currently widespread notion that Quakerism was an equalitarian movement is anachronistic and fictional; within two decades of its founding, the Society of Friends was nothing of the sort. Its nineteenth-century books of Discipline made this long-established hierarchy plain:

> The connection and subordination of our meetings for discipline are thus: Preparative meetings are accountable to the monthly; monthly to the quarterly; and the quarterly to the yearly meeting. *So that if the yearly meeting be at any time dissatisfied with the proceedings of any inferior meeting; or a quarterly meeting with the proceedings of either of its monthly meetings; or a monthly meeting with the proceedings of either of its preparative meetings: Such meeting or meetings ought with readiness and meekness to render an account thereof when required.*
>
> (Kuenning; emphasis added)

DOI: 10.4324/9780429030925-11

Within meetings, this structure was upheld by groups of "recorded" ministers and elders, who served for life, and held private "select meetings". The moves by this "Quaker Establishment" to enforce evangelical orthodoxy in belief, and to silence critics such as Elias Hicks, were the matches that lit the tinder of 1827's conflagration.

After the split, both groups retained the top-down structure (Kuenning). But some nascent Hicksite liberals hoped for a loosening of disciplinary strictures, which were many, and led to frequent individual disownments for what some deemed petty offenses, such as attending weddings that were not Quaker (Palmer 12, 101). One of these hopeful Hicksites was an eloquent young mother, Lucretia Mott, who was born on Nantucket Island but settled with her husband, James, in Philadelphia. Her preaching in meetings was steadily gaining confidence and attracting more attention.

Mott's hopes for change strengthened in the 1830s when she learned about, and was strongly drawn to, the new movement called abolitionism. By then, US Quakers had been against owning, buying, or selling enslaved persons for fifty-plus years. But their corporate stance as to abolishing the institution was hedged about and very equivocal. As a Baltimore Yearly Meeting Elders' epistle in 1842 put it:

> We earnestly and affectionately intreat our Friends and brethren every where, to pause and deeply reflect upon the consequences, before they commit themselves in any degree, by countenancing or entering into associations founded upon principles, or governed by motives, inconsistent with the mild, forbearing, and peaceable spirit of the Gospel. We may rest assured that all attempts to effect the liberation of the slaves, by coercive measures, will be met, as they already have been, by a counteracting force, and if persisted in, will finally lead to violence – perhaps to bloodshed. . . .
>
> May we therefore, beloved Friends, retire to the Divine Gift within ourselves, and seek after that "wisdom that is from above which is first pure, then peaceable, gentle, and easy to be entreated, full of mercy and good fruits, without partiality, and without hypocrisy." May we study to be quiet, and mind our own business; and may we carefully avoid putting forth our hands to a work, to which we have not been divinely called, least like one formerly, we bring death upon ourselves, and be the means of bringing destruction upon others.
>
> *(Fager 2013, 58–64)*

This call to personal purity and group quietism on ending slavery was soon backed up by Hicksite Establishment power: many Hicksites who joined the burgeoning abolitionist groups were disowned or hounded into resigning, in what I have called the Great Purge (Fager 2014, chaps. 2–3, esp. 29–32). Similar warnings were sounded against Quakers joining with other growing reform movements of the era, temperance and women's rights prominent among them ("Admonitory Address").

The reforming spirit was basically at odds with this Quietist Quaker tradition which persisted among both Hicksites and Orthodox. Although she became a recorded minister, and despite the warnings, Lucretia Mott became active in all three movements. She also read widely among insurgent Protestant thinkers, and joined them in questioning aloud biblical literalism and evangelical doctrines, in favor of what she called "practical Christianity" (aka reform) and "the law of progress" as a truer goal than some otherworldly "salvation" (Mott 1848).

This new religious thinking reinforced Mott's doubts about the legitimacy of the hierarchy of the Quaker "select meetings," which ever more firmly and oppressively opposed both the new movements and the new beliefs. As she wrote in 1841 to a close friend:

I have long noticed that difficulties in our Society have had their origin in our Select Meetings, humbling as is the fact. Perhaps if their power were more limited, one cause of dissensions would be removed. 'Tis true we often have good meetings together, but what is there that ought to be regarded as secret? I am more and more prepared for their discontinuance.

(Hallowell, 218)

Her unease did not flag with time. In 1852 Mott complained to her cousin Nathaniel Barney:

What feeble steps have yet been taken from Popery to Protestantism! Our Ecclesiastics, be they Bishops or Quaker Elders, have still far too much sway. Convents we have yet, with high walls, whose inmates having taken the veil, dare not give range to their free-born spirit, now so miserably cramped and shrouded.

(Palmer, 213)

Mott rapidly became nationally known as a public speaker in a time when women speaking in public to mixed male-female (then called "promiscuous") audiences was still seen by most as scandalous (Cromwell, 117; Perry, 160f). But she was not alone in her advancing views. Other liberal Hicksites and her own political skills protected her against several attempts by Establishment elders to silence or disown her (Palmer, 108, 113, 158, 161, 169, 432; Hallowell, 292–294).

Besides which, by 1842, the dissent she spearheaded was taking off on its own, first in Ohio and Michigan. In Ohio's Green Plain Quarterly Meeting, a group of abolitionist-minded reformers, including one named Joseph Dugdale, proposed to their yearly meeting, Genesee, that it abolish their bodies of life-tenured recorded ministers and their closed "select meeting." While that proposal was dismissed out of hand by yearly meeting officials, to the north, Michigan Quarter (another abolitionist hotbed) somehow managed to get the job done, and abolished its "select meetings" entirely (Wilson).

Michigan Quarterly Meeting to Genesee Yearly Meeting, 1843

"This meeting considering the Meeting of Ministers and Elders no longer beneficial to us, have discontinued it, and we cannot feel a duty to resume that Meeting. And we are desirous of having the [Yearly Meeting] Discipline so revised as to make that order no longer obligatory upon us. The women's meeting concurring.

(Bradley)

Both these insurgent Quarterly Meetings paid for such temerity: their "superior" yearly meetings (Indiana for Green Plain, and Genesee in western New York) laid them down (i.e., abolished them; Bradley; Fager 2014, 32–34). But in both locations, the disowned insurgents soon organized new groups, also called "yearly meetings," with the addition of "congregational (i.e., no "Select" hierarchy), or "Progressive", as their revised religious lodestar.

It took Genesee Yearly Meeting's elders six years, until 1848, to bring the hammer down on the Michigan rebels (Wilson). During that time, the United States had won a war with Mexico, which brought several more states into American territory and expanded and intensified the struggle over the expansion of slavery.

When Genesee acted, about 200 of those attending their session walked out and then formed the Waterloo Progressive Friends Yearly Meeting (Bradley, 95–108). They had the support of the rising abolitionist star Frederick Douglass. Also among them were five of the six women who also took time to gather in a kitchen to organize the first national convention on women's rights, in the nearby village of Seneca Falls. One of the five was Lucretia Mott (Palmer, xxiv–xxv, 166–167).

The Progressive movement soon expanded its reach to Philadelphia Yearly Meeting. There it was spurred by conflict among Hicksites over holding abolitionist meetings in meetinghouses (Fager 2013, 5–8). Establishment Friends raised numerous objections: the speakers were typically not Quaker, and such outside connections were still to be shunned; many were "hirelings," preaching for pay, something Friends then abhorred, and their messages typically involved calls to do things like support the Underground Railroad, which were illegal in the South and in danger from mobs in the North (Fager 2013, 58–64, 76f).

The underground was a very live issue around Marlborough Meeting, southwest of Philadelphia. It was close to the borders of Maryland and Delaware, both slave states, from which frequent escapes made for a brisk and tumultuous illicit runaway traffic. In June 1852, the Marlborough elders obtained arrest warrants for Oliver Johnson, an abolitionist speaker, and four local Friends, who were then arrested when they tried to have Johnson speak in the meetinghouse. This incident was not actually violent, but was shocking, and came to be known as the "Marlborough Riot" (Wahl 1975, 45). In the aftermath, several dozen Friends were disowned by Marlborough and nearby Kennett Meeting for abolitionist activism.

The rebel exiles' response was to organize a new Pennsylvania Yearly Meeting of Progressive Friends in nearby Longwood (Pennsylvania 1853). This group became the largest and longest lasting of Progressive Friends outposts, and the only one which built a meetinghouse which still stands. Its clerk for the first ten years was Joseph Dugdale, one of the Friends disowned in the laying down of Green Plain in Ohio. He had also attended the Waterloo Progressive sessions before moving to Pennsylvania (Dugdale 1849).

Longwood was also the group which produced the most detailed Progressive manifesto, the *Exposition of Sentiments* (Fager 2013, 420–433). This remarkable 6500-word document deserves to be much better known. It was as influential in its liberal Quaker stream as was the more famous, only slightly longer, and one might say notorious Orthodox-drafted *Richmond Declaration of Faith* of 1887 (The Richmond Declaration). Besides endorsing such social reforms as temperance, abolition of slavery, and ending war, the *Exposition* also called for sweeping changes in Quaker polity and governance, among them the abolition of "select meetings," an end to the recording of ministers, a rational approach to understanding the Bible and doctrine, and replacing the sacral "peculiar people" Quaker identity with an individual-centered spirituality.

To call the *Exposition*'s program radical is an understatement. The document, though enthusiastically adopted at Longwood's initial session, was binding on no one, and its name was soon forgotten by most. Yet its key tenets persisted and proved seminal and formative for generations.

The Progressives never kept a membership list; one did not join them but simply attended. Annual gatherings at Longwood sometimes drew crowds of thousands to hear speakers such as William Lloyd Garrison and Sojourner Truth. Lucretia Mott was one of many Friends who took part there for years, while still active in her Philadelphia Hicksite meeting, and visiting other Hicksites, where she preached the Progressive gospel along with her other reforms. In this way, the Progressives became not an institutional rival to the Hicksites but an ongoing, spreading influence.

Further, their sessions were not like traditional Quaker gatherings – little time for worship, maximum time for formal lectures and debates over resolutions, called "Testimonies," which were passed or defeated by votes. Topics ranged widely over the varied terrain of reform and its associated interests; a major one for some years was spiritualism (Pennsylvania 1859, 31; cf. also Fager 2013, chap. 5).

Soon enough the Civil War engulfed these Friends, along with the rest of the country. This cataclysm evoked major changes. Longwood Friends had twice appealed to the president and Congress to shut down military bases and disband the navy (Fager 2013, 58; cf. Pennsylvania, 1853, 10; 1857, 15) and many times they had vowed to find a peaceable way to end slavery. But history was now drowning that hope in blood, and soon the tide of their opinion turned inexorably toward supporting Abraham Lincoln's public duty to quell the "treasonable outbreak" of proslavery secession by all available means (i.e., war). In June 1862, they even sent a delegation to Washington, bearing an appeal to the president, which they were able to deliver in person (Pennsylvania 1862, 17–19). It urged Lincoln to issue an Emancipation Proclamation immediately freeing the slaves, as a means of hastening a victorious end to the war. He received them and listened politely to the appeal.

Many young Hicksite males also defied the pacifist elders and joined the Union Army. When the survivors returned, a handful were disowned, but more were accepted back if they asked. The official Quaker condemnation of war remained, but the decision of whether to take part de facto became a matter of individual judgment. This shift in discipline was seismic: it ended the Great Purge and was soon followed by the shedding among Hicksites of most other Quaker "peculiarities" (Fager 2003).

In 1860, the Progressives opened a new front: Joseph Dugdale moved to Iowa and settled in Mount Pleasant. The town's appeal was enhanced by the presence of a Hicksite meeting, under the care of Baltimore Yearly Meeting, nearly a thousand miles east. Mount Pleasant Friends courted Dugdale, whose reputation had evidently preceded him. He told them plainly he remained a Progressive Friend in his views. They were fine with that, and soon he was their clerk, and once again an "official" Hicksite Friend (Dugdale 1863; Palmer, 349).

This restoration proved fateful. In 1875, Mount Pleasant became part of the new Illinois Hicksite Yearly Meeting. Dugdale helped write its first *Book of Discipline* (Fager 2014, 117–120; cf. Illinois Yearly Meeting 1878), which showed a strong Progressive influence, sharply curbing the role and significance of recorded ministers and giving up the practice of disowning those who married "out of unity" (i.e., took non-Quaker spouses). The two other members of that drafting committee were also important figures: Jesse Holmes, another Iowan, who had supported Progressives in Ohio and New York, and whose son, Jesse Jr., born in 1864, was to play an important future role (Wahl 1979, cf. Fager 2014, chaps. 17–26); and Jonathan Plummer, the new Illinois clerk, who conceived and floated the idea of cooperative gatherings (not unlike Progressive annual meetings) among Hicksite yearly meetings (Illinois Yearly Meeting, Minutes 1878, 15). The first of these gatherings was held in Waynesville Ohio in 1882, and Plummer's idea was the seed that grew into Friends General Conference (Warren).

By the 1880s, the other Progressive bodies had dissipated, except for Longwood, which was more of an annual forum for "Progressive" ideas than anything else. But the movement's influence had now become pervasive among Hicksites, its internal reform agenda kept alive and advanced by younger Friends linked to its heritage.

Perhaps the most notable of these younger successors was Jesse Holmes Jr. Raised in Nebraska, he moved east for graduate school and soon joined the faculty of the Hicksite-founded Swarthmore College near Philadelphia (Wahl 1979). There he was a vocal and activist fixture for forty years. He was also a fixture in both Friends General Conference (FGC) and Philadelphia Yearly Meeting. In the Yearly meeting, he was on the committee which in 1918 succeeded in abolishing the recording of ministers (PYM Minutes 1917, 1918; *Friends Intelligencer*, 6th Month 1 1916, 346). And in FGC, he was on another committee which in 1926 produced a *Uniform Discipline* for the then seven Hicksite Yearly Meetings (FGC Central Committee Minutes 1922; cf. *Friends Intelligencer*, 10th Month 28, 1922, 684).

This *Uniform Discipline* quietly codified almost every particular of the Progressive intra-Quaker agenda, as enunciated in the 1853 Longwood *Exposition of Sentiments,* from the abolition of recording, a congregational yearly meeting polity, to rationalist theology and Bible study, and individual-centered religiosity. Most had already been adopted piecemeal by the member groups (*Uniform Discipline*).

Holmes bears one further distinction, almost eerie in its symmetry: in 1927, he became the last clerk of the Longwood Progressive Friends (Wahl 1979), which still held annual meetings in the Longwood meeting house. A kind of apostolic succession can be traced here, from Lucretia Mott who helped launch Longwood; to Joseph Dugdale who first clerked it and then took the ideas to Iowa, where he met and worked with John Plummer and Jesse Holmes Sr. to birth Illinois yearly Meeting and FGC; and now this long circle closed with Jesse Holmes Jr., after helping draft the ratifying Progressive documents, back in Longwood, for what proved to be its final acts (Fager 2014, 185). Its work done, Longwood was laid down in 1940 after eighty-seven years (*Daily Local News*), though the building still stands and is used as a tourist information center (Brandywine). Holmes Jr. died in 1942 (Wahl 1979, 433).

The Progressive Friends, as we have seen, gave short shrift to organizational niceties. Nor did they care much for history: their lodestar was Progress, ever ahead, ever coming to pass, or being impeded by reaction. They did not pause to write their own history. The same goes for other American liberal Friends. Thus it is no accident that most major Quaker histories have been written by authors shaped in the Orthodox streams: they believe in history, sacred history first, with Quaker history – at least theirs – filling small but not trivial chapters thereof.

In mid-1920 an article, "Congregational or Progressive Friends: A Forgotten Episode in Quaker History," appeared in the *Bulletin of Friends Historical Association* (now called *Quaker History*). The *Bulletin* was published at Haverford College, the Orthodox-founded school near Philadelphia, and was written by Haverford professor Allen C. Thomas, its editor. The article is the earliest one I have found in a scholarly journal about Progressive Friends. It is also a prime illustration of the Progressives' poor treatment in Quaker historiography.

Thomas was correct that by 1920, the Progressive Friends groups in western New York and Michigan, which he dealt with, were long gone, and records of their existence and work were few and hard to find.

However, as Thomas's article was being written and put into print, actual living Progressive Friends gathered for their Yearly Meeting less than 25 miles away, at Longwood in June, as they had for more than sixty years. The sessions drew large crowds, and major speakers included socialist leader Norman Thomas and W.E.B. Du Bois. "DuBois," wrote a local reporter with tantalizing understatement, "lived up to his erudite yet militant reputation" (unidentified news clipping dated June 7, 1920, in the Chester County PA Historical Society "Longwood" files).

Forgotten? Indeed not. Beneath notice? The inference is hard to rebut.

In the standard histories, when they are mentioned at all, the Progressive Friends are seen as a minor, mid-nineteenth century separation out of some of the Hicksite yearly meetings, an ephemeral and irrelevant splinter.

Consider: Elbert Russell's *History of Quakerism* gives them one paragraph (Russell, 1942, 1979, 370–371), as does Barbour and Frost's *The Quakers* (Barbour and Frost, 181). Rufus Jones, in *The Later Periods of Quakerism*, Vol. II, relegates them to a summary footnote (Jones, 1921, 596), while neither John Punshon's *Portrait in Grey* nor the evangelical Walter Williams's *The Rich Heritage of Quakerism* mentions them at all.

Most surprisingly, Howard Brinton, whose ancestral Chester County turf includes Longwood, stated flatly – and erroneously – in his perennially bestselling *Friends for Three Hundred (& Fifty) Years*, that "no further separations occurred among [the Hicksites after 1827]" (191). The distinguished scholar Thomas Hamm, in his 2003 survey *The Quakers in America,* continues this tradition, devoting only two paragraphs to the movement. (His book, *God's Government Begun,* which surveyed mid-nineteenth-century utopian community experiments in the Midwest, offers a much better sketch of the early Ohio Progressives. [Hamm 1995, esp. chaps. 3, 6].) For that matter, at the time this chapter was prepared (winter 2021), no scholarly history of the Hicksites had yet appeared, though one is reported to be nearing completion – written, of course, by an Orthodox-oriented historian.

Thus, until very recently, the published remains of Progressive Friends history were scattered and slight, a handful of journal essays and short sketches in a few larger histories. The most detailed studies were by Albert J. Wahl, beginning with his unpublished doctoral dissertation from 1951. Wahl's is a pioneering and deeply researched work, but it deals only with the pre-Civil War period and ignores spiritualism. Wahl extended his account of Longwood in an article (Wahl 1975) and in his biography of Jesse Holmes Jr. (1979).

Wahl does not mention the FGC *Uniform Discipline* of 1926, which codified the Progressive impact. For that matter, by the late 1930s, the *Uniform Discipline* was essentially lost and completely forgotten even by FGC. When accidentally rediscovered in 1999, its existence (indeed, the very concept) was a complete surprise to both the staff of the main archive of Hicksite Quakerism at Swarthmore College and the FGC Centennial Committee (Fager 2000). Not until 2014 did the first volumes appear that encompassed the full arc of Progressive/Congregational Quaker history, from 1842 to 1940, based on original research: *Remaking Friends*, a narrative account, and *Angels of Progress*, a documentary collection, both by this writer.

Yet the Progressives' history and influence are, once seen, undeniable, substantial, and continuing. Further, while the results are, as usual with history, ambiguous and arguable, they are far from played out.

References

"Admonitory Address" to Indiana Yearly Meeting, reprinted as, "Pious Blackguardism," in *The Liberator,* February 2, 1849, p. 17.

Barbour, Hugh & Frost, J. William. *The Quakers.* New York: Greenwood Press, 1988.

Bradley, A. Day. "Progressive Friends in Michigan and New York." *Quaker History* 52 (1963): 95–103.

Brandywine Valley Tourism Information Center, https://tinyurl.com/yypmwwyj

Brinton, Howard. *Friends for 350 Years.* Wallingford, PA: Pendle Hill, 2002.

Cromwell, Otelia. *Lucretia Mott: The Story of One of America's Greatest Women.* Cambridge: Harvard University Press, 1958.

Daily Local News, West Chester PA, September 9, 1940; and Longwood 1940 Program flyer.

Dugdale, Joseph. "Reform among the Quakers." *The Anti-Slavery Bugle,* August 18, 1849. reprinted in *The Liberator,* October 26, 1849, p. 172.

Dugdale, Joseph, letter to William Lloyd Garrison, January 3, 1863, in Joseph Dugdale Correspondence, cdm-HC_QuakSlav-3791, Friends Historical Library, Swarthmore College.

Fager, Chuck. "FGC's 'Uniform Discipline' Rediscovered." *Quaker History* 89 (Fall 2000): 51–59, http://quaker.org/quest/uniform-1.htm

Fager, Chuck. "Speaking Peace, Living Peace: American Quakers Face the Civil War." 2003, Baltimore Yearly Meeting, https://tinyurl.com/y4lh9kl8

Fager, Chuck. *Angels of Progress: A Documentary History of the Progressive Friends.* Durham, NC: Kimo Press, 2013.

Fager, Chuck. *Remaking Friends: How Progressive Friends Changed Quakerism & Helped Save America.* Durham, NC: Kimo Press, 2014.

Friends General Conference (aka FGC), *Proceedings,* 1922, 1926.

Friends Intelligencer, 6th Month 1, 1918.

Friends Intelligencer, 10th Month 28, 1922.

Hallowell, Anna Davis. *James and Lucretia Mott. Life and Letters.* Boston, Houghton Mifflin, 1884, https://archive.org/details/jamesandlucreti00hallgoog

Hamm, Thomas. *God's Government Begun.* Bloomington. Indiana University Press, 1995.

Hamm, Thomas. *The Quakers in America.* New York: Columbia, 2006.

Illinois Yearly Meeting, Minutes, 1875–1890.

Illinois Yearly Meeting. *Rules of Discipline and Advices of Illinois Yearly Meeting of Friends.* Chicago: A.J. Goff & Co, 1878. Online at: http://tinyurl.com/mpobjfe

Ingle, H. Larry. *Quakers in Conflict: The Hicksite Reformation.* Knoxville, TN: University of Tennessee Press, 1986.

Jones, *The Later Periods of Quakerism*, Vol. II. London: Macmillan, 1921, Online at: https://archive.org/details/laterperiodsofqu02joneuoft/page/596/mode/2up

Kuenning, Larry & Licia, Eds. *The Old Discipline: Nineteenth-Century Friends' Disciplines in America.* Farmington, ME: Quaker Heritage Press, 1999.

Mott, Lucretia. "Lucretia Mott, The Law of Progress." May 9, 1848, https://users.wfu.edu/zulick/340/mott.html

Palmer, Beverly, Ed. *Selected Letters of Lucretia Coffin Mott.* Urbana: University of Illinois Press, 2002.

Pennsylvania Yearly Meeting of Progressive Friends (Longwood), *Proceedings,* 1853–1905.

Perry, Mark. *Lift Up Thy Voice: The Grimke Family's Journey from Slaveholders to Civil Rights Leaders.* New York: Penguin, 2001.

Philadelphia Yearly Meeting (Hicksite; aka PYM), *Minutes,* 1917 & 1918.

Russell, Elbert. *The History of Quakerism.* New York: Macmillan, 1942; Richmond Indiana: Friends United Press, 1979, pp. 370–371.

"The Richmond Declaration of Faith, 1887." In *Indiana Yearly Meeting Faith & Practice,* pp. 19–35, https://www.iym.org/file/18660580-ed4f-11ea-8884-cbb086c5411b

Thomas, Allen C. "Congregational or Progressive Friends: A Forgotten Episode in Quaker History." *Bulletin of Friends Historical Association* X (1920): 21–32, http://tinyurl.com/oju4acv

Uniform Discipline, Friends General Conference (aka FGC), 1926, https://tinyurl.com/y64m99yh

Wahl, Albert J. "The Congregational or Progressive Friends in the pre-Civil War Reform Movement." Doctoral dissertation, Ed.D., Temple University, 1951.

Wahl, Albert J. "Longwood Meeting: Public Forum for the American Democratic Faith." *Pennsylvania History* XLII, no. 1 (January 1975): 43–69.

Wahl, Albert J. *Jesse Herman Holmes: A Quaker's Affirmation for Man.* Richmond, IN: Friends United Press, 1979.

Warren, Elizabeth. *Jonathan Wright Plummer, Quaker Philanthropy.* Bloomington, IN: Author House, 2006.

Williams, Walter. *The Rich Heritage of Quakerism.* Newberg, OR: Barclay Press, 1962, 1987.

Wilson, Brian C., Western Michigan University. "The Battle for Battle Creek: Sectarian Competition in the Yankee West." Paper delivered at the Conference of Quaker Historians and Archivists, 2012, Newmarket, Ontario, https://quakertheology.org/the-battle-for-battle-creek/

10

STUBBORN FRIENDS

Quakers and Native Americans in the Long Nineteenth Century

Damon B. Akins

Between American Independence at the end of the eighteenth century and the Great Depression in the twentieth, the relationship between the US government and Native Americans changed from a policy based on eradication or removal to "protection" through assimilation.[1] The expanding settler colonial state pushed the continent's Indigenous people west and then followed them over the Appalachian Mountains into the Ohio, Missouri, and Mississippi River valleys. By mid-century, the United States had acquired the western half of the current territorial extent of the country through war with Mexico and treaties with Great Britain. Settlers traveled to the west coast in search of wealth. Settler communities killed tens of thousands of Native Americans and pushed many more out of their lands. The federal government forced Native people to reservations and other territories in the trans-Mississippi west. By the 1860s, settlers and speculators followed new rushes and railroads back east in a violent backfill of the Great Plains, squeezing Indigenous people at every point and culminating in the explosive violence of that decade.

Indians could no longer be removed beyond the reach of settler greed, and the protests against widespread violence grew more pronounced. Federal policy turned toward assimilation and protection, and Quakers were instrumental in this shift, having long prided themselves on their benevolence in regard to Indigenous people. Quakers' stubborn commitment to peace, honesty, integrity and a universalist approach to religion which recognized the light within all people drove them to resist the unchecked greed and violence of the settler state early on. The earnest, honest, and industrious aspects of Quaker identity meshed easily with industry and industrial agriculture–centered capitalism upon which the assimilation program was based. They sought to uplift and assimilate Indian peoples along lines familiar to them and in sync with their world view and practical experience, which often failed to take into account the needs of the Native people themselves. By 1868, Quakers came to dominate federal Indian policy. While their assistance was often a welcome alternative to the violence Native people faced, it was nonetheless tied to their eventual dispossession and assimilation into the American polity. Peace under the Friends' guidance also included an end to formal treaties between Native people and the United States in 1871, which paved the way for the implementation of allotment policy and deployment of the military to foreclose Indian sovereignty in the 1880s and 1890s.

Native people took what they could use from Quakers but repurposed it to further their own goals. Many welcomed Quaker educational efforts, which often enabled them to resist

DOI: 10.4324/9780429030925-12

acculturation. Many more were shaped by them whether they welcomed them or not. Some Native Americans were interested in the religious practices of the Society of Friends, but most did not convert. Indian communities were resistant to the proscription of *civilization* and the patterns of behavior it imposed on Indian life. As was so often the case when Indigenous people encountered outsiders wishing to help them, they selectively appropriated the help, leveraging it toward *their* own ends, often subtly at odds with the visions of those wishing to help them.

To attempt a concise overview, I have highlighted six "moments" in which the stories of specific places and the people – Quakers, Indians, and others – who interacted around and in those places illustrate this fundamental disconnect between Quaker and Indian goals. The complexity of American Indian history defies easy generalization and can only be captured through case studies that suggest themes or trends but remain attentive to individual differences among (and within) Indian communities. Similarly, the lack of formalized doctrine in the Society of Friends meant that there was significant diversity of beliefs and approaches taken by Friends. Focusing on western New York, western Ohio, Indian Territory (present-day Oklahoma), Kansas, Nebraska, and California, we will roughly follow the path of settler society as it colonized and incorporated the various "wests." These places brought together a variety of people together and tested their ability and willingness to cooperate and compromise. We begin with a very brief overview of Quakers and Indians in Pennsylvania in order to establish the centrality of the image and mythology surrounding Quakers' early interaction with the Lenni Lenape and its role in helping to animate subsequent Quaker actions and beliefs.

First Moment: William Penn's Peace

When William Penn negotiated the Treaty of Shackamaxon in 1682–83 with the Lenni Lenape, in whose territory Penn sought to settle, he established a period of relative peace distinctive among the colonial enterprises of the eastern seaboard. This history is well known, partly because of its distinctiveness, but also because the story provided the Quaker tradition with an illustration – literally – of their benevolence. It was the subject of Benjamin West's famous painting, "Penn's Treaty with the Indians," as well as Edward Hicks' painting "Peaceable Kingdom."[2] The story had value to Quakers.

Penn died in 1718, and his sons and others who followed him into positions of leadership in Pennsylvania were less committed to his policies. As a result, settlers gradually pushed the Lenape north and west. Within twenty years, the infamous and fraudulent Walking Treaty (1737) had damaged his (and Quakers') reputation among Lenape even further, pushing most of them into alliances with the Moravians in Ohio or the French along the Great Lakes. By the middle of the eighteenth century, with the eruption of the French and Indian War, Penn's peace had collapsed entirely. Despite this, its memory was valuable to Quakers, as evidence of their benevolence, and to Native People who leveraged it as a way to force Quakers to honor the past they claimed.

At the turn of the century, Friends from the Baltimore and Philadelphia Yearly Meetings sought to restore their reputation through mission work. They turned to Native People in New York and Ohio, where they provided training in agricultural practices and the domestic arts in which men engaged in close cultivation of managed and fenced fields, while women worked in duties associated with Quaker understandings of keeping a proper home. In the face of intense settler pressure on Native land, Friends believed intensive agriculture would reduce Indian need for land and make them more amenable to parting with the land they no longer needed. At its most charitable, they saw this as a way to defuse a volatile situation peacefully. But Native people quickly recognized the economic value of the land they possessed. Rather than parting with it, they sought to utilize it as an asset to further their own goals of cultural preservation. Thus, despite the fact that Quakers provided what they understood to be "necessary" and "useful" assistance, they still faced a fundamental paradox: the more acculturated Indians became, the better able they were to resist the elements of acculturation that ran counter to their needs.[3]

Second Moment: Early Missions

The Friends' work among the Iroquois (Haudenosaunee) began with the Oneida. Despite the fact that they had sided with the Americans during the Revolution, the new government nonetheless seized Oneida land as part of their effort to punish the Iroquois for their support of the British. Based on the Quakers' reputation, the Oneida sought them out for assistance. Friends from the Philadelphia Yearly Meeting sent a three-man delegation to the Oneida in spring of 1796, where they established a model farm and tried to address the needs of the Oneida *as they saw them*. For their part, the Oneida were interested in assistance, but they were less welcoming of the cultural change the Quakers envisioned. For example, the Oneida purchased food from other Indians. Quakers envisioned Oneida men as small farmers and saw agricultural self-sufficiency as a sign of progress. But in Oneida culture (as with many Native peoples), agriculture was work traditionally done by women. These disagreements, among others, caused the mission to flounder, and the Quakers officially abandoned it in 1798, although individual Friends from the New York Yearly Meeting continued to support the Oneida informally. As they had with the Lenape, Quakers moved on from the Oneida, this time to the Seneca, the westernmost of the Haudenosaunee.

Quaker–Seneca relations had begun when Cornplanter, the powerful Allegany Seneca leader, traveled to Philadelphia in 1790 to negotiate with the US government. While in residence there, he attended a Quaker meeting. When he returned to Burnt House, his residence at Allegany, he wrote to the Philadelphia Yearly Meeting asking them to provide education for Seneca children. He sent his sons to be educated by Friends in Philadelphia. In 1797, Seneca leaders relinquished much of their land in western New York in return for four large reservations (Allegany, Buffalo Creek, Cattaraugus, and Tonawanda), and a few other small settlements. In 1798, at Cornplanter's invitation, Friends settled a mission at Burnt House, which focused on homebuilding and modernizing agricultural practices.[4]

In the summer of 1799, Cornplanter's older brother, Handsome Lake, had a powerful vision.[5] The vision formed the basis of a religion – the Code of Handsome Lake, or the Longhouse Religion – which combined elements of Quaker worship with a partial rejection of white culture in favor of traditional Seneca practices. Cornplanter and Handsome Lake exercised significant influence among the Iroquois in the years leading up to the War of 1812. Their influence buttressed the Quaker mission, which expanded to include a school at Tunesassa in 1803, and a mission to Clear Creek near the Cattaraugus Reservation a few years later. The war interrupted Quaker efforts and Seneca life.

The end of the war in 1815 coincided with the death of Handsome Lake and a shift in power from Cornplanter to Red Jacket (Sagoyewatha), the leader of the Buffalo Creek Reservation. In 1816, Joseph Elkington established a new Friends school at Cold Springs in the Allegany Reservation, but Red Jacket opposed it. In an illustration of the changing power dynamics, Cornplanter acceded to Red Jacket's opposition and ordered the school closed.

Red Jacket's resistance stemmed from growing pressure on Seneca land and a radically changing landscape. The Erie Canal, which came into operation in 1821, dramatically altered land values and use. As non-Indian settlement increased, so too did pressure on the land the Seneca held. In 1826, Red Jacket, Cornplanter, and other Seneca leaders signed a dubious treaty with the United States which surrendered all of their small settlements, leaving the Seneca with only the four primary reservations. The consolidation contributed to power struggles within Seneca leadership. In addition, a schism among Quakers divided efforts in the region between those who followed the teachings of Elias Hicks, focusing on the "Inner Light," and those who called themselves Orthodox and retained a strong commitment to the collectivity of the meeting house. According to historian Laurence Hauptman, the Hicksites saw Indians as a "vanishing race that had to be carefully transformed for their own good. . . . [they] could not long endure because of constant pressures by avaricious and morally corrupt whites."[6] They allied with conservative Whigs in pressing for removal as a way to protect Indians from the far more harsh removal plans of the Democratic administration of Andrew Jackson. Maris B. Pierce, the Cattaraugus chief, who had been educated at the Tunesassa school and Dartmouth College, became a spokesman for what came to be called the "Old Chiefs" group which opposed the Hicksite efforts to consolidate Seneca settlements.

Some Seneca who had migrated west into Ohio in the 1810s sold that land in 1831 for land in Indian Territory, eventually becoming the Seneca-Cayuga Nation. In 1838, Seneca leaders in New York were forced to sign the fraudulent Treaty of Buffalo Creek, which dissolved the four reservations in return for land purchased for them in Kansas. The fraud was so clear that the Seneca, with the help of Hicksite Friends, launched a four-year fight for a new treaty. In 1842, they were able to have land restored to them at Tonawanda, Allegany, and Cattaraugus, and more appropriate compensation for the land they lost. Members of the Allegany and Cattaraugus reservations seceded from the Iroquois Confederacy and formed the Seneca Nation in 1848. The Tonawanda refused to join them and renegotiated a treaty with the United States which recognized them as the Tonawanda Band of Seneca, forming the third of the three federally recognized Seneca people today.[7]

Further west, Friends from the Baltimore Yearly Meeting faced similar challenges. In 1804, a three-man mission to Little Turtle's Miami people southwest of present-day Fort Wayne, Indiana, lasted only one year. Friends sent others to work at the site periodically thereafter. In 1807, Baltimore Friend William Kirk was sent by the federal government as agent for the Miami. Opinions differ as to why, but all agree that the mission under Kirk's leadership was a failure, and he transferred to the Shawnee town of Wapakoneta along the Auglaise River.[8]

Among the Shawnee, Friends found themselves in the heart of the confederacy organized by Tecumseh and his younger brother, Tenskwatawa (The Prophet). In 1805, Tenskwatawa had a vision, similar to that of Handsome Lake. However, while Handsome Lake had integrated aspects of Quaker worship and counseled careful cooperation with whites, Tenskwatawa's message urged Shawnee to reject all contact with white culture. The confederacy was weakened in 1811 after the Shawnee defeat at the Battle of Tippecanoe at the hands of the US Army. Tecumseh was killed in battle two years later. After the war, Tenskwatawa's influence remained, but he ran headlong into Quaker efforts. Lacking the similarities to Quaker worship practices found in the Code of Handsome Lake, many Friends viewed The Prophet's spiritual leadership as witchcraft or superstition.[9]

As it was with the Seneca, the 1820s brought increasingly intense settler pressure on their land. In 1825, the US government purchased land in Missouri on the Kansas River for the Shawnee. Henry Harvey, who took over the school at Wapakoneta in 1830, described the reluctance among Shawnee to improve their land. He attributed the reluctance to the fear that improvement would make it more attractive to white settlers. Harvey wrote that Friends

> would try to allay these apprehensions by assuring them that they need have no fears
> on that account, as they could not believe, for a moment, that the United States would

be so intolerably hard, after the solemn pledges so often made and repeated, that if they would improve their lands and be at peace, that they never should be asked for their land; but alas! what a mistake![10]

In 1831, the Shawnee signed the same treaty as the western Seneca in return for land in the west. By 1833, the Shawnee had been removed.

Third Moment: Removal

Quaker missionaries from Ohio followed the Shawnee west, establishing the Shawnee Mission near Merriam in 1837. As was often the case, removal divided Native people. The Shawnee who were relocated directly to Indian Territory in 1831 form the basis for the Eastern Shawnee Tribe of Oklahoma, with its capital in Wyandotte. Toward the end of the nineteenth century, many of the tribes from the Missouri valley and Ohio, who had already been removed west, were relocated again to Indian Territory with a significant loss of land. The Shawnee relocated to Kansas in 1831 were removed to Indian Territory and now form the Shawnee tribe, with its capital in Miami, Oklahoma. The Shawnee in Missouri formed the basis of today's Absentee Shawnee Tribe, which, after subsequent removals, now has its capital in Shawnee, Oklahoma. These threads, while complicated and tedious, are important in resisting the erasure that so often accompanies stories of removal.

Friends also established missions among the Kaw, Otoe-Missouria, Pawnee, Omaha, and Ponca. The Otoe Agency was established in 1854. Among the Pawnee, Quaker efforts to promote peace did little to resolve the long-standing conflict they had with the Sioux. Friends' efforts to promote civilization contributed to familiar patterns of factionalism: "traditional" versus "progressive" Indians competing for scarce resources. In reality, those labels never accurately captured the diversity of experiences but served as political labels.[11]

Indian–settler interaction had always been characterized by the presence of violence, but the middle of the nineteenth century saw the most abject and public violence yet. The Gold Rush in California initiated a genocidal campaign against California's Indigenous people which lasted for almost thirty years and decimated their population. At the end of the Civil War and after, the US Army sought to remove Indians, primarily northern and southern plains tribes, to reservations under the control of federally appointed Indian agents – appointments which were often nothing more than political spoils. Widespread corruption across many Indian agencies became a public spectacle. Additionally, a series of high-profile and particularly vicious massacres – of Shoshone at Bear River (now Idaho) in 1863, of Cheyenne and Arapaho at Sand Creek (Colorado) in 1864, and of Cheyenne at the Washita River (now Oklahoma) in 1868 – captured public attention.

Fourth Moment: Peace

In response to the dramatic increase of violence in the west in the 1850s and 1860s, Quakers lobbied in the nation's capital to press for a more humane and peaceful Indian policy. What emerged is commonly referred to "Grant's Peace Policy," although the term has been rightly criticized by many for downplaying or ignoring the policy's negative consequences. The policy outlined the ostensibly peaceful (but forced) assimilation of Indians into American culture, particularly through the efficient administration of Indian reservations as a tool to promote western agriculture, private land ownership, education, and the habits of civilized life, many of the same goals first elaborated seventy-five years before.

In 1868, president Grant established the Board of Indian Commissioners (BIC) comprising religious leaders from a variety of faiths. The BIC divided up the nation's reservations and agencies, distributing them to the control of specific denominations. Quakers took on direct control of sixteen reservations, divided between the Hicksite and Orthodox groups. Grant appointed Tonawanda Seneca Ely Parker as the first Indigenous person to serve as Commissioner of Indian Affairs between 1869 and 1871. Orthodox Quaker Enoch Hoag was appointed the superintendent for the Central Superintendency, while Liberal Quaker Barclay White was appointed superintendent of the Northern Superintendency. Each oversaw a diverse group of unrelated people who had been removed to or consolidated into reservations.

In 1869, Lawrie Tatum was appointed the first agent to the Kiowa and Comanche. He stepped into a volatile situation. The 1867 Medicine Lodge Treaty had provided land for the Kiowa, Comanche, and Kiowa-Apache, but within each of these groups, divisions remained. Kicking Bird, Lone Wolf, and Satanta were the leaders of the Kiowa. Kicking Bird advocated for peace, but the other two pushed for military resistance to the reservations. Tatum saw the solution as cultural, and forced the Kiowa and Comanche to abandon cultural practices at odds with reservation life. He was pleased when Satanta was arrested and sent to Texas in 1871. That same year, Thomas Battey, a Vermont Quaker, took a position as agent to the Caddo and Kiowa at the Wichita Agency in Anadarko. In that capacity, he worked closely with Kicking Bird to promote peace. He helped secure the release of Satanta in 1873, something Tatum opposed. As a result, Tatum resigned and advocated the use of military force to compel the Kiowa and Comanche to cease hostilities. Tatum was replaced by James Haworth, who had been moved to enter the Indian service by the massacre at Sand Creek. As agent, he removed soldiers and pursued an explicitly peaceful approach, working with Kicking Bird as well as Comanche leader Quanah Parker to negotiate a cessation of hostilities after the Red River War (1874–75).[12] Today, their descendants make up the Kiowa Tribe of Oklahoma, with its capital in Carnegie, the Comanche Nation, with its capital in Lawton, and the Apache Tribe of Oklahoma, with its capital in Anadarko.[13]

In 1872, Kientpoos led the Modoc people home to the lava beds of the present-day California–Oregon border region from the Klamath reservation, where the US government had placed them. From there, they fought a fierce war of resistance against the US Army that lasted into 1873. When the fighting stopped, the federal government allowed those Modocs who had not participated in the war to return to the Klamath reservation but sent those who had fought to Indian Territory. Steamboat Frank was one of 150 Modoc men, women, and children who came to Indian Territory, where the Indian Office located them on the Eastern Shawnee lands of the Quapaw agency – one of many under Quaker control. Hiram W. Jones and his son Endlsey, working with superintendent Hoag, ran a notoriously corrupt operation. The Jones and Hoag group distributed eleven of the twelve jobs at the Quapaw agency to family members and dealt corruptly with local licensed traders and teachers. At one point, the teachers were receiving $2 per student per week, but students rarely attended and learned even less frequently. Instead, the money went toward real estate purchases. Cattle contracts and purchasing contracts were similarly rife with kickbacks. Numerous investigations failed to root out what historian Albert Hurtado called the "Quaker ring."

While this was happening, Modocs at the Quapaw agency were dying. Of the 150 who were relocated there in 1873, fewer than 100 were alive in 1880, eighty-four in 1890, and fewer than fifty within the first few years of the new century. In hearings looking into the corruption in 1878, Modoc Bogus Charlie testified, "we die; we lose a good many in this country; this land don't suit them. My heart; I tell you what I feel now. We die out; my people."[14] A non-Indian visitor to the Quapaw agency was even more direct in writing to his congressman after the visit, claiming that Hiram Jones should be "indicted for manslaughter, there is very strong testimony to convict him of this latter charge."[15] Steamboat Frank's wife, Alice, died in the early 1880s from tuberculosis. He left his son Elwood with relatives and traveled to Vassalboro, Maine, to study at the Oak Grove seminary. He was a well-known speaker and promising preacher but died of tuberculosis himself, which he had contracted at the seminary, in 1886. Today, the Modoc tribe of Oklahoma has its capital in Miami, Oklahoma.[16]

Fifth Moment: Institutional Organization

In 1877, Poncas were removed from their reservation in Nebraska due to an error in the 1868 Fort Laramie Treaty. The conditions of removal were horrible, causing many Ponca deaths along the way. Conditions did not improve once they reached the Ponca's new home in northern Indian Territory. Against the orders of the Indian Office, Standing Bear led many of the Ponca home to Nebraska, where he was arrested. Capitalizing on the support of Thomas Tibbles and his Omaha wife Susette La Flesche, he brought a habeas corpus suit against the official who arrested him. The lawsuit ultimately failed but made Standing Bear famous. With La Flesche as his interpreter and Tibbles as promoter, Standing Bear toured the nation speaking and raising awareness of the plight of the Poncas and the conditions of Indians in general. In response, a raft of reform organizations formed, among them the Women's National Indian Association (WNIA), formed in 1879 by Amelia Stone Quinton and Mary Bonney. While not Quaker, Quinton worked closely with many Quakers, particularly Albert Smiley, a prominent member of the Board of Indian Commissioners.[17] Three years later, Herbert Welsh founded the Indian Rights Association (IRA) in Philadelphia. Quakers James Rhoads and Phillip Garrett were two early leaders. These groups, among others, came to be called, collectively and loosely, the "Friends of the Indians," and they found an organizational nexus when, in 1883, Albert Smiley and his identical twin brother Alfred organized the annual Lake Mohonk Conference of the Friends of the Indian at their resort hotel in upstate New York. Their commitment to gender equality in terms of representation made the conferences heady meeting places for members of the WNIA, the IRA, and many other organizations.

Inspired by hearing Standing Bear speak, poet and novelist Helen Hunt Jackson, whose husband was a prominent Quaker businessman, took up the Indian cause. In 1881, she wrote (and sent a copy to every member of Congress) her critique of US Indian Policy, titled *A Century of Dishonor*. She moved to California, where she wrote a number of reports outlining the specific conditions of the Mission Indians of southern California. Neither the reports nor a *Century of Dishonor* moved public opinion or federal policy. In 1884, she published a novel, *Ramona*, which accomplished some of what her previous work had been unable to do. Like Harriet Beecher Stowe's *Uncle Tom's Cabin*, Jackson hoped it would animate public opinion to force federal officials to defend Indians from the oppressive power of local racism. It was wildly successful, but it failed in the same way that Stowe's novel did. Both novels freighted the subjects the authors sought to help with powerfully racist stereotypes.

Similarly moved and misdirected by his encounter with Standing Bear, Massachusetts Senator Henry Dawes began his push for the wholesale distribution of Indian land to Indian *individuals*, rather than communal ownership by *tribes*, through allotment in severalty. The Dawes Act passed in 1887, an event described by Herbert Welsh as the beginning of a "new order of things." He praised the fact that the legislation aligned with the goals of the IRA, which he described as

> the immediate adoption of a system for the education of all Indian children, the extension of law over the reservations, for the protection of the rights of both Indians and white men; the allotment of lands to individual Indians, and the breaking up of the tribal organization, which is the real citadel of savagery.[18]

The attack on Indian land as a means to break up tribal organization increasingly involved the intentional destruction of Indian culture. In 1884, Yankton Dakota Zitkala-Ša left her home in South Dakota with Quaker missionaries. The first time she saw a train was the day she boarded one to go east, to the White's Manual Labor Institute in Indiana, which had been founded by an endowment from Josiah White, a wealthy Philadelphia Quaker businessman and Barclay White's uncle, in 1852. The experience, which she recounted in detail in her book *The School Days of an Indian Girl*, was a mixture of excitement and fear. She went on to study at Earlham College, where she garnered great attention and accolades for her writing. She later became an instructor at the Carlisle Indian School in Dickinson, Pennsylvania – the pinnacle of the federal government's assimilationist effort, founded on the principle that, in the words of the school's founder, "all the Indian there is in the race should be dead. Kill the Indian in him, and save the man."[19] Zitkala-Ša lost her enthusiasm for assimilation and suffered a deep sense of cultural dislocation common to many in her position, and which she expressed through her writing, reaffirming her paganism in the face of the religion of the "solemn-faced 'native preacher.'" She wrote:

> A wee child toddling in a wonder world, I prefer to their dogma my excursions into the natural gardens where the voice of the Great Spirit is heard in the twittering of birds, the rippling of mighty waters, and the sweet breathing of flowers. If this is Paganism, then at present, at least, I am a Pagan.[20]

She worked with the Society of the American Indians in the 1910s and co-founded the National Council of American Indians in 1926, which she led until her death in 1938.[21] The National Council was folded into the National Congress of American Indians when it was founded in 1944, and its work is ongoing and important.

Sixth Moment: Quakers in Power

In spring 1929, just before the stock market crashed that fall, Herbert Hoover took office as president. Born into a Quaker family in 1874 and raised among Friends and Indians in West Branch, Iowa, northern Indian Territory and Oregon, Hoover was deeply steeped in Quaker and Indian relations. Lawrie Tatum served as his legal guardian after the death of his mother. To fill the vacancy left when Charles Burke resigned the position of Commissioner of Indian Affairs, Hoover reached back out to the heart of the Quaker reform movement of the east coast, tapping Charles James Rhoads – the president of the IRA, an organization Rhoads' father had helped found – as the new commissioner. Rhoads brought along with him James Henry Scattergood, another IRA Quaker, as his assistant commissioner. These two Quakers brought their vision of an efficient, honest, and peaceful policy of assimilation to Washington, much the same as Friends had done in the 1860s.

Quaker's historical commitment to help Indians is unquestionable and clear. Against the backdrop of violence, dispossession, removal, and genocide, Friends stand out. They worked to make society more just, fair, honest, and peaceful, and toward the goal of Indians as full members of that society. But what was distinctive in the late eighteenth century, and innovative and forward thinking in the mid-nineteenth century, was outdated by the twentieth century. Rhoads' efforts to bring education, farming, mechanical technology, industriousness, punctuality, sobriety, and cleanliness to the nation's Native people encapsulated both the ideal and the problematic elements of Friends' work. In their relationship with Indians, Quakers were generally earnest, peaceful capitalists, devoted to the peaceful assimilation of the Indian, a kinder, gentler alternative to extinction. They encountered Native Americans equally stubborn in their defense of their cultures. In 1933, federal Indian policy shifted dramatically again under what came to be called the "Indian New Deal." Problematic and controversial in many ways, it nonetheless represented a break with the general cluster of policy initiatives that had been so closely associated with Friends since the late eighteenth century.

Notes

1 I will be using the term Native American, Native people, Indigenous people, and Indian essentially interchangeably here. I have written elsewhere, "the language used to refer to people, any people, is both arbitrary and powerful. It is created, and it creates." In many instances the referent here is the conceptual entity that Quakers created – that is, "Indians" as they saw them. In most instances, I have used specific tribal or national identities as they are applicable. Damon B. Akins and William J. Bauer Jr., *We Are the Land: A History of Native California* (Oakland: University of California Press, 2021), 9–10.

2 Benjamin West, "Penn's Treaty with the Indians," (1771–72), Pennsylvania Academy of the Fine Arts; Edward Hicks painted many examples of this image, one of which is "The Peaceable Kingdom, about 1833," in the collection of the Worcester Art Museum, Worcester, Massachusetts. See also Max L. Carter, "John Johnston and the Friends: A Midwestern Indian Agent's Relationship with Quakers in the Early 1800s," *Quaker History* 78, no. 1 (Spring 1989): 37–47.

3 Karim Tiro, " 'We Wish to Do You Good': The Quaker Mission to the Oneida Nation, 1790–1840," *Journal of the Early Republic* 26, no. 3 (Fall 2006), 356. The terms "necessary" and "useful" come from *The Proceedings of the Yearly Meeting for Pennsylvania, &c. reflecting the situation of the Indian Natives in the year 1795* (Philadelphia: Samuel Sanson, 1795), 6: "the purpose of instructing them in husbandry, and useful trades; and teaching their children necessary learning, that they may be acquainted with the scriptures."

4 On the Seneca, see Anthony F. C. Wallace, *The Death and Rebirth of the Seneca* (New York: Vintage, 1972); Daniel Richter, *The Ordeal of the Longhouse: The People of the Iroquois League in the Era of European Colonization* (Chapel Hill: University of North Carolina Press, 1992).

5 Handsome Lake (Sganyadaí:yoh) was Cornplanter's maternal half-brother, but given Seneca matrilineal kinship, it is unclear if the concept of half-brother is appropriate here.

6 Laurence Hauptman, *The Tonawanda Senecas' Heroic Battle Against Removal: Conservative Indians* (Albany: State University of New York Press, 2011), 48.

7 C. Joseph Genetin-Pilawa, *Crooked Paths to Allotment: The Fight over Federal Indian Policy after the Civil War* (Chapel Hill: University of North Carolina Press, 2012), 29–50.

8 Carter, "John Johnston and the Friends," 40–41.

9 Henry Harvey, *A History of the Shawnee Indians* (Cincinnati: Ephraim Morgan & Sons, 1855), 170–175; Patrick Bottiger, *The Borderland of Fear: Vincennes, Prophetstown, and the Invasion of the Miami Homeland* (Chapel Hill: University of North Carolina Press, 2016); Gregory Evans Dowd, *A Spirited Resistance: The North American Indian Struggle for Unity, 1745–1815* (Baltimore: Johns Hopkins University Press, 1993).

10 Harvey, *Shawnee Indians*, 145.

11 For an in-depth treatment of this work, see Clyde Milner II, *With Good Intentions: Quaker Work among the Pawnees, Otos, and Omahas in the 1870s* (Lincoln: University of Nebraska Press, 1982).

12 Thomas Battey, *Life and Adventures of a Quaker among the Indians* (Boston: Lee and Shepard, 1876); Lawrie Tatum, *Our Red Brothers and the Peace Policy of President Ulysses S. Grant* (Philadelphia: John C. Winston & Co., 1899; Lincoln: University of Nebraska, 1970).

13 Clyde Ellis, *To Change them Forever: Indian Education at the Rainy Mountain Boarding School, 1893–1920* (Norman: University of Oklahoma Press, 1996).

14 Albert Hurtado, "The Modocs and the Jones Family Indian Ring: Quaker Administration of the Quapaw Agency, 1873–1879," in *Oklahoma's Forgotten Indians*, ed. Robert E. Smith (Oklahoma City: Oklahoma Historical Society, 1981).

15 Hurtado, "The Modocs and the Jones Family Indian Ring," 102.

16 Boyd Cothran, *Remembering the Modoc War: Redemptive Violence and the Making of American Innocence* (Chapel Hill: University of North Carolina Press, 2014).

17 On the WNAI, see Valerie Sherer Mathes, *The Women's National Indian Association: A History* (Albuquerque: University of New Mexico Press, 2015); and Mathes, *Gender, Race, and Power in the Indian Reform Movement* (Albuquerque: University of New Mexico Press, 2020).

18 Charles C. Painter, "The Present Condition of the Mission Indians of California" (Philadelphia: Indian Rights Association, 1887), 3.

19 Richard H. Pratt, "The Advantages of Mingling Indians with Whites," in *Americanizing the American Indians: Writings by the "Friends of the Indian" 1880–1900*, ed. Frances Paul Prucha (Cambridge, MA: Harvard University Press, 1973), 260–271.

20 From "Why I Am a Pagan," *Atlantic Monthly* 90 (1902): 801–803.

21 Tadeusz Lewandowski, *Red Bird, Red Power: The Life and Legacy of Zitkala-Ša* (Norman: University of Oklahoma Press, 2016).

Bibliography

Battey, Thomas, *Life and Adventures of a Quaker among the Indians* (Boston: Lee and Shepard, 1876).

Bottiger, Patrick, *The Borderland of Fear: Vincennes, Prophetstown, and the Invasion of the Miami Homeland* (Chapel Hill: University of North Carolina Press, 2016).

Carter, Max L., "John Johnston and the Friends: A Midwestern Indian Agent's Relationship with Quakers in the Early 1800s," *Quaker History* 78, no. 1. (Spring 1989): 37–47.

Cothran, Boyd, *Remembering the Modoc War: Redemptive Violence and the Making of American Innocence* (Chapel Hill: University of North Carolina Press, 2014).

Dowd, Gregory Evans, *A Spirited Resistance: The North American Indian Struggle for Unity, 1745–1815* (Baltimore: Johns Hopkins University Press, 1993).

Ellis, Clyde, *To Change Them Forever: Indian Education at the Rainy Mountain Boarding School, 1893–1920* (Norman: University of Oklahoma Press, 1996).

Genetin-Pilawa, C. Joseph, *Crooked Paths to Allotment: The Fight over Federal Indian Policy after the Civil War* (Chapel Hill: University of North Carolina Press, 2012).

Harvey, Henry, *A History of the Shawnee Indians* (Cincinnati: Ephraim Morgan & Sons, 1855).

Hauptman, Laurence, *The Tonawanda Senecas' Heroic Battle Against Removal: Conservative Indians* (Albany: State University of New York Press, 2011).

Hurtado, Albert, "The Modocs and the Jones Family Indian Ring: Quaker Administration of the Quapaw Agency, 1873–1879," in *Oklahoma's Forgotten Indians*, ed. Robert E. Smith (Oklahoma City: Oklahoma Historical Society, 1981).

Lewandowski, Tadeusz, *Red Bird, Red Power: The Life and Legacy of Zitkala-Ša* (Norman: University of Oklahoma Press, 2016).

Mathes, Valerie Sherer, *The Women's National Indian Association: A History* (Albuquerque: University of New Mexico Press, 2015).

Mathes, Valerie Sherer, ed., *Gender, Race, and Power in the Indian Reform Movement* (Albuquerque: University of New Mexico Press, 2020).

Milner, Clyde, [II] *With Good Intentions: Quaker Work among the Pawnees, Otos, and Omahas in the 1870s* (Lincoln: University of Nebraska Press, 1982).

Painter, Charles C., "The Present Condition of the Mission Indians of California" (Philadelphia: Indian Rights Association, 1887), 3.

Pratt, Richard H., "The Advantages of Mingling Indians with Whites," in *Americanizing the American Indians: Writings by the "Friends of the Indian" 1880–1900,* ed. Frances Paul Prucha (Cambridge, MA: Harvard University Press, 1973), 260–271.

Richter, Daniel K., *The Ordeal of the Longhouse: The People of the Iroquois League in the Era of European Colonization* (Cambridge, MA: Harvard University Press, 2003).

Tatum, Lawrie, *Our Red Brothers and the Peace Policy of President Ulysses S. Grant* (Philadelphia: John C. Winston & Co., 1899; Lincoln: University of Nebraska Press, 1970).

Tiro, Karim, "We Wish to Do You Good": The Quaker Mission to the Oneida Nation, 1790–1840," *Journal of the Early Republic* 26, no. 3 (Fall 2006), 356.

Wallace, Anthony F. C., *The Death and Rebirth of the Seneca* (New York: Vintage, 1972).

Zitkala-Ša, "Why I Am a Pagan," *Atlantic Monthly* 90 (1902): 801–803.

11

EVANGELICAL FRIENDS

Jennifer M. Buck

Introduction

The term "evangelical" can be used in a myriad of ways, such as to distinguish Protestants from Catholics in Europe or Puritans and Methodists from Anglicans in England. Grammatically, the term can be an adjective or a noun, and in the 1940s in America, a community emerged that later became known as the National Association of Evangelicals. Distinctly, the term uses itself as a contrast term against other forms of Christianity (Catholic, scholastic, etc.), with the aim being a gospel-centered Christianity distinguishing its Christian witness in the world.

The *euangelion* – the "good news" or "gospel" of Jesus Christ – serves as the basis for the stream of the Christian faith that identifies as Evangelical and becomes known only through God's special revelation in Scripture. Centered off of the New Testament books that interpret Jesus's actions as Messiah, this embodied salvation views biblical doctrine and Christian spirituality through a "gospel" lens. The Wesleyan Quadrilateral centers Scripture as one of four primary norms for understanding the Christian faith, alongside reason, tradition, and experience. Evangelicals in this sense view Scripture as primary. Four attributes appear to be present in the communities that identify as evangelical: biblicism, crucicentrism, conversionism, and activism.[1] Biblicism emphasizes the centrality of Christian Scriptures as normative for theology; crucicentrism stresses the cross of Christ as necessary for salvation and discipleship; conversionism emphasizes life transformation and the process of being born again; and activism focuses on evangelism, outreach, and the preaching of the gospel. Evangelical Friends hold distinction from Roman Catholics, mainline Protestants, and for the sake of this work, unique differences from the other Quaker branches: the Modernist and Liberal Quakers, the Five Years Meeting and Friends United Meeting, and the Conservative Friends.

Evangelical churches, since the Reformation in the sixteenth century, have acknowledged *sola scriptura* ("Scripture alone"), using acknowledged canonical Scripture as the primary source for revelation and theology. Passages such as Gal. 3:23–29, Acts 2:4–38, 1 Cor. 3, Heb. 3:1, Eph. 2:20, and others affirm the biblical foundation for an Evangelical ecclesiology. Evangelicalism traces its origins back to medieval Europe, yet the eighteenth-century revivals in England and figures such as John and Charles Wesley are thought to be its foundations. In the United States, the growth of Evangelicalism came in connection with the Protestant Reformation and American revivalism. State churches and free churches spawned missionary movements, historic

DOI: 10.4324/9780429030925-13

documents to protect the Christian faith such as the Barmen Declaration in 1934, and theological education schools worldwide. The twentieth century saw a rise in "neo-evangelicalism" and a division between the fundamentalist movement and a more moderate, culturally engaged, and intellectually developed evangelicalism.

Within the Quaker context, Evangelical Friends categorizes a movement within the United States that primarily occurred among Gurneyite Friends after 1887, beginning within the Five Years Meeting and then expanding worldwide. After the Gurneyite split, the Modernist/Renewal and Holiness/Revival, including pastoral movements since 1875, saw contemporary Evangelical Friends fall into one of three categories: Friends United Meeting, Evangelical Friends International (now EFCI), or an unaffiliated evangelical grouping. Nearly all Majority World Quakers are evangelical and practice programed worship, as are the majority in both Europe and North America. Evangelical Friends often point back to founder George Fox (1624–1691) as the key founder in the evangelicalism, in particular his view of Christ as the source of complete redemption and conversion. Likewise, Fox's language of a deep study of Scripture and finding inner peace in trusting Jesus as Savior echoes evangelical Friends' convictions. The Faith and Practice book of the EFC Mid-America, for example, viewed Fox's evangelistic zeal in telling others about the spreading of the good news of salvation as key in their own evangelical Quaker origins. Though evangelicalism itself as a reform movement would not yet come for another hundred years or so, Evangelical Friends see the roots of evangelical Quakerism in Fox, Fell, and other Quaker founders from the 1650s.

Historical Context

The eighteenth-century revival movements of John Wesley and George Whitefield directly led to the emergence of Evangelical Friends. Wesley's revival movement within the Church of England later became known as Methodism, arguing for a Christian perfectionism and a counter to predestination, with an evangelicalism deeply grounded in the sacraments as means of sanctification for the believer. George Whitefield likewise continued to further the evangelical movement alongside Wesley, traveling to America and preaching a series of revivals that became part of the Great Awakening movement. Revival meetings began in Iowa in 1867 began affecting the American Friends churches, with the practices of altar calls, conversions, and sanctification as the context for which what later becomes Evangelical Friends Church International and continued into the next century. The 1887 Richmond Declaration of Faith served as a defining document for the Evangelical Friends, with Quakers Joseph Bevan Braithwaite and James Rhodes helping shape the text. Over a four-day period, 95 delegates gathered in Richmond, Indiana, to "consider matters appertaining to the welfare of our branch of the church . . . strengthen the bonds of Christian fellowship . . . promote unity in important matters of faith and practice."[2] These orthodox Friends articulated theological convictions around God, Jesus Christ, the Holy Spirit, the Scriptures, creation, the Fall, justification, sanctification, the resurrection, the final judgment, baptism and communion, public worship, and our relation to local governments. It created a work of unified, reasonable Quaker faith and practice that responded to issues of liberal theology and the Ohio ordinance debate. As Quaker scholar Jon Kershner describes it, the pressures of both Holiness revivalism and modernism led to a stream of Quakerism that introduced the pastoral system, taught the culmination of faith as a fully sanctified life, and incorporated higher biblical criticism and constructive engagement of culture.[3] Evangelism and education became priorities of early branches of evangelical Friends.

Westward expansion saw Quaker migrations in the 1880s, such as Indiana Friends settling in a community in Kansas and naming it after abolitionist Laura Haviland, later forming a Friends Bible College (today Barclay College). Others established roots in Nebraska, starting Nebraska Central College in 1899 (today William Penn University), both areas developing Yearly Meetings as well. Rocky Mountain Yearly Meeting emerged alongside Great Plains Yearly Meeting (FUM), leading the establishment of a sizeable midwestern Friends presence, evangelizing and growing, all while sending missionaries to South America. Up in Oregon, Quakers Henry John and Laura Minthorn helped establish an academy (today George Fox University) in Newberg where their nephew, President Herbert Hoover (1874–1964), was educated. The gold rush of 1849 brought Quakers to California, and the first Quaker yearly meeting in the southwest (Utah, Nevada, California, and Arizona) began in 1895 as an outgrowth of Iowa Yearly Meeting. Down in southern California, a Quaker community established a town and college in Whittier, where a son of Frank and Hannah Nixon, Richard, would later be president as well (1913–1994). A training school for Christian Workers, founded in 1899, later became Azusa Pacific University. Missionary work expanded to Alaska and Central America, and major hubs of evangelical Quakerism continued to grow in the United States, in California, Oregon, Idaho, Ohio, Kansas, and Indiana. For Evangelical Quakers, the emphasis on evangelism and education is of utmost importance, and the start of these Quaker training schools and Bible colleges only continued to reinforce the value that winning and training youth and adults for Christ was a goal of the movement.

Starting as early as 1919, a Friends Evangelistic Band was formed in England. Quaker Evangelists such as George A. Fox, John Fredrick and Alice Hanson, and their son Isaac Hanson moved between the English countryside, Scandinavia, and America as itinerant preachers. Programmed meetings arose from revivals of 1867–1877. Itinerant preachers became settled community pastors with the title "recorded minister," extending pastoral ministry to both women and men. Adoption of pastors, as Quaker scholar Pink Dandelion notes, led to the adoption of programming. By nearly 1875, and substantiated by 1900s, every Gurneyite Yearly Meeting except Baltimore had accepted pastors alongside a Spirit-led pre-programming.[4] A combination of sermons and vocal ministry filled these services, and churches grew to have a paid leadership that administered church business, taught biblical instruction, visited the ill, and built a network of community outreach. Christian education blossomed in larger Friends churches, with youth ministers and other pastoral staff assisting the lead pastor. An hour of Sunday School, preceded by a service for worship and then a possible evening or Wednesday night gathering for youth, became the common pattern among Evangelical Friends churches. Conference sites developed in the early 1900s, such as Quaker Meadow, Quaker Ridge, Quaker Haven, Quaker Knoll, and Quaker Hill, for adults and youth, encouraging evangelism, teaching, and fellowship alongside spiritual retreats. Many churches saw numerical growth for a variety of factors, not least of which was the church growth movement from the 1960s onward, as well as increasing diversity due to primarily Hispanic and Asian families joining congregations in areas such as California and Texas. In the words of Quaker scholar Arthur O. Roberts, "Young Friends, although less precise and articulate in theological formulation than their elders, nevertheless affirmed experientially, and testified by word and deed, that the crucified risen Christ is the Light Within."[5]

The Fundamentalist-Modernist Conflict

Forces continued to shape the diversity of Evangelical Quakerism, such as modernism, holiness spirituality, and fundamentalism. Cultural trends such as the social gospel, Darwinism, end times theology, and Christian Zionism continued to grow and create tensions amongst Quakers, as well as between Quakers and other churches in the United States at the time. The early 1900s saw Friends continuing to discuss affirmations of historic Christian theology while also holding liberty in non-essentials. Several Yearly Meetings left the Five Years Meeting, including churches from Oregon, Indiana, Kansas, and Nebraska. The newly formed Central Yearly Meeting and Rocky Mountain Yearly Meeting emerged from such discussions and disagreements over liberal theology, particularly disagreeing over the role of Scripture and its manner of interpretation.

The conflict evolved into the growing value of furthering theological training spaces for women and men in both the Quaker and Evangelical doctrines. Evangelical Friends, alongside other holiness Christians, helped found Bible schools as effective means of training Evangelical leaders and furthering Evangelical teaching. Examples include Walter and Emma Malone founding Cleveland Bible College (today Malone University) in 1892, Scott T. Clark founding Friends Bible College (today Barclay College) in Haviland, Kansas in 1917, and several Oregon Friends founding Portland Bible Institute in 1919.

Association of Evangelical Friends

In 1927, Edward Mott convened a gathering of eleven Friends in Cheyenne, Wyoming. Concerns were mounting with modernist trends and the impact of the Five Years Meeting all fueling a desire to protect and uplift the evangelical Christian faith. Twenty years later, as another gathering functioned as the first inter–Yearly Meeting conference, Quakers from independent Yearly Meetings, Conservative Meetings, and Friends United Meetings gathered together under a shared stated purpose. The newly articulated Evangelical Friends worked to "provide a possible means of cooperative promotion of evangelical service in various areas such as missions, evangelism, education, publications, youth work, relief, and peace."[6] Drawing inspiration from the Valiant Sixty, early Quakers who travelled in pairs to spread the Quaker message, the Association of Evangelical Friends worked to strengthen bonds of unity among Friends by continuing information organization, increasing visitation and revival, and building a common fellowship. Their desire was for an affirmed peace testimony, robust Christian theology, and a broader Friends Church – both evangelical in nature and worldwide in scope. By 1963, the Evangelical Friends Alliance was formed, with a faith statement and procedural guidelines, which would later evolve into the Evangelical Friends Church International.

Evangelical Friends Church International

In the 1960s, Evangelical Friends International (renamed Evangelical Friends Church International in 1989) formed to "make more and better disciples for Jesus through church planting and active missions efforts throughout the world."[7] EFCI includes over 1000 local churches in over twenty-five countries, divided into five international regions. As of 2018, EFCI represented more than 180,000 Friends, with approximately 140,000 being in the majority world. Africa contains approximately 60,000 members, with the majority being in Rwanda, Congo, and Burundi. Latin America holds similar numbers with around 55,000 Quakers, most in Bolivia and Guatemala. EFCI also includes independent Yearly Meetings, such as five independent Yearly Meetings in Bolivia that total more than 30,000 members.[8]

EFCI defines its purpose "to work together in Christian ministry based on biblical principles to develop personnel and resources that will enable the member regions to fulfill the

Great Commission (Matt. 28:19–20)."[9] The boundaries of theological belief for the Evangelical Friends under the EFCI umbrella include:

1 Trinitarian formula for God as described in the Bible;
2 Jesus is divine, lived perfectly, died sacrificially and was resurrected, and is the "only acceptable payment for the penalty of mankind's rebellion and wrongdoing";
3 The Holy Spirit Empowers believers to follow Jesus's pattern on earth;
4 The Bible is "the written word of God" and "fully authoritative in all it says";
5 Humanity was created for full relationship with God, but that relationship was destroyed through disobedience and can only be repaired through Jesus' sacrifice;
6 The Church is the "living presence of Jesus in the world" as seen in evangelism and service,
(Friends Belief n.d.)

How this evangelical theology is translated into Quaker testimony and practice varies from Evangelical Friends church to church. Liberal and Conservative Yearly Meetings tend to give primacy to unprogrammed worship and other Quaker beliefs, whereas Evangelical Friends tend to prioritize these theological doctrines.

Friends United Meeting

One branch of the tree of Evangelical Friends is the Friends United Meeting (FUM). Not every FUM church is theologically evangelical (though every EFCI member church would identify as such). FUM characterizes itself as a collection of Christ-centered Quakers, but the theological diversity amongst its churches is far vaster than the EFCI churches. Of the 184,000 FUM members, approximately 15,000 are dual affiliated with Friends General Conference, making them likely not evangelical and unprogrammed (or at least semi-programmed).[10] The majority of FUM is pastoral and programmed and identifies as evangelical, whether in the majority world or in the United States. EFCI differentiates from FUM largely because EFCI determines membership around a shared set of beliefs, whereas FUM provides resources and facilitates partnerships for a Quaker Yearly Meetings along a vast theological spectrum with many doctrinal differences amongst them. There have been occasional and inconsistent collaborations between EFCI and FUM due to a variety of reasons, one being the significance of the centrality of evangelicalism to the EFCI leadership. One such example occurred in 1993, when the Southwest Yearly Meeting attempted realignment efforts with FUM; these efforts were ultimately unsuccessful over positions on the authority of Scripture and the deity of Christ, despite historical and spiritual bonds.

Global Evangelical Friends

The global presence of EFCI embodies the Quaker legacy of global missions work through Evangelical Friends Mission. EFM serves as EFC-NA's most involved ministry, and it serves as the ministry that is largest in size, budget, fundraising work, and global evangelistic commission. It works to "fuel a worldwide movement of people who seek first the kingdom of God, planting churches that live and die to carry out the Great commission in the spirit of the Great Commandment" (Evangelical Friends Mission n.d.) Gospel evangelization serves as its primary aim, however Quaker testimonies also function as discipleship practices for the new believers. As early as the 1900s, Friends' evangelistic zeal compelled them to travel to China, India, Alaska, and Guatemala, and later saw ongoing work in Palestine, Madagascar, Jamaica, Rwanda, Congo,

Bolivia, and beyond. Networks of church planting evolved into Yearly Meetings and permanent indigenous-led Quaker work around the globe. Friends' testimonies of peacemaking, gender equality, inner spiritual experience, and sacraments set Quaker missions work apart from parallel mission work from other denominations as the movement continued to establish itself.

Though there is no one stream of global Evangelical Friends, commonalities emerge for majority world Christians out of the Quaker tradition, such as an emphasis on evangelism and personal salvation alongside a more supernatural expression of faith as manifest in healings, visions, and encounters with the angelic or demonic. Global Quakers emphasize poverty and social justice as aspects of the Christian faith lived out and also often highlight the communal dimensions of Scripture. As characterized by Quaker scholar Arthur O. Roberts, Majority World Friends "are less materialistic, more charismatic, more concerned for the second coming, and more empirical in expectations about heaven."[11] Ongoing social issues such as the role of the sacraments, biblical understandings of family, reconciliation, and the role of suffering continue to be areas of formulation for Quakers worldwide.

Evangelical Quaker Theology

As mentioned earlier, the Richmond Declaration of 1887 retained Quaker testimonies of sacraments and peace but also demonstrated the influence of orthodox Christianity and holiness revivals. Though creedal in language, a posture Quakers often disregarded, its words became a backbone for the Evangelical Friends Yearly Meetings. Most continue to include it in their Faith and Practices alongside statements by groups such as the National Association of Evangelicals. Evangelical Quaker authors such as Everett Cattell, Thomas Kelley, and Richard Foster helped articulate an embodied Friends discipleship and holiness-informed theology. Friends' practices such as queries in books of discipline helped hold Quakers to an individual piety (integrity in speech and action, abstinence from addictions, and sexual purity) and to communal demonstrations of faith (earth keeping, reconciliation, peacemaking, and justice concerns). Holiness doctrines continue to inform the Evangelical Friends today, with emphases on faithful living, evangelism, and small-group growth over itinerant ministry.

Contemporary Issues

The significant issues between Evangelical and non-evangelical (Liberal or Conservative) Quakers consist of topics that would fall under what Kershner calls two major categories: (1) spirituality, worship, and authority; and (2) social justice and morality.[12] Orthodox and Liberal Quakers tend to practice non-pastoral, unprogrammed worship, whereas Evangelical Friends continue in the programmed and pastoral manner of services. Evangelical Friends continue to see Quakerism as an aspect of the Christian religion and understand it as salvation through Christ with an evangelistic element, with aspects of Quaker theology and practice incorporated into the faith. One major difference between Evangelical Friends and other branches of the evangelical Christian tradition is the universal ministry or priesthood of all believers and open worship, both areas which open up the congregation to greater participation by everyone.

One of the primary differences between Liberal and Evangelical Quakers is whether they view themselves as Christian primarily, with a Quaker identity being secondary, or if their Quaker identity is primary to any other secondary religious identity (Christian, post-Christian, and non-Christian). Because of this, Liberal Friends tend to define themselves in terms of method/form, whereas Evangelical Friends define themselves in terms of belief. Liberal Friends tend to view theology as more of a movement or activity, whereas Evangelical Friends often see it as more formed and permanent. These differing worldviews relate to disparate views on sexual morality, missions work, and interpretations of Scripture. One such example arose in the 1970s: the charismatic issue separated John Wimber (later founder of the Vineyard Fellowship and adherent to the signs and wonders Pentecostal movement) from the California Yearly Meeting, primarily parting ways over worship style and views on gifts of the Holy Spirit.

Evangelical Friends continue to evolve throughout the twenty-first century. Majority World Evangelical Friends continue to grow numerically and serve as an evolution of their missionary movement heritage that unites much of Evangelical Friends around the world. Developments such as Convergent Friends value the connections between the larger Quaker communion and progressive branches of the Evangelical Friends, be it in North America or more worldwide. Social and theological issues provide areas for disagreement and discussion among churches and Yearly Meetings throughout the Evangelical Friends world, not always resulting in unity or clarity on the sense of the meeting. Two such examples are the split in the Northwest Friends Yearly Meeting (EFC-NA) and the North Carolina Yearly Meeting (FUM) in 2015 over issues of the role of the Yearly Meeting and church autonomy, homosexuality, and biblical authority. The influence and affiliation with larger Evangelical culture remains to guide much of the Evangelical Friends world. The future for smaller evangelical Friends churches remains unknown, and the hope is for more growth. And partnerships with non-English-speaking Evangelical Friends churches continue, both in the United States and worldwide. It could be very likely, as Kershner propones, that majority world Quakers could help Western Evangelical Friends embody a Friends heritage for a post-Christian, post-denominational global context. Evangelical Friends must continue to evolve with a changing globalized Christian communion in order to remain a faithful yet essential manifestation of both the Quaker and evangelical Christian voice.

Notes

1 I borrow this from David Bebbington's widely used definition. McGrath. "The Future Configuration of a Global and Local Tradition," in O'Mahony and Kirwan, eds. *World Christianity* (London: Melisende, 2004), 172.
2 *Faith and Practice of the Evangelical Friends Church Southwest* (Yorba Linda, CA, 2011 edition), 33–47.
3 Jon R. Kershner. "Evangelical Quakerism and Global Christianity," in Angell and Dandelion, eds. *The Cambridge Companion to Quakerism* (Cambridge: Cambridge University Press, 2018), 293.
4 Pink Dandelion. *An Introduction to Quakerism* (Cambridge: Cambridge University Press, 2007), 111.
5 Arthur O. Roberts. "Evangelical Quakers, 1887–2010," in Angell and Dandelion, eds., *The Oxford Handbook of Quaker Studies* (Oxford: Oxford University Press, 2013), 111.
6 Arthur O. Roberts. *Association of Evangelical Friends* (Newberg, OR: Barclay Press, 1975), 2.
7 *Faith and Practice of the Evangelical Friends Church Southwest* (Yorba Linda, CA, 2011 edition).
8 Roberts. "Evangelical Quakers, 1887–2010," in Angell and Dandelion, eds., *The Oxford Handbook of Quaker Studies*, 120.
9 W. Evans. "Evangelical Friends," *Quaker Religious Thought* (2014, 123:4), 75.
10 Kershner. "Evangelical Quakerism and Global Christianity," in Angell and Dandelion, eds., *The Cambridge Companion to Quakerism*, 297.
11 Roberts. "Evangelical Quakers, 1887–2010," in Angell and Dandelion, eds., *The Oxford Handbook of Quaker Studies*, 123.
12 Kershner. "Evangelical Quakerism and Global Christianity," in Angell and Dandelion, eds., *The Cambridge Companion to Quakerism*, 298.

Bibliography

Angell, Stephen W. and Pink Dandelion, eds. *The Oxford Handbook of Quaker Studies*. Oxford: Oxford University Press, 2013.

Angell, Stephen W. and Pink Dandelion, eds. *The Cambridge Companion to Quakerism*. Cambridge: Cambridge University Press, 2018.

Dandelion, Pink. *An Introduction to Quakerism*. Cambridge: Cambridge University Press, 2007.

Evans, Wayne. "Evangelical Friends," *Quaker Religions Thought*. 2014.123:4, 75–84.

Faith and Practice of the Evangelical Friends Church Southwest. Yorba Linda, CA, 2011 Edition.

O'Mahony, Anthony and Kirwan, Michel, eds. *World Christianity: Politics, Theology and Dialogues*. London: Melisende, 2004.

Roberts, Arthur O. *Association of Evangelical Friends*. Newberg, OR: Barclay Press, 1975.

Stackhouse Jr., John G. ed., *Evangelical Ecclesiology: Reality or Illusion?* Grand Rapids: Baker Academic, 2003.

12

RICHARD FOSTER (1942–)

Jennifer M. Buck

Richard Foster is an Evangelical Friend, pastor, professor and author on Quaker Spirituality. He married his wife Carolynn and they had two sons, Joel and Nathan. Foster was born in New Mexico and currently resides in Denver, Colorado. He earned an undergraduate degree from George Fox University in Newberg, Oregon, earning a bachelor of arts degree in religion and philosophy in 1964. He later earned a doctorate of pastoral theology at Fuller Theological Seminary in 1970. For his dissertation, he wrote on Quaker concern in race relations then and now, comparing the Quaker attack on slavery and the present Quaker attitudes on race in both California and the Pacific Northwest.

Foster was formed by an early childhood where he was orphaned and forced into poverty in his early teens due to his father's death from emphysema and his mother's death from multiple sclerosis.[1] In his teens he found community and faith through a local youth group. He converted to the Christian faith in his early high school years through Alameda Friends Church in Garden Grove in Orange County, California. An early mission trip to help build a school for Native Alaskans, which involved an overnight in the gymnasium at George Fox College and spurred his dreaming of the proposition of attending Quaker college, a move that ultimately opened up his future life work.[2] He credits his studying under and being deeply formed by Quaker professor Arthur O. Roberts, whose love of words inspired him to be a writer. Foster went on to pastor on staff at Alameda Friends Church (now Garden Grove Friends Church), Arcadia Friends Church, Woodlake Avenue Friends Church, and Newberg Friends Church. He also counseled at a Family Counseling and Guidance center and was previously a director of an inner-city ministry project.

During his years at Woodlake Avenue Friends Church, Foster developed a friendship with Dallas Willard, a parishioner and respected philosophy professor at the University of Southern California. Out of that friendship grew "a conversation that never stopped" between the two, and their ministry partnership served as a "disciple incubator" – practicing and cultivating the spiritual disciplines in community.[3] Their friendship helped birth a movement encouraging a return to ancient devotional practices that the modern church neglected over the years. Foster described his ministry years as "a period of wilderness wandering, stretching, learning, and transformation," where his desire was to help people grow in Christlikeness more than any church growth or personal recognition. At this small congregation he experienced an influx of genuinely needy people and sought another local pastor to learn much about prayer, an area he

DOI: 10.4324/9780429030925-14

felt severely lacking in during this season of his life. His desire was to integrate "academic 'head knowledge' into a new worldview, a different way of being – what [he] would later call a 'with-God' lifestyle."[4] Willard would teach on the Sermon on the Mount (ideas that would later form the basis for his 1998 bestseller *The Divine Conspiracy*), and the community's liturgical practices of solitude and silence, led by Foster, would form the basis of ideas for his 1978 work *Celebration of Discipline*.[5] This friendship extended and deepened until Willard's death, and through such a model of transformative, renovating relationship did Foster come to see his writings and teachings as fully embodied discipleship experiences worked out in community.

Foster took a pastoral position in Newberg that would allow him to explore the dual vocation of pastor and educator. After serving as an adjunct professor at George Fox College for five years, Foster became a professor of theology and writer-in-residence at Friends University in Wichita, Kansas, beginning in 1979. He later would be the Jack and Barbara Lee Distinguished Professor of Spiritual Formation at Azusa Pacific University in California. He continued to teach later in life at various universities and seminaries on the theme of spiritual formation. Foster would be considered a practical theologian, as his pastoral work and writings on spirituality continue to cultivate the faith of the Christian church through a Quaker lens. Foster's writings have been praised for thoughtful presentation and simplification of diffuse subjects, and crafting writings of devotion that are also accessible and readable for the church worldwide, much like his pedagogical classroom style.

Before writing for a broader audience and accepting the major aspect of his vocation as author, Foster wrote anonymously for *Quaker Life* and similar small publications under the name "John Q. Catalyst."[6] He wrote devotionally and for a non-academic audience, and his thoughtful works reengage Christian mysticism and the Quaker holiness tradition. In speaking of Foster's legacy in shaping Quaker spirituality, Carole Dale Spencer writes: "the first popular and widely-read late twentieth century work reclaiming the Christian mystical tradition for evangelicalism was penned by a Quaker."[7] In *Friends Search for Wholeness* (John L. Bond, ed.), Foster wrote about "Wholeness and the Healing Ministry," beginning an exploration into the healing work of Christ being accessible on every level for the believer – body, mind, will, emotions, and spirit.[8] He saw this illustrated in the early Quaker writings of John Jay, William Dewsbury, Richard Farnsworth, John Banks, and George Fox, all of whom recall radical healing stories at the origins of the Friends movement. Foster understood the healing ministry of the early Children of the Light as paralleling the ministry of Jesus and the early Church – natural, modest, and connected to the power of the Holy Spirit to give them authority over "powerless kingdoms" of political and religious systems of their day. This early publication began to solidify his philosophy of ministry, where the work of the Holy Spirit contains the power to transform and heal every part of the human condition.

Out of his pastoral work, and with some direct encouragement from Quaker author D. Elton Trueblood, Foster sent an unsolicited manuscript to Harper & Row, who took a risk on an unknown pastor. In his proposal for the manuscript, Foster wrote: "this book is for all those who are disillusioned with the superficialities of modern culture, including modern religious culture."[9] Foster's congregation covered his pastoral duties for this season so he could complete this first written work in service of the larger Church. Such an act of support by his Quaker community, alongside such faith in his ideas from Harper & Row along with others, led to a celebrated career where he is best known for his writings. The most famous is *Celebration of Discipline* (1978), which examines the inward (prayer, fasting, meditation, study), outward (simplicity, solitude, submission, service), and corporate Christian disciplines (confession, worship, guidance, celebration). The work opens with these powerful words: "Superficiality is the curse of our age. The desperate need today is not for a greater number of intelligent people, or gifted people, but for deep people."[10] The book went on to widespread critical acclaim, reviving ancient Christian spirituality and the emphasis on the practice of Christian disciplines in twenty-first-century America. *Christianity Today* named the book one of the top ten books of the twentieth century. Translated into 26 languages, the work sold over two million copies and is considered by many to be one of the greatest contemporary works on Christian spirituality. Foster later released a supplemental study guide, intending that the work could continue to serve the church through group exploration.

Foster went on to write *Freedom of Simplicity* (1981), exploring a deeper look at the discipline of simplicity through intentional living and practices. His follow-up work to *Celebration of Discipline* was originally named *Money, Sex and Power* (1985) and was later retitled *The Challenge of the Disciplined Life*. It came out of a study of the monastic vows of poverty, chastity, and obedience as the historical responses to money, sex, and power, but Foster proposed alternative vows: simplicity for money, fidelity for sex, and service for power. He was advocating for a Quaker renaissance involving three elements for spiritual renewal: a great new experience of God, a great new passion for purity, and a great new baptism of power (Quaker Life, 1986, 10–13). He invites a public and private holiness, stemming from our deep legacy of being on the forefront of ethical concerns. He speaks against distraction and technological gluttony as spiritual problems for our day, and emphasizes the value for the Christian in being present in order to listen to God. For Foster, the work of formation is found in the midst of everyday life, never sequestered to the cloister, and most worked out through our home life and our work life.

Another one of Foster's most famous areas of exploration in writing is that of prayer. *Prayer: Finding the Heart's True Home* (1992) found Foster delving further into another Christian discipline, that of prayer, by using the framework of inward (transformation), upward (intimacy), and outward (ministry) as types of prayer. In his words:

> to pray is to change. This is a great grace. How good of a God to provide a path whereby our lives can be taken over by love and joy and peace and patience and kindness and goodness and faithfulness and self-control. The movement inward comes first because without interior transformation the movement up into God's glory would overwhelm us and the movement out into ministry would destroy us.[11]

Prayer was *Christianity Today's* Book of the Year and the winner of the Gold Medallion Award from the Evangelical Christian Publishers Association. Foster went on to compile some of his favorite prayers from Christian history, as well as pen some of his own, in the volume *Prayers from the Heart* (1994). Foster sees prayer as a means to cultivate a posture of holy expectancy and holy obedience, a vehicle to "usher us into the loving heart of God" as we step into the reality which the words signify.[12] Foster believes that "my whole life, in one sense, has been an experiment in how to be a portable sanctuary, learning to practice the presence of God in the midst of the stresses and strains of contemporary life."[13] Out of this desire grew Foster's deep attentiveness to the power and profound work of prayer. Prayer, for Foster, is embodied through our vocations and we teach those around us about prayer, by the way we live.

Foster co-edited two works: *Devotional Classics* (1993, with James Bryan Smith) and *Spiritual Classics* (2000, with Emilie Griffin). Continuing on the theme of guiding the church through the Christian disciplines, Foster and his co-authors curated a year's worth of reading and reflection (52 selections) on the same 12 disciplines explored in *Celebration of Discipline*.[14] The selections pull from classic and current authors from a diversity of Christianity's denominational streams: Catholic, Protestant and Orthodox alike. Quaker authors like George Fox and Thomas R. Kelly are placed alongside voices such as Hadewijch of Antwerp, Simone Weil, and Martin

Luther King Jr. Surrounded with biblical texts and discussion groups, this work helps educate lay congregants on the various Christian traditions while elevating a diversity of historic and modern voices in their spiritual practice. Another work, *Streams of Living Water* (2001), continued mining the resources of the Christian tradition for the local church. In this work, Foster explores the various Christian traditions through a sixfold model: Contemplative: the Prayer-Filled Life; Holiness: The Virtuous Life; Charismatic: The Spirit-Empowered Life; Social Justice: The Compassionate Life; Evangelical: The Word-Centered Life; and Incarnational: The Sacramental Life.[15] Foster explores the case for a less fragmented view of life in Christ by tracing Christian history through these traditions. These six streams have corrected, informed and enlivened each other over time, inviting a wider and deeper Christian faith that ceases to ignore whole planes of life in the Kingdom of God.

After the success of *Celebration of Discipline*, Foster continued to discover the challenges people faced in applying the concepts in the book and began to articulate that deeper transformation was needed through greater encouragement, support, and instruction. Founded in 1988, *Renovaré* became the Christian para-Church organization through which Foster could continue resourcing Christians for a life of discipleship and spiritual growth. The organization equips individuals through print and online materials, spiritual formation opportunities for individuals and communities, and a two-year online and in-person discipleship school called the Institute for Christian Spiritual Formation. The aim serves to help individuals and churches grow in Christ through the practice of spiritual disciplines like prayer, fasting, meditation, and so forth as practices in a variety of settings and styles. Foster sees the organization as a part of a movement committed to the renewal of the church in all of its multifaceted expressions. The *Renovaré* covenant states: "in utter dependence upon Jesus Christ as my ever-living Savior, Teacher, Lord, and Friend I will seek continual renewal through spiritual exercises, spiritual gifts and acts of service." Willard and Foster's friendship continued in the early years of this organization, as Foster articulated that they were teaching themselves at first, rooting the organization in the spiritual disciplines they had been continually practicing together. Foster invested deeply in *Renovaré*, desiring that the organization never turn into a commercial enterprise but serve to support Christians and faith communities in the journey into further spiritual growth by "bringing the Church to the church."

His later career continued Foster's writings and investment in *Renovaré*. He wrote *Life with God: Reading the Bible for Spiritual Transformation* (2008) and co-edited the *Life with God Study Bible* (NRSV) through *Renovaré* alongside Gayle Beebe, Dallas Willard, Walter Brueggemann. He jointly authored *Longing for God* (2008) alongside Quaker author and university president Gayle Beebe.[16] His work with Beebe grew out of a team-taught course on "the History and Practice of Christian Spirituality," as well as their shared desire to articulate the intellectual integrity of Christianity as a means for moving the Christian closer to the heart of God.[17] His later works include *Seeking the Kingdom* (2010); a devotional work, *Sanctuary for the Soul* (2011); and co-edited *A Year with God: Living Out the Spiritual Disciplines* (2016) with Julia L. Roller. As of 2018, Foster had retired from public ministry.[18]

Foster wrote the afterword for *Wisdom Chaser* (2010), a book by his son Nathan, a memoir recalling their father-son relationship and shared mountain climbing undertakings intertwined with Nathan's own grappling with sobriety. In his son's own words describing his father's character supporting him through his journey out of addiction:

> His hours of listening were healing. He didn't bring talent or theological insight; he brought grace. He didn't swoop in or rescue me or fix anything. By simply *being*, he provided a window into the kingdom where guilt was turned upside down and I was able to breath and hope.[19]

Nathan credits his dad with being the most involved in his recovery, asking questions out of encouragement and optimism, never shame, as meaningful accountability.

Though an evangelical Friend himself, his writings found an audience among both liberal and evangelical Quakers, and beyond Quakers to broader Christian and non-Christian religious traditions. Building upon Quaker spiritual writers such as Everett Cattell, Thomas Kelley, and John Woolman, Foster "explored the Christian mystical tradition and reclaimed it as a source of [Quaker] spirituality."[20] Foster counts Dallas Willard and Gayle Beebe as close friends, with Augustine, Teresa of Avila, Julian of Norwich, George Fox, John Woolman, and Dietrich Bonhoeffer as mentors in the faith. *The Cost of Discipleship* by Dietrich Bonhoeffer deeply shaped his early faith and guided the trajectory for his vocation in service to the Church. In his later years, Foster wore his hair, as he said, in a long ponytail as a connection with his Chippewa heritage. His writings and speaking work have called on Friends to work against racism "that dehumanizes those for whom Christ died."[21] Dallas Willard describes the character of Richard Foster in this way:

> Richard has a discipline of simplicity. It comes out of his tradition as a Quaker. It is so deeply rooted and so pervasive. . . . The Quaker writer George Fox – a mentor for both of us – talked about taking people off of men and putting them onto Christ. That's what you see in Richard. He doesn't care to be noticed, and, despite his notoriety, he can actually pay attention to people.[22]

Foster is often cited as an influence in helping shift Quaker holiness language from prescriptive personal conduct to interpersonal actions (justice, reconciliation) through the use of spiritual disciplines along the Christian journey.[23] Alongside other voices like Dallas Willard, Foster believed that modern evangelicalism overly focused on the instance of conversion and the afterlife without teaching Christians about how to cultivate a life with God here and now in their everyday lives. Foster viewed following Christ as an entire life process, where Jesus becomes one's life through their habits, practices, and patterns. His vision for salvation invited Quakerism into a "new order of life in the kingdom of God that encompasses all of human existence, both here and hereafter."[24] His theology invited a broad understanding of salvation that cultivated disciples formed through the power of God through a shared life together. Through his many popular books that include anthologies of spiritual writings from a great variety of spiritual traditions, Foster almost single-handedly retrieved the Christian mystical tradition and the practice of meditation and contemplation from a century of neglect by Evangelical Friends.[25] He continues to be one of the most widely read Quaker authors today, whose writings never cease to advocate for a posture of being mastered by God, entering ever fuller and deeper into Christ-likeness.

Notes

1 Nathan Foster, *Wisdom Chase* (Downers Grove, IL: InterVarsity Press, 2010), 12.
2 Ibid., 13.
3 Tina Fox. "Living a "With-God" Life." *Christian History*. Issue 129 (2019). Accessed September 23, 2020. https://christianhistoryinstitute.org/magazine/article/living-a-with-god-life.
4 Ibid.
5 Dallas Willard. *The Divine Conspiracy* (San Francisco: HarperOne, 1998); Richard J. Foster. *Celebration of Discipline* (San Francisco: HarperOne, 1978).
6 *Quaker Life*. Friends United Meeting. Multiple volumes and editions between 1960 and 1975.
7 Carole Dale Spencer. *Holiness: The Soul of Quakerism* (Eugene, OR: Wipf & Stock, 2007), 235.
8 John Bond, ed. *Friends Search for Wholeness* (Richmond, IN: Friends United Press, 1978).

9 Richard J. Foster. *Celebration of Discipline* (San Francisco: HarperOne, 2018 Special Anniversary Edition), xix.

10 Ibid., (New York, NY: HarperCollins, 1978), 1.

11 Ibid., *Prayer: Finding the Heart's True Home* (San Francisco: HarperSanFrancisco, 1992), 6.

12 Ibid., *Prayers from the Heart* (San Francisco: HarperOne, 1994) xiii.

13 Ibid., i.

14 Richard J. Foster and James Bryan Smith, eds. *Devotional Classics* (San Francisco: HarperOne, 1993) and Richard J. Foster and Emilie Griffin, eds. *Spiritual Classics* (San Francisco: HarperOne, 2000).

15 Richard J. Foster, *Streams of Living Water* (San Francisco: HarperOne, 2001).

16 Richard J. Foster and Gayle Beebe. *Longing for God* (Downers Grove, IL: Intervarsity Press, 2009).

17 Foster and Beebe. *Longing for God*, 10.

18 Richard J. Foster, *Seeking the Kingdom* (San Francisco: HarperOne, 2010); Richard J. Foster, *Sanctuary for the Soul* (Downers Grove, IL: IVP Books, 2011); Richard J. Foster and Julia L. Roller, eds. *A Year With God* (San Francisco: HarperOne, 2009).

19 Foster, *Wisdom Chaser*, 109.

20 Spencer, *Holiness,* 235.

21 Quoted in Thomas Hamm, *The Quakers in America* (New York, NY: Columbia University Press, 2003), 157. Also Sean Patterson, "Finding Foster." *George Fox Journal* (Summer 2014). George Fox University. Accessed September 11, 2020. https://www.georgefox.edu/journalonline/summer14/feature/finding-foster.html.

22 Agnieszka Tennant, "The Making of the Christian: Richard J. Foster and Dallas Willard on the Difference between Discipleship and Spiritual Formation," *Christianity Today* (October 2005), 44.

23 Arthur O. Roberts, "Evangelical Quakers, 1887–2010," in Stephen W. Angell and Pink Dandelion, eds. *The Oxford Handbook of Quaker Studies* (Oxford: Oxford University Press, 2013), 114. Also Mark Galli, "A Life Formed in the Spirit." *Christianity Today*. (September 17, 2008). Accessed September 23, 2020. https://www.christianitytoday.com/ct/2008/september/26.41.html

24 Richard J. Foster, "Salvation Is for Life," *Theology Today* 61 (2004): 308. Also Kelli. B. Trujillo, "Richard Foster: Effort Is Not the Opposite of Grace." *Christianity Today* (October 2018), 64.

25 Carole Dale Spencer, "Quakers in Theological Context," in Angell and Dandelion, eds. *Oxford Companion,* 154.

Bibliography

Angell, Stephen W. and Pink Dandelion. *The Oxford Handbook of Quaker Studies*. Oxford: Oxford University Press, 2013.

Bond, John, ed. *Friends Search for Wholeness*. Richmond, IN: Friends United Press, 1978.

Foster, Nathan. *Wisdom Chaser*. Downers Grove, IL: InterVarsity Press, 2010.

Foster, Richard J. *Freedom of Simplicity*. San Francisco: HarperCollins, 1981.

Foster, Richard J. *The Challenge of a Disciplined Life: Christian Reflections on Money, Sex and Power*. San Francisco: HarperCollins, 1989.

Foster, Richard J. *Life with God: Reading the Bible for Spiritual Transformation*. New York, NY: HarperOne, 2008.

Foster, Richard J. *Celebration of Discipline*. New York, NY: HarperCollins, 1978. And special anniversary edition, 2018.

Foster, Richard J. and Gayle Beebe. *Prayer: Finding the Heart's True Home*. San Francisco: HarperSanFrancisco, 1992.

Foster, Richard J. and Gayle Beebe. *Prayers from the Heart*. San Francisco: HarperOne, 1994.

Foster, Richard J. and Gayle Beebe. "Salvation Is for Life." *Theology Today* 61 (2004): 297–308.

Foster, Richard J. and Gayle Beebe. *Longing for God: Seven Paths of Christian Devotion*. Downers Grove, IL: InterVarsity Press, 2009.

Foster, Richard J. and Emilie Griffin. "Toward a Quaker Renaissance." *Quaker Life* (May 1986): 10–13.

Foster, Richard J. and Emilie Griffin. *Streams of Living Water: Celebrating the Great Traditions of Christian Faith*. San Francisco: HarperCollins, 2001.

Foster, Richard J. and Emilie Griffin. *Spiritual Classics: Selected Readings for Individuals and Groups on the Twelve Spiritual Disciplines*. San Francisco: HarperOne, 2000.

Fox, Tina. "Living a 'With-God' Life." *Christian History*. Issue 129 (2019). Accessed September 23, 2020. https://christianhistoryinstitute.org/magazine/article/living-a-with-god-life.

Galli, Mark. "A Life Formed in the Spirit." *Christianity Today*. September 17, 2008. Accessed September 23, 2020. https://www.christianitytoday.com/ct/2008/september/26.41.html

Hamm, Thomas. 2003. *The Quakers in America*, New York, NY: Columbia University Press.

Patterson, Sean. "Finding Foster." *George Fox Journal*. Summer 2014. George Fox University. Accessed September 11, 2020. https://www.georgefox.edu/journalonline/summer14/feature/finding-foster.html.

Spencer, Carole Dale. *Holiness: The Soul of Quakerism*. Eugene, OR: Wipf & Stock, 2007.

Tennant, Agnieszka. "The Making of the Christian: Richard J. Foster and Dallas Willard on the Difference between Discipleship and Spiritual Formation." *Christianity Today*. October 2005, 42–44.

Trujillo, Kelli. B. "Richard Foster: Effort Is Not the Opposite of Grace." *Christianity Today*. October 2018, 63–66.

Willard, Dallas. *The Divine Conspiracy*. San Francisco: HarperOne, 1998.

13

MOVEMENTS WITHIN QUAKERISM – LIBERALISM

Isaac Barnes May

In the contemporary United States and United Kingdom, Quakerism has an outsized influence on the religious left. Quakerism's lack of a fixed creed, its focus on individual revelation rather than scripture, openness to religious truth being found in non-Christian traditions, and gender egalitarian conception of ministry made it particularly conducive to the growth of religious liberalism. Liberalism first flowered in the Religious Society of Friends during the nineteenth century, and by the beginning of the twentieth century liberal theology had come to dominate London Yearly Meeting in the United Kingdom and the newly formed Friends General Conference (FGC) in the United States. In the twenty-first century, these liberal Friends constitute a visible minority of the world's Quaker population, their combined membership numbering slightly under 50,000 people in a global religious community of approximately 370,000 Friends.[1]

The Quakers who embraced religious liberalism were part of a wider intellectual movement in Christianity, Judaism, and other religious groups. Religious liberals attempted to adapt their religious convictions to social, scientific, and cultural developments that dramatically were transforming industrializing societies in the nineteenth century. New scientific ideas, such as Darwinian evolutionary theory, challenged conventional understandings of scripture and offered an account of human creation that did not necessitate belief in God. The development of historical criticism of the Bible, which understood that it was the historical product of an ancient culture rather than a revealed religious text, worked to undermine the authority of scripture. The further development of capitalism and mechanized industry atomized individuals and tended to undermine traditional religious institutions.[2] Religious liberals wanted a faith that could stand up to the scrutiny of reason and still offer meaning and purpose. Religion scholar Gary Dorrien has written that for Christians, religious liberalism offered a "third way between a regnant orthodoxy and an ascending 'infidelism.'"[3]

Quakers offered a distinctive contribution to this movement's ideas, particularly with their emphasis on the "inward light" and divinity to be found in each individual and through an emphasis on silence and mysticism. Yet Quakers also borrowed and adapted ideas from outside the boundaries of Quakerism, taking freely from Anglicans, Free Religionists, and Unitarians. The rise of liberal Quakerism was the result of Quakerism becoming more open to the surrounding culture and a diversity of intellectual and theological influences.

DOI: 10.4324/9780429030925-15

Hicksites and Progressive Friends

The roots of Quaker religious liberalism go back to at least the early nineteenth century. In 1827, Quakerism in the United States broke apart into two rival factions, each claiming that they were the only authentic Quakers. Both factions represented a departure from the Quietist period of Quakerism in the eighteenth century, which had seen Friends embrace prolonged silences in meeting for worship, focus more on internal discipline, and clarify their theological ideas.[4] The Orthodox faction, and their most numerous descendants, the Gurneyites, are often depicted as being inclined towards evangelicalism, in part because of their engagement with other Christians in ecumenical work on temperance and missions. Their foes, dubbed the Hicksites because they rallied around Long Island farmer and Quaker minister Elias Hicks, were theologically a diverse lot. As Hicks's followers would include religious liberals and conservatives, both groups could plausibly claim to be his intellectual heirs.

Hicks could appear as either a startling religious innovator or a devoted traditionalist to different audiences. While Hicks maintained that scripture was divinely inspired, he also warned against holding scripture in such esteem that it became an idol. Theologically, Hicks denied the trinity as being incoherent and unbiblical. He held an adoptionist Christology, believing that Jesus Christ was not born as the anointed son of God but had been chosen by God to become Christ when he was baptized in the Jordan River.[5] Yet Hicks combined these radical theological ideas with a hostility to innovation and modern technological developments. In analyzing the Hicksite separation, sociologist Robert W. Doherty perceptively observed, "Some, probably many, rural Friends saw Hicks as a preserver of eighteenth-century Quietist Quaker ideals."[6] Based on his religious convictions, Hicks decried the construction of the Erie Canal, lamented the creation of public schools, and maintained that cities were a distraction from a virtuous rural lifestyle. While consistent and legible to his contemporaries in his theology, Hicks's adherence to precepts that could reliably be called "liberal" is hazy in a modern context.

The liberal strain of Quakerism was more clearly exemplified in the career of Hicksite minister Lucretia Mott. A feminist leader at the Seneca Falls Convention and a vocal abolitionist, Mott combined these radical political ideas with a theology to match. In one memorable 1849 sermon, Mott invoked the words of William Penn to explain her beliefs: "it is time for Christians to be judged more by their likeness to Christ than their notions of Christ." The specifics of Christian doctrine mattered less than "holy principles of peace, justice, and love." Mott went on to explain that modern knowledge was just as vital as the Biblical text, telling her audience: "Let us not hesitate to regard the utterance of truth in our age as of equal value to that which is recorded in scriptures."[7]

Religious liberalism proved to be contentious among Hicksites. Mott found herself frequently challenged by her fellow minister George White, who denounced abolitionism and advocated a return to Quietism, with its greater focus on internal Quaker matters. White feared that involvement with social reform movements and abolitionism would bring Quakers into too-close contact with outsiders, and potentially lead them to abandon their distinctive practices and embrace paid ministry.[8]

White's perception of Hicksite radicals as strongly shaped by movements outside Quakerism was accurate. Mott and many of her allies were influenced by Unitarianism and the closely affiliated Transcendentalist movement. She was an admirer of Boston minister William Ellery Channing, whose sermon, *Unitarian Christianity*, had led American Unitarians to embrace that label. Mott praised Transcendentalist Theodore Parker's sermon, *The Transient and Permanent in Christianity*, which argued that Christianity could discard nonessential doctrines to remain viable in the modern era. One of Mott's most cherished possessions was a book by Blanco

White, a former Catholic priest who had become an English Unitarian minister.[9] Henry David Thoreau once remarked that a sermon he heard by Mott had been "a good speech, – Transcendentalism in its mildest form."[10] Intellectual influences could also flow in the other direction. Ralph Waldo Emerson referred with great warmth to Quaker minister Edward Stabler and Quaker-turned-Unitarian Mary Rotch.[11] Beyond these encounters, Emerson read Quaker books, particularly the works of George Fox and William Penn, and spoke of Fox in his lectures.

The tension between the religious liberals and Quietists within Hicksite Quakerism reached a crisis point by the late 1840s. The central issue was the liberals' ties to the abolitionist movement, especially their involvement with the Garrisonian wing of that movement, which espoused socially radical ideas about immediate abolition and equal rights for women. The liberals also were increasingly resentful of the power of ministers and elders within Quakerism, who they felt often stifled innovation and spiritual freedom. A portion of Hicksite liberals would ultimately break away from their Hicksite Yearly Meetings and found Yearly Meetings of the Congregational or Progressive Friends. Progressive Friends freely exchanged ideas with both the most liberal Hicksites, as well as with Unitarians, Free Religionists, and other religious radicals.[12]

Beyond their dedication to antislavery activism, this new group of Quakers would zealously embrace other social reform causes. Progressive Friends from near Waterloo, New York, would form the majority of the attenders at the nearby 1848 Seneca Falls Convention, the first US conference on women's rights. In 1853, Waterloo Friends would resolve that "every member of the human race, without regard to color or sex, possesses potentially the same faculties and powers capable of like cultivation and development, and consequently has the same rights, interests and destiny."[13]

The emerging willingness to challenge established orthodoxies meant that many American Quakers were particularly receptive to new metaphysical religious ideas. One of the ideas that spread the fastest was spiritualism, the belief that people could receive communications from the dead. Spiritualism first emerged in upstate New York after two sisters, Margaret and Kate Fox, reported hearing noises, which they described as "rappings," which they later claimed were communications from the spirit world. Spiritualism spread using networks of Progressive Friends and reformers as one more new innovation and cause for them to champion. Some of the Progressive Friends ultimately left Quakerism to devote themselves wholeheartedly to spiritualism, while others rejected spiritualism as contrary to Quaker beliefs, and at least a few Friends sought to combine them.[14] While the Progressive Friends would significantly decline in the late nineteenth century, many of their ideas, particularly the belief that ministry should be open to all and not just a formally "recorded" ministry, found their way back into Hicksite Quakerism.

British Friends and the Turn to Liberalism

Religious liberalism would also make inroads among British Quakers, though its progress was gradual due to opposition from evangelical Friends. In 1860, the publication of *Essays and Reviews*, an Anglican text that grappled with the impact of Biblical criticism and new developments in the natural sciences, was felt even within the Religious Society of Friends. The following year, David Duncan, a Scottish-born convert to Quakerism, gave a series of lectures on the book at the Friends Institute in Manchester. Duncan's call for religion to adapt to new knowledge and emphasize the importance of the Inward Light rather than scripture excited a group of young Quakers in Manchester and simultaneously caused serious concerns among the evangelical leaders, such as Joseph Bevan Braithwaite in London Yearly Meeting.

After a lengthy process, Duncan was disowned from Quakerism for his views in 1871 and died almost immediately afterward of smallpox. The final breaking point had been Duncan's choice to extend a speaking invitation to Charles Voysey, a former Anglican priest turned universalist who questioned the validity of the Bible and the divinity of Christ. Duncan's liberal supporters were horrified that he was disowned, and they argued that because Quakerism had no creed, it was a violation of freedom of conscience to oust Duncan for heresy.[15]

The actions against Duncan did little to stamp out a growing liberal movement. In 1884, three Quakers anonymously published *A Reasonable Faith*, which stated its goal was to "present a view of Christianity which is at all events intelligible and reasonable."[16] The book extolled the Inner Light as a way to get direct access to God and suggested the atonement should be seen as a loving act of reconciliation by God to humanity, rather than a substitute for humanity's sins by a wrathful deity. At London Yearly Meeting the next year, Joseph Bevan Braithwaite challenged the authors of the book to step forward to defend it; Francis Firth, William Pollard, and William E. Turner did so. The liberals survived the contentious debate intact, and *A Reasonable Faith* became popular among younger Quakers.[17]

In 1895, British Friends gathered in Manchester for a conference that was put on by the Home Missions Committee of London Yearly Meeting. Manchester proved to be a crucial moment where the liberal faction within London Yearly Meeting moved to the fore. Speeches extolled how the Quakers should engage with the world, particularly on projects of social reform. Historian Thomas C. Kennedy noted that "many who recalled the Manchester Conference fixed upon the address of John Wilhelm Rowntree as its decisive moment." Not yet thirty, Rowntree advocated a vision of a modern and yet still religiously vital Society of Friends.

Mysticism and Activism

Rowntree would find a partner to help him with his liberal vision on the other side of the Atlantic: Haverford College philosophy professor Rufus M. Jones. Jones had been raised in Maine by Gurneyite Quakers, one of the branches that had come out of Orthodox Quakerism. In the late nineteenth century, a series of revivals caused many Gurneyites to embrace holiness theology and Biblical inerrancy. Jones's upbringing initially made him a surprising advocate for religious liberalism, which was more strongly associated with the Hicksites. Yet perhaps because of this more traditional background, Jones was particularly driven to reconcile religion with modern life. As an undergraduate at Haverford College in the 1880s, he devoured the works of Ralph Waldo Emerson, and attending Harvard as a graduate student in 1900, he studied with philosophers Josiah Royce and William Ernest Hocking. In his numerous books, Jones's theology ultimately drew heavily on the pragmatism of Royce and William James.

Jones would meet Rowntree in 1897 while in Switzerland. They would hatch plans to produce a grand history of Friends that would serve as an intellectual blueprint for modern Quakerism. However, Rowntree died in 1905, leaving Jones to work with other British Friends to finish the project. The resulting seven-volume collection would be known as the Rowntree series in his honor.[18] In his work for that series and his prolific other writings, Jones depicted Quakerism as a mystical religious tradition. For Jones, Quaker worship was particularly suited to invoking religious experiences and connecting with a universal sense of the divine.[19]

Mysticism was ultimately a liberal religious apologetic, a way to have a verifiable experience of God without appealing to scripture or miracles. Jones's ideas attracted a mass audience and a small circle of academic followers. These followers, including Douglas Steere, Howard Brinton, and Thomas Kelly, were part of an emerging modernist wing of Gurneyite Quakerism, which attempted to carry forward Jones's idea of a mystical Quakerism that would be fully compatible with modern knowledge.[20]

By the early twentieth century, some Quakers, increasingly skeptical about the prospect of coming to a consensus around theology, sought to find unity and purpose in service work. After it was formed to coordinate the efforts of several Hicksite Yearly Meetings in 1900, the annual meetings of FGC became a frequent site of talks about various social issues, ranging from the need for world peace to the desire to create a just economic order.[21] During the First World War, British Friends formed the Friends Service Committee under the authority of London Yearly Meeting, and in 1917, Quakers from most of the denomination's branches in the United States jointly created the American Friends Service Committee (AFSC). Jones served as the AFSC's first chairman. The AFSC allowed Quakers, especially men of draft age engaged in alternative service, to participate in efforts to reconstruct and aid Europe after the First World War. After that conflict, Quaker service work would expand to become a worldwide enterprise, involving a host of causes such as providing food aid to Germany and efforts to improve race relations in the United States.[22]

Patricia Appelbaum has noted that liberal Quakers exerted a disproportionate influence on the broader Protestant pacifist culture emerging in the interwar years.[23] The Peace Testimony began to be interpreted in novel ways by liberal Quakers, who sought not just to avoid their own participation in war, but to alleviate and prevent violent conflict through diplomacy. For some liberal Friends, peace would become the central focus of their faith. In 1955, the AFSC published *Speak Truth to Power*, which argued that an ethic of love could provide a way to bridge Cold War divisions. Yet the pamphlet also deliberately eschewed religious vocabulary, framing what it saw as a Quaker message around mostly practical arguments.[24]

Expanding the Boundaries of Liberal Quakerism

After the First World War, some liberal Friends began to move in theologically radical directions, advocating for a unitarian Quakerism that did not see Jesus as divine, or even a Quakerism that redefined God. Jane Rushmore, the clerk of the newly unified Philadelphia Yearly Meeting, published a number of books on Quakerism that expressed her unitarian religious perspectives and argued that because Quakerism had no creed, the specifics of Quaker theology were ultimately up to each individual to decide for themselves. Swarthmore philosophy professor Jesse H. Holmes, with the assistance of FGC, published a public letter in 1928 calling on religious skeptics to consider joining the Religious Society of Friends. In the letter, Holmes suggested that "God" could be thought of as a metaphor for human relationships.[25]

The limits of who could be considered a Quaker also expanded to allow a broad range of religious views. Jones created the Wider Quaker Fellowship, which was designed to recruit non-Quakers into a kind of sympathetic affiliation with Friends. Quakers were hopeful that Gandhi might join, though he never did. Arthur Morgan, the president of Antioch College and a prominent Friend, began to contemplate the idea of non-Christians holding membership in Quaker meeting, arguing that the Inner Light did not differ based on outward religious forms. During the Vietnam War, Friends found themselves supporting the legal case of Daniel Seeger – an agnostic, Quaker meeting attender and AFSC employee – as he struggled for the right to be considered a religious conscientious objector under the law. After successfully winning his case, Seeger would officially join the Quakers while remaining an agnostic.[26]

By the 1980s and 1990s, liberal Quakerism included growing groups of Friends who identified themselves as having multiple religious belongings, among them Quaker neo-pagans, Quaker Buddhists, and Quaker Jews. The Quaker Universalist Fellowship, founded in 1983, espoused the idea that Quakerism should draw insights from many religious traditions. There were also nontheistic Friends, who publicly proclaimed that they did not believe in God or regarded the question of God's existence as unanswerable. Nontheistic Friends have had events at Quaker gatherings and study centers, and in 2006 published an edited collection, *Godless for God's Sake*.[27] The existence of nontheistic perspectives and plural religious belonging within Quakerism continues to elicit mild controversy, but there has been little official condemnation of these identities. This expansion of permitted views means that contemporary liberal Quakers do not have a shared theology. The question of whether Quakerism is Christian or even theistic continues to elicit debate.

Though theology has proven divisive, liberal Friends have been in general agreement on a variety of political and social causes. One of the most dramatic shifts has been the growing acceptance of gay and lesbian Friends. In 1963, the Friends Home Service Committee published *Towards a Quaker View of Sex*, an essay that argued for the decriminalization of homosexuality in Britain and suggested that "an act which expresses true affection between two individuals and gives pleasure to them both, does not seem to us to be sinful by reason *alone* of the fact that it is homosexual."[28] Monthly meetings in the United States began to perform same-sex commitment ceremonies and marriages by the 1980s. In 2009, British Friends became the first religious organization in the UK to recognize same-sex marriage. The acceptance of same-sex marriage and the issue of LGBTQ acceptance became a key division between liberal Friends and their evangelical co-religionists and has been a factor in numerous Yearly Meeting schisms in the United States.[29]

Within liberal Quakerism there is still considerable internal unity. Liberal Friends are devoted to similar social causes, share a history, practice unprogrammed worship, and make use of the same religious vocabulary. Rhetorically, they emphasize the importance of the Inner Light. Liberal Quakerism provides considerable latitude for its members on matters of theology, but it has understood itself to be in continuity with prior generations of Friends.

Notes

1 Stephen W. Angell and John Connell, "Quakers in North America," in *The Cambridge Companion to Quakerism*, ed. Stephen W. Angell and Pink Dandelion (New York: Cambridge University Press, 2018), 162; FWCC (2017); Yearly Meeting of the Religious Society of Friends (Quakers) in Britain, *Tabular Statement* (Compiled for Yearly Meeting Gathering, 2017); Map, "Finding Quakers Around the World," Available as a PDF. Quaker demographics are not kept to a consistent standard and are fairly imprecise, thus these figures represent a rough estimate.
2 Eugene McCarraher, *The Enchantments of Mammon: How Capitalism Became the Religion of Modernity* (Cambridge, MA: The Belknap Press of Harvard University Press, 2019); William R. Hutchinson, *The Modernist Impulse in American Protestantism* (Durham, NC: Duke University Press, 1992).
3 Gary Dorrien, *The Making of American Liberal Theology: Imagining Progressive Religion, 1805–1900* (Louisville, KY: Westminster John Knox Press, 2001), xiv.
4 Thomas D. Hamm, *The Quakers in America* (New York: Columbia University Press, 2003), 29–33; Robynne Rogers Healey, "Quietist Quakerism, 1692–c. 1805," in *The Oxford Handbook of Quaker Studies*, ed. Ben Pink Dandelion and Stephen W. Angell (New York: Oxford University Press, 2013), 47–62.
5 Paul Buckley, *The Essential Elias Hicks* (San Francisco, CA: Inner Light Books, 2013); Bliss Forbush, *Elias Hicks: Quaker Liberal* (New York: Columbia University Press, 1956), 25.
6 Robert W. Doherty, "Non-Urban Friends and the Hicksite Separation," *Pennsylvania History: A Journal of Mid-Atlantic Studies* 33, no. 4 (1966): 442.
7 Lucretia Mott, "Likeness to Christ," September 30, 1849, https://quaker.org/legacy/mott/likeness.html.
8 Brycchan Carey and Geoffrey Plank, eds., "George F. White and Hicksite Opposition to the Abolition Movement," in *Quakers and Abolition* (Urbana, IL: University of Illinois Press, 2014), 43–55.

9 Carol Faulkner, *Lucretia Mott's Heresy: Abolition and Women's Rights in Nineteenth-Century America* (Philadelphia, PA: University of Pennsylvania Press, 2011), 57–58, 121–22.

10 Henry David Thoreau quoted in Frederick B. Tolles, "Emerson and Quakerism," *American Literature* 10, no. 2 (1938): 144, https://doi.org/10.2307/2920611.

11 Robert D. Richardson Jr, *Emerson: The Mind on Fire* (Berkeley: University of California Press, 1995), 78, 157–163; Tolles, "Emerson and Quakerism"; Elizabeth Addison, "Compensation and the Price of Purity: An Old Quaker Impresses the Young Emerson," *Studies in the American Renaissance* (1992): 107–120; Murray Gardner Hill, "'A Rill Struck Out From the Rock': Mary Rotch of New Bedford," *Bulletin of Friends Historical Association* 45, no. 1 (1956): 8–23.

12 Christopher Densmore, "From the Hicksites to the Progressive Friends: The Rural Roots of Perfectionism and Social Reform among North American Friends," *Quaker Studies* 10, no. 2 (2006): 243–255; Chuck Fager, *Remaking Friends: How Progressive Friends Challenged Quakerism & Helped Save America* (Durham, NC: Kimo Press, 2014); A. Day Bradley, "Progressive Friends in Michigan and New York," *Quaker History* 52, no. 2 (1963): 95–103, https://doi.org/10.1353/qkh.1963.0004.

13 Waterloo Proceedings quoted in Bradley, "Progressive Friends in Michigan and New York," 100.

14 Ann Braude, *Radical Spirits: Spiritualism and Women's Rights in Nineteenth-Century America*, Second Edition (Bloomington, IN: Indiana University Press, 2001), 10–14; Robert S. Cox, *Body and Soul: A Sympathetic History of American Spiritualism* (Charlottesville, VA: University of Virginia Press, 2003), 11.

15 Thomas C. Kennedy, "Heresy-Hunting among Victorian Quakers: The Manchester Difficulty, 1861–73," *Victorian Studies* 34, no. 2 (1991): 227–53; R. K. Webb, "The Limits of Religious Liberty: Theology and Criticism in Nineteenth Century England," in *Freedom and Religion in the Nineteenth Century*, ed. Richard J. Helmstadter (Stanford, CA: Stanford University Press, 1997), 146–148.

16 [Francis Firth], [William Pollard], and [William E. Turner], *A Reasonable Faith, Essays, by Three "Friends"* (London: Macmillan, 1884), 2.

17 Thomas C. Kennedy, *British Quakerism, 1860–1920: The Transformation of a Religious Community* (New York: Oxford University Press, 2001), 102–106.

18 Alice Southern, "The Rowntree History Series and the Growth of Liberal Quakerism," *Quaker Studies* 16, no. 1 (September 2011): 7–73.

19 Matthew S Hedstrom, "Rufus Jones and Mysticism for the Masses," *Cross Currents* 54, no. 2 (2004): 31–44; Leigh Eric Schmidt, *Restless Souls: The Making of American Spirituality*, Second Edition (Berkeley, CA: University of California Press, 2005), 230–240; Guy Aiken, "Beyond Liberalism: Rufus Jones and Thomas Kelly and the History of Liberal Religion," *Quaker Theology* 11, no. 2 (Fall 2012): 74–90.

20 Schmidt, *Restless Souls: The Making of American Spirituality*, 240–260.

21 Douglas Gwyn, *A Gathering of Spirits: The Friends General Conferences 1896–1950* (Philadelphia, PA: Friends General Conference, 2018).

22 Allan W. Austin, *Quaker Brotherhood: Interracial Activism and the American Friends Service Committee, 1917–1950* (Champaign, IL: University of Illinois Press, 2012).

23 Patricia Appelbaum, *Kingdom to Commune: Protestant Pacifist Culture between World War I and the Vietnam Era* (Chapel Hill, NC: The University of North Carolina Press, 2009), 5.

24 "Speak Truth to Power: A Quaker Search for Alternatives to Violence" (American Friends Service Committee, 1955).

25 Jane P. Rushmore, "Our Basis of Faith," *Friends Intelligencer* (1953): 134; Jane P. Rushmore, *Testimonies and Practices of the Society of Friends* (Philadelphia, PA: Friends General Conference, 1945); Jane P. Rushmore, *The Quaker Way* (Philadelphia, PA: The Representative Committee of Philadelphia Yearly Meeting, 1951); Jesse H. Holmes et al., "To the Scientifically Minded" (FGC Advancement Committee, 1928), RMJ Papers, Box 27, Quaker Collection, Haverford College.

26 Isaac Barnes May, "God-Optional Religion in Twentieth-Century America: Quakers, Unitarians, Reconstructionist Jews, and the Crisis Over Theism, 1920–1965" (PhD Dissertation, University of Virginia, 2020).

27 *Godless for God's Sake: Nontheism in Contemporary Quakerism,* ed. David Boulton (Dent, Cumbria [UK]: Dales Historical Monographs, 2006).

28 *Towards a Quaker View of Sex: An Essay by a Group of Friends*, Revised Edition (London, England: Friends Home Service Committee, 1964), 41; Mark D. Jordan, *Recruiting Young Love: How Christians Talk about Homosexuality* (Chicago, IL: University of Chicago Press, 2011), 87–91.

29 Meetings that divided over LGBTQ issues include Indiana, Northwestern, Wilmington, and North Carolina.

14

THE LIFE AND THOUGHT OF RUFUS JONES (1863–1948)

Richard Kent Evans

When Quakers point to the founders of their faith, they usually point to George Fox or Margaret Fell. They are not incorrect to do so. But it may very well be the case that Liberal Quakers, who tend to live in North America and Europe, practice a form of seeker spirituality that owes less to Fox or Fell than it does to the American philosopher, activist, and mystic Rufus Jones. Few Friends match Jones's influence over Quaker history. Through his voluminous public writing, his prolific social activism, and his genius for institution building, Jones offered a new direction for the Society of Friends in the twentieth century – one that asked Friends to put aside the doctrinal disagreements of the nineteenth century and focus instead on mysticism and seeker spirituality, to abandon quietist peculiarity for ecumenical social activism, and to replace skepticism towards the world and its wisdom with an enthusiastic embrace of modernism (Punshon, 1984, p. 10; Watt, 2016, pp. 218–224).

Rufus Jones was born on January 25, 1863, in South China, Maine, into an unusually active and religious family with deep roots in the Society of Friends (Vining, 1958, pp. 17–31). His aunt and uncle, Sybil and Eli Jones, travelled frequently as missionaries. The Jones home regularly hosted visiting itinerant Quaker ministers. These connections to the wider Quaker world counterbalanced his rural and somewhat provincial upbringing. With the help of scholarships and family connections, he was educated at a series of Quaker boarding schools, including the Moses Brown School.[1] In 1882, he enrolled at Haverford College, where he became a protege of Pliny Chase, who nurtured his interests in philosophy and mysticism, and Isaac Sharpless, who facilitated his introduction to Quaker intellectual life. After graduating in 1885, Rufus Jones taught at Quaker schools in New England. In 1888, he married Sallie Coutant, who was also a teacher. Their son, Lowell Coutant Jones, was born in 1892. In 1893, Isaac Sharpless invited Jones and his family to move back to return to Haverford to teach courses in psychology and to take over as editor of *Friends' Review* (Alten, 1985, pp. 41–48).[2]

Jones spent the rest of his professional life as a professor of philosophy at Haverford College, though the college gave him ample rein to travel as his career as a Quaker intellectual and social activist grew increasingly demanding. Those demands became especially pressing during wartime. In 1917, Rufus Jones played a leading role in founding the American Friends Service Committee (AFSC), in part to protect Haverford students and other pacifists from conscription or imprisonment. He was instrumental in that organization's relief efforts during the interwar

DOI: 10.4324/9780429030925-16

period – feeding five million German children at risk of starvation – and served in leadership positions for most of his life.

People who knew Jones marveled at his perennial optimism, his cheerfulness, and his kindness towards others – facets of his personality that are all the more admirable considering the many tragedies he suffered. His mother died when he was sixteen. His wife Sallie died in 1899, leaving Rufus to care for their young son, Lowell. Over the summer of 1900, Rufus Jones fell in love with Ellen Wood.[3] They decided to marry but elected to postpone the announcement of their engagement until after Ellen returned from a trip to Europe. She contracted typhoid fever on the trip and died (Vining, 1958, pp. 82–83). In 1902, Rufus Jones married Elizabeth Bartram Cadbury, a brilliant Quaker intellectual in her own right and the sister of the important New Testament scholar Henry Cadbury. Rufus and Elizabeth would remain happily married until Rufus's death in 1948. A year into their marriage, alas, Rufus Jones's son Lowell died. Despite these many tragedies, Rufus Jones's personality remained upbeat and gregarious, though he did suffer intense bouts of depression in his later years.

At the time Rufus Jones was beginning his professional career, a new intellectual movement, Liberal Quakerism, was emerging within the Society of twentieth-century Quakerism and would propel him to the forefront of American Christianity (Frost, 2013, pp. 78–91). In 1895, a group of young Quakers met in Manchester, England, to discuss the future of Quakerism. Out of this meeting emerged an influential cadre of young, progressive Quakers who were determined to counteract the influence of evangelicalism within British and American Quakerism, which they viewed as a deviation from the teachings of early Friends (Jones, 1921). Modernist Quakers, or Liberal Quakers, as this movement came to be known, believed that the Society of Friends had erred when they, along with large swaths of British and American Protestantism, embraced evangelicalism during the Great Awakening. Influenced externally by Methodism and the evangelical revivals underway in the Church of England, and internally by evangelical Quaker ministers such as David Sands and Job Scott, Quakers in the mid-eighteenth century embraced doctrines that, according to the Liberal Quaker historical interpretation, were new to, and perhaps distinct from, Quakerism. Jones did have some good things to say about evangelicalism. He praised evangelicalism for inspiring Quakerism to "an awakened, intensified, religious faith, marching forth in the power of experience to the conquest of sin in the name of a Saviour who really saves" (Jones, 1921, p. 276). He noted that Quakers became much more interested in alleviating human suffering after their evangelical awakening, and he believed that evangelicalism forced Quakers to articulate more clearly doctrinal positions he agreed with: the divinity of Jesus and the need for redemption from sin through grace, for example (Aiken, 2011, pp. 37–53). But Jones believed that Quakers had made a mistake in embracing the evangelical doctrine of human depravity, which he viewed as difficult to reconcile with the Quaker doctrine of the Inner Light. He also criticized evangelicalism for introducing to Quakerism a formulaic "plan of salvation," dependent on the efficacy of the historical atonement, and for deeming vast and complex systems of doctrine essential for salvation. The result of the evangelical influence, Jones wrote, was that by the nineteenth century some Quakers had begun to practice "a type of Christianity . . . which is in strong and radical contrast to the mystical movement inaugurated by George Fox" (Jones, 1921, p. xiv).

In Jones's interpretation of Quaker history, evangelicalism arose, in part, as a response to the inadequacies of Quaker quietism. The quietist opponents of evangelicalism had "pushed much further than any Friends before them had done in the direction of an attempt to make Christianity square with reason" (Jones, 1921, pp. 292–293). Rufus Jones believed that in reaction to evangelicalism, Quakers turned inward and were more interested in preserving their own sectarian particularities than they were in "the continuous vital and authoritative work of Christ in the human soul" (Jones, 1921, p. 437). As Rufus Jones put it, nineteenth century Friends had been "content with a more humble mission" (Jones, 1921, p. 101). According to Jones, it was this fundamental split between evangelical Friends, Hicksite Friends, and quietist Friends that had caused the schisms of the nineteenth century. In their minds, Liberal Quakers like Jones were attempting to heal these schisms by restoring Quakerism to its roots. To their critics, the liberals' embrace of biblical criticism, their emphasis on mystical experience, their tendency to demythologize Biblical texts, and their rejection of some evangelical doctrines made their Quakerism – perhaps even their Christianity – suspect.

As his stature grew within the world of American Quakerism, Rufus Jones played a prominent role in building a new denominational structure, the Five Years Meeting, which furthered his goal of uniting American Quakerism under the banner of Liberalism. In 1897, the Third Conference of Friends discussed a proposal, written mostly by Jones, for uniting North American Yearly Meetings under a centralized organization and a uniform discipline (Hinshaw, 2013, pp. 93–107). To compose the section on belief for the uniform discipline, Rufus Jones and his collaborators (he worked particularly closely with James Wood) drew from two documents favored by evangelical Friends: the Richmond Declaration of Faith and George Fox's 1671 Letter to the Governor of Barbados. The resulting statement of belief struck a middle ground that satisfied neither the most evangelical and pastoral parties (Ohio Yearly Meeting, which had embraced outward embodiments of the sacraments, rejected the discipline on theological grounds) nor the most liberal (the Wilburite-majority Philadelphia Yearly Meeting did not even consider it.) But eleven Yearly Meetings in North America adopted Jones and Wood's proposal, and the majority of American Quakers united, beginning in 1902, under the Five Years Meeting (Alten, 1985, p. 45).

The harmony was short-lived, however, as the theological disagreements that Liberal Quakers like Jones were trying to repair were not so easily brushed aside. The sticking point within the Five Years Meeting was what to make of the Richmond Declaration of Faith. That document had been written in 1887 by a group of evangelical Quakers who gathered in Richmond, Indiana, under the leadership of prominent British evangelical Quaker Joseph Bevan Braithwaite (whose son, William Charles Braithwaite, was a prominent Liberal and worked with Jones on the Rowntree Series; Vining, 1958, p. 50). These Friends produced a document that they believed reflected the historical faith of the Quakers (Hinshaw, 2013, p. 98). The Richmond Declaration of Faith stated, among other things, that the Bible was "given by inspiration of God" and that "there can be no appeal from them to any other authority whatsoever." The Richmond Declaration was (and is) controversial because it brings to the fore the central theological problem in Quakerism; that is, the question of which source of spiritual authority deserved primacy, the Bible or the Inner Light. Jones struggled against the Richmond Declaration for decades. At the Five Years Meeting in 1912, he successfully pushed for an important caveat to be added to the Richmond Declaration, that it was "not to be regarded as constituting a creed." By 1922, many Western Quakers were advocating for Five Years Meeting to strongly affirm the Richmond Declaration as a creedal statement. This time Jones lost, and the line "not to be regarded as constituting a creed," was removed from the Richmond Declaration of Faith (Hinshaw, 2013, p. 99).

Rufus Jones spent much of the first two decades of the twentieth century laying the intellectual foundation for Liberal Quakerism through the Rowntree Series of Quaker histories. The Rowntree Series had been the idea of John Wilhelm Rowntree, who had emerged as a leading voice of Liberal Quakerism after delivering an address at London Yearly Meeting in 1892 on the difficulties Friends of his generation faced reconciling their faith with the modern world (Southern, 2011, p. 16). When Rowntree died unexpectedly in 1905, the task of organizing the project fell to Jones, his close friend. Jones had little training as a historian. As a student at Haverford, he had taken such a heavy course load that he had completed the coursework for a degree in philosophy by the end of his junior year. He received permission from the college to spend his senior year pursuing a master's degree in history under Allen Thomas, and he wrote a thesis, based entirely upon secondary sources, on the history of Christian mysticism in Europe (Vining, 1958, p. 40). Jones brought to the Rowntree Series his deep reading in the history of Christian mysticism, and he made the argument in his volumes of the series that the intellectual roots of Quakerism could be found in medieval continental mysticism.

The first book to appear in the Rowntree Series was Jones's 1909 *Studies in Mysticism*. Jones would go on to write *Spiritual Reformers in the Sixteenth and Seventeenth Centuries* (1914); *Later Periods of Quakerism* (1921), which appeared in two volumes; and co-authored *The Quakers in the American Colonies* (1911) with Amelia Mott Gummere and Isaac Sharpless. He edited all of the books in the series (the other two books, *Beginnings of Quakerism* [1912] and *The Second Period of Quakerism* [1921] were written by William Charles Braithwaite). Jones considered his *The Flowering of Mysticism* (1939) to be a part of the Rowntree series, though officially it was not (Livezey, 1970, pp. 176–185).

In Jones's interpretation, Quakerism was founded upon a mystical experience (when George Fox climbed Pendle Hill in 1652 and saw a "great people to be gathered") and was, from its beginning, an experiment in group mysticism that owed an intellectual debt (perhaps indirectly) to continental mystics like Jacob Boehme (Kent, 1987, p. 259). Jones argued that Christian mysticism had undergone a revival and reinterpretation in the radical reformers of the seventeenth century. Groups including the Spiritualists, the Family of Love, the Seekers, the Familists, and the Ranters made a radical break with the Protestant tradition, represented by the Puritans, in favor of a more direct encounter with the divine. Jones had drawn a hard line separating Quakers from Puritans. As the historian Melvin Endy argued, Jones believed the essence of Quakerism to be the "direct and first-hand experience of God." The essence of Puritanism, to Jones, was the belief that "God's Word to the human race was . . . to be found, and to be found only, in the volume of the Scriptures." Jones believed "Puritanism and mysticism were antithetical" (Endy, 1981, p. 6). As Alice Southern points out, early Friends, as portrayed in the Rowntree Series, look an awful lot like Liberal Friends at the turn of the twentieth century: they are committed to social activism, they are rational and take a critical approach to the biblical texts, they are dedicated mystics yet outward looking and energetic, and they have a generally optimistic view of human nature.[4] The point of the Rowntree Series was not just to narrate the history of the Society of Friends; it was meant to provide Liberal Friends like Jones with a telling of Quaker history that would prove useful to fight against twin foes of evangelicalism and quietism (Southern, 2011). That is, the point was not to merely to recount the past but to create a *usable* past with which liberal Quakers, who fully embraced modernism, could forge a new, modern, liberal Quakerism for the twentieth century (Kent, 1987, p. 256).

Jones's interest in mysticism was not confined to his study of Quaker history. The foundation of all of Rufus Jones's thought was his belief that people could and did have direct experiences of the divine. He called these moments, which felt "like a thrust from beyond," mystical experiences, and he called the mode of religious life that seeks these intimate, personal connections with the divine "mysticism" (Jones, 1941, p. 60). By "mysticism" Jones meant "the type of religion which puts the emphasis on immediate awareness of relation with God, on direct and intimate consciousness of the Divine Presence." Mysticism, to Jones, was "religion in its more acute, intense and living stage" (Livezey, 1970, p. 180).

Jones claimed to have had three mystical experiences. The first was in 1887 when he was twenty-four years old. He was at the time spending a month in the south of France, at the foothills of the Alps. He was hiking alone (retracing the trails that Huguenots and Waldensians had used to flee to Switzerland and Germany after Louis XIV revoked the Edict of Nantes three centuries earlier) and ruminating about his purpose in life when he "felt the walls between the visible and the invisible suddenly grow thin." Recounting the experience forty-two years later, Jones wrote that he became

> conscious of a definite mission of life opening out before me. I saw stretch before me an unfolding of labor in the realm of mystical religion, almost as clearly as Francis heard himself called at St. Damiens to "repair the church."
>
> *(Jones, 1929, pp. 159–160)*

His second mystical experience was in 1903, near the end of a transatlantic voyage. Jones had left his eleven-year-old son Lowell behind to recuperate from a mild bout of diphtheria as he and his wife, Elizabeth Cadbury Jones, sailed to England to celebrate the opening of Wood-brooke Study Centre. The night before their arrival, Jones awoke with a "strange sense of trouble and sadness" (M.H. Jones, 1986, p. 15). He soon found himself "surrounded by an enfolding Presence and held as though by invisible Arms." He felt a deep comfort, as though his "entire being was fortified." When the ship landed, Rufus and Elizabeth learned that Lowell had died. His third mystical experience was in 1922, when he was struck by a car and thrown twenty feet. He suffered a concussion, broken ribs, and a leg fracture, and he tore the ligaments around his knee. His injuries left him bedridden in his study. (His classes at Haverford continued unabated; he taught from a hospital bed in his study on the top floor of his house on campus.) Nine years later, he wrote about his recovery as its own mystical experience: "There was no single moment of invasion or of uprush. I discovered that a new life and power *had come* to me without my knowing precisely *when it came*" (Vining, 1958, p. 99). Rufus Jones believed that he "had entered into an unexpected tranquility and peace" which left him "more joyous and radiant," gave him more energy for his work, and made him more certain of the reality of God and of mystical experiences (Vining, 1958, p. 201).

Jones wanted everyone to have these mystical experiences. His career as a public intellectual was premised on the idea that mystical experiences were an attainable pursuit for the burgeoning American middle class. In the words of historian Matthew Hedstrom, Jones was unafraid "to market himself to the masses" (Hedstrom, 2004, pp. 31–44). His most widely read books were autobiographical. He wrote prolifically for popular outlets including *The Atlantic Monthly*, *Christian Century*, and *Time* magazine. He delivered hundreds of speeches, lectures, and sermons every year. He was a tireless reviewer, editorialist, and editor. And he still found time to write fifty-three books: the first, a biography of Sybil and Eli Jones, was published in 1889; he finished editing the proofs to his last book, *A Call to What Is Vital*, on the day he died (Livezey, 1970, p. 183).

In his public writing, Jones was careful to distinguish between the kind of mysticism he advocated, which he called "affirmation mysticism," and the mysticism practiced by Meister Eckhart and John Tauler, which he called "classical mysticism" or "negation mysticism." Jones worried that classical mysticism sought to negate the human personality. When done right, in Jones's reading, classic mysticism dissolved the individual into a depersonalized God, the "Abstract Infinite," or a "nameless Nothing" (Livezey, 1970, p. 183). Jones worried, too, that classical mysticism was designed to cultivate ecstatic experiences, something that he, drawing on the influential work of William James, viewed as counterproductive at best and dangerous to mental health at worst.

It may be the case that Jones's affirmation mysticism owes as much to Transcendentalism as it does to classical Christian mysticism. As Leigh Eric Schmidt has noticed, Rufus Jones's study provides a clue as to Jones's intellectual heroes. Jones kept a portrait of John Greenleaf Whittier above his desk, beneath a set of prints of Ralph Waldo Emerson and Thomas Carlyle. The largest image in the room is another portrait of Emerson as a young man. (Jones also kept two portraits of George Fox and one of the liberal mystic Harvard theologian Charles C. Everett.) Jones had a deep affinity for Walt Whitman, and he named his son after the poet James Russell Lowell. The Transcendentalists found kindred spirits in George Fox and the Early Friends. As Jones explained, his "studies of Emerson led on into an extensive reading of Carlyle and both these men planted in me a new idea in reference to the significance of the Quakerism in which I had been nurtured." Through the Transcendentalists and other writers, Jones rediscovered his own faith tradition, albeit mediated through Romantic treatments by Emerson, Robert Alfred Vaughan, and Thomas Carlyle (Schmidt, 2005, pp. 231–232).

One wonders what role Transcendentalism may have played in Jones's widely influential reinterpretation of the Inner Light. In an introduction to a 1903 abridged edition of Fox's Journals, Rufus Jones isolated the phrase "that of God" in every person as a cornerstone of Fox's thought. This phrase, as Jones interpreted it, is as close to a creed as one will find in Liberal Quakerism (Benson, 1970, pp. 2–25). The phrase indeed originates in one of Fox's epistles but had fallen out of disuse before Jones appropriated it. As Lewis Benson argued, Fox meant something quite different from the phrase than Jones did. For Jones and Liberal Friends today, Fox's phrase has been interpreted to mean that "there is something Divine, 'something of God,' in the human soul," and that the work of being a Quaker is to cultivate that divine spark, sometimes called the Inner Light (Jones, 1904, pp. 167–168). It seems, however, that Fox's quote (in context), and indeed his theology, is hard to square with Jones's interpretation. Some scholars, engaged in a theological debate as much as a historical one, argue that Jones's reinterpretation of the phrase tends towards a humanistic "self-deification" that was "the exact opposite of what Fox intended." Historically speaking, they may well be right (Cooper, 2005, p. 33).

Rufus Jones retired from teaching in 1934, though his was an active retirement. He continued to write at a breakneck pace, averaging more than one book per year. (Much of Jones's prolificacy is thanks to the work of his wife, Elizabeth Cadbury Jones, who researched and edited for her husband, in addition to caring for their daughter and attending to Rufus's many other needs. Elizabeth Jones ought to be considered a co-author of many of Rufus Jones's works. Their daughter, Mary Hoxie Jones [1904–2003], also assisted her father with his research and writing and went on to make noted contributions to Quaker intellectual life in her own right.)[5] Jones also travelled a great deal on behalf of the AFSC, having resumed the chairmanship of that organization in 1935 (Vining, 1958, p. 263). In 1938, after *Kristallnacht*, he and two other Friends travelled to Berlin to confer with Nazi officials about how Quakers might provide relief to Jews living in Germany. Quakers eventually rescued around 5700 people. But Jones's meeting with the Gestapo deserves a closer look. He made it clear to the Nazis that the Quakers were not there "to judge or criticize" their actions, and he seemed to believe that Quaker love and goodwill had "melted the hearts" of the Nazi officials. He continued to believe this even after the extent of Nazi brutality – and the impotence of his meeting with the Gestapo – had become evident (Aiken, 2017, pp. 209–231).

Jones remained in fairly good health into his eighties. He lived to see the end of World War II, and he delighted in the fact that the AFSC was awarded the Nobel Peace Prize in 1947 for the organization's postwar relief efforts. He died on June 16, 1948, peacefully in his home at Haverford College (Vining, 1958, p. 314). By the time he died, he was one of the most famous theologians of the century. He earned many admirers and students during his lifetime and beyond, including Aldous Huxley, Christopher Isherwood, Gerald Heard, and Thomas R. Kelly (Schmidt, 2005, p. 231). Harry Emerson Fosdick discovered Jones's theology as a young man, and he credited Jones for both saving his faith and laying the foundation for the liberal Christian theology Fosdick would make famous. Fosdick invited Jones to preach at his well-known Riverside Church on numerous occasions, and Fosdick helped spur a revival of interest in Jones in 1961 when he edited a popular collection of Jones's writings (Fosdick, 1961). Howard Thurman came across Jones's *Finding the Trail of Life* (1929) almost by accident as a young man and decided to study with Jones at Haverford (Massey, 1972, pp. 190–195). At the time, Haverford College did not admit African American students, but through a particular arrangement, Thurman became a "special student" of Jones's during the spring semester of 1929.

Within the history of Christianity in the United States, Rufus Jones serves an important intellectual bridge connecting the Transcendentalist Seekers of the nineteenth century to the countercultural turn to seeker spirituality and the emergence of the New Age in the 1960s and 1970s. To Quakers, Jones's legacy looms even larger. He is one of the key architects of Liberal Quakerism, both intellectually through his popular interpretations of Quaker history and his public writing, and institutionally, through organizations such as the AFSC and Friends General Conference. Rufus Jones was looking for the common denominator that he hoped could heal the Quaker schisms of the nineteenth century. In the process, he found, in mysticism, the theological vocabulary to articulate a new vision of Quakerism: one that was at peace with modernism, that prioritized humanitarianism over missions, and that paved the way for emergent post-Protestant, post-Christian, and non-theist Quaker spiritualities (Schmidt, 2005, pp. 230–232).

Notes

1 At the time Rufus Jones attended, the school was called Providence Friends School.
2 *Friends' Review* soon merged with the Western and evangelical *The Christian Worker* under the title *American Friend*.
3 Ellen Wood's father, James Wood, worked closely with Rufus Jones constructing the Five Years Meeting.
4 In Southern's reading, Braithwaite gives more credence to the dualistic view of human nature that seems to be shared more by early Friends than does Jones.
5 Those include two histories: *Swords into Ploughshares: An Account of the American Friends Service Committee, 1917–1937* (1971), and *The Standard of the Lord Lifted Up: A History of Friends in New England from 1656–1700, Commemorating the First Yearly Meeting Held in 1661* (1961), as well as books of poetry *Beyond This Stone* (1965) and *Mosaic of the Sun* (1975). Her papers are held at Haverford College.

Bibliography

Aiken, G., 'Who took the Christ out of Quakerism? Rufus Jones and the person and work of Christ', *Quaker Religious Thought* 116 (2011), 37–53.
Alten, D., 'Rufus Jones and the American Friend: A quest for unity', *Quaker History* 74 (1985), 41–48.
Benson, L., "That of God in every man' – what did George Fox mean by it?', *Quaker Religious Thought* 24 (1970), 2–25.
Bernet, C., *Rufus Jones (1863–1948): Life and bibliography of an American scholar, writer, and social activist* (New York: Peter Lang, 2009).
Cooper, W. A., 'Reflections on Rufus M. Jones: Quaker giant of the twentieth century', *Quaker History* 94 (2005), 25–43.
Endy, M. B., 'The interpretation of Quakerism: Rufus Jones and his critics', *Quaker History* 70 (1981), 3–21.
Fosdick, H. E., *Rufus Jones speaks to our time* (New York: The Macmillan Company, 1961).
Frost, J. W., 'Modernist and liberal Quakers', pp. 78–91, in Angell, St. and Dandelion, B. P. (eds.), *The Oxford handbook of Quaker studies* (New York and Oxford: Oxford University Press, 2013).
Hedstrom, M. S., 'Rufus Jones and mysticism for the masses', *Cross Currents* 54 (2004), 31–44.
Hinshaw, D., *Rufus Jones: Master Quaker* (New York: G. P. Putnam's Sons, 1951).

Hinshaw, G. P., 'Five years meeting and friends united meeting, 1887–2010', pp. 93–107, in Angell, St. and Dandelion, B. P. (eds.), *The Oxford handbook of Quaker studies* (New York and Oxford: Oxford University Press, 2013).

Jones, M. H., 'Rufus Matthew Jones: Mystic', *Mystics Quarterly* 12 (1986), 15.

Jones, R., *Social law in the spiritual world: Studies in human and divine inter-relationship* (New York: George H. Duran Company, 1904).

Jones, R., *Spirit in man* (Stanford: Stanford University Press, 1941).

Jones, R., *The later periods of Quakerism*, 2 vols. (London: Macmillan, 1921).

Jones, R., *Finding the trail of life in college* (New York: The Macmillan Company, 1929).

Kent, S. A., 'Psychological and mystical interpretations of early Quakerism: William James and Rufus Jones', *Religion* 17 (1987), 251–274.

Livezey, W. E., 'Rufus M. Jones: Apostle of the friendly way', *Journal of Thought* 5 (1970), 176–185.

Massey, J. E., 'Bibliographical essay: Howard Thurman and Rufus M. Jones, two mystics', *Journal of Negro History* 57 (1972), 190–195.

Punshon, J., 'Rufus Jones and mystical Quakerism', *Friends Journal* (1984), 10.

Schmidt, L. E., *Restless souls: The making of American spirituality* (New York: HarperCollins, 2005).

Southern, A., 'The Rowntree history series and the growth of liberal Quakerism', *Quaker Studies* 16 (2011), 7–73.

Vining, E. G., *Friend of life: The biography of Rufus M. Jones* (Philadelphia: J. B. Lippincott Company, 1958).

Watt, D. H., 'Philadelphia, Rufus Jones, and the reinvention of Quakerism', pp. 218–224, in Alvarez, E. H. (ed.), *Religion in Philadelphia* (Philadelphia: Temple University Press, 2016).

15

H. LOUISE BROWN WILSON (1921–2014)

Exemplary North Carolina Conservative Friend

Lloyd Lee Wilson

Each of the three surviving Conservative yearly meetings[1] has a unique origin story, separated for distinctly different reasons, and has demonstrated a unique set of characteristics or qualities over the generations between those separations and the present day. North Carolina Yearly Meeting was the last of the "Conservative" separations, in 1903–1904 – two generations after the first Wilburite separations began in 1842. Earlier Conservative separations had focused on theological, doctrinal, or liturgical issues. North Carolina Friends survived those challenges as a united body, only to founder on the rocks of ecclesiastical polity, specifically the struggles over adoption of the Uniform Discipline,[2] which came to a climax in North Carolina in 1902. The combination of regional history, yearly meeting history, and specific reasons for the separation, as well as changes in the secular culture over the generations generated a recognizable "personality" for Conservative Friends in North Carolina different from other Conservative yearly meetings.

In the decades leading up to the Civil War, trying to live a moral life in the midst of a slave-owning society had been a relentless challenge to Friends in the south. Each new tactic for freedom was met by a legislative response that often seemed to leave the enslaved people worse off than before. In the decades leading up to open conflict, thousands of North Carolina Friends emigrated to free states or territories, leaving Quaker meetings in the state significantly weakened.

During the war years, the religious pacifism and abolitionist sentiments of Friends made them objects of suspicion by all sides. At the war's end, Friends in North Carolina were physically, emotionally, and spiritually impoverished. They were open to accept the physical support offered by northern Friends through initiatives like the Baltimore Association and ready to listen to new ideas about how best to revive the spiritual vitality of meetings in North Carolina.

As a result of focused evangelical efforts much aided by northern Friends affiliated with the Baltimore Association, North Carolina Friends membership nearly doubled in the years following the Civil War. Some means was needed to teach all these newcomers the full extent of the faith and practice of Quakers, and some agreement on the specific content of that faith and practice was felt necessary as well. Compromises and working arrangements were found in many areas, but the effort to codify orthodox Quaker faith and practice, in the form of a single Uniform Discipline, proved the breaking point in North Carolina.

DOI: 10.4324/9780429030925-17

After the separation into two yearly meetings, the group that would later be called Conservatives were a collection of extended families in rural, agricultural settings. They continued a history of strong support for the education of their children. In spiritual matters they maintained an apophatic spirituality, avoiding trying to insist on specific words, looking instead to the greater reality to which all such words point.

Helen Louise Brown Wilson[3] exemplified the distinctive qualities of North Carolina Yearly Meeting (Conservative) throughout its first century (1904–2004); over the course of her life she played a leadership role in changing some of those distinctives in very significant ways.

Family

At the time of its first annual sessions in 1904, the Conservative yearly meeting was made up of monthly meetings that were each composed of a very small number of extended families. In West Grove, 86% of the founding members were named Newlin; at Piney Woods, 68% were from the Chappell family. Rich Square Monthly Meeting, the "mother meeting" of conservative Friends in North Carolina, was the largest monthly meeting but still drew most of its membership from just three families: the Parkers, the Outlands, and the Browns. Albert Brown was men's clerk of the new yearly meeting for its first 11 years. He was succeeded by Walter Brown for the next seven years. In 1950, David H. Brown was named clerk of the yearly meeting (no longer separated into men's and women's meetings), and served for 11 years. David H. Brown was at this time also serving as clerk of Rich Square Monthly Meeting, a position he held for a total of 25 years.

Helen Louise Brown, the daughter of David H. Brown, was born in 1921. She and her brothers, David Jr. and Benjamin, carried on the family history of long and dedicated leadership in their monthly meetings and the yearly meeting. Louise and Benjamin were recorded as ministers, and David Jr. was named an elder. Like their father and other close relatives before them, David Jr. and Louise both served as clerk of the yearly meeting[4] and of their respective monthly meetings.

Education

Unlike some other Conservative yearly meetings ,[5] formal education was valued, not stigmatized, by the Conservative Quakers in North Carolina. David Brown Sr. and other Friends and relatives had gone to Westtown School[6] in Pennsylvania to finish high school, and in her turn Helen Louise went also. After graduation, she enrolled at Guilford College, a Quaker institution in Greensboro, NC.

Very early in the life of the monthly meeting Helen Louise founded in Virginia Beach, Virginia, Friends there determined to start a new Friends school. She was instrumental in the success of this endeavor, serving as teacher, driver, head of the school, financial supporter, and cheerleader for all concerned. The school opened before there was any building to house it; the first classes were held on the sand dunes by the oceanfront. Eventually it grew to cover the full range of ages pre-kindergarten through high school graduation, with a roomy campus and several academic buildings located next to the Virginia Beach Friends meeting house.

It is appropriate to note that Friends School in Virginia Beach was initiated and has always been operated not as a "guarded education" for Quakers seeking a hedge from the world but as a place to embody the best principles of education and to serve the wider non-Quaker community. Alumni of the school have gone on to successful careers in academics, public service and the arts; probably the most famous of these is B.J. Leiderman, who composed theme music for several NPR programs that has been familiar to listeners for 40 years.

Rural to Urban Transition

In the first decades after the separation in North Carolina, all the meetings belonging to what is now called the Conservative yearly meeting were in rural areas of the state. Twentieth-century growth among liberal unprogrammed Friends, in contrast, was concentrated in urbanized areas, especially after World War II. Some observers have speculated that the Conservative faith and practice could find no foothold in these cities and larger towns. When Helen Louise and her new husband, Robert Wilson, relocated to booming Virginia Beach, Virginia, she was given a vision that changed all that. Following the instructions of that vision,[7] she established a new meeting in Virginia Beach in 1954 that was quickly accepted into North Carolina Yearly Meeting (Conservative). This new monthly meeting grew rapidly and thrived spiritually; in a very short time, its members had founded a new Quaker secondary school as well.

Before Virginia Beach Friends Meeting was established, Helen Louise would later observe, Conservative Friends in North Carolina assumed no one not already a Conservative Friend would be interested in their faith and practice.[8] With this new meeting in their midst, they had to rethink their assumptions; the effect on the yearly meeting has been profound. While rural Conservative meetings in North Carolina have struggled, new meetings in urban centers have joined the Conservative yearly meeting, including Durham, Greensboro, Greenville, Wilmington, Fayetteville, and Davidson. Even as liberal yearly meeting alternatives have developed in North Carolina, these urban meetings have reaffirmed their commitment to remain in the Conservative yearly meeting. Helen Louise Wilson literally led the way in transforming Conservative Friends in North Carolina from a rural to a largely urban faith and practice.

Ecumenical Vision: Maintaining Unity of Spirit in the Bond of Peace

All separations among Friends can be said to embody a certain narrowness of ecumenical vision. This was certainly true of the Great Separations of the nineteenth century, including the one in North Carolina which spilled over into 1903. In its early decades the Conservative yearly meeting in North Carolina shared in this general narrowness of vision. This is demonstrated by the yearly meeting's endorsement of *A Brief Synopsis of the Principles and Testimonies of the Religious Society of Friends*[9] adopted by the seven Conservative yearly meetings in 1912, and the widely publicized protest of Holly Spring Monthly Meeting against participation in the newly formed Friends World Committee for Consultation.[10]

This sectarian perspective was always at odds with the deep-rooted desire of Friends in North Carolina generally to want to get along with each other. This is most clearly articulated in the classic phrase at the conclusion of the Conservative yearly meeting *Advices* on the importance of "endeavoring to keep the unity of the Spirit in the bond of Peace" (Ephesians 4:3, KJV).[11] In the decades leading up to the North Carolina separation, one could see this desire for overall unity in the arrangements made to avoid direct conflict inside the yearly meeting. When Friends of a more evangelical inclination wanted to sponsor tent meetings, or revivals, and more traditional Friends were opposed, an agreement was reached in which those meetings who were in favor of these activities paid the entire cost of carrying out the project, and those who were opposed were not asked to bear any of the expense. Even the separation itself was conducted civilly, without the lawsuits or discharge of firearms that marked separations in other yearly meetings. In some localities, evangelical and traditional meetings shared a meeting space for years following the separation.

Helen Louise Wilson tapped into this desire and expanded it by introducing North Carolina Conservatives to a wide variety of Christian resources beyond Conservative hedges and often outside of the Religious Society of Friends, while in her own travels she introduced non-Conservative Quakers to some of the richness of the Conservative tradition. In the early years of Virginia Beach Friends Meeting, she invited articulate, seasoned Friends from the Philadelphia yearly meetings, as well as Ohio Yearly Meeting, to visit Virginia Beach, to share worship and their personal experience of Quakerism with the new Friends there.

Helen Louise's gifts in the spoken ministry had been formally recognized (by Rich Square Monthly Meeting) in 1955,[12] the year Virginia Beach Friends Meeting was established.[13] These gifts were exercised faithfully in the new meeting, and also to a wider audience, both Friends and others. The yearly meeting minutes record some of her travels in the ministry, including the 1954 conference on "Church and Ministry" in Detroit, Michigan, and service at the yearly meeting sessions themselves, including a plenary presentation in 1961. Her spontaneous ministry during a Representative Body meeting for business in 1960[14] was minuted as follows:

> Helen Louise Wilson spoke very feelingly on the need of Friends to go to the source of all power for knowledge which will govern our actions in the present situation. We should listen with great care and then we will know what to do. We should come up with a common concern to learn to love one another and we as individuals must learn to love and act in love. This is our real peace testimony. The Power of God is the real source of all good.

Nearly 30 years later, one contemporary Friend summed up Louise Wilson's ministry in these words:

> Louise's talk this afternoon was well presented and well received. Her style is very much herself, and if the listener is willing to uncover that tender spot we all have near our heart, Louise's words and presence can't help but have a powerful effect. It is possible to be unmoved by her testimony, but only by choosing to be hard. Yet when one looks at her offerings intellectually, there is no immortal prose or poetic imagery in her words; it is instead the obvious testimony of her whole being that lends power to what she says. Louise has let God have His way with her, and it shows. Her spoken words are simply the carrier waves by which His message is transmitted.[15]

Summary

Helen Louise Brown Wilson exemplified the distinctives of North Carolina Friends Meeting (Conservative) and showed how those distinctives could be adapted to maintain their relevance in a new generation. Her commitment to education continued a long tradition in the yearly meeting; founding Friends School in Virginia Beach showed the value of continuing the tradition of Quaker schools in the era of a state-run public school system. She made the transition from a rural childhood to being named First Citizen of the City of Virginia Beach; by founding Virginia Beach Friends Meeting and situating it firmly in the Conservative tradition she broke old thought patterns and made a vibrant faith accessible to many individuals and families across the state. In her ministry and witness she continued the long-held desire to maintain unity in a bond of peace; her spiritual teaching expanded the boundaries of that unity by recognizing that all spiritual vocabulary is no more than a pointer directing one to the Truth that is beyond expression in words.

Notes

1 Ohio Yearly meeting, Iowa Yearly Meeting (Conservative), and North Carolina Yearly Meeting (Conservative).

2 *The Constitution and Discipline for the American Yearly Meetings of Friends*, a single ("Uniform") document adopted by four Gurneyite yearly meetings in 1897 and subsequently by seven more between then and 1902.

3 Helen Louise Wilson (née Brown) was known by a variety of names during her life, depending on who was speaking to or about her: Helen, Helen Louise, Louise Brown Wilson, and so on. She will be referred to in this chapter by these various designations, as she was in life.

4 David Jr. for five years, 1978–1982; Louise for three years, 1984–1986. Minutes of North Carolina Yearly Meeting of Friends (Conservative), 1978, 1979, 1980, 19812 1982, 1984, 1985, 1986, no publisher, no printer named.

5 Cf. Bill Taber's description of the distrust of formal education in Ohio Yearly Meeting in *The Eye of Faith*.

6 Westtown was the Quaker boarding school for Orthodox Friends. Hicksites attended George School.

7 Louise Wilson, *Inner Tenderings*. Friends United Press (Richmond, IN) 1996.

8 Personal communication, c. 2005.

9 http://www.snowcamp.org/brief/brief.html, accessed 6/27/2022.

10 Holly Spring Monthly Meeting of Friends, "A Protest Against Joining with the Friend's World Conference," *Friendsville Current*, Vol. 12, No. 6 (6/1937), 2–4.

11 North Carolina Yearly Meeting (Conservative), "Advices," *Faith and Practice – Book of Discipline of the North Carolina Yearly Meeting (Conservative) of the Religious Society of Friends,* 1983 Revision, https://docs.google.com/document/d/1u-CBMAfe46DW33Yit9tpC45KTset2SE8zDh68vL0uKI/edit.

12 **Third** Month 19, 1955: "Answers to the Queries from Eastern Quarterly Meeting of Friends," *Minutes of North Carolina Yearly Meeting of Friends Held at Cedar Grove in the Town of Woodland, North Carolina*, 1955, p. 11.

13 Wilson, Helen Louise Brown, *A View from My Window: History of Virginia Beach Friends Meeting and School,* self published, 1995, pp. 12–13.

14 *Minutes of North Carolina Yearly Meeting of Friends Held at Cedar Grove in the Town of Woodland, North Carolina,* 1960, pp. 12–13, and *Minutes of North Carolina Yearly Meeting of Friends Held at Cedar Grove in the Town of Woodland, North Carolina,* 1961, p. 39.

15 Lloyd Lee Wilson (no relation), personal journal entry, December 8, 1989.

Bibliography

Hickey, Damon D., "Traditionalists Challenge Southern Quakerism's New Order," *Sojourners No More: The Quakers in the New South 1865–1920,* Greensboro, NC: North Carolina Yearly Meeting of Friends and North Carolina Friends Historical Society, 1997, pp. 59–80.

Holly Spring Monthly Meeting of Friends, "A Protest Against Joining with the Friend's World Conference," *Friendsville Current*, Vol. 12, No. 6 (6/1937), 2–4.

North Carolina Yearly Meeting and six other Conservative yearly meetings, *A Brief Synopsis of the Principles and Testimonies of the Religious Society of Friends,* approved 1912 and distributed 1913,

North Carolina Yearly Meeting (Conservative), *Faith and Practice – Book of Discipline of the North Carolina Yearly Meeting (Conservative) of the Religious Society of Friends,* 1983 Revision, https://docs.google.com/document/d/1u-CBMAfe46DW33Yit9tpC45KTset2SE8zDh68vL0uKI/edit, accessed 12/11/2019.

North Carolina Yearly Meeting of Friends held at Cedar Grove in the town of Woodland, *Minutes,* Woodland, NC: n.p., 1955.

Perry, David Neil, "A Visitor's Observations about North Carolina Yearly Meeting (Conservative)," *Journal of the North Carolina Yearly Meeting (Conservative),* No. 5 (Summer 2006), 30–36.

Taber, William. *The Eye of Faith: A History of Ohio Yearly Meeting, Conservative*. Ohio: Religious Society of Friends, 1985.

Wilson, Lloyd Lee, "A Conservative Yearly Meeting is Born," *Quaker Theology*, Issue #11, Vol. 6, No. 2 (Spring–Summer 2005), 78–91.

Wilson, Lloyd Lee, *The Remnant of Like Faith: The First Fifty Years of North Carolina Yearly Meeting (Conservative)*, Richmond, IN: MA Thesis, Earlham School of Religion, 2009.

Wilson, Louise, *Inner Tenderings*, Richmond, IN: Friends United Press, 1996, 0-944350-37-2.

Wilson, Louise B., *A View from My Window: History Virginia Beach Meeting and School*, Virginia Beach, VA: self-published, 1995.

16

THE INCORPORATION OF COMMITTEES

The Development of Quaker Institutions

Robin Mohr

The Quaker world is a complex mixture of individuals and institutions, each with a role to play in the world. In general, the development of Quaker institutions, large and small, has come through the incorporation of Quaker committees. By this I mean both senses of incorporation, from the Latin, *incorporare*: embodying a concept or concern, and legal recognition by governments. An institution is, by dictionary definition,[1] an organization devoted to promotion of a cause. Another way to look at an institution is as the incarnation of a cause, the legal structure for a commitment by people to a cause. As C. Wess Daniels once said about the Incarnation, the physical expression of the Divine will in the human body of Christ Jesus, "the medium is the message."[2]

Quakers have typically expected that Quaker institutions will be run by Quakers and either for the benefit of Quakers or for some other social need. This has not always been the case, particularly in the late twentieth century when Quaker social service agencies endeavored to employ representatives of the populations served and engage them in their governance.[3] In these cases, the question arises whether they are still Quaker institutions or if they are instead Quaker founded or Quaker inspired.

Internal Structures

The first Quaker institutions were the local congregations of Friends that met for worship, beginning in the 1650s.[4] The monthly meeting was the name given to the local congregation that met to do business every month. This body was responsible for the right holding of meetings for worship, weekly and more often. At the same time, yearly meetings have been part of the infrastructure of the Religious Society of Friends since the first General Meeting in Rhode Island, now New England Yearly Meeting. George Fox encouraged the development of these institutions to counter a tendency to excesses of exuberance and also to take better care of Friends who were incarcerated because of their Quaker faith and practice. A yearly meeting is

> A body consisting of Monthly Meetings from a geographically extended area, whose members are invited to gather in annual session to worship and conduct business together. This term is also used to denote the total membership of the constituent Monthly Meetings of a designated Yearly Meeting.[5]

DOI: 10.4324/9780429030925-18

Among Friends, a monthly meeting or Friends church (these two terms are synonymous) is the local decision-making body holding authority for approving memberships and conducting marriages. As might be expected, this group typically meets monthly to conduct business in the manner of Friends. A yearly meeting is frequently divided into quarterly meetings, by geographic regions, and has varying amounts of power and authority over monthly meetings. This degree of authority varies by the yearly meeting and by the century. Within the Quaker denomination, a yearly meeting is the body with the authority to publish or designate a book of discipline, often called the Book of Faith and Practice, for its member meetings. However, a yearly meeting is more than its denominational infrastructure. The true and proper purpose of a Quaker yearly meeting is to assist Friends and their local meetings to align their will, their values, and their understandings with God's.[6]

The Rise of Committees

However, many matters of importance to Friends could not wait for a monthly or yearly event. And so more frequent meetings of small groups for specific purposes were created. One of the most long-standing and far-reaching of these meetings was known as the "Meeting for Sufferings" of Britain Yearly Meeting. In Britain, starting in 1676, "the meeting was not restricted to the efforts to obtain redress in particular 'Cases of Suffering' (though this was the first item in the minutes until about 1750)".[7] In the nineteenth century, it became the central locus of various subcommittees on the slave trade, missions and other foreign relations, peace, the drug trade, and many more. While growing in responsibilities over the years, since approximately 1965, "Meeting for Sufferings is the standing representative body entrusted with the care of the business of Britain Yearly Meeting through the year."[8] In other yearly meetings, today this might be called Representative Meeting, Interim Meeting, or the Permanent Board.

This growth of committees at the yearly meeting level was mirrored at the local level or at monthly and quarterly meeting levels. Friends around the world recognize committee service as an essential element of Quaker governance, although the role, number, and composition of committees varies in each meeting. Today, all levels have a plethora of volunteer positions that no one wants to fill and a plurality of people who want to help but do not know how.[9]

The Rise of Direct Service Organizations

Quakers have long valued primary education for both girls and boys. Because they were excluded from English institutions for failure to pay mandatory tithes, Friends began to set up Quaker schools. George Fox encouraged Friends to start schools as early as 1668 in England.[10] The vast majority today are in Kenya, and secondly the United States, but there are also Quaker schools in Britain, Ireland, Jordan, Palestine, Australia, Japan, Guatemala, El Salvador, Peru, and Bolivia. Most were originally for Quaker children but are now open to others in their communities. Most have a Quaker element in their governance and retain an explicit Quaker ethos.[11]

As the concerns of Friends grew beyond caring for their own members, and as the wealth of members grew along with the stability and lack of persecution, Friends, like the outside world, began to found institutions.

The first Quaker hospital was founded in the United States in 1751.[12] In Kenya, early twentieth-century missionary work led to the founding of Quaker hospitals at Kaimosi and Lugulu.[13] Later in the twentieth century, retirement communities in the United States[14] and orphanages in Africa were additional forms of social service.

Friends were also instrumental in founding non-Quaker institutions like Oxfam[15] and contributed to the establishment of international governance institutions like the World Bank.[16]

The Rise of Associations

In the 1800s, as the Quaker movement grew and spread, the work of the elders (individuals appointed to support the spiritual welfare and discipline of the community) to hold it all together failed. Worldly socio-economic dynamics mixed with theological window dressing and drove a wedge into the American Quakers. In Britain, the smaller region allowed more coherence, avoiding the early splits and leading to a wholesale change from an evangelical and orthodox approach to a more liberal modern theology at the turn of the twentieth century.[17] Friends Church Kenya was established in 1986 to bring together the growing number of yearly meetings in that country.[18]

The history of the splits in the American Quaker movement has been detailed elsewhere.[19] Even as they moved apart as institutions, there was still significant intervisitation, family relationships, and multiple attempts at reconciliation.

The Five Years Meeting, founded in 1902,[20] now Friends United Meeting, became a conduit for communication and coherence in faith and practice and in mission work in the United States, Kenya, Uganda, Tanzania, Jamaica, Cuba, and Palestine.[21] The Friends General Conference, founded in 1900,[22] was originally a collection of Friends from multiple yearly meetings discussing shared interests in religious education and other topics and now spans 16 yearly meetings in the United States and Canada.[23] The Association of Evangelical Friends, founded in 1947,[24] now Evangelical Friends Church International, arose as an association of yearly meetings that were further called to a more coherent faith and practice, in line with the broader evangelical and fundamentalist Christian movements, and now includes Friends churches in 36 countries.[25] The Friends World Committee for Consultation was founded at the 1937 World Conference of Friends to bridge these distinctions and foster communication.[26]

Particularly in the early twentieth century, as communication and transportation options improved, Friends found a desire to collaborate on projects like war relief and foreign missions and educational institutions. Formal institutional collaborations like the American[27] and Canadian Friends Service Committees,[28] Evangelical Friends Missions,[29] United Society of Friends Women,[30] Friends Disaster Service,[31] and Quaker Earthcare Witness[32] arose to meet specific needs.

Many advantages accrue from greater collaboration. There are more pre-existing channels for good work to flow through. These channels are more resistant to disruption and ready to serve as needed. The downside of establishing structures is that people become attached to the structure. With greater stability, there can be a loss of flexibility. Quakers, like other humans, are prone to turf protecting. When separated from the context when and where they arose, institutions become self-serving rather than Christ serving.[33]

Whither Quaker Institutions?

What institutions do Friends need going forward? In the twenty-first century, most Quaker institutions are struggling.[34] The variety in size and complexity of Quaker institutions is both a strength and a burden. As patterns of work, organizational development, communications, and transportation change, how are Quakers, or any religious institutions, following the changes in their context?

> The Quaker tradition, like all large scale traditions in late Modernity, is in a constant
> state of flux. It is increasingly difficult to talk about the Quaker tradition as a monolith

given the global, theological, and practical diversities within Quakerism today. In the West Quakerism has begun to drift and decrease in terms of numbers and impact. More importantly, meetings (congregations in Quaker speak) and yearly meetings are struggling to adjust to the current cultural and spiritual landscapes of our people. Set adrift because of diminishing understanding of identity, practice, and theology, Quaker communities struggle to meet the needs of those within its organizations, let alone the needs of the larger communities and world.[35]

Quaker meetings, and associations of meetings, are wrestling with the meaning of membership. What is the core identity of a Quaker body? Membership in all religious denominations is declining in the United States, Western Europe, and Australia,[36] causing anxiety and complicating the response of members. In other regions, religious affiliation is growing, especially in non-traditional denominations. Across the branches, Friends struggle to see each other as Quaker. One hundred years ago, they would have denied the others as Friends.[37] Today there is a little more tolerance but not much understanding or collaboration. There is a rich opportunity to work together on the social concerns that Friends have – to run schools, prison ministry, disaster relief, and environmental witness. And none of these institutions is monolithic. There are Friends in each branch that have more in common with each other than with the extremists in their own branch.[38]

Given the demographic shift by 2001 to an African majority among Friends,[39] how can Quaker institutions founded in Anglo-American culture reflect the diverse reality of Quaker membership? Another troubling dynamic is the disproportionate wealth held in some areas compared to the distribution of membership. How will a new generation of representative leadership take up the management of Quaker institutions?

Are there institutions that have finished their useful life or outgrown their original mission? Some, like Friends Services Alliance[40] and Pendle Hill Conference Center,[41] are wrestling with whether they are to focus on serving Quaker constituencies or to be responsive to wider audiences. How can Quaker institutions be both authentically Quaker and authentically responsive to other participants?

The true purpose of any Quaker institution is to carry out God's will. Some have a specific role to play, a mission focused on a particular part of God's will. For many, that mission is primarily the formation of human beings in the vocation of being the Quakers the world needs.[42] In Taber and Drayton's writing,[43] the purpose of Quaker worship is to align one's will, values, and understanding with God's will. For a monthly or yearly meeting, the purpose is to assist Friends in that process. It is this author's opinion that an institution that does not have as an explicit part of its mission the continuation of the Quaker community and religion, the Quaker body – to put it another way, the sustenance and formation of Quakers as a living body of Friends – will cease to be a Quaker institution within a generation. Half measures can prolong this process, but not forever.

In the twenty-first century, Quaker institutions continue to incorporate the gifts and the challenges of the Religious Society of Friends, and Friends Church, at large.

Notes

1 Random House Webster's College Dictionary, 1991.
2 Daniels, C. Wess. Spontaneous remarks, FWCC Section Meeting, workshop on convergent Friends, 2007.
3 Hamm, pp. 175–178.
4 Hamm, p. 18.

5 Mohr, 2018, p. 25, "The True and Proper Purpose of Yearly Meetings," *QRT #130*.
6 Mohr, 2018.
7 Britain YM, https://qfp.quaker.org.uk/chapter/7/.
8 Britain YM, https://www.quaker.org.uk/our-organisation/meeting-for-sufferings.
9 Jackson.
10 Hamm, p. 109.
11 Hamm, pp. 110–114.
12 https://www.uphs.upenn.edu/paharc/features/creation.html.
13 Abbott, p. 32.
14 Abbott, pp. 87–88.
15 http://www.quakersintheworld.org/quakers-in-action/313.
16 Personal conversations with Jack DeBeers, San Francisco Monthly Meeting.
17 Abbott, pp. 164–165.
18 Gunya, Catherine. https://www.friendsunitedmeeting.org/news/what-is-friends-church-kenya.
19 Hamm, *The Quakers in America*, 2003 or Hugh Barbour and J. William Frost, *The Quakers*, 1988.
20 Abbott, pp. 111–113.
21 https://www.friendsunitedmeeting.org/about-us/yearly-meetings.
22 Abbott, pp. 110–111.
23 https://www.fgcquaker.org/about/affiliated-yearly-and-monthly-meetings.
24 Abbott, pp. 94–96.
25 https://efcinternational.org/.
26 https://fwcc.world/about-us/mission-history/.
27 https://www.afsc.org/content/history-afsc.
28 https://quakerservice.ca/about-cfsc/history/.
29 https://friendsmission.com/affiliations-and-sponsors/.
30 http://usfwi.net/history.
31 https://www.quakersintheworld.org/quakers-in-action/323/Friends-Disaster-Service.
32 https://quakerearthcare.org/about-us/.
33 Niebuhr.
34 McCormick.
35 Daniels, C. W., in Mohr, R., ed., 2020 FWCC Americas grant proposal, unpublished.
36 https://www.pewresearch.org/fact-tank/2015/05/13/a-closer-look-at-americas-rapidly-growing-religious-nones/ and https://www.pewresearch.org/fact-tank/2017/04/07/why-people-with-no-religion-are-projected-to-decline-as-a-share-of-the-worlds-population/.
37 Hamm, p. 12.
38 Kelley.
39 Abbott, pp. 319–322.
40 https://www.fsainfo.org/about.
41 https://pendlehill.org/pendle-hill-at-90-looking-forward/.
42 Mohr, 2015.
43 Drayton, pp. 92–93.

Bibliography

Abbott, Margery Post, Mary Ellen Chijioke, Pink Dandelion, John William Oliver, Jr. *Historical Dictionary of the Friends (Quakers)*. Lanham, MD: The Scarecrow Press, 2003.

Drayton, Brian & William Taber. *A Language for the Inward Landscape: Spiritual Wisdom from the Quaker Movement*. Philadelphia, PA: Tract Association of Friends, 2015.

Hadley, Herbert. *Quakers World Wide: A History of the Friends World Committee for Consultation*. London: Friends World Committee for Consultation, 1991.

Hamm, Thomas D. *The Quakers in America*. New York: Columbia University Press, 2003.

Jackson, Johanna. "Visions of a Strong Quaker Future" *Friends Journal*, October 2021. https://www.friendsjournal.org/visions-of-a-strong-quaker-future/

Kelley, Martin & Robin Mohr. "Eight Questions on Convergent Friends" *Friends Journal,* January 2012. https://www.friendsjournal.org/eight-questions-convergent-friends/, accessed, 12/12/21

McCormick, Don. "Can Quakerism Survive?" *Friends Journal*, February 2018. https://www.friendsjournal.org/can-quakerism-survive/

Mohr, Robin. "Quakercraft: Becoming the Quakers the World Needs" *Western Friend*, September 2015. https://westernfriend.org/media/quakercraft-becoming-quakers-world-needs, accessed 12/7/2020

Mohr, Robin. "The True and Proper Purpose of a Quaker Yearly Meeting" *Quaker Religious Thought*, Vol. 130, 2018.

Niebuhr, H. Richard. *The Social Sources of Denominationalism*. New York: Henry Holt and Company, Inc., 1929, renewed 1957.

17

THE RELIGIOUS ROOTS OF THE QUAKER WAY

Stuart Masters

Introduction

Members of the early Quaker movement were deeply suspicious of the received Christian tradition. In opposing what they regarded as an apostate faith, the first Friends proclaimed that 'Christ is come to teach his people himself' (Benson 1976: 3). This preoccupation with direct divine revelation, and rejection of human notions, is reflected in George Fox's *Journal*. Here, one of the founders of the movement claimed that his understanding of the true faith came 'in the pure openings of the Light without the help of any man' (Fox 1997: 33). Without seeking to undermine the crucial role of revelation in the emergence of the Quaker way, this chapter identifies four themes and, within them, eight characteristics that were both visible in early Quakerism and present in movements of popular piety and radical religious dissent dating back to the late medieval period. The proposition is not that the beliefs and practices associated with these earlier groups determined the nature of Quakerism, but rather that they formed a radical religious milieu within which the spiritual experiences of the first Friends were interpreted and acted on.[1]

Theme One: The Turn Inwards

There was a tendency in late medieval and Reformation radical religion to downplay the importance of physical images, sacraments and ceremonies in favour of a turn inwards that emphasised the inward and spiritual in the religious life. This is revealed in the mystical and spiritualist characteristics.

Mystical

Medieval Catholicism placed significant emphasis on outward imagery, liturgy and the sacraments. However, towards the end of the thirteenth century, an expression of Christian mysticism emerged in northern Europe, popular piety, which focused on a direct and intimate inward experience of the divine, leading to the birth of God within. Rather than stressing participation in outward religious ceremonies, this form of mysticism promoted a contemplative

DOI: 10.4324/9780429030925-19

spirituality of inward passivity and surrender to God's will (Davies 2006: 30–117). It was associated with beguines[2] such as Hadewijch of Brabant, and Mechthild of Magdeburg and with the Dominicans Meister Eckhart, Johannes Tauler, and Henry Suso. During the sixteenth century, this mysticism informed the development of the radical wing of the Reformation, especially via the anonymous treatise, the *Theologia Germanica* (Blamires 2003). It influenced the theology and spirituality of Thomas Müntzer and various Anabaptist[3] groups, particularly in South Germany and Austria (Packull 1977). The mystical aspects of the Radical Reformation later helped frame the development of a radical form of Puritanism in early seventeenth-century England (Hessayon & Finnegan 2011: 91). Mysticism, rooted in late medieval Europe and transmitted into English Puritanism via the writings of the Radical Reformation, probably helped fashion the spirituality of the early Quaker movement. This can be seen in its preference for unmediated inward spiritual experience over outward images and liturgy and in a spirituality of passive surrender of the human will. In addition, the three key stages of mystical experience – illumination, purgation and union – closely resemble the overall shape of early Quaker transformation experiences described in their convincement narratives. The mystical dimension of the Quaker way was promoted in the early twentieth century by Rufus Jones (Jones 1936).

Spiritualist

Spiritualism questions the need for material mediators between God and the individual believer.[4] In its most radical expression, Spiritualism denies the necessity of all outward forms including the Church, the sacraments and the Bible. Late medieval mysticism prompted a spiritualising tendency within European religious culture. Beguines such as Marguerite Porete and Na Prous Boneta were condemned and executed for questioning the need for the sacraments. Porete wrote, 'nothing stands between the soul and God: not reason, virtue, good works, or even the sacraments' (Swann 2016: 156, 166). R. Emmet McLaughlin notes that 'the Reformation as a whole "spiritualised" much of medieval Catholicism. As a result, all of the Reformers were "spiritualists" to one degree or another' (McLaughlin 2007: 119). However, those on the radical wing of the Reformation tended to take this spiritualising trajectory further than their mainstream opponents. This can be seen in the radical spiritualism of Casper Schwenckfeld and Sebastian Franck and in the spiritualist Anabaptism of Hans Denck and David Joris (McLaughlin 2007: 124–140, Dipple 2007: 256–297). This kind of Spiritualism influenced the development of radical Puritanism in early seventeenth-century England. For example, Nigel Smith suggests that during the 1620s and 1630s, the English radical Puritan minister John Everarde helped make 'German mysticism and radical Spiritualism part of a native inheritance' (Smith 1989: 136–141). The early Quaker movement embraced a spiritualist orientation and, from the late seventeenth century onwards, became its principal surviving expression. In his study of William Penn, Melvin Endy explored the spiritualist currents which helped form the religious milieu in which Quakerism emerged (Endy 1973).

Theme Two: The Kingdom's Come

There was a tendency in late medieval and Reformation radical religion to reject the 'yet to come' and 'after death' emphasis of mainstream Christianity in favour of an affirmation of the possibility of living in the kingdom of God, at least partially, in the here and now. This is associated with the perfectionist and endonomian[5] characteristics.

Perfectionist

A belief in Christian perfection or deification implies the possibility of real transformation in this life, so that the divine will and nature is revealed in human lives. Perfectionist tendencies in the late medieval period were associated with both mysticism and the *vita apostolica* movement.[6] The Church regarded this ascetic way of life as a special vocation and, fearing the challenge of popular piety, sought to confine it within authorised religious orders (Leff 1967: 13–22). Perfectionist principles were common on the radical wing of the Reformation, which tended to reject the Lutheran and Calvinist doctrine of total depravity.[7] Deification formed an important part of the spirituality of both Thomas Müntzer and those Anabaptists who were influenced by him. Müntzer wrote that 'we must believe that we fleshly, earthly men are to become Gods through Christ becoming man' (Matheson 1994: 278). The perfectionist aspects of the Radical Reformation seem to have re-emerged in England within early seventeenth-century radical Puritanism (Como 2004: 38–39). A belief in the possibility of deification was common among radical religious groups during the English Revolution. For example, the Digger Gerrard Winstanley affirmed the perfectibility of human nature (Bradstock 1997: 131). Such tendencies are clearly visible in the early Quaker vision. Like other radical religious groups, early Friends proclaimed that, by the indwelling of Christ, a person's life could be transformed, and that through a process of spiritual death (of the life in Adam) and new birth (in the life of Christ), they would be brought into a perfectly reconciled relationship with God. Such perfectionism often implied that the regenerated had been restored to the prelapsarian state of Eden. The holiness dimension of Quakerism has been emphasised in the work of Carole Spencer (Spender 2007).

Endonomian

Endonomianism is based on the apostle Paul's distinction between the constraining role of the law in the old covenant and the guided life of faith in Christ in the new covenant (Galatians 3:22–26, King James Version). Those living in the new birth no longer need to be constrained by the outward law, because they are ruled inwardly by Christ. This is understood as the fulfilment of the new covenant promise that God's law would be written within human hearts (Jeremiah 31:33–34). During the late medieval period, religious groups who sought a degree of independence and gave priority to direct inward spiritual guidance were often viewed with suspicion by the Church. For example, the beguines were accused of being part of a libertine movement labelled the 'heresy of the free spirit' and suffered persecution as a result (Leff 1967: 314–316). Many individuals and groups on the radical wing of the Reformation linked perfectionism with endonomianism. For example, the Spiritualist Anabaptist Hans Denck wrote that 'whoever has received God's new covenant, that is, whoever has had the law written into his heart by the Holy Spirit, is truly righteous' (Klaassen 1981: 73). David Como has shown how, in the early seventeenth century, a reaction against the perceived legalism of English Puritanism produced a radical 'antinomian' alternative (Como 2004: 24–72). Like these groups, early Friends made an unequivocal distinction between the outward law of the old covenant and the inward rule of Christ in the new covenant. As James Nayler makes clear, this was not about the abolition of the law but rather its inward fulfilment (Nayler 2007: 120–125). The belief that inward spiritual guidance, if properly discerned and followed, leads to a life of righteousness and holiness has been a key feature of Quaker spirituality (Birkel 2013: 247).

Theme Three: Spirit Empowered and Embodied

There was a tendency in late medieval and Reformation radical religion to prioritise the agency of the Holy Spirit over the authority of Tradition and Scripture, leading individuals and groups to exhibit a spirit-empowered life and a visibly embodied witness. This is represented by the charismatic and prophetic characteristics.

Charismatic

The term 'charismatic' is used to describe those who assert that the empowerment and gifts of the Holy Spirit witnessed in the early Church remain available today. This is often associated with prophecies, healings, miracles and a strongly embodied spirituality. There is a long-standing tension within Christianity between the order and structure of the Church as an institution and the free and uncontainable movement of the Spirit. Many dissenting groups, like the Montanists, were motivated by a sense of charismatic power (Trevett 1996). The women of the beguine movement found that the work of the Holy Spirit gave them an authority that was not dependent on powerful men. Laura Swann has argued that beguine worship was charismatic in nature, and included spontaneous Spirit-led ministry, singing and dancing (Swann 2016: 86–87). During the Reformation, many Anabaptist groups were charismatic (Murray 1995). In 1527, the Austrian Anabaptist Leonhard Schiemer wrote that believers receive 'a power about which they have to say that things that were once impossible are now possible' (Klaassen 1981: 75). Again, within the context of English Puritanism, radical groups such as the Grindletonians were associated with 'powerful, even ravishing, subjective experiences'[8] of a charismatic nature (Como 2004: 277). Early Quakers claimed the gifts of the Holy Spirit. The very name Quakers, given to the movement in scorn, reflected the strongly embodied and charismatic behaviour associated with the first Friends. In justifying themselves against opponents, they argued that all the holy people of the Bible had quaked and trembled in the presence of the Lord. In 1653 James Nayler wrote, 'search the Scriptures, and you shall find that the holy men of God do witness quaking and trembling, and roaring and weeping, and fasting and tears' (Nayler 2003: 186). While the charismatic aspects of Quakerism have often been obscured, they have influenced Spirit-led individuals and groups throughout history (Alexander 2006).[9]

Prophetic

The New Testament refers to prophecy as one of the gifts of the Holy Spirit (Romans 12:6). A prophet is a vessel through whom God communicates in words, actions and signs. Walter Brueggemann has suggested that the role of a prophet is to evoke an alternative consciousness and perception to that of the dominant culture (Brueggemann 2001: 81). It is not surprising, therefore, that radical groups have tended to identify with the prophetic vocation, giving judgement on the powerful and offering an alternative vision of God's kingdom. In the late medieval period, the beguine Christine the Astonishing physically acted out her prophetic preaching (Swann 2016: 146). Mechthild of Magdeburg felt called to condemn the corruptions of the church, writing that 'God calls the cathedral clergy goats whose flesh stinks of impurity with regard to eternal truth' (Swann 2016: 146). Similarly, during the Reformation, the Dutch Anabaptist leader Menno Simons denounced the unjust and exploitative practices of the wealthy. He wrote that 'the wicked merchants and retailers, together with all those who are out to make money and to make their living that way, are so bent on accursed profit that they exclude God wholly from their hearts' (Klaassen 1981: 242). The role of a prophet continued to offer women a degree of religious authority during the Reformation and in seventeenth-century England.[10] The early Quaker movement was strongly prophetic in orientation. For a short period, Friends became notorious for their public acts and signs (Carroll 1977: 70–84). The prophetic aspect of Quakerism lives on in Friends' understanding of testimony and in the belief that vocal ministry during worship is an act of divine utterance passing through the speaker. This characteristic of the Quaker way has been given particular attention in the work of Lewis Benson (Benson 1943).

Theme Four: Looking Back and Looking Forwards

There was a tendency in late medieval and Reformation radical religion to condemn and reject the corruptions of the Church and seek inspiration instead, either by looking back to the purity of the early church or by looking forwards to the promised transformation of all things in the final age.[11] This is related to the primitivist and apocalyptic characteristics.

Primitivist

Christian primitivism involves a rejection of the perceived corruptions associated with the Christendom Church, and a desire to return to the purity and simplicity of the first-century apostolic example. Primitivists tend to be anticlerical and critical of the association of Christianity with wealth and power. The popular piety of the late medieval *vita apostolica* movement was a primitivist attempt to live a life of voluntary poverty and service modelled on the way of Christ and the apostles (Leff 1967: 51, 162, 165). In England, the Lollards, inspired by the thought of John Wycliffe, sought to reform the church along New Testament lines (Leff 1967: 573–585). The European Reformation as a whole was founded on a primitivist orientation (Goertz 2007: 1–44). Persecuted radical groups, such as the Anabaptists, identified themselves with the early church martyrs and associated their persecutors with the Roman Empire (Snyder 2004: 159–169). The Puritans wanted to purify the English church of the corruptions it associated with Catholic Christendom. However, radical Puritans tended to be Primitivists of a more Spiritualist sort, who regarded the true church as an invisible *ecclesia spiritualis* which might include Jews, Muslims and Pagans, as well as professing Christians. Early Friends also adopted a spiritualist approach to primitivism, linking the apostasy of the church to a loss of the direct rule of Christ in Spirit and a turn instead to human and textual authorities. In promoting this position, early Quaker leader William Penn claimed that the Quakers were an example of 'primitive Christianity revived' (Penn 2018).

Apocalyptic

'Apocalypse' is a Greek word meaning to reveal or disclose. It points to the unveiling of things that have previously been hidden or unknown. The Bible contains apocalyptic literature such as the book of Daniel and the book of Revelation. Since the late medieval period, European radical religion has tended to include an apocalyptic element. Social upheaval and the perceived corruptions of the Church were often interpreted as signs of the coming end times. In the thirteenth century, the thought of Joachim of Fiore fuelled apocalyptic expectations, including speculation about when the final age of the Spirit would come and who would be the agents of such a transformation (Leff 1967: 68–83). During the Reformation, many radicals shared this apocalyptic outlook, including Thomas Müntzer and Anabaptists operating in Germany,

Austria, and the Netherlands (Snyder 1995: 30–31, 75–77, 143–147). In England, a growing preoccupation with the end times was prompted by rapid social change and growing political and religious conflict, interpreted through the lens of apocalyptic biblical literature. This had an impact on Puritans of all types (Bradstock 2011: xvii). Early Quakerism was also apocalyptic: Friends believed that Christ was being revealed within them (the 'apocalypse of the Word') and was revealing the way of God to them. This was interpreted as a sign that the kingdom of God was about to be established, and that they should join the Lamb's war in a spiritual struggle to finally defeat all opposition to the rule of Christ (Nayler 2009: 1–20). Douglas Gwyn has paid particular attention to the apocalyptic dimensions of Quakerism (Gwyn 1986).

Conclusion

The four themes and eight characteristics form part of the spiritual DNA of Quakerism. However, across time, and in different places, Friends have promoted some of these elements while downplaying others. In England, after the Restoration of the monarchy in 1660, and in the context of intensified persecution, Quakers defended the mystical, spiritualist, endonomian and primitivist characteristics while discouraging the public expression of the perfectionist, charismatic, prophetic and apocalyptic aspects, due to the association of the latter with religious enthusiasm (Dandelion 2007: 37–48). The Evangelical form of Quakerism, which emerged during the nineteenth century, has generally downplayed the mystical, spiritualist and endonomian elements in favour of orthodox Protestant doctrine and biblical authority. On the other hand, throughout the twentieth century, the Liberal and pluralist branch of Quakerism has tended to emphasise the mystical, spiritualist and endonomian characteristics while progressively distancing itself from orthodox Christianity. The charismatic features of early Quakerism have remained marginal throughout most of the movement's history. However, during the past century, the significant growth of Quaker communities in the global south and, in particular, within West Africa, has seen the development of a distinctively charismatic faith and practice.[12] No expression of Quakerism today combines all these themes and characteristics in quite the same way as the first generation.

Notes

1 The contents of this chapter draw on material taken from Masters 2021.
2 The beguines were lay women who formed independent religious communities based on the apostolic example of voluntary poverty and service. Laura Swann has written a useful introduction to the movement. See Swann 2016. For information about the relationship between the beguines and the male Rhineland mystics, see, McGinn 1997.
3 The Anabaptists were radical Christian groups that emerged during the European Reformation. They rejected the state-church alliance of Christendom, infant baptism and a territorial definition of the church in favour of a voluntary association of believers. They suffered severe persecution at the hands of both Catholic and Protestant authorities. Modern Anabaptist groups include the Mennonites, Hutterites, Amish, the Church of the Brethren and the Bruderhof.
4 This form of Spiritualism is associated with the radical wing of the Reformation. It is quite distinct from the Spiritualist movement that emerged in the nineteenth century, which focuses on making contact with the spirits of the dead.
5 The label 'antinomian' was often applied pejoratively to radical religious groups by those in power. This word is problematic, because it implies that such groups rejected all moral and ethical standards. The word 'endonomian' is used here instead, since it seeks to convey the inward and spiritual fulfilment of God's law in the new covenant as described in Jeremiah 31:33 and Hebrews 8:10.
6 The *vita apostolica* was a medieval movement of popular piety influenced in particular by St. Francis of Assisi, which regarded the way of voluntary poverty, powerlessness, and service associated with the life of Christ and the apostles as the norm for all authentic Christians.

7 The doctrine of total depravity asserts that, as a result of the fall, all humans are enslaved to sin and can do no good in their own wills. In the Reformed theology of Puritanism, this tended to imply that liberation from sin was not possible in this life.
8 The Grindletonians were a radical Puritan group founded by Roger Brearely, the curate of the chapel at Grindleton, near Clitheroe, Lancashire (at the time, part of the West Riding of Yorkshire). They were active in Northern England during the 1620s and 1630s.
9 For example, John Wimber, the founder of the neo-charismatic Vineyard Church, began his ministry in an Evangelical Friends Church.
10 Examples include Ursula Jost and Barbara Rebstock of Strasbourg (Snyder and Huebert Hecht 2002: 273–287) and Anna Trapnel (Mack 1994: 87–124).
11 Douglas Gwyn has argued that there was a tension within early Quakerism between 'A' type seekers, who looked back to the purity of the early church, and 'B' type seekers, who looked forward to the coming of God's kingdom (Gwyn 2000: 69–96).
12 For an overview of the differences between the various branches of contemporary Quakerism, see Dandelion 2007: 184–220.

References

Alexander, Paul. 2006. "Historical and Theological Origins of Assemblies of God Pacifism." *Quaker Theology*, Number 12, Fall–Winter.
Benson, Lewis. 1943. *Prophetic Quakerism*. Philadelphia, PA: Friends Book Store.
Benson, Lewis. 1976. *What did George Fox Teach About Christ?* Reading: George Fox Fund.
Birkel, Michael. 2013. "Leadings and Discernment." In Stephen W. Angell and Pink Dandelion. *The Oxford Handbook of Quaker Studies*. Oxford: Oxford University Press, 2013.
Blamires, David. 2003. *The Book of the Perfect Life: Theologia Deutsch: Theologia Germanica*. Walnut Creek, CA: AltaMira Press.
Bradstock, Andrew. 1997. *Faith in the Revolution: The Political Theologies of Müntzer and Winstanley*. London: SPCK.
Bradstock, Andrew. 2011. *Radical Religion in Cromwell's England: A Concise History from the English Civil War to the End of the Commonwealth*. London: I.B. Taurus.
Brueggemann, Walter. 2001. *The Prophetic Imagination*. Minneapolis, MN: Fortress Press.
Carroll, Kenneth L. 1977. "Quaker Attitudes to Signs and Wonders." *The Journal of the Friends Historical Society*, Volume 54.
Como, David, R. 2004. *Blown by the Spirit: Puritanism and the Emergence of an Antinomian Underground in Pre-Civil War England*. Stanford, CA: Stanford University Press.
Dandelion, Pink. 2007. *An Introduction to Quakerism*. Cambridge: Cambridge University Press.
Davies, Oliver. 2006. *God Within: The Mystical Tradition of Northern Europe*. New York: New City Press.
Dipple, Geoffrey. 2007. "The Spiritualist Anabaptists." In John D. Roth and James N. Stayer. *A Companion to Anabaptism and Spiritualism, 1521–1700*. Leiden: Brill.
Endy, Melvin B. 1973. *William Penn and Early Quakerism*. Princeton, NJ: Princeton University Press.
Fox, George and Nickalls, John, L. 1997. *The Journal of George Fox*. London: Quaker Books.
Goertz, Hans-Jürgen. 2007. "Karlstadt, Müntzer and the Reformation of the Commoners, 1521–1525." In John D. Roth and James N. Stayer. *A Companion to Anabaptism and Spiritualism, 1521–1700*. Leiden: Brill.
Gwyn, Douglas. 1986. *Apocalypse of the word: The Life and Message of George Fox*. Richmond, IN: Friends United Press.
Hessayon, Ariel and Finnegan, David. 2011. *Varieties of Seventeenth- and Early Eighteenth-Century Radicalism in Context*. Farnham: Ashgate.
Jones, Rufus M. 1936. *Studies in Mystical Religion*. London: Macmillan.
Klaassen, Walter. 1981. *Anabaptism in Outline: Selected Primary Sources*. Waterloo, ON: Herald Press.
Leff, Gordon. 1967. *Heresy in the Late Middle Ages: The Relation of Heterodoxy to Dissent, 1250–1450*. Manchester: Manchester University Press.
Mack, Phyllis. 1994. *Visionary Women: Ecstatic Prophecy in Seventeenth-Century England*. Berkeley, CA: University of California Press.
Masters, Stuart. 2021. *The Rule of Christ: Themes in the Theology of James Nayler*. Leiden: E.J. Brill, 2021
Matheson, Peter. 1994. *The Collected Works of Thomas Müntzer*. London: T.& T. Clark Ltd.

McGinn, Bernard. 1997. *Meister Eckhart and the Beguine Mystics*. New York: Continuum.

McLaughlin, R. Emmet. 2007. "Schwenckfeld and Franck and their Early Modern Resonances." In John D. Roth and James N. Stayer. *A Companion to Anabaptism and Spiritualism, 1521–1700*. Leiden: Brill.

Murray, Stuart. 1995. "Anabaptism as a Charismatic Movement." *Anabaptism Today*, Number 8.

Nayler, J. and Kuenning, L. 2003. *The Works of James Nayler – Volume 1*. Glenside, PA: Quaker Heritage Press.

Nayler, J. and Kuenning, L. 2007. *The Works of James Nayler – Volume 3*. Glenside, PA: Quaker Heritage Press.

Nayler, J. and Kuenning, L. 2009. *The Works of James Nayler – Volume 4*. Glenside, PA: Quaker Heritage Press.

Packull, Werner O. 1977. *Mysticism and the Early South German-Austrian Anabaptist Movement, 1525–1531*. Scottdale, PA: Herald Press.

Penn, William and Buckley, Paul. 2018. *Primitive Christianity revived; translated into modern English by Paul Buckley*. San Francisco, CA: Inner Light Books.

Smith, Nigel. 1989. *Perfection Proclaimed: Language and Literature in English Radical Religion, 1640–1669*. Oxford: Oxford University Press.

Snyder, C. Arnold. 1995. *Anabaptist History and Theology: An Introduction*. Kitchener, ON: Pandora Press.

Snyder, C. Arnold. 2004. *Following in the Footsteps of Christ: The Anabaptist Tradition*. London: Darton, Longman & Todd.

Snyder, C. Arnold and Huebert Hecht, Linda A. 2002. *Profiles of Anabaptist Women: Sixteenth-Century Pioneers*. Waterloo, ON: Wilfred Laurier University Press.

Spender, Carole D. 2007. *Holiness: The Soul of Quakerism*. Milton Keynes: Paternoster Press.

Swann, Laura. 2016. *The Wisdom of the Beguines: The Forgotten Story of a Medieval Women's Movement*. New York: Blue Bridge.

Trevett, Christine. 1996. *Montanism: Gender, Authority and the New Prophecy*. Cambridge: Cambridge University Press.

18

QUAKERISM IN THE EIGHTEENTH CENTURY

Andrew Fincham

The eighteenth-century Quaker has always presented the historian with something of a conundrum: preceded by the millennial 'Enthusiasts' who became the founding Friends,[1] and developing into leaders of the emerging Social Gospel of the Victorian era, the challenge is to identify the enduring constituent elements which enabled the society to evolve while providing continuity in more than name. Much of the problem remains the legacy of early twentieth-century attempts to do just this, when a cadre of Quaker historians led by Rufus Jones and J. Rendel Harris promoted their mystical interpretation of Quaker continuity: the Quaker insistence that personal (inner) experience of spiritual 'Truth' was of greater importance than doctrinal learning (derived from tradition or authority) became for Jones the resurgence of a European tradition of mystical Platonism antithetical to Puritanism (Endy, 6–12; Punshon, 226–229). Through superficial similarities in the advocation of silence, and the subsidiary nature of the importance of the priesthood, the term 'Quietist' (from the seventeenth-century Roman Catholic heresy in which an antinomian ethic predominated)[2] was subsequently attached to the Quakers of this period (Healey). Ultimately, Jones' labelling required Friends to have ever subscribed to a single, comprehensive theology, and one which was heavily influenced by Continental connections; neither claim is sustained by historical evidence or subsequent research (Rock; Wright).[3] Robynne Healey, in a recent and comprehensive survey, finds the application of this designation creates a Quietist paradox for Quakerism, characterised by Friends seeking 'spiritual awareness by rejecting all temporal desires and distractions' while going on to champion social reform; Healey's somewhat innovative solution proposes that such inconsistencies were held by Friends 'in tension' (Healey, 48). Melvin Endy, noting that Friends under Fox (while spiritual) had ever been 'conservative by instinct' offers a simpler view: Jones, by ignoring 'the mixed signals emitted by the early Quakers . . . failed to convey the complexity of the movement' (Endy, 12). Endy's conclusion is that their doctrine was shaped pragmatically by the 'promise of a reprieve from sufferings if they could squeeze [their Christian Denominational status] under the Toleration Act's minimal fence of orthodoxy' (Endy, 12).

By simultaneously abjuring the 'Quietist' appellation, and embracing a wider spectrum of Friends' beliefs at the turn of the eighteenth century, the Quaker paradox dissolves to reveal a Society at its zenith: upwards of 50,000 Friends in the British Isles, and many thousands more across the colonies, preoccupied with preserving the Kingdom they had built while seeking to make a living in peace (Fincham).[4] The next generation of Elders seem to have managed

DOI: 10.4324/9780429030925-20

rather than led the Society, seemingly content to superintend Friends' adherence to a 'hedge' of 'peculiar' customs, by which the group identity was kept separate from the world (Dandelion, 6, 77). While more readily understandable, this transition at the same time represents a much reduced aspiration when compared with Fox's desire to build God's Kingdom on earth in a world religion of universal salvation. Yet from such a point of departure, the development of the Society on both sides of the Atlantic during the century may be followed as a coherent stream of consequences arising from two factors which pre-dated the Enlightenment but which acted consistently in the context of that reasonable age.

The first of these (and probably the most profound) was the Quaker desire to avoid all unnecessary strife, a product of the experience of civil wars and one which persisted throughout the century on both sides of the Atlantic. The earliest apocalyptic expectations of Friends had largely evaporated when, in 1689, Protestant Dissenters were given rights to worship (Braithwaite, 160),[5] and the leadership of the Society in London responded with a more circumspect and accommodating approach to the wider world. The annual 'Epistle' of advice from London Yearly Meeting (LYM) urged Friends everywhere to give 'no offence nor occasions to those in outward government, nor way to any controversies, heats or distractions of this world, about the kingdoms thereof' (Braithwaite, 44–45). Such advice would characterise the uniformly pacific, intra-Societal focus of Friends' community governance throughout the century. This reconsidered alliance with the world was installed alongside the 'ancient testimonies' of refuting church taxes, oath-taking, and warfare, which shaped the development of Quakerism in both the Old World and the New. The Society of Friends had every reason to believe that cooperation with those in power would bring benefits, for by 1696 they had successfully lobbied for the Quaker (Affirmation) Act to mitigate the consequences of their testimony against oath-taking. This oath of loyalty was demanded in numerous situations where it might help identify sectaries (initially Catholic, later Jacobite); Friends taken to court over other matters (such as non-payment of tithes) needed to escape the sterner penalties devised to trap the disloyal, thus the act removed a major cause of sufferings. Such exclusions as remained – participation in criminal cases, or holding Crown office for profit – were comparatively unimportant to those in London who had little use for either the cumbersome criminal justice or the onerous patronage system. Across the Atlantic, different rules prevailed in each colony: New England attracted Friends from their inception, with a yearly meeting established as early as 1661 (Jones, 149–154); since 1681 Quakers had also widely settled in Pennsylvania, where the Frame of Government allowed them to dominate a Provincial Council which ran (under the Governor) largely along Quaker lines, and often relied on Quaker monthly business meetings to resolve civil issues and take action (Tolles, 63–84). The Quakers deputies of Philadelphia answered to electors and would run their government for the first half of the next century; by contrast, London Friends had felt obliged to appoint a committee as its key leadership body, known as the 'Meeting for Sufferings' – nominally a quarterly meeting of representatives from all regions but which from 1702 also met weekly in London. The significance of this for British Quakerism was a repositioning of the centre of decision-making from its peripatetic origins in the northern English heartlands to the capital, where the Friends faced more cosmopolitan issues and were additionally required to manage an interest group in parliament to support the Quaker cause. Subsequent efforts to manage business in favour of Friends led to a renewal and subsequently permanent Act for Affirmation (1712 and 1722) – albeit after much internal wrangling (Dixon, 238–247). Less successful were the attempts to excuse Quakers from paying tithes on the grounds of conscience, which found expression in the Quaker Tithe Bill of 1736 (Hunt; Taylor). In the colonies, Friends in Maine and Massachusetts petitioned for half a century for exemption from the 'Priest Rate', eventually granted (on petition to George I) in

1724 (Jones, 153–154).[6] Such attempts took place in the context of a wider desire by the British Prime Minister Walpole to mobilise anti-clerical feeling in Parliament, not least in those of the Whig party who were aligned with the opposition: the Quaker lobby were offered support on condition they made no attempt to attack the Test Act of 1673, which required both oaths and taking the sacrament from those holding civil or military office (Taylor, 56).[7] The extent (if not always the success) of Friends' lobbying over this sustained period is one indication of the extent to which they accepted 'temporal desires and distractions' when the cause brought worldly benefit (Healey, 48). The London lobbyists' remaining victory in the century was the 1754 Marriage Act, significant for specifically recognising Quaker rights to marry without Anglican participation.[8] While this regularised what had been practice for almost a century, it also legitimised inheritance, so removing one reason why Quakers might transgress by 'marrying before a priest'. One further area remains of importance when considering the testimonies of Friends and their engagement with the world – that of the militia. The Friends had traditionally refused to arm their merchant ships – a pacific gesture which also significantly reduced the likelihood of their being pressed into naval service at times of crisis. They similarly objected to the burden of military service, which proved simpler in the Old world than the New, for in the colonies both life and personal property lay often at higher risk. Here, issues arose frequently with Friends who not only refused to serve, but to shoulder their share of the costs of fighting: in the French and Indian War under Queen Anne, both fines and imprisonment were used to force military service on recalcitrant Quakers; mid-century, the Louisburg Expedition (1758–59) found the Massachusetts Quakers obliged to hire substitutes, with property distrained to cover the amount if they refused. As with tithes, the amount taken was customarily several times the sum assessed in order to offset poor auction prices; any surplus could be (and sometimes was) returned. The crisis came with the Revolutionary War, in which the Quaker simply could not win: the Friends' pacifist stance hastened their already waning power, and a new assembly saw Pennsylvania's first militia law in 1777; those Friends who took arms on either side were almost invariably disowned (Jones, 149–151). For Friends under the LYM, the greatest threat came with the formulation of the Militia in 1757 under threat of French invasion (Fontana, 131). While a general ballot determined who should join, Quakers (along with Roman Catholics) were excluded from service but remained liable to pay the substitute fine: whether this was a final victory for Friends remains an open question.

The trend towards centralisation can be considered the second major factor in the development of eighteenth-century Quakerism. The century began less than a decade after the death of Quaker founder George Fox, a figure of such magnitude that, having once stamped his personality on the Society, he became not only its leader but final arbiter in matters of dispute.[9] His successor, George Whitehead, never sought such status, and it is significant that on his death in 1723, LYM found no need for a replacement figurehead. It was partially this passing of the last of the original Friends that opened the door to change. Not only in terms of a gradual re-interpretation of what Quakerism stood for, but with no replacement for Fox, the eighteenth-century transatlantic Quaker community lost the one figure who had stood equally on both sides of the ocean: henceforth, the very different contexts which prevailed on either side would inevitably find it easier to loosen the bonds. Centralisation must be seen in the context of the Society of Friends' hierarchical organisational structure: at the turn of the eighteenth century, the Society was still growing as individuals seeking independence in matters spiritual along with access to the interdependent Quaker world network could see multiple advantages in membership. Having accepted the Quaker testimonies – which amounted to a policy of non-cooperation with regard to oaths, tithes, church taxes, the militia, while avoiding social ostentation – the new Friend found 'from first to last *the group was the unit* and the individual found his life and his leading in the Life and Light of the formative spiritual group' (Jones, 141). The reality of this very local quality in Quaker experience can be easily overlooked when considering the movement as a whole, but is amply illuminated by a consideration of the all-important Quaker discipline. This began as collections of advice issued periodically by the annual gatherings: LYM sent 'Epistles' of advice to subordinate meetings worldwide from the last quarter of the seventeenth century. These were passed down the hierarchy to be transcribed into books of advice in which were recorded the collected resolutions of more local bodies; inevitably, over time these collections varied much in content (Hall, 506–507). Differences in early versions of the discipline – in or outside London, and across the Atlantic – show early Friends coexisting with differing priorities, and even occasionally a desire for alternative directions for the movement (Fincham, 2021). The lack of clarity prompted LYM to create a central committee to agree on a single set of Advices, which was eventually produced in 1737 – almost eighty years after Fox began the movement. This was sold (in manuscript form) to the Quarterly Meetings, who were then required to keep it updated with each Annual Epistle. It seems that such meetings also added in their own Advices, such that local variations persisted for another half century.

It is of the first importance to realise that these efforts of LYM in no way restricted the colonial Quakers from issuing their own advices, and a review of those from Pennsylvania produced at the same time as the manuscript London collection reveals many more differences than similarities (Fincham, 2021). However, as the century reached its midpoint, such diversity became a source of contention for those managing the Society of Friends everywhere, who responded with a desire to promote a stricter adherence to the Discipline. The motivations for this are unclear: in London it coincided with the discovery that the Society had, by 1740, lost half its peak membership; but this was far from the case in the colonies, where record attendances could be observed (estimated at 5000 Friends at the Yearly Meeting in Newport, Rhode Island, in 1743; Jones, 129). Notwithstanding, a stricter interpretation of their rules of Discipline was felt necessary on both sides of the Atlantic: Jack Marietta's study terms this the 'reformation' of American Quakerism and shows that a substantial increase in gross numbers of disownments occurred in the third quarter of the century (although the increase in actual incidence is harder to estimate in the absence of reliable figures for the total numbers of Friends; Marietta, 7–14). Figures for London were collated by the meeting dealing with delinquency, they reveal a steady increase from the 1740s and a trebling of disownments in the decade following 1759 (Beck and Ball, 123). However, this needs to be considered in context: there were somewhere under 10,000 London Friends, and disownments increased from around ten per year to an average of twenty-five; the largest group were expelled for marrying before a priest, rather fewer for drinking or gaming, and fewer still for immorality, bankruptcy or failing to observe the testimonies. Some were even removed for repeated failure to attend meetings, which suggests they may have already left, while a handful of resignations appear towards the end of the century. It is worth noting that doctrinal issues do not appear to have been of any significance in these disownments: unlike its predecessor, scarred by the endless cut and thrust of theological exchanges, the eighteenth century increasingly considered religious debate highly unfashionable as it was replaced by the science of reason by which Punshon saw theology 'relegated to the intellectual scullery' (Punshon, 159–161). One area where perhaps more attention might have been paid was the in the growing concern of some Friends over slavery. Yearly Meetings on both sides of the Atlantic had advised Friends not to trade in slaves (Pennsylvania in 1712, London in 1727); however, given the extent of Quaker slaveholding in the colonies (which remained legal throughout the century), ownership of slaves was a more complex matter. In 1758 the LYM Epistle restated their abhorrence of the trade, which drew and admission from Virginia Friends as to their 'unease' at the practice, and the more equivocal response from Pennsylvania, where a large duty on importing slaves was passed into law – an act they urged London to lobby the Board of Trade to ratify (Jennings, 24–25). Ultimately, the Revolutionary War made slavery a wider issue, and the Proclamations of 1775 (Lord Dunmore) and 1779 (Philipsburg) promised freedom for all slaves who joined the royal forces – resulting in tens of thousands choosing to escape (Schama). Trading in slaves by then had become a national issue, and Quakers were joined in leadership by groups as diverse as the 'Saints' of the Clapham Sect and the Rational Dissenters, who together would ensure the eventual triumph of the abolitionists in 1807 (Page). Such national developments influenced a further revision of the collected LYM Advices, which was eventually printed in London in 1783;[10] this was issued not only to the Elders of the Society but was intended to be made available to the membership, an innovation which the introduction notes would assist conformity! In parallel to the development of the Advices, the Disciplines on both sides of the Atlantic contained a set of Queries to which subordinate meetings were required to respond on an annual basis. Meetings were obliged to consider diverse aspects of their prosperity, such as conformity to tithe testimony, recruitment of members, and suppression of disagreements; in such a manner, the potential for Societal conflict arising from local individualities was addressed through sustained (and later systematic) attempts to reduce local differences and enforce a central discipline.

Conclusion

Within this context, what is to be said of the eighteenth-century Friends themselves? Any generalisation across two continents and 100 years needs to reflect a reality that would be recognised by the Quakers themselves. The eighteenth century began with Dissent established by official toleration, and the practical religion of the Quakers (never unduly concerned with outward forms) allowed them to take advantage of the multitude of opportunities to build their Kingdom on earth – a labour in which not a few became very wealthy. Politically fostered schisms within Anglican communities, and the evangelical movements that blossomed in the Old world as Methodism and as the 'Great Awakening' in the New, largely passed them by until the final quarter, when Christian denominations of all forms began to realise the Deist consequences of a domineering scientific rationalism (Domínguez). Quakerism had never been overly intellectual, and perhaps Healey's dynamic 'holding diversity in tension' was rather the product of simple Friends who neither enquired nor required a rigorous logical consistency to govern their undivided secular and spiritual mind (Healey, 31). In this respect, most of the well-known figures frequently drawn from the period are highly atypical – whether the great campaigner John Woolman (1720–1772), or his embattled (and frequently disowned) counterpart Benjamin Lay (1682–1759). In England, it was Quaker industrial families such as those of Lloyd, Derby, Pease, and Reynolds who dominated: first iron and later railways; merchant-aggregators produced some of the largest bankers in the Gurneys, Lloyds and Barclays; and there arose a new cadre of professionals, including medical practitioners John Fothergill (1720–80) and John Lettsom 1744–1815; Cantor). Great wealth was achieved by many in all lands: the Philadelphia Grandes were legendary (Tolles), as were those of Bristol and London, but one can find John Strettell (1721–1786) in Canada, Moses Brown (1738–1836) in New England, and Anthony and Isaac Sharp in Dublin. Of great ministers there appear very few, Samuel Fothergill (1715–72) being perhaps England's likeliest candidate, although known as much for his published diary as his preaching; Josiah Forster (1693?–1763) remains almost as unknown as his half-century of publications on Barclay's theology. In America, Elias Hicks (1748–1830) would need the next century to lead his schismatics, while Ireland's John Rutty kept his theology (simple as it was) modestly confined to his Journal. A single example might stand for the best of the values that the Society represented: William Tuke (1732–1822) was born into the Society and became a successful provincial grocer of some standing; he engaged with the development of the Society's Discipline in London but is now best known for establishing the more humane treatment of mental health by setting up The Retreat in York, England. His concern for all made him a friend to many outside the Society, and it is in his involvement with the wider Anglican Evangelicals in the Bible Society and through his practical philanthropy that he lights the path along which Quakerism would take its steps in the following century.

The average Friend across the century, as with the mainstream in every place and time – must remain largely unsung. An analogy can be found in the parable of the talents given in the New Testament book of Matthew (25:14–30), where an unequal distribution of assets is assigned to three servants of the lord. If the Quakers of the seventeenth century had the greatest religious gifts, and those of the nineteenth century developed a wider awareness that informed the social reform of their evangelical philanthropy, then perhaps the average eighteenth-century Quaker might be regarded as the least spiritually endowed. Yet as Punshon noted, they kept alive the flame of Quakerism – even if somewhat hidden from sight – during a transformative period in which modern Quakerism began to be formed.

Notes

1 'Enthusiasm' was a contemporary term of disapprobation in Christian terms, denoting a spiritualism at odds with rationality; the Social Gospel movement coalesced from Victorian concerns over the effects of mass industrialisation on the working population.

2 Quietism originated in the teachings of Miguel de Molinos (c. 1640–1697), a Catholic Spanish divine condemned for mystical heresy in placing inward revelation above scripture. It has been placed in opposition to Evangelism, to denote the period dominated by intra-Societal introspection; see also William J. Frost, 'George Fox's Legacy: Friends for 350 Years', *Quaker History*, Vol. 93, No. 1 (Spring 2004), iii–viii; also Rufus Jones, *The Later Periods of Quakerism* (London: Macmillan, 1921), Vol. 1, 57–58 note 1.

3 Jones' claim rested on a Societal adherence to the theology contained in Robert Barclay's 1678 *Apologia*, the introduction of which states that Quaker Christianity followed 'the certain rule of the Divine Light, and of the Holy Scriptures', and hoped to thereby establish their acceptability to Charles II.

4 For a detailed exploration: Alan Gilbert estimates the number of Quakers in 1800 at 20,000, having fallen from Braithwaite's figure of 40,000 at the start of the previous century while the population of England rose from some 5 million to around 8 million; Alan Gilbert, *Religion and Society in Industrial England: Church, Chapel and Social Change, 1740–1914* (London: Longman, 1976); William Braithwaite suggested a 40,000 total by assuming about 50% of adult male Quakers were jailed during the 1661 Fifth Monarchy uprising, then multiplying that figure by between five and seven for families (*Beginnings of Quakerism* (London: Macmillan, 1912), 512; all these estimates appear more or less valid. Figures for Colonial Quakers remain obscure, but likely to number many tens of thousands by 1700, in contrast to the very small groups of Friends sparsely scattered elsewhere.

5 'Act Exempting their Majestyes Protestant Subjects dissenting from the Church of England from the Penalties of certaine Lawes' (1 Will & Mary c 18).

6 Permanent exemption by law in Massachusetts was not finally achieved until 1747.

7 The tithe continued to exist for a further century, when it was replaced by the 'corn rent' derived from the average price of grain.

8 Known as Lord Hardwicke's Marriage Act (26 Geo. II. c. 33).

9 Perhaps coincidentally, 1702 marked the death of Fox's wife, Margaret Fell.

10 Printed as *Extracts from the Minutes and Advices of the Yearly Meeting of Friends Held in London from Its First Institution* (London: J. Phillips, 1783).

Bibliography

Beck, W. and Ball, T. F., *London Friends Meetings* (London: F. Bowyer Kitto, [1869] 2009).
Braithwaite, William C., *Second Period of Quakerism* (London: Macmillan, 1919).

Cantor, Geoffrey, *Quakers Jews and Science'* (Oxford: Oxford University Press, 2005).

Dandelion, Pink, *An Introduction to Quakerism* (Cambridge: Cambridge University Press, 2007).

Domínguez, Juan Pablo, 'Introduction: Religious Toleration in the Age of Enlightenment', *History of European Ideas,* Vol. 43, No. 4 (2017), pp. 273–287.

Endy, Melvin B., Jr (1981) 'The Interpretation of Quakerism: Rufus Jones and His Critics', *Quaker History*, Vol. 70, No. 1 (Spring 1981), pp. 3–21.

Fincham, Andrew, 'Faith in Numbers – Re-quantifying the English Quaker Population during the Long Eighteenth Century', *Religions*, Vol. 10, No. 2 (2019), p. 83.

Fincham, Andrew, 'Friendly Advice – The Making and Shaping of Quaker Discipline', in Robynne Healey, ed., *Quakerism in the Atlantic World in the Long Eighteenth Century* (Pennsylvania: Penn State University Press, 2021).

Fontana, V. J. L., 'The Political and Religious Significance of the British/Irish Militias Interchange', *Journal of the Society for Army Historical Research*, Summer 2006, Vol. 84, No. 338 (Summer 2006), 131–157.

Hall, David J., 'Christian and Brotherly Advices', *The Friends' Quarterly* (July 1981).

Healey, Robynne Rogers, 'Quietist Quakerism 1692-c.1805', in Steven Angell and Pink Dandelion, eds., *Oxford Handbook of Quaker Studies* (Oxford: Oxford University Press, 2013).

Hunt, N. C., *Two Early Political Associations. The Quakers and the Dissenting Deputies in the Age of Sir Robert Walpole* (Oxford: Oxford University Press, 1961).

Jennings, Judith, 'Mid-eighteenth Century British Quakerism and the Response to the Problem of Slavery', *Quaker History*, Vol. 66, No. 1 (Spring 1977), pp. 23–40.

Jones, Rufus, *The Quakers in The American Colonies* (London, Macmillan, 1911).

Marietta, Jack D., *The Reformation of American Quakerism 1748–83* (Philadelphia: University of Pennsylvania Press, 1984).

Page, Anthony, 'Rational Dissent, Enlightenment and Abolition of the British Slave Trade', *The Historical Journal*, Vol. 54, No. 3 (Sep. 2011), pp. 741–772.

Punshon, John, *Portrait in Grey: A Short History of the Quakers* (London: Quaker Books, 2006)

Rock, Hugh, 'Rufus Jones Never Did Establish that Quakerism is a Mystical Religion', *Quaker Studies*, Vol. 21, No. 1 (2016).

Schama, Simon, *Rough Crossings: Britain, the Slaves and the American Revolution* (London: BBC Books, 2005).

Taylor, Stephen, 'Sir Robert Walpole, The Church of England, and the Quakers Tithe Bill of 1736', *The Historical Journal*, Vol. 28, No. 1 (Mar. 1985), pp. 51–77.

Tolles, Frederick B., *Meeting House and Counting House: The Quaker Merchants of Colonial Philadelphia, 1682–1763* (Institute of Early American History and Culture at Williamsburg, VA: University of North Carolina Press [1948] 1963).

Wright, Stephen, 'An Investigation into the Possible Transfer of Theology and Practice from Continental Anabaptists to the First Quakers', PhD thesis (University of Birmingham, 2013).

19

ELIZABETH FLETCHER

The Youngest of the Valiant Sixty

Barbara Schell Luetke

Elizabeth Fletcher (October 1639–1658), who my calculations of known birthdates indicate was the youngest of the Valiant Sixty, was born in Kendal, Westmorland, England. The little that is known about her is pieced together from mention of her accompanying other "first Friends" between 1652 and 1654, from an assault on her in Oxford, England (1654), from when Edward Burrough was in Ireland (1655), and when she died (1658). Authors of the letters in which accounts of the plight of Elizabeth Fletcher is reported were men who were reporting back to Margaret Fell at Swarthmoor Hall. Original sources are quoted in the histories of Quakerism, the reproduction of only some of which were available to me. Therefore, I have relied on the scholarship of historians such as Barbour and Roberts (1973), Besse (1753), Brailsford (1915), Mack (1992), Penney (1907), Sewel (1722), Vipont (1976), Wagstaff (1845), and Wright and Rutty (1751). A fictional account of Elizabeth Fletcher was told in *The Kendal Sparrow* (Quakerbooks, 2019).

Penney (1907) stated that Elizabeth Fletcher was "a virtuous maid of considerable family" (258) and perhaps this is why Mack (1992) described her as a woman "of means" (p. 145). However, contradictory evidence appeared in *Quaker Women: 1650–1690* by Brailsford (1915). She documented that according to the accounts kept at Swarthmore Hall (Ulverston, England), Elizabeth's "means" did not allow her "to travel upon her own purse." A hat and shoes were provided to her by the "Kendal Fund," a fund established to support those Quakers who traveled in ministry. It is unknown where in Kendal Elizabeth lived, who her parents were, and if she knew Elizabeth ("Lizzie") Leavens or Thomas Holme, two other contemporary Friends from Kendal.

Elizabeth was convinced by George Fox when she was 14 years old and began preaching when she was 15. According to Vipont (1976; p. 114), she, Lizzie, and Thomas (and many other of the itinerant Quaker ministers) were "ordinary" people, "not ministers with any special training," who wanted to share their "new awareness."

Elizabeth first traveled in ministry in 1654 with John Camm, John Audland, Edward Burrough, Thomas Holme, and Lizzie Leavens. According to Penney (1907), the group of them came zealously into Cheshire (p. 16), south of Kendal, often under strange workings of 'the power,' the people rude and violent, the authorities alarmed at what they could not understand. "Not surprisingly," wrote Mack (1992) "considering their youth and that they travel together as unmarried men and women, sadism towards Quaker women was laced with sexual innuendo and public frivolity" (p. 248).

DOI: 10.4324/9780429030925-21

According to Besse's (1753) *Book of Sufferings* (pp. 562–654), Elizabeth and Lizzie went by the leading of the Spirit (Grubb, 1917; p. 181) to Oxford, the first to bring the Quaker message there. At the time, Oxford was where young men were trained to become ministers of the Church of England. It was June 20, 1654, when Elizabeth and Lizzie arrived and "went through the streets and into the colleges and steeple and tower houses, preaching repentance and declaring the word of the Lord to the people" (Penney, 1907; p. 210). Five days later (on June 25), they were moved to go to St. Martin's at the Crossroads of Cornmarket Street to the north, High Street, to the east, Queen Street to the west, and St. Aldate's to the south.

Penney (1907) stated that "at the backside of the city, the women met 'a black tribe of scholars' and spoke to them (p. 210; 258). The students 'fell on them very violently,' and the women suffered 'as is almost a shame to relate, considering the place and persons that acted upon the two innocent, comely, young maids' (p 258). They dragged them through a dirty pond or pool and afterwards tied them back to back, their mouths held in an endeavor to pump water into them until they were almost dead" (Penney, 1907; Besse, 1753, chap. 29).

Besse (1753; p. 563) reported that the students inhumanely dragged the women up and down near St. John's College in what Thomas Ellwood (Sewel, 1722) described as "a disgraceful riot" (vol. ii, p. 227). Vipont (1976) concurred: "two Kendal girls . . . suffered savage treatment from the authorities at Oxford and the most inhuman mob violence from the students" (p. 44).

The author of the *Kendal Chronicle*, as reported by Penney (1907; pp. 210, 258), wrote that "free from all restraint by the magistrates, the students, backed by the townsmen, abandoned themselves to an orgy of horse-play and shameful abuse." Wagstaff (1845) wrote that the women "were cruelly and shamefully beaten and mistreated in every manner" (p. 48).

"A few days after this," reported Besse (1753; p. 563), "the same women went to one of the places of public worship, and after the priest was finished, one of them spoke something to the clergy and people gathered there. A woman named Ann Andrew thrust Elizabeth Fletcher over a gravestone "in the yard outside St. Giles Church where a corpse was to be buried" (Penney, 1907; p. 258). Penney (1907) concluded that the gravestone event "bruised [Elizabeth Fletcher] so sore that she never recovered but complained of it as a principle cause of her lingering weakness," a "hurt she felt until her dying day" (p. 258). Thomas Camm blamed the "schollars and rable" who attacked her for the fact that she "was never so well againe in health" (Penney, 1907; pp. 259–260).

Besse (1753; p. 563) reported that two justices of the peace were present at St. Giles and, "because of the tumult," they ordered the women (finding them at fault for the commotion) be immediately sent to the Bocardo prison where felons and murders were housed (Penney, 1907). The cells were in a bridge over the road that formed part of the North Gate of the Oxford. It was attached to the Tower of St. Michael's. As of 2019, the prison is gone, but the church tower still stands.

According to Besse (1753; p. 563), there was a hearing for Elizabeth and Lizzie the day after they were imprisoned. The women were asked their names and places of abode, and they made the proper answers. Some of what they were asked was recorded:

- Why were you in Oxford? – They were commanded by the Lord to come thither.
- What did you come to do? – To declare against sin and ungodliness, as pride, lust, and "all manner of self-righteousness, and failed worship, which both priests and people live in, contrary to the comments of God."
- How did you know you were called of God? – One of them replied that they knew the Voice of God, and that they were called of him.

- The vice chancellor said that they had blasphemed the name of God and asked whether they read the Scriptures. – One of them said that they did.
- Then he asked if they were obedient to the power of the magistrate. – One of them answered that they were obedient to the power of God, and to the power, as it was of God, their souls were subject for conscience's sake.

Besse (1753; p. 563) reported that the vice chancellor declared that the women "profaned the word of God" and that he feared they knew not God, though they talked so much of him. Besse (1753; p. 563) also explained that it was the custom that before any sentence or corporal punishment was executed, the mayor had to sign the petition as well and put the seal of his office on the order. In this case, the mayor refused to do so and instead offered the women food and money if they would leave town. They refused. "But so eager were the Vice-Chancellor and some others that they informed [the mayor that] that if he would not sign their sentence, they would execute it without him" (p. 563).

The next morning, Elizabeth and Lizzie were whipped out of the city. "The consciousness of their innocence did so move the hearts [of the people watching], even of the executioner," that he performed his job with reluctance. As the lashing occurred, "many of the sober inhabitants, who observing the innocence of their testimony, acknowledged them as servants of the living God, and in much love a tenderness accompanied them out of the city" (Besse, 1753). According to Penney (1907), the women "were received by Mary Clewer, Elizabeth Digby, and Jane Bettris, some of the first to be convinced in Oxford, being honorable women, faithful to the truth" (p. 258). It is recorded in Oxford Quaker history that the first Meeting was held in the Bettris home.

At some point, Elizabeth went naked through the streets (Penney, 1907; pp. 258–259). Barbour and Roberts (1973, p. 593) reported that although she was

> a very modest, grave, young woman, yet contrary to her own will or inclination, in obedience to the Lord, she went naked as a sign against the hypocritical profession [the students] then made there, being then fledgling priests – Presbyterians and Independents. She told the students that the Lord would strip them, so that their nakedness should appear, which shortly after, at the return of King Charles II, her prophesy was fulfilled.

The act of "going naked" is based on a passage in Isaiah in the Bible, Isaiah 20:3, New Living Translation ("Then the LORD said, 'My servant Isaiah has been walking around naked and barefoot for the last three years. This is a sign – a symbol of the terrible troubles I will bring upon Egypt and Ethiopia.'"). Thomas Holme, Elizabeth (Lizzie) Leavens, and others are also recorded as going naked for a sign during this same time period, attesting to the Pentecostal nature of the first Friends. Brailsford (1915; p. 151) noted that Friends were willing to proclaim Truth at all costs.

Thomas Holme and Lizzie Leavens were married in Chester shortly after Elizabeth and Lizzie were in Oxford. This may have been the first wedding in the manner of Friends. From jail, just prior to the event, Thomas wrote of the two Elizabeths: "They are such as the like of them I know not. By their ministry Friends grow exceedingly and meetings are kept up gallantly. Friends are kept fresh and green here always" (p. 5).

Although it is unclear how much after Oxford it occurred, Thomas Camm (his account mentioned in Brailsford, 1915) wrote that Elizabeth's mind was unhinged for a while by her cruel sufferings in Oxford, reporting that she brooded over the hypocrisy of the students of religion who had abused her. According to this account, Elizabeth was never well again, though for some time after she did travel according to the ability of her weak and bruised body (Penney, 1907; p. 258). Thomas Camm claimed also that her "childish body was so weakened and injured by the rough handling in Oxford that the remainder of her short life was one of struggle with pain and weariness" (Penney, 1907; p. 259).

Brailsford (1915) wrote elsewhere that with "the marks of her brutal flogging in the market place yet fresh upon her, she set out upon her mission to Ireland. . . . With a mind smarting under these indignities, and a body unhealed of its wounds, little Elizabeth Fletcher crossed over to Dublin in early 1655" (Brailsford; 1915; p. 179), the year following her preaching in Oxford.

In Dublin, Elizabeth Fletcher preached in St. Audoen Church and was arrested. By order of the Lord Mayor (Brailsford, 1915), she was imprisoned in Newgate prison, which was located on Cornmarket Street on the south side of the Liffey River. This was originally the site of one of the city gates. Elizabeth was most probably with another woman, Elizabeth Smith at this time. As was Quaker practice, the women refused to pay the rates for bed, food, and drink. Those who could not pay were stripped and beaten and kept on a side of the building that only had "loopholes" for lights. Brailsford (1915) wrote that "the friendship of the women sustained them and that upon their release they stayed a while to preach" (p. 180), "spreading their message, perhaps in less obtrusive ways" (p. 179). Wright and Rutty (pp. 83–39 and p. 92) concurred, reporting in *History of the Rise and Progress of the People Called Quakers in Ireland from the Year 1653 to 1700* that the first Quaker Meeting was in Dublin with ministry from the women at the chamber of Richard Fowkes, a tailor in Polegate (a part of Dublin). There are some documents that indicate that a Meeting also was held in the home of George Latham near Polegate (Myers, 1902).

Brailsford (1915) stated that "Francis Howgill and Edward Burrough came over from London and worked in Dublin for three weeks" (p. 180). It seems they crossed paths with the women, Edward Burrough writing to Margaret Fell (in January 1655), "Our dear sisters Elizabeth Fletcher and Elizabeth Smith are also in the west [Ireland], valiant for the truth" (Brailsford, 1915; pp. 181–182). Braithwaite (1912) noted that the men were helped in their work by 'little' Elizabeth Fletcher of Kendal (p. 214; written in a letter by Howgill to Margaret Fell). Brailsford (1915; p. 214) added that "their ignorance of Gaelic might have presented an unsurmountable difficulty but they seemed to have felt no desire to reach out to the unhappy natives who were casually stigmatized by Howgill as being 'robbers and murderers'" (pp. 181–182). According to a manuscript written by Edward Burrough (Swarthmoor MSS., iii. i6, as recorded in Brailsford [1915; p. 182]), after three weeks, Francis Howgill and Elizabeth Smith left Dublin to work elsewhere.

Once Elizabeth Fletcher was without a companion, Edward Burrough sent a "forlorn letter" to Margaret Fell (Swarthmoor MSS., iii. i6), stating that

> little Elizabeth Fletcher is at present here, but I know not how long she can stay; her dear love is to you . . . truly I suffer for her, she being as it were alone, having no other woman with her, in this ruinous nation, where it is very bad travelling every way on foot, and also dangerous (but we are much above all that). If it were ye will of ye lord and any women were moved to come over to her. There's at Dublin six of our brethren and sisters, in bonds [four men, whom he names], Elizabeth Morgan and Rebecca Ward, taken without anything being laid against them.
>
> *(in Brailsford, p. 182)*

All of these first Friends were English, having come to Ireland as Valiant Sixty to spread the faith. It is true that Howgill and Burrough were forced out of Dublin and not allowed to return.

It is unknown how many times Elizabeth went back and forth from England to Ireland, but reported that she "returned" to Ireland in 1657 and was with Elizabeth Morgan there (Braithwaite 1912, p. 388). This is reported to have been when Francis Howgill recommended her to Friends:

> I am glad that my dear friend and beloved sister, Elizabeth Fletcher (who is a helper and worker in the Lord's vineyard) is moved to come to you again, who is found, honest, precious, and of good report in the family of God, who I know will be serviceable to the Lord and to you, in this His day, wherein He is spreading His name throughout the nations.
>
> *(Braithwaite 1912, p. 388)*

Brailsford (1915) noted that from Dublin Elizabeth Fletcher and Elizabeth Morgan traveled south into Munster, holding meetings in the towns through which they passed. Declaring Truth in the marketplace at Youghall, a large and satisfactory meeting was held (Wright & Rutty, 1751). The evidence of Elizabeth now being an accomplished Quaker minister is stated by several sources and paraphrased by Wright and Rutty (1751): "The young girl, still only 18 years of age, spoke . . . from the text in the Prophet Joel, which is so familiar to all leaders of revival: "Your sins and your daughters shall prophesy" . . . At the close of the service, an Independent teacher stood out from the crowd and began vehemently to oppose the preaching of women. The girl preacher listened without reply, weary with the effort of addressing that great company, and conscious that she had already said all that needed be said in pounding her own text. The two men began to argue on her behalf, carrying the meeting with them and 'Truth prevailed'" (Wright and Rutty, 1751; p. 93 and pp. 120–121 from Edmundson's Journal, reprinted in Wright and Rutty).

Fletcher was recorded as the first Friend to preach in Cork and was well received there. Perhaps about this time, she authored (wrote or dictated) one tract, *A Few Words in Season to All the Inhabitants of the Earth . . . to Leave off Their Wickedness* (1660). It was a warning in which she described herself as "a servant who has known his terror for sin." The text gives a flavor of her strong urging as she invoked the wrath and indignation against the proud and greedy, whom she believed must reform immediately or suffer for all eternity.

Several authors reported that Elizabeth was sent back to England in 1658 and constrained to stay with her aunt Elizabeth Mansergh in Kirby Lonsdale. Her health was failing (Penney, 1907; p. 259). In her dying days, Elizabeth Fletcher was reported as saying that "it was that crush that she got upon that grave stone that was the ground cause of her illness, praying that the Lord might forgive and open the eyes of all her blind persecutors" (Penney, 1907; pp. 209–211).

As she died, Elizabeth was visited by many Friends and she enjoyed their company, glad and resigned in her decline. It is reported that she was "much at peace and contentedness of mind, blessing the Lord that had raised her up to bear testimony to His name and Truth; that she was counted worthy to suffer for the same" (Penney, 1907; pp. 259–260). She died on July 2, 1658, and Friends accompanied her body to Kendal, eight miles away. She was buried two days later in what is believed to be the Birkrigg Friends burial ground in Kendal, as Quakers were forbidden burial in "consecrated ground" or in church-connected graveyards. Her grave is unmarked, as was Quaker tradition at the time. The gravesite in Kendal is a little walled, rocky enclosure that can be found two miles southeast towards Kirby Lonsdale (it is neither in Sunbrick where Margaret Fell is buried near Swarthmore Hall nor in the Sepulchre Lane Quaker burial ground).

Elizabeth Fletcher was 19 years and 9 months old at the time of her death. "Her life counted as dear" and her loss lamented as she "was so young and so excellently qualified, affected with testimony that made her service great and greatly valued, but filled with wisdom to divine the word aright and greatly exemplary in her virtuous innocence and chaste conversation" (Penney, 1907; pp. 209–211).

An historical novel based on the life of Elizabeth Fletcher and other young adults is available at Quakerbooks of FGC.

References

Barbour, H. & Roberts, A. (1973). *Early Quaker Writings 1650–1700*. Grand Rapids: William Eerdmans.

Besse, Joseph (1753). A Collection of the Sufferings of the People called Quakers, for the Testimony of a Good Conscience, From The Time of their being first distinguished by that Name in the Year 1850, to the Time of the Act, commonly call the Act of Toleration, granted to Protestant Dissenters in the Fifth Year of the Reign of King William the Third and Queen Mary in the year 1689. Taken from Original Records and other Authentic Accounts. Printed and sold by Luke Hinde, at the Bible in George-Yard, Lombard Street.

Braithwaite, W. (1912). *The Beginnings of Quakerism to 1660*. London: Macmillan.

Brailsford, Mabel (1915). *Quaker Women: 1650–1690*. London: Duckworth.

Fletcher, Elizabeth (1660). *A Few Words in Season to All the Inhabitants of the Earth . . . to Leave Off Their Wickedness*. [Re-printed and sold by Robert Wilson in London in 1660 and available on microfiche.]. http://name.umdl.umich.edu/A39790.001

Grubb, E. (1917). *What is Quakerism? An Exposition of the Leading Principles and Practices of the Society of Friends, as Based on the Experience of "the Inward Light"*. London: Swarthmore.

Luetke, B. (2019). *The Kendal Sparrow*. Philadelphia, PA: FGC Quakerbooks.

Mack, P. (1992). *Visionary Women: Ecstatic Prophecy in Seventeen Century England*. Berkley, CA: University of CA.

Myers, A.C. (1902). *Immigration of the Irish Quakers into Pennsylvania (1682–1750); With Their Early History in Ireland. Found on the Internet*. Published by the author in Swarthmore, PA and available on the Internet.

Penney, Norman (Ed.) (1907). The Frist Publishers of *Truth; Being Early Records* (now first printed) of the *Introduction of Quakerism into the Counties of England and Wales*. London: Headley Brothers, 14, Bishopsgate Without. Philadelphia: Herman Newman; New York: D.S. Taber.

Sewel, William (1722). *The History of the Rise, Increase, and Progress of the Christian People called Quakers, Intermixed with several Remarkable Occurrences*. London: J. Sowle.

Vipont, E.F. (1976). *George Fox and the Valiant Sixty*. Hamilton: Hamish.

Wagstaff, W. (1845). *A History of the Society of Friends: Compiled from Its Standard Records, and other Authentic Sources. Part I*. New York: Wiley and Putnam.

Wright, T. & Rutty, J. (1751). *History of the Rise and Progress of the People called Quakers in Ireland a History of the Rise and Progress of the People Called Quakers in Ireland from the Year 1653 to 1700*. Dublin: I. Jackson.

20

BIOGRAPHY OF
MARGARET FELL

Kristianna Polder

Considered today one of the central founders of Quakerism, Margaret Fell (1614–1702), has garnered the moniker of "mother of Quakerism" due to her leadership and voluminous writings which provided a conceptual foundation, as well as much-needed organization, to the early Quaker movement of the latter half of the seventeenth century.[1] Fell used both her social standing and her estate not as a shield from persecution per se but rather as a means to guide, aid, defend, and protect fellow Quakers and their civil rights throughout her lifetime. She was not an itinerant preacher like other well-known early Quaker women but was radical in her own right as she risked the well-being and safety of herself, her family, and her estate for the sake of her spiritual convictions.[2] Fell rejected the established Church of England and its various practices refused to follow laws that prevented Quakers from meeting and worshipping, while sustaining social derision and suspicion from fellow countrymen and women, as well as from those in power. Her voluminous writing in defense of Quakerism and her organizational activity within the early Quaker movement led to her quickly emerging as a prominent leader.

Fell (née Askew) was born at Marsh Grange, Dalton-in-Furness, Lancashire, in 1614. She was educated by her gentleman father, John Askew, and at the age of 17 married Judge Thomas Fell (1598–1658), barrister and chief magistrate in Ulverston, Cumbria (previously a part of Lancashire). Fell was a gentlewoman of significant social standing who had a keen interest in spiritual and religious thought and activity. Her life took a turn in 1652 when she met with the itinerant preacher George Fox (1624–1691) at her estate, Swarthmoor Hall. She subsequently invited him to preach at her local Church of England Ulverston parish two days later. Fox admonished the congregants to awaken to the indwelling Light of Christ. Fell later recalled her reaction to Fox's preaching: "I saw perfectly Just then that wee were all wrong, & that we were but Theives, that had stollen the scriptures. which caused me to shed many tears. And I satt down in my pew & wept all the while".[3] After her abrupt spiritual conversion (or convincement), she invited Fox back to Swarthmoor, and her eight daughters, one son, and several servants became Quakers.[4] This marked the beginning of Fell's life as a leader within the emerging Quaker movement, as her household became a center of Quaker activity in the northwest.

Fell's convincement not only began her ministry but seemed to have set off a lifetime trajectory of conflicts and confrontations with the predominantly male authority of the political and ecclesiastical realms, as well as among her family and local community. When the parish rector William Lampitt attempted to have the churchwarden throw Fox out of the church,

DOI: 10.4324/9780429030925-22

Fell recalled, "I stood up in my pew & lookt att the Churchwarden; and he stood behind G F: & let him alon [alone]".[5] One can see the power struggle here among social status. With an assured stare, Fell exercised authority over the ecclesiastical power structure. When gentleman neighbors confronted Fell's husband on his return from circuit, informing Judge Fell that his household had been "undone" and his wife bewitched by Fox, he was not initially accepting of Fell's conversion to Quakerism.[6] Fell confessed to feeling conflicted: "any may think what a condition I was like to be in, that either I must displease my husband, or offend God".[7] Yet she persisted and that evening had what she described as a powerful spiritual experience in front of her husband. She recalled, "And whilst I was sitting, the power of the Lord seized upon me; and he was struck with amazement, and knew not what to think".[8] Judge Fell agreed to speak to the stranger Fox and acquiesced rather quickly to his wife's newfound beliefs. While he never became a Quaker himself, the Judge allowed Fox and Fell to establish Quaker meetings at Swarthmoor, and he likewise at times provided legal aid to the Quakers.[9] Yet it was Fell's exercise of authority over the rector, gentlemen neighbors, and her husband that resulted in a dramatic shift in the use of their domestic realm, resulting in Swarthmoor being a fixed mark of non-conformist activity. As Fell moved forward in her work and ministry, there seems to be little evidence of concern on the part of Fell for spousal obedience.[10]

After her convincement, Fell's agency was effectively rooted in her experience of the inward light of Christ in the conscience. This divine manifestation within herself and fellow Quakers she understood to be the ultimate authority over earthly power structures. Fell, like Fox and fellow Quakers, believed everyone – regardless of age, social status, education, or gender – had equal access to the indwelling Christ through silence and "turning inward" and its empowerment all to freely preach and prophesy.[11] In practice, Fox regarded himself and other Quakers as the new Adam and the new Eve, where men and women were freed from the curse of being ostracized from God's presence. Fell's status as mother within the movement therefore took on a radical, apocalyptic tone as the mother of the New Jerusalem, where God's divine breaking into humanity's presence was occurring in their present new age.[12]

As a spiritual matriarch, she challenged strictures normally attributed to the maternal. She was not meek, or a mother simply working from within, or protecting her domestic sphere. She was bold in her speech, writings, and engagement with patriarchal leaders. Fell was a social outsider, declining social invitations from neighbors for social gatherings and resisting accusations of witchcraft. She encouraged her daughters to marry late, putting ministry first, and to choose a fellow Quaker as a husband, rather than marry for family dynasties or fortune.[13] Unlike many gentlewomen at the time, Fell also encouraged her daughters to breastfeed. Shunning seventeenth-century landed gentry beliefs that breastfeeding inhibited intercourse and thus the husband's pleasure, Fell's promotion of breastfeeding could be seen as an act of defiance against male pleasure.[14] Fell also likely viewed breast milk as a symbol of spiritual nourishment – imagery frequently used by seventeenth-century Quakers. Thus, Fell's understanding and experience of the indwelling light led her to countercultural behavior in her domestic world as a physical and spiritual mother.

As she emerged as a leader within the movement, this empowerment through the indwelling Christ, particularly as a female writer, is evident. The most prolific female writer within early Quakerism, Fell's corpus of writing includes over 20 pamphlets, which both defended Quakerism and laid much of the conceptual framework of Quaker spirituality and theology, as well as over 164 letters.[15] Many newly convinced Quakers looked to her for guidance, as there is evidence that she received at least over 500 letters.[16] Her letters include personal letters, ones admonishing political leaders, and finally those that were epistle-like to be read aloud in Quaker meetings. One of her first letters as a Quaker was addressed to Justice John Sawrey, who had Fox thrown out of the Ulverston parish on the day of Fell's convincement. Accusing him of being affected by the devil and perpetuating lies about her she wrote:

> Oh Thou seeming professor, but rayally [really] A parsecutor of the truth of god, & A peearcer [piercer] of Jesus Christ wwhich will be to thy utter Trying and destruction, except thou repent. . . . The devill is the father of lyes, and thy famyly practices much in that trade.[17]

In not so searing tones but with a confident rhetoric nonetheless, Fell also wrote to men in power, including Oliver Cromwell, King Charles II, and King William III. Throughout these letters, she makes it clear that her first authority on earth is Christ. Not interested in overturning political structures, actions akin to the Ranters or Levellers, she nevertheless admonished and petitioned political authorities to release Quakers from prison, to allow free meeting for worship, and admonished these male authorities to repent and follow the inward light.[18]

Fell also wrote a number of pamphlets, publishing her first three in 1656, just a few years after her convincement. In her first, *To All the Professors of the World* (1656), she attempts to persuade other dissenters to follow the way of Quakerism and the inward light.[19] On its heels was *A Testimony of the Touchstone for All Professions*, encouraging Protestants, including members of the Church of England, to listen to the Word within as well as the Bible to test Quaker beliefs.[20] In the apocalyptic fervor of the early movement, Fell believed the inward presence of Christ within was a sign of the eminent Second Coming of Christ in the flesh, leading her to pen *A Loving Salutation to the Seed of Abraham Among the Jews*, urging the European Jewish community to see the fulfillment of the Hebrew scriptures and the coming of the Messiah.[21] Fell, like other Quakers, advocated Jewish readmission to England, with the aim of witnessing the completion of the Second Coming already in process.[22] In 1660, Fell was the first sectarian to write a peace testimony. In a declaration against the violence against and persecution of Quakers, titled *A Declaration and an Information from the People of God Called Quakers*, Fell defended Quaker beliefs in peaceful living and outlined reasons why Quakers opposed oath-taking and the payment of tithes.[23] Traveling to London to secure the release of Fox from prison, she delivered this declaration directly to King Charles II, using both her social status and writing skills to defend Quakers against those in power.

Fell is perhaps best known for her groundbreaking work *Women's Speaking Justified* (1666 and 1667), the earliest comprehensive Biblical defense for women preaching and prophesying. She organizes her argument topically and cites biblical passages, symbols, and stories she knows by heart, and with which she assumes her contemporaries will be familiar.[24] Defending a woman's right to preach publicly, she bases her argument on biblical examples of powerful women in the Old Testament and on women prophesying (some of whom were quite literally women sent by Jesus) in the New Testament, appealing to the biblical proof often demanded by her fellow Protestants.[25] While not a feminist (such an assertion would be anachronistic), Fell recovers biblical authority for women in her defense of women preaching, leading to a careful re-examination today within feminist scholarship.[26] Her writings which consistently advocated an abolishing of gendered hierarchy of authority in preaching, coupled with the way she lived her life with agency and oftentimes refusing to follow laws frequently instated by male authority makes her both a radical and a pioneer for women's rights in the public domain.

Along with the help of her household, Fell's organization of the movement was largely based from Swarthmoor Hall, which became a harbor for itinerant preachers, a letter correspondence hub, and a place for Quaker meetings. Her daughters, particularly Sarah Fell, worked fervently alongside her, evincing the importance of female collaborative ministry.[27] They frequently traveled together, visiting Quakers in prison and other Meetings, welcomed visitors, sorted mail correspondence among the Quaker itinerant network, and administered meetings.[28] Fell likewise provided crucial guidance to Quakers in regards to the process of marriage. In 1656, in her letter *To Friends, an Epistle on Marriage*, she instructed her fellow Quakers to draw up a certificate documenting that the marriage was done before witnesses and to take this certificate of marriage to the local magistrate.[29] This helped to ensure the legality of Quaker marriages, preventing Quakers from accusations of adultery and affirming the legitimacy of children born from these unions. In 1671, Fell also worked in the north to establish the earliest Women's Meetings outside London and their process of business. Her influence on the structure of meetings is noted today as central to the Quaker meeting process.[30]

When Judge Fell died in 1658, Fell was a powerful widow over her own estate but was also more vulnerable to attacks from both political and familial male authority.[31] After the Restoration in 1660 and the subsequent increasing persecution of Quakers, Fell paid heavy fines for conducting Quaker meetings, and when she refused to desist, she was eventually put on trial and imprisoned for four years in 1663.[32] Shortly after her release, she married George Fox in 1669, a marriage of the father and mother of Quakerism that was seen by some as an apocalyptic symbol of the marriage between Christ and his church. It also raised some eyebrows as Fell was 11 years his senior and a social superior. Perhaps the most crushing criticism came from her son George Fell. George Fell had become disenchanted with Quakerism after his move to London to become a lawyer, was embarrassed by his mother's marriage, and attempted to remove Swarthmoor Hall from her and his sisters' possession.[33] Through political maneuvering on the part of her son, Fell was imprisoned in April 1670 under praemunire, a sentence which lasted for over a year. With George Fell's eventual failure to secure the estate and his untimely death, the estate stayed in the hands of the daughters. Fell remained silent on her estrangement from her son. After she was eventually released from prison, apart from several journeys to London, she remained largely rooted to her estate until her death in 1702.

Fell's long lifespan witnessed political upheaval and transitions which she aptly navigated. By the end of her life, her popularity waned, as the center of Quaker activity and authority largely shifted to a younger generation in London where Fox himself resided until his death in 1691. Outliving most of the "Valiant 60", a non-Londoner whose earlier apocalyptic writings were seen as a remnant of an age no longer relevant, and her refusal to follow the emerging calls for Quaker plain in attire fell on deaf ears in a new generation of Quakers.[34] Her daughters published her writings and autobiography in 1710, in which Fell actively sets out to paint herself as politically active and religiously acute.[35] Thanks to her work, and the renewed interest of modern scholarship, Fell's enduring countercultural and radical influence on Quakerism – evinced through her writings, organizational activity, and her defiance of social norms and laws – continues to be considered in its deserved light today.

Notes

1 While George Fox is usually considered as the founder of Quakerism, Margaret Fell, William Penn, and others are increasingly gaining importance in the founding of the early Quaker movement. See Ingle, *First Among Friends*; Kunze, *Margaret Fell and the Rise of Quakerism*.
2 Polder, 'Margaret Fell, Mother of the New Jerusalem,' pp. 186–201.
3 Ross, *Margaret Fell: Mother of Quakerism*, p. 11; Glines (ed.), *Undaunted Zeal*, p. 430.
4 Kunze, *Margaret Fell*, p. 13.
5 Glines (ed.), *Undaunted Zeal*, p. 430.
6 Ibid., p. 4. Judge Thomas Fell was a barrister who was elected to Parliament in 1645 and served as chancellor to the Duchy of Lancaster in Oliver Cromwell's Commonwealth.

7 Ross, *Margaret Fell: Mother of Quakerism*, p. 15.

8 Ibid.

9 Kunze, *Margaret Fell*, p. 36. A letter from Fell to her husband, imploring him to accept and allow her publications, indicates Judge Thomas Fell may have not always been accepting of Fell's religious activities and might have hesitated in allowing her to publish.

10 Kunze, *Margaret Fell*, p. 37.

11 Bruyneel, *Margaret Fell and the End of Time*, pp. 107–108.

12 Polder, 'Margaret Fell, Mother of the New Jerusalem', p. 187.

13 Ibid., p. 196. Fell's daughter Sarah married at age 39, compared to Fell's own marriage at age 17.

14 Ibid., p. 197. Fell's encouragement of breastfeeding could have been seen by her gentry neighbors as an act of rebellion of wife against husband, because nursing was thought to diminish sexual intercourse as sexual relations were thought to contaminate breast milk. Breast milk was also seen as a powerful symbol of authority. Fox was called the nursing father of the Quaker movement, while other political figures including James I and Oliver Cromwell were also referred to as nursing fathers.

15 Elsa Glines recently published 164 of Fell's known extant letters in *Undaunted Zeal*.

16 Glines, *Undaunted Zeal*, p. xvii.

17 Ibid., pp. 13–14.

18 Glines, *Undaunted Zeal*, pp. 35, 282, 464.

19 Fell, *To All the Professors of the World, 1656* in *A Brief Collection of Remarkable Passages and Occurrences Relating to . . . Margaret Fell* (1710), pp. 73–91; Donawerth and Lush (eds.), *Women's Speaking Justified*, p. 5.

20 Ibid., p. 6.

21 Bruyneel, *Margaret Fell and the End of Time*, pp. 119–120; Donawerth and Lush (eds.), *Women's Speaking Justified*, p. 6.

22 Donawerth and Lush (eds.), *Women's Speaking Justified*, p. 41; Bruyneel, *Margaret Fell and the End of Time*, pp. 138–140. Fell had her pamphlet translated into Hebrew, likely by the Jewish philosopher Baruch Spinoza. A further look into Spinoza's writings after his encounter with Fell reveals she most probably influenced his own wrestling with Jewish tradition. See Clausen-Brown, 'Spinoza's Translation of Margaret Fell' (2019).

23 Kunze, *Margaret Fell*, p. 137; Glines, *Undaunted Zeal*, pp. 282–284. Fell traveled to London and delivered her letter *To King Charles II; James, Duke of York; and Henry, Duke of Gloucester June 1660* in person to the king.

24 Mack, *Visionary Women*, p. 137.

25 Donawerth and Lush (eds.), *Women's Speaking Justified*, p. 34.

26 Thickstun, 'Writing the Spirit', 269.

27 Kunze, *Margaret Fell*, p. 37.

28 For an excellent overview of Margaret Fell's involvement in the creation of the Quaker letter network, see Marjon Ames's recent work *Margaret Fell, Letters and the Making of Quakerism* (2017).

29 Polder, *Matrimony in the True Church*, p. 48; Glines (ed.), *Undaunted Zeal*, pp. 194–195.

30 Ingle, *First Among Friends,* p. 252. The role of Women's Meetings in preserving some equality of power is outlined by Catie Gill in *Women in the Seventeenth-Century Quaker Community: A Literary Study of Political Identities, 1650–1700* (2005), pp. 164–171.

31 Kunze, *Margaret Fell*, p. 7.

32 Donawerth and Lush (eds.), *Women's Speaking Justified*, pp. 137–149. Fell's trial of 1663 was recorded and published as *The Examination of Margaret Fell.*

33 Bruyneel, *Margaret Fell and the End of Time*, p. 51.

34 Ibid., p. 56.

35 *A Brief Collection of Remarkable Passages and Occurrences Relating to . . . Margaret Fell* (1710).

Bibliography

Ames, Marjon, *Margaret Fell, Letters, and the Making of Quakerism* (London: Routledge, 2017).

Bruyneel, Sally, *Margaret Fell and the End of Time: The Theology of the Mother of Quakerism* (Waco, TX: Baylor University Press, 2010).

Clausen-Brown, Karen, 'Spinoza's Translation of Margaret Fell and his Portrayal of Judaism', *The Seventeenth Century*, vol. 34, no. 1 (2019), 89–106.

Donawerth, Jane and Rebecca M. Lush (eds.), *Margaret Fell: Women's Speaking Justified and other Pamphlets* (Toronto, Ontario: ITER Press, 2018).

Fell, Margaret, *A Brief Collection of Remarkable Passages and Occurrences Relating to the Birth, Education, Life, Conversion, Travels, Services, and Deep Sufferings of [. . .] Margaret Fell* (London: J. Sowle, 1710).

Gill, Catie, *Women in the Seventeenth-Century Quaker Community: A Literary Study of Political Identities, 1650–1700* (Aldershot, UK and Burlington, VT: Ashgate, 2005).

Glines, Elsa (ed.), *Undaunted Zeal: The Letters of Margaret Fell* (Richmond, IN: Friends United Press, 2003).

Ingle, H. Larry, *First Among Friends: George Fox and the Creation of Quakerism* (Oxford: Oxford University Press, 1994).

Kunze, Bonnelyn, *Margaret Fell and the Rise of Quakerism* (London: Macmillan, 1994).

Mack, Phyllis, *Visionary Women: Ecstatic Prophecy in Seventeenth-Century England* (London: University of California Press, 1994).

Polder, Kristianna, *Matrimony in the True Church: The Seventeenth-Century Quaker Marriage Approbation Discipline* (London: Routledge, 2015).

Polder, Kristianna, 'Margaret Fell, Mother of the New Jerusalem', *New Critical Studies on Early Quaker Women, 1650–1800* (Oxford: Oxford University Press, 2018), 186–201.

Ross, Isabel, *Margaret Fell: Mother of Quakerism* (York: William Sessions Ltd., 1996).

Thickstun, Margaret Olofson, 'Writing the Spirit: Margaret Fell's Feminist Critique of Pauline Theology', *Journal of the American Academy of Religion*, vol. 63, no. 2 (1995), 269–279.

PART II

Spirituality

21

QUAKER SPIRITUAL AUTOBIOGRAPHY

Andrew Pisano

This chapter is an introduction to Quaker spiritual autobiography, an important facet of Quaker history that continues to inspire readers to find peace in their own spiritual journeys among the challenging ebb and flow of daily life. While this is certainly not an exhaustive study of the genre, I do hope to offer readers, especially those new to Quakerism, a sense of the rich and often complex, even messy legacy of Quaker life-writing.[1] My particular focus is on eighteenth-century Quaker autobiography as a foundational period for the genre, not only in narrative structure but in its antidotal conception. Like contemporary Quaker life-writing, eighteenth-century Quaker writers saw personal writing as a way of making sense of their world, of husking away the chaos of social and political turmoil in order to find God's voice within. These early texts were intended to bring order to readers' spiritual yearnings, to salve the wounds of day-to-day suffering and doubt, and to encourage pause in life's joys. Modern Quaker life-writing continues to explore these characteristics, keeping readers' spiritual well-being, regardless of their station in life, at the heart of the narrative. Like eighteenth-century writings, contemporary Quaker autobiography offers antidotal properties intended to bring clarity and peace to readers.

In his recent book *Living the Quaker Way*, Philip Gulley invites readers of all religious and non-religious stripes to consider the values held sacred by many Quakers. This is not a dense theological treatise or reprimanding of lapsed believers. Rather, it is a deeply personal, autobiographical account of his travels, ministries, personal struggles, and lessons learned articulated in a conversationalist tone intended to draw in and educate readers. These narrative details avoid the trappings of recruitment rhetoric and instead invite readers not "to church but to a life."[2] For Gulley, the purpose of the book seeks to introduce or, perhaps, to reaffirm readers' conceptions of simplicity, peace, integrity, and equality as a foundation for living one's life.[3] It also challenges the notion that an uptick in interest in Quakerism is simply a trend, a drift towards a Christian conviction that has more in common with some Eastern faiths than most Christian denominations. Instead, Gulley asserts that renewed interest in Quakerism hinges on the premise that "its focus on the inner life" is an "antidote to the complexities and challenges of modern life."[4] His use of the term "antidote" is especially striking here, as it directly recalls the historical legacies of the genre of Quaker spiritual autobiography.

Like Gulley's *Quaker Way*, Gil Skidmore's 1996 book *Turning Inside Out: An Exploration of Spiritual Autobiography* presents a Quaker genre of writing still alive and vibrant speaking to seekers of inner faith and those who struggle to make sense of an ever-turbulent world. Where

DOI: 10.4324/9780429030925-24

Gulley explores the self as a means of imparting wisdom to readers, Skidmore uses anecdotal reflection as context for positing actual lessons in writing one's own spiritual autobiography. She clarifies her intent when she writes:

> I also felt a growing conviction that if present-day Friends could be helped to see themselves as part of a continuing tradition of spiritual autobiography, stretching from the seventeenth century to the twentieth, they might be encouraged to continue that tradition into the future.[5]

The tradition of life-writing for Quakers runs long and deep. Indeed, as noted with Gulley's book, there is a recognizable antidotal quality to Quaker spiritual autobiography that stretches back to the eighteenth century. And as Gulley's and Skidmore's books demonstrate, modern Quaker spiritual autobiography continues to inspire a probing and nurturing of the Inner Light and the practice of socially conscious living. But these motifs had to start somewhere, and a glimpse at eighteenth-century Quaker writing will give us some sense of those beginnings and perhaps offer perspective on the continuing tradition of life-writing in Quaker communities.

The eighteenth century was a period when Quakerism in Britain and the Americas found increased economic and social stability following the confusion and difficulties experienced by the first few generations of Quakers. While there were hostilities directed towards Quakers, mostly from Anglican officiants in England and Puritans in the American colonies, there was also a much-needed coalescing of identity. The autobiographical writings of eighteenth-century Quakers not only attempted to chart the ebb and flow of personal spiritual growth but sought clarity of purpose for the faith. What did it mean to be a Quaker? Is there a shared identity in the vast Atlantic world? These questions were especially pressing to eighteenth-century Quakers because the previous century was so fraught with political strife, inconsistent views of scripture and its purpose in meetings, and the role of silence and utterance when listening for the divine moving within one's heart.[6] In the mid-sixteenth century, especially following the restoration of Charles II in 1660, English meeting houses tended to be more concerned with member recruitment under the pressure of apocalyptic expectations of ushering in a new kingdom of God, like other outlier denominations fearing the approach of a new millennium.[7] However, by the end of the century, tensions in England eased; tolerance for non-Anglican worship increased considerably. The influx of Quaker immigrants to North America encouraged Quaker writers to see travel and fellowship as manifestations of Godly grace. Quakers on both sides of the Atlantic devoted more attention to establishing a unified, coherent sense of purpose and direction.[8] Thus, the era of "Quietism," a period from 1690 to 1820, saw Quakers throughout the transatlantic world turning inward and aspiring to carve out what Thomas D. Hamm calls an "outlook that focused on the preservation of group discipline and fear of what Friends referred to as 'creaturely activity.'"[9]

The writers who came out of this period of Quietism not only worked to articulate and unite shared religious values; they also recognized that the struggle for inner peace with the divine was directly connected to their engagement with the material worlds they inhabited.[10] They were, in fact, developing a spiritual antidote to contend with the difficulties of their lives. Addressing social justice concerns became increasingly important to practicing one's Quaker beliefs. There was a marked interest in gender roles, discrimination against Native Americans, and the abolition of the African slave trade, among other social reforms. Therefore, by the first decades of the eighteenth century, Quaker life-writing began to take on a recognizable pattern, a narrative form that would remain mostly intact well into the nineteenth century and ultimately imprint itself on Quaker writing into the present day.

In the seventeenth century, Quaker autobiographers such as George Fox, Margaret Fell, Katherine Evans, and Sarah Chevers depicted a turbulent, even apocalyptic world in which Quaker values were constantly tested against the perils of regicide, incarceration, and community exile. But they also spoke of clarification; moreover, they elucidated the importance of equal gender roles in meetings. For example, Fell writes:

> I see in the Eternal Unchangeable Light of God, that all and every members, who are of the body, ought to be serviceable in their places, and to administer freely, according to their ability, as they have received of the Lord freely.[11]

Fell's conclusion about Friends' participation in meetings addresses not only the early egalitarian impulses of Quaker worship and business but also indicates the importance of shared spiritual values. Gil Skidmore observes that these writings took into account "the individual's spiritual journey for the encouragement of others who might benefit from it . . . experiences of individuals, whatever their background, were seen as valuable to others looking for their own 'truth.'"[12] While notable male Quaker writers continued this tradition into the eighteenth century, women authors presented a more dynamic range of personal and professional experiences that helped ground Quakers' faith, ensure their survival in the Americas, and offer one another a spiritual antidote to the perilous, dangerous worlds they traveled in.

English Quaker women wrote with a familial conviction that was often missing from men's writings. These women writers conceptualized a range of peoples as a type of family unit, at times inspired by their own struggles at home, most often a result of a husband's or son's alcohol abuse. Writers such as Lydia Rawlinson Lancaster and Ruth Alcock Follows are two notable examples of women who struggled to balance personal and ministerial obligations while continuing to travel around Britain.[13] Meanwhile, Sarah Tuke Grubb is notable for traveling around Britain and North America preaching and reaffirming a sense of shared familial Quakerism.[14] When read together, these women's narratives weave a transatlantic Quaker ministry inspired by personal struggle and the desire to impress upon readers and congregants, a sense of familial unity that transcended – and perhaps healed – the disunity they experienced at home.[15] Skidmore observes that the writings of these women and others

> illustrates the personal links which existed between travelling ministers and between Quaker women in the eighteenth century. The network of encouragement and support built up through women's meetings and women traveling together as companions in the ministry, tougher with the hospitality offered in one another's homes, contributed much to the continuation of Quakerism in the eighteenth century as a vital force.[16]

In some ways, Quaker women writers sought to provide a sense of clarity and community to an increasingly global Quaker faith base.

As seventeenth-century Quaker autobiography waded through social and political upheaval, the eighteenth century brought about a more stable narrative form, especially from Quakers living in North America.[17] By the mid-eighteenth century, American Quaker life-writing exhibited a pattern of expression that was characterized by a focus on personal experience, even the most banal, as a search for universal truths pertaining to the divine in the material world. Furthermore, these texts tended to be didactic, positing the need for readers to moderate or even negate one's individual wants and needs in order to render the self empty and thus available to the Spirit.[18] Perhaps the most famous of these American accounts is John Woolman's *Journal*, published in 1774.

Woolman's *Journal* is the most studied and widely anthologized American Quaker document before 1800 and a defining example of the Quietist era. His writings reflect the narrative structure common in spiritual autobiography during the eighteenth century but also stand apart from other personal religious writings of the day in its charting of how the health of one's inner faith is contingent on social justice. His focus on everyday experience as a pursuit for truth led him to question the institution of slavery. For example, Woolman recounts a trip to North Carolina in 1757 where his attempts at centering down into silence for worship left him filled with concern. He writes that a "deep and painful exercise came upon me." He explains:

> As the people in this and the Southern Provinces live much on the labor of slaves, many of whom are used hardly, my concern was that I might attend with singleness of heart to the voice of the true Shepard, and be so supported as to remain unmoved at the faces of men.[19]

For Woolman, the fear is that in his search for the inner light, he might somehow ignore the human suffering all around him. There is a recognition in this particular passage of his own white privilege, a position he was already self-conscious of from his time working as a merchant and tradesman in New Jersey, where he drew up wills for slave owners. Woolman carefully extracted universal truths from his personal experiences and articulated them in ways his readers could relate to. Although he did not live to see his *Journal* published, readers since have found observations regarding his pathway to spiritual conviction to be inspiring, especially in its manifestation as advocacy for social justice. In many ways, Woolman's *Journal* stands apart from other eighteenth-century forms of spiritual life-writing in its careful deliberation on the inner workings of faith; that is, his writing possesses a uniqueness in its manifestation of mindfulness of faith in struggle with doubt, and notions of social justice as demonstrative ideas of faith-in-practice forged out of this conflict.[20] For Woolman, Fell, Lancaster, Follows, Grubb, and others, personal experience is a defining catalyst for spiritual growth and illustrative of God's work in one's life.

By focusing on the inner spiritual life of the mind, oftentimes sparked by illness, personal tragedy and triumphs, engagements with a turbulent material world, or even the banality of one's life, Quaker spiritual autobiography is an antidotal tradition. As Philip Gulley and Gil Skidmore observe, modern Quaker and non-Quaker readers and writers continue to find solace, inspiration, and encouragement in the genre. These narratives provide some sense of clarity and purpose in the face of a seemingly chaotic and random material world, even when notions of "spirituality" differ from person to person. As Skidmore rightly points out, the concept of "spiritual" is not a monolithic notion; it means different things to different people.[21] But just like the eighteenth-century Quaker writers who toiled over the negation of the self in order to understand the inner light, contemporary Quaker writers look to how personal experience shapes one's sense of self and, from there, work to set it aside in order to hear the divine within.

Notes

1 For detailed analyses of Quaker spiritual autobiography, see D. Shea, *Spiritual Autobiography in Early America* (Madison: University of Wisconsin Press, 1968) and S. Wright, "'Gaining a Voice': An Interpretation of Quaker Women's Writing, 1740–1850," *Quaker Studies* 8, no. 1 (2003). For a detailed study of Christian autobiography, conversion narratives, and autobiographical narrative theory, see D.B. Hindermarsh, *The Evangelical Conversion Narrative: Spiritual Autobiography in Early Modern England* (Oxford: Oxford University Press, 2005).

2 P. Gulley, *Living the Quaker Way: Timeless Wisdom for a Better Life Today* (New York: Convergent Books, 2013), 5.

3 Ibid., 4.

4 Ibid.

5 G. Skidmore, *Turning Inside Out: An Exploration of Spiritual Autobiography* (Reading: The Sowle Press, 1996), 7.

6 For a detailed history of Quakerism in the transatlantic world, see T. Hamm, *The Quakers in America* (New York: Columbia University Press, 2003).

7 T. Hamm, Introduction to *Quaker Writings: An Anthology, 1650–1920*, ed. Thomas D. Hamm (New York: Penguin Books, 2010), xii–xiv. For more on English Quakerism and Millenarianism, see H.L. Ingle, "George Fox, Millenarian," *Albion: A Quarterly Journal Concerned with British Studies* 24, no. 2 (1992). For discussion of colonial American Quakerism and apocalyptic thinking, see M. Ward, "Transformative Faith and the Theological Response of the Quakers to the Boston Executions," *Quaker Studies* 21, no.1 (2016).

8 Ibid., xv.

9 Ibid.

10 Ibid.

11 M. Fell, *A Brief Collection of Remarkable Passages, Quaker Writings* (ed.) T. Hamm, 47.

12 G. Skidmore, *Strength in Weakness: Writings by Eighteenth-Century Quaker Women* (Walnut Creek, CA: Altamira Press, 2003), 17.

13 Ibid., 12–13; Both Lydia Lancaster and Ruth Follows experienced considerable personal anxiety which informed their respective ministries. Lancaster's husband Brian, for example, was most likely an alcoholic and often accrued significant debt through gambling. Follows's two sons drank excessively and often ran into trouble in public places. These experiences, too, influenced Follows's ministry.

14 Writings by Lancaster, Follows, and Grubb appear in Skidmore's *Strength in Weakness*. Their writings were published posthumously. For Lancaster, see "Letter from Lydia Lancaster to Gilbert Thompson, 1729," "Letter from Lydia Lancaster to her niece Mary Rawlinson, 1743," and "Letter from Lydia Lancaster to Susannah Fothergill, 1755," 38–40, 46–47. For Follows, see *Ruth Follows's Spiritual Autobiography and Journal* and "Letter from Ruth Follows to her son, 1777," 49–54, 59. For Grubb, see "Extracts from published letters (with years but no indication of recipient)," 86–90.

15 Ibid., 33–47, 48–62, and 84–102.

16 Ibid., 15.

17 D. Shea, *Spiritual Autobiography in Early America*, 4–5.

18 R. Banes, "The Exemplary Self: Autobiography in Eighteenth Century America," *Biography* 5, no. 3 (1982): 228.

19 J. Woolman, *Journal of John Woolman, Quaker Writings,* (ed.) T. Hamm, 171.

20 For more on the uniqueness of Woolman's writings, see D. Anderson, "Reading John Woolman," *Early American Literature* 51, no. 3 (2016).

21 Skidmore, *Turning Inside Out*, 18–19.

Bibliography

Banes, Ruth A., "The Exemplary Self: Autobiography in Eighteenth Century America," *Biography* 5, no. 3 (1982).

Fell, Margaret, *A Brief Collection of Remarkable Passages and Occurrences Relating to the Birth, Education, Life, Conversion, Travels, Services, and Deep Sufferings of That Ancient, Eminent, and Faithful Servant of the Lord, Margaret Fell, Quaker Writings: An Anthology, 1650–1920*, ed. Thomas D. Hamm (New York: Penguin Books, 2010).

Gulley, Philip, *Living the Quaker Way: Timeless Wisdom for a Better Life Today* (New York: Convergent Books, 2013).

Hamm, Thomas D., Introduction to *Quaker Writings: An Anthology, 1650–1920*, ed. Thomas D. Hamm (New York: Penguin Books, 2010).

Shea, David B., *Spiritual Autobiography in Early America* (Madison: University of Wisconsin Press, 1968).

Skidmore, Gil, *Turning Inside Out: An Exploration of Spiritual Autobiography* (Reading: The Sowle Press, 1996).

Skidmore, Gil, *Strength in Weakness: Writings by Eighteenth-Century Quaker Women* (Walnut Creek, CA: Altamira Press, 2003).

Woolman, John, *The Journal of John Woolman, Quaker Writings: An Anthology, 1650–1920*, ed. Thomas D. Hamm (New York: Penguin Books, 2010).

22

BAYARD T. RUSTIN

The Faith of a Conscientious Objector in the 1940s

Carlos Figueroa

Introduction

The 1940s was transformative for the United States and the world, with events like World War II, the Holocaust, the Bretton Woods World financial systems conference, India's independence from the British, the signing of the Universal Declaration of Human Rights, the North Atlantic Treaty Organization compact, and China's Communist Revolution, among others (Brinkley, 1993; Foner, 1998). Yet, we must remember that the 1940s, like any other decade, does not consist of coherent narratives, consistent social and political actions, or inevitable outcomes. As Timothy W. Luke (1986) observed, "a decade serves as the fungible containerization of uniquely diverse social upheavals, cultural innovations, and political struggles. Significance is marked in differences" (p. 246). This chapter considers the different ways Bayard T. Rustin was shaped by the vibrant 1940s while serving as a conscientious objector against war, broader social violence, and racial segregation guided by his *pragmatic Quaker faith* (Figueroa, 2022).

Rustin balanced personal dilemmas and social upheavals by providing more explicit faith-based justifications for his critical anti-war and anti-violence actions. His efforts were criticized by adversaries yet recognized, praised, and encouraged by Quakers, fellow pacifists, and family along the way. All this led to Rustin eventually committing more deeply to his religious faith and his becoming an official member of the Religious Society of Friends in 1943. Rustin's commitments to his pragmatic Quaker faith permitted him to advocate a pacifist nonviolent message more effectively with opportunities for broader discussions about the importance of resisting the evils of injustice and violence around the world on moral-religious grounds.

"Discuss an Issue . . . Only When . . . Calm": Rustin and the "Promises of God"

Rustin's grandmother Julia (Wilson) – who attended Quaker Meetings and was an active member of the African Methodist Episcopal Church along with his grandfather Janifer Rustin – raised and educated him about the importance of God, Jesus, and the Judeo-Christian traditions (Figueroa, 2022). Rustin gained self-confidence, which he took into the broader social world as an openly gay black man. Julia frequently reminded Rustin to rest on the "Word of God" whenever experiencing any doubts in his social and political activities, often quoting

DOI: 10.4324/9780429030925-25

from the Old and New Testaments as scriptural authority while also alluding to the "Light Within" as another source for living within a mostly secular world of politics that attracted Rustin.

Rustin's varied religious education drew from liberal and evangelical Quakerism, Gandhian philosophy, and the Holy Scriptures (Bible). With his diverse philosophical and theological perspective, Rustin navigated both the private and public spaces challenging injustices wherever he witnessed them (Figueroa, 2022). Yet, love, peace and concrete strategic action together made change. Frederick B. Tolles (1961) wrote about John Woolman's "universal love" informing his Quakerism.

> The only effective dissolvent of the love of power . . . was the power of love. Not the "*amor intellectualis dei*" of Spinoza, not the metaphysical "love to being in general" of Jonathan Edwards, not the violently emotional "holy love" of John Wesley and the Evangelicals, but "the pure flowing of divine love," a tender, pulsing sympathy with all [humankind] and all created things, arising from a secret inward spring and spreading its fructifying, refreshing streams over the plains of daily life every direction.
>
> *(pp. v, xi)*

This "universal love" also characterized Rustin's religious faith, social thinking, and political action, especially within the complexities of the 1940s, although expressed differently in both form and content. Charles L. Cherry (2013) informs us:

> Quakers believe that there is God in every person, an indwelling power whose expression should not be hindered by any form of physical or mental oppression. That power may be described differently by believers, but it is central to Quakers' "inward encounter with God."
>
> *(p. 397)*

Rustin pursued the secular world with the knowledge and awareness that the Light of Christ and thus "power of love" would guide and protect his every endeavor (Figueroa, 2022).

Rustin shares how his Quaker faith helped him deal with the world around him in a meditative way.

> We were told that we should never discuss an issue when we were wrought up, but only when we were calm. We were taught that it was too tiresome to hate, and that we should never go to sleep without first reconciling differences that had occurred during the day. We should never raise the question as to who had caused a dispute, for nothing constructive was to be gained by arguing over who started what.
>
> *(cited in Dixon, 2013)*

This was a lesson Rustin learned from his grandmother Julia, that *calmness* would not only help him control his emotions but also increase his *clarity of thought* while working on mobilizing and organizing people for social justice causes.

Rustin's calm, open, nonviolent demeanor was described in a note by John Nevine Sayre, co-chair of the Fellowship of Reconciliation (FOR), sent to Rustin's grandmother Julia on her birthday in 1944. Sayre recognized Rustin's kindness, humility, and spirituality as her grandson sat in a maximum-security prison at Ashland, Kentucky, "for refusing to serve in [the] U.S. military or accept alternative service as a conscientious objector" (Podair, 2009, p. x).[1]

He has a combination of gifts in singing voice, dramatic recital of experiences, and personality inspired by loving nonviolence. I believe that these gifts will take him very far. . . . if he can maintain his inner sweetness and humility of spirit, on the one hand in the face of the bitter sufferings of the Negro race and himself at the hands of White prejudice, and on the other hand against the adulation which will come his way because of his talents and personality.

(Long, 2012, pp. 13–14)

Sayre captured Rustin's precocious and charismatic personality informing his nonviolent spirit. But Sayre believed Rustin faced a potential dilemma: he thought Rustin had to find a way through his "inner sweetness and humility of spirit" to balance his dealing with "the sufferings of the Negro race . . . at the hands of White prejudice" and the equally dangerous personal adulations that "will come his way."

Julia responded to Sayre, as she often did to Rustin, by reference to the scriptures. She shows her intimate knowledge of both the Old Testament with the poetic Psalms and the Pauline Epistles with the book of Romans from the New Testament.

It is very comforting and heartwarming to have so many kind expressions from Bayard's friends. In a letter to me [Bayard] asked that at 1 o'clock P.M. I read 56th Psalm and he would be reading it at the same time. Also in Romans 8:28 [God] has promised that all things work together for good to those who love God. So Mr. Sayre while I am concerned and anxious about Bayard, I have no real fear as I live in the promises of God. And I love the 91st Psalm – "He that abideth in the secret places of the Most High, shall dwell under the shadow of the Almighty."

(Long, 2012, p. 14)

Rustin embraced his profound spiritual connections with his grandmother while he was physically away in prison. They shared the power of scripture and "promises of God" by engaging in what I would call *shared holy readings in time* that seemed unique to them.[2] By referencing Psalms 56, Julia showed how Rustin trusted in God to guide him through the worst of times. For example, several passages from Psalms 56 appropriately validated Julia's confidence in the "promises of God" vis-à-vis Rustin's well-being.

When I am afraid, I will trust in you. In God, whose word I praise, in God I trust; I will not be afraid. What can mortal man do to me? Then my enemies will turn back when I call for help. By this I will know that God is for me. In God, whose word I praise, in the Lord, whose word I praise – in God I trust; I will not be afraid. What can man do to me? I will present my thank offerings to you. For you have delivered my soul from death, and my feet from stumbling, that I may walk before God in the light of Life.

(Thompson Chain-Reference Bible, 1983, pp. 585–586)

Although historians and biographers have suggested or presumed that Rustin "was a lifelong Quaker" (Hamm, 2003, p. 172) and "a Quaker by birth" (D'Emilio, 2003, p. 65), he did not receive official membership however into the Religious Society of Friends until March 1943. By the time Rustin gained membership, he had been attending the 15th Street Monthly Meeting (Manhattan) since shortly arriving in New York City to study at City College of the City University of New York in 1937.[3] After a long-time attending Quaker Meeting and embodying a pragmatic Quaker sensibility throughout his early life, Rustin decided to pursue membership. Rustin submitted his initial inquiry to the New York Preparative Meeting responsible at the time for bringing business items, such as membership requests and applications, to the Monthly Meetings. The New York Yearly Meeting (NYYM) minutes announced: "The committee appointed to give attention to the request for membership of Bayard Rustin recommends that his request be granted. The recommendation is approved, and he is received into membership."[4] Rustin was informed of the NYYM decision immediately when "the Clerk . . . [was] directed to notify him of this action, and the Recorder [was] requested to add his name to [the] Register."[5] Thus, Rustin was not a birthright but a convinced Friend.[6]

Rustin's pragmatic Quaker faith may have been partly shaped by the merger process of the NYYM that included the 15th Street Monthly Meeting. The merger process started in the 1920s and ended with the final unification in 1955 opening a dialogic relationship between the Quaker Orthodox, Hicksite, and Gurneyite branches (Hinshaw, 2013, p. 100). Yet, Rustin did not describe his reasons why he sought membership into the Religious Society of Friends when he did. This fact does not deny, however, Rustin's long-standing, deep-rooted Quaker sensibilities and Judeo-Christian values that inspired his "oneness of the human family" perspective tacitly framing his social thought and political action (Figueroa, 2022).

A Committed Quaker Under God's Protection During World War II

The so-called European war was in its second year after Hitler's Germany invaded Poland in September 1939. The United States had not entered the war efforts but did provide assistance to allies indirectly with the Neutrality Acts (1935–1939) to appease the isolationists in the federal government, but more directly with the Lend-Lease policy (1940) that provided weapons-borrowing privileges to Britain and later the Soviet Union (Brinkley, 1993, pp. 719–720). In retaliation for the United States "having broken Japanese [military] codes," President Roosevelt freezing "all Japanese assets in the" country that severely limited "Japan's ability to purchase needed American supplies," and following a change in Japan's administration where Prime Minister General Hideki Tojo took reign, Japan attacked the United States "naval base at Pearl Harbor in Hawaii on December 7, 1941" (pp. 721–722). This attack led the United States to declare war on Japan, while Germany and Italy followed suit, declaring war on the United States as Japan's European allies (p. 722). President Roosevelt had already anticipated entering the United States into the war, and so in September 1940, the Selective Training and Service Act (or Burke-Wadsworth Act) was passed, establishing "the first peacetime military draft in American history" (p. 718).

In late 1940, Rustin submitted his Selective Training and Service questionnaire, choosing *conscientious objector* status and planned to serve at a Civilian Public Service (CPS) camp. Then, on November 16, 1943, Rustin sent a letter to the Federal Local Board No. 63 with reasons for taking a critical stance on military conscription and war. Rustin's courageous nonviolent strategy, leading to eventual imprisonment, was guided by his pragmatic Quaker faith. As a recently convinced Quaker, Rustin acknowledged the underlying faith-based motives of his political objections.

> For eight years I have believed war to be impractical and a denial of our Hebrew-Christian tradition. The social teachings of Jesus are: (1) Respect for personality; (2) Service the "summum bonum";[7] (3) Overcoming evil with good; and (4) The brotherhood of man. These principles . . . are violated by participation in war. Believing this, and having before me Jesus' continued resistance to that which he considered evil,

I was compelled to resist war by registering as a Conscientious Objector in October, 1940. However, a year later, September 1941, I became convinced that conscription as well as war equally is inconsistent with the teachings of Jesus. I must resist conscription also. I wish to inform you that I cannot voluntarily submit to an order springing from the Selective Service and Training Act for War.

(Rustin, 2011, p. 153)

Even serving as a conscientious objector seemed to imply acceptance of the conscription policy. Rustin cites the teachings of Jesus and thereby providing his evangelicalism as another source to his pragmatic Quaker faith compelling him toward a form of self-absolution from military conscription or engaging in any war-related activities, violent or otherwise. Rustin's "oneness of the Human family" framework implied in his use of the "brotherhood of man" notion offered the premise to his rhetorical arguments. Rustin expressed his "oneness" principle by alluding to how federal government power undercuts an individual's political rights and moral responsibilities but more problematically the country's commitments to its citizens, the public good, and democracy.

In one of his more explicit decrees, Rustin shows how and why his pragmatic Quaker faith and "oneness" principle infused his civil disobedience against the US government's conscription policy. Three interrelated reasons to resist authoritative power, Rustin argues, stem "from the basic spiritual truth that men are brothers in the sight of God" (pp. 153–154).

(1) War is wrong. Conscription is a concomitant of modern war. Thus, conscription for so vast an evil as war is wrong.

(2) Conscription for war is inconsistent with freedom of conscience, which is not merely the right to believe, but to act on the degree of truth that one receives, to follow a vocation which is God-inspired and God-directed. Today I feel that God motivates me to use my whole being to combat by non-violent means the ever-growing racial tension in the United States; at the same time the State directs that I shall do its will; which of these dictates can I follow – that of God or that of the State? Surely, I must at all times attempt to obey the law of the State. But when the will of God and the will of the State conflict, I am compelled to follow the will of God. If I cannot continue in my present vocation, I must resist.

(3) The Conscription Act denies brotherhood – most basic New Testament teaching. Its design and purpose is to set men apart – German against American, American against Japanese. Its aim springs from a moral impossibility – that ends justify means, that from unfriendly acts a new and friendly world can emerge.

(pp. 153–154)

Rustin discloses his understanding of a core Quaker theological notion, "that of God in everyone," by referencing a New Testament teaching "brotherhood [of man]" that has been violated by human-made law. The law is designed to separate people, which violates "brotherhood" and is contrary to "the will of God"; thus Rustin has no choice but to resist. In his use of the New Testament, Rustin seems to accept the Christian Scriptures as an authoritative source for his political critiques and strategies against the federal government.[8] Rustin's vocation was to follow "the will of God" and challenge "racial tension in the United States." He concludes:

In practice further, [the Act] separates black from white – those supposedly struggling from a common freedom. This means that I must protest racial discrimination in the armed forces, which is not only morally indefensible but also in clear violation of the Act. This does not, however, imply that I could have a part in conforming to the Act if discrimination were eliminated. Segregation, separation, according to Jesus, is the basis of continuous violence. It was such an observation which encouraged him to teach, "It has been said to you in olden times that thou shalt not kill, but I say unto you, do not call a man a fool" – and *he might have added*: "For if you do call him such, you automatically separate yourself from him and violence begins." That which separates man from his brother is evil and must be resisted. I admit my share of guilt for having participated in the institutions and ways of life which helped bring fascism and war. Nonetheless, guilty as I am, I now see as did the Prodigal Son that it is never too late to refuse longer to remain in a non-creative situation. It is always timely and virtuous to change – to take in all humility a new path. Though joyfully following the will of God, I regret that I must break the law of the State. I am prepared for whatever may follow. I herewith return the [materials] you have sent me, for conscientiously I cannot hold a card in connection with an act I no longer feel able to accept and abide by.

(pp. 153–154)

Rustin expresses his vulnerability and fallibility as the "Prodigal Son" recognized his sin/wrong-doing and now seeks repentance, thus showing the strength of a redemptive spirit amid fascism, racial discrimination, and war. Rustin finds three aspects of the human-made law objectionable: (1) military conscription, (2) segregation of blacks and whites in the armed forces, and (3) war in general. All three undermine "the will of God" that lies at the center of Rustin's commitments to social fairness, equality, and justice. So, war and racial segregation are equally violent acts. But taken together are real obstacles to achieving the "will of God." Rustin shows a Quaker leading in his stance for the concern of others; that is, he has and will forever be led by "the will of God" in all political thought and action against unjust laws. Rustin's Quaker leading is closely tied to a familiar biblical passage, John 4:24, which states, "God is spirit, and those who worship him must worship in spirit and truth" (Thompson Chain-Reference Bible, 1983, p. 1087).[9]

Pragmatic Quaker Faith in Action at Federal Prison, Ashland, Kentucky, 1944–1946

In January 1944, Rustin was arrested for "his defiant reply to the draft board" and "found guilty of violating the Selective Service Act and sentenced to three years" (Anderson, 1997, p. 99). After spending time at a detention center, Rustin eventually landed at the Ashland, Kentucky, maximum security penitentiary on March 9, 1944. He was not the only conscientious objector who was placed either in prison or a civilian labor camp, however. Rustin engaged in resistance strategies often used by other radical anti-war pacifists. These strategies were generally supported by Rustin's mentor A.J. Muste of the FOR, among others (p. 100). Rustin was already nationally known as a successful labor activist and war resister and thus was respected among radical pacifists. Rustin accepted leadership positions – although some thought too soon – while in prison because of his extensive experiences. For instance, Rustin led hunger strikes against racial segregation in the prison facilities that would land him in solitary confinement (p. 100).

Despite ending in prison for his anti-violence and anti-war work, and later solitary confinement for his prison activism, Rustin kept his focus on the larger goals of the movement. But Rustin had already recognized that "the prospect of incarceration offered the opportunity to remain on the front lines of pacifist conviction and to forge an even tougher stance against the coercive power of the war-making state" (D'Emilio, 2003, p. 74). Thus, Rustin was prepared to partake in prison reform activities, stating, "I go to prison with high hopes of making some contribution" that may include protests, if necessary, although not his preference (Anderson, 1997, p. 101).

However, Rustin often remained close to anonymous as a Quaker and pacifist because of his penchant for working behind the scenes (Figueroa, 2022). Yet, on occasion Rustin's religious convictions were acknowledged by Quakers and non-Quakers alike. In June 1944, Doris Grotewhohl, a close friend of Rustin, shared a note while he sat in prison after she had met his grandparents (Julia and Janifer): "I can now understand the source of your insight into people and [your] faith in something greater than any one of us" (Anderson, 1997, p. 106). Last, in a memo of March 29, 1946, Howard E. Kershner, clerk of the *New York Yearly Meeting*, wrote of Rustin's courage and integrity as a Quaker and conscientious objector:

> [We send our] affectionate greetings to those of [our] members in prison for conscience' sake. You are carrying on the noble tradition of those who have chosen to suffer for their convictions rather than deny the Light. May the peace and love of God comfort and strengthen you. "They that wait upon the Lord shall renew their strength. They shall mount up on wings as eagles. They shall run and not be weary, they shall walk and not faint."

> *(Friends Historical Library)*

Unfortunately, Rustin's many attempts at desegregating the dining hall in Ashland failed spending more time in solitary for his efforts. He was then sent to Lewisburg, Pennsylvania, with other "pacifist coconspirators" for his civil disobedience and homosexual behavior (Anderson, 1997, p. 108; Long, 2012, pp. 68–87). Rustin continued his prison activism, however, to his detriment landing in the hospital where A.J. Muste later visited and asked him to "moderate his behavior in order to secure an early release" because he was needed in the larger peace movement and thus "more valuable as a free man" (Podair, 2009, p. 25). Rustin finally heeded Muste's strong message and was released early in June 1946. A.J. Muste had written Rustin on several different occasions with similar emotional and religious-based pleas (Long, 2012). Overall, these experiences solidified Rustin as a seasoned moral force for social and racial justice leading to more opportunities, not only to work on national civil disobedience campaigns with FOR, such as the 1946 Journey of Reconciliation project that became the model for the 1960s Freedom Rides (Anderson, 1997, p. 110), but also to share his pragmatic Quaker faith and Gandhian nonviolence philosophy more broadly.

"In Apprehension How Like a God": Rustin Gives Prestigious William Penn Lecture

In March 1948, Rustin in his capacity as secretary of the Racial-Industrial Department of the FOR was honored with the opportunity to deliver the William Penn Lecture as part of the Young Friends Movement of the Philadelphia Yearly Meeting (PYM). Since its inception in 1916, the William Penn Lecture had been given by several Quaker luminaries.[10] The lecture, titled "In Apprehension How Like a God," drawing on Shakespeare's *Hamlet*, provided many of the Quaker values but, more importantly, the moral and pragmatic lessons Rustin had learned while incarcerated for two years in Kentucky and Pennsylvania federal prisons for refusing induction into the military. In his lecture, Rustin reminded Friends to uphold their moral responsibility whenever witnessing and confronting any domestic or global social injustices but with *integrity* as individuals and within the community. He implored those in attendance toward consistency and truthfulness in the face of violence, war, and oppression.

Rustin's William Penn Lecture was given in the Cold War context of national and international uncertainty. To the extent that Quakers could navigate such uncertainty, Rustin's aim rested on the hope "that [the] spark of God in each of us is not all but completely smothered" by war, violence, and apathy (Rustin, 1948, p. 3). He feared that the competing global nationalisms and the now entrenched US military conscription policy would enhance an already seemingly fixed procrustean world politics.

In this new post–World War II environment, Rustin was concerned that Quakers and broader humanity had "become cynical and frustrated" and therefore suspicious of the unknown other, from the provincial to the international level (p. 3). Rustin reveals his commitment to the power of human creativity *in community* despite cultural and other social differences but through a metaphor that reflects his "oneness" principle and broader pragmatic Quaker faith.

> The spark, the potential, is indeed still within us, but in our reliance on violence we have misused our energies and sapped the strength from our moral muscles. At this moment each man in the world possesses a limited energy for social action. Let us consider this quantity similar to the contents of a drinking cup. If we use a portion of this energy in fear, another portion in frustration, and still another in preparation for violent aggression, soon we shall discover that our power is greatly diminished. But, if we can discipline ourselves – and that is a matter requiring a practical, willing, and thorough-going devotion – we can remove fear, hatred, bitterness and frustration. Then the cup will overflow with energy, a great deal of which can be used in finding a creative solution to our problems.
>
> *(p. 4)*

Rustin's "content of a drinking cup" metaphor represents the vessel that contains the "limited [positive] energy for social action." Rustin's solution is for everyone to practice "discipline" towards a renewed revelation; that is to say, he thinks "a practical, willing, and thorough-going devotion" to the *Inner Light* will change the content of the cup from negative to positive, and from limited to abundance. Rustin suggests that the people's collective power remains in their individual commitment or perhaps recommitment to the Inner Light, and not in the outer world of problems producing fear, distrust, and hopelessness often distorting who we really are as a caring human community. Required was discipline, creativity, and a willingness to devote ourselves, our resources, and our collective spirit to resolving our shared problems.

Rustin tells Friends that the moral imperative should be guiding their thoughts and actions. Although Rustin did not offer any systematic theology, he did however extend a moralistic message (perhaps a Niebuhrian moral realism) that he later shared with Dr. Martin Luther King Jr. during the 1960s Civil Rights Movement. Rustin rationalizes:

> If it is true that violence destroys our liberty, it is also possible to offer some evidence that violence causes inconsistencies that are tantamount to moral suicide. The moral man is he who is opposed to injustice per se, opposed to injustice wherever he finds it; the moral man looks for injustice first of all in himself. But in the process of creating and utilizing modern weapons, one cannot really be concerned with injustice wherever it appears. Certainly, many who use violence wish to be so concerned, and begin with a broad sense of community; but they end in opposing injustice when it touches them, having become capable of rationalizing when they use it against others.
>
> *(pp. 9–10)*

Rustin issues a clarion call to Quakers and others to rethink accepting violence, in the present Cold War context, as a strategy for opposing any injustice. He sees the use and threat of violence for the sake of justice as equivalent to "moral suicide." To Rustin, any violent act – coming from either a totalitarian regime or a supposed democratic one – minimizes real concerns to overcome injustice. Rustin finds hypocritical US policies that attempt to justify conscription when preparing to fight adversaries as a moral necessity while challenging others (non-democratic regimes, especially) who use the same logic against the United States for similar reasons. Rustin believes violence and the threat of violence are equally immoral.

> In the thirties, we argued that conscription in peacetime was wrong in principle, that Italy and Germany, by conscription, were depriving young men of a most sacred freedom – freedom from military domination. Arguments which appeared in American newspapers and journals condemned totalitarian leadership which then conscripted youth. Yet today, many responsible men would conscript our young men in peacetime, and would be embarrassed to reread the things they once wrote. Military preparedness has led to its logical conclusion, as it did in Germany and Italy. We are opposed to conscription when others prepare to fight us, but can justify it when we are preparing to fight them.
>
> *(p. 11)*

Rustin made several critical observations about the US government's unnecessary use of the atomic bomb in Japan (August 1945) as a sign of weak moral integrity. For instance, Rustin states:

> We . . . observe the eternal truth proclaimed by Laotse, Buddha, Jesus, St. Francis, George Fox and Gandhi: the use of violence will destroy moral integrity – the very fundamental of community on which peace rests. We cannot remain honest unless we are opposed to injustice wherever it occurs, first of all in ourselves.
>
> *(p. 13)*

This is a viewpoint he later shares with Dr. Martin Luther King Jr. during the civil rights movement in the 1950s and 1960s.

Rustin reiterates his position on the importance of *individual responsibility* and *moral integrity* to holistic communities, especially when challenging unjust laws but in nonviolent ways.

> Individual responsibility is the alternative to violence; individual responsibility is capable of overcoming fear; it is capable of converting nation-worship back to the Judeo-Christian tradition and ethic; it is capable of re-establishing moral integrity. How can we begin? We can begin by opposing injustice wherever it appears in our daily lives. As free men we can refuse to follow or to submit to unjust laws which separate us from other men no matter where they live, nor under what government they exist.
>
> *(p. 18)*

Rustin explicitly sought to persuade others into considering civil disobedience as a social democratic tool or strategy for pursuing structural and policy change, not unlike his letter to the Federal Local Board No. 63 in 1943. Rustin advocated for a humanitarian, communal, and moralistic approach to change, thus disregarding an individual's political affiliation, geographic location, or government system. Drawing on Mahatma Gandhi's work, Rustin made a distinction between an individual's *duty* and *right* to protest and resist unjust laws propagated by a state or government. He proclaimed:

> One has not the right to rebel against the state. One has not the right to resist the social group of which he is a part. This is particularly true where decisions made have been reached after extensive democratic discussion. One has, on the other hand, a duty to resist, and one resists because the state is poorly organized and one's everlast-ing aim is to improve the nature of the state, to disobey in the interest of a higher law. Hence, one has the duty but not the right to rebel.
>
> *(p. 19)*

Rustin makes a strong argument in emphasizing duty over right for a morally based social democracy with active citizens at the helm of the decision-making process. Rustin privileges the moral integrity of the people (*ithikós demos*) over unjust laws (*ádikos Kratos*) but on natural (*providential/theóstaltos*) grounds.

> There have been many great men in history who have been civil resisters. All who have resisted have seen clearly that social progress is made through simultaneous change in men and in the environment in which men find themselves. Thus, these men have not only sought to behave with integrity, but they have resisted secure in the faith that their opposition ultimately would influence society in the direction of those condi-tions which make it possible for other men to see issues clearly enough to press for a more abundant economic, social, and political life. These men recognized that there is "individual responsibility for collective guilt."
>
> *(p. 21)*

Resistance politics leads to individual and community change. People must be made aware of the conditions that prevent social progress. The duty to resist is part of Rustin's hope that suc-cessful oppositional protest politics would eventually result in positive societal changes. Indi-vidual responsibility is essential to a collective shift in attitude, public policies, and structural adjustments, although Rustin does anticipate some challenges to his pragmatic Quaker views against war preparations, war funding, and war itself.

> One may question that a minority could stop war, but certainly one cannot question that disobedience both to military service and to payment of taxes for war would reveal to the state that a segment of the population cares enough to pay a price for peace. Wide-spread resistance to war preparations and the willingness of resisters to face imprisonment would have to be taken seriously by the state and ultimately would have a profound effect on American foreign policy.
>
> *(p. 23)*

Peace is the goal, sacrificing for peace even in prison could serve as an effective strategy, as Rustin previously thought while at Ashland penitentiary. Rustin insisted on the use of civil disobedience as an equally effective social democratic means for producing more humane policy outcomes moving away from fear, and closer to his "oneness of the human family" idyllic world.

> Civil disobedience is not advocated as a cure-all, nor is it urged as an alternative to world government. It is not itself equal to the adjustment of social, political and

economic displacements which have produced first depression and then dictatorship and war. Such adjustments are in reality the means of peace. But in our fear, when we behave as if the truth were not true, the real problem, the struggle to provide men with bread, beauty and brotherhood, has been relegated to a second place. Our fears have brought about an armaments race and until we have broken the vicious cycle of this race with the Soviet Union, there cannot be attention, energy and money given to the basic causes of war and injustice. It is important to realize that such competition can be ended when the United States is willing to disarm completely. We have within us as individuals the responsibility and power to help achieve this task. We have the power to disarm the United States by one gun if we refuse to carry one; we have the power to take a gun from another if we refuse to pay for it by refusing to pay that part of taxes used for war.

(pp. 25–26)

Rustin believes Quakers have also fallen into the trap of blind patriotism because of fear while ignoring "the real problem" that is "the struggle to provide men with bread, beauty, and brotherhood." Our *individual* and *collective* moral responsibility should be, according to Rustin, to disarm the United States through civil disobedience and the constant pursuit of Truth. Rustin sees citizens as the real representatives of the United States because people can refuse to carry guns and pay the war taxes. This strategy would bring humanity back from the brink of self-destruction that useless material capitalist competition perpetuates, and gradually into the "brotherhood of man."

In concluding his lecture, Rustin reminds Friends to muster the courage, intellectual, and revolutionary strengthen to return to a time where they relied on the normative precepts of the Christian ethic. Rustin thinks Friends, if not broader humanity, have the potential to change the course of history if only they could use discipline and listen to the *Light within*. He trusts that each person can still understand at the level of God (as rational moral beings) to do the right thing for the whole of humanity. Quakers must once more grasp the urgency of the times and stop complying to (even implicitly) the use of weapons, engaging in violence, and worshiping capitalism (considering the Cold War context and the rise of communism). Nonviolent civil disobedience was the way to achieving "the will of God."

We cannot convert nation-worship back to Christianity again unless we care enough, unless we can believe that man is in apprehension like a god, unless we are able so to revolutionize and to discipline ourselves that those who behold us exclaim of us, "In action how like an angel!," unless like Jesus and Gandhi we attain that spirit which makes it possible for us to stand with arms outstretched, even unto death, saying "You can strike me, you may destroy my home, you may destroy me, but I will not submit to what I consider wrong; neither will I strike back." Many will question the practicality of such a course, but has not the life, the work, the death of Gandhi demonstrated in our time that one man holding fast to truth and to non-violence is more powerful than ten thousand men armed? Yet even though failure should seem certain, the faith we profess demands allegiance. But how are we different from the heathen if we strike back or submit to unjust demands and laws; or what have we left to protect if in the process of defending our freedom we give up both democracy and principle? How can we love God, whom we have not seen, if we cannot, in time of crisis, find the way to love our brothers whom we have seen?

(pp. 28–29)

For Rustin, the idea of defending our "freedom" through violence was unacceptable since it meant abandoning our social democratic values while destroying our moral and religious foundations. He insisted that Friends ought to believe in their intellectual capacity – inherent in the Inner Light ("like a god") – to restore peace and "brotherhood." Friends should use their agency ("in action like an angel") to make individual and collective change by heeding their Light. Last, Rustin asked, "How can we love God, whom we have not seen, if we cannot, in time of crisis, find the way to love our brothers whom we have seen?" to convince Friends that to achieve real "brotherhood" requires accepting the theology of "that of God in everyone" no matter the context or circumstances.

Conclusion

During the 1940s, Rustin closely aligned his religious values to his political rhetoric and social actions. Rustin officially received membership into the Religious Society of Friends in 1943, committing himself profoundly to his Quaker faith. Rustin's faith-based approach to politics, during the transformative 1940s, could be understood in terms of (1) a strong spiritual devotion to *Truth* as one sees it guided by the *inward light* of consciousness, (2) a real commitment to *integrity* and *universal love* spurring purposeful social and political action, and (3) an intimate allegiance to *peace, equality*, and *community* when pursuing substantive policy goals. This framework helped Rustin in the struggles against racial discrimination, war, and political oppression but also elevated him to various leadership positions, especially within the FOR. Last, Rustin's faith-based message for civil disobedience and non-violent action was in full display as he gave the prestigious William Penn Lecture in 1948 at the Race Street Meeting House in Philadelphia, Pennsylvania. The lecture provided Rustin a platform to address his Quaker community more directly about the importance of "brotherhood," demonstrating his commitment to his pragmatic Quaker faith that would carry him into the 1950s and 1960s civil rights movement and beyond.

Notes

1 Rustin was released from Ashland on June 11, 1946, and greeted by his joyful grandmother Julia at New York Penn Station (D'Emilio, 2003, p. 120).
2 What I am calling the *shared holy readings in time* method to affirm the "promises of God" was initiated by Rustin as another way to remain connected to his religious faith in community. There is no evidence of a broader similar practice or norm at the time within or outside the Quaker world.
3 In fact, Rustin had been active in the *New York Yearly Meeting* (NYYM) since 1937 but became disappointed that many Quakers were discussing "the possibility of providing U.S. soldiers with hospitality service" after the Pearl Harbor attacks. Rustin wrote a letter to the NYYM showing his opposition to Friends' position. Rustin writes, "Dear Friend, [s]ince it is possible that I will not be at the . . . meeting, I offer the following . . . for your consideration. The problem before us is not an easy one. We must decide whether or not . . . to assist the government in making men into efficient soldiers. We must decide whether . . . to cooperate in an essential phase of war waging. We must face with reality the fact that rights we now enjoy as a society came because of our traditional peace testimony. We must discover our peculiar world task in these times and answer this question in light of this duty. The truth is that war is wrong. It is then our duty to make war impossible first in us and then in society. To cooperate with the government in building morale seems inconsistent with all we profess to believe. Indeed, from the professional militarist's [perspective], 'morale' is that which makes it possible for one willing to do without moral qualm, if not with some moral justification, many things he previously has felt wholly wrong. If morale and recreation are essential military needs for waging battle effectively, let us avoid relieving the government of its responsibility. Let us avoid the possibilities of spiritual suicide. The moral letdown following the last war was due in part to the lack of faith the world had in a church which had cooperated in waging war" (Long, 2012, pp. 1–3).

4 Quote from the March 1943 New York Yearly Meeting Minutes; the original New York Monthly Meeting where Rustin's application was discussed: 221 East Fifteenth Street, Manhattan, NYC on July 13, 1942. (Rustin papers, *Friends Historical Library*, Swarthmore College, PA).
5 March 1943, New York Yearly Meeting Minutes.
6 Pink Dandelion (2007) shares, "Convincement . . . was about (a) a powerful in-breaking of God, (b) a sense of conviction of sin, (c) a choice, repentance, and (d) being born again into perfection, or a measure of perfection. Ultimately, this experience would lead to (e) the convinced gathering together . . . and in the years which followed, (f) calling 'the world' towards a new mode of religious experience" (pp. 23–24). However, it is not clear whether Rustin experienced or went through these stages of convincement as described above.
7 Although Rustin did not provide a source for the use of this ancient Latin philosophical concept (meaning the *highest good*), it appears related to common Jewish and Christian ideals of virtue and ethical action.
8 Pink Dandelion (2007) points out that "the variety of primary authority for belief and action lies on an axis between scriptural authority and the authority of inward revelation" (p. 184).
9 One of Rustin's contemporaries, Quaker Thomas R. Kelly, observed in 1941 that concern for others starts with trusting God: "A concern is God-initiated, often surprising, always holy, for the life of God is breaking through into the world. Its execution is in peace and power and astounding faith and joy, for in unhurried serenity the Eternal is at work in the midst of time, triumphantly bringing all things unto God's self." Likewise, Quaker Howard H. Brinton, in 1948, put the Quaker leading principle in terms of a concern for both the well-being of individuals and a community. "Throughout Quaker journals we find frequent reference to the absence of inward peace as a sign that some 'concern' possibly to undertake a journey [or] engage in some effort for social reform, had been laid upon the individual. . . . It is not essential that the undertaking be successful for inward peace to result. It is only necessary that the individual feel that he or she has done all that they are able to do to carry out the requirement. . . . God only demands that we live up to our capacity." Thus, in Rustin's case he often attempted to "live up to [his] capacity" in making clear that the Inner Light or God's Will came before human-made law (quoted in Whitmire, 2001, pp. 134; 131–132, respectively).
10 Notable *William Penn Lecturers* prior to Rustin included Norman Thomas (1917), Douglas V. Steere (1937), Thomas Kelly (1939), Howard H. Brinton (1938), Rufus M. Jones (1919 and 1941), and D. Elton Trueblood (1947).

Bibliography

Anderson, J. (1997) *Bayard Rustin: Troubles I've Seen, A Biography*. New York, NY: HarperCollins.
Brinkley, A. (1993) *The Unfinished Nation: A Concise History of the American People*. New York, NY: Knopf.
Cherry, C. L. (2013) 'Quakers and Asylum Reform', in Stephen W. Angell and Pink Dandelion, Eds., *The Oxford Handbook of Quaker Studies*. Oxford: Oxford University Press, 2013, p. 397.
Dandelion, P. (2007) *An Introduction to Quakerism*. Cambridge, UK: Cambridge University Press.
D'Emilio, J. (2003) *Lost Prophet: The Life and Times of Bayard Rustin*. New York, NY: Free Press.
Dixon, M. E. (2013) 'Bayard Rustin's Civil Rights Legacy Began with Grandmother Julia Rustin', *Main Line Today*, 19 September: http://www.mainlinetoday.com/Main-Line-Today/October-2013/Bayard-Rustins-Civil-Rights-Legacy-Began-with-Grandmother-Julia-Rustin/
Figueroa, C. (2022) 'The Political Activist Life of Pragmatic Quaker Bayard T. Rustin', Chapter 39, in C. W. Daniels and R. Grant (eds.), *The Quaker World*. London: Routledge Press
Foner, E. (1998) *The Story of American Freedom*. New York, NY: W. W. Norton & Company, Inc.
Friends Historical Library, Bayard Rustin papers, Swarthmore College, Swarthmore, PA.
Hamm, T. D. (2003) *Quakers in America*. New York: Columbia University Press.
Hinshaw, G. P. (2013) 'Five Years Meeting and Friends United Meeting, 1887–2010', in S. W. Angell and P. Dandelion (eds.), *The Oxford Handbook of Quaker Studies*. Oxford, UK: Oxford University Press, pp. 93–107.
Long, M. G. (2012) *I Must Resist: Bayard Rustin's Life in Letters*. San Francisco, CA: City Lights Books.
Luke, T. W. (1986) 'What's Left? An Exchange', in Adolph Reed, Jr. (ed.), *Race, Politics, and Culture: Critical Essays on the Radicalism of the 1960s*. Westport, CT: Greenwood Press, p. 246
Podair, J. (2009) *Bayard Rustin: American Dreamer*. Lanham, MD: Rowman & Littlefield.
Rustin, B. (1948) 'In Apprehension How Like a God!', *William Penn Lecture*, The Young Friends Movement of the Philadelphia Yearly Meetings, pp. 3–29.

Rustin, B. (2011) 'Letter to His Draft Board', in Harold D. Weaver, P. Kriese and Stephen W. Angell (eds.), *Black Fire: African American Quakers on Spirituality and Human Rights*. Fitchburg, MA: Quaker Press of FGC, pp. 153–154.

The Thompson Chain-Reference Bible (1983) New International Version, Frank Charles Thompson (ed.). Indianapolis, IN: The B. B. Kirkbride Bible Company, Inc.

Tolles, F. B. (1961) 'Introduction', in J. Woolman (ed.), *The Journal of John Woolman and A Plea for the Poor – The Spiritual Autobiography of the Great Colonial Quaker*. New York, NY: The Citadel Press.

Whitmire, C. (2001) *Plain Living: A Quaker Path to Simplicity*. Notre Dame, IN: Sorin Books, Ave Maria Press.

23

THOMAS KELLY'S MYSTICAL ITINERARY AS A SPIRITUAL ORIENTATION FOR PERSONAL SPIRITUALITY

David Pocta

On the morning of January 17, 1941, Quaker philosophy professor Thomas Kelly wrote an acceptance letter to Eugene Exman, religious book editor for Harper, stating, "I am very glad to have your favorable reaction on the possibility of building a small book out of the lectures that I sent you."[1] After writing the letter he expressed to his wife, Lael, "Today will be the greatest day of my life."[2] While drying the dishes that evening, Kelly suffered a massive heart attack and died in his home at the age of forty-seven. Although he never witnessed the publication of the book he envisioned, twenty-two of Kelly's essays have been compiled and published posthumously. Douglas Steere, friend and colleague of Kelly's from Haverford College gathered four of Kelly's essays and the beginning chapters of the devotional book intended for Harper. He added a brief biography of Kelly before submitting it. Harper published it in April 1941 under the title *A Testament of Devotion* (hereinafter *Testament*).

Thomas Kelly's *Testament* quickly became and continues to remain a unique and undying gift of spiritual devotion. HarperCollins prints the text and states, "Since its first publication in 1941, *A Testament of Devotion*, has been universally embraced as a truly enduring spiritual classic."[3] *Testament* enjoys favour across wide variances of Quaker practice and has stretched far beyond Quaker circles. E. Glenn Hinson, a spirituality professor at a Baptist seminary states, "In classes on classics of Christian devotion which I have taught since the early 1960s, students without fail have voted *A Testament of Devotion* the classic that helped them most to find a meaningful way to live out their commitment to God in all of life."[4]

Thomas Kelly was two different men in his adult life: one up until the end of 1937, and the other from early 1938 until his death in 1941. Before 1938, Kelly's adult life was filled with uneasiness as he struggled to find fulfillment in the academic world. At great cost to his personal health and against the better judgement of his wife and academic mentors, he pursued a second doctorate at Harvard after already possessing a PhD in philosophy from Hartford Theological Seminary, believing these new credentials would propel his career. After unsuccessfully defending his dissertation due to a psychological episode which left him woozy and unable to remember its content, he was denied completion of his degree.[5]

Being denied his second doctorate spun Kelly's life around and he cascaded into darkness and depression. The zenith of his academic pursuit had ended in failure. He had made many significant sacrifices, including uprooting his family multiple times and incurring significant

DOI: 10.4324/9780429030925-26

debt. His health also suffered. Kelly was lost and directionless. His wife was deeply concerned about his mental stability and his son Richard summarized his father's life up to this point as "a lifetime of struggle and inner turmoil."[6]

It was during this wilderness period of Kelly's life that something radically began to change. Sometime in the next couple of months, around November or December 1937, Kelly began experiencing an overwhelming presence. He almost immediately seemed to be a different man. Douglas Steere said,

> No one knows exactly what happened, but a strained period in his life was over. He moved toward adequacy. A fissure in him seemed to close, cliffs caved in and filled up a chasm, and what was divided grew together within him.[7]

After this period Kelly wrote differently, in both personal correspondences and in his spiritual writings. Rather than philosophical expositions, his work was personal, authentic, and spiritual. His concerns shifted. Academic pursuits paled in comparison to the newfound experience and exuberance of the Light Within. Kelly began delivering messages at Quaker meetings that he said, "wrote themselves."[8] He assured his listeners that "God *can* be found."[9] He wrote to his friend and mentor Rufus Jones, "The reality of Presence has been very great at times recently. One knows at first hand what the old inquiry meant, 'Has Truth been advancing among you?'"[10]

Kelly's friends and family attribute the transformation to mystical experiences over a period of several months from the end of 1937 through the summer of 1938. Kelly himself referred many times to these months of spiritual ecstasy in personal letters. In one letter sent to his family from Strasbourg, France, dated August 16, 1938, Kelly described this discovery in what he called "'the experiences of Presence' or as 'an increased sense of *being laid hold on* by . . . a gentle loving, but awful Power, 'resulting in a 'new sense of unreserved dedication of oneself to a life of child-like dedication to God.'"[11] Kelly began writing the essays contained in *Testament* during this period. The first one, "The Eternal Now and Social Concern," was composed in early 1938.

So, what makes *Testament* so unique? How does it compare to spiritual writings within the larger mystical tradition? Christian historian Bernard McGinn defines the mystical element in Christianity as "that part of its belief and practices that concerns the preparation for, the consciousness of, and the reaction to what can be described as the immediate or direct presence of God."[12] The Thomas Kelly that emerged in *Testament* was a mystic in the strictest sense. In his last years he was devoted to living and teaching others to live simultaneously both in the world and in the presence of God. The wide appeal of *Testament* can be attributed to its accessibility. Kelly's mystical itinerary is available. In other words, he guides the individual sojourner to orient and realign themselves in such a way that is attainable, while living in the surrounding secular world.

Kelly journeys with his listeners. He addresses the spirituality of the common person, and yet his education speaks with ease through casual references to Eckhart, Grou, Fichte, and the *Upanishads*. He speaks as a pedagogue, a poet, and even as a Quaker apologist, but his personal experience never appears detached. His writing emanates from personal conviction and, as good preachers often do, he commonly addresses the audience as "we." Kelly speaks to himself as he shares his insights with others, "I mean this literally, utterly, completely, and I mean it for you and for me – commit your lives in unreserved obedience to Him."[13]

Testament occasionally refers directly to scripture, a biblical narrative, or a biblical character, but more frequently the allusions to scripture are welling up in the background. For example, the opening paragraph of *Testament*'s section "The Light Within" contains ten sentences, the first one being a quote from Meister Eckhart. The remaining nine sentences of the paragraph allude to more than just as many scriptures which include "the inner sanctuary" (Heb 6:19), "eternity is at our hearts" (Eccl 3:11), "warming us with intimations" (Eph 2:6–7), and "a seed stirring to life if we do not choke it" (Matt 13:7–8). Kelly's seminary training and personal devotional life exude throughout his work.[14]

One of Kelly's highlights when studying at Harvard was a philosophy course with Professor Alfred North Whitehead. He was particularly intrigued by the way Whitehead crafted words to explain experiences.[15] Kelly borrowed this practice in his work, building layers of expressions for the Divine. Some of the titles he uses for God's Presence include the Divine Centre, the Inward Light, the Holy Whisper, the Voice, the Root of all living, the Eternal Now, and the Shekinah of the soul. In fact, Kelly trains his readers to watch for capital letters. It quickly becomes evident when reading *Testament* that when unfamiliar nomenclature is capitalized (such as in the "Holy Whisper"), Kelly is signifying another expression of the Divine.

Kelly's style varies, but the four essays written for public lectures possess a strong sermon quality. They are didactic and often exhortative. Even though each essay addresses profound and intimate spirituality, Kelly reveals the evangelical preacher of his younger days in these works. In "The Simplification of Life," Kelly challenges, "Do you really want to live your lives, every moment of your lives, in His Presence? Do you long for him, crave him?" He continues, "I know I'm talking like an old-time evangelist. But I can't help that, nor dare I restrain myself and get prim and conventional. We have too long been prim and restrained. The fires of the love of God, of our love toward God, and of His love toward us, are very hot."[16] Although Kelly is stronger in this composition than others, it is not uncommon to see "the revivalist preacher" appear in his writings, particularly in the four essays that began as lectures.

"The Light Within" is different. It operates as a mystical itinerary. Kelly develops a common Quaker theme in this essay, an inward spirituality; and he walks his readers through the methods of living connected to the Light Within. For Kelly, the "inner sanctuary of the soul" is a place within all people where the Divine resides.[17] The "Light Within," "Presence" or "Slumbering Christ" is stirring to be awakened. This is where real spiritual work is done. Kelly believes that authentic value "lies in that call to all men to the practice of orienting their entire being in inward adoration about the springs of immediacy and ever fresh divine power within the secret silences of the soul."[18] This theme, goal, or lifestyle permeates every dimension of Kelly's work. It is his linchpin. Without understanding this concept, it would be nearly impossible to grasp Kelly's spirituality.

> "Our real problem, in failing to centre down, is not a lack of time; it is, I fear, in too many of us, lack of joyful, enthusiastic delight in Him, lack of deep, deep-drawing love directed toward Him at every hour of the day and night. I think it is clear that I am talking about a revolutionary way of living.[19]

In fact, all of Kelly's writings in *Testament* revolve around this core value, the Presence, each of them putting into dialectic a different aspect of the spiritual life. "Holy Obedience" proposes the entire "outer pageant of history" is determined by the inner life of humankind, thereby calling people to live in utter obedience to the Holy for the betterment of the world.[20] Kelly teaches that "The Blessed Community" only exists through a mutual understanding of intimacy with the Divine as he states, "Persons in the Fellowship are related to one another through Him, as all mountains go down into the same earth."[21] The essay "The Eternal Now and Social Concern" establishes the relationship between contemplation and action. For Kelly, as with most mystics, living in fellowship with the Light Within only finds fulfilment when shared with a world in need. He states, "But there is more to the experience of God than that of being plucked out of the world. The fuller experience, I am sure, is of a Love which sends us out into the world."[22] And finally, the "The Simplification of Life" addresses the complex and overcrowded lives lived in the modern world by calling individuals back to the Light Within:

> Life is meant to be lived from a Center, a divine Center. Each one of us can live such a life of amazing power and peace and serenity, of integration and confidence and simplified multiplicity, on one condition – that is, *if we really want to*. There is a divine Abyss within us all, a holy Infinite Center.[23]

Testament refrains from holding mystical gifts or ecstatic experiences as the goal of the spiritual journey. It is also not particularly concerned about mystical visions. Kelly's own experiences with the mystical are not described in his writings in the first person. When he does refer to them, he makes general comments, describing them as if they are attainable by any sojourner attempting participation in Divine fellowship. In "Holy Obedience," he states, "It is an overwhelming experience to fall into the hands of the living God, to be invaded to the depths of one's being by His presence."[24] Kelly makes a general observation, as if it is a common experience to be "invaded to the depths of one's being." Writing in this manner, Kelly normalizes the mystical experience, as if inviting participation. Mystical union with the Light Within is Kelly's baseline ambition in his spirituality.

Kelly walks through his simple but challenging mystical itinerary in "The Light Within" by describing two levels of existence: the first level or upper level, and the second level or deep level. The upper level is the outside world, the daily routine, or the common experience. Kelly teaches, "The secular world of today values and cultivates only the first level, assured that *there* is where the real business of mankind is done."[25] Kelly sees the limitations and fruitlessness of a life lived at this level. He says, "But the light fades, the will weakens, the humdrum returns. Can we stay this fading? No, nor should we try, for we must learn the disciplines of His will, and pass beyond this first lesson of His Grace."[26] Kelly does not propose that we ignore the outside world, but rather he acknowledges its limitations. The will fades and the routine becomes dry without an internal renewal.

> Let us explore together the secret of a deeper devotion, a more subterranean sanctuary of the soul, where the Light Within never fades, but burns, a perpetual Flame, where the wells of living water of divine revelation rise up continuously, day by day and hour by hour, steady and transfiguring.[27]

Kelly draws the attention of his reader into hope, life, and energy. He calls us to the deep living and abiding Presence of the Eternal. The Christian's goal is to learn how to *live here*.

> What is here urged are internal practices and habits of the mind. What is here urged are secret habits of unceasing orientation of the deeps of our being about the Inward Light, ways of conducting our inward life so that we are perpetually bowed in worship.[28]

For Kelly, the inner depths are not to only be visited on Sundays. The practices of "praying the office," "having a Quiet Time," or stopping to meditate during the day all fall woefully short of the vision Kelly holds for the spiritual man or woman. Kelly bids, prods, and encourages his readers to breathe and bathe at the inner level, "He who is within us urges, by secret persuasion, to such an amazing Inward Life with Him, so that, firmly cleaving to Him, we always look out upon all the world through the sheen of the Inward Light."[29]

For Kelly, living at the subterranean level of the soul changes the way the world looks at the outer level. Someone effectively and simultaneously living on both planes is able to process the outer-world experience differently. The lens changes. The perspective shifts. Kelly says:

> For the religious man is forever bringing all affairs of the first level down into the Light, holding them there in the Presence, reseeing them and the whole of the world of men and things in a new and overturning way, and responding to them in spontaneous, incisive, and simple ways of love and faith. Facts remains facts, when brought into the Presence in the deeper level, but their value, their significance, is wholly realigned. Much apparent wheat becomes utter chaff, and some chaff becomes wheat.[30]

Through this realignment, the significance of everyday life presents itself in new colours. Events or issues that may at first seem daunting can lose their sting. Seemingly trivial happenings or interactions might gain newfound priority.

Where some mystics may value the deeper levels of spirituality and downplay the importance of the external world, Kelly perceives them in a symbiotic relationship. For it is this outer world that "supplies the present-day tools of reflection" and also "furnishes us with those culture-patterns of our group which are at one and the same time the medium and the material for their regeneration, our language, our symbols, our traditions, and our history."[31] In other words the outside world creates the framework for understanding the inner world. Without a proper understanding of light and dark, the concept of the Light Within would lack substance. The notion of an inner sanctuary gains dimension and colour when in the upper level a safe place provides refuge in one of life's storms. Kelly calls us to appreciate the semiotic nature of the physical world. The upper level also provides an egress for the outpouring of Presence. Spirituality mandates love. The outer world provides the canvas for love's expression.

This divine attendance or fruitful interplay requires practice and discipline. In order to develop an inward orientation, Kelly calls us to act immediately and "offer your whole selves, utterly and in joyful abandon, in quiet glad surrender to Him who is within."[32] He explains that we keep contact with the outside world and "walk and talk and work and laugh with your friends. But behind the scenes, keep up the life of simple prayer and inward worship."[33]

Recognizing the radical shift in daily routine, Kelly explains two conditions, alternating and simultaneous. The novice naturally gets distracted: "Lapses and forgettings are so frequent. Our surroundings grow so exciting. Our occupations are so exacting."[34] This is what Kelly calls a state of alteration, attention shifting between outer things and the Inner Light. The apprentice engages the Light Within but then loses focus, one moment engaged and the next distracted. Kelly directs: "Admit no discouragement, but ever return quietly to Him and wait in His Presence."[35] Within the graceful recognition of faltering, Kelly pushes, "yet what is sought is not alternation, but simultaneity, worship undergirding every moment, living prayer, the continuous current and background of all moments of life. Long practice indeed is needed before alteration yields to concurrent immersion in both levels at once."[36] Maturity does not come easily, and yet "the hunger of the committed one is for unbroken communion and adoration."[37]

Testament imparts a critical equilibrium in its spirituality. Kelly values both the cataphatic and apophatic. Sometimes he calls for action, application, and response. He may charge "begin now," or "long practice is needed." At other times he advises surrender and the emptying of self: "surrender *self*-confidence and *self*-centered effort . . . and let the Eternal be the dynamic guide."[38] He is aware of the potential polarity of either extreme, a skill that was most likely born through ministry experience rather than academic training. Just when the pressure of high expectation and performance appears to mount on the journey to simultaneity and unending connection to the Presence of God, Kelly counters:

> For if the least taint of spiritual pride in our prayer-growth has come, it is well that He humble us until we are worthy of greater trust. . . . For God himself works in our souls, in their deepest depths, taking increasing control as we are progressively willing to be prepared for His wonder.[39]

Kelly knows the wisdom of struggle and surrender, when to fight and when to relinquish. The practitioner must wrestle with the nuance themselves to discover this pathway.

Kelly paints an image of a life lived in constant devotion to the Eternal while fully engaged in the world concurrently. Walking this path requires passion and patience, persistence and submission. What lies at the end of this route for Kelly? "Here is not ecstasy but serenity, unshakableness, firmness of life-orientation. We become what Fox calls 'established men.'"[40] Living in union to the Light Within provides the simplified life of radiant joy. As Kelly says, "He who is in Fellowship is in the Kingdom."[41]

For Kelly, as with many mystics, the goal of the spiritual life is to encounter the Divine in such a way that it overflows into others. The man who wrote *Testament* zealously practiced and taught a life infused with the Eternal Now, the Holy Presence. Kelly's contribution to the mystical tradition is unique. The Quaker spirituality witnessed in his orientation around the Light Within combined with his broad philosophical education and his personal devotion attending to simultaneously living in Divine Presence while engaging the world around him inspires a deeply thoughtful yet accessible mysticism. His writing in *Testament* provokes its readers to respond as Richard Foster did as he penned the introduction for the 1992 edition of the book: "Each time I leaf through the pages of this book, I know I am in the presence of a giant soul."[42]

Notes

1 Richard Kelly, *Thomas Kelly: A Biography*, p. 122.
2 Richard Kelly, *Thomas Kelly: A Biography*, p. 122.
3 https://www.harpercollins.com/9780060643614/a-testament-of-devotion/.
4 Hinson, "The Impact of Thomas Kelly on American Religious Life," 11.
5 Richard Kelly, *Thomas Kelly: A Biography*, p. 90.
6 Richard Kelly, *Thomas Kelly: A Biography*, p. 11.
7 Thomas Kelly, *Testament*, p. 18.
8 Thomas Kelly, *Testament*, p. 18.
9 Thomas Kelly, *Testament*, p. 18.
10 Thomas Kelly, *Testament*, p. 19.
11 Paul Kelly, "Thomas Kelly Encounters Nazi Germany: His Letter from Strasbourg, 1938," 183.
12 McGinn, *The Foundations of Mysticism: Origins to the Fifth Century*, p. xvii.
13 Thomas Kelly, *Testament*, p. 52.
14 Quotations are from *Testament* and parenthetical scripture references refer to this writer's assessment of where the biblical allusion originates.
15 Thomas Kelly, *Testament*, p. 9.
16 Thomas Kelly, *Testament*, p. 119.
17 Thomas Kelly, *Testament*, p. 29.
18 Thomas Kelly, *Testament*, p. 34.
19 Thomas Kelly, *Testament*, p. 121.
20 Thomas Kelly, *Testament*, p. 51.
21 Thomas Kelly, *Testament*, p. 83.
22 Thomas Kelly, *Testament*, p. 106.

23 Thomas Kelly, *Testament*, p. 116.
24 Thomas Kelly, *Testament*, p. 56.
25 Thomas Kelly, *Testament*, p. 35.
26 Thomas Kelly, *Testament*, pp. 30–31.
27 Thomas Kelly, *Testament*, p. 31.
28 Thomas Kelly, *Testament*, p. 31.
29 Thomas Kelly, *Testament*, p. 32.
30 Thomas Kelly, *Testament*, pp. 36–37.
31 Thomas Kelly, *Testament*, p. 37.
32 Thomas Kelly, *Testament*, p. 38.
33 Thomas Kelly, *Testament*, p. 39.
34 Thomas Kelly, *Testament*, p. 39.
35 Thomas Kelly, *Testament*, p. 39.
36 Thomas Kelly, *Testament*, p. 40.
37 Thomas Kelly, *Testament*, p. 40.
38 Thomas Kelly, *Testament*, p. 99.
39 Thomas Kelly, *Testament*, p. 41.
40 Thomas Kelly, *Testament*, p. 42.
41 Thomas Kelly, *Testament*, p. 86.
42 Thomas Kelly, *A Testament of Devotion* (1992), x.

Bibliography

Birkel, Michael, *Quakers Reading Mystics* (Leiden: Brill, 2018).

HarperCollinsPublishers. https://www.harpercollins.com/9780060643614/a-testament-of-devotion/. Accessed May 20, 2020.

Hinson, E. Glenn, 'The Impact of Thomas Kelly on American Religious Life', *Quaker Religious Thought* 85 (1995), 11–22.

Kelly, Paul M, 'Thomas Kelly Encounters Nazi Germany: His Letter from Strasbourg, 1938', in *Seeking the Light: Essays in Quaker History in Honor of Edwin B. Bronner*. Edited by J. William Frost and John M. Moore, pp. 183–208 (Wallingford & Haverford, PA: Pendle Hill Publications, 1995).

Kelly, Richard M, 'New Light and Inner Light', *Quaker Religious Thought* 85 (1995), 43–57.

Kelly, Richard M, *Thomas Kelly: A Biography* (New York: Harper & Row, 1966).

Kelly, Thomas R, *A Testament of Devotion* (New York: Harper & Brothers, 1941).

Kelly, Thomas R, *Reality of the Spiritual World* (Whitefish, MT: Kessinger Publishing, 1942).

Kelly, Thomas R, *The Eternal Promise: A Sequel to A Testament of Devotion* (Richmond, IN: Friends United Press, 1988).

Kelly, Thomas R, *A Testament of Devotion* (New York: HarperOne, 1992).

Kelly, Thomas R, *The Sanctuary of the Soul: Selected Writings of Thomas Kelly* (Nashville: Upper Room Books, 1997).

Macy, Howard R, 'Thomas Kelly: At Home in the Blessed Community', *Quaker Religious Thought* 85 (1995), 33–42.

McGinn, Bernard, *The Foundations of Mysticism: Origins to the Fifth Century* (New York: Crossroad, 1991).

Prevallet, Elaine M, 'A Testament of Devotion: An Appreciation', *Quaker Religious Thought* 85 (1995), 23–31.

Schmidt, Leigh Eric, *Restless Souls: The Making of American Spirituality* (Berkeley: University of California Press, 2012).

24

HANNAH WHITALL SMITH

Nineteenth-Century Free-lance
Quaker Heretic

Carole Dale Spencer

On her sixty-ninth birthday, popular spiritual writer Hannah Whitall Smith announced to her wide circle of friends in her usual indomitable style:

> Not to be outdone by the younger generation, I too am preparing something for publication. . . . It is the story of my soul life from my early Quaker days, on through all the progressive steps of my experience until I reach that peace which cannot fail to come to the soul who has "discovered God"! – I am putting all my heresies into my story, and am trying to show the steps that have led to them; and I flatter myself that it is going to be very convincing! So if you feel afraid of becoming heretics, I advise you not to read it.[1]

This chapter explores the life and thought of noted nineteenth-century religious writer, celebrity preacher, and free-spirited product of Orthodox Quakerism, Hannah Whitall Smith. It also examines the Quaker writing culture that shaped her calling and vocation, which she passed on to her children and grandchildren. It will outline her journey from Quietist Quakerism to the emerging evangelicalism and revivalist camp meetings, at the same time propelling her into a more radical universalism and feminism, leadership in the Women's Suffrage and Temperance Movement, and finally across the Atlantic into the British literary and intellectual world of her free-thinking adult children. Her narrative reveals how Quakerism informed her writing and vocation, and it demonstrates both the tensions and the fluidity of Quaker identity in the transitional period of the nineteenth century.

Smith's life spanned a period of profound transformation in the Society of Friends and the changing religious, social, and political culture at large. As she explored the evolving religious landscape and pushed for new opportunities for women in the broader culture, she struggled with how to enact change in the traditional Quaker culture she deeply valued but often found narrow and reactionary. Her life embodied multiple identities and contradictions as she sought to expand her horizons and find a public voice and vocation within radical emergent ideas but also the constraints of the Victorian age. She observed the splintering and gradual enculturation of a large portion of the Society of Friends in the long nineteenth century, and she happily resided as a "heretic" on the outside edge of the Quaker world on both sides of the Atlantic. Calling herself a religious "free lance," she explored and critiqued, often with amusement, her

DOI: 10.4324/9780429030925-27

inherited Quaker tradition, and the many emerging spiritualities, revivals, faith healing, and mind cures of her times. She drifted in and out of the Society of Friends, but Quaker values remained central to her identity throughout her life. She wrote over a dozen books but is best known today as the author of *The Christian's Secret of a Happy Life*, a Victorian self-help book. Her book became an instant bestseller in 1875, was translated into several languages, and is continually reprinted in modernized versions and still in print today. It became a classic of evangelical Christianity. Yet at the same time, it was a book praised by the famous agnostic Harvard philosopher and pioneer in psychology, William James, a close friend of the Smith family. James called her "the mother of pragmatism."[2] Revered for generations by evangelical women, her fierce feminism and unconventional views would surprise and confound most conservative Christians today.

Hannah Whitall Smith was born in Philadelphia into a devout Orthodox[3] Quaker family on February 7, 1832, and died May 1, 1911, in Oxford, England, at age seventy-nine. She was raised in a tight-knit, separatist Quaker community, surrounded by an unusually warm and doting family but also a family of privilege and wealth. Her early journals reveal a loving and happy childhood but also strictly plain. Plain meant following peculiar Quaker customs of plain dress and plain speech distinct from the larger culture and the avoidance of the arts, music, theater, and fictional literature. After graduation from a Quaker day school (the extent of her formal education), she took her first step outside the Quaker fold by joining a reading club, a group of young women who met for education and entertainment. She also began a process of self-education by reading voraciously history, philosophy, natural science, theology, and mysticism, including forbidden fiction,[4] and she began to expand her cultural horizons. But her lifelong regret was that she was never able to become "a thoroughly educated woman,"[5] and she made sure her daughters received the finest college education available for women of the time. Mary attended Radcliffe Annex, the subsidiary institution to the all-male Harvard College, and Alys attended Bryn Mawr College, where Hannah's favorite niece, M. Carey Thomas, was the president. Hannah announced to her close friend, Anna Shipley, in 1873, in her typical forthright style:

> Girls have a *right* to a college education. They ought to be *made* to get it even if it had to be done at the point of the Bayonet. But since the world is not yet sufficiently advanced for that the least parents can do is to open the door very wide to every girl who feels the least desire for it herself. I regret my own loss in this respect every day of my life and the world has cause to regret it too, for as I will be a rather public character and will insist on undertaking to teach, it is a monstrous pity that I have this great lack – of want of education. You don't any of you know what I might have been if I had had it; I do![6]

After her marriage in 1851 to Philadelphia Quaker Robert Pearsall Smith and the death of her first child in 1856, she experienced a crisis of faith, struggled with the idea of eternal damnation, and, for a time, skepticism of all religion. She also became an early supporter of women's rights by joining the Bloomerites, a feminist dress reform movement, promoting a costume that included pants under a shorter skirt, which only a few daring women had the courage to wear at that time. She writes to her sister Carrie in 1857: "Robert & I have become confirmed Bloomerites in our principles. The outrage inflicted upon women by their present style of dress is shameful – they are crippled by it all their lives far more than they know."[7] (It is not known if Hannah ever actually wore bloomers.)

In 1858 at age twenty-eight, she had a life-changing spiritual experience during a public "noon-day prayer meeting" in Philadelphia, which she describes in these terms:

> Then suddenly something happened to me. What it was or how it came I had no idea, but somehow an *inner eye* seemed to be opened in my soul, . . . I do not remember anything that was said. I do not even know that I heard anything. A tremendous revolution was going on within me that was of far profounder interest than anything the most eloquent preacher could have uttered. God was making Himself manifest as an actual existence, and my soul leaped up in an irresistible cry to know Him.[8]

She names this experience her "conversion." A year later she resigned from the Society of Friends, finding Philadelphia Orthodoxy too restrictive and unresponsive to change. While initially traumatic for the family, they soon reconciled.

After her conversion, feeling selfish that she was now among the privileged few, her struggle with the idea of eternal torment intensified. Resolution of her struggles occurred sometime in the 1860s while riding a tram in Philadelphia, when she was given a powerful revelation of the infinite love of God, which would save everyone. In her 1903 autobiography, she describes in three detailed chapters how this inner conviction of what she termed "the restitution of all things" came about. Deemed too controversial for her readership, it is edited out of all subsequent editions of her autobiography. She was convinced that a loving God would not condemn anyone to eternal torment, and she was certain her interpretation of scripture confirmed her revelation.

In 1864 her husband, Robert, became manager of her father's glass company in Millville, New Jersey, a rustic factory town where she was to discover a very different religious and social culture. The mill workers were mainly Methodists, and joining them in their meetings she was introduced to their teaching on sanctification called "The Second Blessing," a crisis experience subsequent to conversion. Holiness advocates viewed sanctification as a breaking in of the Holy Spirit that empowered the individual to live a righteous, obedient, and sin-free life. This experience was often referred to as the "Baptism of the Spirit," a phrase familiar to Hannah and early Quakerism but which she had never understood before. She began attending Holiness revivals, called "camp meetings," and soon became a popular speaker at these events. She felt she had discovered the true inner meaning of Quakerism and became an evangelist for the movement among Friends. But she lamented to her friend Anna in 1871, "My unsectarian position is splendid for giving me an open door among all denominations and I never feel any difference anywhere except when among Friends who are so unreceptive it is like ploughing through mud to talk to them."[9] But eventually, the Holiness revival did transform a large portion of the Religious Society of Friends into the Friends Church, but her tribe, Philadelphia Quakers, remained the most resistant to change.

Although she initially reveled in the emotional drama of the camp meeting experience, in her writings she always warned against trusting one's emotional experiences and emphasized instead the power of convictions and the strength of "the will" (a major theme in all of her books). By 1873 she had become a prominent female religious figure, an international celebrity preacher and best-selling author, and most renowned as a "Bible teacher," and she published several popular books on interpreting scripture. Her fame arose despite the fact that she stood far outside the theological mainstream in holding a universalist view of salvation. Although she did not write about or teach her "heretical" views (until publicly revealed in her autobiography), her universalism was generally known and rarely an obstacle to her speaking invitations or book contracts. She explains:

> It seemed likely that the holding of what was considered by many to be such a grave heresy, might have proved a hindrance to my Christian work; and I dare say it may have been so in some quarters. But as I always had far more openings for work await-ing me than I could possibly fill, I never experienced any difficulty. . . . I was never willing to sail under false colours, nor speak anywhere without its being perfectly well known beforehand what a heretic I was, I enjoyed for the most part all the freedom I desired.[10]

In England and Europe, the Holiness movement became known as the Higher Life Move-ment and later as the Keswick Movement. In its earliest form it was shaped by Hannah and her husband, Robert Pearsall Smith, who also became a popular lay preacher, as they brought their version of the American Holiness movement to England from 1873 to 1875. The Smiths' teach-ing on holiness became known as the "Keswick teaching" and was heavily flavored with Quaker spirituality in its earliest iterations. Hannah's "Bible Readings" were often considered the high-light of their meetings, attended by both women and men, unusual for the time, and despite her known "heresy" of final restitution. The Smiths preached to audiences of thousands, made up of Oxford and Cambridge students, Anglican and Free Church ministers, poets, writers, and English aristocrats. Earnest striving after holiness embodied the religious version of the Roman-tic impulse in Britain. The large gatherings took place in the Lake District of England, where poetry and natural beauty abounded and the intense spirituality of the movement resonated with the romanticism of the Lake poets. Progressive (for the time), inclusive, and ecumenical, it was not doctrinally rigid. Although controversial in its beginnings, it gradually became the epitome of respectable evangelicalism in England in the twentieth century.

But in 1875, just before the fourth large gathering, when the Smiths' were at the pinnacle of fame, scandal erupted when a woman claimed that Robert Pearsall Smith had behaved inappro-priately when he counseled her in a hotel room. Smith claimed that "I do not think my inten-tions would have been more pure to my own daughter."[11] But the rumor mill exploded and led to the immediate departure of the Smiths from England. Robert never recovered from the shame and trauma of his banishment, though many of his friends proclaimed his innocence.[12] He withdrew from public life, lost his faith, and fell into a deep depression. Hannah was loyal and resolute, defending him from what she claimed was libel.[13] After their departure, Keswick spirituality gradually became less open and more conservative, as it was shaped by the forces of fundamentalism in the 1920s.

Returning to the United States from England after speaking at the Higher Life conferences she admits to her friends that "my orthodoxy has fled to the winds. I am Broad, Broader, Broadest."[14] Despite the scandal that caused her husband to lose his faith and withdraw from public life, Hannah proved to be resilient. She turned her attention to the Women's Christian Temperance Union (WCTU), which she viewed as a powerful women's liberation movement, teaching women leadership skills and providing an outlet for a public life of social reform. She became an early leader and long-time friend of Frances Willard, the architect of the movement. Together they steered the WCTU, an evangelical women's social movement, into accepting the radical platform of women's suffrage in 1882 and aligning with the National Women Suffrage Association.[15]

Joining the WCTU in 1874 became a major turning point for Hannah in her life. She was enthralled by the religious, social, and political activism of temperance women. They walked daringly in urban working-class neighborhoods, places they would never ordinarily go, and spoke to people with whom they would normally not interact. Once she shifted her energies to the Women's Christian Temperance Movement, her interests broadened from preaching almost exclusively on sanctification and the inward life to preaching on the outward fruits of a socially aware holiness that addressed issues of social injustice.

Smith became spiritual counselor, guide, and mentor to hundreds of women in her lifetime, who met with her one-on-one, or whom she counseled through her letters.

Her many experiences of listening to the grievous stories of women's abuse and oppression motivated her radical liberationist rhetoric, which comes through forcefully in her letters. She writes to her daughter Mary:

> I wish thee could have heard some of our women. Two new [leaders] have been devel-
> oped during the past year – two grand good women, whose lives had been lived in
> a little narrow circle with no scope for their gifts, until our WCTU came along and
> gave them an outlet. . . . Neither of them are married – they were not willing to go
> into slavery, they declare, let it be ever so gilded.[16]

Smith's feminism had been shaped from her childhood within her Quaker community, which provided women a greater degree of independence and public life as traveling ministers than most religious traditions. From childhood she imagined herself as a minister preaching and traveling across the ocean, and often spoke with great admiration for the Quaker women who modeled such a life for her. She writes, "the perceptible guidance of the Holy Spirit was one of the most priceless of all the gifts that my Quaker inheritance has brought me." And with a strong expression of female agency, she asserts that "no male Quaker, not even the most tyrannical, could curtail the liberty of his womankind, if only they could say they 'felt a concern' for any course of action."[17] To feel a concern was to announce that the spirit was speaking to her and leading her to a course of action that could not be countered by male domination.

She gave her first official public speech on women's suffrage in 1882 and, writing to her daughter, Mary, she relates how she came to this conviction:

> In my speech I said I had come to the advocacy of this reform by the way of the gos-
> pel, that Christ came to break every yoke and set free all that were bound, and that
> I wanted to follow in his steps and share in his work. I said the gospel did not arbitrar-
> ily upset the existing order of things, but it put a mine under all wrong and oppression
> that finally blew it up. And that therefore women were made free by the working out
> of the principles of Christ who had declared there is neither male nor female in Him.[18]

For Hannah, the matter was settled through her reading of the New Testament.

In her autobiography she conveys how she was able to resolve and synthesize the various shifting currents into a meaningful life narrative and reaffirms the core of her Quaker identity at the cusp of a new cultural era. She came full circle back to her Quaker roots and understood their meaning anew:

> Nearly every view of divine things that I have since discovered and every reform
> I have since advocated, had, I now realize, their germs in the views of the Society; and
> over and over again, when some new discovery or conviction has dawned upon me,
> I have caught myself saying, "Why that, was what the early Friends meant, although
> I never understood it before."[19]

She describes her spiritual evolution in these words:

> I feel myself to have gotten out into a limitless ocean of the love of God that overflows all things. My theology is complete, if you but grant me an omnipotent and just creator I need nothing more. "God is love," comprises my whole system of ethics. There is certainly a very grave defect in any doctrine that universally makes its holders narrow and uncharitable, and this is always the case with strict so-called orthodoxy. I find that every soul that has traveled on this highway of holiness for any length of time, has invariably cut loose from its old moorings.[20]

Hannah believed that Quakerism contained universal truths found in every religion though expressed in different ways. In a letter to a friend much earlier in 1879 she declared:

> The pure spirituality of Quakerism is the only thing I believe fitted to meet successfully the demands of the thoughtful minds of this century of doubt and questioning. The 19th century must have a religion that exists *behind* all creeds, and dogmas, and forms.[21]

A Quaker Family Writing Culture

Quaker women from the beginnings of the movement were expected to keep journals, write epistles, and maintain careful records of every kind. Hannah's great grandmother, Ann Cooper Whitall, was a formidable Quaker matriarch and heroine, who left a historically significant journal that details her resoluteness and indomitable spirit during the Revolutionary War. Her legendary great-grandmother's journal captures the sense of divine agency felt by early Quaker women and passed down through the generations. Hannah was raised among Quakers who idealized home and family, but she was also endowed with a fierce spirit of female independence by following her "inward guide." Hannah wrote volumes, both published and unpublished, from devotional bestsellers and bible studies to biography, autobiography, and daily epistles to friends and family. The Smith family wrote daily letters to each other, each one carefully preserved. Over 20,000 family letters are archived, 6000 from Hannah.[22] Autobiographical and biographical writing became a family tradition. Hannah's first major publication was a biography of her son, Franklin, who died suddenly at age eighteen.[23] In 1879, a few years after the surprising success of *The Christian's Secret*, she wrote another biography, this time of her father.[24] Although religious writing ended with her generation, she passed on biographical and autobiographical writing to succeeding generations. Her son Logan Pearsall Smith (1865–1946) was a noted essayist and literary critic. He is most known today for his autobiography, *Unforgotten Years*.[25] He also edited his mother's letters to create a biographical account of her life, *A Religious Rebel: The Letters of "H.W.S." (Mrs. Pearsall Smith)*.[26] Smith's eldest daughter, Mary, married Bernard Berenson, a noted art historian. Mary became a renaissance scholar who wrote pamphlets and scholarly articles on art history.[27] Hannah's second daughter, Alys, did not become a writer but was known for her relief work organizing. She married the acclaimed writer and philosopher Bertrand Russell in 1894, in a Quaker meetinghouse in London.[28] (They eventually separated and divorced, but she adored him her entire life.) All three of Hannah's children and her husband, Robert, befriended the poet Walt Whitman in his later years, and he became a close family friend. (Hannah, however, never quite approved of him, though she became more conciliatory as time went on.)[29]

Hannah's eldest granddaughter, Ray (Mary's daughter), also became a writer, as well as a feminist politician, mathematician, engineer, and artist. She married Oliver Strachey, and thus into the Bloomsbury literary group. She is best known for her book, *The Cause: A Short History of the Women's Movement in Great Britain*. Ray also wrote several novels; one, *Shaken by the Wind*, is a story of religious fanaticism based in part on research, documents, and material collected by her grandmother, Hannah. Later in 1928, she edited Hannah's years of research into new religious movements and published them as *Religious Fanaticism*. Ray also published a biographical account of Smith's life, *A Quaker Grandmother*, in 1914, as well as the biography *Frances Willard: Her Life and Work*,[30] who was one of Hannah's closest friends and colleague in temperance and suffrage work. Hannah's granddaughter, Karin (second daughter of Mary), married into the literary Stephens family, marrying Adrian Stephen, the brother of Virginia Woolf. Karin became one of the first female psychoanalysts and wrote scholarly articles in the field of psychology.

Smith's great-granddaughter, Barbara, eldest daughter of Ray, also married into a literary family. She married Oliver Strachey, the brother of biographer Lytton Strachey of the Bloomsbury Group. Barbara Strachey also wrote *Remarkable Relations: The Story of the Pearsall Smith Women*,[31] which highlighted the lives of the matriarchal family of strong feminist Whitall women. She also wrote the foreword to her mother's work *The Cause: A Short History of the Women's Movement in Great Britain*.

Hannah's niece, Helen Thomas Flexner, daughter of her sister, Mary Thomas, a prominent Quaker minister and also a feminist, wrote *A Quaker Childhood*, in which Hannah as beloved aunt plays a major role.[32] Helen Thomas was professor of English at Bryn Mawr College where her sister, M. Carey Thomas, was the president. Hannah was mentor of M. Carey Thomas and a fierce advocate for women's education. She encouraged and supported her niece, Carey, not only to go to college but also to pursue a PhD in Europe.

The prodigious output of Hannah Whitall Smith and her daughters drew on that "fluid literary space" between public and private in letters, diary, and family biographies that made writing a practice that drew women into deeper community.[33] Hannah's letters were to be circulated to select reading circles and opened up a literary space for recording and valuing women's lives, and also deepened the bonds of a female community and culture. A tradition of strong female agency was passed on through the family writing culture. A resistance to gender norms was handed down, but in ways Hannah did not always anticipate nor welcome. Mary, who left her first husband to travel in Italy with her lover, admitted perceptively to her mother:

> Of course the danger is that I have (I think) no orthodox standards of any kind. Thee, who is such a rebel against orthodoxy in religion, cannot be surprised or shocked if I am a rebel against orthodoxy in conduct. Frank [her first husband] is quite right in saying that the one heresy leads to the other in the next generation at least.[34]

Hannah, though disapproving of Mary's choices, was fiercely loyal to her family, and wrote to Mary:

> I must give you the same liberty I want for myself. . . . I am on *thy side* against the whole world, and even against myself, if this last could be possible, which however I do not think is, for thy side *is* my side always, I guess.[35]

Conclusion

In her sixties Hannah raised her two granddaughters, Ray and Karin, after their father died, and Mary pursued her unconventional life in Italy with Berenson. Hannah went to court, fought to get custody, and won after she agreed to raise them in the Catholic faith of their father, a promise she faithfully kept.

Hannah's radical optimism, captured in her final book titles published in 1906, *Living in the Sunshine* and *The God of All Comfort*, sustained her through the deaths of four of her seven children and into old age and physical disability. Despite the constraints of the Victorian age, including failure of the vote for women in her lifetime, she never lost her chutzpah even at the end of life. She confidently claimed in her autobiography:

> I have always rather enjoyed being considered a heretic, and have never wanted to be endorsed by any one. I have felt that to be endorsed was to be bound, and that it was better, for me at least, to be a free lance, with no hindrances to my absolute mental and spiritual freedom.[36]

Hannah Whitall Smith passed on her independent spirit, her mental freedom, her tireless activism, and her fierce feminism to her daughters and granddaughters, but not her enlightened Quaker faith, or even her buoyant but pragmatic Christian faith. For Hannah, religion was always the great romance of her life. She passed on a Quaker writing culture, the art of letter-writing and memoir to her descendants, most of whom published many books, but none of her children or grandchildren (whom Hannah dutifully raised Roman Catholic) found meaning or solace in religion. Their pursuits and passions instead were directed toward the arts, and high culture, arenas that had been forbidden to Hannah's Quaker generation, but which she cautiously explored in later life with her beloved children and grandchildren.

Her pursuit of holiness never waned but turned into new, pragmatic channels, from the seeking of internal experiences to a reality undergirding all of life, from a focus on personal holiness to the holiness of God who was infinite mercy and love. Her certainty of the theological reality of "the mother-heart of God"[37] and the "restitution of all things" enabled her to maintain an irrepressible faith that gave her no fear of death. She concluded her autobiography by declaring "I await the moment with joy."[38]

Notes

1 L. P. Smith, *Philadelphia Quaker*, 1950, 141.
2 Qtd. in B. Strachey, *Remarkable Relations*, 1982, 73.
3 In 1828 Quakerism split into two branches, the Orthodox and the Hicksite. The Orthodox tended toward a doctrinal and Bible-centered spirituality and the Hicksites toward the Inward Light as the wholly sufficient authority. Both branches valued the nurturing of the inward life and traditional silent worship.
4 Quakers considered the arts, including the reading and writing of fiction, as frivolous, vain, and untruthful from their beginnings and throughout most of the nineteenth century.
5 B. Strachey, 1982, 21.
6 Smith to Shipley, August 14, 1873, Asbury Seminary Library Special Collections.
7 Smith to Carrie, June 10, 1857.
8 H. W. Smith, *My Spiritual Autobiography*, 1903, 172.
9 Smith to Shipley, October 27, 1871.
10 H. W. Smith, 1903, 221.
11 M. J. D. Roberts, "Evangelism and Scandal in Victorian England: The Case of the Pearsall Smiths," *History*, October 2010, Vol. 95, No. 4, 445.
12 For more detailed interpretations of this event, see Carole Dale Spencer, "Hannah Whitall Smith's Highway of Holiness," in Jon R. Kershner, ed., *Quakers and Mysticism: Comparative and Syncretic Approaches to Spirituality* (New York: Palgrave Macmillan), 2019 and M. J. D. Roberts, *History*, 2010, 437–457.

13 B. Strachey, *Remarkable Relations*, 1982, 48.

14 Smith to Mary Beck, August 8, 1876, Box 9. Lilly Library, Indiana University.

15 Frances Willard, *Glimpses of Fifty Years,* 1889, 380.

16 Smith to Mary, January 29, 1882, Asbury Seminary Library Special Collections, Wilmore, KY.

17 H. W. Smith, *The Unselfishness of God*, 1903, 82.

18 Letter to daughter, November 11, 1882.

19 H. W. Smith, 1903, 55–56.

20 H. W. Smith, 1903, 120.

21 Letter to Prisca, December 14, 1897.

22 B. Strachey, 1982, 14.

23 Smith, *The Record of a Happy Life: Memorials of Franklin Whitall Smith,* 1873.

24 Smith, *John M. Whitall: The Story of His Life,* 1879.

25 L. P. Smith, *Unforgotten Years* (Boston: Little, Brown & Co.), 1938.

26 Published in the United States as *Philadelphia Quaker, The Letters of Hannah Whitall Smith, 1949.*

27 She co-wrote *The Venetian Painters of the Renaissance* with her husband, Bernard, though her name was omitted by the publisher.

28 Sheila Turcon, *A Quaker Wedding: The Marriage of Bertrand Russell and Alys Pearsall Smith*, https://mulpress.mcmaster.ca/russelljournal/issue/view/175.

29 For more on the complex relationship between Whitman and the Smith family, see Joann Krieg, "'Don't Let Us Talk of That Anymore': Whitman's Estrangement from the Costelloe-Smith Family," *Walt Whitman Quarterly Review*, Winter 2000, Vol. 17, 91–120 and B. Strachey, 1982, 65–70, 98–99.

30 R. Strachey, *A Quaker Grandmother*, 1914; *The Cause: A Short History of the Women's Movement in Great Britain* (London: G. Bell and Sons, Ltd.), 1928; *Shaken by the Wind,* (London: Faber & Gwyer), 1927; *Frances Willard: Her Life and Work* (London: Fleming H. Revell Company), 1913; Ray Strachey, ed., *Religious Fanaticism: Extracts from the Papers of Hannah Whitall Smith* (London: Faber and Gwyer Ltd.), 1928.

31 B. Strachey, 1982.

32 Flexner, *A Quaker Childhood*, 1940.

33 See M. L. Tarter and C. Gill, *New Critical Studies on Early Quaker Women*, for a detailed analysis of this dynamic in the writing of eighteenth-century Quaker women.

34 B. Strachey and J. Samuels, eds., *Mary Berenson*, 47.

35 B. Strachey, 1982, 70.

36 H. W. Smith, 1903, 220.

37 H. W. Smith, 1903, 214–16. See also "God as our Mother," in Smith, *The Open Secret*, 1885; *Every-day Religion*, 1893, 177–183.

38 H. W. Smith, 1903, 311.

Bibliography

Flexner, Helen Thomas. *A Quaker Childhood*, New Haven: Yale University Press, 1940.

Smith, Hannah Whitall. *The Record of a Happy Life: Memorials of Franklin Whitall Smith,* Boston: Willard Tract Repository, 1873.

Smith, Hannah Whitall. *The Christian's Secret of a Happy Life*, New York: Fleming H. Revell, 1875.

Smith, Hannah Whitall. *John M. Whitall: The Story of His Life,* Philadelphia, 1879.

Smith, Hannah Whitall. *The Open Secret*, New York: Fleming H. Revell Co., 1885.

Smith, Hannah Whitall. *Every-day Religion*, New York: Fleming H. Revell, 1893.

Smith, Hannah Whitall. *My Spiritual Autobiography or How I Discovered the Unselfishness of God*, New York: Fleming H. Revell, 1903.

Smith, Hannah Whitall. *The God of All Comfort and the Secret of His Comforting*, London: J. Nisbet., 1906.

Smith, Hannah Whitall. *Living in the Sunshine*, New York: F. H. Revell Co., 1906.

Smith, Logan Pearsall. *Unforgotten Years*, Boston: Little, Brown & Co, 1939.

Smith, Logan Pearsall (Ed.). *Philadelphia Quaker: The Letters of Hannah Whitall Smith,* NY: Harcourt. Brace and Company, 1950. Published in England as *A Religious Rebel: The Letters of "H.W.S." (Mrs. Pearsall Smith)*, London: Nisbet & Co., 1949.

Strachey, Barbara. *Remarkable Relations: The Story of the Pearsall Smith Women*, New York: Universe Books, 1982.

Strachey, Barbara and Jayne Samuels (Eds.). *Mary Berenson: A Self-Portrait from her Letters and Diary*, London: Hamish Hamilton, 1983.

Strachey, Ray. *A Quaker Grandmother*, New York: Fleming H. Revell Co., 1914.

Strachey, Ray (Ed.). *Religious Fanaticism: Extracts from the Papers of Hannah Whitall Smith*, London: Faber and Gwyer Ltd., 1928.

Tarter, Michele Lise and Catie Gill. *New Critical Studies on Early Quaker Women, 1650–1800*, Oxford: Oxford University Press, 2018.

Willard, Frances. *Glimpses of Fifty Years*, Chicago: H.J. Smith & Co., 1889.

Archival Collections

Hannah Whitall Smith Collection, Asbury Theological Seminary, B.L. Fisher Library, Wilmore, KY.

H. W. Smith Mss, Lilly Library, Indiana University, Bloomington, IN.

25

LOVING "THAT OF GOD"

Participatory Love and the Quaker Way

Matt Boswell

Friends' affirmation that there is "that of God" in every person may be the closest thing to a fundamental, unifying concept in Quaker spirituality. This notion is at least a convenient starting point in a discussion of what makes Friends distinct from other religious streams in the Christian tradition. While it has echoes of perhaps more familiar theological anthropological affirmations – the "imago Dei" or the "priesthood of all believers," to name a couple – the notion of "that of God" communicated a specific and nuanced message about the human person, God, and the relationship between the two when it was first used in seventeenth-century England. Its meaning has certainly evolved over time, with present appeals to "that of God" often drifting (usually quite innocently) from the original usage but arguably retaining much of its initial spirit. While a failure to precisely replicate the spirituality of early Friends (if that were even possible) does not indicate a failure in present-day Quakerism, it is for many reasons worthwhile and responsible to understand "beginnings" – even if later appropriation of this embryonic language has seemingly proven meaningful and fruitful.

This chapter examines the ways "that of God" has been used in the Quaker tradition, from its emergence among early Friends in the seventeenth century to, after being mostly unused for two centuries, its renaissance in the twentieth century. Furthermore, while I will remain faithful to the spirit of early Friends, I will also creatively expand on their understanding of "that of God." In *The Way to Love: Reimagining Christian Spiritual Growth as the Hopeful Path of Virtue*, I presented a model of spiritual formation that conceives of the Christian life as the experience of being trained in the art of Love.[1] George Fox writes in 1656, "then you will come to walk cheerfully over the world, answering that of God in every one."[2] What is "that of God"? Simply put: *it is Love*. How, then, do we answer that of God? Once again: *with Love*.

Margaret Hope Bacon describes "that of God" as the "religious basis for a holy community in which no one had dominance over another," as well the basis for Friends' opposition to war, use of plain speech without titles, and refusal to take oaths.[3] The term certainly implies a sense of universal reverence and respect. The common use of the term in the last century has sustained and emphasized this affirmation of fundamental human worth. For example, the American Friends Service Committee (AFSC) states that "every AFSC program is an expression of the Quaker belief that each person has 'that of God' in them – everyone is equal and should be treated with dignity."[4] AFSC rightly finds energy and direction for its social actions in the Quaker emphasis on human goodness and sacredness. Similarly, the Sierra-Cascades Yearly

DOI: 10.4324/9780429030925-28

Meeting of Friends (SCYMF) speaks of the urgency of a robust response to racial injustice as reflective of "our underlying Truth as Friends: to recognize God in all people."[5] SCYMF's anti-racist statement appeals to this same fundamental truth: that every person (with Black Americans in sharp focus, in this instance) deserves respect because they are of inestimable worth. Yet the extent to which immigrants, racial minorities, and incarcerated persons, for example, are "othered" reveals that this basic truth is easily forgotten. To affirm and answer "that of God" in each contains a call that goes beyond mutual respect. It is a call to *nurture* something sacred within each person. To co-become. To grow into Love, together. "That of God" *is each individual's actual and potential embodiment of God's Love*, flowing from the presence of God within *every* individual.

Puritan Calvinism – the theological context of early Friends – emphasized, among other things, human depravity (a theological underpinning by no means extinct). Despite Puritans' and Quakers' shared critiques of their ecclesial parent (the Church of England), Quakers rejected the "low" Puritan view of the human person, an anthropological assessment that consequently made God, in a way, both relationally and morally inaccessible. To affirm "that of God," in contrast, is to draw God near and to emphasize the goodness of the human person. God is not *confined* to the human person, a claim that might deify the individual in a way that undermines God's transcendence, but God is also not solely outside of the person. To use terms foreign to early Friends, affirming that of God in each person is an implicit critique of theism (God is wholly other than and unbound by humans) that also avoids pantheism (the world, including humans, is identical with God), instead looking more like panentheism – the belief that God is *in* all things and in some ways inextricable from those things, even if God is *not* those things.

God has become flesh in Jesus Christ; the risen and eternal Christ has become and *is becoming* flesh in each person. Early Friends believed each person had something like a "God potential" in them. This is not to say that each person has the potential to become God but that within every person is a potentiality that can be nurtured and developed. This potential is not a pale imitation of God or only *seemingly* God but *truly* God among and within. That certainly makes each individual sacred! But more than that, it implies a sacred *responsibility*: each person is invited to steward God's gracious, unmerited gift of God's own presence. God's grace is thus more than a transaction or declaration from without, but a coming-to-be-within. We might even say that God is *vulnerably* with us, putting God's own agency at the mercy of ours. While God may be, in one sense, "complete" as is, in another sense we are invited to help "grow God" by minding that of God in one another, allowing the Divine Life to grow in and among us.

George Fox writes: "Let your lives and conversation preach, that with a measure of the spirit of God you may reach to that of God in all."[6] Fox urges folks to "mind the seed of God and the life of Christ" within them.[7] He encourages others to "keep in the life, that ye may answer that of God in every man upon the earth."[8] Reaching, minding, answering – these are words that convey attentiveness and responsiveness. "Waiting" is a common motif in many Friends practices, from worship to group discernment. In a way, Fox's exhortations are a call to just that: to wait. To wait long enough to see the Truth in each other, perhaps not evident without slowing down to see it. Something is rising, bubbling up in each person, Friends might say; we are invited to find that "something" and to celebrate it, affirm it, and support its continued rising.

Another term used somewhat interchangeably with "that of God" among early Friends is "the Seed of God." Robert Barclay, arguably the first Quaker systematic theologian, speaks of the Seed as "an invisible principle" in each that "draws, invites, and inclines the individual toward God."[9] We can "hurt" and "wound" this Seed, but where the Seed "is received in the heart and allowed to bring forth its natural and proper effect, Christ is resurrected and takes shape."[10] This Seed can "produce the kingdom of God if it receives its proper nourishment . . .

if it is cherished and received in love."[11] Barclay clarifies that the "seed or light . . . may be quenched, bruised, wounded, pressed down, or slain and crucified," but that God "cannot be resisted, hurt, wounded, crucified, or slain."[12] In other words, God is One worth counting on, since God can outlast the moral failures of humans. We cannot kill God. And yet, we have a *responsibility* and *opportunity* to grow the God-that-is-growing-in-every-one. We are at God's mercy, and yet, paradoxically, as a divinely willed act of grace, God is at ours.

Rufus Jones, writing in the early twentieth century, identifies Jesus Christ as a "person who made the supremacy of Love vivid and vocal and victorious" and a revelation of "what the Heart of God is like."[13] Jones also affirms that "human nature *can* become an organ for the Life of God since it *has been* such an organ."[14] Jones thus fuses together divinity and humanity in a way that retains the distinctiveness of each while uniting them. God is revealed through humanity, and humans find who they truly are through "the Life of God."[15] For Jones, humans have a fundamental nature that gives rise to the possibility and reality of Christ and carry with us that same potential to express "the life of God" (whether or not any person has expressed that Divine Life quite like Jesus Christ). Jones thus affirms the present *and* potential goodness of the human person: we are "good" as we are and have unrealized goodness waiting to emerge.

Friends are a theologically diverse group, of course, and some would later take issue with Jones's characterization of "that of God" as something inherent to human nature. Lewis Benson, in 1970, critiques Jones (and by extension AFSC, heavily influenced by Jones) for misunderstanding Fox. Benson argues that a true and faithful understanding of Fox would recognize "that of God" as "a means of knowing that can be described as seeking counsel of the Creator."[16] Benson claims that God's goal in each of us is not "reactivating a dormant spiritual potential in man" but "re-establishing the link of communication between man and his Creator."[17] Benson bristles at the way he believes many twentieth-century Friends centered an affirmation about the human person as the fundamental Quaker belief rather than the work of Christ in each person. Friends are potentially at risk of spiritual hubris either way – whether displaying moral overconfidence ("just look at how good I could become!") or theological exclusivity ("only those who happen to worship and believe like *we* do have truly encountered the living God"). Benson concludes that we lose the Christ-centered and evangelistic nature of Fox's use of "that of God" by making it a universal affirmation about human nature and would argue that Fox wants people to discover that of God in them as a *pathway* to Christianity.

George Amoss Jr. is critical of both Jones and Benson, offering a more incarnational understanding than the deifying approach of Jones and the knowledge-centered approach of Benson. Amoss identifies that of God as "the indwelling Christ, the divine Logos, the very nature (i.e., love) and righteousness-power of God which can show us our dark condition and lead us into a new, holy life of light, peace, justice, and generosity."[18] Mark Russ echoes Amoss, using the concept of "Shekinah" to suggest "that of God" is "the indwelling of God in all creation" – an approach that Russ believes retains God's unity (not breaking God up into pieces in each one of us), God's otherness (we are not God), and God's nearness (God is present in each one).[19]

One gift of Amoss's and Russ's conceptions of "that of God," beyond being something of a synthesis or "middle way" between the more liberal and evangelical approaches of Jones and Benson, respectively, is how they are conducive to a less hierarchical understanding of "obedience" in Quaker spirituality. Obedience language in Christian spirituality often indicates a low view of the human person, reflecting a deontological ethic in which exemplary morality is expressed through rule or command following. An ethic of virtue, on the other hand, emphasizes human growth while also recognizing that the human, while sacred, is not "good just as they are." In other words, to overemphasize human goodness risks moral complacency. To overemphasize divine otherness can lead Quakers to simply mimic the Calvinist thought to which they reacted. An incarnational approach, emphasizing the free choice of Christ to dwell in the human person, honors the otherness and nearness of God simultaneously. It suggests we possess both *actual* goodness and *potential* goodness, holding these two affirmations in a healthy tension. Thus, to obey "that of God" within is to listen for how the Love that resides in each person is longing to grow and find expression and to, consequently, give ourselves over to this burgeoning "love force" rising within and among us. As Isaac Penington writes, "there is a pure seed of life which God hath sown in thee . . . wait daily to feel it, and to feel thy mind subdued by it, and joined to it."[20] We do not *obey* the God-Who-Commands-From-Above; we *respond* to the God-Who-Is-Love-Within.

Marcelle Martin speaks of the transformative power of this indwelling presence as "God's law written on their hearts" that enables people to receive "divine guidance to change their lives in very specific ways."[21] Put differently, people are *wired* to love. Martin echoes early Friends like Francis Howgill who took the message of Romans to heart: "Ever since the creation of the world his eternal power and divine nature, invisible though they are, have been understood and seen through the things he has made" (Rom 1:20, NRSV).[22] Or in the words of John: "The true light, which enlightens everyone, was coming into the world" (John 1:9). There is "that of God" in all people, primed to become ever more visible and vibrant. Given the presence of this Seed, what then, ought we to do?

In Fox's words, Quakers *answer* it. Elton Trueblood clarifies: "[Fox] apparently meant that it is possible to nurture and bring to fulfillment the vague yearnings toward the divine, which are in all [people], but which are often underdeveloped."[23] The Friends Committee on National Legislation (FCNL) states that their "lobbying starts with listening, seeking that of God in policymakers and partners."[24] FCNL is, in this case, speaking not simply of respecting those in question (policymakers and partners) but of appealing to their compassionate instinct or "love impulse" in hopes of tapping into that impulse. To answer that of God in policymakers and potential co-advocates is to recognize the desire to Love in others, however overshadowed by other concerns, and then to create conditions that give rise to the expression of that Divine Love in tangible ways.

Friends can also turn to Quaker books of Faith and Practice, which, in addition to outlining the norms and practices of a particular regional networks of Quaker meetings, offer queries – questions of self-examination intended to help people find spiritual clarity and direction for action. Consider two queries from Britain Yearly Meeting's book of Faith and Practice: "2. Are you open to the healing power of God's love? Cherish that of God within you, so that this love may grow in you and guide you"; and, later, "17. Do you respect that of God in everyone though it may be expressed in unfamiliar ways or be difficult to discern? Each of us has a particular experience of God and each must find the way to be true to it.[25] The first query implies a synonymous relationship between "that of God" and "Love" and invites each person to be responsive to that Love, that it might grow. The second query affirms the unique way each person is poised to Love; "that of God" in a person is their irreplicable way of expressing God's love. To respect others is to make oneself open to discovering the ways others are equipped to love and then to participate in that Divine Love by celebrating it, receiving it, and nurturing it.

In the Christ-centered yet pluralistic perspective I have presented here, what is at stake is not others' eternal salvation. Something many would call "Christ" is on the cusp of becoming a guiding, formative reality in each person, if they would but awaken to it. The goal of "answering that of God in every one" is not about Christian or Quaker expansion but about nurturing and caring for the Seed of Love in each person – a truly universal, present reality. Quakers do not "bring" Christ to others; they help others see the Christ already present within who is teaching – or, more aptly stated, *training* – people in the ways of Love.

Friends also help liberate people from the oppressive social conditions that would otherwise stifle a person's ability to listen attentively and respond emphatically to that Love within. Friends' ministry of loving "that of God" in others entails a love that is *profoundly* participatory. To say that love is "participatory" is to emphasize one's active engagement in the life of another in a way that affirms and nurtures the Seed of God, empowering it to grow. Friends have testified through their actions that impact carries more weight than intentions and that theology *lived* is more crucial than theology *articulated*. By discovering Love and listening to the leadings of that Love within them, Friends have yielded to that Love by participating in the liberating work of Love through a variety of ways. This is and always has been the true work of Friends, even if the language to express this basic truth has been varied: to learn Love, to cultivate Love, and to responsively and obediently follow that fundamental impulse to Love. This "Love impulse" is more than a fleeting emotion or a self-interested pursuit; it is Christ within, loving the world through the actions of willing collaborators with that Love.

Many Friends have tangibly testified to this sacred responsibility to let that Love within manifest itself. George Fox refused a position in the army of Oliver Cromwell in seventeenth-century England, affirming that he lived "in the virtue of that life and power that took away that occasion of all wars."[26] Fox chose in a very tangible way to be guided by "that of God which is Love" rather than by the envious and lustful motives that undergird war or by mere social conformity. Fox did not follow "a rule" prohibiting participation in war; he permitted Love to shape his imagination and inclinations. This inward journey of transformation created the conditions for his refusal to join the army and laid down a pattern that has energized generations of conscientious objectors to follow who have believed that war is at odds with the inward-dwelling Spirit of God who lives in both those who would kill and destroy and those whose Spirit-dwelling bodies are threatened by war.

Hannah Barnard, an early nineteenth-century Friend who lived not long before Quakers began fracturing into the various streams that exist today, bore witness to that "Love Within" by quite radically rejecting those facets of Scripture that portrayed God as anything but truly loving in a life-affirming way (and was disowned by her meeting for it – a worthwhile reminder that Quakers have often initially rejected those who contemporary Friends have "recovered" and come to celebrate). Barnard questioned biblical portrayals of God as a leader of war, suggesting that the God she knew through lived experience could not have commanded the Israelites to make war on other nations.[27] Her biblical hermeneutic, while non-violent, was also out of step with an emerging fundamentalism in the Christian and Quaker churches whose biblical literalism (albeit a *selective* literalism) made space for such a warmongering God. Her "heresy" (a powerfully undermining word in the hands of anxious defenders of the status quo) arose from her responsiveness to "that of God" within her, a God of Love fundamentally opposed to violence and dominance.

Lucretia Mott, a mid-nineteenth-century Quaker, bore witness to that of God in herself and others. Mott challenged two of the most fundamental elements of the way of the world in her time – the institution of slavery and the belief that women were less entitled to shape their world than men. She rejected two gods at once – the god called "White Supremacy" and the god called "Patriarchy" – living instead in faithfulness to the God of Equality, Inclusion, and Love. Such faithfulness was expressed through her public opposition to wage inequality, her anti-slavery efforts, her traveling ministry, and her critical organizational and vocal role in women's suffrage. Mott, in a speech in Boston in 1841, said that

> when truth directs us, there will be no longer assumed authority on one side, or
> admitted inferiority on the other; but that as we advance in the cultivation of all our

powers, physical as well as intellectual and moral, we shall see that our independence is equal, our dependence mutual, and our obligations reciprocal.[28]

This "guiding truth" of which Mott speaks is "that of God," a power which, when cultivated, leads to justice and equity between genders.

Elizabeth Fry, an early nineteenth-century Quaker (and sister of Joseph John Gurney, the man at the heart of one of the mid-nineteenth-century Friends "splits" that led to the emergence of evangelical Quakerism), bore witness to that of God in every person by answering that of God in prisoners. Fry believed in both the fundamental worth of incarcerated persons and in their need for an environment conducive to true rehabilitation and growth, rather than an environment of neglect and unsanitary living conditions. Fry worked tirelessly on behalf of prisoners. She spent the night in prison to experience it firsthand; she brought clean clothes and food; she helped cultivate self-respect in the prisoners; she cared for the women and children of female prisoners, children who were often products of rape. Fry was also an advocate for other kinds of social reform but also very hands-on, expressing her concern for the poor by visiting the sick, establishing a nightly shelter in London, and teaching poor children to read.[29] Fry's fundamental belief of "that of God" in each person undergirded her tangible efforts to protect, advocate, and nurture the "least of these" (Matt 25:31–46), seeing something truer about such persons beyond the pejorative and dehumanizing labels bestowed by either legal processes or public opinion.

There are many other examples of Friends who were responsive to the leadings of "that of God" within. John Woolman's responsiveness to the leadings of that of God within himself led him, in the eighteenth century, to bear witness to this Love by traveling door-to-door to persuade slaveholders to free their slaves and to avoiding paying for any product of service that involved cruelty to humans or animals. Bayard Rustin manifested this Love by collaborating with Martin Luther King Jr. to promote nonviolent resistance and end racial discrimination before then, later in life, advocating for more dignifying treatment of the LGBTQ+ community, of which he himself was a part – answering that of God in Black and LGBTQ+ folks. Pedro Sosa, a Guatemalan immigrant to the United States who now works for the AFSC and directs the Portland Project Voice Immigrant Rights Foundation, works as an advocate for and protector of immigrants, answering that of God in every newcomer to the United States through organized hospitality and protective advocacy that communicates "you are welcome here." Ruah Swennerfelt (New England Yearly Meeting) is an active participant and leader in the "Transition Movement," a movement focused on "respecting one another and Earth, looking for a transition from a fossil fuel-based consumer society, to one that cares deeply for healthy relationships, walking gently on the earth, and rising to action on behalf of all that lives."[30] Swennerfelt lovingly honors that of God in herself through personal and radical care for the earth; she answers that of God in others by awakening people to God's Love for the earth, inviting them to participate in God's movement to liberate and tend to our entire ecosystem.

Even those "uncelebrated Quakers," faithfully following the Quaker way in their own meetings, have developed established ways of honoring "that of God" in one another. The conviction that every member of the meeting is a minister, expressed through the opportunity for participation in crucial committee work, through vocal ministry in unprogrammed worship, or through a meeting's frequent willingness to follow the leadings of a member to take some collaborative social action – these Quaker practices that testify to the universality of Christ's presence, ministering through each person. When a Friend ministers to others, the unique way "that of God" has taken shape in them empowers that individual's participation in the lives of others. As another example, Quaker meetings for clearness presume that one's inner Teacher is the most qualified teacher.[31] These meetings are composed of folks who help a person find clarity on a "concern" or question when the best way forward is unclear to that person. Discerning this way forward invites others to ask questions that will help the individual come to clarity about the right next step(s) without being imposing or overly directive. Others, in this case, *love* the individual seeking clearness by empowering them to listen to the voice of Love within themselves.

The affirmation that there is "that of God" in every person is a fundamental part of Quaker spirituality, inviting an active response from those who affirm it. Friends are invited to participate in that of God in others and in themselves – affirming its presence, awakening its potential, nurturing its growth, and expressing its sacred beauty in ways that uplift and set free. "It," most plainly put, is the Love of God, dwelling within and among us.

Notes

1 See Matt Boswell, *The Way to Love: Reimagining Christian Spiritual Growth as the Hopeful Path of Virtue* (Eugene, OR: Cascade Books, 2018).

2 George Fox, "The Journal," in *Quaker Spirituality: Selected Writings*, ed. Douglas V. Steere (Mahwah, NJ: Paulist Press, 1984), 93.

3 Margaret Hope Bacon, *Mothers of Feminism: The Story of Quaker Women in America*, 2nd ed. (Philadelphia: Friends General Conference, 1986), 10.

4 American Friends Service Committee, "Quaker Action: Resisting the Continuing Cost of War (Spring 2020)." https://www.afsc.org/resource/quaker-action-resisting-continuing-cost-war-spring-2020.

5 From a "Minute for Black Lives" approved June 13, 2020, at SCYMF's Annual Sessions. https://static1.squarespace.com/static/59791f3537c581de3f155d87/t/5eea707cc6747b0842061865/1592422524509/SCYMF_Minute+for+Black+Lives_2020.pdf.

6 George Fox, "Epistle 319, 1675," in Steere, 134–35.

7 Ibid., "Epistle 52, 1653," in Steere 129.

8 Ibid., "Epistle 150, 1657," in Steere, 131.

9 Robert Barclay, *Barclay's Apology in Modern English*, ed. Dean Freiday (Newberg, OR: Barclay Press, 1991), 85.

10 Ibid., 85.

11 Ibid., 108.

12 Ibid., 85.

13 Rufus Jones, *Quakerism: A Spiritual Movement* (Philadelphia: Philadelphia Yearly Meeting of Friends, reprint edition, 1963), 127.

14 Ibid., 128.

15 Ibid., 136.

16 Lewis Benson, " 'That of God in Every Man' – What Did George Fox Mean By It?" in *Quaker Religious Thought*, Vol. 24 (1970): 5.

17 Ibid., 4.

18 George Amoss Jr. "That of God: A Quaker Reading of Romans 1:16–20," September 2, 2013. https://postmodernquaker.wordpress.com/2013/09/02/that-of-god-a-quaker-reading-of-romans-1–16–20/.

19 Mark Russ, "What Is 'That-of-God' In Everyone?" September 25, 2019. https://jollyquaker.com/2019/09/25/what-is-that-of-god-in-everyone/.

20 Isaac Penington, "The Letters: To Dulcibella Laiton, 1677," in Steere, 147.

21 Marcelle Martin, *Our Life Is Love: The Quaker Spiritual Journey* (San Francisco: Inner Light Books, 2016), 39.

22 See Francis Howgill, *The Invisible Things of God: Brought to Light by the Revelation of the Eternal Spirit Who Was an Ey-witness of the Wonders of the Lord in the Beginning* (London: Printed for Thomas Simmons, 1659).

23 Elton Trueblood, *The People Called Quakers* (Richmond, IN: Friends United Press, reprint, 1971), 36–37.

24 The Friends Committee on National Legislation, "Quaker Lobbying." https://www.fcnl.org/updates/quaker-lobbying-122.

25 *Quaker Faith and Practice*, 5th ed. https://qfp.quaker.org.uk/passage/1-02/.

26 George Fox, "The Journal," in Steere, 74.

27 Barnard, in the same spirit, called Friends to question several sacred beliefs, including some of Jesus' miracles and the "vicarious atonement for the sins of mankind" (David W. Maxey, "New Light on Hannah Barnard, a Quaker 'Heretic,'" *Quaker History* 78.2 [Fall 1989], 64). More than just an emblematic "liberal," that of God within Barnard drove her discovery of a Love-centered theology that discarded what was either too violent (like many atonement theories) or too peripheral (like an overemphasis on miracles).

28 Bacon, *Mothers of Feminism*, 112.

29 Katherine Murray, "Social Justice and Sustainability," in *The Cambridge Companion to Quakerism*, eds. Stephen W. Angell and Pink Dandelion (Cambridge, UK: Cambridge University Press, 2018), 91–92.

30 Ruah Swennerfelt, "Finding Hope," *Nonviolence Magazine*, August 3, 2016. https://nonviolencemag.org/finding-hope-9b6e886d5f79.

31 For a brief but helpful overview of meetings for clearness, see "How to Have a Quaker Clearness Committee," October 13, 2016. https://quakerspeak.com/video/quaker-clearness-committee/.

26

HOW FAR THE THEOLOGICAL MESSAGE OF LIBERAL BRITISH QUAKERISM HAS CHANGED OVER THE LAST FIFTY YEARS

An Analysis of Key Introductory Texts for Enquirers

Hugh Jones

Introduction

This case study presents and discusses recent research into whether, and how far, the liberal[1] Quaker theological message has changed over the past fifty years, as evidenced in four Quaker introductory texts for newcomers and enquirers published in Britain between 1969 and 2011.

The focus was on two current topics of particular research interest:

1   Quaker belief in God (however defined); and
2   Continuing Quaker identification as a Christian religious Society.

At a time of increasing secularisation in the West, the diversity and flexibility of liberal British Quakerism can seem for many a more welcoming spiritual home than more doctrinal religions: a declining majority of Quakers in Britain still profess to believe in a God of some kind, and only a minority still identify as Christian. Does this mean that traditional 'God language', and references to Christ and Christianity, in key Quaker outreach publications are giving way progressively to more neutral, spiritual[2] language?

In fact, quite the opposite was found. Despite increasing secularisation and continuing diversity of Quaker beliefs, over the period, very little dilution in religious language was observed, and all four texts presented consistently robust and positive messages on both issues.

The case study is divided into two parts: Part A surveys the context of Quaker theological and belief patterns, compared with British belief trends, over the period, and Part B describes the Quaker message presented by the four texts.

DOI: 10.4324/9780429030925-29

The Key Texts and Definitions

The four key texts analysed were published between the mid-twentieth century and the first quarter of the twenty-first century:[3]

George Gorman, *Introducing Quakers* (1969)
Geoffrey Hubbard, *Quaker by Convincement* (1974)
Harvey Gillman, *A Light That Is Shining* (1988)
Geoffrey Durham, *Being a Quaker* (2011).

All four were written by well-known Quaker authors of the time and were recommended and distributed free by the Society of Friends in Britain to enquirers and newcomers to Quakerism. Each book devoted considerable space to Quaker religious beliefs.

'Quakers' (or 'Friends') and 'Quakerism' are used here to refer solely to British liberal Friends and British liberal Quakerism.

Part A: The Context

A1: Quaker Theology Over the Past Fifty Years

The liberal British Quakerism that emerged in 1895 reflected modernist Friends' need for a faith that acknowledged modern scientific knowledge. It was nevertheless still then 'a distinctively Christian . . . form of religion' (Martin Davie, 1997:137–138). Pink Dandelion links the liberal thinking, and openness to new light, with 'Progressivism': the idea that God's revelations to humanity are gradual and appropriate to each age (2007:132). It also re-affirmed the foundational Quaker insight, linked directly to the authority of direct experience, now popularly known as 'That of God in Everyone'.

From the 1960s onwards, Davie saw growing liberalism leading to a more general diversity of belief (1997:268). Dandelion, similarly, identifies a definite shift to 'Pluralism' (2007:133).

This permissive and constantly adaptable approach to religious belief, characterised by Dandelion as 'liberal-Liberal Quakerism' (2007:134), ultimately led to a Quaker theology in which whether Friends called themselves Christian or not almost ceased to matter: as Janet Scott put it in the 1980 Swarthmore Lecture: 'what matters to Quakers is not the label by which we are called or call ourselves, but the life' (1980:70).

In the first quarter of the twenty-first century, this growing diversity is a continuing characteristic of British Quakerism. This does not mean, though, that, even in 'liberal-Liberal' Quakerism, 'anything goes'. Dandelion (2007) points out that increasing theological diversity has steadily been balanced by what he describes as a Quaker 'behavioural creed' that manages the right ordering of Quaker Meetings, and equally how Liberal Friends 'live' their faith. For Dandelion, this amounts to a tacit but effective Quaker 'double culture' (2007:137–139), in which British Quakerism is held together not by *what* it believes but by *how* it believes (2007:152).

A2: The British Quaker Survey 2013

The latest statistics for Quaker beliefs indicate a significant general trend towards secularisation, and a corresponding decline both in belief in God and self-identification as Christian. In recent analysis, Dandelion traces a decline in key Christian or religious beliefs amongst British Quakers over three surveys conducted between 1990, 2003 and 2013 (2018). The respective declines were striking:

* Levels of belief in God dropped from 74% in 1990 to only 57% in 2013 – a dramatic decline (but still a majority).
* Levels of self-identification as Christian fell from 51% in 1990 to 36.5% in 2013 (Dandelion, 2018:2).

It is notable how much further self-identification as Christian has declined than belief in God. This is consistent with Dandelion's (2007) characterisation of 'liberal-Liberal Quakerism' (above) and Scott's (1980) argument that denominational labels matter less than 'the life'. However, 36.5% is still a substantial minority, and at the time of writing, the latest (fifth) edition of Britain Yearly Meeting's book of discipline *Quaker Faith and Practice* (2013) is still sub-titled a book of 'Christian' discipline.

A3: British Belief Trends Compared

Although 'the Quakers are not typical of the British population as a whole but represent a very particular demographic' (Dandelion, 2018:2), recent belief statistics for Britain as a whole are not very different. Robin Gill (1999) traces a decline in belief in God from 79% in the 1960s to 68% in the 1990s (1999:509), while the *British Social Attitudes* surveys 2008–2010 report a further decline to 62%.

Gill highlighted contrasting responses on *belief in a personal God* (declining over 12% from 43% in the 1940s to 31% in the 1990s) to those on *belief in God as a Spirit or Life Force* (increasing 2% over the same period, from 38% to 40%; Gill, 1999:509). This supports the view that, in Britain, as Grace Davie (2015) put it: 'there is a continuing shift away from those who believe in a personal God towards those who prefer a less specific formulation' (2015:73).

Linda Woodhead (2016), citing the latest (2013) *British Social Attitudes* survey, reports that those who self-describe in surveys as belonging to 'no religion' have actually now become the majority religious category in Britain: 50.6% in 2013 (2016:246). Woodhead characterises this as mainly due to their youthful age profiles, whereas Christians are much more likely to be older: 'In that sense, Christianity [in Britain] is literally dying out, whereas "no religion" is expanding' (2016:247).

There seems to be little argument that older people are much more likely to profess a religious belief than their children or grandchildren, and Quakers are a significantly older demographic. This is likely to remain a significant factor in any attempts to predict future Quaker belief patterns.

A4: Future Trends

Gay Pilgrim (2003) predicted that diverging tendencies within Quakerism would ultimately lead to schism, with two (or even three) separate Yearly Meetings within Britain by 2050 (2003:156). Although this has not (yet) happened, the prediction of divergence is strikingly similar to Jennifer Hampton's (2014) analysis of the 2013 Quaker survey which identified three distinct tendencies amongst the respondents:

> Traditional Quakers: 32% of the total, 90% of whom believe in God and are more likely to self-identify as Christian;

Liberal Quakers: the largest group with 50%, only 55% of whom believe in God;

Nontheist Quakers: the smallest group at 18%, who do not necessarily self-describe as athe-ist, but may be agnostic or humanist or adhere to spiritual beliefs.

The nontheist movement, in particular, has stimulated much debate about the future identity of liberal Quakerism, particularly about 'God-language', reflected in a 2017 consultation book-let *God, Words and Us* (Rowlands, 2017) sent to all British Meetings.

Part B: The Quaker Message in the Four Texts

B1: How Belief in God Is Presented

Despite all the evidence mentioned above, of decline in respect for traditional religion and widespread doubts about God that characterised the half-century over which the four texts were written, they all presented a remarkably consistent message to newcomers about Quaker belief in God. In fact, 'God' (however defined) is still confidently present in all of them, albeit in the universalist context of 'That of God in Everyone'.

Diversity of Quaker definitions of God is a theme common to all four books. Despite Gor-man's frequent use of 'God language', he is at pains, even in 1969, to stress that not all Quakers share the same belief in God. Hubbard, a former humanist, echoes this a decade later:

For some, [That of God in Everyone] is an extension of the divine presence into the human existence; a linking of man with God through the presence in every man of the Holy Spirit, the still small voice. For others this is not their view, nor their experi-ence. Nevertheless, those who express their experience in very different terms identify a basic shared belief, knowing that they are finding words for the transcendental, that the experience on which belief is based is fundamentally non-transferable.

(1974:69)

Gillman's description of 'a creative, loving power in all people in the world and in the world around' also reflected equal diversity throughout the 1990s:

Many call it God, though it is beyond all names. Everyone can become aware of it directly by listening to its promptings in their hearts and in the hearts of others. . . . The experience of quiet waiting upon God gives [Quakers] strength to go back into the world, the better to serve their fellows.

(1988:17)

While highlighting Quaker diversity, all four books are remarkably inclusive about others' views. Durham, in the twenty-first century, presents 'God language' within Quakerism in nota-bly positive and inclusive terms:

While Quakers have no corporate statement of belief, they are none the less united, all of them, in one great truth: that the human spirit gains resilience, courage and power as a result of communion with the Divine. It is the experience of Quakers that strength and grace come from guidance which is given when they live in single-minded contact with the force for good that many people call God.

(2011:42)

He is particularly inclusive about nontheist Friends who reject the traditional, 'transcendent'[4] concept of God entirely, but he notes 'at the same time their reverence for the life force, for nature, for humanity, [finds] expression in the ways of Quakers' (2011:20).

B2: How Far Quakers Are Presented as Christian

All four authors present a strikingly consistent message about the extent to which Quakers may be described as Christian, while seeing it less as a doctrinal label than as a historic underpinning of Quaker belief. For all of them, it represented a fair characterisation of where many Quakers still felt their religious home to be.

Gorman uses much Christocentric language on Jesus: 'in him we have a window into God, for in his life the love that is God is most clearly seen. Thus Jesus disclosed God to men' (1969:19). Even on the central topic of Christ, however, he emphasises liberal Quaker diversity:

> The Society has never required its members to conform to a particular view about Jesus, holding that the only valid test of Christians is whether they live in the spirit of Christlike love, and not what they say they believe.
>
> *(1969:18)*

Hubbard identifies an underlying Christianity in the Quakerism of his time that for him, despite his humanist background, justifies a positive description of Quaker views of Jesus:

> One interpretation of Christianity we can all accept: we recognise Jesus as a man through whom the divine light shone undimmed . . . wholly God yet not the whole of God. We can accept his teaching, insofar as we have it, and seek to follow it as best we can.
>
> *(1974:78)*

At the same time, he allows for Quaker inclusivity on the subjects of both Christianity and Jesus:

> Friends have re-affirmed repeatedly that they are a religious Society and a Christian Society; [but] they have accepted into membership people whose views cover an exceptionally wide spectrum, including [many] who . . . will not concede any uniquely divine character to Christ.
>
> *(1974:75–76)*

Gillman's book is remarkable in the way it combines a deep knowledge of Quakers and Quakerism with a distinctive empathy for Christianity, particularly in its mystical and monastic traditions. He notes, though:

> However Quakers define Christianity, and there are differences between them, they all see it as making for an open, inclusive community. There are a few who prefer not to use the Christian language at all and even maintain that they are Quaker, not Christian. Certainly very few Quakers in Britain today would accept the conservative evangelical view. Most would say that for them the teachings and life of Jesus of Nazareth were central to the view they have of God. For some Jesus is God in a trinitarian sense; for others he is the human being who has reached his divine potential.
>
> *(1988:25)*

Durham addresses the question 'Are Quakers Christian?' as follows:

> [Although] a large number of Quakers describe themselves as Christian . . . it is prob-
> ably the case that most of these Christian Quakers don't take a literal view of certain
> parts of the Bible, tending to consider some of its narrative to be symbolic of the
> human search for God rather than the actual truth. Yet I also know Quakers for whom
> particular episodes [for example, the resurrection] are a literal truth, a living reality on
> which they base their lives. And the point is that no one is arguing about it. People's
> beliefs are personal to them: often shared, sometimes questioned, but never decried.
> Quakers learn from each other.
>
> *(2011:48)*

He also describes his own initial

> deep, unyielding scepticism [about Jesus] but in the stillness of my first Quaker meet-
> ing, I felt a wound beginning to heal. I still fail to understand the divinity of Jesus but
> I am relaxed in the company of many Quakers for whom it is a given . . . it has helped
> me to know who I am. . . . And I am astonished to find myself acknowledging today
> that I am a Christian Quaker.
>
> *(2011:48)*

For these reasons, he describes most Quakers in 2011 as comfortable with 'Christ-language', but like all the other authors, he stresses 'what matters to most Quakers is not what you say or think, but what you do' (2011:49).

Conclusion

As foreseen in the introduction, the initial hypothesis underlying this research (that comparison of four introductory texts written over fifty years of secularisation might reveal a gradual dilution of 'God' and 'Christian' language) has decisively *not* been realised. On the contrary, all the texts presented a robust and consistent message on both key issues.

Belief in God, in the universalist context of 'That of God in Everyone', is consistently presented as a feature of liberal Quakerism in all four books, although each one stresses the diversity of belief and definitions of God among British Friends.

Equally, each author presents a strikingly consistent message about the extent to which inclusive liberal Quakers may be characterised as Christian, albeit in the context of an underlying Christian ethos that values the way Quakers live their lives more than doctrinal labels.

This surprising constancy in expression of two key Quaker beliefs has been maintained despite the evidence of declining Quaker belief patterns over the period.

Perhaps one explanation for this continuing constancy may lie in recognition that even liberal British Quakers are a significantly older demographic than the population as a whole, and as such are statistically more likely to believe in God (or at least feel spiritually at home within a religious group many of whose members do).

Overall, the message presented of liberal British Quakerism is of a diverse, inclusive Society of Friends that still seems to be finding unity in its foundational belief in 'That of God in Everyone' (despite varying definitions of God), and which at the time of writing continues to self-describe as both a 'religious' and a 'Christian' Society.

Notes

1 As defined at Part A1.
2 As opposed to 'religious' (particularly in the orthodox or doctrinal sense): see Gill's alternative characterisation of belief in God as a spirit or life force at Part A3.
3 Full publication details for each book are listed in the References section.
4 In the sense of having independent or objective existence (especially as a 'transcendent' creator or supreme ruler 'up there' or 'out there'), as opposed to a purely human creation, myth or symbol.

References

British Quaker Survey (2013): see Hampton (2014) below, and www.woodbrooke.org.uk/data files/ CPQS/initial_findings_Quaker_ Survey 2013 pdf.pdf

British Social Attitudes Survey 2013: at www.brin.ac.uk/british-social-attitudes-2013

British Social Attitudes Surveys (2008–2010): at www.brin.ac.uk

Dandelion, P.: *An Introduction to Quakerism*, Cambridge, Cambridge University Press (2007).

Dandelion, P.: *The British Quaker Survey 2013: Believing and Belonging in a Secularising Society*, Birmingham, UK, Woodbrooke (2018).

Davie, G.: *Religion in Britain: A Persistent Paradox* (2nd edition), Oxford, Blackwell (2015).

Davie, M.: *British Quaker Theology since 1895*, Lewistown, NY, Edwin Mellen Press (1997).

Durham, G.: *Being Quaker*, London, Quaker Quest (2011).

Gill, R. [and Hadaway, K. and Marler, P.]: 'Is Religious Belief Declining in Britain?' *Journal for The Scientific Study of Religion* (1999), pp. 507–516.

Gillman, H.: *A Light That is Shining: An Introduction to Quakers*, London, Quaker Books (1988).

God, Words and Us, see Rowlands.

Gorman, G.: *Introducing Quakers*, London, Quaker Home Service (1969).

Hampton, J.: 'The British Quaker Survey: Examining Religious Beliefs and Practices in the Twenty First Century' *Quaker Studies* (2014), 19/1.

Hubbard, G.: *Quaker By Convincement*, Harmondsworth, UK, Penguin Books (1974), and London, Quaker Home Service (1985).

Pilgrim, G.: *The Quakers: Towards an Alternate Ordering* (ch.12 of Davie, Woodhead and Heelas: *Predicting Religion*), Aldershot, Ashgate (2003).

Quaker Faith and Practice (2013): see Yearly Meeting of the Society of Friends (Quakers) in Britain.

Rowlands, H.: *God, Words and Us: Quakers in Conversation about Religious Difference*, London, Quaker Books (2017).

Scott, J.: *What Canst Thou Say? Towards a Quaker Theology*, The Swarthmore Lecture, London, Quaker Books (1980).

Woodhead, L.: 'The Rise of 'No Religion' in Britain: The Emergence of a New Cultural Majority' *Journal of the British Academy* (2016), 4, pp. 245–261.

Yearly Meeting of the Religious Society of Friends (Quakers) in Britain: *Quaker Faith and Practice* (5th ed.), London, Religious Society of Friends (2013).

27

QUAKER DECISION-MAKING MEETINGS THROUGH THE AGES

Consistency and Variation

Judith Roads

Quakers have been making decisions collectively for over three hundred years, guided by the 'sense of the meeting'. What is this distinctively radical approach? How has it endured, and how has it evolved over that time? This chapter answers these questions primarily through the lens of internal evidence provided by minute books that have come down to us since the late seventeenth century. Most of the findings refer to principles and practices adopted by Quakers in Britain, but the underlying consistency is clear in Quaker business meetings across the anglophone world. My analytical approach is more linguistic than historical, and the flavour of this case study reflects that. Minutes written in other languages may present a greater variation to the principle. The chapter explores typical preoccupations of Quaker meetings in past eras inferred from internal evidence in archived minuting texts and reviews usage of 'God' language retrieved from the data through corpus-based textual analysis.

Much of my data comes from British sources, and I am not able to scale up reliably to make generalisations about present-day practice worldwide. However, I believe the theological basis for the 'method' to be broadly common to all Friends, no matter the varieties of tradition among the Quaker world's Yearly Meetings.

Underlying Principles

Decisions are taken collectively, and all those present have equal authority through reliance on listening to God. A potential variety of theological positions appears to be no barrier to working through agenda item issues no matter the Quaker tradition of any particular meeting. There is no chair, but the Friend steering the process, called the clerk, is expected to follow the collective wishes of the meeting which itself is dependent on following the guidance of the Spirit at the time. Individuals may with permission of the clerk offer spoken contributions that facilitate the emerging final outcomes. In many Quaker traditions the practice is based on silence, but clerks have the temporary authority given to them to ensure collective and personal discipline during the meeting as a core practice. Friends present know that they are seeking not consensus or unanimity but *unity*, sometimes referred to as the Truth. I return to this point later.

DOI: 10.4324/9780429030925-30

Each decision or outcome is recorded by an unusual process of collective drafting and editing during the meeting. The meeting comes to one mind both for the content to be recorded and for the detailed wording, with the clerk obediently making editorial changes following the wishes of the group. Typically, minutes written in English (even in early modern times) use the present tense for decisions (e.g., *this meeting agrees . . .*), indicating the contemporaneous nature of the collective minute drafting. The ensuing authority resides with the agreed minute(s), not with any one individual or group, and no subsequent changes to the wording may be made. There is no voting, as that would create majorities and minorities and perceived power gaps. Later in this chapter we will inspect sample minutes from various periods in Quaker history.

The approach set out above is still radical today, both in terms of process and where power lies or does not lie. In past centuries, this departure even from Christian decision-making groups would have been seen as even more radical. No paid priests were present in Quaker meetings to lead the faithful; instead there was a sense that all had equal standing within the membership. All had equal access to hearing the will of God and thus the right to speak in the meeting and be heard. Having said that, from a social perspective the existence of separate women's meetings for much of Quaker history means that what earlier Friends understood by 'equality' may not be the same as present-day Friends see it. Women could act as clerks in their own meetings, but their meetings had to defer to the men's meetings for many of the issues (see, e.g., Polder 2015).

Differences Found in Early Quaker Minutes

My evidence for much of the description of practices in past Quaker business meetings in Britain comes from a collection (or *corpus*) I have made of minutes from several local, regional and national Meetings, clerked by different Friends over the years and ranging across three centuries until the mid-nineteenth (see Roads 2019). Software analytical techniques enable a degree of generalisation to be indicated and interpreted, and my findings in this chapter derive from these investigations. I claim to infer from the internal evidence of the historical minutes that the principles and procedures just outlined differ little today from the earliest days of the Society. Nevertheless, there are cultural and contextual differences in terms of the business being considered and the various concerns of earlier Meetings. I grouped these under broad headings of behaviour; persecution, imprisonment, and other sufferings; financial matters and relief of hardship; premises and meeting house matters; distribution of printed material such as tracts; routine or required business matters such as nominations, membership and deaths; and of course spiritual commentary. Some of these issues are dealt with by meetings still today, but many have disappeared from the record.

To give a flavour of these, I offer below some examples, not by category but by types of minute. Let me explain. In the Britain Yearly Meeting present-day tradition, clerks typically draw on a variety of minuting formats and styles to deal with matters that appear on the agenda. These include variations on these broad types. Naturally, real-life minutes rarely conform neatly to categories:

- Administrative minutes of record (merely noting brief facts);
- Minutes of exercise (a more discursive style where elements of the preceding discussion might be noted by the meeting, as well as outcomes and future actions);
- Administrative minutes of nomination and membership (noting appointments to roles and release of service), recording admission of new members to the Society, births, marriages, deaths and funerals.

The selection below is drawn from local, regional, yearly, elders meetings and Meeting for Sufferings in London, and is illustrative of minutes from the entire span of dates 1669–2014.

Minute of record – finance.	John Fly gives an account that there is in his hand five pounds for poore friends. [Ratcliff Monthly Meeting 1685]
Minute of exercise.	This meeting has been introduced into a lively exercise on this deeply interesting subject. Under a deep sense of the solemn responsibility which rests upon us, as individuals and as a church, we would commend this subject to the serious thoughtfulness and sympathy of our members; desiring that, in dependence upon heavenly guidance in all efforts for the good of others, they may humbly yet earnestly seek for ability to do all the Lord's will, in spreading among the unenlightened, whether abroad or at home, the knowledge of the unsearchable riches of the Gospel of Christ. Under this feeling it is concluded to refer the further consideration of this important subject to the following Friends, to report to our next Yearly Meeting. [Meeting for Sufferings 1860]
Continuing minute of record of intention of marriage.	John Lindoe Son of Thomas & Sarah Lindoe of Norwich and Margaret Ellington of Epping, Daughter of Thomas Ellington deceas'd & Margaret his Wife him Surviving, appear'd at this Meeting and openly declared their Intention of taking each other in Marriage. The Young Man produced a Certificate Signifying his Father & Mothers Consent, also a Certificate from Friends in their Monthly Meeting at Norwich Testifying his Clearness in Respect to Marriage & Sober Conversation. The Young Womans Mother being present, gave her Consent, this Meeting Appoints John Squirrel and William Blacaby to Enquire into the Young Womans Clearness and Report to next Meeting. [Enfield Monthly Meeting 1748]
Minute of record and action regarding poor behaviour.	It was ordred & agreed that Thomas Tudway Thomas Curtis or Joseph Coale goe to him, & sharply reprove him for it, & advise him to owne his condemnation before those men whom he so misdemeand himselfe: to the disshonoure of that holy truth which he hath some time made profession of. [Reading Elders 1669]
Minute of discipline and backsliding contrary to Quaker practice.	It being signifyed to this Meeting that Johanna Fletchter – widow, is gone into the World for a housband [husband], & is marryed by a Priest, Joan Woodcock, & Martin Fisher, is desired to speake to her & to report to the next Meeting his answer. [Westminster Quarterly Meeting 1683]
Administrative minute of report and future action.	It is reported that some of those Friends which are Appoynted to doe theire in[derver] to keepe the dores [doors] quait [quiet] from rude boys and other rude Multitude do not theire duty therein therefor it is desierous that they be put in mind the next Monthly Meting to be more carefull therein. [Ratcliff Monthly Meeting 1684]
Minute of exercise and spiritual counsel.	God has preserved us as a faithful remnant, and yet God does not intend that we be stuck in the past. We need to allow the Holy Spirit to show us where and how to move ahead, how and what to think outside the box. . . . We take to heart the Scripture "You have not chosen me, [Jesus], but I have chosen you." We may be given opportunities for service at any time. We seek to strengthen our sense of community, of being a body in Christ's service, and to instill that sense in our children and the people who join us as adults. [Ohio Yearly Meeting 2014]

Minute of record – sufficings	The business of the Friends in prison in Southwark for refusing the sword in the . . . Courts of power to propose oaths is now questioned and lies before the Judges of the Kings Court to determine, and it's left with the prisoners immediately concerned to retain Counsel to argue the matter or other wayes and to Report the case for further consideration to the 6 Weekes Meeting. [Meeting for Sufferings 1678]
Minute of record of a death and burial.	We record that . . . of xxx Meeting who died on xx November was buried at Wanstead Burial Ground on 30th November. We send our love to his wife and family at this time. [North East Thames Area Meeting 2014]

Answers to Queries

In London (now Britain) Yearly Meeting the process of regularly responding to routine and rigidly defined Queries became a large part of the business of all types of regional and local Quaker meetings. The 'Answers to Queries' was the dutiful completion each year of what surely became a very tedious exercise as the tick-box requirement became more and more empty. This activity emerged around the end of the seventeenth century and remained – as something of a burden – until well into the nineteenth century. Rufus Jones (1921) sets out a comprehensive summary of the practice by overseers in 17th-century meetings of providing a series of *Advices*, collected organically over time, and of expecting *Answers* on a regular basis. The aim initially was the regulation of the outward manner of living by members.

> At first the Queries were formal questions asked for the sake of securing information in reference to the number of members suffering under persecution . . . for the first 100 years answered only once a year to give definite information to the Yearly Meeting, for example: "Does Truth prosper among you?"[3]

This is what London Yearly Meeting in 1759 was moved to minute:

> We observe with sorrow by several of the answers from the respective Quarterly Meetings that notwithstanding there is too much Unfaithfulness in some respecting the maintaining many of our Christian Testimonies yet it does not appear that all the Monthly Meetings take care to advise and Admonish such. It is therefore the earnest request & desire of this Meeting that whenever any deficiency appears in particular persons in not maintaining or coming up in our Ancient Testimonies, that due Care be taken by the Monthly Meetings in proper time to Admonish & deal with such, in the Wisdom of Truth.
>
> *(London Yearly Meeting 1759)*

As time went on this practice became ever more cumbersome as increasing numbers of Queries were formulated and needed replies. The Yearly Meeting in 1755 revised and enlarged these questions but by 1792 they had developed into a single uniform set, with provision for written answers and for the next hundred years:

> Answers were minutely drawn up, scanned, discussed, considered, revised until almost every member knew the Queries off by heart and could forecast the answers with almost unerring precision.[4]

Rufus Jones muses that such a formal detailed way of answering the Queries was 'almost certainly a mistake.' At any rate, the practice led to the bloating of many sets of Quaker minutes. As the fifth edition of *Quaker Faith and Practice* (Britain Yearly Meeting) explains, in 1833 the set of *Advices and Queries* was completely re-written and expanded. Their purpose was no longer mainly disciplinary but became more of a set of pointers for Friends' personal use. The present practice of collecting and periodically revising the *Advices and Queries* today in many Yearly Meetings is a happy solution to that outdated burden from the past.

'God' Language in Minutes

Quaker business meetings differ from secular committee, political or workplace meetings in consciously working under the guidance of God. One would therefore expect to find this recognition stated clearly and often in the minutes. Well, yes and no. This section looks at the frequency or otherwise of the mention of *God* or *the Lord* over the centuries and what terminology was used in the past in British meetings. An analysis of my collection of minutes covering the three centuries before the present hundred years shows that the most frequent alternative word for *God* or *Lord* was *(the) truth*. The item *Jesus (Christ)* occurs very infrequently, as does *(the) Light*. Other near synonyms such as *the seed* and the *inwardguide* are not present in the data. This does not mean that clerks never used them – my collection is not exhaustive – but that scaling up the numbers from my sample would indicate likely frequency.

According to Rex Ambler (2007), there were several senses of truth as used by seventeenth-century Friends in the minutes:

- 'Reality itself' – that is, not merely a version of the truth that is merely imitation or misrepresentation (perhaps an early instance of putting a spin on an element of the truth);
- An expression of reality as observed in an image or a statement – so more a semiotic symbol than reality itself (perhaps comparable to Plato's (2007) allegory of the cave, in which the inhabitants took the shadows of unseen reality beyond the cave for the truth itself);
- A realisation of reality as applied to human life (perhaps the modern equivalent would be integrity).

Ambler claims that George Fox saw *truth* as 'the reality beyond our deceit and selfish distortion'.

As this is becoming rather metaphysical, let us return to the evidence of the minutes for examples of usage by Quaker clerks. The following phrases or clusters occur reasonably frequently, and an inspection of the contexts leads me to interpret them in this way:

- *Friends in Truth*: the Quaker community; the title they often applied to themselves;
- *Truth's prosperity*: the religious life of the community; furthering God's will;
- *The general cause of Truth*: Friends' message and witness in their personal and community lives;
- *The wisdom of Truth*: what God is telling Friends to do and to be;
- *(In) the service of Truth*: actions stemming from the leadings of God;
- *Preservation and growth in the Truth*: being faithful to following God after the manner of Friends.

Unfortunately, space precludes providing extensive examples of most of these in their contexts, but we can consider one phrase that presents itself with relatively high frequency in the minuting corpus, the two-word cluster *of truth*.[1] The corpus analysis software I use (*WordSmith Tools*) has a feature that can generate concordance lines of all the occurrences of a chosen word or phrase. Figure 27.1 presents a selection of these, and when the full list is retrieved, patterns can be detected as well as raw frequencies. In the case of the selection shown in Figure 27.1, the lines are sorted alphabetically by first left of the central phrase and then by second left. These examples bring up both *truth* and *the truth*. The word was not always capitalized back in the seventeenth-century and in any case had no underlying significance one way or the other.

Before we leave this exploration of lexical items that broadly denote a sense of *God*, there is one concept that is central to Quaker decision-making with reliance on the Spirit, and that is *the sense of the meeting* – mentioned in the introduction to this chapter. It is commonly heard during present-day business meetings and occasionally included in the minuted text. Here is an extract explaining the understanding of this concept in the current (fifth) edition of *Quaker Faith and Practice* as adopted by Britain Yearly Meeting:

> Our meetings for church affairs, in which we conduct our business, are . . . meetings for worship based on silence, and they carry the . . . expectation that God's guidance can be discerned if we are truly listening together and to each other, and are not

N	Concordance
1	our hands to promote the general Cause of Truth, it is recommended to Friends to stand
2	in the behalfe of John Jigger For Friends of Truth in Barksheire These /Deare/ Freinds &
3	, Friezland & Gilderland there is a breaking out of truth, some hath some drawings that way, &
4	that he may experience the quickening power of truth, and that such a happy change may be
5	. Showing how contrary it is to the Principle of Truth, and the great sufferings that comes on
6	Meeting, or Travel amongst them in the service of Truth. That, in each Monthly Meeting, there be
7	to Admonish & deal with such, in the Wisdom of Truth. A proposition for the Encrease of Unity.
8	to such thoughts & reasonings as are not of the Truth, but against it; the Lord would yet shew you
9	it. And Therefore haveing a tender regard unto the truth of God and all who in any measure are
10	Guns and Bearing Armes Act contrary to Truth, being not agreeable thereto. And therefore

Figure 27.1   Selected concordance lines showing instances of the phrase *of truth*

N	Concordance
1	Marriage, laid down last year. It is the sense of this meeting, that all Friends
2	left to their consideration." And it is the Sense of this Meeting that Friends of
3	Whitehead to read over, & and give the sense of it to this meeting. W.Bennet
4	it, desiring it to be the Judgement or Sence of this Yearly Meeting, &
5	and Judgement of this meeting. It is the sence & Judgement of this meeting that
6	part, & stil eaten out the good sense & inclinations, that God in his
7	this Meeting have declared their Sence and Judgment is that G.K. hath
8	the Kindred, and to have regard to the sence and Judgment of the Yearly
9	unanimously agree & have it to be the Sence and Judgement of this meeting.
10	Meeting House the 13, 3 mo. 1695. The Sence and Advice of the last Yearly
11	and opposed the great Travell tender Sense and Desire of the said Yearly
12	the matter, I desire to give my contrary sence and desire to keep to the
13	whether he has answered those the Sense and Advice which, in the name
14	friends have throughly ... weighed, the sense & advice of the Meeting was,

Figure 27.2   Selected concordance lines for collocations of *sense/sence*

blinkered by preconceived opinions. It is this belief that God's will can be recognised through the discipline of silent waiting which distinguishes our decision-making process from the secular idea of consensus. We have a common purpose in seeking God's will through waiting and listening, believing that every activity of life should be subject to divine guidance.

(*Quaker Faith & Practice 2013, para 3.02*)

Was the concept or even the phrase commonly used by earlier generations? A search in the corpus retrieves several instances, and Figure 27.2 presents a selection plus their adjacent contexts. So the answer is yes: it was there from the start though with spellings and collocating phrases that would rarely or never be found today. (A definition of *collocation* is the juxtaposition of a particular word with another word or words with a frequency greater than chance.) There are some interesting pairings here: *judgement, advice, desire* and so on.

Present-Day Practices and Variations

Many of the core preoccupations that Meetings deal with today have been with Friends since the earliest days: membership matters, finance and hardship issues, spiritual exhortation or acknowledgement of the necessity of waiting on God for guidance. The practice still endures of drafting, agreeing and recording minutes that must not be subject to change outside the meeting. But what do Quakers typically no longer see in most yearly, local and committee minutes? One dominating one is the reproof of backsliding and insisting on correct behaviour that the Queries engendered. Anecdotal evidence in the modern era indicates a less rigid approach to the insisting of adhering to many customs 'after the manner of Friends', as the old phrase has it. So marrying out of the Society or 'marrying before a priest' are no longer reasons for disowning a Friend or terminating membership.

Wearing a sword is a custom lost by time, but the Peace Testimony is broadly kept to in more subtle ways, such as through conscientious objection. Friends in many (but not all) countries no longer have to pay tithes to the established church, but they commonly refuse to swear an oath on the Bible if the law of the land does not offer affirmation as an alternative. Some will choose punishment rather than comply, so suffering for conscience sake is still widely a possible action before Friends. Integrity and strict adherence to Truth is characteristically a Quaker trait, both collectively and individually. Discipline and discipleship is encouraged by meetings but not punitively. Friends still do not vote to determine the way forward for a meeting. Meetings still expect to wait on God, mostly on the basis of silence and spoken contributions, in order to be led to the sense of the meeting and thus to right action; many would describe this in terms of following the will of God. Meetings around the anglophone Quaker world may have different theological language to describe and explain what is going on in these gatherings, but the outward conduct appears to be a precious practice familiar to all Friends. In essence, the Quaker method of conducting decision-making meetings is a long-standing custom that endures.

Summary

The collection of earlier minute books that form the basis of my corpus of historical Quaker minutes in English makes for a plentiful pool in which to fish for a greater understanding of the principles and practices of Quaker decision-making through the ages. The chapter has explored contextual preoccupations that have no modern relevance, as well as an investigation into specific language usage in minutes. By contrast, it has offered a nuanced and reassuring look at strands of religious and pragmatic practices that are recognisably similar to those experienced in many of today's Quaker business meetings. I conclude with a quote from George Fox in which he gives timely advice for those embarking on decision-making together:

> Now dear Friends, let there be no strife in your meetings, nor vain janglings nor disputings. In all matters of business, or difference, or controversies, treat one another in such things kindly and gently, and be not fierce, or heady and high minded. Be careful in all your meetings that they be kept peaceable, in the wisdom of God, which is pure, peaceable and easy to be entreated, that, being ordered by the pure, gentle, heavenly peaceable wisdom, easy to be entreated, they may be holy and virtuous examples to all others. Let all be careful to speak shortly and pertinently to matters in a Christian spirit and dispatch business quickly and keep out of long debates and heats; and with the help of the Spirit of God, keep that down which is about questions and strife of words and tends to parties and contention.'
>
> *(George Fox, Epistle, 1683)*[2]

Notes

1 Also frequent is the cluster *of God*; for example: *wisdom of God / fear of God / sight of God / love of God / assistance of God*.
2 Fox, G. 'To the Quarterly Meeting at York'. Ed. Nickalls (Epistle 383, in Works, v 1:67–93). (1831). https://esr.earlham.edu/qbi/gfe/index.htm
3 Jones, R. *The Later Periods of Quakerism* (London: Macmillan, 1921), Vol. 2, p. 128.
4 Jones, R. *The Later Periods of Quakerism* (London: Macmillan, 1921), Vol. 2, p. 140.

Further Readings

Ambler, R. *The Truth of the Heart: An Anthology of George Fox*, revised ed. (London: Quaker Books, 2007), p. 169.

Fox, G. 'To the Quarterly Meeting at York'. Ed. Nickalls (Epistle 383, in Works, v 1:67–93). (1831). https://esr.earlham.edu/qbi/gfe/index.htm

Jones, R. *The Later Periods of Quakerism* (London: Macmillan, 1921), Vol. 2, pp. 128–145.

Muers, R. and Burton N. 'Can We Take the Religion Out of Religious Decision-making? The Case of Quaker Business Method'. *Philosophy of Management* 18 (3) (2018), 363–374. http://eprints.whiterose.ac.uk/132292.

Plato. *Republic*, trans. Desmond Lee, 2nd ed. (London: Penguin Random House, 2007).

Polder, K. *Marriage in the True Church: The Seventeenth-century Quaker Marriage Approbation Discipline* (Farnham: Routledge, 2015).

Quaker Faith and Practice, 5th ed. (London: Britain Yearly Meeting, 2013). paras 1.04, 3.02.

Quaker Life, Britain Yearly Meeting. *How Quaker Meetings Make Decisions* (2006). www.quaker.org.uk/documents/how-quaker-meetings-make-decisions-2006

Quakers and Business. *The Quaker Business Method*. https://qandb.org/resources/publications/150-quaker-business-method

Roads, J. *Sweetness in Unity: Three Hundred Years of Quaker Minuting* (London, 2019). [Details of the minute books corpus are listed here].

Scott, M. *WordSmith Tools* 5.0, *A Suite of Programmes for Corpus Analysis* (2008). http://lexically.net/word smith/version6/index.html

28

QUAKER DECISION-MAKING PROCESS

The Case of Burundi Yearly Meeting

David Niyonzima

The Burundi Yearly Meeting

Quakers in a given region unite to form a Yearly Meeting which is usually named after the geographic area. For example, Quakers in Burundi are referred to as being under the Burundi Yearly Meeting, meaning that they gather yearly to have a business meeting to deal with issues relevant to its members as an organization.

Before going as a missionary to Burundi, Arthur Chilson served as superintendent of Kansas Yearly Meeting of Friends. In its meeting at Lawrence, Kansas, in 1932, the Kansas Friends decided to send Arthur Chilson, his wife, Edna, and daughter Rachel for mission work. They arrived at Kibimba, Burundi, on April 20, 1934, according to Arthur Chilson's diary (Choate 1965:7).

The decision-making process for sending the Chilsons revealed the state of decision-making practices among Kansas Friends. Seeing that the process was not new to the Chilsons, it was their turn to teach it to Burundi Quakers. Those who joined the Burundi Yearly Meeting soon discovered that the business meeting in which decisions were made was an integral part of the life of Quakers as a denomination and part of their worship. They learned early on that "the goal is to be gathered by Christ into a common understanding of his will for the group, and when that happens, it truly is a 'spiritual gathered' event" (Anderson 2006:39).

Quakers in Burundi believed that the same Holy Spirit who gathers in worship also leads in the decision-making process (Anderson 2006:15). Since Quakers in Burundi believed that the Holy Spirit could direct both the individual and the group "to reach right policy decisions", actions were normally taken on approval rather than by voting (Roberts 2006: 9).

Concerning the governance of Quakers in the early days of their work in Burundi, it was evident that it emphasized that the decision-making process was to be exercised in a way that eliminated the possibility of any individual authority. "Individual leadings were to be tested against the corporate discernment and were ultimately subordinate to the authority of the gathered meeting" (Halliday 2010:10). Quakers in Burundi believed that only the authority of the group acting by the leading of God was valid, because they had time to pray together (Brinton 2002:123). The most important element in the Burundi early Quakers' decision-making process was to consider the authority of the group to be essential. Some consider this

DOI: 10.4324/9780429030925-31

equivalent to what Halliday called "corporate discernment", which is often advocated by Quaker groups.

Values of Decision-Making Process on Which Quakers in Burundi Built

The Quaker decision-making process sought to stand on principles and values just as every community has its own guiding principles. Those values were crucial in that they determined their interaction as community. One of the forgotten things, especially in the religious communities, is that knowing the values is not enough until they are acted upon and applied. Regardless of the gap that has been evidenced among the Burundi Yearly Meeting, the values, adapted from Fendall et al. in *Practicing Discernment Together: Finding God's Way Forward in Decision Making* (2007), were considered as important for their growth as a community.

The Process

For Quakers in Burundi, the process of decision-making as practiced during meetings for business has a listening component as a central feature. According to Fendall, listening includes three practices that facilitate decision-making: (1) worship sharing groups; (2) threshing meetings; and (3) clearness groups. These practices have been so crucial to the decision-making processes. Please consider the following details pertaining to each one.

1   A worship sharing group session focuses on a question of a particular interest. If the group is small enough, all members may speak and the session may even be organized as a go-round. There is no discussion following contributions. Worship sharing is particularly useful for opening up an issue, enabling feelings and thoughts to be shared without the expectation of a particular decision. Quakers usually exercise this type of practice to ease tensions among elders, especially when they realize that an arisen issue has the potential to divide the local meeting leadership.

2   Threshing is an expression that is used in the perspectives of Quaker decision-making processes. It is a term that is well understood by agriculturalists, especially when they are harvesting their dry crops. They thresh their crop by removing the coverings of wheat or rice. The concept is that issues have layers, and that not all the layers are necessary. Just as it is understood that the threshing of the grain separates the edible part from the stalks, so is the process helps the participants to analyze what can be taken and accepted or what cannot be good for them. This practice is used especially when a controversial decision has to be made. A threshing group meeting may build on the worship sharing group in which a session is done to provide an opportunity for participants to discuss a topic of a controversial nature. It can simply be facilitated in a way it takes a question–and–answer format. However, as surprising as it can be, this threshing session, according to the Quaker tradition, does not have the capacity to make decisions, even when a good direction is elicited! The point is to enable participants to hear each other's point of view on issues, explore arguments as put forward, test out their own thinking on each other to find out how they are taken, whether negatively or positively, and deepen their understanding of the issues. Threshing normally precedes a formal business meeting where a decision is to be taken.

Sometimes, when an item before a business meeting turns out to be controversial, a threshing session may be arranged to allow for detailed discussion and exploration in small groups where everyone may have an opportunity to express themself at ease. The item is then brought back to a later business meeting, and the decision becomes often much easier because the tension might have cooled down during the smaller threshing groups.

3   Clearness groups are another practice that is used among some Quakers. Even though they were not very much used in the Burundi Yearly Meeting, they contribute to the smoothness of the decision-making process. These groups are used to support an individual rather than to practice corporate discernment. A small group of Quakers meets with a person seeking to make a decision to support them in reaching a certain clearness. The intention is not for the group to make the decision for the individual. In fact, the participants are discouraged from giving any advice. The process usually starts with a person explaining the decision being considered. Fendall et al. (2007:131) says:

> Early Quakers had "meetings for clearness"; some still follow this practice today. On one level, the meaning of the clearness is the same as clarity, but there is a richer meaning that indicates the absence of any hindrance to discernment, inwardly or outwardly. Individually and in the groups, we come to clearness by the patient process of discernment of the Holy Spirit's leading.

The idea is that participants in the group get involved mainly by asking questions to the person who is considering a particular decision and to encourage them to look at different dimensions before the decision is taken. The questions do not necessarily need to be answered right then in the session, and the person may not make the decision until later at their convenience. Sometimes a clearness group meets several times, depending on when the question is or is not explored, to the satisfaction of the one who has requested for it.

The Facilitation

Quakers in general have a common process through which decisions are made, known as the Quaker Business Meeting. This process includes aspects that are becoming commonly used in the consensus approach. The uniqueness of this process is that it involves a special inner discipline. The Quaker understanding of this method is that it facilitates a discovery of God's will or allows the participants to discern God's direction, which is the leading of the Spirit or the "sense of the meeting" (Willcuts 1992:75). Other religious groups or religious denominations use the expression "a sense of God's presence at any time in the meeting" (Williams 1997:58).

Decision-making during a Quaker business meeting is always facilitated by a clerk, almost similar to an executive officer who chairs an assembly. As well defined in *Practicing Discernment Together*: "We have taken the term *clerk* from the traditional Quaker word for the presiding officer. As expressed in this book, the leadership of the clerk is a spiritual exercise, a very different process from serving as chairman" (Fendall 2007:131). Along with the spiritual exercise in the process, the responsibilities of the clerk, with the assistance of a co-clerk, include the preparation of the meeting for business. This preparation entails a careful planning of the items to be considered and the projected time the meeting will take. The clerk prepares the draft agenda and makes sure that the participants receive it well ahead of the meeting, sometimes two weeks or even a month in advance.

In the next phase of the business meeting, the clerk has to introduce the draft agenda and make any changes as they are suggested by participants. The clerk is careful, and encourages participants to maintain their focus on the items in hand. They ensure that the time is kept according to what was set in the beginning. The harder part of the clerking is when it comes to putting together ideas of the participants in order to make a decision. The "minutes"[1] are carefully drafted in a way they reflect what everyone seems to be agreeing on. Once they are announced, the participants are invited to make comments on them.

It is the responsibility of the clerk to listen to what the participants are saying and draft a minute that captures the leading of the Spirit. This "leading" therefore becomes a position or a point of view around which the participants can unite. It might occur that such a position is given by one participant, but most commonly, the minute is drafted based on many contributions presented at the meeting. The minute is usually agreed upon by the participants at the time of drafting, but sometimes the clerk may work on it during a break and bring it back for consideration and approval. Once it is agreed upon, it is not changed and therefore becomes a resolution of the participants to which they all adhere. Traditionally, there is no voting in the process, although in the course of history, some Quakers, like those in Burundi, vote during all the decision-making processes.

The decision-making facilitation is the ability to arrive at a decision after due consideration of all the factors involved. People need guidance from God about how they should make up their minds on difficult issues. The clerk skillfully facilitates the process in such a way that participants do not attach themselves to personal positions but accept the sense of the meeting. This is usually not easy on the part of the participants. It has happened in the past that a leader might want to introduce their personal "leading" or a point to be implemented and sought the meeting to simply "bless" it. This has often led to disagreements and participants feeling that they are being used or forced to support a personal bias. It has been hard, especially among those who use voting as a way to settle on minutes.

In such a situation, the difficulty is to know whether those who vote for the resolution have really taken time to listen worshipfully and discern the leading of the Spirit or the sense of the meeting. Those voting against the suggestion of the leader are often viewed as unsupportive of the leadership, as unfortunately has been witnessed in the past among Quakers. This is perhaps why Willcuts (1984:77) believed that voting was an invitation to division, in the sense that "the secret ballot only allow anonymity instead of unity". It is the duty of the clerk to work on the minutes until they are accepted by the participants. If an individual has a serious doubt about the minutes, Quakers usually allow an opportunity to express it.

The minutes may record that one or more Quakers were uncomfortable with the decision, that they have indicated their willingness to respect the sense of the Meeting and stand aside. If even one Quaker indicates that he or she cannot possibly agree to the minutes, the decision should not be taken, and the Meeting should minute that it has been unable to reach a decision. In such a case, an alternative such as this suggested by Dean and Shelley, is considered: "Sometimes, if we still don't have oneness of opinion, we'll table the matter for another meeting. This gives time for emotions to cool, facts to be assembled, and more prayer to be offered" (Dean et al. 1984:39). It is better to table the matter than to take a hasty decision that will not be owned by the participants.

The sad thing occurs when, during the facilitation, the views of those against the minutes are marginalized, ignored and rejected. This often leads to painful breaking of relationships or sometimes even splits among the participants. The clerk is considered as a servant leader of God and of the participants during the whole process. They must not be attached to whatever outcome and must be careful not to introduce personal interests. They must obey what God is saying through the people and facilitate unity.

The Role of Participants

Participants have a number of qualities that are expected of them. Just as the clerk comes to the meeting for business prepared, also the participants are expected to come to the meeting with a certain discipline. This discipline entails the following qualities:

1   Come well prepared, that is, having reflected on the agenda. It must be remembered that the agenda for the meeting has been sent to them well in advance. The hope is that they have had an opportunity to pray about and explore items to be discussed before they come to the meeting. Usually, when the participants are not prepared, the process takes longer than necessary.

2   Come to the meeting with an open mind and heart, with a readiness and willingness to change their own point of view and to listen and adhere to the "leading of the Spirit." The open heart of the participants is of great significance because it prevents the participants from coming to the meeting with a hidden agenda, a position to defend and a leader's idea to support, as it sometimes has been observed, regrettably.

3   Be careful not to interrupt others' contributions. Just like in the worship, the understanding is that contributions that people bring forth are from the leading of the Holy Spirit. This is where respect of each other is exercised, seeing that Quakers hold that "there is that of God in every human being." In respecting each other, Quakers who feel shy or who are reluctant to contribute will be encouraged to say what is on their minds. But when they are interrupted, they will be prompted to stop and assume that their contributions are not important.

4   Seeing that the spoken contributions come from the Holy Spirit, participants try their best not to speak from prepared contributions. This is where the discipline of listening is exercised. Prepared contributions usually come from hidden agendas, especially when participants have come with a plan to push forward. When this happens, the leading of the Holy Spirit is blocked and people end up following their own minds.

5   Stand to speak only if they have a substantive addition to make to what has gone before. As far as possible, contributions should be constructive, seeking to build on previous contributions or offer a different view rather than to debate the points others have made or to justify one's own points. This discipline is rather hard for those who think they should be heard on any point that is brought forward. These persons sometimes do not even care for what others have said previously and never give any credit or acknowledgement to prior discussants.

Much of the discipline of Quaker business meetings is quite subtle and it is best conveyed through experience rather than in writing. Barry Morley comments that the business method cannot be taught, but it can be learned (Morley 1993:307). For example, contributions are normally considered and offered without strong emotion, making space for alternative points of view. The Wiltshire Quarterly Meeting in 1678 set down advice on the conduct of Quaker business meetings and gives ideas that could guide participants' attitude during a meeting in which decisions are made:

> For the preservation of love, concord and a good decorum in this meeting, 'tis earnestly desired that all business that comes before it be managed with gravity and

moderation, in much love and Amity, without reflections or retorting, which is but reasonable as well as comely, since we have no other obligation upon each other but love, which is the very bond of our society: and therein to serve the Truth and one another; having an eye single to it, ready to sacrifice every private interest to that of Truth, and the good of the whole community.

(Britain Yearly Meeting 1995:19)

Spiritual Discernment as an Answer

A return to a spiritual discernment that has always characterized the Quakers could be an answer. Spiritual discernment is a channel that brings God's directions to the seeking hearts. "A group discernment process is essentially a process of listening carefully to God. . . . As we listen for God's voice, we do not at the same time compose our next words, as though we needed to rebut our opponent's statements in a debate" (Fendall et al. 2007:43–44).

This is a discipline that is expected of the participants in the decision-making processes. Anderson (Anderson 2006:39–45) gives us very significant elements concerning discernment that must be taken into consideration in the Quaker decision-making process: (2) The matters that concern the direction of the entire community deserve the searching of all. (2) Because business is for worship, the question should be "what is the leading of Christ in our midst?" (3) Because no individual possesses all of God's truth, the contribution of each who has something to say is essential. (4) Where there is a conflict of perspective, the issue must be sorted until the genuine issue(s) of disagreement is (are) clarified. (5) Friends must agree to wait until there is clarity of leading and then support the decisions made in unity. (6) Not all concerns and understandings are of equal weight, but the important thing is for people to feel that their views are attended and understood by others. (7) The goal is not to make a particular decision, but to come together in unity in aspiring to follow Christ's leading above all else.

While these elements, principles and values do not guarantee a successful decision-making process always, they are at least a tool through which the Spirit facilitates Quakers to make decisions that are according to God's will and leading. Those values will not only usher the smoothness of the meeting during a decision-making process but also will help the participants maintain healthier relationships as they depend on God's direction to make their decisions.

Note

1 "The singular word *minute* is not normally used, but some Quakers speak of a minute as the individual statement capturing the discussion and the action that follows in the discernment process" (Fendall et al. 2007, 132).

References

Anderson, Paul. (2006). "The Meeting for Worship in Which Business is Conducted – Quaker Decision-Making Process as a Factor of Spiritual Discernment," *Quaker Religious Thought* 107: 26–47.

Brinton, Howard. (2002). *Friends for 350 Years, Pendle Hill Pamphlet*. Wallingford, PA: Pendle Hill Publications.

Britain Yearly Meeting of the Religious Society of Friends. (1995). *Quaker Faith and Practice*. London: Britain Yearly Meeting.

Choate, Ralph. (1965). *Dust of His Feet*. Mweya, Burundi: Grace Memorial Press.

Fendall, Lon, Jan Wood and Bruce Bishop. (2007). *Practicing Discernment Together: Finding God's Way Forward in Decision Making*. Newberg, OR: Barclay Press.

Halliday, Robert. (2010). *Mind the Oneness: The Foundation of Good Quaker Business Method*. Euston Road, London: Quaker House.

Merrill, Dean and Marshall Shelley. (1984) *Fresh Ideas for Administration & Finance*. Carol Stream, IL: Christianity Today; Word Books.

Morley, Barry. (1993) *Beyond Consensus: Salvaging the Sense of the Meeting*. Wallingford, PA: Pendle Hill Publications.

Roberts, Arthur. (2006). *The People Called Quakers*. Newberg, OR: Barclay Press.

Willcuts, Jack L. (1984). *Why Friends Are Friends*. Newberg, OR: Barclay Press.

Willcuts, Jack L. (1992). *The Sense of the Meeting*. Newberg, OR: Barclay Press.

Williams, Dan. (1997). *Starting (and Ending) a Small Group*. Lifeguide Bible Studies. Downers Grove, IL: InterVarsity.

29

THE WORK OF EQUALITY

Supporting Quaker Women in Ministry

Ashley M. Wilcox[1]

> Do we honor Friends' traditional testimony that men and women are equal? How
> do we work to make these ideals a reality?
>
> *New York Yearly Meeting, Faith and Practice (2001: 85)*

Since its early days, the Religious Society of Friends has held forth the promise of equality for
women in ministry.[2] However, equality is easier said than done. In this chapter, I will begin by
describing some of the ways early Friends tried to support women's equality, through traveling
ministry, the women's meeting, and recording women as ministers. These efforts had inconsistent results: they solved some problems while creating others. Next, I will discuss some current
attempts to support women in ministry, through women's gatherings for mutual support and
a renewed interest in recording. These efforts to support Quaker women in ministry also have
benefits and downsides. If Friends are to fulfill the promise of equality, we must be clear about
our past and present and actively pursue ways to support women who are called to ministry in
the Religious Society of Friends.

Early Friends' Support for Women in Ministry

Traveling Ministry

One of the early ways that Quaker women found support in ministry was through the practice of traveling ministry. These traveling ministers were called "Public Friends" and included
women who were unmarried, married, and those with children. They journeyed in pairs and
preached in places other than meetinghouses, including town halls and courthouses – places
traditionally for men (Larson, 1999: 11). According to Rebecca Larson, "There were an estimated thirteen hundred to fifteen hundred women ministers active in the transatlantic Quaker
community during the first three-quarters of the eighteenth century" (1999: 63). The expectation was that their preaching and influence would go beyond Friends to the non-Quaker world
(Pullin, 2018: 234).

These women felt called to traveling ministry by the Holy Spirit, but there were mechanisms
in their home meetings to regulate their ministry – in particular, the traveling minute. When

DOI: 10.4324/9780429030925-32

a woman had a leading to travel in the ministry, she would appear before the ministry committee of the meeting, which would decide whether to grant her a traveling minute based on her ministry, health, and family obligations (Bacon, 1986: 33). The request would then go to the quarterly and yearly meeting. Once the meeting provided a traveling minute, the minister's home meeting was responsible for her expenses, with the expectation that the meetings she visited would provide hospitality. This financial support made the traveling ministry possible, but it could also be a form of control (ibid.).

Women's Business Meeting

Another way that early Friends supported the equality of women was through the creation of a separate women's business meeting that had the same structure and met simultaneously with the men's business meeting. This was an imperfect solution. On one hand, the women's meeting allowed women who did not travel to learn new skills, through writing their own minutes and in their roles as clerks and treasurers, as well as giving them the freedom to control their own agendas, funds, and discipline (Pullin, 2018: 14). These separate meetings also gave women a space to speak on matters of business when they might have been too timid to do so in the presence of men (Bacon, 1986: 21). But on the other hand, these separate meetings gave the men's meeting more formal power by giving the men's meeting final authority to make decisions, taking power away from women (Gill, 2005: 164).

The process of creating a separate women's meeting was not always smooth. When the proposal was brought forth in 1753 to have a women's meeting in London Yearly Meeting, some Friends resisted it, arguing that a body could not have two heads. In response, Rebecca Jones, a preacher from Philadelphia reminded Friends that the head of the church is Christ, and male and female are one in Christ (Larson, 1999: 229–30). The women's meeting in London Yearly Meeting was finally established in 1784, following the example of women's meetings in America (ibid., 230).

The power these women's meetings held varied from place to place. Generally, the responsibilities of the women's meeting were to watch over the members' moral behavior, provide for the poor and ill, examine couples' readiness for marriage, and educate the children (Bacon, 1986: 43). The women's meeting advised the men's meeting but did not have the power to ensure the outcome of their decisions (Holton, 2007: 11). Because these meetings ultimately proved unequal, women pressed for the merging of the men's and women's meetings in the late nineteenth and early twentieth centuries (Bacon, 1986: 181).

Recording

A third way that early Friends supported women's equality and gifts of ministry was by recording women as ministers. Friends believed that only God could make a minister, and Friends would recognize (not ordain) the gifts of ministry given through these individuals (Larson, 1999: 59). After a Friend had spoken several times in meeting for worship, the monthly meeting would discern whether it was in unity with the ministry, which would then go to the quarterly meeting. Elders encouraged developing preachers and would watch for weakness in ministers or ministers outrunning their gifts (ibid., 62–63).

In London Yearly Meeting, a visitor would write their name in the book, and if no one challenged the name, the minister was accepted as a member of the meeting of ministers (Kershner, 2017: 9). In America, ministers with a certificate could minister in other meetings and sit on committees of ministers and elders (ibid.). But as with other attempts at equality, some opposed women having equal status in ministry. In London Yearly Meeting, conservatives tried to exclude female preachers from the meeting of ministers and elders (Larson, 1999: 229). Others tried to subdue women who spoke too long or with too much passion in mixed assemblies for worship, arguing that these women prevented men from service (ibid., 39; Bacon, 1986: 23).

Recording gifts of ministry continues in many Friends meetings and churches, but some Liberal Friends have discontinued the process. Some argue that laying down recording ended a two-tier system of membership that consolidated power in the ministers and elders, while others point to this as a shift from Quakerism as a mystical spirituality to a Society of Friends based on ethics and duty (Spencer, 2007: 227). Some yearly meetings that still make provision for recording in their Faith and Practice have functionally discontinued the process without providing for alternative systems of support and accountability for those called to public ministry (Chestnut Hill Friends Meeting, 2012).

Current Support and Challenges for Quaker Women in Ministry

Although there are more opportunities for women in ministry across denominations now than at times in the past, there are still a lot of voices telling women that they cannot do ministry. According to a 2017 study, 85% of the pastors in the United States are men, even though women are much more likely to pray, attend services, and say religion is important to them (Quealy, 2017). Many Quaker women in ministry came from other denominations; some say that the fact that Quakers allow women in ministry attracted them to Friends (Wilcox, 2011: 1–2).

Women's Gatherings

Ministry can be lonely work, and women have found formal and informal ways to provide mutual support. More informal ways include spiritual friendships, mentorships, and ongoing mutual support groups. Gatherings such as the Pacific Northwest Quaker Women's Theology Conference and the United Society of Friends Women International Triennial Conferences provide more formal support for Quaker women in ministry.

The Pacific Northwest Quaker Women's Theology Conference began in 1995 with the goal of bringing together women from the Evangelical and Liberal Friends traditions (Abbott, n.d.). The conference has continued to meet every other year since and has become a place where women support each other in ministry, using narrative theology to share their faith and understanding. In preparation for the 2020 conference, the organizers noted that this type of "women only" space "continue[s] to be necessary given the harmful nature of our larger patriarchal and misogynistic social climate" (Pacific Northwest Women's Theology Conference, 2020). The organizers also explicitly named that the conference is for all self-identified women, including cis and trans women and people whose gender is more fluid (ibid.). This conference is in many ways like the women's business meeting, a place where women can discern and develop their gifts, and those who are further along can help them find their voice.

The organization known as the United Society of Friends Women International (USFWI) began in 1881 to support Quaker women in missionary work (United Society of Friends Women International, n.d.). The mission of USFWI includes meeting in local churches, meetings, and homes for study and supporting mission programs. USFWI also holds triennial conferences in various locations for members to meet globally. Gatherings like these conferences provide much-needed support for Quaker women in ministry, but they are limited by geography, size, and branch of Friends.

Recording

Another way to support Quaker women in ministry, as in the past, is through recording. Recording is an issue of gender equality. As Johan Maurer says, "The *denial* of recognition of public ministry, especially when denying people who by social stereotype are not seen as carrying spiritual authority, can represent the opposite problem – a form of marginalization" (Maurer, 2007). He goes on to say that the story of gender equality among Friends "could probably not be told without knowing how many women never even considered the possibility of being pastors for lack of encouragement or role models" (ibid.). By strengthening the recording process, Friends support women's ministry.

In theory, recording is a simple concept: the meeting observes the minister and records their gifts of ministry. However, recording processes now span from nonexistent to overly complex. As noted above, some yearly meetings have laid down the practice of recording entirely. Others have overly complex processes that can take many years and include requirements that are more stringent than a seminary degree. At worst, recording processes can get bogged down in political, social, or theological disagreements (Kershner, 2017: 13), with meetings refusing to record people from particular demographics (particularly women and LGBTQ+ people). In addition, because recording processes are so inconsistent, if a minister is recorded in one meeting and moves to another, the minister may have to give up their recording or go through an entirely different recording process. Protracted recording processes can be traumatic, especially for women who have been told in other contexts that they are unfit for ministry.

Considering the inconsistencies and trauma involved in recording, why not give up the practice entirely? One reason that Friends have not eliminated recording is that many Friends today feel called to work as chaplains. Even meetings that say they do not record ministers will provide a minute recording the ministry of a person who needs one for chaplaincy certification. Chaplains are an example of the type of calling that ministers feel – an echo of the early Friends who would leave their homes and families for months to follow a leading to share Friends' message inside and outside of the Religious Society of Friends.

Even in meetings that do not formally record ministers, Friends recognize that some people feel called to ongoing public ministry. There is a vast difference between feeling led to speak in meeting occasionally and feeling called to a life of sustained, public ministry. Some meetings have recognized this sense of call in Friends who feel led to ministry, especially when the ministry extends beyond the meeting and lasts longer than one trip (Chestnut Hill Friends Meeting, 2012). In situations like this, the meeting may give the minister a minute of service or an ongoing traveling minute. Although the meeting may not call this recognition of ministry a recording process, that is essentially what it is. Friends are recording while saying that they do not record, and it would be more straightforward to just call this a recording process.

There are many other reasons that increased support for recording would be beneficial for Friends. Generally, recording provides support and accountability for people who are called to sustained public ministry. Recording provides a path for mutual support: ministers who are doing the same work can identify and find each other. These relationships can include role models, mentors, and those who feel called to educate people feeling called to ministry. Recording creates a historical archive of those who are active in ministry among Friends. In addition, recording creates a parallel to ordination for Friends called to ecumenical ministry. Recording is a way to recognize the gifts of ministry that God has given to the meeting and the Religious Society of Friends through individuals. Expanding the recording practice makes space to recognize a diversity of ministers and gifts.

Recording also benefits the meeting where the minister is a member. By recording, the meeting gives its backing to ministers as they go out, letting others know that the minister is a member of the meeting in good standing and the meeting has recognized their gifts. The meeting can ask ministers to provide regular reports on their work – a place to reflect, inform, and connect with the home meeting. This oversight protects people from ministers who have outrun their guide and may do harm. It is also a way to protect ministers from harm, which may be physical, sexual, spiritual, or emotional – the minister has a way to report harm or the fear of it to their meeting. At heart, recording should be about recognizing gifts of ministry and nurturing these gifts for the good of the Society. This is not about raising up individuals, but rather a way to recognize gifts of ministry that are central to Friends' message.

Conclusion

I began this chapter with a query from New York Yearly Meeting: "Do we honor Friends' traditional testimony that men and women are equal? How do we work to make these ideals a reality?" (2001: 85). Equality does not just happen; we have to do the work. Friends have done and continue to do some of the work of equality, but we still have work to do. Fortunately, supporting women in ministry benefits the Religious Society of Friends as a whole. Let's do the work of equality so that people of all genders may flourish in ministry.

Notes

1 I am grateful to the archives at Guilford, Earlham, and Swarthmore Colleges for their research assistance, as well as Emily Provance, Peggy Senger Morrison, and Lloyd Lee Wilson, who sent resources. Thanks to everyone who helped me shape the ideas in this chapter, especially Troy Winfrey. In memory of Patty Levering.
2 Note on gender and location: historically Friends had a generally binary understanding of gender (cis men/women, although one in the Holy Spirit). This understanding of gender has evolved for many Friends. When I talk about support for women in ministry, my intention is to have an expansive definition of women, including cis and trans women and non-binary femmes. My hope is for a Religious Society of Friends where people of all genders can flourish. In addition, this chapter focuses primarily on the experiences of Quaker women in England and America. I recognize that Quaker women's experiences globally differ from the ones depicted here, and that women of color face particular challenges in these contexts.

Bibliography

Abbott, Margery Post, 'Brief History of the Evolution of the Pacific Northwest Quaker Women's Theology Conference,' https://www.pnwquakerwomen.org/conference/a-brief-history-of-pnwqwtc.

Bacon, Margaret Hope, *Mothers of Feminism: The Story of Quaker Women in America* (San Francisco: Harper & Row Publishers, 1986).

Chestnut Hill Friends Meeting, 'History of Minuting Ministry Among Friends' (2012), https://www.quakercloud.org/cloud/minutes/history-minuting-ministry-among-friends.

Gill, Catie, *Women in the Seventeenth-Century Quaker Community: A Literary Study of Political Identities, 1650–1700* (Aldershot, UK: Ashgate Publishing Ltd., 2005).

Holton, Sandra Stanley, *Quaker Women: Personal Life, Memory and Radicalism in the Lives of Women Friends, 1780–1930* (London: Routledge, 2007).

Kershner, Jon R., 'A Brief History of the Quaker Practice of "Recording"' (2017).

Larson, Rebecca, *Daughters of Light: Quaker Women Preaching and Prophesying in the Colonies and Abroad, 1700–1775* (New York: Alfred A Knopf, Inc., 1999).

Maurer, Johan, 'Recording Ministers; Calling Pastors' (June 14, 2007), https://blog.canyoubelieve.me/2007/06/recording-ministers-calling-pastors.html.

New York Yearly Meeting, *Faith and Practice: The Book of Discipline of the New York Yearly Meeting of the Religious Society of Friends* (New York: New York Yearly Meeting, 2001).

Pacific Northwest Quaker Women's Theology Conference, 'Widening the Circle,' http://www.pnwquakerwomen.org/conference/widening-the-circle-for-2020.

Pullin, Naomi, *Female Friends and the Making of Transatlantic Quakerism, 1650–1750* (Cambridge: Cambridge University Press, 2018).

Quealy, Kevin, 'Your Rabbi? Probably a Democrat. Your Baptist Pastor? Probably a Republican. Your Priest? Who Knows,' https://www.nytimes.com/interactive/2017/06/12/upshot/the-politics-of-americas-religious-leaders.html.

Spencer, Carole Dale, *Holiness: The Soul of Quakerism* (Milton Keynes: Paternoster, 2007).

United Society of Friends Women International, 'History of USFWI,' http://usfwi.net/history.

Wilcox, Ashley M., 'Gifts to Share: Stories of Women Who Are Recorded Ministers' (2011).

30

WILLIAM PENN'S PRAGMATIC CHRISTOLOGY

A Christian Philosophy of Religion(s)

Benjamin J. Wood

Introduction: The Meaning of Pragmatism

What theological resources do contemporary Quakers have for living in a religiously plural world? The discussion in this chapter attempts to answer this question through an extended dialogue between the Pragmatic philosophy of William James (1842–1910) and the Christology of the early Quaker polemicist William Penn (1644–1718). The goal of this unlikely fusion of personalities is to recover a distinctively Quaker approach to the philosophy of religion in general, and inter-religious conversation in particular. In both Penn and James, we have two generous interlocutors who force us to think carefully about matters of religious belonging and co-existence. Penn has long been identified by Quaker historians as a great systematiser of the early movement's thought by drawing on a wide range of philosophical and theological sources. At the heart of Penn's theological work is the insistence that the Spirit of Christ transcends the division of creeds, sects, and religions. The Risen Jesus who is experienced by Friends in silent Worship is, in principle, graspable by all human beings. Summarising Penn's theological character in his study of early Quaker theology, Doug Gwyn has observed that for Penn, religion is 'the noblest end of an individual's life and the best bond of human society. It is *false* religion – both enthusiasm and persecution – that make people furious and unnatural' (Gwyn, 1995:325–326). Behind this definition lies Penn's claim that religion springs from the shared impulse of natural reason, the activity of universal revelation, and the conscientious search for 'subjective truth' (Gwyn, 1995:327). Thus, thinks Penn, it can be said that 'the humble, meek, merciful, just, pious, and devout souls are everywhere of one religion' (Penn, 1902:166). While Gwyn does not approve of the liberal and relativising implications of these theological moves, he vividly illustrates their impact on Quaker thought. By adopting general categories of universal reason and revelation, Penn reveals himself as an insider who is always reaching beyond the bounds of his community. Appeals to other ways of seeing and thinking give Penn's arguments a general, even disinterested quality which sets him apart from the earlier partisan Puritan milieu of George Fox, Margaret Fell, or James Nayler.

But such a radical conception of legitimate plurality leaves many loose ends untied. Who is this Universal Christ Penn worships? What does Penn's Christological language imply for matters of religious identity and difference? And how might contemporary Quakers live in the light of this assumed unity of religion? William James is significant for advancing and clarifying

DOI: 10.4324/9780429030925-33

such a project in two important ways. Firstly, he offers a fluid and inclusive definition of religious expression which avoids excessive abstraction. In James' nineteenth-century world, it was habitual for philosophers and theologians to define religion according to abstruse principles, naturalistic reductions, or elaborate metaphysical arguments. James' great contribution to the philosophy of religion was his insistence that these rarefied methods failed to appreciate the essence of religious commitment. For James, the religious individual is chiefly characterised, not by intellectual beliefs, but by a certain orientation towards existence. The religious personality is chiefly defined, says James, by 'the feelings, acts, and experiences of individual men in their solitude, as far as they apprehend themselves to stand in relation to whatever they call divine' (James, 1982:31). While these experiences frequently generate communities, 'the founders of every church owed their power originally to the fact of their direct personal communion with the divine' (James, 1982:30). This starting point has profound implications for how we imagine and grasp the religious life. When we encounter the sacred convictions of an individual or a people, we are presented, not with hypotheses about nature, but attempts to express a profound reverence for life. To make religious claims subject to some grand philosophical theory is to unhelpfully disentangle them from the person who loves, reasons, and senses through them. When we meet religious difference, the problem is not a philosophical one (a matter of argument or intellectual foundations), but rather a question of biography and psychology. If we understand the abiding goals of a life, we will comprehend the substance of its faith. This decisive turn to primal spiritual experience leads us to consider James' second important contribution; namely, his turning towards practical outcomes in the analysis of religious claims. James insists that the nature of religion must be understood, not merely as a system of beliefs, but as a method of knowing that draws the full range of human capacities into itself. The ultimate validity of any theological turn must be ascertained according to the results it furnishes for individuals and communities. If religious claims have predictive power or else make our experiences coherent, they must possess the mark of truthfulness. Thus, statements concerning the meaning of existence, or the applicability of a given moral ideal, cannot be proved by abstract speculation, but only by the test of concrete action (James, 2000:131). Thus, one cannot speak of God, Spirit, or soul without sketching out what 'use' these words have for their users. The work they do in the life of the believer constitutes their only measurable reality. The more one uses these words, clarifies their accompanying sensations, and gauges their applicability to one's own life or community, the more we are able to ascertain their truthfulness.

As I will go on to show, Penn is both a contributor and a precursor to this Pragmatic approach to religion that James so vividly describes. Far from a rigid insistence on grand theories, Penn's focus upon lived experience permits his Quaker theology to break from the bonds of a single culture and find dignity in difference. When we consider the implications of this practical approach, we face something more than a parochial Quaker artifact. Penn's sense of Christ's universality implies, albeit tentatively, a Christian philosophy of religions. Before we consider the nature of this project in some detail, it will be necessary to briefly sketch out Penn's sources and theological preoccupations. In the opening discussion, Penn's complex range of sympathies with ancient Greek philosophers, Protestant Reformers, and Catholic contemplatives will be considered. In writings peppered with a rich hinterland of sacred sources, Penn offers a compelling program for ecumenical and inter-religious cooperation for the fractured landscape of seventeenth-century Europe. What does this project mean for our world of radical religious diversity? The second part of this discussion evaluates the significance of Penn's Christology by placing his work within the history of Pragmatism. Through a close comparison between Penn and the Church Father Augustine of Hippo, I will seek to show the revolutionary applications of the early Quaker emphasis on practice. I conclude by offering an extended reflection on the complex relationship between Penn's life and thought.

Penn and the Christological Question

From its very inception, Quakerism held as self-evident that all inherited notions of religious identity were profoundly suspect. Whatever outward authorities claimed on behalf of their followers, it was God, not institutions, that determined the criteria for faithful belonging. Recalling his stunning revelations to that effect in the mid-1640s, George Fox recalled:

> About the beginning of the year 1646, as I was going to Coventry, and entering towards the gate, a consideration arose in me, how it was said that all Christians are believers, both Protestants and Papists; and the Lord opened to me that, if all were believers, then they were born of God, and passed from death to life, and that none were true believers but such; and though others said they were believers, yet they were not.
>
> *(Fox, 2007:6–7)*

Such a radical break with institutional Christendom demanded not merely a revolutionary reorientation of Christian identity but a comprehensive re-description of religion in general. If those who called themselves Christians were not always Christian, was it possible that some who did not call themselves Christians belonged to Christ? Fox's answers, in accord with the thought-world of first-generation Quakers, were framed by the notion of the eschatological covenant and Christ's radical indwelling in history. In this first ecstatic phase, Friends saw themselves as the Universal Church reborn, renewed in the Apostolic commission to sweep over the earth. All people who heeded Christ would be called from their outward forms to the true religion of inward Truth. Consequently, in old age, Fox could still say with confidence: 'Christ hath enlightened every man that comes into the world, he hath enlightened the Turks, Jews, and Moors, with the light, (which is the life in him the word) that all the light might know God and Christ' (Fox, 1831:235). But, despite such a generous treatment of cultural others, early Friends were not ethnologists, patiently seeking out the presence of God in each group, culture, or religion. Such statements were expressions of first-generation evangelical urgency, not theological inquiry. In the outpouring of God's Spirit on all flesh, such questions would soon be irrelevant. But, as persecution lengthened and apocalyptic expectation dimmed, Friends had to adjust to the mundane reality of existing as one sect, among others. How could Quakerism maintain its spiritual urgency in the world beyond ecstatic vision?

Resolving this quandary required a new attentiveness to early Quaker claims to represent a universal revelation, in particular answering afresh the classic Christological question: "Who do you say I am?" (Matt. 16:15). William Penn emerged as a prominent member of the Religious Society of Friends at the very moment this issue became pressing. Penn's resolution was not to break with the convictions of the first generation, but rather to reinterpret them in the light of a less expectant age. Penn returned to Fox's most universalist insights and radicalised them. If Friends worshiped an inward and Universal Christ, the Risen Lord was not the property of any Church, sect, or faith. Such gestures had profound implications for Quaker self-understanding. Perhaps the most significant consequence was a collapse in concepts of space and time. For Penn, Friends were not merely primitive Christianity revived but the latest manifestation of the Eternal Christ, who has sought the salvation of the world throughout the Ages. Much as the Patristic apologist Justin Martyr had pinpointed the Eternal Christ in the lives of pre-Christian Greek thinkers like Socrates and Heraclitus (Martyr, 1997:55), Penn placed Quakerism in a universal history that spanned churches, traditions, and religions. In Penn's thought, Christ appears as the timeless Son who, epoch after epoch, draws human lives towards a formless religion of the heart, a faith without ceremonies, temples, or priesthoods. Before Christ came in the flesh, this inward religion had many practitioners. Like Justin, Penn revered Socrates as one who 'died for the one true God' (Penn, 1825a:284). Alongside Heraclitus and Socrates, Penn placed Anaxagoras (Penn, 1825a:259), Zeno (Penn, 1842a:282), Epictetus (Penn, 1825c:472), Plato, Sophocles (Penn, 1825a:266), Seneca (Penn, 1825c:472), and Plotinus (Penn, 1825c:472) among those who had partly grasped the nature of the Inward Light. Yet, what of the vast expanse of Christian history? Were Friends the only inheritors of this sublime revelation since the Apostles? Refuting any suggestion of such exclusivity, Penn endeavoured to pinpoint other lives that exemplified the formless peaceful religion of Friends. Among them, Penn includes the Rhineland contemplative Thomas à Kempis and the Dominican mystic Johannes Tauler (Penn, 2002). While these men hailed from an Apostate Church, their hearts belonged to the true religion of love that Christ had founded in diverse hearts throughout the ages. Yet Penn's generosity did not terminate at the borders of an old Christendom. Alongside Catholic mystics, Penn was a generous reader of the reforming Humanist Erasmus of Rotterdam, as well as Luther, Melanchthon, and Calvin (Penn, 1825b:580). Taken together, these inclusions constituted a tender ecumenicalism, underpinned by a revolutionary affection that attempted to bridge the chasms between religions and peoples. While Penn's theology had certainly enlarged and extended embryonic Quaker preoccupations, pressing questions remained. If the Quaker vision could include religious and philosophical communities radically separated by time and space, what were the frontiers of such a mystical communion? And how were its inhabitants to be identified? It is here, in generating a criterion of belonging, that Penn's pragmatic conception of religion comes firmly into focus.

The Coherence of Love in Action

Where then should Penn's work be placed in the history of Pragmatism? James, in his genealogy of this perspective incorporates many great philosophical thinkers, including Socrates, Aristotle, Locke, and Hume. But unlike such sceptical-empiricists, Penn's appeal to practice was sustained by a searching use of the Hebrew and Greek Scriptures. This fact alone places Penn's work in fascinating alignment with one of the great exegetes of the early Church, Augustine of Hippo (354–430 CE). In summarising his contribution to the tradition of religious Pragmatism, C. C. Pecknold has suggested that Augustine was engaged in the construction of a 'a genuinely scriptural form of pragmatism aimed at healing the world through the Word' (Pecknold, 2005:60). When Augustine seeks to establish the proper use of Scripture in the life of the believer, he attends to the concrete results that flow from the act of biblical interpretation. Since the Word became flesh to heal the world, words of Scripture are rightly applied if the words of the text come to reflect and embody the original character of the Word. As Pecknold expresses this imperative in Augustine's thought: '[Human mediation] . . . must be read as the mediation of the Word of God made flesh in the reading community who performs this Word, (as Christ's body). Readers must themselves become a textual replication; a living salvic text made flesh for the healing of the nations' (Pecknold, 2005:56). Thus, for Augustine, to be a Christian is to be practically formed by the story of Christ. The Logos is bound to time so that the things of time can reflect the things of eternity. In this scheme of replication, love is the primary bridge between text and the Word (Pecknold, 2005:56). By directing their love towards the deep needs of the neighbour, Christians mirror the character of the Saviour they worship.

While Augustine was one of the most articulate advocates of this vision of lived interpretation, it would be rediscovered many times in the proceeding centuries, not least by early Friends. Penn's contribution to this rediscovery took the form of a profound extension of the universal possibilities of this stance. For Penn, the Word not only manifests in the lives of devout Christian readers but also among those who possess the Word engraved on their hearts (Rom. 2:15). As Penn observed in his 1696 tract *Primitive Christianity Revived*: 'there is a dispensation of grace which we declare has appeared to all, in various measures, teaching all who will receive it, "to deny ungodliness and worldly lusts"'(Penn, 2018:77). In this charitable spirit, Penn claims that many sages of classical antiquity apprehended something of the Inward Light, confirmed by the quality of their conduct. In contrast to their intemperate Christian peers, the demeanour of these refined pagans mirrored Paul's fruits of the Spirit: 'love, joy, peace, patience, kindness, generosity, faithfulness, gentleness, and self-control' (Gal. 5:22–25). The effects of the Spirit are more central than any mere recitation of theological belief. In this vein, Penn is comfortable telling his co-religionists:

> How little the Christians of these times are true philosophers and how much more these philosophers were more Christian than they, let the Righteous Principle in every conscience judge. But is not then intolerable that they should be esteemed Christians, who are yet to be good Heathens.
>
> *(Penn, 1825a:543)*

Using this insight as his foundation, Penn comes to a startling conclusion:

> The humble, meek, merciful, just, pious, and devout souls are everywhere of one religion; and when death has taken off the mask they will know one another, though the divers liveries they wear here makes them strangers. This world is a form; our bodies are forms; and no visible acts of devotion can be without forms. But yet the less form in religion the better, since God is a Spirit; for the more mental our worship, the more adequate to the nature of God; the more silent, the more suitable to the language of a Spirit.
>
> *(Penn, 1902:166)*

Here the divides of religion and ethnos fall away, leaving only an expectant soul, gravitating towards what is eternal. This force of spiritual attraction manifests in the visible world as a personality filled with virtue. Life is always the answer to the demands of the Spirit. But for Penn, this is not a mere statement of passive sympathy. It represents a sweeping program of theological repair. Just as Augustine had insisted on the priority of healing in the reading of Scripture, Penn argued that the primacy of love means a fundamental reordering of Christian priorities, away from abstract doctrinal formulations and towards the immediacy of concrete life. Like many other Friends of the period, Penn's spiritual life had been defined by an atmosphere of pious sectarianism, at home and abroad. The fragmentation of Christendom had precipitated violent altercations between the populations of Catholic and Protestant kingdoms. Doctrine had become a bloody litmus test of political loyalty. Applying his Pragmatic theology to this sorrowful context, Penn concludes that no reconciliation of humanity is possible under God unless Christians first trust their direct experience of the divine world. Penn refutes the suggestion that spiritual things in principle function differently from ordinary things. Since everyday

experience is never fully disclosive, but cumulative, objects of the spirit also possess this incre-
mental dimension. As Penn suggests in one illuminating passage in *No Cross No Crown*:

> To have religion upon authority and not upon conviction is like a finger watch, to be
> set forwards or backwards as he pleases that had it in keeping. It is a preposterous thing
> that men can venture their souls where they will not venture their money; for they
> will take their religion upon trust but not trust a synod about the goodness of half a
> crown. Wait and watch unto His daily and hourly visitations to your souls. Don't bow
> down thyself before thy old experiences but behold the arm that has helped thee and
> that God who has often delivered thee. Remember that the manna descended from
> heaven daily; that is daily must be gathered and eaten, and that manna that was gath-
> ered yesterday cannot serve today for food.
>
> *(Penn, 1825b:390)*

Like the phenomena of outer life, spiritual reality should intrude into our consciousness, not as
a function of our will, but as an unfurling of spontaneous encounter. We do not force the table
in our kitchen into being every morning, nor are the table's qualities directly dependent upon
our fleeting faith in those attributes. We comprehend the table quite intuitively, according to
the capacity of our senses at a given moment. For Penn, the life of the Spirit is no different. To
traverse the spiritual world through involuntary symbolic mediation or second-hand belief is
to fall 'from experience to tradition and worship from power to form' (Penn, 1825b:33). Here
Penn introduces us to a distinctive feature of his theological phenomenology. While the manifold signs of tradition appear to consciousness as a succession of fixed solidities ('special garments
and furniture, perfume, voices and music'; Penn, 1825b:33), their apparent hardness masks their
relative unreality. For Penn, the essence of things is not constituted by outward form, but rather
depends upon the capacity of the phenomenon to reach into the deepest inward regions of
ourselves. Things have truthful solidity if they impress themselves upon us. Illusions are those
things that captivate us for a moment but leave us much as they found us. In this vein, outward
things are like lights that do not illuminate and food that does not nourish. Much as James insists
that life, not axioms, validate our beliefs, Penn desires that Christians return to living water, of
which dogma is a mere residue. But what does such an approach mean for the promulgation
of key Christian doctrines such as the Trinity? Here Penn diagnoses the malady of his times.
Dogmatic utterance has been severed from the living truth of Christ. Before Christians contend
for this or that opinion of divine matters, Penn insists that they must learn to walk in the love
of Christ. As Penn exhorts:

> They [Quakers] believe in the Holy Three, or Trinity of Father, Word, and Spirit,
> according to Scripture. . . . But they are very tender of quitting Scripture terms and
> phrases for schoolmen's, such as distinct and separate persons or subsistences are, from
> which people are apt to entertain gross ideas and notions of the Father, Son and Holy
> Ghost. And they judge that a curious enquiry into those high and Divine relations,
> and other speculative subjects, though never so great truths in themselves, tend little
> to godliness, and less to peace; which should be the chief aim of true Christians. And
> therefore they cannot gratify that curiosity in themselves or others.
>
> *(Penn, 1874:23)*

It is not axiomatic consistency that exercises Penn, but the fruits of practice. If there is to exist
a correspondence between human words and the Word, the work of doctrine cannot manifest

as disputation or controversy, but must serve to heal and comfort, educate, and edify. It is here that we see a clear bridge between Quaker universalism and James' pragmatic understanding of religious experience. Once we discover the manifold virtues of concrete lives lived, we will turn away from abstruse matters of theoretical principle and towards the unfolding of practical ideals. As James summarises this shift of priorities:

> For the philosophy which is so important in each of us is not a technical matter; it is our more or less dumb sense of what life honestly and deeply means. It is only partly got from books; it is our individual way of just seeing and feeling the total push and pressure of the cosmos.
>
> *(James 2000:7)*

Once this distinctly personal dimension of human life is granted its proper significance, it is easily conceded that productive interchange with others requires the sensitive comprehension of the wholeness and complexity of each personal story, the unique facts that animate their thoughts and actions. What might such pragmatic practice have to teach the contemporary Quaker world? In prioritising the influence of formless but dynamic love, Penn's theology not merely dismantles doctrinal, ethnic, and sectarian boundaries, but suggests the necessity of a Quaker ethnography. The character of the Quaker story asserts that in order to uphold the universality of Christ's work, Quakers must learn to view the Other as an intrinsic part of their own story and proclamation. As Penn conceives it, the Quaker posture assumes a potential deep resonance in all persons addressed by the Gospel, whether or not they are in intellectual agreement with it. Propositional knowledge is never the point. Ancient pagans or Catholic contemplatives might baulk at the puritan garb of Quakerism, but as Penn maintains, beneath outward form, there is deep communion of experience and practice. Penn refuses to remove any community from his theology of dialogue merely on account of cultural remoteness. It is not enough for the evangelical task to come from above in order to perfect a world below. The universality of the Word demands something more. To articulate the radicality of the Good News of Christ is to acknowledge that *he is present already*. In this account, the stories of others are portals to the divine love Quakers seek, and tender instruments of ongoing discovery. Implied in such a project of recognition is a cluster of virtues: tenderness, deep listening, and a capacity to see oneself mirrored in difference.

The Janus Face of William Penn: The Problem of Words and Fruits

In good Pragmatic fashion, Penn's convictions found plentiful expression in outer life, in his commitment to religious toleration, his petitioning on behalf of the persecuted, and his famed proposal for European unification. But in underscoring his significance for Quaker thought, a judicious historical eye should caution us against an excess of admiration that might transform a complex life into a bland hagiography. Penn was indeed an eloquent progenitor of a humane universalism, which advanced the cause of generous religiosity in a divided West. But alongside Penn the writer of common sympathy is Penn the artful property manager and state builder. It is in this much more mundane and hard-nosed character that we confront an unsettling fact. It was the cultural critic Walter Benjamin who observed: 'There is no document of civilization which is not at the same time a document of barbarism' (Benjamin, 1968:200). So it is with the gentle William Penn. This theological boundary crosser was an owner of slaves. This fact is not tangential to Penn's Christology, for it draws into stark relief the limits of his conception of cherishing the other in the name of love. Despite his capacity to recognise the uncontested humanity of numerous cultural and religious Others, this did not lead Penn to the practical rejection of slavery when he oversaw his Holy Experiment in Pennsylvania. It was an ostensibly permanent part of his world that his theology did not of itself force him to examine. For all his imaginative empathy, Penn's creative dedication to human unity was not qualitatively different from the Roman Stoics. These sages of quiet moderation spoke of universal brotherhood, while unfree men and women toiled on their vast country estates. Like them, the hours Penn spent dreaming about new worlds of tolerance were underwritten by enclosed and shrunken lives. In this way, both the Stoic villa and the Quaker plantation expressed the perennial temptation of the idealist, of the work of the lips being undone by the careless hand or the avaricious eye.

So it is for many of us in the post-industrial West, with our mass imports and leisure economy. Penn knew the names of those he held in bondage. We, with our vast supply chains, are deprived of even this. While Western societies continue to repudiate the ownership of fellow human beings in the name of Universal Human rights, our cut-price consumer economies depend in large part upon forms of wage slavery – which are kept meticulously out of sight. In this respect, Penn presents contemporary Quakers with a pertinent Janus-faced legacy. With his talk of love and tolerance, Penn is the best of his world and ours. But in his yawning moral silences, he reveals the all-too contemporary affliction of ethical complacency. In facing these painful facts of power and privilege, any meaningful use of Penn in contemporary Quaker theology requires the capacity to read Penn against Penn. Our author must be condemned, corrected, and absolved through the principles he himself espoused. When we read Penn's exhortations of spiritual harmony we must hear in them, not self-congratulatory pieces of Quaker progressiveness, but stern rebukes that encourage contemporary Quakers to examine the practical results of their words. In esteeming Penn's image of boundless fraternity, Friends should be pricked by the demand to live out what Penn himself failed to do. If embarked upon with seriousness, such internal criticism will amplify the validity and urgency of Penn's theology of difference, not disgrace it. In our deeply interconnected world of collapsing space and plural cultures, the generosity represented by a pragmatic Christology appears as a life raft, rescuing our religious life from the cold waters of cultural relativism and fundamentalist insularity. By approaching early Quaker experiments in inter-cultural Christology through Pragmatic lenses, we may yet find the road to a redemptive mode of life, capable of responding faithfully to the challenges and gifts of spiritual diversity.

Bibliography

Benjamin, Walter. 'Theses on the Philosophy of History', in *Illuminations*, ed. Hannah Arendt (New York: Mariner Books, 1968).

Fox, George. *A Collection of Many Select and Christian Epistles, Letters and Testimonies on Sundry Occasions, Vol. II* (Philadelphia: Marcus T. Gould, 1831).

— *The Journal of George Fox*, ed. Norman Penney (New York: Cosimo, 2007).

Gwyn, Douglas. *The Covenant Crucified: Quakers and the Rise of Capitalism* (Wallingford: Pendle Hill Publications, 1995).

James, William. *The Varieties of Religious Experience* (London: Penguin, 1982).

— *Pragmatism and Other Writings* (London: Penguin, 2000).

Martyr, Justin. *The First and Second Apology*, trans. Leslie Williams Bernard (New York: Paulist Press, 1997),

Pecknold, C. C. *Transforming Postliberal Theology: George Lindbeck, Pragmatism and Scripture* (London: T&T Clark, 2005).

Penn, William. *No Cross, No Crown: A Discourse Showing the Nature and Discipline of the Holy Cross* (London: Darton & Harvey, 1842).

— *The Political Writings of William Penn*, ed. Andrew R. Murphy (Indianapolis: Liberty Fund, 2002). https://oll.libertyfund.org/titles/penn-the-political-writings-of-william-penn/simple#lf6418_label_277

— *Primitive Christianity Revived*, ed. Jason R. Henderson (Akron: Market Street Fellowship, 2018).

— *The Select Works of William Penn*, Volume 1 (a) (London: William Philips, 1825a).
— *The Select Works of William Penn*, Volume 3 (b) (London: William Philips, 1825b).
— *The Select Works of William Penn*, Volume 5 (c) (London: Janes Philips, 1825c).
— *Some Fruits of Solitude* (New York: HM Caldwell Co, 1902).
— *A Testimony to the Truth of God, as Held by the People Called Quakers* (Manchester: William Irwin, 1874).

31

LIBERAL QUAKER PNEUMATOLOGY

Christy Randazzo

Exploring Liberal Quaker theology from an intentionally systematic framework – such as using the explicitly systematic term of 'pneumatology' – is an uncommon move. Liberal Quakers are far more likely to speak about their personal experience of what they define as 'Spirit', an exceedingly broad term which could mean anything from Trinitarian Christian conceptions of the Holy Spirit to any personal experience with any supernatural entity that could be understood as divine. Instead, Liberal Quakers would explain the ways in which they experience 'Spirit' at work in the world, such as in meeting for worship or in the practical work of living Quaker testimony through the actions of Quaker communities. Thus, due to this traditional Liberal Quaker aversion to the explicit categorisation and definition of its theology, very few theologians from outside the Quaker tradition have engaged with Liberal Quaker theological content, let alone anything related to pneumatology. This chapter therefore has an intentional focus on outlining frameworks upon which to build future explorations of Liberal Quaker pneumatology which could more easily 'translate' to traditional Christian systematic categories.

Liberal Quakers balance their unique theological anthropology of God as an experienced reality, immanent within creation and interdependent upon the creation – encapsulated within the dizzyingly expansive metaphorical theology of Light – with the traditional Christian theological anthropology categories of the Trinity, particularly those which explore the complex relationship between Christ and Spirit. Liberal Quakerism expresses an interchangeability between Christ and Spirit in its language, due to the insistence that God takes the form of Spirit, whether the Spirit of Christ or the Spirit of a universal consciousness. The imprecision around the language delineating Spirit from Christ is reflective of the insistence on founding theology upon the base of experience. As Liberal Quaker experience of the Spirit and of Christ is sometimes challenging to differentiate, any subsequent theology would also be ambiguous about the difference between them.

Quakers have a global presence, and reflecting that geographic diversity is a similar diversity in theology and practice across the various branches of religious communities who trace their roots to the Quaker tradition.[1] These include several broad categories, of which Liberal, Conservative, Pastoral, Evangelical, and Pentecostal are only a few. There are other ways of categorising Quaker communities, including worship style (programmed/unprogrammed), links

DOI: 10.4324/9780429030925-34

to historical divisions (Hicksite/Orthodox/Gurneyite, amongst many others), or even whether they refer to worship communities as 'meetings' or 'churches'. The particular branch known as Liberal Quakerism developed its particular theological approach in the application of liberal theology within Quaker thought in the late nineteenth century.

It must be noted at the outset that there exists quite a considerable diversity in Liberal Quaker theological thought. Recent scholarly work has shone a light on this diversity from a variety of perspectives. Christy Randazzo has explored divisions between those with explicitly Christian theological perspectives from those with what has been termed a 'Universalist' approach,[2] as well as the development of a self-defined non-theist Quakerism.[3] Randazzo has also used argued that Liberal Quaker theology can be approached systematically, and used to develop both a uniquely Liberal Quaker reconciliation theology,[4] as well as ecotheology.[5] Rhiannon Grant has examined Liberal Quaker theology from the perspective of the language they use – both general patterns as well as specific words, metaphors, and phrases employed – to explain their experience of the Divine.[6] Most recently, Grant has also interrogated Liberal Quaker theological method, using the official Books of Discipline/Faith and Practice from yearly meetings around the world as a means of developing a framework for discerning Liberal Quaker theological method.[7] Suffice it to say, there is considerable diversity in theological thought and expression amongst Liberal Quakers, and one should be cautious when making universal claims about a single, definable 'Liberal Quaker theology'.

In an effort to actually say something about Liberal Quaker theology without being drowned in a sea of caveats, however, I propose the following framework: that a 'Liberal Quaker' approach to the development of theology and its subsequent expression of is dominated by two main aspects:

> One, the negative dictum that Quakers reject any theological statement or structure which resembles a 'creed', and two, the positive dictum that theological 'truth' is to be known 'experimentally', or through the interaction between the experience of individuals and the community in worship and the testing of these experiences in the lives of both individual Quakers and the community of Quakers.[8]

With our throats thoroughly cleared, let us proceed.

Liberal Quakers recognise the transcendence of God beyond creation as an inherent aspect of what could be considered divinity, yet due to their emphasis on the epistemological primacy of direct religious experience of the Divine, Liberal Quakers stress the immanence of God within the creation to a much greater degree. This stress on immanency colours their view of the Christian anthropological categories, causing them to place greater emphasis on anthropological theories of interdependence, immanence within the creation, and intimate love of the creation. Pneumatology, it could be argued, is more foundational to Quaker anthropology than Christology, particularly through metaphors of divine/human interdependence. This is due to the significant import placed upon the experience of God, a category in which Quaker theology views the Spirit playing the main role.

This chapter provides an overview of the main elements of Liberal Quaker pneumatology, with an emphasis on exploring the theological methods and metaphorical frameworks which Liberal Quaker theology uses to construct its pneumatology, including metaphorical theologies of Light that engage both Christian and Universalist models of Divine Immanence, towards the end of presenting potentialities for the future development of a Liberal Quaker systematic pneumatology.

Authority and Experience in Liberal Quaker Theology

Liberal Quakers place religious experience as the primary locus for theological reflection and development. Liberal Quakerism makes the claim that theology must be contextual, dynamic (i.e., continuously open to change), non-universal, and developed through the dialogic interplay between the interpretation of the religious experience of individuals and the community. Liberal Quakers therefore draw from multiple sources in a continuous effort to develop language to comprehend their complex communal experience of the Divine. These multiple sources are placed alongside each other, with varying levels of authority granted to each source depending both on the importance and value each individual Liberal Quaker places on the available sources, all interpreted through the communal discernment of experience within each Liberal Quaker community, or meeting. As Liberal Quakerism is rooted in its original Christian witness and heritage, many of the sources they look to are Christian ones – including biblical passages and the writings of historical and communally respected, or 'weighty', Quakers – which inevitably imprints a Christian framework on any resulting theological thought. The primary source, however, is the experience of Quakers themselves, whether experiencing the Divine in worship or in the testimony of their lives, as they embody Quaker values and theology through their actions. For Quakers, therefore, 'testimony' is an essential concept encapsulating the experience of encountering God at all times of one's life and reflecting that encounter in one's every action.[9]

Thus, the construction of theology will bring all potential aspects of analysis to bear upon an experience: the history of how such experiences have been interpreted within Quakerism generally, correspondence with Scriptural passages (generally Judeo-Christian scriptures, yet with increasing regularity scriptures from other faith traditions), alignment with the written narratives and stories of respected Quakers throughout Quaker history, sociological analysis of how other Liberal Quakers interpret and apply similar experiences, and even examination of the experience in light of socio-political realities.

Liberal Quakers insist that bringing individual experience of God into conversation with the communal experience of God, including the Bible and theological tradition, must not lead towards granting any inherent authority in the communal experience and any doctrine which might emerge from such experience. Liberal Quakers must therefore keep the tools and aspects of Quaker heritage, including the Bible, from becoming authoritative and thus serving as the main means of maintaining the cohesion of the community.[10]

Liberal Quaker theology has always emphasised the tension which must exist in holding the balance between the experience and needs of both the individual and the community. Liberal Quaker theology therefore exists at the point where the individual and community meet: individual theology is tested by the community, stems from the experience of individual existing within the community, and must be seen as having some claim over the lives of the community. Liberal Quaker theology is broad, reflecting the variety and diversity of individual experiences of the Divine, while also allowing for some boundaries in the way that Quakers establish common corporate frameworks for explaining the meaning and purpose of those experiences for the entire Liberal Quaker community. By granting the community some substantive influence over the individual, Liberal Quaker theology can avoid placing the individual as the sole seat of authority and influence in interpreting the meaning of the Divine experience.

Christ and Spirit in Quaker Theology

This section addresses the theology of Liberal Quakers who either self-identify as Christian or who use Christian theological categories to frame their theological worldviews and beliefs. As noted above, Liberal Quaker theology is incredibly internally diverse, and many Quakers who might willingly self-identify as universalist or non-theist might reject the value or necessity of 'Christ' as a theological category to explain their experience of the Divine. For those who use such terms as 'Christ' and 'Holy Spirit', Liberal Quaker theology expresses an interchangeability between Christ and Spirit, due to the insistence that God takes the form of Spirit, whether the Spirit of Christ or the Spirit of a universal consciousness. The imprecision around the language delineating Spirit from Christ is reflective of the dynamic tension which exists between individuals and the community: individual experience continually tests communal witness, which in turn strives to incorporate individual experience. As Liberal Quakers struggle to differentiate between Spirit and Christ in their experience of the Divine, their Christology and Pneumatology is also inherently ambiguous.

Liberal Quakers tend to accept the position that a divine Spirit moved within Jesus in complete union, where Jesus' will was closely aligned with the will of the divine. Liberal Quakers who consider themselves Christian often base their Christology on the Logos of Johannine theology, where Jesus completely embodies the divine life, a life lived as Spirit.[11] Trinitarian thought is present here, yet intentionally outlined in very imprecise terms. A minute from Yorkshire Quarterly Meeting represents this imprecision, claiming that Jesus demonstrated 'the divine life humanly lived and the human life divinely lived'.[12] This perspective certainly exists in Christian theology, yet it creates the challenge of defining the unique role of the Spirit and of Jesus in God's relationship to humanity. The imprecision of Quaker theological language about this relationship leads to a wide spectrum of approaches to the relationship.

This focus on paradox and inconsistency suggests a profoundly apophatic strain in Quaker theology. This aversion to reflect with any specificity on the nature and action of the Spirit seems strange in light of the profoundly Spirit-focused aspect of the Quaker experience of God and the consistent use of Spirit language to narrate that experience. As George Gorman argues, Liberal Quakers often emphasise that any theological statement about the nature of God must prioritise reflection on the interplay between the manifestations of the Spirit in silent worship and the process by which the Spirit draws humanity into greater union with God and God's will.[13] This interplay of the Spirit and humanity is an experienced reality first, which is then imperfectly slotted into an area of theological inquiry. As one Friend relates, this feeling is most often experienced intentionally, especially during Meeting for Worship.[14] An account from another Friend speaks of the meeting as an expression of the universal conscience, reflecting the Universalist strain of Liberal Quakerism.[15]

The experience is not often a product of daily existence, instead occurring as the gathered meeting welcomes the Divine Presence in silence. Quakerism recognizes that the Spirit is always present, yet humanity is not able to fully comprehend and recognize the presence in the busyness of daily existence. The gathering together is essential, therefore, to reconnect with the Spirit and to reflect on the morals and ethics of daily existence that stem from the mystical union with the Spirit.[16] The experience of unity in meeting also serves to remind Friends in a very palpable way that the Spirit brings all of creation into unity with God.

This lack of precision extends to the lack of a clean and clear division between the actions of Jesus the Logos and Jesus the Spirit. This has deep roots in early Quakerism. Rosemary Moore notes the confusion that the imprecision of Quaker language created for other theologians, particularly relating to that famous Quaker construction: 'that of God within'.[17] Early Quakers were faced with explaining whether this construction represented a fourth aspect of God, particularly as Quakers insisted 'that of God' was not specifically the Father, the Son, or the Holy Spirit, individually, yet was somehow representative of all three concurrently. For

Quakers, this vague concept was almost analogous to the action of the Holy Spirit moving within the person.[18]

This aversion to specificity continued into the early twentieth century, with one Quaker, William Littleboy, stating unequivocally that Quakers 'dare not dogmatise on the manner of the Parousia'. Littleboy then appears to reject his previous statement and outlines a realising eschatology where the Spirit is both the 'very self' of Christ and a separate emanation active in a post-resurrection world.[19] This demonstrates an ambiguity latent in Quaker theology, rooted in the line that Quakers straddle between the need to narrate their experience of God to the community, while also not establishing concrete and definitive boundaries on the meaning and purpose of that experience. Liberal Quakers insist that they experience God as appearing to exist everywhere and within everything while also remaining mysteriously unknowable.

Rufus Jones, one of the most important early Liberal Quaker theologians, made a link between Jesus Christ and the Holy Spirit; or as Jones terms it, the 'Divine Spirit'. Jones appeared to subscribe to a procession theory of the Spirit, claiming that the 'real presence' of Jesus exists as the Spirit, continually emanating from Jesus into the lives of people and demonstrating God's care for all of creation.[20] Jones claimed that the most important and central tenet of Quakerism is this theme of the 'real presence' of Christ in the Spirit. This imprecision in early Liberal Quakerism became a subsequent theme, such that Quakers are generally vague as to the relationship between the persons of the Trinity. They even question whether 'Trinity' is the most accurate way to describe the different ways that God exists and interacts with humanity.

As noted above, the method of apprehending these aspects of the Divine is far less important for Liberal Quakers than apprehending them in the first place, allowing them to guide human behaviour towards peaceful action. This is reflected in what I argue is an inherent ambiguity in Liberal Quaker theological concepts.

Light and the Holy Spirit

Liberal Quakers often use metaphor in a creative attempt to explain their experience of God and the forms that God takes in their understanding as a result of that experience. The Light is one such central metaphor, yet Inner Seed, Inner Guide, Light of Christ, and Inner Light are also attempts to explain the Liberal Quaker experience of an immanent God who is concomitantly connected to all of creation.[21] This use of images reflects the difficulty that Liberal Quakers often have in expressing the fullness of their experience of the Divine, resulting in metaphors that might not work beyond specific circumstances, or for all people. This is not to argue against the use of such metaphorical language, however. Liberal Quakers argue that metaphorical language and models of God are necessary tools for framing the complexity of the experience of God, as long as they are – reflecting Liberal Quaker theological conventions – vessels for moving human understanding towards the deeper reality of the God which was experienced and are not held to as definitive statements of the fullness of the reality of God.[22]

One of the most consistent models in Quaker theology is the language of 'Light'. The theological meaning of this language has not remained static across Quaker history, however. Henry Cadbury argued that while the early Quakers tended towards more explicitly Christological language in their constructions of the Light, the constructions themselves were still rather vague in terms of their theological content and meaning. This vagueness reflected the experiential theology which inspired the vision of God as Light.[23] Early Quakers did not understand the Light in terms of a constant, ever-present 'Inner Light', as many Liberal Quaker models of the

Light claim. It did not act as a form of conscience or a guide, the presence of which a person could decide whether or not to recognize. It was more of a potential for actual union with God or Christ which, if attended to, could help the person attain a level of perfection where the person could resist temptation and thus did not sin.[24] The access to the divine Light lay dormant within a person until it was awakened by faith. It would then reveal sin and work to purify the person through a process of sanctification, restoring the original, holy image of God within the person.[25]

The inherent vagueness of Liberal Quaker theology influences their visions and constructions of the Light, emphasising experience and metaphor as the main interpretive tools employed by Liberal Quakers to envision the Light and to construct theologies of the Light. In the history of Quaker theology, the term 'Inward Light' has a very specific meaning, relating to the Light of Christ which shines from God inward towards the person.[26] Reflecting the general Liberal Quaker trend towards a flexible and open approach to theological language, where even Quaker theological terms with a specific meaning began to shift and morph as Liberal Quakers struggled to explain their experience of God and used whatever tools were at their disposal, the early Quaker concept of 'Inward Light' morphed into 'Inner Light', which carries a variety of theological meanings. The Light is thus an expansive term for the interdependence of God and humanity, and for the human experience of being in relationship with God that includes Christian and Universalist constructions.

Liberal Quakerism assumes the greatest possible divine immanence within the creation, an Incarnation which infuses every particle of the creation. The challenge Liberal Quakers encounter is whether they can actually claim that divine immanence leads to an inherent goodness and sacredness of the entire creation, with the corollary that humanity must therefore be inherently good, or whether this view fails to acknowledge the human potential for evil. In general, the Light is understood as active in the process of human transformation, striving to guide humanity towards a greater awareness of Light's presence, and the subsequent ethical consequences. Liberal Quakers view this intimate guidance to be the truest expression of human freedom, for it allows humans to develop faith in the presence of the Light, on their own terms. Liberal Quakers admit that this construction is vague, yet wrestle with whether the vagueness is a flaw to be mended or an inherent feature to be praised.

This reflects the Liberal Quaker emphasis on Pneumo-presentism, with an amorphous Spirit representing the Divine that is immanently present throughout creation. This Spirit can be understood as the Holy Spirit incarnated in the creation, and thus inherently the form of God that Liberal Quakers mean when they refer to the mystical experience of God.[27] Liberal Quakers thus often conflate Light and Holy Spirit, assuming that as Light is the presence of the Divine within the creation, and as the Divine *is* Spirit, then Light and Spirit must in some way be the same thing. For example, Richenda Scott states that the Light 'is Christ, or the Holy Spirit, the power and grace of God', overlapping the terms and dismissing the need for a distinct personality or role for Christ and Holy Spirit. The Light is itself God, therefore, and not just an avenue for accessing the presence of God.[28] Similarly, Peter Eccles terms the divine 'God, the Holy Spirit, the Inner Light', simply listing them in such a fashion where their equivalence is assumed.[29] Even when Liberal Quakers acknowledge that God and Light can have different meanings, they still see a general equivalence between them, enough to be comfortable allowing them to overlap each other, without spending much effort attempting to explore the different meanings between the terms further.[30] As Grant notes, this propensity to use etymological diversity as a form of theological method to attempt to encompass the diversity of theology and belief is inimical to the Liberal Quaker tradition.[31]

Conclusion

It is in these spaces between terms, where Liberal Quakers allow their metaphorical theology to simply exist without exploring their definitional meaning, that Liberal Quaker theology demonstrates both its greatest strengths and most challenging flaws. If the metaphor of Light can represent both the experience of human inter-relationality with the Divine as well as the Divine itself, then that allows for both a breathtaking theological diversity amongst Friends, but also the potential for a diversity so vast that it could fall apart under its own weight. At some point a term must have some general meaning to a community or else it ceases to be meaningful for teaching what beliefs and ideas unify a community, and instead simply becomes a shibboleth, a phrase which connotes identity in a community, but nothing more.

It is precisely this need for some definitional framework which has animated much of the recent work in Liberal Quaker theology, including the development of systematic approaches to Liberal Quakerism. Simply approaching Liberal Quaker theology from a systematic framework – such as this chapter – demonstrates that a community's pneumatology need not be precise in order to exist and have value. The future of Liberal Quaker pneumatology will most likely wrestle with these issues of the 'definition', 'meaning', and 'experience' of the Divine as Spirit.

Notes

1 Randazzo, *Liberal Quaker Reconciliation Theology*, 15.
2 Randazzo, 'Christian and Universalist?'
3 Randazzo, 'Non-Theism'.
4 'Universalist is understood in this sense to mean, as Quaker Universalist Ralph Hetherington explained, a "doctrine of universal salvation or redemption". Hetherington argues that in the context of Liberal Quakerism, Universalism stems initially from William Penn's claim that belief that the "Light of Christ" is present in all people everywhere leads to enlightenment and salvation. This could then extend to all belief systems, where the Christian vision of God is not the only "true" understanding of the nature, and framework, of God.' Randazzo, 'Christian and Universalist?', 33.
5 Randazzo, 'The Divine Light of Creation'.
6 Grant, *British Quakers and Religious Language*.
7 Grant, *Theology from Listening*.
8 Randazzo, *Liberal Quaker Reconciliation Theology*, 15.
9 Rachel Muers has written extensively on the role that testimony plays in Quaker theology and practice, most recently in Muers, *Testimony*.
10 Braithwaite, *Spiritual Guidance*, 26.
11 Brinton, *The Religious Philosophy of Quakerism*, 66.
12 Yearly Meeting, *Quaker Faith and Practice*, 26, 56.
13 Gorman, *The Amazing Fact of Quaker Worship*, 71.
14 Dandelion, *The Liturgies of Quakerism*, 90.
15 Dandelion, *The Liturgies of Quakerism*, 89.
16 Scott, Janet, *What Canst Thou Say?* 3.
17 Moore, *The Light in Their Consciences*, 109.
18 Ibid.
19 Littleboy, *The Day of Our Visitation*, 18.
20 Jones, *Quakerism*, 17.
21 Grant, 'Understanding Quaker Religious Language', 268.
22 Allen, *Ground and Spring*, 25.
23 Cadbury, *Quakerism and Early Christianity*, 38.
24 Moore, *The Light in Their Consciences*, 21.
25 Spencer, 'Early Quakers', 43.
26 Dunstan, *Quakers and the Religious Quest*, 25.
27 Randazzo, *Liberal Quaker Reconciliation Theology*, 65.
28 Scott, Richenda C., *Tradition and Experience*, 71.

29 Eccles, *The Presence in the Midst*, 64.
30 Scott, Janet, *What Canst Thou Say?* 4.
31 Grant, *British Quakers and Religious Language*, 15.

Bibliography

Allen, Beth, *Ground and spring: Foundations of Quaker discipleship* (London: Quaker Books, 2007).

Braithwaite, William C., *Spiritual guidance in the experience of the Society of Friends* (London: Headley Brothers, 1909).

Brinton, Howard, *The religious philosophy of Quakerism: The beliefs of Fox, Barclay and Penn as based on the gospel of John* (Wallingford, PA: Pendle Hill Publications, 1973).

Cadbury, Henry J., *Quakerism and early Christianity* (London: George Allen and Unwin, Ltd., 1957).

Dandelion, Pink, *The liturgies of Quakerism (*Aldershot: Ashgate Publishing Limited, 2005).

Dunstan, Edgar G., *Quakers and the religious quest* (London: George Allen & Unwin, 1956).

Eccles, Peter J., *The presence in the midst: Reflections on discernment* (London: Quaker Books, 2009).

Gorman, George H., *The amazing fact of Quaker worship* (London: Friends Home Service Committee, 1973).

Grant, Rhiannon, 'Understanding Quaker religious language', *Quaker Studies* 19/2 (2015), 260–276.

Grant, Rhiannon, *British Quakers and religious language* (Leiden, The Netherlands: Brill Publishing, 2018).

Grant, Rhiannon, *Theology from listening* (Leiden, The Netherlands: Brill Publishing, 2020).

Jones, Rufus, *Quakerism: A religion of life* (London: Headley Brothers, 1908).

Littleboy, William, *The day of our visitation* (London: Headley Brothers, 1917).

Moore, Rosemary, *The light in their consciences: Early Quakers in Britain, 1646–1666* (University Park, PA: The Pennsylvania University Press, 2000).

Muers, Rachel, *Testimony: Quakerism and theological ethics* (London: SCM Press, 2015).

Randazzo, Christy, 'Christian and universalist? Charting liberal Quaker theological developments through the Swarthmore lectures', *Quaker Religious Thought* 131 (2018), 33–42.

Randazzo, Christy, 'Non-Theism', in *The Cambridge companion to Quakerism*, Stephen W. Angell and Pink Dandelion (eds.) (Cambridge, UK: Cambridge University Press, 2018).

Randazzo, Christy, '"The divine light of creation": Liberal Quaker metaphors of divine/creation interdependence', in *Quakers, creation care and sustainability*, Cherice Bock and Stephen Potthoff (eds.) (Longmeadow, MA: Full Media Services, 2019).

Randazzo, Christy, *Liberal Quaker reconciliation theology* (Leiden, The Netherlands: Brill Publishing, 2020)

Scott, Janet, *What canst thou say? Towards a Quaker theology* (London: The Swarthmore Press, Ltd., 1980).

Scott, Richenda C., *Tradition and experience* (London: George Allen and Unwin, Ltd., 1964).

Spencer, Carole Dale, 'Early Quakers and divine liberation from the universal power of sin', in *Good and evil: Quaker perspectives*, Jackie Leach Scully and Pink Dandelion (eds.) (Hampshire, UK: Ashgate Publishing Limited, 2007), 43–58.

Yearly Meeting of the Religious Society of Friends (Quakers) in Britain, *Quaker faith and practice* (London: Britain Yearly Meeting, 1994).

32

BAPTIZED WITH THE HOLY SPIRIT

Emma Condori Mamani

Introduction

Nowadays, the belief and practice of being baptized with the Holy Spirit has been fading among Friends in the wider Quaker World. There are few Yearly Meetings that still preserve the practice of the baptism of the Spirit as much as the early Friends did. As time has passed the Quaker Movement has grown. Some Friends teachers and pastors have started reinterpreting the Holy Scriptures unalike to the previous Friends tradition regarding baptism of the Holy Spirit and baptism of water, which caused some Friends to adopt the practice of being baptized with water or forget the importance of being baptized with the Holy Spirit.

Early Friends held that the teaching of Jesus about baptism was clear: he said, "For John baptized with water, but in a few days you will be baptized with the Holy Spirit" (Acts 1:5). One of the yearly meetings that keeps this teaching in its religious and spiritual life is the yearly meeting called Iglesia Evangelica Misión Boliviana de Santidad Amigos (Bolivian Mission Evangelical Church of Holiness Friends). Its members have the biblical, theological and experiential foundation to support the belief and practice of baptism of the Holy Spirit. Thus, in the new dispensation of the Gospel all followers of Jesus Christ are baptized with the Holy Spirit that is the baptism of Christ, to live out a life in holiness.

As followers of Jesus Christ, Friends need to understand the will of God, which consists of living a life in holiness. The Lord has not called believers to practice outward religious rites or ceremonies but to welcome the Lord into their hearts and lives so that the Light of Christ dwells in them through the Holy Spirit. It is said in 1 Thessalonians 4:7: "For God has not called us to uncleanness, but to sanctification." The new dispensation of the Gospel has been opened to all human beings through the life and death of Jesus. So, if one believes in and is saved by Jesus Christ, he or she is invited to be baptized with the Holy Spirit in order to partake fully in the dispensation of the Gospel. In the Sacred Scriptures, converts are commanded to live out a life of holiness and purity, which is accomplished by being baptized not with the baptism of John but with that of the Holy Spirit. That is the baptism of Christ. Thus, the teaching about Christ's baptism is at the core of Quaker faith and practice, even though this teaching is understood as a mystical aspect of Quaker spirituality, but it is not connected to the traditional religious outward sacraments of baptism and supper (also called communion or eucharist).

DOI: 10.4324/9780429030925-35

Friends and the Sacraments

Friends have avoided using the term "sacraments" as part of their spiritual practice and religious ceremonies. The term "sacrament" is not found in the Bible, and its origin is related to secular life. Early Quaker theologian Robert Barclay says that this word sacrament "was borrowed from the military oaths used by pagans."[1] According to church history, both Catholics and Protestants adopted the word "sacraments" as one of their observances. For them, this term is often defined as the outward visible sign for receiving the grace of God. Among the most practiced sacraments is baptism.

The understanding of sacraments is controversial for Catholics and Protestants. The term "sacraments" does not cause any trouble within Christian community when it is considered only as an outward symbol of something sacred. However, when a group of Christians affirms that a sacrament is an outward sign that represents inward grace or that confers grace on people, the others disagree with that statement. Unlike Catholics and other Protestant Christian groups, Quakers do not involve in this controversy because Friends worship God "in spirit and in truth." Thus, Quakers practice a worship service without any outward rites, ceremonies or physical symbols.

Quakers, known as Religious Society of Friends, have denied any outward sacrament since the beginning of the Quaker movement in the seventeenth century. Robert Barclay, one of the first academic Friends, worked as a lawyer for Charles II, king of England. Before Barclay became a Friend, the king asked him to investigate the illegal practices of the Quakers. During that investigation, Barclay converted to Jesus Christ (to Quakerism) and wrote "An Apology" about the faith of the Friends, in which he gave a theological explanation regarding the principles and doctrines of Quakers. Robert Barclay's "Apology" was published in 1672 and presented to King Charles II in 1675, and in it Barclay defends Friends' position on the sacraments such as baptism and communion.[2] Barclay declared in his "Apology" that Catholic and Protestant Christians had degenerated the true form of worship to God in truth and in spirit, "because man, in his fallen state, is prone to exalt his own inventions and mix his own work and ideas in the service of God."[3]

Today, Friends disagree with other Christians, both Protestant and Catholic, regarding the outward elements of the sacraments (bread, wine and water). These elements are used in Christian worship for remembering and celebrating the life, death and resurrection of Jesus Christ. But Quakers don't accept that point of view, because for them the true worship consists in experiencing the love, power and transformation of Lord Jesus Christ in the soul. To Friends, "worship is only efficacious insofar as one touches and experiences God directly in the act, and no ceremonial re-enactment will suffice."[4] For George Fox and the other early Friends, for example, the sacramental elements wine and bread did not bring the risen Christ into people's lives. Fox stated that "the practice of ordinances [or sacraments] was spiritually barren and an invitation for people to mistake the substance for the form."[5]

The term *sacraments* is not used by Friends, but if they would like to give a definition to this word, they might say that invisible sacrament is the living sign of the invisible presence of God our Lord Jesus Christ himself, who lived and died in our midst and now dwells within us through the Holy Spirit. Those who experienced the presence of God in truth and in spirit at worship time cannot follow the tradition of the sacraments like others Christians do. Thus, Quakers have objected to practice of the sacraments strongly, including baptism.

The Baptism

The New Testament, which was written first in the Greek language, guides us to understand better the term *baptism*. Baptism originates from the term "baptize," which comes from the

Greek word βαπτιζω (*baptídsö*). The term baptism is used in different contexts because in Greek it means "plunge" and "dip in," "left in the middle or covered with something." When there is an objection stating that the word baptism indicates immersion and washing with water, and alleging that water baptism is divinely appointed, Quakers would reply that

> even though the word baptism was used among the Jews to signify only washing with water, nevertheless John, Christ, and his apostles all speak of being *baptized with the Spirit and with fire*. And it is this latter type of baptism which they speak of as Christ's baptism as distinguished from John's, which was with water.[6]

Baptism of Water

John the Baptist baptized with water according to the records in the Holy Bible, but he ministered it because baptism of water was one of the specific parts of John's ministry. He baptized many people including Jesus, who went to him to be baptized. He explains the reasons why he had to baptize Jesus, saying, "I myself did not know him; but for this I came baptizing with water, that he might be revealed to Israel" (John 1:31). He had to minister water baptism in order to introduce Jesus to the Jewish people. And in John 3:30, he declares that his water baptism must decrease and Christ's baptism must increase. Thus, John's baptism had to stop so that the baptism of Christ may be revealed in the new dispensation.

Some Christians claim that baptism of water is a commandment. They state that in Matthew 28:19, Jesus commanded to baptize: "Go therefore and make disciples of all nations, baptizing them in the name of the Father and of the Son and of the Holy Spirit." But in this biblical reference, the phrase *baptizing them with water* is not mentioned. Moreover, the phrase *in the name* in Greek is written in various ways and has different meanings; for example, in the great commission this term is written εις το ονομα (*eis to ónoma*), which means "within the name." The modern Quaker theologian Édgar Amílcar Madrid Morales states this term's true translation in Spanish "would look like this: *Go therefore, and make all people disciples, by immersing them [or baptizing them] within the name of the Father and of the Son and of the Holy Spirit*. Then, it must be understood that immersing them within the name of the Father, the Son and the Holy Spirit, means let them be covered with the name and power of God, in the three divine persons."[7] Thus, baptism in the great commission refers to what Jesus said that by receiving Him, the believer receives his Father, too (John 13:20).

The Scriptures reveals to us only one baptism that Christians need to experience spiritually. In his proposition XII, *On Baptism*, Robert Barclay defends the faith and practice of Quakers by declaring: "Just as there is "one Lord and one faith," so is there "one baptism" (Ephesians 4:5), which is not "a removal of dirt from the body but . . . an appeal to God for a clear conscience, through the resurrection of Jesus Christ" (1 Peter 3:21). This baptism is a pure and spiritual thing (Galatians 3:27); namely, the baptism of the Spirit and of fire, by which we are buried with Him (Romans 6:4; Colossians 2:12), so that being washed and purged of our sins, we may "walk in the newness of life" (Romans 6:4).[8] Also, the words written in the Bible that teach, rebuke, correct and train people in righteousness describe the cessation of the rites under the law so that people in the new dispensation of Gospel are not justified anymore by the law of Moses. Colossians 2:12–14 states that those who accepted the Lord "were buried with him in baptism" and were "raised with him through faith," because on the cross Jesus Christ abolished any legal bond to the old law. Therefore, Christians already rejoice in this inner Christ's baptism.

Baptism of Christ

Water baptism is not the baptism of Christ for those whose lives were transformed by the Holy Spirit. If John the Baptist were alive now, he would agree with them because he differentiates between the two baptisms by saying: "I baptize you with water for repentance, but he who is coming after me is mightier than I, whose sandals I am not worthy to carry; he will baptize you with the Holy Spirit and with fire" (Matthew 3:11). He clearly affirms that those who already received the baptism of water would be baptized with the Holy Spirit that is the baptism of Christ. Being baptized with the Holy Spirit was reconfirmed when the Lord Jesus Christ himself spoke about it, in Acts 1:4–5, by commanding people who had received John's baptism to wait in Jerusalem to be baptized with the Holy Spirit that is the divine promise of God. Robert Barclay, in his disapproval to practice water baptism, points out this statement of Jesus Christ by writing, "For Christ concedes altogether that John's baptism was complete, both in regard to its manner and to its substance."[9] Thus, these biblical passages corroborate the one baptism that is the baptism of Christ.

Baptizing With the Holy Spirit and the Yearly Meeting IEMIBSA

The yearly meeting Iglesia Evangélica Misión Boliviana de Santidad Amigos – IEMIBSA, which began in 1919, has had a clear difference between water baptism and the baptism of the Holy Spirit. In the book of faith and practice IEMIBSA, it is written regarding their position about baptism,

> We believe that the rites had their use under the Jewish dispensation, but they are not divinely instituted for observance in the dispensation of the church, because the experience of the presence of Christ in the midst of his church is not determined by a sign nor any outward representation, but by a real spiritual communion.

For this group of Friends, the practice of water baptism that has its roots in Jewish ceremonies opposes the teachings of Jesus Christ about the one baptism. The Lord himself spoke to people about the baptism of the Holy Spirit, and so did his apostles. In Acts 1:4, our Lord Jesus Christ reaffirms what John the Baptist said about the baptism with the Holy Spirit. Friend Jack L. Willcuts says, "The Friends Church concludes from these and other similar statements that Christian baptism is the baptism with the Holy Spirit."[10] And at this yearly meeting, Friends have a testimony about being baptized with the Holy Spirit. Therefore, these Friends hold the belief of the *one baptism of Christ*, so that they practice the baptism with the Holy Spirit.

Jesus and the Baptism

The members of this yearly meeting obey what they understand to be Jesus Christ's teaching about being baptized with the Holy Spirit. The Lord who died on the cross and was raised by the Almighty God gave the instruction on the baptism with the Holy Spirit before his ascension to be together with his Heavenly Father. He said, "For John baptized with water, but in a few days you will be baptized with the Holy Spirit" (Acts 1:5). It is believed that this passage teaches the importance of being baptized with the Holy Spirit. In Matthew 28:19–20, the great commission consists of teaching about and ministering baptism of Christ until the end of the church age. Thus, the Inner Light of Christ guides people to fulfil this command regarding the baptism of Christ.

Friends at this yearly meeting deny that Jesus was baptized with water to give a model of water baptism. In spite of the fact that Jesus followed all the Jewish rites and ordinances because he was born into the Jewish community and the prophesy had to be fulfilled, people who convert to Jesus Christ do not need to be baptized with water or to be circumcised just like Jesus was. Barclay wrote, Jesus "observed Jewish feasts and rites and kept the Passover. But it does not follow that because he did so Christians must do so now."[11] Although John humbly told Jesus, "I need to be baptized by you, and do you come to me?" But Jesus answered him, "Let it be so now" (Matthew 3:14–15). In this reference, the time is required to be fulfilled, therefore, "they should have done so, because it was necessary that Jesus fulfilled everything, being baptized for the sinner, just as it was convenient for John to fulfill the task that God gave him to introduce Jesus."[12] The explanation for this fulfilment is found in Colossians 2:10–14, which declares to believers that Jesus was circumcised and baptized because of their sins.

Apostles' Position Regarding the One Baptism of Christ

It is said that the Catholic Church and other Christian churches follow the apostolic practice of water baptism. Indeed, the apostles baptized converts with water in the days of the early church because they lived in a period of transition between the law and the grace time. The apostles' points of views are found in the Bible regarding this transitional period and the Christ's baptism.

At first the disciple Peter, an outstanding disciple of Jesus, struggled to welcome fully the converted Gentiles into his faith community because their traditions were not according to the law of Moses. Actually, he forced the Gentiles to be circumcised and keep other Jewish observances. In one occasion the apostle Paul publicly rebuked him by saying, "I said to Cephas before them all, "If you, though a Jew, live like a Gentile and not like a Jew, how can you compel the Gentiles to live like Jews?" (Galatians 2:14). Moreover, in the story of Peter at Cornelius' home, God sent Peter to the Gentiles. When he preached to them, the Holy Spirit was poured on all those who were in the house of Cornelius, who had not been baptized in water or circumcised; seeing this situation, Peter commanded them to be baptized with water (Acts 10:47–48). However, later when there was already a council at the Jerusalem Church, he rectifies this error of imposing a Jewish rite on the Gentiles by explaining what happened in Cornelius' house. He said to the Council,

> As I began to speak, the Holy Spirit fell on them just as on us at the beginning. And I remembered the word of the Lord, how he said, "John baptized with water, but you shall be baptized with the Holy Spirit."
>
> *(Acts 11:15–16)*

This incident confirms Christians that "baptizing with the Holy Spirit that is administered by Christ has taken the place by replacing John's baptism that was baptizing with water."[13]

According to Acts 2, the apostle Peter's advice was clear about being baptized with the Holy Spirit. When he preached after the day of Pentecost with the power of God, the hearers of the sermon felt moved by the Holy Spirit, so they asked him and the other apostles what they should do to turn their lives toward God's will. Peter's response to these new converts was "repent, and be baptized every one of you in the name of Jesus Christ for the forgiveness of your sins; and you shall receive the gift of the Holy Spirit" (Acts 2:38). In this reference, first, the apostle does not say "be baptized with water"; second, the phrase "in the name of Jesus Christ" comes from the Greek word *ejpiv tov ojnovmati* (*epí tó onómati*), which means "within the name" and not "in the name," referring to uJpevr (*jupér*), so that in this biblical quotation the apostle states the baptism with the Holy Spirit. Therefore, the baptism of Christ was witnessed by the apostle Peter when he saw the Holy Spirit working in the three thousands of new converts' lives after his sermon.

The apostle Paul experienced baptism with the Holy Spirit. On the story of the calling and consecration of Saul, who was later called Paul, it is written that he arose and was baptized (Acts 9:18). The disciple Ananias did not baptize Saul with water, because at that time water baptism required the action of descending, but in this biblical story Saul rose to receive the baptism with the Holy Spirit. After that spiritual experience Paul became the great apostle to the Gentiles about fulfilling the commandment to preach the Gospel.

What does the apostle Paul say about his calling to be an apostle? As he started his ministry, he clarified that God did not command him to baptize with water. He mentioned that he only baptized with water a few early Christians because Christ sent to him to preach the Gospel and not to minister water baptism (I Corinthians 1:14–17a). Paul thanked God that he had not practiced water baptism anymore, but he had preached and taught about the baptism of Christ. For example, on his journey to Ephesus as a missionary according to Acts 19:2–5, Paul asked the new disciples whether they received the Holy Spirit after they accepted to follow Jesus Christ. When they told him that they did not hear about being baptized with the Holy Spirit, he exhorted them by saying that John's baptism was for repentance, but John himself urged people obey Jesus Christ. After that the new disciples were baptized with the Holy Spirit.

Baptizing With the Holy Spirit Is an Invisible Seal

Christians need the seal of the Holy Spirit, which is granted when someone is baptized with the Holy Spirit. Robert Barclay, in denying the baptism with water, talks about the "seal" of Spirit. For Barclay, "nothing except the Spirit of God is called the seal and pledge of our inheritance in the scriptures."[14] According to the apostle Paul, people who heard the Gospel and believed in Jesus Christ were sealed with the Holy Spirit, which was a promise that the Lord made for the ones who follow him (Ephesians 1:13,14). The seal of the Spirit cannot be compared with outward baptism, that is water baptism, in order that people's soul, spirit and body be cleansed and sanctified of all sins. And people who receive this "seal" of Spirit inherit all the promises of God together with Jesus Christ.

Baptism with the Holy Spirit is manifested within the life of a consecrated Christian. Christians who experienced the baptism of Christ live by the Spirit and walk by the Spirit. The fruits of the Holy Spirit govern their inward and outward lives; for example, they obey God in all their paths, speak with integrity, live a simple life and feel uneasy before any injustice. They know that they are children of God, because they felt to be "baptized into Christ are clothed with Christ" (Galatians 3:27). Thus, under the dispensation of Gospel the baptism of Christ transforms an individual to have a pure and sincere conscience to worship and serve God.

Conclusion

To conclude, the baptism of the Holy Spirit must be administered within the Christian Church. The traditional belief of water baptism as an ordinance does not have any more value for the believers of the new Gospel dispensation. The Holy Scriptures, our Lord Jesus Christ, the Disciples and Apostles reaffirmed that water baptism is not the baptism of Christ. At the core of Christians' spiritually, the one baptism, that is, Christ's baptism, is commanded to be obeyed in order to "Pursue peace with everyone, and the holiness without which no one will see the Lord" (Hebrew 12:14). Friends who are members of the Holiness Yearly Meeting have testified to be filled and transformed with the Holy Spirit. One Friend testified about being baptized with Holy Spirit by saying that while in prayer sincerely she was asking God that she can walk with and serve Him forever, the power of God's love searched her soul and her body in spirit, making her feel alive in Christ. And the Holy Spirit was felt inside her then like a huge light. Her body felt pure and soft, and her heart became vast land of peace, joy and love. This spiritual experience allows them to get a daily transformation to live out a life full of "love, joy, peace, patience, kindness, goodness, faith, meekness, self-control" (Galatians 5:22–23). Thus, baptizing with the Holy Spirit is an inward experience that brings a complete inner change in the life of a Christian to live in communion with God.

Notes

1 Dean Freiday, *Barclay's Apology in Modern English* (Newberg, OR: Barclay Press, 1998), 303.
2 Édgar Amílcar Madrid Morales, *Historia de los Amigos* (Chiquimula, Guatemala: Editorial "Setegu", 2002), 39.
3 Excerpts from the "Apology" by Robert Barclay, p. 10.
4 Wilmer A. Cooper, *A Living Faith: An Historical Study of Quakers Beliefs* (Richmond, IN: Friends United Press, 1990), 88. Historical Dictionary of Friends, p. 251.
5 Margery Post Abbott, *Historical Dictionary of Friends (Quakers)* (Lanham, MD and Oxford: The Scarecrow Press, Inc., 203), 251.
6 Dean Freiday, *Barclay's Apology in Modern English* (Newberg, OR: Barclay Press, 1998), 320.
7 Édgar Amílcar Madrid Morales, *Porque Jesús fue bautizado* (Chiquimula, Guatemala, 2013), 9.
8 Dean Freiday, *Barclay's Apology in Modern English* (Newberg, OR: Barclay Press, 1998), 301.
9 Ibid., 307.
10 Jack L. Willcuts, *A Family of Friends* (Newberg, OR: The Barclay Press, 1977), 30.
11 Dean Freiday, *Barclay's Apology in Modern English* (Newberg, OR: Barclay Press, 1998), 315.
12 Édgar Amílcar Madrid Morales, *Porque Jesús fue bautizado* (Chiquimula, Guatemala, 2013), 16.
13 Ibid., 12.
14 Dean Freiday, *Barclay's Apology in Modern English* (Newberg, OR: Barclay Press, 1998), 304.

33

LANGUAGE, LABELS AND BEYOND

The Shifting Foci of Concerns Over Adequate Representation in the Liberal Quaker 'Theism-Nontheism Debate'

Stewart David Yarlett

This chapter begins by considering the manner in which Liberal Quakers operate a suspicion around theological language. This is related to a characteristic Quaker view of language as insufficient for capturing the substance of religious experience and to typical Quaker assumptions around the religious experience as having a universal, pre-linguistic origin but being ultimately ineffable. The assumption of ineffability is often deployed to explain diverse expressions of belief. Thus, these assumptions have previously acted to facilitate, cover and accommodate the group's pluralism (Grant 2014a:37–38, 2015:261, 2018:8, 15–18). The chapter will examine the emergence of Quaker nontheism, some forms of which directly challenge these accommodating assumptions. Subsequently, the chapter will demonstrate that Quaker discussions over theism–nontheism still exhibit concerns over the accuracy and adequacy of labels. However, on both sides of the debate, there is a perceivable shift in motivation for the concerns Quakers display; namely, that Quakers are not simply concerned with the representation of a presumed common, religious experience but also with accurately representing their personal views. This includes a recognition of the differences between such views. This is a marked shift away from the formerly accommodating assumption that Quakers are using different words to express an experience of common origin; that is, Quakers are beginning to explicitly note that they are not necessarily all talking about the same thing. This is relatable to the group's pluralism and associated valuing of individualism. Additionally, it connects with the shift from a concern for the 'transcendent' to the 'subjective', delineated in Paul Heelas and Linda Woodhead's *The Spiritual Revolution* (2005). However, the Quaker context diverges from that of Heelas and Woodhead's subjective 'spirituality' in two ways: (1) Quakers are still incentivized to maintain their cohesion as a group; and (2) some views expressed push beyond a subjective 'spirituality'. The emerging desire to explicitly recognize their differences thus presents a challenge to group cohesion with which Quakers are currently grappling.

Language: Suspect and Secondary

The typical attitudes Liberal Quakers hold around 'theological' language have been usefully delineated, in broad terms, by Pink Dandelion (2008), and in a more specified manner, by

DOI: 10.4324/9780429030925-36

Rhiannon Grant (2014a, 2015, 2018). Dandelion argues that Quakers have typically operated a 'culture of silence', which he describes as involving

> The devaluation of language, the value of silence, and the consequent rules governing the breaking of silence with speech . . . the caution given words and the philosophical caution towards theology as a sufficient description of experience.
>
> *(2008:22)*

It is under the 'mask' of this 'culture of silence' that Dandelion holds Liberal Quakerism's belief culture was able to diversify and become post-Christian (ibid.). There are now numerous Quakers (63.5%) who understand their in-group identity outside of an explicitly Christian framework (Hampton 2014:36), potentially as, for example, Quaker Buddhists, Hindus, Muslims, Jews, Pagans, or simply as 'Quakers' with no further modifiers (Boulton 2006; Dandelion and Collins 2008; Huber 2001; Vincett 2009).

Grant's work further illuminates the types of assumptions and attitudes Liberal Quakers hold around the relation between religious experience and language; how and why they view theology as an insufficient descriptor of said experience; and how these assumptions may act to facilitate and, to a degree, accommodate, Quaker diversification. Grant delineates three major Quaker assumptions concerning the relationship between language and experience:

(1) That language is secondary to a primary experience.
(2) That language is inadequate for describing an ultimately ineffable experience.
(3) That language (i.e. the diversity of Quaker religious expression) nonetheless refers to a universal experience of common origin.

(Grant 2014a:37–38, 2015:261, 2018:8, 15–18)

With similarities to Dandelion, Grant contends that concerns about the inadequacy of language, as a secondary medium for describing a primary, ineffable experience, provoke a (Quaker) pattern of 'reticence' about expressing theological views (2018:14). Crucially, she highlights that Quakers generally maintain that there is a unity in their experience, what Quaker Rex Ambler denotes as the 'mysterious and finally inexpressible common ground' (1994:29). Grant notes that the assumption of inadequacy is often employed by Quakers to explain their diverse belief culture whilst allowing the assumption of unity to be maintained (2014a:38).

Grant also details how Quakers will often employ a metaphor of 'translation' when interacting with divergent expressions of belief (2018:18). She points to an example of Dandelion writing internally as a Quaker where he asks readers to ' "translate" or hear where the words come from' when he chooses to use traditional God-talk (2010:3). Grant contends that this metaphor of 'translation' feeds into a process whereby Quakers look to express and represent belief within the community by constructing 'list-format remarks', comprising 'apparent synonyms' for the religious experience (2018:10). Much of what Grant demarcates concerning Quaker assumptions around language is validated throughout the group's popular literature. However, a particularly stark example comes from John Lampen's pamphlet *Finding the Words*:

> There is something more in reality than whatever we can perceive with our senses and hold . . . in our minds. . . . This . . . is not merely the object of belief; it is experienced by the individual. . . . It is not simply an individual experience since we can also meet it as a group. . . . This is the experience which has been given such names as 'God', 'The Light', 'The Tao' . . . 'The Spirit'. . . . It is not the naming which is important

but the experience. . . . The 'something more' is essentially indescribable. Theologies, at best, can only point towards it. . . . tolerance should be the rule in religious discussion. . . . there is nothing incongruous in people worshipping together who have wildly differing beliefs-systems, if they are trying to experience together the reality which underpins all creeds.

(2007:6)

Thus Grant gives a fuller account (than the 'culture of silence') concerning how Quakers *will* talk, in a certain manner, about their theological beliefs; that is, with reticent patterns in place involving 'hedging and qualifications', 'lists' and so forth (2018:14). Notably, her initial delineation indicates that Quakers operate a general, theological rationale, that there is a universal experience that cannot be adequately (singularly) linguistically represented. It appears to be this 'universalist' rationale (when left unquestioned) that acts to accommodate, limit (and possibly mask) Quaker diversity, as Grant has formerly suggested:

The . . . universalist position . . . within Quakerism . . . can be thought of as taking . . . [a] kind of second-order role. . . . in other words, it tells you the kind of things that can be said within the . . . game at hand.

(2014a:178)

Caroline Plüss has likewise contended that Quakers will typically respond to an apparent lack of consensus by affirming a collective view that the basis for their worship is 'mystical' and that 'words are inadequate to express what is believed to be a shared experience' (2007:265). Significantly, both Grant and Plüss imply at least two different major motivations behind the adoption of this rationale:[1]

1   Ostensibly original theological concerns about difficulties in accurately representing a 'mystical' experience in words.
2   Ostensibly secondary social concerns about (a) maintaining group cohesion whilst (b) being inclusive to theological diversity. (Grant 2018:2;15; Plüss 2007:265)

This chapter looks to demonstrate that the emergence of Quaker nontheism has directly challenged these accommodating assumptions, pressuring Quakers to (not mask but) explicitly confront their internal group tensions and jeopardizing group cohesion (2a). However, because of a sustained social desire to be inclusive (2b), the emergence of nontheism has not resulted in a breakdown but rather discussions between the different subgroups. These dialogues reveal complexities and general shifts in what Quakers are concerned about accurately representing in their linguistic expressions of belief (1).

The Subjective Turn

These shifts may be helpfully elucidated by first considering the formulations of Heelas and Woodhead in *The Spiritual Revolution* (2005), along with their treatment of Liberal Quakerism within that work. In the work they draw upon the claims of Charles Taylor (1991) relating to a 'major cultural shift', whereby individuals moved from living their lives primarily with reference to external authorities and systems to living their lives primarily with reference to the authority of 'one's own subjective experiences . . . [and] feelings'. This shift is also framed as being 'a turn away from "life-as" . . . a dutiful wife, father, husband . . . self-made man etc. . . . a member of a community or tradition . . . to "subjective-life"' (Heelas and Woodhead 2005:2–3). Heelas and Woodhead apply this framework to developments in religion and spiritual belief. They draw a distinction between 'life-as religion' and 'subjective-life spirituality'. They characterize the former as sacralizing life-as living in reference to an external authority, by 'subordinating subjective-life to the "higher" authority of transcendent meaning . . . the latter invokes the sacred in the cultivation of . . . subjective-life' (2005:5).

John Knox (2016) has expanded upon this framework suggesting additional 'Sacro-States' (i.e., religious/spiritual 'systems' where people sacralize different referents of authority and/ or significance). Knox demarcates 'Sacro-theism' and 'Sacro-egoism' as approximate equivalents to Heelas and Woodhead's transcendent religion and subjective spirituality respectively. However, he adds the (interrelated) categories of 'Sacro-communalism'; where the lay community becomes sacralized and 'Sacro-clericalism'; where tradition becomes sacralized (2016:6–18). These may be understood as alternative forms of 'life-as religions', in that they still concern people understanding their religious life in reference to an external authority but the primary reference point is not necessarily transcendent or theistic. This insight that 'life-as religion' may also develop into alternative forms (involving alternative 'social' reference points) is useful for understanding developments in Liberal Quakerism, as shall be returned to later.

Regarding Heelas and Woodhead's specific treatment of Liberal Quakerism, they position the group within 'congregations of experiential humanity', on the edge of the 'life-as religion' category (2005:17–18). They hold that whilst Quakers emphasize the importance of an internal religious experience – which is noted to synthesize well with an individualistic viewpoint (Campbell 1978) – Quakers still understand this experience via a transcendent reference point, external to their subjective lives. Given the limiting and accommodating assumptions discussed in the previous section, concerning *the* experience having a universal, pre-linguistic origin, it seems fair to claim that Quakers generally view their religion as based on an external 'transcendent' authority.

More recently, however, Dandelion (2019) has affirmed that 'Heelas and Woodhead are right to include organizational Quakerism at the experiential end of religion but wrong not to have its popular expression overlapping into their "holistic milieu"' of subjective spirituality (2019:129). He contends rather, that a growth of subjective spirituality has occurred 'within a nominally transcendent religion' (2019:9). This is a helpful way to conceptualize the type of shifts this chapter is interested in exploring (along with consequent implications and developments for the group's dynamics) through an examination of some of the internal framings and discussions produced within the 'theism-nontheism debate.'

Nontheism and the Elevation of Language

Quaker nontheism is an umbrella term which refers to a growing component of Liberal Quakers who explicitly state they do not hold theistic beliefs yet still identify as Quakers. The term is intended to reflect the subgroup's own diversity; involving 'agnostics, atheists and skeptics' and so forth (Boulton 2006:5–6, 2012:35–36). Since the early 2000s there has been an increasingly visible 'organised nontheist presence within Liberal Quakerism' (Boulton 2012:5). The 2013 British Quaker survey found that those respondents reporting no belief in God to have more than doubled to 14.3% from 7% in 2003 (Hampton 2014:7–43); a dedicated website was set up in 2004; numerous dedicated workshops and conferences have taken place, and 2011 saw the establishment of the Nontheist Friends Network UK, which Britain Yearly Meeting have accepted as a Quaker Recognised Body (Boulton 2012:5–7).[2] The debate around nontheism and whether it can authentically be incorporated within Quakerism, has been further brought to a head by the currently ongoing revision process for the group's Book of Discipline.[3] A consultation of Quaker Meetings in 2015 found that the theism-nontheism divide was identified by Quakers as the key issue in need of resolution before a revision could proceed (Boulton 2016:57), consequently a think-tank took place in February 2016 resulting in the publication *God, words and us* (Rowlands 2017a).

A number of Quaker responses to the divide fall in line with the typical assumptions and responses outlined in the opening sections, that the divide is superficial and really about linguistic expression; theist and nontheist Quakers are talking about the same phenomenon but express it with inadequate language; and they have a common external reference point of transcendent experience, however, some Quakers prefer not to speak to this experience using the term 'God' or theistic language. Under Grant's framework, such problems may be resolved by adding extra 'synonyms' to Quaker list-format remarks. Indeed, this typical response may be perceived as having a high likelihood of reconciling the divide; it seems to reflect a component of beliefs held within Quaker nontheism (Dandelion 1996:157–158; Nontheist Friends 2005) and has been entertained by both 'theist' and nontheist commentators such as Paul Anderson and David Rush, respectively:

> Most of the contributors believed in some sort of spiritual reality we might term 'God' but had problems with particular descriptions of that reality. . . . I'm not sure they should see themselves as strict atheists or nontheists.
>
> *(Anderson 2012:4)*

> One very important gap in knowledge concerns what Quakers mean when we speak of God. . . . This writer senses that the theist/non-theist divide is far more fluid than we have supposed, and that we will find this divide often to be a false one.
>
> *(Rush 2006:106)*

However, there are other forms of Quaker nontheism that are less likely to be reconciled by the 'universalist' theological rationale. Significantly, this primarily concerns the form promoted by David Boulton; the most prominent exponent of Quaker nontheism. Boulton's views are heavily influenced by the non-realist thought of theologian Don Cupitt. Cupitt advocates a view of the relationship between experience and language which appears to be a complete inversion of the typical Quaker assumptions. He elevates language to a primary position. For Cupitt it is through language that people construct and access a secondary experience in any meaningful sense, as he makes clear in writing:

> Language comes first. . . . it prescribes the shape of the various 'realities' . . . amongst which we move, and not the other way round. Reality does not determine language: language determines reality.
>
> *(1985:220)*

Boulton positively refers to Cupitt numerous times in his writing. He places Cupitt as a key initial influence on the development of his nontheist views saying: ' "God" once meant something clear and definite . . . Cupitt was forcing me to rethink. . . . Language didn't work as I had . . . naively supposed' (2005:65). And in a review of Cupitt's book *Mysticism After Modernity* (1998),

Boulton gives an explicit endorsement of the view of experience as secondary to linguistic construction:

> The notion of non-linguistic experience or non-verbal thought has been . . . comprehensively demolished. . . . The notion that there are or can be . . . extra-linguistic psychological states or experiences that verify beliefs about God will not bear scrutiny. To think it, we'd have to 'put it into words', which would drag it down into language. . . . We cannot think ourselves clear of language. Only language can turn an event into an experience of something.
>
> *(Boulton 1998)*

Through an engagement with Cupitt, Boulton promotes a form of nontheism that directly opposes the accommodating view of a universal pre-linguistic experience.

This Boulton-Cupitt view does not necessarily hold that there are no experiential phenomena (or events) prior to language, but rather that they are formless, without meaning and entirely subjective (Grant 2021). There is no meaningful way of establishing that there is a common experience between people, as linguistic/communicative systems inadequately capture or (more accurately) reshape subjective realities. Notably, this concern for the inadequacy of language for capturing experience seems to fit very closely with the typical Quaker view. However, there is a shift whereby the concern is no longer about language's inadequacy for representing a divine, transcendent experience, but rather its inability to convey subjective life without reshaping it. Indeed, for Cupitt, the very purpose of religion becomes about creatively directing this reshaping, to promote self-actualization: 'the religious task has become the task of attaining true selfhood. The formation of a creative artist is the best image for this task' (1985:266). The development of the Boulton-Cupitt form of nontheism therefore seems to resonate with Heelas and Woodhead's view of an emerging subjective spirituality.

However, both Quaker (Grant 2015, 2018, 2021; Russ 2017; Wood 2016a, 2016b) and non-Quaker (Ward 2005:329) commentators have criticized the adoption of individualism within such a non-realist conceptual framework as inconsistent. The suggestion being that language is communal, so even if peoples' access to each other's subjectivities is shaped and/ or limited by language they can still reach points of consensus, and develop common, cultural and/or traditional ways of speaking (or 'grammars') within a linguistic-type system. Such responses may be linked to Knox's concepts of Sacro-communalism or Sacro-clericalism (2016:6–18) and will be returned to shortly. First, though, it is pertinent to examine further ways in which nontheists have presented themselves, and significantly, been responded to within the Liberal Quaker group, which do potentially indicate the development of a more general subjectivization.

General Subjectivization

The more general concern nontheists show for the accurate representation of their individual views can be observed in the discussion between nontheists concerning the labelling of their movement, described in Boulton's introduction to *Godless for God's Sake* (2006), a book compiled by 27 Quaker nontheists. Before this description, it is noted that 'labels are nearly always problematic' (2006:6), which seems like a typical Quaker sentiment. However, the description makes it clear that concerns around language and labels have little to do with notions of an ineffable transcendent experience, but rather that their group's label accurately represents (and sits well) with individual views held amongst the group.

The introduction also affirms that it is necessary to have a label distinguishing nontheists from theists:

> Religious labels have the useful function of distinguishing one group from another . . . it makes sense for clarity to distinguish between theist and nontheist. . . . Those who charge that this is unnecessarily divisive are often simply wishing that the distinctions were not there. . . . Far better . . . to acknowledge our diversity . . . celebrate it, and – for the sake of clarity and integrity – label it.
>
> *(Boulton 2006:7)*

The characterization of 'simply wishing that the distinctions were not there' may too easily dismiss the nuances of typical Quaker approaches to resolving theological conflict. It is not simply that the distinctions are ignored or wished away but that there is an active theological rationale around the ineffability of religious experience that explains the differences as superficial and linguistic. However, it is notable that explicitly recognizing difference and distinctions is framed as being inclusive to diversity. Quakers typically value inclusiveness highly, but given a parallel desire to prevent division and maintain cohesion (Grant 2018:15), this inclusiveness has historically been facilitated and bracketed by a universalist rationale. The manner in which Boulton characterizes an honest acknowledgement of diversity challenges this bracketing.

Significantly, a number of 'theist' Quakers responding to nontheism have taken an amiable stance to this more radical inclusiveness with its acknowledgement of a real divide between the two groups. Demonstrations of this can be found throughout the *God, words and us* (Rowlands 2017a) publication that came out of the think tank specifically set up to discuss the theism-nontheism divide:

> Diversity of belief and language among friends is real and should be acknowledged.
>
> *(2017a:55)*

> The Quaker community needs to engage in open dialogue on a continual basis. . . . If labels are needed to describe people's belief they should be self-chosen and not imposed on others.
>
> *(2017a:2)*

> If someone self-describes with a label such as 'Christian' or 'nontheist', it is important to explore what that label actually means for them – it is very easy to jump to conclusions that are not what they meant.
>
> *(2017a:17)*

In a follow-up talk on the think-tank process and complementary publication, editor Helen Rowlands stated that the participants were clear that they were not necessarily using different language to describe the same experiences (2017b). This seemingly demonstrates a more general breakdown of the accommodating assumptions discussed in the opening section.

Notably, during the think tank, 'theist' Quakers also voiced concerns over the accuracy of how their personal beliefs were being labelled. Many claimed that they had never held conventional or traditional views of God or theistic beliefs to begin with, and that they were only being defined in opposition to the nontheists. Those present therefore adopted the label 'non-non-theists' (Rowlands 2017a:49, 55, 67). In emphasizing the complexities and unconventionalities of their 'theistic' beliefs these 'non-nontheists' may be understood as intimating that the divide is potentially not as large as is perceived; similar to the earlier quoted reflections of Anderson (2012) and Rush (2006). However, in responding in this way these 'non–non-theists' feasibly allow for the discussion on both sides to be focused on the treatment of personal subjective views, thereby (perhaps inadvertently) encouraging a further shift towards subjectivization.

This potential aspect of the shift within Quaker thought is highlighted by Quaker philosopher Jeffery Dudiak in his discussion of the theism-nontheism debate (2012). Dudiak argues that the modern age has not simply seen a turn away from the transcendent and towards the subjective in relation to religiosity. But rather, ' "subjectivity" has undergone a transformation' in the very way it is understood (2012:27–28). Dudiak holds that a pre-modern understanding of God and subjectivity placed subjects as 'subject to' God and living in 'God's world'; faith was an 'ontological' concern for the subject about recognizing 'What *is* is lived as gift' out of God. Under a modern understanding, the subject is elevated to 'rational epistemic subject, who is capable of adjudicating . . . existence or non-existence' and belief in God becoming epistemological question to be assessed by said active subject. Dudiak claims that the very labels and oppositional categories of theism-nontheism are 'modernist, rationalist invention[s]' (2012:28):

> What they share is . . . the claim that it is . . . possible . . . [and] of central importance, that we make a judgment about whether God . . . exists. . . . Theism and atheism, as 'options' open to us as subjects endowed with the volition to make such a judgment, are . . . modern possibilities.
>
> *(2012:27)*

He suggests that engaging in this very debate instigates a greater valuing of nontheism (and perhaps subjective-life spirituality) than a faithful life lived out of God:

> God is dead . . . as soon as we argue for or against God, rather than from out of God . . . atheism has perhaps already won . . . even among the most strident theists . . . insofar as . . . [the] modern . . . places the centre of gravity in the believing subject . . . as prior to that which is believed or disbelieved.
>
> *(2012:29)*

Dudiak thus can be seen as proposing that the subjective turn is both subtler and more comprehensive than Heelas and Woodhead (2005) suggest. Categorizing people as either valuing the authority of their subjective realities or, living life-as religion in reference to an external transcendent authority, does not fully follow through on the implications of the modern mindset for Dudiak. According to Dudiak, the very notion that that individuals can make a choice between the two favours the subjective-life and undermines the possibility and legitimacy of living such a life-as religion.

Indeed, this resonates with the views Taylor later developed in *A Secular Age* (2007), which Dudiak references directly. Taylor discusses how the shift away from a pre-modern context, where a live engagement with God was 'naively' assumed, to a modern context, where believing in God is an option, has cause an uncertain setting even amongst believers, whereby they are simultaneously split:

> Between two standpoints: an 'engaged' one in which we live . . . the reality our standpoint opens to us; and a 'disengaged' one in which we are able to see ourselves as occupying one standpoint amongst a range of possible ones.
>
> *(2007:12)*

Even 'engaged' religious believers have to hold an awareness of this pluralistic framework, which, in line with Dudiak, may give secularity the advantage. In José Casanova's terms: 'Secularity . . . tends to become . . . the default option, which can be naively experienced' (2010:226).

There may be intellectual space to question Dudiak and Taylor's characterization of pre-modern religion. However, in relation to the Quaker case the insight that simply placing non-belief as an option next to belief, undermines life-as religion and promotes subjectivization (and potentially secularity) amongst all parties, may be considered more pertinent. For Quakers are seemingly inviting the need for a disengaged standpoint specifically into their own space for religious engagement. It is not simply that they have to adopt a disengaged stance when recognizing the plurality of wider society but their internal diversity as well. It may be said that Quakers had to recognize internal diversity before the increased emergence of nontheism. However, as discussed above, this diversity was previously accommodated under the assumption that it was superficial and due to language; Quakers still saw themselves as engaging in the same ineffable, 'transcendent' experience. In explicitly interlocuting with views that directly challenge these accommodating assumptions, Quaker 'non-non-theists' have to *internally* contemplate and defend their engagement with transcendence as a potential (total not partial) subjective reality. This may engender a more generalized subjectivization (and/or concern for accurate representation of their subjective views), which may actually undermine cohesion and raison d'être of the Liberal Quaker religion.[4]

Beyond (or Between) Subjective 'Spiritualities'

However, Dudiak also suggests that there may be a way of moving beyond the labels and oppositional conceptual framework of the theism-nontheism divide, and its central focus on the subject's judgement. He advocates that Quakers should seek to push 'through to a hyper-critical, self-aware "second naivete"' – wherein, Quakers do not 'abandon modern rationality' but do not 'give it the last word' (2012:32), allowing themselves to move beyond the theist-nontheist framework. Casanova similarly suggests that modern individuals have now become so familiar with the dynamics of secularity that they may be able to move to a reflexive (self-aware) post-secularity (2010:280–281). These types of suggestions, framed in this manner, seem to have some traction amongst Quakers as a response to nontheism. Dudiak has been referenced extensively and positively as a possible reconciliatory response in recent treatments of Quaker nontheism (Kershner 2018:63–64; Randazzo 2018:284–286). However, there is a question of what this move beyond an oppositional framework of subjectivities would actually entail. Accordingly, this final section briefly outlines and examines some of the ways Quakers may, or are attempting to move beyond this framework.

Practice and Action

Dudiak's characterization of faith, as something that is lived rather than epistemically assessed, chimes with some typical Quaker sensibilities, sensibilities which are captured by Quaker theologian Janet Scott's declaration that 'what matters to Quakers is not the label by which we are called . . . but the life' (1980:70). Indeed, another reason Grant gives for Quakers being suspicious of language is that they favour action over what is perceived as intellectual pontification (2018:15). This connects with Dandelion's sociological claim that Liberal Quakerism is cohered via an implicit 'behavioural-creed' rather than one prescribing the content of belief (2008:25–33). I have previously discussed how both nontheists, and Quakers in general, showcase a growing reflexive internal affinity for the notion that Quakerism is a religion based on what is practiced, on what is done (Yarlett 2020).

This move may be seen to offer Quakers a way out of the theism–nontheism oppositional framework, as it shifts the focus from debates about individual beliefs and towards the Quaker identity, represented via practice and action. In her forthcoming publication, Grant makes reference to David Cooper's *God Is a Verb* (1998) to suggest that it may not be useful to understand God as a noun; a labelled 'thing' one makes judgements about, but rather a verb – 'godding' being potentially a thing one does.

There is a necessary note of caution here, however; Dandelion's 'behavioural-creed' was a sociological formulation concerning Liberal Quakers' conservativism, specifically over their method of worship. However, within the Quaker community what counts and Quaker practice is potentially open to idiosyncratic interpretation and expansive lay-theologizing (Collins 2002:151; Yarlett 2020:217). It is not necessarily a static or stable basis for consensus.

Indeed, considering Grant's formulations around Quaker list-making, such list-making may itself be understood as a Quaker practice and/or a 'speech-act' (2018:39). However, here Grant's work also points to a way in which there may be potential for cultivating consensus via 'grammatically/linguistically' structured type practices. For as was mentioned previously, language and grammar are produced communally, and points of consensus can still be reached within those systems, indeed they must be for communication to be possible. And again, Quakers writing internally have suggested that a path to reconciliation may be to focus on Quaker shared narratives and traditions in order to develop a sense of Quaker 'grammar' (Russ 2017; Wood 2016a, 2016b) – again resonating with Knox's additional 'Sacro-states' (2016). However, one potential problem with this response is it again seems to jar with Quakerism history as an experiential religion, and there are still questions over how stable any reference points for a sense of Quaker tradition can be (Russ 2017).

Intersubjectivity and Listening

However, what Grant and these other Quaker commentators are pointing towards may be understood as intersubjectivity. The concept of intersubjectivity relates to how meaning, consensus, culture and relationships between subjects are mutuality constructed by individuals. It notes that this very process queries the possibility of objective external knowledge – including about the transcendent, but denies that this leaves questions of meaning 'entirely up to the individual' (Chandler and Munday 2011:223–224). The concept seems to play exactly into Dudiak's call for a 'self-aware "second naivete"'.

The framing also indicates the possibility of Quakers moving past a framework of oppositional subjectivities by emphasizing, not the representation of their own subjectivity, but rather the need to attend to the subjectivities of others, and the relationalities between members of their community. Such an aspiration to switch emphasis in this manner could be seen as a factor in the 2016 think tank's adoption of a 'radical inclusiveness'.

Liberal Quakerism may also be well placed in conceptual resources to perform such a shift. Grant (2014b) and Quaker theologian Rachel Muers (2004) have previously explored Nelle Morton's (1985) feminist theological notion of 'hearing to speech'; the framing of hearing as an active practice. Muers supplements this notion with the philosophy of Gemma Fiumara, who places listening as *The Other Side of Language* (1990) and seeks to give it priority over speech, as making speech possible. From this Muers builds a theology with a central understanding of God as one that listens. Grant has supplemented this by suggesting this listening should be reciprocal, and that listening to God is a foundational Quaker practice (2014b). The centrality of listening to Quaker theology and practice has been a prominent theme in some of Grant's most recent theological work (2020, 2021). Notably, Dudiak similarly suggests that metaphors of hearing, of 'being attuned' to God's voice or the music of religious moments, may be a way of moving beyond a framework

> of 'seeing', i.e . . . the active judging . . . of objective facts, and [towards] a commitment to cultivating a more passive sensibility . . . developing . . . 'ears to hear'. Such a commitment seems to me commensurate with corporate Quaker practice, and consistent with historic Quaker faith.
>
> *(2012:31–32)*

Such talk of listening to God may be viewed as likely to be dismissed by nontheists. However, in Dudiak's terms the crucial point is 'cultivating a more passive sensibility', which is unfortunate phrasing given the above mentioned feminist framings of hearing and listening being a more active practice. But, the manner in which listening is being employed in these cases is still similar, in that they are trying to promote a 'de-centring' of the priority given to a subject's rational formulations and expression of their individual beliefs. The suggestion seems to be that this de-centring would involve promoting an attention to alterity,[5] or in other words, other-centeredness.

Woodhead has previously produced work with Eeva Sointu on women's approaches to subjective spirituality. Wherein they argued that women's spirituality tended to involve a negotiation between ' "living life for others" and "living life for oneself"' (2008:259). Woodhead and Sointu raise some interesting complexities to consider regarding the dynamics of what one might call an 'intersubjective spirituality', although there is not space for a full exploration here. However, I believe it is illuminating to consider this shift to a more 'passive sensibility' suggested in Dudiak's work, in light of the work of the philosopher Emmanuel Levinas, with which Dudiak himself engages (Dudiak 2012:31).

Ethics and Alterity as Experience

Levinas' work looks to create an account of an experiential ethics; an experiential response to alterity or; an 'intersubjective responsibility' as a first philosophy, meaning that Levinas looks to challenge the traditional philosophical understanding of theology or ontology (i.e., being) as the most fundamental discipline for understanding the universal principles of life (Bergo 2019).

The basis for Levinas' challenge to ontology as first philosophy is an argument around the experience of encountering the other. Levinas claims that the 'other' places an infinite demand of responsibility on our subjective sense of being. This demand comes from a place of vulnerability and involves a call not to destroy or cast out the other but rather to be radically hospitable or radically inclusive. Levinas admits that one may ignore this call to infinite responsibility. However, he maintains that the call persists, it 'haunts' and informs our understanding of our own ontology; keeping us 'awake' to our own sense of being (Bergo 2019; Levinas in Kearney 2004:78–79).

Whether or not one agrees with Levinas' account of a primordial ethical experience is not precisely the concern of this chapter. Rather, what I wish to draw attention to is the similarities between Levinas' attempt to place ethics (rather than ontology or theology) as a first philosophy, and Knox's suggestion that one can conceive of different Sacro-states where different reference points are being emphasized and sacralized. Levinas' work could be understood as suggesting another Sacro-state, one where other-centeredness is sacralized, what might be called Sacro-alterity.

The philosopher Jacques Derrida contended that Levinas' account of ethical experience breaks down the distinction 'between the infinite alterity of God and the . . . infinite alterity of every human' (2008:84). Notably, having the option to understand this alterity as relating to theistic or nontheistic concepts may attract Quakers to 'Sacro-alterity' as having the potential to reconcile the theism-nontheism divide. The fact that Levinas understands ethics in experiential terms may also be attractive to Quakers. By following such a trajectory, the caution (or 'reticence') Quakers operate around expressing one's subjective beliefs and the 'radical inclusiveness' emerging from the interactions between diverging Quaker subgroups, may be placed as (actually) constitutive of the Quaker religious or spiritual experience. Under this framework, Quaker concerns around language may be understood to increasingly involve concerns around inadequacies in properly representing the beliefs of others, and also allowing space for others to express their beliefs without being silenced.

This type of Levinassian ethical experience and the related other-centred 'listening' discussed previously may also appeal to Quakers as they seem to synergize well with other Quaker practices and values, such as silence and nonviolence (Muers 2015:58; Levinas 1991:203). This discussion may be connected with work in my other chapter in this volume (Chapter 57), which gives some further consideration to how an openness towards others is being 'sacralized', in reference to nonviolence by some commentators (particularly Rock and Gillman) in attempts to reconcile the theism-nontheism divide.

Indeed, the compelling resonances between Quakers and Levinas are such that when previously reflecting upon them, Rachel Muers posed the question: 'Is it possible to say that Quakers, like Levinas, begin with ethics?' (2010:56). At the time, Dudiak responded in the negative, saying:

> I myself am not convinced that Quakers (at least traditionally) begin with ethics; our 'ethics' rather testify to the God whose proximity finds expression in them, so that 'the power of the Lord can be over all'.
>
> *(2010:40)*

Nevertheless, it is notable that Dudiak added the caveat 'at least traditionally' in brackets. It contains the suggestion that the primary concern of Quakerism may shift. Accordingly, in Dudiak's piece directly addressing the issue of theism-nontheism a few years later, he is suggesting such a shift, beyond old frameworks. He makes reference to Levinas, a 'passive sensibility', and having 'ears to hear', but it is not clear whether he is concerned with Quakers being passive in hearing God's voice, whether God is being used as a metaphor for Quakers attending to each other, or both. It seems that, as Derrida suggested with Levinas, the distinction between human and divine alterity is somewhat blurred in Dudiak's piece.

I believe this is to be (somewhat) expected as, sacralizing ethics or a generalized appreciation of alterity, is an avenue of thought that avails itself to a group like the Liberal Quakers, a diverse group which is looking to reconcile a disparate – at points contradictory – belief culture, including nontheistic elements. The shift of focus towards attending to the subjectivity of others is a possible response to the generalized development of a more individualistic subjectivization.

It is beyond the scope of this chapter to assess whether such a shift to focusing on alterity is likely to be successful in renewing Liberal Quakerism. However, I believe this chapter and my other one in this volume (Chapter 57) demonstrate that (influenced by a variety of factors) such responses are emerging within the Liberal Quaker discourse.

Conclusion

This chapter began by exploring the typical assumptions Liberal Quakers have operated around the relation between religious experience and its linguistic expression, following the argument that Quakers have generally understood that they have a common, mystical experience of pre-linguistic origins that cannot be adequately expressed in language. The assumption of the inadequacy of language is used to explain theological diversity within the group. Thus, the chapter claimed that this assumption acted as a 'universal' theological rationale that accommodated and limited Quaker diversity. The chapter held that this aligned with Heelas and Woodhead's characterization of Liberal Quakerism as a religion with an emphasis on experience, but ultimately based around a transcendent reference point rather than people's 'subjective spiritualties', with Quakers being ostensibly concerned over the representation of a universal divine experience and this giving them some sense of cohesion.

However, the chapter argued that with the emergence of nontheism (particularly the form espoused by Boulton), this accommodating rationale is being directly challenged within the group, with a chief importance now being given (by elements of the group) to the role of language is cultivating a representing one's subjective reality. In examining the way other Quakers have reacted to these directly challenging viewpoints, by explicitly interlocuting with them and trying to be inclusive, the chapter argues that a more general subjectivization can be seen as occurring within the group; with 'non–non-theists' shifting to focus on the representation of their own subjective views rather than that of a common transcendent experience. This development was seen to fall align with formulations in Taylor's work and notably Quaker philosopher's Jeffery Dudiak's framing of the theism-nontheism debate.

The final section reflected upon ways in which Liberal Quakers may be responding to this subjectivization in light of Dudiak's call for Quakers to in a self-aware manner move beyond the oppositional theism-nontheism framework. In light of this, the section considered Quaker's tendency to focus on practice and action above labels, and pointed to some commentators who suggest Quaker practice may be more expansive than physical behaviour, including, for example, a sense of consensus around ways of speaking. The section argued that such formulations were liable not to remain stable but be open to further interpretative work within the Quaker community. In line with this, the section considered the ways in which the practice of 'listening' and an explicit other-centeredness (or Sacro-alterity), concerned not with the accurate representation of one's own beliefs but a caution around the representation, others could be seen as potentially emerging within the group, framed as a possible response to a more individualistic subjectivization.

Notes

1 Grant also details additional reasons Quakers give for their suspicion theology and theological language, such as a preference for action, which is considered later in the chapter. Grant, *British Quakers and Religious Language*, p. 15.
2 Quaker Recognised Bodies are attached to but not directly under the organizational mandate of Britain Yearly Meeting.
3 The 'closest thing Quakers in Britain have to an authoritative text', which is 'revised . . . approximately once in each generation'. Grant, *Wittgensteinian Investigations*, pp. 28–29.
4 This all connects with Dandelion's theory of internal secularization (2019) which is more thoroughly considered in my other chapter in this volume.
5 Alterity is a term used primarily in the disciplines of continental philosophy and anthropology to refer to 'otherness'.

References

Ambler, R. (1994). *End of Words: Issues in Contemporary Quaker Theology*. London: Quaker Books.
Anderson, P. (2012). 'Is "Nontheist Quakerism" a Contradiction of Terms?'. *Quaker Religious Thought*. **118**(1), 5–20.

Bergo, B. (2019). 'Emmanuel Levinas'. In: Zalta, E. N. (ed.), *The Stanford Encyclopedia of Philosophy* [online]. Fall 2019 edition. [Viewed 2 March 2021]. Available from: https://plato.stanford.edu/entries/levinas/

Boulton, D. (1998). 'What on Earth is Mysticism?'. *Sea of Faith Magazine*. Spring [online]. [Viewed 31 May 2020]. Available from: https://www.sofn.org.uk/reviews/mystic.html

Boulton, D. (2005). *The Trouble with God: Building the Republic of Heaven*. 2nd ed. Winchester; New York, NY: O Books. [2002].

Boulton, D. (ed.) (2006). *Godless for God's Sake: Nontheism in Contemporary Quakerism*. 1st ed. Dent, Cumbria: Dales Historical Monographs.

Boulton, D. (2012). 'Nontheism among Friends: Its Emergence and Meaning'. *Quaker Religious Thought*. **118**, 35–44.

Boulton, D. (2016). *Through a Glass Darkly: A Defence of Quaker Nontheism*. Dent, Cumbria: Dales Historical Monographs.

Chandler, D. and Munday, R. (2011). *A Dictionary of Media and Communication*. 1st ed. Oxford: Oxford University Press.

Collins, P. (2002). 'Habitus and the Storied Self: Religious Faith and Practice as a Dynamic Means of Consolidating Identities'. *Culture and Religion*. **3**(2), 147–161.

Cooper, D. (1998). *God is a Verb: Kabbalah and the Practice of Mystical Judaism*. New York, NY: Berkley Publishing Group.

Cupitt, D. (1985). *The Sea of Faith*. Paperback ed. London: BBC. [1984].

Cupitt, D. (1998). *Mysticism After Modernity*. Oxford: Blackwell.

Dandelion, P. (1996). *A Sociological Analysis of the Theology of Quakers: The Silent Revolution*. Lampeter: Edwin Mellen Press.

Dandelion, P. (2008). 'The Creation of Coherence: The "Quaker Double-culture" and the "Absolute Perhaps".' In: Dandelion, P. and Collins, P. (eds.), *The Quaker Condition: The Sociology of a Liberal Religion*. Newcastle: Cambridge Scholars Publishing. 22–37

Dandelion, P. (2010). *Celebrating the Quaker Way*. 2nd Revised ed. London: Quaker Books. [2009].

Dandelion, P. (2019). *The Cultivation of Conformity: Towards a General Theory of Internal Secularisation*. Oxford and New York, NY: Routledge.

Dandelion, P. and Collins, P. (eds.) (2008). *The Quaker Condition: The Sociology of a Liberal Religion*. Newcastle: Cambridge Scholars Publishing.

Dudiak, J. (2010). 'A Response to Muers and Wood'. *Quaker Religious Thought*. **115**(1), 39–40.

Dudiak, J. (2012). 'Quakers and Non/Theism: Questions and Prospects'. *Quaker Religious Thought*. **118**(1), 25–34.

Fiumara, G. C. (1990). *The Other Side of Language: A Philosophy of Listening*. Trans. Lambert, C. London: Routledge.

Grant, R. (2014a). *Wittgensteinian Investigations of Contemporary Quaker Religious Language*. PhD thesis. University of Leeds.

Grant, R. (2014b). 'Speaking from Silence: A Quaker feminist Understanding of Revelation'. Paper presented at the society for the Study of Theology conference. n.d. [Viewed 31 May 2020]. Transcript available from: https://orwhateveryoucallit.wordpress.com/speaking-from-silence/

Grant, R. (2015). 'Understanding Quaker Religious Language in its Community Context'. *Quaker Studies*. **19**(2), 260–276.

Grant, R. (2018). *British Quakers and Religious Language*. Leiden: Brill.

Grant, R. (2020). *Theology from Listening: Finding the Core of Liberal Quaker Theological Thought*. Leiden: Brill.

Grant, R. (2021). *Hearing the Light*. London: Christian Alternative.

Hampton, J. (2014). 'British Quaker Survey: Examining Religious Belief and Practices in the Twenty-first Century'. *Quaker Studies*. **19**(1), 7–136.

Heelas, P. and Woodhead, L. (2005). *The Spiritual Revolution: Why Religion is Giving Way to Spirituality*. Oxford: Blackwell.

Huber, K. (2001). 'Questions of Identity among "Buddhist Quakers"'. *Quaker Studies*. **6**(1), 80–105.

Kearney, R. (2004). *Debates in Continental Philosophy: Conversations with Contemporary Thinkers*. New York, NY: Fordham University Press. [1985].

Kershner, J. (2018). 'Comparisons and Divergences in Contemporary Quaker Theology and Philosophy'. In: Daniels, C. W. Healey, R. R. and Kershner, J. (eds.), *Quaker Studies: An Overview – The Current State of the Field*. Leiden: Brill, 51–83.

Knox, J. (2016). *Sacro-Egoism: The Rise of Religious Individualism in the West*. Eugene, OR: Wipf and Stock.

Lampen, J. (2007). *Finding the Words: Quaker Experience and Language*. Stourbridge: The Hope Project.

Levinas, E. (1991). *Totality and Infinity: An Essay on Exteriority*. 4th ed. Pittsburgh, PA: Duquesne University Press. [1969].

Morton, N. (1985). *The Journey Is Home*. Boston: Beacon.

Muers, R. (2004). *Keeping God's Silence: Towards a Theological Ethics of Communication*. 1st ed. Oxford: Blackwell.

Muers, R. (2010). 'Levinas, Quakers and the (in) Visibility of God: Responses to Jeffrey Dudiak and Corey Beals'. *Quaker Religious Thought*. **114**(1), 53–56.

Muers, R. (2015). *Testimony: Quakerism and Theological Ethics*. London: SCM Press.

Nontheist Friends (2005). 'Report From Nontheistic Friends Workshop at FGC 1976' [online]. *Nontheist Friends*. [Viewed 31 May 2020]. Available from: http://www.nontheistfriends.org/article/report-from-nontheistic-friends-workshop-at-fgc-1976-2

Plüss, C. (2007). 'Analysing Non-doctrinal Socialization: Re-assessing the Role of Cognition to Account for Social Cohesion in the Religious Society of Friends'. *British Journal of Sociology*. **58**(2), 253–278.

Randazzo, D. C. (2018). 'Quakers and Non-theism'. In: Angell, S. W. and Dandelion, P. (eds.), *The Cambridge Companion to Quakerism*. Cambridge: Cambridge University Press, 274–289.

Rowlands, H. (2017b). 'Presentation' presented at 'The Impact of Diversity of Belief on Quaker Practice: Discernment, Decision Making, Worship Event'. 25–28 September.

Rowlands, H. (ed.) (2017a). *God, Words and Us: Quakers in Conversation about Religious Difference*. No location given: Quaker Books.

Rush, D. (2006). 'Facts and Figures'. In Boulton, D. (ed.), *Godless for God's Sake*. Dent, Cumbria: Dales Historical Monographs, 101–111.

Russ, M. (2017). '"I'm Religious Not spiritual": Postliberalism for Quakers' [online]. *Jolly Quaker*. 17 September. [Viewed 31 May 2020]. Available from: https://jollyquaker.com/2017/09/17/im-religious-not-spiritual-postliberalism-for-quakers/

Scott, J. (1980). *What Canst Thou Say? Towards A Quaker Theology*. London: Quaker Home Service.

Sointu, E. and Woodhead, L. (2008). 'Spirituality, Gender and Expressive Selfhood'. *Journal for the Scientific Study of Religion*. **47**(2), 259–276.

Taylor, C. (1991). *The Ethics of Authenticity*. Cambridge, MA: Harvard University Press.

Taylor, C. (2007). *A Secular Age*. Cambridge, MA: Harvard University Press.

Vincett, G. (2009). 'Quagans: Fusing Quakerism with Contemporary Paganism'. *Quaker Studies*. **13**(2), 220–237.

Ward, G. (2005). 'Postmodern Theology'. In: Muers, R. and Ford, F. D. (eds.), *The Modern Theologians: An Introduction to Christian Theology since 1918*. Malden, MA: Blackwell Publishing, 322–338.

Wood, B. (2016a). 'Boulton, Lindbeck and Rorty: Imagining Quakerism without Metaphysics (part 1)' [online]. *Armchair Theologian*. 30 May. [Viewed 5 April 2020]. Available from: https://summeroflove85.wordpress.com/2016/05/30/boulton-lindbeck-and-rorty-imagining-a-quakerism-without-metaphysics/

Wood, B. (2016b). 'Boulton, Lindbeck and Rorty: Imagining Quakerism without Metaphysics (part 2)' [online]. *Armchair Theologian*. 30 May. [Viewed 5 April 2020]. Available from: https://summeroflove85.wordpress.com/2016/05/30/boulton-lindbeck-and-rorty-imagining-a-quakerism-without-metaphysics-part-2/

Yarlett, S. D. (2020). *The Accommodation of Diversity: Liberal Quakerism and Nontheism*. PhD thesis. University of Birmingham.

34

WORSHIPPING AT THE EDGE OF WORDS

The Work of Silence and Speech in Meeting for Worship

Ann Wrightson

Silent Worship as practised by Quakers is both paradoxical – how can silence be worship? – and a fiercely guarded treasure.

A quick read through extracts 2.01 through 2.17 in Britain Yearly Meeting's *Quaker Faith & Practice* (which is easily accessed online; Britain Yearly Meeting, 1995–2015) provides ample evidence that to those experiencing Silent Worship – especially where this tradition of Quaker worship is a regular practice – silence in Meeting for Worship is more than simple absence of speech, and speaking and hearing in the context of that silence is more than simply speaking to and being heard by the other people in the room.

In 2015 I undertook a series of short text analysis studies on volumes 1–4 (2010–2013) of the magazine *Quaker Voices*, published by Quaker Life of Britain Yearly Meeting (Wrightson, unpub.). One of the outcomes was a list of words used distinctively frequently when writing about Silent Worship. The word cloud (Figure 34.1) shows all these keywords, with the size of each word indicating how often it turned up associated with silence and being quiet, in passages concerning Quaker worship.[1]

But how does Silent Worship *work*? The extracts in Quaker Faith and Practice mention various activities and experiences and provide moving accounts of value and benefits both to individuals and to the worshipping community. However, neither these extracts nor the guidance for Elders[2] also published by the Yearly Meeting (Gross, 2015) throws much light on how and why these specific practices of Silent Worship enable Meeting for Worship to operate as a place and a practice enabling encounter and revelation beyond individual experience and simple gathering in community – in short, a functional liturgy.

Rowan Williams' 2013 Gifford lectures provided a key for me to unlock this mystery. Williams takes a journey through various uses of language, including many examples of how and why different patterns of speaking and hearing serve to shape, help and hinder communication, to focus finally on silence – silence as simultaneously a place or situation (a locus), an example and a medium for communication that is pushed to and beyond the edge of what words can accomplish. Surely this is exactly what is happening in Meeting for Worship?

That thought sent me on a journey of investigation and reflection, applying Williams' perspective on silence as a way of exploring how and why the practical details of Silent Worship operate to create a functional liturgy. In the traditional spirit of Quaker seeking, I am not

DOI: 10.4324/9780429030925-37

Figure 34.1

making any claim to a uniquely valid or authoritative account, just offering an insight or pattern that may be helpful to fellow seekers for understanding.

Quotations and page references are from the book form of Williams' lectures (very aptly titled *The Edge of Words*; Williams, 2014) unless otherwise indicated. Double quotes in the text are used to indicate words and phrases given specific meanings by Williams; single quotes (outside a quotation) are used to highlight characteristically Quaker usage of words and phrases.

What Silence Betokens and Enables

Williams' discussion of silence in his final lecture focusses strongly on the communicative power of silence, communication that arises from what some particular silence betokens (points to, witnesses to) through how it is established and surrounded. So let us start at the beginning: how is the particular kind of silence in Silent Worship achieved?

The Bare Facts: Silence Assumed, Silencing

> To talk about silence, I would argue, is always to talk about what specifically we are not hearing.
>
> *(p. 157)*

General social chatter and purposeful conversations are set aside until after Meeting for Worship has finished. Non-verbal social communication is also largely silenced through stillness. For an individual taking part, 'settling' into the quiet of the meeting also means inner silencing of distractions and preoccupations. Considered as organized worship, Silent Worship also silences the predetermined words and actions of a typical denominational liturgy.

Although spoken ministry is allowed and expected to occur in the silence, it is (or should be) carefully weighed before speaking, so that inappropriate spoken ministry is silenced by an individual choosing not to speak it. Spoken ministry is received in silent attention, silencing normal conversational response and discussion. Inner silence and receptiveness are also advised, silencing discursive thinking on what has been said. For Williams, the freedom to "go on" in a conversation, that another thing can always be said, is fundamental to the nature of language – indicating that this practice of intentionally refraining from going on is a very significant piece of silencing.

Within the group that is meeting, Elders take responsibility for due process and faithful performance, and an Elder may act as a servant of the meeting to silence inappropriate speaking. For example, if a sequence of spoken offerings is becoming more like a debate, an Elder may rise and speak to recall the meeting to proper practice, typically by saying a few words about reflecting in silence on what has been said. In an extreme case, such as a lengthy disorganized rant or prepared speech, an Elder may stand in silence in order to silence someone who is still speaking; he or she may be joined by others standing in silence to strengthen the resistance to the inappropriate speaking.

What Is Being Betokened or Represented?

> Silence betokens in the context of speech and image . . . how silence actually and particularly criticizes and modifies speech and thus itself 'says' something.
>
> *(p. 157)*

Taking a step onward from the bare fact of silencing, what does this silence then betoken?

The silence of Meeting for Worship is different from a group committing to be in silence together for a period, for example to sit together for silent prayer or meditation. There is an ever-present potential for spoken ministry, even in a Meeting for Worship that is silent from end to end. 'Gathered' silence, or 'tarrying in the Spirit' in older Quaker language, creates a space that enables something to participate, to "go on" in the conversation.

Tentative language ('can', 'may') is a distinctive flavor of Quaker speaking and writing, together with reluctance to use doctrinally loaded names to name what is encountered. Although sometimes taken as simply indicating drift away from belief (Pink Dandelion, 2005, p95ff), not speaking definitively is another way in which there is no end to the conversation about encounter and revelation. The word cloud in Figure 34.1 and the extracts cited from Quaker Faith and Practice show a little of how Quakers speak or write about what they find or encounter in the silence. Rhiannon Grant's more recent work demonstrates how British Quakers are bringing a wide variety of faith-related, philosophical and other perspectives into play to make sense of all this, with language continually proving inadequate to the task (Grant, 2019).

Acknowledging this inadequacy, I need to use some reasonably concise language and want to facilitate a perspective on Silent Worship as a kind of functional liturgy analogous to, as well as profoundly different from, the denominational Christian liturgies that have developed in many branches from common roots in the second and third centuries (Hurtado, 2003). So, while acknowledging with honour the diversity of language and sense-making witnessed by Grant, my closing summary for this section uses traditional Christian language (grounded in the usage of early Friends).

- Meeting together in silence witnesses to the equality of all present: before each other, as a witness to others, and before the living 'Presence in the Midst' of Jesus the Messiah (Christ). This is an equality of 'tarrying' or 'waiting', with something of the sense of a servant standing by quietly until needed, so betokening service or subservience as a member of the people of God to howsoever encounter or revelation may manifest on this occasion.
- Functionally, this is a group of individuals committed to waiting together quietly for a space of time during which they are open to being called, whether the call may be to speech, insightful understanding, or action in the world. (There was a particularly memorable piece

of ministry in meeting that was widely shared then and is still occasionally recalled: we are not God's sheep but his sheepdogs, waiting patiently for the whistle.)

- All are equal before God and in the presence of Christ Jesus – who speaks to us individually, 'to our condition' (Fox, 1647). All are equally called to wait and serve, to speak and to be silent.

- All the things that are silenced, taken together, are not what matters; they are not what those gathered here are paying attention to, committed to at this time.

Language in Silence, Under the Pressure of Silence

A central point of Williams' exposition is how language can, under pressure at its "edge" or extremes, represent (point to, witness to, betoken) what is otherwise beyond its ability to convey. The intentional blocking of ordinary speaking and "going on" in conversational ways puts the use of language in Meeting for Worship "under pressure". This is often enacted physically through the custom of standing to speak, then waiting a second or two after standing before speaking (during which it is quite acceptable to sit down again). Standing and waiting for a moment enacts and signifies a significant threshold to cross when moving from silence to speech.

This reticence may be experienced by the speaker as being overcome by an opposing pressure from an undeniable call or power. Sometimes this feeling is expressed physically through visible agitation or trembling ('quaking'), and the resulting speech may struggle to be coherent.

When all speech is silenced then the silence itself may be experienced as a medium or place of encounter and revelation – becoming 'deep' or 'gathered', customary Quaker words for an experience otherwise beyond words.

As with the long quest to understand the workings of human bodies and minds, the ways that things go wrong can help with understanding how it all works.

If the Crucible Cracks, the Metal May Leak Away

There are various well-known ways in which speech in Silent Worship can be recognizably inappropriate, for example a conventional statement supporting some activist position, a reading selected beforehand for some purpose, or to-and-fro responses debating a point (Gross, 2015). These particular practices are recognized as inappropriate through experience; that is, from how such speech and its effects are experienced by those present as weakening the distinctive character of Silent Worship.

Take the example of a contentious statement followed by responses that although received in silence are forming an extended debate or discussion. Even those receiving all of this ministry in outward silence will tend to settle into thinking about the issue in question, perhaps preparing to offer their own contributions in turn. By weakening the silencing of ordinary conversation and thinking, this reduces the "pressure" highlighted by Williams. It may feel comfortable because it does reduce the "pressure", however it also closes the space that was being created and sustained for encounter and revelation to "go on" in the conversation. With timely intervention by an Elder and renewed commitment to silent waiting-on by the worshipping group, there can be a shared experience of return to 'depth' and a 'gathered meeting'.

Another example is ministry that imitates, quotes or is merely conventional – 'not in the life', in older Quaker language. This is neatly illustrated by Williams' discussion of saying the same words again not amounting to saying the same thing ("There's a mouse in the kitchen"; p. 67). As an example from Quaker worship, early in my life as a Quaker I attended very small meeting where the only elder felt she was responsible for ensuring there was some spoken ministry, and usually read a carefully selected paragraph or two from a Quaker publication at around twenty-five minutes into the meeting. For all the goodwill and care it represented, it was an interruption, though the regular few were well used to it and re-settled quickly afterwards. I remember talking about this with a more experienced Friend and hearing – very helpfully for me at the time – that it was common for a Meeting for Worship to lose its focus for a while, however it would usually come back if I (and all) waited quietly 'in the Light'.

Traditional denominational ('programmed') liturgy can be an example of such merely conventional repeated speech, however traditional Quaker polemic against any programmed liturgy is probably best left in its original social and political situation in the seventeenth century. Williams highlights other factors at work in programmed liturgy, including a different kind of fruitful silencing analogous to the engaged silence of the audience in a theatre, purposeful and committed quiet observation that is enriched and extended through aspects of bodily participation including but not limited to ritual speaking (p. 84).

Trying Too Hard, With Unintended Consequences?

Paradoxically for a tradition that has so consciously moved away from programmed worship, this quality of worship as performance with silent observation and routinized participation the norm for most of the group can be yet another way that Silent Worship may move away from being 'in the life'. Such a Meeting for Worship becomes more of a ritual performance or prescribed liturgy of achieving and sustaining 'deep' silence (with occasional rather predictable spoken parts), then closing with the elders' handshake and handshakes all round. (Any Meeting may have periods with little or no spoken ministry in meeting – here I am talking about a settled pattern.)

Interestingly, one of the ways this situation can develop is through concern to safeguard the quality and appropriateness of spoken ministry in meeting. For example, Elders may emphasize elements of the older Quaker tradition that speak of compelling inspiration to speak, and the role of spoken ministry in expressing insight, guidance and discernment that is valuable to the community. There may be a focus on positive experience in the silence ("What a lovely deep meeting we had today"; "It was very rich, very rich indeed") or on process (Is it ever right to have ministry in the first ten minutes, the last ten minutes? When should someone read from Advices and Queries?), and so on.

The obvious weakening here is in 'free ministry'; that is, that speaking in meeting is open to all and not restricted to approved or licensed ministers. A subtler loss is that Silent Worship becomes a group activity of meditation or contemplative prayer, with spoken contributions supporting the group activity. The traditional 'free ministry' is not only about who speaks; it is about free and open access to encounter and revelation, maintaining as broad and open a channel as possible for the Spirit to "go on" in the conversation.

Not Quite Worship

In the relatively recently established Quaker practice of 'worship-sharing', disciplined listening in silence provides a safe worship-like space for individuals to speak in and to a group, outside a formal Meeting for Worship. Worship-sharing has become part of the usual Quaker toolkit; a typical example would be a study group going into worship-sharing to share personal experiences relevant to their topic.

There is certainly some "pressure" here in Williams' sense, derived from silencing that is outwardly similar to Silent Worship. Typically, the session leader will speak to open and close a series of contributions, each contributor will speak in their turn, and there is no other speaking. A Quaker group that is worship-sharing may end with a different kind of silence, often delimited by saying "let's close with a few minutes of silence". Worship-sharing has been around for a few decades – I remember encountering it in the early 1990s – however I'm meeting it more often, and in a wider range of contexts, in recent years.

Afterwords

The practice often called 'afterwords' (also 'bridging time') is a period of worship-sharing immediately after Silent Worship. Afterwords provides a worship-like community safe space in which to share a personal event such as a bereavement, or to express a personal concern. It is also a natural bridge both out of and into participation in Silent Worship – for example, children's meeting may regularly speak in afterwords about their meeting, and Elders may encourage those who feel a call to speak in Silent Worship but don't have the courage, to respond to the call – and practice in afterwords to gain confidence.

A growing practice of 'afterwords' indicates concern to build a supportive community in the Meeting. However, more recently I have seen more of an emphasis on afterwords as the right place to say things that are not quite ministry, that don't make the grade to come out in Meeting proper. This suggests that quality-managing the traditional 'free ministry' and valuing gathered silence in its own right may be going a little too far, moving Silent Worship towards intentional silent prayer and meditation and away from waiting together quietly in patient expectation of encounter and revelation – and accepting that may be neither comfortable nor as expected.

Again here we see the risk involved, the potential danger of doing what is comfortable; it is more comfortable to meditate in silence in Meeting and speak my mind in afterwords than to engage in a team task of being open to the Light in the silence of worship, with the freedom and responsibility of recognizing a call to speak, working at discerning what should be said, and breaking through the pressure of silence to say it as well as I can.

What Is Made Possible by and in Silent Worship?

The practice of Quaker Silent Worship, with its combination of silencing and "language under pressure", frames and enables a range of experience and activity related to encounter and revelation. When Quakers talk about what happened in Meeting, experience that is beyond words is made accessible to shared understanding through conventional expressions that point beyond the usual reach of words towards ("represent", in Williams' sense) what is done and experienced. Individual experiences of encounter and revelation in the context of Silent Worship are given a validating context with community support through the shared understanding and experience of the 'gathered meeting'. Grant's work has shown that the shared and community validated experience of the 'gathered meeting' is a key factor in supporting a remarkable unity of fellowship and action alongside, or rather deeply embedded within, a wide diversity of language and conceptual understanding.

In Silent Worship, there is a kind of conversation free of human judgement and debate that includes a space and role for encounter and revelation, including a speaking part (spoken ministry). "A God who acts . . . gives Himself to be known . . . through . . . the human self" (early in the spoken words of Williams' first lecture) is intentionally given an opportunity to break in and act, enabled by a particular discipline of silence and speech, an embodied activity in community that opens the way (as cleaning a window rather than switching on the sun).

This is why – or perhaps more appropriately how – Silent Worship is considered sacramental in Quaker tradition.

Notes

1 For readers who want the technical details: keywordness is ranked using a log–likelihood measure, and the diagram includes all keywords significant at p <0.01, excluding the focus words used to seed the search. The diagram was prepared using Feinberg's Wordle tool.
2 Elders are experienced Quakers with a responsibility for worship and spiritual nurturing, though they do not lead worship in the sense common in liturgical worship.

References

Britain Yearly Meeting of the Religious Society of Friends (1995–2015), *Quaker Faith and Practice: The Book of Christian Discipline of the Yearly Meeting of the Religious Society of Friends (Quakers) in Britain*. https://qfp.quaker.org.uk/

Fox, George (1647) as quoted in Britain Yearly Meeting (1995–2015), extract 19.02.

Grant, Rhiannon (2019), *Telling the Truth About God* (London: Christian Alternative Books).

Gross, Zelie (2015), *With a Tender Hand: A Resource Book for Eldership and Oversight* (London: Quaker Books).

Hurtado, Larry W. (2003), *Lord Jesus Christ: Devotion to Jesus in Earliest Christianity* (Grand Rapids, MI: Eerdmans).

Johns, David (2013), 'Worship and Sacraments', in Ben Pink Dandelion and Stephen Angell (eds.), *The Oxford Handbook of Quaker Studies* (Oxford: Oxford University Press), 260–273.

Pink Dandelion, Ben (2005), *The Liturgies of Quakerism* (Aldershot: Ashgate).

Williams, Rowan (2014), *The Edge of Words* (London: Bloomsbury Continuum).

Wrightson, Ann (unpublished), The study referenced here was presented at the Quaker Studies Research Association conference, Woodbrooke, Birmingham 2019.

35

TESTIMONY AS CONSEQUENCE

The Reinvention of Tradition

Pink Dandelion

All social groups, including religious ones, adapt themselves to changing contexts and in line with changing interpretations of their own tradition over time. What scholars of religion do is chart the history, content and dynamics of that change. Quakerism can be portrayed as a story of continual change, as well as one of some constants. Quaker witness in some ways has constant threads around the opposition to war and the desire for social justice running across the group's history. However, but it is also possible to chart subtle shifts in the way that 'testimony' has moved from being portrayed as a consequence to the spiritual life in the early years to, within the Liberal Quakerism this chapter focuses on, a set of aspirational values in the twentieth and twenty-first centuries. This chapter first defines testimony, then charts early shifts in its framing, and finally discusses how testimony sits within Liberal Quakerism today.

Defining Testimony

Testimony is the term used to describe the expression of the collective experience of Quaker faith, the experience of the group as its tries to remain 'faithful'. In some ways, then, it is about the everyday manifestation of the consequences of faith. In this way, it can be seen as similar to the way those in evangelical settings will 'share testimony'; that is, give an account of how the holy has impacted a person's life. Quakers also use 'testimony' in terms of written accounts detailing the manifestation of faith in someone's life, describing a spiritually focused biography of a Quaker written after their death as 'a testimony to the grace of God in the life of . . .' It is all about the manifestation of the consequences of faith. Collectively, for Quakers, that is often most visible in lifestyle choices and campaigning work (Dandelion, 2014, p. 21, pp. 53–57). For Quakers historically, words have been less important than action, and testimony can be most easily identified in terms of the outworkings of the spiritual life (possibly a paradox given the emphasis on the interior spiritual life). Any words about Quaker testimony are a reflection of the experience. There are no definitive written statements outlining Quaker testimony, just reflections of how Quakers have understood their attempts to be faithful in everyday life. New aspects of testimony are not agreed by a committee but become established over time through the actions of Quaker groups and, after the fact, written reflections on those actions. We can see this in the way that new formulations of Quaker witness have been developed, such as simplicity and peace.

DOI: 10.4324/9780429030925-38

The earliest British 'books of discipline' (the authoritative texts denoting the way of the faith) consisted almost entirely of the collective understandings of how Quakers were to enact their faith. The 1783 British Book of Extracts is an alphabetical listing of elements of Quaker practice and performance, with no explicit doctrinal elements at all. It reminded Quakers of the time not to use the pagan-derived names for days of the week or months of the year, not to use the deferential 'you' rather than 'thee', not to erect gravestones, or to mark Christmas as any more special than any other day. It was about presenting and preserving spiritual purity. It was public and identifiable as Quaker. Testimony in this way is rooted in the spiritual life and is not discrete. In an ideal theologised form, Quakers may claim that testimony is about the impellation of God's will upon the group but more pragmatically, all of Quaker life and all of the lives of Quakers can be seen to enact 'testimony', the expression of the faithfulness – and sometimes faithlessness – of the group and its members.

Since the 1950s, Liberal Quakers have tended to use a shorthand for testimony, initially designed to help teach the Quaker way to newcomers and to express key Quaker understandings to non-Quakers (Brinton, 1952). This shorthand takes the form of a list, refined in the 1990s to STEPS in Britain (simplicity, truth, equality, peace and stewardship; Wood, 2021) and SPICE in North America (simplicity, peace, integrity, community and equality). SPICES has added 'sustainability' or 'stewardship' as the sixth 'testimony' in recent years (https://www.friendsjournal.org/s-p-i-c-e-s-quaker-testimonies/). These lists have become very popular, and most Quakers today will talk of 'the testimonies' rather than the singular 'testimony'. Within the group, some commentators have seen these lists as unhelpful, suggesting that different parts of the spiritual life are options, differentiated from other aspects (Dandelion, 2014, pp. 53–57). The list also fails to account for the way the whole of Quaker practice can be framed as testimony. The very way most Quakers understand and practice worship is a testimony to the equality of all, the free ministry, the priesthood of all believers, inward communion and baptism, the authority of direct revelation, and a testimony against any form or practice which undermines or opposes these key Quaker understandings. Rachel Muers' work has very helpfully articulated the singular nature of Quaker testimony, as well as the way it both advocates for and proscribes against (Muers, 2015). Testimony in this way is about the positive, as well as the negative. For example, Quaker testimony is both for peace and against war and the preparation for war.

The content of testimony has changed over time. Gravestones and exogamy were allowed, and plain dress and speech became optional in the decades after the 1850s. Plainness became reformulated in terms of 'simplicity' at this time and the 'witness against war' recast in terms of peace in the twentieth century (Dandelion, 2014, p. 54). These changes reflect a different interpretation of the spiritual life, for Quakers, but not the spiritual basis of testimony itself. One of the challenges for the group with the list, especially when used as a teaching tool to those outside Quakerism and possibly all faith affiliation, is that it can be presented and received in purely secular terms. This can become normative in a group with high levels of adult recruitment, as is true of the Liberal tradition of Quakerism, and potentially lead to the phenomenon of internal secularisation by which the importance of religion and spirituality diminishes within the faith group, rendering it a value-based organisation (Dandelion, 2019: chap. 7). Instead of testimony as a consequence of the spiritual life, it can become an aspirational set of collectively agreed social values. The list, then, is also potentially undermining of the core purposes of Quakerism in that it can downplay the spiritual and allow the re-presentation of the tradition in terms of the political or psychological. Another practice, such as Anarchism, also includes not voting, not having a fixed leadership, campaigning for peace, simplicity but as an ideology not a spirituality.

The Changing Nature of Testimony

In the mid-seventeenth century, distinctive Quaker practice developed quickly, with the adoption of plain speech and dress and a particular liturgical form, the refusal to use titles or swear oaths or pay tithes, or to be married or buried using church rites, and the clarity that fighting and killing, as well as social hierarchy and etiquette, was un-Christian. Quaker spirituality was played out in public. Thomas Ellwood, one of the first generation of Friends, met his friends in Oxford one day and they took off their hats, bowed before him and greeted him In the familiar form, only to find him still standing upright with hat still on. So they repeated their greeting and then, bemused, one finally realised what was happening and slapped him on the back, 'What, Tom, a Quaker!' (Ellwood, 1714, pp. 33–34). This highly performative aspect of Quaker religion appears in the Quaker texts as a corollary to Quaker spiritual experience. It is consequential to spiritual encounter and transformation. Thomas Ellwood refuses to take his hat off and greet his former friends because of his transforming convincement experience. At the same time, this witness reaffirms his faith.

In the eighteenth century, two Friends waited twenty-three years before marrying. They had to be sure that they were doing the right thing at the right time. John Conran saw a woman across the room and felt inwardly that this woman was to be his wife.

> I fell into company with a young woman Louisa Strongman: the first time I saw her at a Friend's house, I felt, in silence, a strong draft of love more than natural, and a secret intimation impressed my mind that she would be my wife; this I hid in my heart, and it was nearly two years before I felt at liberty to disclose it to any one, waiting as I apprehend the Lord's time to communicate it . . . when I felt the way open to proceed in it at that time, it was nearly six years after this before we were married.
>
> *(Damiano, 1988, p. 184)*

He told her this only two years later, and they were married a full six years later. It is similar to the discernment Quakers face when called to share vocal ministry (Quaker Faith and Practice, 1995, 2.55). There is the 'what' and the 'when'.

At the same time, the increasing formalisation of the Society in the eighteenth century meant that there was an increasing list of proscribed and prescribed activities. The consequences of the experience of the first generation of Friends became rules, what Margaret Fell called a 'silly poor gospel' ministry (Quaker Faith and Practice, 1995, 20.31), to help nurture the second and third generations who had been raised as Quakers but who were still waiting for the inward spiritual transformation their parents and grandparents had experienced. During the eighteenth century when Quakers sought to be 'a peculiar people' (after Paul's Letter to Titus 2:11), testimony became the measure of integrity and membership, and breaking testimony led to disownment. Testimony was the outward means for Quakers of expressing their desire for inward encounter; remembering and being reminded of what they were about and how they should go about it. An individual could be disowned for marrying before a priest, becoming bankrupt, taking another Quaker to court, publishing without permission, or even owning a piano (Dandelion, 2019, p. 62). Testimony had moved from a consequence of spiritual encounter to part of normative Quaker culture functioning to safeguard the remnant and display 'true religion' to wider society.

Testimony and Liberal Quakerism

Liberal Quakerism, established within a part of the Quaker world at the beginning of the twentieth century (as described in chapters by Isaac Barnes May and Chuck Fager in this volume), is most popularly characterised as pluralistic, as celebrating a diversity of beliefs. We know today that there are many Quakers who are not Christian but who may be Hindu, Muslim, non-theist and so forth. Liberal Quakerism has developed into a seeking religion, suspicious of theology (because the words can never match the experience) and of theological certainty (because the spiritual search is ongoing; Dandelion, 1996; Grant, 2018).

Alongside this permissive attitude towards belief, it is the form of Quakerism, the way in which the group is religious, that binds Liberal Quakerism together. Liberal Quakers are conservative and conformist about the way they are Quaker. Worship and worship for business has hardly changed in 350 years, whilst the theology of the group has changed six or seven times and continues to be in flux (Dandelion, 1996). Belief is slippery, individual and marginalised; the form of Quakerism is solid and defined. Lives not labels, deeds not creeds, seem more authentic to Liberal Quaker participants. So where does that leave testimony? Is testimony now as diffuse or suspect as belief in the Liberal tradition?

Today, testimony within the Liberal Quaker setting works in two ways. First, it is part of how Quakerism defines itself. As an expression of corporate experience/witness (i.e., as part of the form of Quakerism almost as doctrine or as a given principle), it is part of the conservative and conformist way in which Quakers are Quaker. Second, as an area of interpretation, it is open to pluralistic individualism in a way which would not have been possible a hundred years ago. During the 1991 Gulf War, there were many ideas offered about the best way forward. None challenged the existence of the testimony as a principle, but there was a whole variety of possibilities for action, including one suggesting assassinating Saddam Hussein (Dandelion 2014, p. 39). This was an interpretation of the peace testimony as minimisation of suffering. So in terms of the content of testimony, the expression of Quakerism is now individualized and varied.

As Elaine Bishop and Jung Jiseok have cogently argued (2018), there are four aspects to this in terms of testimony.

First, there is a loss of specificity in the move to testimony as principle. For example, plainness is much easier to define than simplicity. The move from plainness to simplicity has major consequences. Plainness was about everything visible being unadorned, whether furniture or dress. Friends in the 1850s claimed they could maintain that testimony inwardly, and the word 'simplicity' came in to replace it (Dandelion, 2014, p. 54). Simplicity is a much more diffuse term, and we can interpret it in different ways. Does it mean owning a car which may never break down, or a bicycle? Similarly, peace is a much more diffuse concept than being against war. As the Gulf War example shows, what is peace?

Secondly, the pluralism of belief has meant Liberal Quakers are less rooted in a single-faith tradition, so there is no longer a single theological tradition informing Quaker faith.

Thirdly, the new aspects of Quaker testimony of the twentieth century are less prescribed. The emphasis on seeking means that 'Truth' has become truth or truths, and Liberal Quakers are less sure about what is definitely not Quaker. One-third of eligible Quaker men in Britain joined up in the First World War. Many Quakers in Britain celebrate Christmas now, and most no longer use the plain dress or plain speech. These are no longer seen as critical to the faith, to what God wants of God's people, of how God wants Quakers to remain faithful. Equally, if some still feel these are important issues, that is also accepted. Liberal Quakers believe they can maintain spiritual integrity within a more permissive attitude.

Fourthly, testimony is less enforced: although in many communities individuals are still appointed as Elders with responsibility for the spiritual welfare of the group, those Elders no longer visit Quakers in their homes to check up on participants, and disownment today is rare.

Testimony no longer functions as an automatic consequence to spiritual experience as it did for Thomas Ellwood and seventeenth-century Friends or as a rule of life in the way that it did in the eighteenth century. Testimony as a necessary corporate category has become smaller, as less is collectively agreed on as vital, and also as the corporate experience reduces more and more to what happens at meeting for worship, with the home life outside the control of the meeting community. When in the late 1850s and early 1860s Quakers relaxed the rules about marriage and about plain dress and plain speech, Quakers could be invisible and inaudibly distinct outside of the meeting house. Quakers have had the option to be private about what happens outside the meeting house and generally the meeting acts as if that is a present-day preference. Individuals now decide what aspects of their 'private' life they wish to share with their Meetings. In this way, that aspect of agreed corporate witness in the book of discipline reduces in line with the increased freedoms afforded by Liberal Quakerism. We can see this in the difference between, say, the early books of discipline of 1783 and 1802 and the later twentieth-century variants (Book of Extracts, 1783; Quaker Faith and Practice, 1995). It is the completion of the shift in the operation of testimony from consequence to rules to values.

The challenge of the freedom to be private about theology and life choices is that Quakers can be left feeling isolated. Liberal Quaker Meetings rarely feel confident to venture into what is now seen as a 'private life' outside of the meeting. Couples experiencing difficulties have complained that they feel unsupported (Dandelion, 2014, p. 30), but I suggest that it is often that meetings do not know how far they can get involved with life outside of the meeting house.

Some have also felt the lack of accountability and a lack of willingness on behalf of the Meeting to engage with personal discernment. Some modern Liberal Quakers have turned to spiritual directors and accompaniers from outside of Quakerism for support. For some, modern liberal Quakerism is not serious enough about its corporate spirituality. For earlier Friends, spiritual integrity and church purity was at stake, with salvation the ultimate goal. Today, Liberal Friends are more relaxed about the spiritual life, less worried about original sin and redemption. Testimony today, as I have said, is reduced both in size and as ultimate import within the Liberal Quaker tradition.

These are not inevitable or irreversible tropes. Liberal Quakers could rediscover a strong spiritual core and/or reclaim a specific and explicit spiritual language to offset internal secularization. The very freedoms that have led to the present situation can also accommodate shifts in different directions. Testimony could move again from its popular expression as a list of values to a direct consequence of spiritual encounter, with those ascribing Quaker social action to purely human impulse finding themselves in tension with the wider Quaker culture. Liberal Quakerism could again become collectively and spiritually certain and in this, potentially more aligned with majority Quakerism. Everything is possible within this mutable religious form, hence the way it remains compelling to sociologists of religion.

References

Bishop, E. and Jung, J. (2018). 'Seeking peace: Quakers respond to war' in Angell, S. W. and Dandelion, P. eds., *The Cambridge Companion to Quakerism*. Cambridge: Cambridge University Press, pp. 106–128.

Book of Extracts. London Yearly Meeting, 1783.

Brinton, H. H. (1952) *Friends for 300 Years; The History and Beliefs of the Society of Friends Since George Fox Started the Quaker Movement*. New York, NY: Harper.

Damiano, K. A. (1988). 'On Earth as it is in heaven: Eighteenth century Quakerism as realized eschatology.' Unpublished PhD thesis, Union of Experimenting Colleges and Universities, Cincinnati, OH.

Dandelion, B. P. (2014). *Open for Transformation: Being Quaker*. London: Quakerbooks.

Dandelion, P. (1996). *A Sociological Analysis of the Theology of Quakers: The Silent Revolution*. Lampeter: Edwin Mellen Press.

Dandelion, P. (2019). *The Cultivation of Conformity: Towards a General Theory of Internal Secularization*. London: Routledge.

Ellwood, T. (1714). *The History of the Life of Thomas Ellwood*. London: J. Sowle.

Grant, R. (2018). *British Quakers and Religious Language*. Leiden: Brill.

Muers, R. (2015). *Testimony: Quakerism and Theological Ethics*. London: SCM.

Quaker Faith and Practice: The Book of Christian Discipline (1995). London: Britain Yearly Meeting.

Wood, J. G. (2021). *In STEP with Quaker Testimony: Simplicity, Truth, Equality and Peace – Inspired by Margaret Fell's Writings*. https://www.friendsjournal.org/s-p-i-c-e-s-quaker-testimonies/, accessed 8/11/21

PART III

Embodiment

36

NETWORKED TO FREEDOM, BUT NOT MY NEIGHBOR

Complicating Legacies of Quakers and the Enslaved Population of North Carolina

Krishauna Hines-Gaither

Northern Friends were willing to pledge generous donations to help remove slaves of the Yearly Meeting from North Carolina, but would not encourage the migration of blacks to their own communities.

Reluctant Slaveholders, *Peter Kent Opper (1975)*

The matter of slavery was so divisive that it ultimately fueled the US civil war – a war that pitted sibling against sibling, citizen against citizen and Friend against Friend. To this end, Levi Coffin, the proclaimed president of the Underground Railroad and devout Quaker abolitionist, wrote: "A few leading members [of the North Carolina Manumission Society] were colonizationists, some were gradualists, and many were led to believe that there was some disgrace about abolitionism . . . and they fell in with the current opposition" (L. Coffin, 2014, p. 120). Quakers questioned to what extent, if any, they should involve themselves in the cause of manumission. This chapter affirms the anti-slavery gains by early Friends while also examining the complexities of the movement. As the title of the chapter indicates, networking African Americans to free lands did not always equate to loving thy neighbor as thyself. Further evidence of these blurred lines include the lack of African American membership in eighteenth- and nineteenth-century Quaker Meetings, despite anti-slavery work. African Americans in North Carolina did not become members of Quaker meetings in any noticeable numbers, "nor would they have been welcome in most" (Hilty, 1993 cited in McDaniel and Julye, 2009). Though many anti-slavery practices and gains of nineteenth-century Friends are noteworthy, their conflicting practices and complicated legacies also merit equal weight and interrogation.

Early Friends' Positions on Slavery

Although Quakers were relatively quiet on slavery until the eighteenth century, English Quaker founder George Fox spoke out against the evils of slavery as early as 1671. While he did not call for an immediate emancipation, he admonished enslavers to train the enslaved "in the fear of God" and to be mild and gentle toward them. He also recommended that the enslaved

DOI: 10.4324/9780429030925-40

be manumitted after a certain number of years (Fox cited in Bland, 1968). It would be over 100 years before Quakers would heed Fox's admonition as a collective movement.

According to Linda Adams Bland, "As a unified group, North Carolina Quakers had not always opposed slavery. For almost a century the official policies of the North Carolina Yearly Meeting did not condemn slaveholders" (Bland, 1968, p. 5). That said, North Carolina was home to some of the earliest opponents of slavery. By the mid-eighteenth century, New Garden Quakers of Guilford County were becoming increasingly uncomfortable with slavery. They began enacting a practice of disownment[1] for Friends who participated in the buying and selling of the enslaved; however, "the fellow members of the Society of Friends in eastern North Carolina did not share their views" (New Garden Monthly Meeting Minutes, I, pp. 215, 218, 219). In 1768, western Friends requested that the Yearly Meeting take up the issue of slavery. Although western Friends requested it be prohibited to buy and sell the enslaved, those who already owned enslaved property were at liberty to maintain ownership. Conversely, New Garden Friends called for an absolute abolition of slavery. However, the Quarterly Meeting advised Friends to make the enslaved Africans' lives as easy as possible. From this response, it is evident that the Quarterly Meeting fell short of taking an anti-slavery position.

Similar to George Fox's earlier admonition, Friends were instructed to make the enslaved comfortable. Friends in western North Carolina felt that Friends should only buy or sell enslaved persons to another Friend. The only exception was in order to prevent the separation of the enslaved family. The western North Carolina Friends stated unequivocally that Friends were prohibited from selling the enslaved to those who "make a practice of buying and selling them for the sake of gain" (New Garden Monthly Meeting Minutes, I, p. 274 cited in Bland, 1968). Although Friends made some strides, slavery as an institution remained supported by North Carolina Friends.

Direct abolition of slavery met strong opposition amongst Friends. In 1774, "Thomas Nicholson submitted a tract titled 'Liberty and Property' to the [North Carolina] Yearly Meeting urging the emancipation of slaves" (Minutes of the North Carolina Yearly Meeting cited in Bland, 1968). Bland asserted, "Both Newby and Nicholson were from the eastern region of North Carolina, but their protest against slavery did not reflect the prevailing attitudes or actions among Friends in that area" (Bland, 1968, p. 31). By 1779, the Yearly Meeting forbade Friends from "importing, buying or selling"; however, it was permissible to rent the enslaved from other Friends (Swaim and Sherwood, 1848, cited in Wright, 1974). The practice of hiring the enslaved as late as 1779 reveals the entanglements with which Friends continued to engage in the slave empire.

Barbara Wright clarified that Friends only purposed to rid the Society of Friends from the sin of slavery, however, they did not seek to abolish slavery throughout the state or the nation. Wright declared:

> The [North Carolina] Yearly Meeting did not intend to encourage the general emancipation of slaves. There is not a single mention of abolition or general emancipation of blacks in North Carolina in the Yearly Meeting minutes or petitions during the period of 1758–1824. Friends merely wished to have the freedom to manumit their own slaves and to give the same liberty to others.
>
> *(Wright, 1974, p. 16)*

The Yearly Meeting compromised by only proclaiming abolition "where it had control" (Wright, 1974, p. 16). We will never fully know the cost of Quaker insularity versus pushing for abolition beyond Quaker borders. "Thus, with their own members free from personal guilt, the Society of Friends rested their case against slavery" (Bland, 1968, p. 5).

From Anti-slavery to Manumission

While the first period of Quaker involvement in anti-slavery work occurred between 1758 and 1816, the second wave transitions from anti-slavery to abolition from 1816 and 1832. "[W]hen the issue of slavery was of greatest concern to North Carolina Friends their center of activity was in the western part of Guilford County near the place where Guilford College now stands" (Bland, 1968, p. 3). The next phase in the cause of anti-slavery came through the North Carolina Manumission Society. In 1816, local manumission societies of Guilford and Randolph Counties joined forces to form the North Carolina Manumission Society. The Society was heavily led by Quakers but was open to anyone who opposed slavery. Notwithstanding, "membership was limited to free white males" (Weeks, 1968, p. 235). It is unfortunate that the Society did not afford membership to other oppressed groups, such as free blacks or women, nor did they engage the very people they intended to liberate. The preamble to the Society's constitution read in part, "The human race, however varied in color, are justly entitled to freedom and that is the duty of nations as well as individuals enjoying the blessings of freedom to remove this dishonor of the Christian character from among them" (Bland, 1968, p. 35). Although the preamble and overall goal of manumission were honorable, these were unfunded mandates. The Society of Friends renounced any financial support given that the Manumission Society's stated goals were to spread the good news of manumission and not to serve as a fundraising body. Facing these limitations, the Manumission Society was "completely retarded in accomplishing its objectives" (Wright, 1974, p. 36). In an attempt to gain some backing, the Manumission Society joined with the Colonization Society. Both enslavers and anti-slavery advocates held membership in the Colonization Society. The goal of the Colonization Society was to remove free African Americans from North Carolina and resettle them in free lands, both in the northern and western states and abroad.

In 1817, the two societies joined forces and they amended the formal title to the Manumission and Colonization Society. At that time, Levi Coffin led the New Garden Manumission Society. Of the amalgamation, Coffin wrote:

> This produced a sharp debate. Many of us were opposed to making colonization a condition of freedom, believing it to be an odious plan of expatriation concocted by slaveholders, to open a drain by which they get rid of free negroes, and thus remain in more secure possession of their slave property. They considered free negroes a dangerous element among slaves. . . . When the vote was taken, the motion was carried by a small majority. We felt that the slave power had got the ascendency in our society, and that we could no longer work in it.
>
> *(L. Coffin, 2014, p. 45)*

Levi Coffin and his small band of anti-slavery Friends left the convention following the vote and did not return. The concerns voiced by Levi Coffin regarding colonization would be fulfilled in the coming years. Before launching into the failures and ethics of forced colonization, one must understand the Trustee system among Friends.

Trustee System

Friends sought consultation from Judge William Gaston. Thereby, Friends learned that according to an Act of 1796, it was lawful for the Meeting "to elect trustees to have full power to receive donations and purchase and hold in trust any property for the benefit of the Society"

(Weeks, 1968, p. 224). Having solicited the North Carolina legislature to no avail to allow the legal manumission of the enslaved, and seeing that "laws relating to slavery were constantly more oppressive," some Friends moved west and north, preferring to live in a free state (L. Coffin, 2014, p. 45). Some who remained implemented the Trustee Plan of Slaveholding in the early 1800s.

In 1808, Quaker Meetings held collective ownership of the enslaved. Those who wished to manumit their enslaved property could sign them over in trust to a Meeting. The Meeting would become their legal owners. According to a 1741 North Carolina law, it was illegal for "any Negro or mulatto slave to be set free, upon any pretense whatsoever, except for meritorious service" (Bassett, 1896 cited in Bland, 1968). They had to depart or risk being re-enslaved. Although the African Americans remained legally enslaved, the Quaker meetings had found a legal loophole via the Trustee system. Many Quaker enslavers found the request to free their property and turn them over to the Meeting discordant, especially Friends in the eastern part of the state where slaveholding was more prevalent.

Recalling the tension amongst Friends regarding manumission, Addison Coffin (cousin to Levi Coffin) wrote, "When Friends freed their slaves . . . many others promised their slaves freedom when they died, but heirs refused to let them go" (A. Coffin, 1894, p. 122). At different points in time, Quakers held over 1000 African Americans, making the Yearly Meeting one of the largest slaveholders in the state. Though African Americans remained legally enslaved but nominally free under the Trustee system, some were treated better by the Quaker Meeting than non-Quaker enslavers. They worked for wages as hired hands (although the funds largely went to their care and litigations), and a few purchased land. Such a large undertaking was bound to produce divisions.

> The Friends, however, disliked this system. They realized that it was an evasion of duly constituted law. In addition the trustee slaves in their unsupervised lives sometimes ran afoul of the law. Also many elderly slaves had to be supported by the Yearly Meeting, and the females constantly proved their worth by presenting the trustees with new charges. In view of these problems the yearly meeting repeatedly petitioned the North Carolina legislature for modification of the slave code.
>
> *(Minute Book of the North Carolina Yearly Meeting cited in Sowle, 1965)*

Positioning the enslaved as criminally delinquent and the women as promiscuous is a problematic framing that is rooted in white supremacy and still prevalent today. That said, this quote reveals the schisms within Quaker spaces regarding the Trustee program. The treatment under the trustees was intended to be a better system than slavery; however, the plan did not always yield laudable results.

Blurred Lines: Failures of North Carolina Manumission and Colonization

Not all of the enslaved had their needs met. Some Friends freed their bondsmen without turning them over to the Trustees, and did not make provisions for them once freed. Quaker Joseph Hoag wrote, "Many Quakers who had removed from eastern North Carolina to the West had freed their slaves and then left them unprovided for. . . . In 1825 the number thus left neglected was put at ninety-five" (Weeks, 1968, p. 229).

Far away from the slave empire, Friends sought freedom in the North, while not affording the same freedom to those left behind. Although the Trustee system was meant to serve as a remedy against the ills of slavery, in practice there were inconsistencies. "Most of the Quakers' enslaved Africans were under the care of the Meeting, so that the only blacks that remained with families were minors" (Wright, 1974, p. 14). The Society believed the minors needed to be separated in order for them to be "instructed in virtue, morality and useful employment" (Weeks, 1968, p. 226). We know from later accounts related to colonization that the enslaved community was unyielding in wanting to keep their families together. Therefore, this separation of adult African Americans from minor children most certainly would have caused unrest for the parents and children alike. In any assistance they accepted from Quakers, African Americans "discovered that they lost independence in making decisions concerning their own families" (Soderland cited in McDaniel and Julye, 2009).

Another blurred line between slavery and manumission was that of literacy. Although the Society of Friends recommended the enslaved held in trust be taught to read and write, "this suggestion was not enthusiastically received . . . and nothing was done to further the matter" (Minutes of the North Carolina Manumission Society cited in Wright, 1974). Furthermore, the attitude of some Friends regarding the enslaved in their care bore the same stain of white supremacy as their non-Quaker counterparts. Joseph Hoag recalled in his memoirs, "When I talked with some Friends on the subject, they replied that if they gave them learning, it would make them saucy and they would feel themselves as good as white folks" (Hoag, 1861, cited in Wright, 1974). By comparison, Levi Coffin wrote that non-Quaker enslavers presented a very similar argument. Coffin wrote, "Some of the neighboring slaveholders . . . said that [teaching them to read] made their slaves discontented and uneasy, and created a desire for the privileges that others had" (L. Coffin, 2014, p. 43). Although the Meetings encouraged alphabetization, Friends did not put forth serious efforts to realize this goal. Education is a key tenet of liberation; however, Friends failed, and in many cases refused, to educate their bondsmen. Nor did many Friends wish for the enslaved to live among them.

Although some Friends were actively working towards manumission, they had not accepted the enslaved as their neighbors. According to Addison Coffin:

> What to do with the negro when freed was the serious question, various plans were before the people, the colonization of Africa was advocated by many, others were decidedly in favor of sending them to Hayti, while some were in favor of French Guiana. None seemed willing for them to remain in the state, many of the most conscientious anti-slavery men and women were strongly opposed to their remaining, many would rather they remain in slavery.
>
> *(A. Coffin, 1894, p. 71)*

That Friends would allow their freedom seekers to be returned to slavery rather than live in their midst leads one to question the motives of their anti-slavery work. Nothing speaks more clearly to this revelation than the forced colonization that follows.

Networked to Freedom, but Not My Neighbor: An Unwelcomed Reception by Northern Friends

Levi Coffin saw the fate of the liberated as the most critical question. Believing that forced colonization was slavery by another name, Levi dissented from the North Carolina Manumission and Colonization Society. The financial burden of caring for so many African Americans became prohibitive under the Trustee system. "Before the idea of foreign colonization had gained momentum, Friends began to think of emigration to free states as a solution to the tremendous burden caused by the Trustee slaves" (Wright, 1974, p. 52).

The enslaved held in trust faced constant threat of re-enslavement. Many of the former masters' heirs brought legal suits to reclaim their property. These lawsuits kept the Meetings in legal entanglements. Friends in the Deep River area of Guilford County made a request to the Yearly Meeting to devise a plan to rid themselves of the enslaved held in trust. The solution soon became the system of colonizing African Americans to free territories. According to an 1830 report summarizing their expenses, the Meeting for Suffering reported 652 African Americans had been colonized to free governments costing $12,769.51 (over $350,000 in today's currency) (Weeks, 1968, p. 228). In 1830, there remained under Quaker care 402 African Americans. By 1834, there remained 300 under care in the Eastern Quarter. In the same year, 133 were sent to Indiana. In 1856 the "African fund" only held $353.12 (almost $11,000 in today's currency) (Weeks, 1968, p. 228). In that year, there remained 18 African Americans under Friends' care. As the enslaved were sent to Indiana, they faced great prejudice from both non-Quakers and Quakers alike.

On April 8, 1826, Samuel Charles wrote to North Carolina Friends that "the prejudice against a coloured population was as great in Indiana as in North Carolina." The missive went on to reveal, "there is as much prejudice in the minds of our Society as in other people" (Charles, 1826, p. 28). Northern Friends feared that their white counterparts would look upon them with disdain for bringing African Americans into their states. They also feared the freedom seekers would make life harder for them financially; others simply did not wish to live among African Americans due to racial prejudice. Philadelphia Friends sent strong discouragement to the North Carolina Yearly Meeting against immigrating African Americans to Philadelphia by attacking their character. The letter stated African Americans "mingle with the lowest class and remain in a degraded state" (Cook, 1827 cited in Wright, 1974). These correspondences expose the unwelcomed reception that African American freedom seekers received from non-Quakers and Friends alike.

Opting not to adhere to these admonitions, North Carolina Quakers arranged for African Americans to sail to Philadelphia aboard the ship *Julius Pringle* for Pennsylvania. George Swaim, a Quaker attendant aboard the vessel, wrote the following account of the violence he encountered by Friends upon attempting to dock the ship in Philadelphia.

> The menacing were all ready at the sight of me to break out and fire their big guns, he later reported. The menacing crowd included Quakers. . . . Philadelphia Quakers were determined that none of the blacks aboard the Julius Pringle should disembark. A man whom Swain described as a "very influential Friend" threatened the emigrant party with a lesson from history, declaring "that if they undertook to land . . . he should not think [it] strange if they shared the fate of the Boston tea."
>
> *(Sheppard, 1832 cited in Opper, 1975)*

Friends were willing to resort to violence to keep the freedom seeking African Americans from living among them. As tensions rose in free states, Friends set their sights on foreign missions.

Colonized With or Without Consent

The president of Haiti, Jean-Pierre Boyer, agreed to receive African Americans and assist with the fees of their transport. Haitian resettlement seemed to be an optimal plan that would afford Quakers a solution to their financial troubles. An issue that soon arose was that of consent. Few

African Americans actually wanted to go to Haiti, and even fewer to Liberia given how long the journey was. Also, there was the matter of preference. Some of the enslaved wished to join relatives in a particular state and refused to settle anywhere else.

> Slaves not only changed their minds on the eve of voyages to Liberia but did so before overland journeys to the free states as well. James Peele, of the Rich Square Monthly Meeting, who experienced a desertion of blacks on his 1834 expedition, was enraged by those who "after giving an expectation that they would go and were fitted up with clothes . . . put them selves out of the way."
>
> *(Peele, 1834)*

The North Carolina Yearly Meeting decided that the enslaved "might be made to go for their own benefit" (Ratcliff, 1828 cited in Wright, 1974). The Meeting's plan to colonize without consent, even to places ill-equipped to care for the African Americans, demonstrated that "Quakers were at least partially motivated by self-interest" (Wright, 1974, p. 57). Of the 776 enslaved Africans held in trust, Quakers settled 420 to Liberia. The rest went to other free governments including Haiti and northern states. Conversely, the African Americans regularly reported mistreatment in Haiti resulting from being seen as outsiders. They also reported not having received the wages and land promised to them by the Haitian government, as well as overall discontentment. Hannah Elliot, an African American woman from North Carolina who had relocated to Indiana, penned a letter in 1829 during the heart of the colonization era. She wrote to the Parkers in North Carolina, a white Quaker family. Her letter reads:

> We are well contented better satisfied than in Carolina. . . . [Mary] wants to know where her Brother Samuel and his wife is, she wants to know . . . where her Brother Robert is whether he gone to *Lydera* [Liberia] or not. . . . Hannah wishes to know whether her mother's Husband has gone to *Lyberia* with his wife or not.
>
> *(Elliott, 1829)*

Hannah Elliott felt that her living situation was better in Indiana than it had been in North Carolina. Simultaneously, Mrs. Elliott inquired of several relatives and friends, uncertain of their whereabouts or final destinations. This correspondence demonstrates how African American families were impacted by colonization.

Closing

The role of Quakers for the cause of anti-slavery and abolition is one of complexity. While Friends joined in collective silence for almost a century, their African American siblings suffered through one of the most barbaric systems known to humankind. Their silence was fueled by many of the same politics that were at play within the larger white non-Quaker community. From the earliest dialogues related to anti-slavery, Quakers never had full consensus. Although Friends in North Carolina were some of the earliest to lend their voices to the weighty matter of slavery, there was still great division among them. Quakers' anti-slavery efforts led to the manumission of hundreds of enslaved Africans. Save twelve to fifteen, the North Carolina Yearly Meeting had resettled most of the 779 African Americans enslaved by the Trustee plan. Although some African Americans reported greater quality of life resulting from resettlement, many suffered resentment, violence and a poorer quality of life. The most telling is that many were colonized without their consent, an unfortunate practice akin to their lack of agency within the slave community. While honoring the stand that Quakers took for manumission, it is necessary to also interrogate their practices. A rewriting of Quaker history must give voice to these unbearable truths.

Note

1 Disownment was a meeting's action making clear that an individual's behavior does not honor Friends' witness. Although the individual could continue to attend services, they would not be permitted to engage in church governance.

Bibliography

Bassett, J.S. (1896). *Slavery and Servitude in the Colony of North Carolina 1867–1928*. Baltimore: John Hopkins Press.

Bland, L.A. (1968). Guilford County Quakers and Slavery in North Carolina. Master's Thesis. Wake Forest University.

Charles, S. (1826). Letter to Jeremiah Hubbard and Henry Ballinger, 8 April, Record of Correspondence, 28.

Coffin, A. (1894). *Early Settlement of Friends in North Carolina: Traditions and Reminiscences 1894*. North Carolina: North Carolina Friends Historical Society, Typed in 1952.

Coffin, L. (2014). *Reminiscences*. Missouri: Richard Buchko.

Cook, J. (1827). Letter to Friends, 26 October.

Crawford, M.J. (2010). *The Having of Negroes Is Become a Burden*. Florida: University Press of Florida.

Elliott, H. (1829). "Josiah Parker Papers Letter 30," *Earlham Exhibits*, accessed June 8, 2020, https://exhibits.earlham.edu/items/show/142.

Hilty, H. (1993). *Toward Freedom for All: NC Quakers and Slavery*. Richmond: Friends United Press.

Hoag, J. (1861). *Journal of the Life of Joseph Hoag*. Auburn: Knapp and Peck.

McDaniel, D. & Julye, V. (2009). *Fit for Freedom, Not for Friendship: Quakers, African Americans, and the Myth of Racial Justice*. Philadelphia: Quaker Press of Friends General Conference.

Minute Book of the North Carolina Yearly Meeting, 1794–1837, passim, Guilford College Archives, Guilford College.

Minutes of the North Carolina Yearly Meeting, I, Guilford College Archives, Guilford College.

Opper, P.K. (1975). 'North Carolina Quakers: Reluctant Slaveholders', *North Carolina Office of Archives and History*, 52(1), pp. 37–58.

Peele, J. (1834). Letter to Jeremiah Hubbard, 25 October, Meeting For Suffering Correspondence.

Ratcliff, S. (1828). Letter to Meeting for Sufferings, 11 December.

Sheppard, M. (1832). Letter to George McGill, 19 April, Moses Sheppard Collection, Manuscripts Division, Swarthmore College Library, Swarthmore, Pennsylvania.

Sowle, P. (1965). 'The North Carolina Manumission Society 1816–1834', *The North Carolina Historical Review*, 42(1), pp. 47–69.

Swaim & Sherwood. (1848). A Narrative of Some of the Proceedings of North Carolina Yearly Meeting on the Subject of Slavery Within Its Limits, Greensborough, NC.

Wagstaff, H.M. (1934). *Minutes of the North Carolina Manumission Society, 1816–1834*, Chapel Hill: University of North Carolina Press, 62–63.

Weeks, S.B. (1968). *Southern Quakers and Slavery*. New York: Bergman Publishers.

Wright, Barbara. (1974). North Carolina Quakers and Slavery. Honors Thesis. UNC Chapel Hill.

37

SARAH MAPPS DOUGLASS

An American Saint

Abigail Lawrence

Sarah Mapps Douglass (1806–1881), an educator, activist, painter, and Quaker,[1] was some-one who embodied religion in an incredibly pure form: faith. The granddaughter of formerly enslaved Cyrus Bustill (1732–1806), Sarah Douglass lived the first six decades of her life in a country where atrocities were committed against people simply for being African American, just like her. Despite the discrimination and hate, Sarah Douglass never lost faith in her God, nor did she rely upon her God to be the harbinger of change. Sarah Mapps Douglass was an exceptional example of a human being who, when permitted a few basic human rights, used those rights to risk her life in order to end enslavement, educate others, and to contribute to the world in the very best way she could: by being herself.

Born to two prominent abolitionist families, both of the few wealthy free Black families in Philadelphia descended from slaves, Sarah Mapps Douglass inherited history with her Bustill blood and Douglass blood. Devout Quaker Grace Bustill (1782–1842), Sarah Douglass's mother, was one of the eight children of Cyrus Bustill and the Delaware Indian/English Elizabeth Morey (1746–1827).[2] Cyrus Bustill was born into enslavement; his parents were the Quaker lawyer Samuel Bustill (1710–1742) and Parthenia, who was enslaved by Samuel Bustill. Cyrus Bustill was a baker who had baked bread for George Washington's troops, and he managed to purchase his freedom (after his father's death) in 1774[3] or was freed by a Friends Meeting in 1769,[4] depending on the source. In 1787, he cofounded the Free African Society (first African American charity in America), and in 1803 he founded a school for Black children in his Arch Street home in Philadelphia (an example which his daughter and granddaughter would follow). That same year, Reverend Robert Douglass Sr. and Grace Bustill married.

On September 9, 1806, Sarah Mapps Douglass was born. As a child, she received an exceed-ingly strong education at the hand of tutors, eventually integrating into a school which was founded in 1819 by her mother and a wealthy shipbuilder named James Forten.[5] From there, she attended college and briefly taught in New York City before returning to teach at her mother's school in Philadelphia.[6] In 1827 Sarah Douglass opened her own school for Black girls, where she began her fifty-year career as a principal and teacher at her own school and, later, the (Quaker) Institute for Colored Youth. During that same period, she wrote prose and poetry about religion, slavery, and prejudice, and painted botanical watercolors under the pseudo-nym Zillah and possibly Sophonista, Sophanista and/or Ella.[7] In 1831 she founded the Female Literary Association and fundraised for the abolitionist *Liberator* newspaper; one year later she

DOI: 10.4324/9780429030925-41

gave her famous "The Cause of the Slave Became My Own" speech (which described what is debatably the most important turning point in her life: her decision to combat enslavement in any way she could), and two years later she cofounded the interracial Philadelphia (later Pennsylvania) Female Anti-Slavery Society with her mother and others.[8] In the 1850s, Sarah Douglass studied female hygiene, reproductive health, and other "indelicate" topics at the Female Medical College of Pennsylvania and the Pennsylvania Medical University.[9] In 1855 she married Reverend William Douglass (no relation) of St. Thomas Episcopal Church; he died in 1861. The marriage was henceforth referred to by Sarah Douglass as "that School of bitter discipline, the old Parsonage of St. Thomas."[10] Further continuing her advocacy for the self-education of Black women, she founded the Sarah M. Douglass Literary Circle in 1861, at the beginning of the Civil War.[11] During and after the war, she helped lead the Pennsylvania Branch of the American Freedman's Aid Commission, which provided aid to formerly enslaved people. She also lectured, advocated reform, established a geriatric and indigent care home for Black people, and taught at the Institute for Colored Youth. In 1877, she retired from the Institute, where she had been the head of the primary department for over two decades. In 1882, she died, ending her half-century career as an educator and activist.

Sarah Mapps Douglass fought for the abolition of enslavement at every opportunity. It may even be said that when there were no opportunities, she made her own. However, she did not oppose enslavement so fiercely at the behest of a church or an organization. The Quaker meeting she attended as a child held segregated meetings, as she describes:

> I am free to say, that my Mother and myself were told to sit there, and that a friend sat at each end of the bench to prevent white persons from sitting there. And even when a child, my soul was made sad by hearing five or six times, during the course of our meeting, this language of remonstrance addressed to those who were willing to sit with us. "This bench is for the black people," "This bench is for the people of color" – and often times I wept, at other times I felt indignant and queried in my own mind, are these people Christians? Now it seems clear to me, that had not that bench been set apart for oppressed Americans, there would have been no necessity for the often repeated and galling remonstrances, galling indeed because I believe they despise us for our color.[12]

The passage clearly states that Sarah Douglass did not consider the Quakers as the epitome of humanity but rather relied on her own inward truths for direction. Interestingly enough, this rejection of outward messages in favor of inward light and connection to God is the principle upon which Quakerism was founded.[13] She stopped attending Quaker meetings during her young adulthood but reconciled with the community by the 1840s. Sarah Douglass found that, as Emma Lapsansky so neatly put it, "'anti-slavery' was not always the same as "pro-black,'"[14] even in a Quaker meeting house.[15] Additionally, the passage demonstrates Sarah Douglass's intense conviction of the wrongfulness of race-based hate and discrimination, for which she risked her life. One example of a common threat directly addressed to those perceived to be rebelling against slavery was:

> You have taken up arms against your masters, and have burnt and plundered their houses and buildings . . . all who are found at the rebels will be put to death without mercy. You cannot resist the king's troops. . . . All who hold out will meet certain death.[16]

Every word spoken, every letter written, every meeting attended, and every time Douglass dared to defy social norms, she knowingly put herself in danger. She frequently wrote under pseudonyms along with a group of Black female friends, which was likely a result of such imminent danger. The strength of Sarah Douglass's conviction and determination against enslavement enabled her treacherous actions.

Sarah Mapps Douglass taught with a passion in her heart and bones, and she would risk anything to give the power of knowledge to those who desired it. She was given education, and education she would give. In one essay, titled *Family Worship* and written under the pen name "Sophonista," Douglass earnestly waxed poetic about the beauty and necessity of education:

> The voice of the mother falls like sweet music on the ear, as she reads a portion from the book of books and the meek and loving expression on the countenances of her children bears witness, that it is happiness to be those employed. O, lady, would that we might see all the families of our people so engaged! How would the sunshine of such an example disperse the mists of prejudice which surround us! Yes, religion and education would raise us to inequality with the fairest in our land.[17]

Douglass all but outright states that she views education as a perfectly positive, near-universal solution to the issues of prejudice of her time. By conveying her belief in the benefits of learning, Douglass elucidates part of that which drives her Quaker beliefs: her faith in enlightenment through education. Her life reflects this belief, having "continued lecturing into her old age and only stopped teaching when she was no longer physically able to get to the school."[18] She taught for half a century, founded a school, and even went to medical school to learn how to teach more advanced knowledge. If actions spoke louder than words, then Douglass was singing at the top of her lungs. She committed her life to teaching, learning, and enlightenment.

Sarah Mapps Douglass recognized that in a realm where people of her color and sex were considered sub-human, she had to show her humanity to the world and herself, for if the oppressors suppressed her creativity, they suppressed some of her humanity as well. She frequently expressed herself through poetry, in lyrical prose such as is exhibited in "Moonlight," as follows:

> I have a melancholy pleasure in looking upon the moon in a cloudless night, when she hangs like a lamp of silver in the sky, and throws her pure light abroad on spire and cottage, hill and dale. Oh! It is on such a night as this that memory brings before me all the friends I have ever loved, all I have lost."[19]

Though perhaps productive as well, this exhibition of creativity radiates pure, unadulterated joy despite the topic. It appears to definitively depict Douglass's clear and conscious choice to ensure that her human creativity was unleashed upon the world, showing her humanity through writing for pleasure, not persuasion. Douglass was also a visual artist; her pieces are thought to be the first paintings discovered signed by an African American woman. She would frequently include lines of prose or verse which she wrote or selected with her paintings, such as in the example which follows.[20]

The simplistic, elegant, colorful illustrations which Douglass created are not thought to have been published during her lifetime. Her paintings appear only in letters to her dear friends, who preserved them.[21] As someone so wholly motivated to better society and fight oppression, it seems almost unthinkable that Sarah Douglass would have a "guilty pleasure," an unproductive, private hobby. However, it can be inferred that Douglass realized that in order to best contribute to society, she would need to be true to herself and not stifle herself by limiting all activities to those strictly practical. Although perhaps this intent alone tips the activity into practicality, the paradox is hardly relevant. Douglass enjoyed writing, painting, and likely other pastimes lost to time, and so she wrote and painted.

Douglass was a person given an inch who moved a mile. Her story is so heartening, so enlivening, so inspirational, and so informative that people may recognize her and study her life and admire her faith in God. Her gift for teaching has outlived her: people continue learning. As a woman centuries ahead of her time, she said of her faith that "[she has] no hope in man, but much in God – much in the rock of ages."[22] This statement of her beliefs about humanity, combined with her determination to follow her inward truths and her dedication to education, illustrate the spirit which completely permeated her life. As an individual, Douglass never showed difficulty with ascertaining the right course of action, despite facing the near-insurmountable opponent of hate as a product of ignorance. With unparalleled resolve, Douglass fought for her own rights and the rights of others. The courage and compassion displayed by Sarah Mapps Douglass remains inspirational to this day. She may have been dealt a hand of few cards, but she used every bit of that hand to fight for a better world.

Notes

1 Marie Lindhorst, "Politics in a Box: Sarah Mapps Douglass and the Female Literary Association, 1831–1833," *Pennsylvania History: A Journal of Mid-Atlantic Studies* 65, no. 3 (1998): pp. 263–278, https://www.jstor.org/stable/27774117.

2 Margaret Hope Bacon, "Learning from Sarah Douglass," *Friends Journal* 48, no. 1 (January 2002): pp. 17–19. https://www.friendsjournal.org/wp-content/uploads/emember/downloads/2002/HC12-50991.pdf.

3 Brian Temple, *Philadelphia Quakers and the Antislavery Movement*, illustrated, reprint (Jefferson, NC: McFarland, 2014), https://books.google.com/books?id=dAGhAwAAQBAJ&vq=cyrus+bustill&source=gbs_navlinks_s, 55.

4 Donald Scott, *Remembering Cheltenham Township*, illustrated (Charleston, SC: History Press, 2009).

5 "Sarah Mapps Douglass," Women's History Blog (History of American Women, May 29, 2020), https://www.womenhistoryblog.com/2008/02/sarah-mapps-douglass.html.

6 Herb Boyd, "Sarah Mapps Douglass, Ardent Abolitionist, Teacher and Painter," *New York Amsterdam News*, March 10, 2021, p. 20.

7 Marie Lindhorst, "Politics in a Box: Sarah Mapps Douglass and the Female Literary Association, 1831–1833," *Pennsylvania History: A Journal of Mid-Atlantic Studies* 65, no. 3 (1998): pp. 263–278, https://www.jstor.org/stable/27774117; Julie Winch, "'You Have Talents – Only Cultivate Them': Philadelphia's Black Female Literary Societies and the Abolitionist Crusade," in *The Abolitionist Sisterhood: Women's Political Culture in Antebellum America*, ed. John C Van Horne and Jean Fagan Yellin (Ithaca, NY: Cornell University Press, 1994), pp. 101–118.

8 Stacy M. Brown, "Grace Bustill Douglass Co-Founded Female Anti-Slavery Society in Philadelphia," *The Washington Informer* (March 4, 2021), https://www.washingtoninformer.com/grace-bustill-douglass-co-founded-female-anti-slavery-society-in-philadelphia.

9 Alissa Falcone, "Examining Drexel's Ties to the First African-American Women Physicians," *DrexelNow* (Drexel, February 26, 2016), https://drexel.edu/now/archive/2016/February/African-American-Women-Physicians/.

10 "Sarah Mapps Douglass," Women's History Blog (History of American Women, May 29, 2020), https://www.womenhistoryblog.com/2008/02/sarah-mapps-douglass.html.

11 Ibid.

12 Sarah Mapps Douglass, n.d.

13 Pink Dandelion, "Who Are the Quakers?" in *The Quakers: A Very Short Introduction* (Oxford: Oxford University Press, 2008), pp. 1–18.

14 Emma J. Lapsansky, "New Eyes for the 'Invisibles' in Quaker-Minority Relations," *Quaker History* 90, no. 1 (2001): pp. 1–7, https://doi.org/10.1353/qkh.2001.0004.

15 Margaret Hope Bacon. "New Light on Sarah Mapps Douglass and Her Reconciliation with Friends." *Quaker History* 90, no. 1 (2001): 28–49. https://doi.org/10.1353/qkh.2001.0011.
16 N. Y. Dai. Ado., "Insurrection in Jamaica, Baltimore, Feb. 7," *The Liberator*, February 18, 1832, Vol. II edition, sec. No. 7, p. 26.
17 Dorothy Sterling and Sarah Mapps Douglass, "Daughters of Africa/Daughters of America: Selection from *Family Worship* by Sarah Mapps Douglass," in *We Are Your Sisters: Black Women in the Nineteenth Century* (New York: W. W. Norton & Company, 1997), p. 112.
18 "Sarah Mapps Douglass (1806–1882)," LCP Album Project (Library Company of Philadelphia, July 25, 2014), https://lcpalbumproject.org/?p=137.
19 Sarah Mapps Douglass, "The Liberator," in *The Liberator* (Philadelphia, PA: William Lloyd Garrison and Isaac Knapp, 1832), p. 56.
20 Sarah Mapps Douglass (Philadelphia, PA, n.d.).
21 See image found at the Library Company of Philadelphia's website: https://digital.librarycompany.org/islandora/object/Islandora%3A64975.
22 Sarah Mapps Douglass, "The Cause of the Slave Became My Own" (1832), in *The Black Abolitionist Papers*, ed. C. Peter Ripley (Chapel Hill: The University of North Carolina Press, 1991), 116–117.

Bibliography

Bacon, Margaret Hope. "New Light on Sarah Mapps Douglass and Her Reconciliation with Friends." *Quaker History* 90, no. 1 (2001): 28–49. https://doi.org/10.1353/qkh.2001.0011.
Bacon, Margaret Hope. "Learning from Sarah Douglass." *Friends Journal* 48, no. 1 (January 2002): 17–19. https://www.friendsjournal.org/wp-content/uploads/emember/downloads/2002/HC12-50991.pdf.
Boyd, Herb. "Sarah Mapps Douglass, Ardent Abolitionist, Teacher and Painter." *New York Amsterdam News*, March 10, 2021.
Brown, Stacy M. "Grace Bustill Douglass Co-Founded Female Anti-Slavery Society in Philadelphia." *The Washington Informer*, March 4, 2021. https://www.washingtoninformer.com/grace-bustill-douglass-co-founded-female-anti-slavery-society-in-philadelphia/.
Cadbury, Henry J. "Negro Membership in the Society of Friends." *The Journal of Negro History* 21, no. 2 (April 1936): 151–213. https://doi.org/10.2307/2714569.
Dandelion, Pink. "Chapter 1: Who Are the Quakers?" Essay. In *The Quakers: A Very Short Introduction*. Oxford, England: Oxford University Press, 2008, 1–18.
Douglass, Sarah Mapps. Letter to The Liberator. "Moonlight." *The Liberator* II. Philadelphia, Pennsylvania: William Lloyd Garrison and Isaac Knapp, April 7, 1832.
Douglass, Sarah Mapps. Letter to William Bassett, December 1837. (Held in the Theodore D. Weld Collection at the William Clements Library, University of Michigan.)
Douglass, Sarah Mapps. "The Cause of the Slave Became My Own." June 1832. In *The Black Abolitionist Papers*, edited by C. Peter Ripley. Chapel Hill: The University of North Carolina Press, 1991, 116–117.
Douglass, Sarah Mapps, and Amy Matilda Cassey. *Watercolor of Flowers with Lines of Prose Written below.* 1314 Locust Street, Philadelphia, PA: The Library Company of Philadelphia, 1833. Library Company of Philadelphia. Philadelphia, Pennsylvania.
Dunbar, Erica Armstrong. "Voices from the Margins: The Philadelphia Female Anti-Slavery Society 1833–1840." Essay. In *A Fragile Freedom: African American Women and Emancipation in the Antebellum City*. New Haven, CT: Yale University Press, 2008, 70–95.
Falcone, Alissa. "Examining Drexel's Ties to the First African-American Women Physicians." *DrexelNow*. Drexel, February 26, 2016. https://drexel.edu/now/archive/2016/February/African-American-Women-Physicians/.
Genovese, Holly. "Not a Myth: Quakers and Racial Justice★." *Quaker Studies* 19, no. 2 (2015): 243–59. https://doi.org/10.3828/QUAKER.19.2.243.
Gonzalez, Aston. "The Art of Racial Politics: The Work of Robert Douglass Jr., 1833–46." *The Pennsylvania Magazine of History and Biography* 138, no. 1 (January 2014): 5–37. https://doi.org/10.5215/pennmaghistbio.138.1.0005.
Kelley, Mary. "'Talents Committed to Your Care': Reading and Writing Radical Abolitionism in Antebellum America." *The New England Quarterly* 88, no. 1 (March 2015): 37–72. https://doi.org/10.1162/tneq_a_00435.
Lapsansky, Emma J. "New Eyes for the 'Invisibles' in Quaker-Minority Relations." *Quaker History*, African-Americans and Quakers, 90, no. 1 (2001): 1–7. https://doi.org/10.1353/qkh.2001.0004.

Lindhorst, Marie. "Politics in a Box: Sarah Mapps Douglass and the Female Literary Association, 1831–1833." *Pennsylvania History: A Journal of Mid-Atlantic Studies*, African Americans In Pennsylvania, 65, no. 3 (1998): 263–278. https://www.jstor.org/stable/27774117.

N. Y. Dai. Ado. "Insurrection in Jamaica, Baltimore, Feb. 7." *The Liberator*, February 18, 1832, Vol. II edition, sec. No. 7.

"Sarah Mapps Douglass." Women's History Blog. History of American Women, May 29, 2020. https://www.womenhistoryblog.com/2008/02/sarah-mapps-douglass.html.

"Sarah Mapps Douglass (1806–1882)." LCP Album Project. Library Company of Philadelphia, July 25, 2014. https://lcpalbumproject.org/?p=137.

Scott, Donald. *Remembering Cheltenham Township*. Illustrated. Charleston, SC: History Press, 2009.

Sterling, Dorothy. *We Are Your Sisters: Black Women in the Nineteenth Century*. New York, NY: W. W. Norton & Company, 1997.

Sterling, Dorothy, and Sarah Mapps Douglass. "Daughters of Africa/Daughters of America: Selection from Family Worship by Sarah Mapps Douglass." Essay. In *We Are Your Sisters: Black Women in the Nineteenth Century*. New York, NY: W. W. Norton & Company, 1997, 112.

Temple, Brian. *Philadelphia Quakers and the Antislavery Movement*. *Google Books*. Illustrated, reprinted. Jefferson, NC: McFarland, 2014. https://books.google.com/books?id=dAGhAwAAQBAJ&vq=cyrus+bustill&source=gbs_navlinks_s. 55.

Winch, Julie. " 'You Have Talents – Only Cultivate Them': Philadelphia's Black Female Literary Societies and the Abolitionist Crusade." Essay. In *The Abolitionist Sisterhood: Women's Political Culture in Antebellum America*, edited by John C Van Horne and Jean Fagan Yellin. Ithaca, NY: Cornell University Press, 1994, 101–118.

38

QUAKER ADVOCACY FOR PEACE

From Grassroots to Congress

Diane Randall

Quaker Roots of Faithful Advocacy

The Friends Committee on National Legislation (FCNL) has faithfully lobbied the US Congress and various administrations to advance peace, justice, opportunity, and environmental stewardship since its founding in 1943. It was established at a gathering in Richmond, Indiana, attended by 52 Friends from 15 Quaker Yearly Meetings, mostly from the Midwest because of the war. FCNL began by lobbying against military conscription and for aid to war-torn Europe during World War II.[1]

As the oldest registered religious lobby in Washington, DC, FCNL advocates for government policies guided by issues and priorities determined through a regular process of discernment by Quaker meetings, churches, and Friends. In recent decades, the policies have been published as *The World We Seek: A Statement of Legislative Policy*. Every two years – coinciding with a new session of Congress – FCNL considers and refreshes its legislative priorities through engagement with Friends meetings, churches, and in accordance with FCNL's vision:[2]

> We seek a world free from war and the threat of war
>> We seek a society with equity and justice for all
>> We seek a community where every person's potential may be fulfilled
>> We seek an earth restored.

The *we seek*s express FCNL's mission of living Quaker "values of integrity, simplicity and peace, and to build relationships across political divides to move policies forward." FCNL's current priorities focus on such areas as peacebuilding, global militarism, nuclear disarmament, solutions to the climate change crisis, environmental justice, economic justice, health care access, ending gun violence, criminal justice reform, election integrity, immigration and refugees, and Native American policy.

FCNL's approach to changing public policy relies on the expertise of registered lobbyists in Washington, DC, and the deep commitment of thousands of advocates around the country who are willing to talk to their members of Congress about legislation that advances peace and justice. FCNL trains volunteer advocates to build personal relationships with members of Congress and their staff, regardless of political leaning.

DOI: 10.4324/9780429030925-42

The persistence of FCNL's national network of advocates and supporters follows Quaker faith and practice, enabling them to press forward no matter which political party controls the government. This practice of nonpartisan political engagement is, for many people, a matter of faith and a way to exercise civic engagement. By writing letters to their members of Congress, visiting congressional offices on Capitol Hill and in their districts, and speaking out through print, broadcast and social media, advocates share their stories of why they care. This witness influences their elected officials.

To support its cause, FCNL has also long recognized the need to train young people to be effective advocates. Beginning with an internship program in in 1970s, FCNL's young adult programs have grown to offer opportunities for thousands of young adults. Launched in 2006, Spring Lobby Weekend has offered young adults the opportunity to come to Washington for training and lobbying on one of FCNL's legislative priorities. The event has grown over 15 years to include as many as 500 young people annually from across the country.

In 2015, FCNL launched a new young adult program, the Advocacy Corps, a dynamic cohort of passionate advocates. FCNL selects 20 young people annually, providing them with training, coaching, and connections, along with a monthly stipend. They lead organizing and advocacy efforts in their local communities. These organizers motivate others in their communities to advocate on one of FCNL legislative priorities – immigration, climate change, gun violence prevention, and police militarization – to help drive public policy changes in Congress (FCNL, 2020).

Activism and advocacy are not new concepts; concerned people have heeded the call to serve and have leveraged their voices for justice throughout history. The practice of speaking truth to power has long been a practice of Quaker faith. Its roots date back to the early days of the Religious Society of Friends, when early Quakers confronted political power both in England and the United States, leading movements for social justice and peace. Friends peacefully objected to laws that violated their conscience, resulting in their imprisonment, abuse, and death. They have also routinely objected to the misapplication of the law.

In *A Theological Perspective on Quaker Lobbying*, Margery Post Abbott describes the Quakers' early and persistent opposition to injustice:

> Their consistency in the face of unjust application of the law, public declaration of their case, and willingness to accept the consequence of standing up to brutal actions of the government meant that they were not easily controlled or intimidated.[3]

Although its priorities may change and new tools may be used, the steadfast commitment to peace and justice that shaped FCNL's early days continues today.

Peacebuilding and Violence Prevention

> At a time in history when so much blood and treasure is poured out in war, there need to be insistent voices for peace. When there is so much fear and suspicion and hatred, the Church should be seeking paths of reconciliation, understanding, cooperation, and forgiveness.
> – E. Raymond Wilson, first executive secretary of FCNL (1943–1961)[4]

FCNL's founding executive secretary, E. Raymond Wilson, could have written this quote in 1944, 2001, or today. Similarly, as George Fox and other leading Quakers stated in 1661, "We utterly deny all outward wars and strife and fightings with outward weapons, for any end or under any pretence whatsoever."[5] This peace testimony, as well as the belief that there is that of God in every person, fuels FCNL's legislative policy to this day. Friends' commitment to peace has governed FCNL's work to prevent war, minimize the threat of war, and violent conflict since its beginning.

During its first 30 years, FCNL advocated to prevent the US engagement in war, eliminate universal conscription for military service, and address the root causes of war by changing public policy through the US Congress. The organization has remained steadfast in its commitment to Quaker peace testimony – from promoting laws that provided relief to Europe during and after World War II, to defeating congressional proposals for mandatory military training for young men, to playing a significant role in advocating for the creation of the Peace Corps in 1961, and to passing the 1964 Civil Rights Act.[6]

FCNL remains at the forefront of advocacy for nuclear disarmament, peacebuilding, and violence prevention. In 1985, it organized the US-Soviet Working Group, which compiled a draft "Exchange for Peace Resolution" in consultation with members of Congress and State Department officials. FCNL lobbied the US ambassador and the State Department to consider the draft resolution ahead of the Reykjavik summit between President Ronald Reagan and Soviet Union President Mikhail Gorbachev in Iceland in 1986. The draft resolution contributed to thawing nuclear relations between the Soviet Union and the United States. The summit also paved the way for the 1987 Intermediate-Range Nuclear Forces Treaty (INF) and the 1991 Strategic Arms Reduction Treaty (START I).[7]

By the time the Cold War ended in 1991, FCNL had played a significant role in building congressional support for a series of international treaties to reduce the number of nuclear weapons and lessen the threat of war. In 1993, FCNL led a coalition to help pass legislation that required the United States to adopt a code of conduct on arms transfers, which it achieved in 1998. In 2015, FCNL successfully advocated for support of the 2015 Iran nuclear deal. FCNL continues its advocacy for arms control, nuclear non-proliferation, reduction of arms sales, and a reduction in all forms of militarism today.

Despite the international treaties, US militarism is deeply embedded in both foreign and domestic policies. In 2001, the 9/11 terrorist attacks marshalled a response to punish an enemy and fortify the country. On September 12, 2001, and over the ensuing months and years, FCNL urged the United States not to respond to the violence of 9/11 with more violence.[8]

Even though FCNL actively opposed them, Congress subsequently passed two Authorizations for Use of Military Force (AUMF) in 2001[9] and 2002,[10] which sanctioned the US invasion of Iraq and expanded military operations in Afghanistan and beyond in the "war against terror." Through these widely permissive laws, Congress essentially ceded to the president its constitutional power to decide whether and when the United States enters military conflict. It also shunted aside the role of diplomacy, development, and peacebuilding as effective ways for the United States to engage in the world.

The decision of Congress to invade Iraq, fight a war in Afghanistan, and fund military interventions across the globe was the inspiration for FCNL's adoption of Dr. Martin Luther King Jr.'s powerful statement, "War Is Not the Answer." Using an iconic design created by Atlanta Friends Meeting, this slogan became a campaign for FCNL, with bumper stickers and signs in peoples' yards and at marches and protests at the time President George W. Bush declared war on terror. Most importantly, it fueled a campaign for a congressional response to endless war.[11]

By 2020, three US presidents – George W. Bush, Barack Obama, and Donald Trump – had used the AUMFs as blank checks to launch more than 40 military conflicts in 19 countries. This period, spanning nearly two decades, is the longest that the United States has ever been at war. It has been longer than World War II, World War I, and the Civil War combined.[12]

Since the passage of the 2001 and 2002 AUMFs, the FCNL community has actively advocated to repeal both bills. After more than four legislative attempts, FCNL's Advocacy Teams – groups of local advocates working together – led a national effort in 2019 that resulted in the House of Representatives voting to repeal the 2001 AUMF. This bill authorized military action against Al-Qaeda and other terrorist groups which perpetrated the 9/11 attacks. Although the measure failed in the Senate, passage by the full House was a historic victory.

The US expansion of militarism and using a war-first approach to terrorism is also reflected in the constant growth of the Pentagon budget. Today, the United States spends far more on the military than every other country, including all potential adversaries, even after accounting for inflation and countries' varying purchasing power.[13] Congress and the Trump administration agreed to spend more than $2 billion every day on wars and the military for the fiscal year that ran through September 2020.[14]

This excessive spending on militarism is not limited to international engagements. For years, the Pentagon has transferred bayonets, weaponized combat vehicles, and other war equipment to local police in the United States. By 2014, more than 8000 local law enforcement agencies had benefited from what is called the 1033 Program. More than $5.1 billion in military materiel was transferred by the Department of Defense since 1997.[15]

Through another program, the Department of Homeland Security gave over $34 billion in grants to police forces since 9/11. They were used to buy drones, mine-resistant ambush protected vehicles, and other military materiel.[16] This contributed to rising police violence in local communities.

Thanks to the faithful advocacy of thousands of constituents nationwide, the National Defense Authorization Act (NDAA) of December 2020 banned the transfer of some war equipment to local police. There is still much work to be done to restore justice in policing, but this was an important step in the years long effort to end police violence.[17]

Despite setbacks along the way, FCNL's long-term strategy recognizes the essential requirement of persistence in advocacy. Diplomacy, development, and peacebuilding remain effective ways for the United States to engage with the world. However, the problems of racism and militarism within the United States are extended through US hegemony as a foreign policy that perpetuates militarism and racism. Fortunately, the growing bipartisan drumbeat against war and militarization and the recognition of addressing systemic racism is gradually impacting the policy debate.

Making "Never Again" Plausible

While the government waged a War on Terror after 9/11, FCNL persisted in its efforts to shift the foreign policy focus in Congress from fearful response to the peaceful prevention of violent conflict.

The shift gained traction when the United States failed to address atrocities in Darfur in 2003.[18] Over the course of two decades of tireless advocacy and in the face of ongoing atrocities around the world, FCNL sought to answer the questions, "If war is not the answer, what is? How do we end and prevent war and violent conflict?" FCNL's staff and its network of advocates listened, learned, and acted on the Quaker peace testimony in trying to shape US foreign policy to establish a new orientation to global conflict and terror.

To mark the 60th anniversary of the UN Convention on the Prevention and Punishment of the Crime of Genocide, the bipartisan Genocide and Atrocities Prevention Task Force released its violence prevention recommendations in 2008.[19] FCNL decided to advance these recommendations and organized the Prevention and Protection Working Group. This is a coalition of human rights, religious, humanitarian, and peace organizations dedicated to preventing violent conflict and averting mass atrocities.

FCNL was at the forefront of educating members of Congress with the concept of violence prevention. In 2010, the Senate unanimously passed a resolution urging the improvement of prevention efforts. Together with its partners, FCNL pressured the Obama administration to implement key recommendations of the 2008 task force. In 2012, President Obama created the Atrocities Prevention Board, a White House-led interagency body to help prevent mass violence. Four years later, he issued an executive order committing the United States to the goal of preventing atrocities and genocide.

Though Congress did little to further advance violence prevention, change was on the horizon. Every year, hundreds of Quakers, representatives of Yearly Meetings, and friends from across the country gather to advocate for a more just and peaceful world at FCNL's Annual Meeting and Quaker Public Policy Institute (FCNL, 2020). In November 2015, the participants descended on Capitol Hill to lobby Congress to pass a law on atrocities prevention. Their lobby visits catalyzed the creation of a bipartisan bill in 2016 – also a result of FCNL's lobbyists' work with Congress and the State Department to build the US capacity and investment in peacebuilding.

The 115th Congress passed the Elie Wiesel Genocide and Atrocities Prevention bill (P.L. 115–441) in 2018. The bill was signed into law by President Donald Trump on January 14, 2019.[20] Named after Holocaust survivor and 1986 Nobel Peace Laureate Elie Wiesel, the law ensures coordination among US government departments to prevent global atrocities from occurring and mandates training for American diplomats to identify early warning signs of genocide. It is a good example of how FCNL's advocates, staff, donors, and partners raised the need for such a bill, helped to write it, gathered congressional support for it, and lobbied Congress to vote on it. Most importantly, the Elie Wiesel Act substantiates that "War Is Not the Answer."[21]

The concerns of the Religious Society of Friends span both international and domestic policy issues on which FCNL lobbies. The results are sometimes not as straightforward as the Elie Wiesel Act, but FCNL remains steadfast in its efforts to educate and empower Friends and those who share its concerns to participate in the political process as voters, advocates, and elected officials. FCNL continues to focus on root causes and long-term consequences of injustice, inequality, economic disparity, disproportionate power, and violence.[22]

Taking Steps on Criminal Justice

While FCNL had lobbied on criminal justice reform for decades, it focused on ending mass incarceration as a racially unjust policy in 2012 in its priorities for the 113th Congress.[23] Quakers call for a transformation of the US criminal justice system, which is used today principally as an instrument of retribution. This runs contrary to Quaker faith, which historically emphasizes rehabilitation and restorative justice over punitive measures.[24] In 2014, FCNL broadened this priority to "advance policies that reduce mass incarceration," a version of which has been included in the organization's priorities since.[25]

More than 2.2 million people – mostly Black and brown – are incarcerated for nonviolent drug offenses. Over the last 40 years the US prison population has increased by 500%.[26] One of the major drivers of this growth in mass incarceration is sentencing, especially mandatory minimum sentences, the most controversial of which are for drug-related crimes.[27]

FCNL focused its advocacy on legislation to reduce long federal prison sentences for non-violent crimes and to provide better rehabilitation programs for those in prison. The legislative vehicle for this was the FIRST STEP Act (P.L. 115–391), or the Formerly Incarcerated Reenter Society Transformed Safely Transitioning Every Person Act.

Ultimately, another mass incarceration bill, the Second Chance Reauthorization Act (S. 3635), was incorporated into the FIRST STEP Act. The bill provides much needed funding to community-based organizations helping people leaving prison. Lawmakers passed the revised FIRST STEP Act at the end of the 115th Congress, and it was signed into law by Donald Trump in December 2018.[28]

Although FCNL supported the FIRST STEP Act as a whole, it contains certain provisions that the organization does not support. The bill fails to apply certain sentencing reductions retroactively, making people in prison serve sentences Congress would have deemed unfair. The lengthy exemptions for people to participate in rehabilitation programs mean that many who need help will not receive it.[29]

The decision on these compromises was difficult for FCNL lobbyists, but the FIRST STEP Act was an important legislative step bill to reform the US criminal justice system.

Remaining Open to God's Leading

> A good end cannot sanctify evil means; nor must we ever do evil, that good may come of it.
>
> *William Penn, 1693*

The successful advocacy of Quakers, FCNL staff, lobbyists, and friends towards the passage of the Elie Wiesel Genocide and Atrocities Prevention Act and the FIRST STEP Act demonstrates two important demands of advocacy. First, legislation must be kept alive in Congress – introduced and persistently reintroduced for years – before victory can be won. Second, legislation often requires compromises. Sometimes legislation does not pass, as in the 2019 attempt to repeal the 2002 AUMF. Other times, bills pass, but without each of the provisions for which FCNL advocated, as with the 2020 NDAA (Point, 2020).

Nevertheless, FCNL maintains that lobbying from a place of faith is about remaining grounded and not being riled or thrown off track by the response of government officials. As FCNL's first executive secretary, E. Raymond Wilson said, "We ought to be willing to work for the causes which will not be won now, but cannot be won unless the goals are staked out now and worked for energetically over a period of time."[30]

Engaging in this work requires presenting accurate research as fully as possible to give the public as well as government officials access to information not otherwise readily available to them. It is about advancing government policy to move toward a more powerful, just, and whole world.[31]

FCNL lives at the intersection of faith and politics. Integrating its inward leadings of a world with peace, justice, and an earth restored requires us to be act in hope and possibility. FCNL helps Friends and friends in the United States to participate in government policy making as informed and engaged citizens.

As the world faces profound challenges and great opportunity, FCNL speaks from its Quaker faith and advocates for a new vision of how the global community can live together more peacefully and justly, and with greater care for each other and our shared world.

As our statement of legislative policy, the World We Seek, states: "We are convinced by our faith and experience to continue building the peaceful, just, equitable, and sustainable global community we seek. Above all, we seek to remain open to where God's spirit leads us."[32]

Notes

1 Friends Committee on National Legislation. 2018. *Prophetic, Persistent, Powerful: Working for the World We Seek, 1943–2018*. Washington, DC: FCNL, pp. 10–16.

2 Ibid.

3 Abbott, M. 2014. *A Theological Perspective on Quaker Lobbying*. 2nd ed. Washington, DC: FCNL Education Fund, p. 13.

4 Abbott, M. 2014. *A Theological Perspective on Quaker Lobbying*. 2nd ed. Washington, DC: FCNL Education Fund, p. 21.

5 Abbott, C. 2020. *Quaker: A Quick Guide*. Washington, DC: FCNL Education Fund, p. 38.

6 Friends Committee on National Legislation. 2018. *History*. https://www.fcnl.org/about/history.

7 Ibid.

8 Friends Committee on National Legislation. 2016. *Statement on the Attacks on the World Trade Center, Pentagon, and Civilian Aircraft, September 12, 2001*. https://www.fcnl.org/updates/statement-on-the-attacks-on-the-world-trade-center-pentagon-and-civilian-aircraft-42.

9 Weed, M. 2018. *Presidential References to the 2001 Authorization for Use of Military Force in Publicly Available Executive Actions and Reports to Congress* [Memo]. Washington, DC: Congressional Research Service. https://fas.org/sgp/crs/natsec/pres-aumf.pdf.

10 U.S. Government Publishing Office. 2002. *Authorization for Use of Military Force against Iraq Resolution of 2002*. Washington, DC: P.L. 107–243.

11 Friends Committee on National Legislation. 2020. *War Is Not the Answer: MLK's Words Endure as an Anti-War Sign*. https://www.fcnl.org/resources/war-not-answer.

12 Brandon-Smith, H. 2019. *Why Congress Needs to Reassert Its Power to End Endless War*. https://www.fcnl.org/updates/why-congress-needs-to-reassert-its-power-to-end-endless-war-2466.

13 Wier, A. 2017. *Get the Facts: Pentagon Spending*. https://www.fcnl.org/updates/get-the-facts-pentagon-spending-956.

14 Friends Committee on National Legislation. 2020. *Pentagon Spending*. https://www.fcnl.org/issues/us-wars-militarism/pentagon-spending.

15 Poynton, A. 2014. *Military & Civilian Resources: Doing More with Less*. Domestic Preparedness. https://www.domesticpreparedness.com/preparedness/military-civilian-resources-doing-more-with-less/.

16 Golan-Vilella, M. 2018. *1033 Program & Police Militarization*. https://www.fcnl.org/sites/default/files/documents/1033_and_police_militarization_fact_sheet_3_23_18.pdf.

17 Point, K. 2020. *Congress Took a (Small) Step to Demilitarize Police. What's Next?* Friends Committee on National Legislation. https://www.fcnl.org/updates/2020-12/congress-took-small-step-demilitarize-police-whats-next.

18 Human Rights Watch. 2008. *Q&A: Crisis in Darfur*. https://www.hrw.org/news/2008/04/25/q-crisis-darfur.

19 Albright, M. and Cohen, W. 2008. *Preventing Genocide: A Blueprint for U.S. Policymakers*. https://www.ushmm.org/m/pdfs/20081124-genocide-prevention-report.pdf.

20 U.S. Government Publishing Office. 2018. *Elie Wiesel Genocide and Prevention Act of 2018*. Washington, DC: P.L. 115–441.

21 Keny-Guyer, N. 2018. *Conflict Is Reshaping the World. Here's How We Tackle It*. World Economic Forum. https://www.weforum.org/agenda/2018/01/conflict-is-reshaping-the-world-mercy-corps/.

22 Friends Committee on National Legislation. 2021. *Our Approach*. https://www.fcnl.org/about/world-we-seek/our-approach.

23 Friends Committee on National Legislation. 2021. *Transforming Justice*. https://www.fcnl.org/about/policy/issues/criminal-justice/incarceration.

24 Quakers in the World. 2021. *Crime and Justice*. http://www.quakersintheworld.org/quakers-in-action/20/-Crime-and-Justice.

25 Friends Committee on National Legislation. 2014. *FCNL Legislative Priorities for the 114th Congress*. https://www.fcnl.org/sites/default/files/documents/114th_congress_-_nov_2014.pdf.

26 Sterling, E. 2016. *Drug Laws and Snitching: A Primer.* https://www.pbs.org/wgbh/pages/frontline/shows/snitch/primer/.

27 ACLU. 2020. *Fair Sentencing Act.* https://www.aclu.org/node/17576.

28 Friends Committee on National Legislation. 2018. *Quaker Lobby Celebrates Congressional Passage of the FIRST STEP Act.* https://www.fcnl.org/updates/quaker-lobby-celebrates-congressional-passage-of-the-first-step-act-1826.

29 Lee, A. 2018. *The FIRST STEP Act Passed: What's in It?* Friends Committee on National Legislation. https://www.fcnl.org/updates/the-first-step-act-passed-what-s-in-it-1814.

30 McBride, A. 2020. *Systems, Relationships, and History: Advocating for Peace Today.* https://www.fcnl.org/updates/2020-09/systems-relationships-and-history-advocating-peace-today.

31 Friends Committee on National Legislation. 2021. *Our Approach.* https://www.fcnl.org/about/world-we-seek/our-approach.

32 Friends Committee on National Legislation. 2018. *Prophetic, Persistent, Powerful: Working for the World We Seek, 1943–2018.* Washington, DC: FCNL, pp. 10–16.

39

THE POLITICAL ACTIVIST LIFE OF PRAGMATIC QUAKER BAYARD T. RUSTIN

Carlos Figueroa

Introduction

In 1986, toward the end of a long and extraordinary life, Bayard Taylor Rustin reflected upon his overall philosophy guiding his community organizing, and social justice work for poor and working-class people, against racial discrimination and other oppressions in the United States and abroad. Rustin wrote:

> My activism did not spring from my being gay, or, for that matter, from my being black. Rather, it is rooted fundamentally in my Quaker upbringing and the values that were instilled in me by my grandparents who reared me. Those values are based on the concept of a single human family and the belief that all members of that family are equal. Adhering to those values has meant making a stand against injustice, to the best of my ability, wherever, and whenever it occurs. The racial injustice that was present in this country during my youth was a challenge to my belief in the oneness of the human family. It demanded my involvement in the struggle to achieve interracial democracy, but it is very likely that I would have been involved had I been a white person with the same philosophy. Needless to say, I worked side-by-side with many white people who held these same values, some of whom gave as much, if not more, to the struggle than myself.
>
> *(cited in Long, 2012, p. 460)*

Rustin's religious faith based on two important Quaker values – *equality* and *community* – served him profoundly throughout his life within what he referred to as "the oneness of the human family." He longed to "achieve interracial democracy" in the United States by fighting for political and social rights and economic equality for all. Yet, he was never quite explicit, with a few exceptions, in how his Quaker theology offered him specific support for the different social issues that he purposefully confronted over his political life – for example, when challenging unfair government actions, and discriminatory political and economic policies at home and abroad.

Rustin's life, written work, and activism has garnered much attention recently. Biographies, articles, short and long essays, and edited volumes have been written with intriguing accounts

DOI: 10.4324/9780429030925-43

of his labour radicalism, supposed anarchistic tendencies, unmatched organizing capabilities, charismatic personality, and impeccable ability to build alliances, among others (Anderson, 1997; Levine, 1999; Podair, 2009; Long, 2012; Wiley, 2014; Houtman, Naegle and Michael, 2014; Naegle, 2014; Hirschfelder, 2014). However, Rustin's religious beliefs as it relates to his political life have been taken for granted by most. Philosopher and Quaker Newton Garver recently observed:

> What most of [Rustin's] biographers have not recognized is that he had a deep spiritual grounding, with religious as well as worldly wisdom. [This] is mentioned in neither major biography and is omitted from the collection of Rustin's writings. [His] spiritual depth has been widely overlooked and deserves to be brought back to our attention.
>
> *(Garver, 2012)*

Rustin's religious faith drew from multiple sources and traditions (Western and Eastern), including liberal and evangelical Quakerism, while fundamentally rooted in his practical experiences living in an integrated environment in West Chester, Pennsylvania, in the 1920s and 1930s.

In this chapter, I explore Rustin's life and faith more broadly, drawing mostly on his own words and deeds focusing on his "oneness of the human family" conception that guided his pragmatic Quakerism (Figueroa, 2011, 2012). Rustin's Quaker theology, premised on the principles of oneness and unity, was often expressed in mostly tacit ways throughout his activist life by reference to traditional Quaker testimonies while bearing witness to the different social and political problems of his time, as he on occasion expressed his religious values in speeches and written works.

"Chronicles of My History": Growing Confidence Within Integrated West Chester, Pennsylvania

Bayard T. Rustin was born on March 17, 1912, and raised in West Chester, Pennsylvania, in a mostly white neighbourhood. Rustin graduated from racially integrated West Chester High School in June 1932. Later that fall, Rustin attended Wilberforce University in Ohio and then the Quaker-founded Cheyney State Teachers College (currently the Cheney University of Pennsylvania), two historically black colleges. Rustin briefly continued his studies in 1937 at City College of the City University of New York, but his political and social activism prevented him from graduating and earning his degree. He had a spirited tenor singing voice, wrote poetry, and played sports (track and football). Rustin described West Chester as "a town rich in the history and culture of Negro Americans [with] a strong Quaker tradition [that was also] an important stop on the Underground Railroad in the period leading up to the Civil War" (Rustin, 1976, p. 22).

Rustin was raised within a progressive middle-class environment by his grandparents, Julia (Davis) and Janifer Rustin, in an extended household with eight other children who were his aunts and uncles. During most of his childhood, Rustin thought his biological mother Florence Rustin (who could not raise him after his father Archie Hopkins left before Rustin's birth) was his older sister. Rustin never knew his father, who was a West Indian immigrant, and he was eventually adopted by his grandparents who also gave him his name. Julia attended Quaker meetings but was mostly active in the African Methodist Episcopal (AME) Church.[1] She was also a charter member, in 1910, of the National Association for the Advancement of Colored People (NAACP). While his grandfather Janifer was also an active member of the AME Church, Rustin's early political thinking was essentially shaped by his grandmother's broad Christian values and her social activism, as she taught him the importance of ecumenical collaborative work. These early lessons gave Rustin the confidence to partake in future anti-war protests and nonviolent direct action for social justice and economic rights in the 1940s through the mid-1980s.

Rustin, in his book *Strategies for Freedom* (1976), wrote that

> while West Chester was certainly no utopia of interracial harmony – indeed, "segrega-tion" and "discrimination" were two of the first words that had significant meaning for me – [however] the extent of racism was not so deep as to prevent a black youngster from becoming aware of his cultural and historical heritage.
>
> *(pp. 22–23)*

Rustin appeared to understand *race* not in biological terms but rather as a category of cultural and social difference. For Rustin, *racism* seemed to mean living under a political and economic structure and related policies – based on a notion of alleged white superiority – that determined not only the civic worth but also the kinds of treatments blacks experienced in the United States. He claims that despite such an often-limiting environment, blacks in West Chester were still cognizant of their heritage and were able to draw on it in their lives. Rustin captured the complexity of living in an integrated northeastern Quaker town while surrounded by a larger Jim Crow (segregated) environment in the 1920s and 1930s,

> West Chester was not the [Deep] South, with its rigid, enforced Jim Crow and its shambles of an educational system. Nor was it the archetypical northern ghetto, with its malignant pattern of social dislocation. The high school I attended was integrated, and while – because of my blackness – I was deprived of [honours] I had earned, my intellectual and athletic achievements were recognized. Moreo-ver, West Chester's black community was economically and socially heterogeneous. It included occasional representatives of the "black bourgeoisie," mainly business-men and property owners; working-class blacks, some of whom were struggling to break the bonds of impoverishment; and others who had given up the struggle – down-and-outers.
>
> From these diverse people and their diverse experiences, I learned about my own heritage. They sang me Negro ballads, quoted me Negro poetry, and recited folktales told by slaves. I met black ministers, black political leaders, and black visionaries. And through all these encounters, I gained an understanding of the Negro struggle. This happened simply because these indigenous forms are about precisely that. They tell of the struggles of blacks, first against slavery and then against discrimination. They are, in short, chronicles of my history.
>
> *(Rustin, 1976, p. 23)*

Rustin recognized the political-economic conditions shaping his "blackness" and broader skin-color bias as another expression of white racial prejudice in the United States while equally acknowledging the heterogeneity found within the black community in West Chester. Accord-ingly, it seems that within this environment blacks were free to cultivate a distinctive race culture drawing on past but also present American struggles against social and political discrimina-tion and economic domination. Hence, Rustin saw his cultural heritage not from an African diasporic perspective but rather within an American context where black struggles for political/civic freedom and social/economic equality were indigenous forms.

Labour and Civil Rights Activism in and Outside Religious Organizations

Rustin's successes in the late 1930s through the mid-1940s brought him into contact with key labour and civil rights leaders in the 1950s–1970s. Rustin was active in several critically important civil and labour rights organizations, some affiliated with Quakers or other religious groups, and all involved in the broader peace, social justice, and anti-war movements: American Friends Service Committee (AFSC), Congress of Racial Equality (CORE), Fellowship of Reconciliation (FOR), and Southern Christian Leadership Conference (SCLC). Although it originally served as an alternative to military service for conscientious objectors in 1917, the AFSC subsequently moved to improving "racial relations" and toward the "unfinished business of democracy" (Hamm, 2003, p. 171; Austin, 2012). As an integrationist, Rustin's goal was to build an *interracial democracy* in the United States, and the work of the AFSC aligned well with his overall vision. Rustin provided inspiration for these kinds of egalitarian social justice efforts at home and abroad with "his spirit and his efficient handling of race relations" (Austin, 2012, p. 145). Rustin's underlying "spirit" seemed grounded in his West Chester experiences and pragmatic Quaker faith that required open deliberation, and a candid look at the larger political structures with the hope that the repressive human conditions would change gradually but through collaborative work.

Rustin spent several years with the Young Communist League fighting for racial and social justice until the United States entered World War II in December 1941. Yet, earlier that year, A. Philip Randolph, founder of The Brotherhood of Sleeping Car Porters and Maids, asked Rustin to organize the first of many March on Washington (MOW) mass protest movements.[2] Rustin thereafter began building a reputation as an effective organizer and gaining national credibility (Farmer, 1985, p. 239). The 1941 MOW was set to occur during the early preparations for US potential engagement in the war (considering the federal government had been aiding European allies since at least September of 1940) and was thus planned as a strategy to pressure the government into desegregating the armed forces and also into providing employment opportunities to black Americans after military service. However, the March was cancelled after President Franklin D. Roosevelt signed "an executive order establishing the Fair Employment Practices Committee and prohibiting job discrimination not only in the federal government but in defense industries as well" (D'Emilio, 2003, p. 58).

The 1940s proved as important a decade to Rustin's spiritual and political growth as any other. Rustin gained additional experiences in the nonviolent direct-action tactic through his close association with well-known white pacifist and fellow Quaker A.J. Muste, a founding member of the FOR.[3] Rustin joined FOR in 1941 as a staff member and served as a conscientious objector during World War II. After years of attending Quaker meetings, Rustin officially became a member of the Religious Society of Friends in March of 1943 (Figueroa, 2022). In 1947, as a member and treasurer of the CORE, Rustin along with George Houser led 16 men (both black and white) into the Deep South under the Journey of Reconciliation direct-action project to challenge segregation practices in interstate travel. This trip served as the model for the Freedom Rides of the 1960s. James Farmer, fellow activist and friend, describes in his autobiography how he and Rustin were the only "two black faces" in the founding meeting of CORE. He writes:

> In addition to me, there was Bayard . . ., a thirty-one-year-old Quaker with a clipped, British accent, an impressive, deliberate speaking style, and a beautiful, lyric tenor singing voice. Bayard, who was called Rusty, had just been brought on FOR staff

as youth secretary by A.J. He obviously was very close to A.J. and there was a deep affection between them. John Swomley jokingly referred to them as Muste and Rusty.

(Farmer, 1985, p. 102)[4]

Clearly, by the late 1950s and early 1960s, Rustin had already been quite experienced in protest politics. Not surprisingly, in the early 1960s, Dr. Martin Luther King Jr. and Rustin would cross paths in a serious way. Rustin advised Dr. King on several political and social strategies – for example, how to engage in effective nonviolent tactics to combat social injustices (Cazden, 2013, pp. 360–361). Subsequently, Rustin provided some reasoning for a new or different civil rights organization drawing on his own pragmatic Quaker values that eventually became the SCLC. As David R. Goldfield (1990) observed:

> Rustin . . . believed that a new civil rights organization was in order since CORE had failed to interest the black masses in the South and the NAACP remained wary of boycotts and demonstrations. King, fresh from his Montgomery experience, required little persuasion. The group of about sixty agreed to establish the Southern Leadership Conference on Transportation and Nonviolent Integration and resolved to meet again the following month at an expanded gathering to launch the new organization.
>
> *(p. 104)*

Arguably, Rustin may have been partly "responsible for launching the international reputation of [Dr.] King, Jr. and his daring dream for America" (Long, 2012, p. xiv).

Yet, despite his involvement in numerous social justice and egalitarian mass protest movements and becoming a prolific writer of critical political commentary, Rustin is best known for serving as chief organizer of the 1963 March on Washington for Jobs and Freedom (under the leadership of A. Philip Randolph), which focused on civil rights from a moral perspective and economic equality for all, as well as providing a national platform for Dr. Martin Luther King Jr. and his now famous "I Have a Dream" speech (Rustin, 1973, pp. 224–227; Steinberg, 1997; Cazden, 2013). William P. Jones (2013) points out that "Despite King's emphasis on nonviolence and his familiarity with Gandhi, Rustin found that the minister had 'very limited notions about how a nonviolent protest should be carried out'" (p. 106). Rustin also opened other Quaker-founded spaces for the noted civil rights leader. For example, Elizabeth Cazden (2013) observes that Rustin through the AFSC was able to initiate "the first mass distribution of [Dr. King's] letter from the Birmingham Jail" (p. 361). Finally, Cazden also notes that King was provided yet another platform to spread his message of nonviolence, which Rustin had a major role in teaching King about – at the Friends General Conference gatherings and the 1967 Friends World Conference (p. 361).

However, Rustin endured early harsh public criticism and personal attacks as an anti-segregationist and gay man that may have jeopardized his career and the broader civil rights movement if not for his moral integrity as a pragmatic Quaker. For instance, Rustin served on a chain gang in 1947 for thirty days after protesting North Carolina's segregated schools by sitting in the front seat of a bus on religious and moral grounds (a strategy later used by Rosa Parks during the Montgomery, Alabama, bus boycott) and then arrested on a "morals" charge in 1953 (Anderson, 1997, p. 251). The latter charge led to long-time South Carolina Senator Strom Thurmond's moral crusade against Rustin that lasted through much of the 1960s. Perhaps more significant was Thurmond introducing Rustin's previous record of left-wing radicalism, if not communism, into the congressional record that many believed was an attempt to weaken the broader Civil Rights movement (D'Emilio, 2003, pp. 346–347; Podair, 2009, pp. 58–59).

To his credit, Rustin was able to construct a coalition of disparate labour, civil, and political activist organizations, and he managed conflict within and between them by drawing on a traditional Quaker decision-making method as he understood it. Rustin stated in an interview:

> As a Quaker, I started out by saying that I thought we had to make all decisions by consensus. Consensus does not mean that everybody agrees. It means that the person who disagrees must disagree so vigorously . . . that he is prepared to fight with everybody else.
>
> *(cited in D'Emilio, 2003, p. 342)*

Yet, the nonviolent approach to social reform was not only based on Rustin's *pragmatic Quaker faith* but also on his studying closely of Mahatma Gandhi's philosophy and activist work in India in the early twentieth century. Rustin shared key lessons from his Gandhian studies (Rustin chaired the Free India Committee in 1945, and he participated in the 1948 World Pacifist meeting in India where he met Jawaharlal Nehru, an associate of Gandhi): (1) that "a social movement relying on the tactics of nonviolence cannot succeed unless it is able to convince a full majority of the people that its cause is just", and (2) "that, in a situation where the objective of a social movement are accepted as valid by the majority, protest becomes an effective tactic to the degree that it elicits brutality and oppression from the power structure" (Rustin, 1976, p. 24).

In terms of what I have been calling his pragmatic form of Quaker faith, Jerald Podair shares how Rustin handled the organizing of the 1963 March on Washington for Jobs and Freedom.

> Rustin presided over the March organizing process during July and August like a maestro. Calm and collected amid the chaos of the brownstone on 130th Street . . . issuing orders with clipped authority . . . [he] left nothing to chance. "If you want to organize anything," Rustin once said, "assume that everybody is absolutely stupid. And assume yourself that you are stupid."
>
> *(Podair, 2009, p. 56)*

In a prophetic Christian way, Rustin showed self-criticism and humility with the use of the word "stupid." However, Rustin's use of the word was more than just proclaiming ignorance in others or himself to get things done; rather his language seems consistent with a core Quaker testimony: *simplicity*. Although the word "stupid" is not equivalent to *simplicity* in the secular sense, this is how Rustin attempts to tell us about the need for individuals to focus closely on and attempt to intimately apprehend the essence of an activity or action but from an egoless position adhering to such guiding moral imperative.

Emma J. Lapsansky tells us that *simplicity* as an early Quaker value has been understood and interpreted differently since the seventeenth century.

> Over time, many Quakers have embraced the idea of "simplicity" or "plainness" (sometimes described as "humility" or "modesty") as one strategy for nurturing a posture that promotes balance between secular and sacred lives. But, like much of Friends theology, which is grounded in the New Testament focus on visionary experience and continuing "revelation," simplicity and plainness have been subject to a diversity of interpretations.
>
> *(Lapsansky, 2013, p. 336)*

Moreover, Thomas D. Hamm reminds us too that early Quakers "spoke in terms of simplicity, which they saw as allowing themselves to live more fully in the world, yet not be of it" (Hamm, 2003, p. 103). Thus, in Rustin's case, it meant that everyone regardless of socioeconomic status, secular or sacred moral beliefs, political affiliations, ideological orientation, sexuality, and other ascriptive social markers or identities, ought to begin political or social activism with *humility*, open to revelations and often unfamiliar or unexpected experiences *in community* for the betterment of the human family.

However, Rustin was not only a well-sought out activist and organizer, but he was also a prolific writer of social and political commentaries that appeared in academic journals, books, magazines, and newsletters.[5] In probably his most-referenced *Commentary* article "From Protest to Politics: The Future of the Civil Rights Movement" in 1965, along with his lesser-known book *Strategies for Freedom: The Changing Patterns of Black Protest* in 1976, Rustin shared his critical perspectives on civil rights and black power politics. These critiques were made within his pragmatic Quaker perspective as he claimed the Civil Rights movement was originally based on three important *strategic imperatives* that had been forgotten: (1) the need for a framework of integration in pursuit of real *community*, (2) the importance of *peace* and nonviolence, and (3) the necessity of building social *alliances* and political coalitions. He adopted a more *gradualist* "integrationist" social-democratic approach to transformative politics. Yet, his pragmatic Quaker approach to structural and policy reforms based on his "oneness of the human family" conviction was often challenged by other black intellectuals, elected officials, and activists, such as Malcolm X, with whom he debated at Howard University in 1961, and Congressman Adam Clayton Powell, who supported "War on Poverty" legislation as part of President Lyndon B. Johnson's "Great Society" initiative (a set of social programs in 1964–1965 attempting to lessen domestic economic crises). Rustin's 1960s coalition building steered by his Quaker faith, if not broader his Judeo-Christian sensibilities, may have also been informed by the New Deal and post-scientific racism context in which the private sector was implored to collaborate with government institutions trying to meet the economic and social demands of the American public (Reed, 2020, p. 121).

Responding to President Johnson's "War on Poverty" program was another of Rustin's major contributions within his "oneness" principle, a ten-year plan to end poverty for all Americans "regardless of colour." The 1966–1968 "Freedom Budget for All Americans" (supported and signed by A. Philip Randolph, Dr. King, and several prominent economists) aimed to directly address the economic inequalities in rural America and urban centres where most blacks and whites lived and were facing low wages, high unemployment, dilapidated housing, underfunded public schools, and inadequate healthcare. Rustin made it clear that the labour movement even with its shortcomings was still the most effective way to resolve issues facing all Americans, including Northern black and Southern white workers, consistent with his "oneness of the human family" ideal (Rustin, 1971).

> The [labour] movement has not abolished poverty, and could not by itself have been expected to, but it has lifted more American people out of poverty than any other institution or agency organized to that end. I do not mean to say the [labour] movement could not have done more for Negroes. But it is worth noting that discrimination now persists only in a minority segment of the [labour] movement. In any event, that past history tended to obscure an equally important truth – that, despite discriminatory practices, the [labour] movement was, and remains, the most integrated institution in our society.
>
> *(Rustin, 1968)*

Rustin made similar arguments in a December 1966 *New York Times* letter to the editor, where he tells of his coalition-integrationist strategy reflecting his pragmatic Quaker outlook as he critiques the head of the Student Nonviolent Coordinating Committee (SNCC) Stokely Carmichael and his "Black Power" form of black nationalism as an empty "slogan" for addressing the "Negro social, economic and political struggles":

> I am for Negroes forming alliances with liberal and religious organizations and with trade unions. I think that "Black Power" is a politically reactionary and divisive slogan, while [Carmichael] thinks that it is psychologically progressive and will unify the Negro community. He thinks that the violence and disturbances in Watts and Harlem are signs of new militancy. I believe they are the tragic outgrowth of societal negligence. I advocated the economic program of the "Freedom Budget for All Americans" [and] Mr. Carmichael, in turn, asked that his name be removed from the list of those endorsing the budget. [I] advocated nonviolence, democratic social change, and integration. Mr. Carmichael did not comment on nonviolence; he offers no program for democratic social change; and he believes "integration is irrelevant."
>
> *(Long, 2012, pp. 326–327)*

Rustin distinguishes his integrationist social-democratic perspective grounded, although implicitly, on his "oneness of the human family" belief, which is what he meant by "forming alliances with liberal and religious organizations and with trade unions . . . [and the goal of] unifying the Negro community" (Long, p. 327). Later, in a 1972 *New York Times* column, Charles V. Hamilton, who also co-authored *Black Power: A Politics of Liberation* with Carmichael (1967), captures Rustin's integrationist political-economic approach by way of a tacit critique:

> While recognizing the existence of racial prejudice and discrimination, Rustin believes that "poverty," and all the evils attached to it, is not due solely or even largely to racism, but to an economic system already weighted to those with wealth and power.
>
> *(Hamilton, 1972, p. 38)*

Clearly, neither Carmichael nor Hamilton appreciated or even recognized Rustin's *pragmatic Quaker faith* informing his broader social outlook and political-economic perspective on the needs of black and working-class Americans.

However, Rustin suggested that the "Freedom Budget for All Americans" within the broader labour movement was the way to accomplish the needs of black Americans – political, social, and economic – within the larger society.

> Today, as the focus of the Negro struggle has shifted from constitutional issues to economic and political equality, the [labour] movement remains the only major institution in our society that articulates the economic demands that are now at the heart of the Negro struggle. It is certainly the only major institution that wholly subscribes to, and substantially embodies in its own program, the proposals and priorities outlined in the *Freedom Budget for All Americans*.
>
> *(Rustin, 1973, pp. 227–228)*

Rustin acknowledges the shift from framing black struggles in constitutional terms to political and economic equality concerns by offering the Freedom Budget as a model for labour institutions to follow. Rustin continued to think that the times required more integration of working-class people across racial and geographic spaces. Rustin's holistic framing of the black struggles in political and economic terms was consistent with his "oneness" principle because the labour movement included everyone regardless of race, class, gender, and religion. Finally, in a letter dated August 6, 1969, Rustin expressed his "oneness of the human family" once again but now within the larger context of a waning Civil Rights Movement:

> I think it is my responsibility and the responsibility of all of us who want [an] integrated and just society to make our demands known, and to criticize those who would settled for a piece of the action for themselves. Believe me, nobody yearns more for unity than I do. I am only painfully aware that the great *March on Washington*, 1963 could not have taken place except for the fact that CORE, SNCC, SCLE, Urban League and the NAACP were able to agree on a human program. That march moved Congress to pass the Civil Rights Bill, and had many good effects. I strive for that unity, but it can only come on the basis of a program that will benefit all the people.
>
> *(Friends Historical Library, n.d.)*

Rustin's hope for "unity" and call for a true democratic community showed his consistent *egalitarian* stance as aligned with his larger pragmatic Quaker faith. Throughout the 1970s and 1980s, Rustin continued criticizing any "all-black strategies" as antithetical to community-building, coalition politics, and interracial democracy more broadly. For example, in a 1973 essay in the *Journal of American Labor*, Rustin commented:

> The labor-liberal approach to social problems has been vindicated time and again over other narrow, sectarian, "all-black" strategies. In the coming period, therefore, we cannot be content to define economic programs in racial terms. To pursue purely "black" issues at a time when our needs increasingly converge with those of the larger working class is to perpetuate political isolation. Thus, our agenda should consist of the basic demands of the March on Washington and the Freedom Budget. Full employment is probably the single most basic issue. But we should also work for programs to ensure that all Americans have adequate housing, decent medical care that they can afford, the opportunity to pursue higher education regardless of financial circumstances and a minimum wage sufficient to guarantee a life of dignity.
>
> *(Rustin, 1973, p. 227)*

Rustin thought that a "narrow race consciousness" perspective or "spurious black agenda" would undercut what he considered as the most effective and realistic way to deal with black and other working-class people's political, social, and economic needs – an integrationist approach that would enhance black Americans' already maturing electoral political life post-civil rights movement (Rustin, 1972, p. 297).

"[The] World Was His Home": Rustin's "Oneness" Beyond the US Context

Rustin was known to engage the world around him in a blithesome yet intense manner. He pursued international affairs in the final fifteen years of an incredible political life differently but still guided by his "oneness" principle and social democratic values. Rustin focused less on pacifism and more on humanitarianism as he joined two groups advocating for democracy and human rights worldwide, Freedom House and the International Rescue Committee (IRC;

D'Emilio, 2003, pp. 478–483). In general, Jervis Anderson (1997) characterizes Rustin as a person who "was . . . unsuited to the wielding of political power" because of his complex personality (p. 4). Yet, Rustin's complexity pushed him towards dealing with hard social, economic, and political problems wherever he found them, and thus preferring "the life of a trouble-shooter – an itinerant strategist, tactician, and organizer," as an advocate and less an administrator or a bureaucrat (p. 4). As Anderson suggests, Rustin was often "running off here and there, cultivating his interest in art and antiques" that he found "more appealing . . . than presiding steadily at an office desk" (p. 4). Rustin often "took issues seriously, but not himself; the alleviation of social problems was more interesting to him than the exercise of authority" (p. 4). Thus, Rustin was committed to the larger societal issues that often crossed different classes, people, countries, and ideological perspectives, leading to some controversial positions. For example, in the early 1970s, Rustin supported Israel's position under Zionism, to the disdain of some other civil rights leaders. Rustin commented, "To me Zionism is beautiful. It is the struggle of a people for a land where they can live in dignity."[6] Rustin seemed to contradict his principles when he showed support for Zionism abroad and his disdain for Black Nationalism at home in the late 1960s and early 1970s. Yet, for Rustin Zionism was about *dignity* as part of an Israeli nationalism seen in cultural terms that needed protection and Black Nationalism was more about asserting a "Black Power" ideology and less about protecting the national interests and civil rights of black Americans.

In 2013, Walter Naegle, who was Rustin's last partner during the final ten years of his life (1977–1987), shared his perspective on what made Rustin a complex figure during his lifetime: "Being black, being homosexual, being a political radical, that's a combination that's pretty volatile and it comes along like Halley's Comet. Bayard's life was complex, but at the same time I think it makes it a lot more interesting."[7] Later, Naegle provided a glimpse of Rustin's malleable *pragmatic Quaker* spirit while they travelled abroad:

> I accompanied Bayard on some of his travels and was amazed at how the world was his home. Whether in a refugee camp or an ambassador's residence, he treated everyone as an equal. His [demeanour] was welcoming and open and he had deep respect for the human personality, regardless of cultural differences. His principles were grounded in faith, but over time he learned a practical, political lesson that served him well in a country that was rapidly becoming a nation of minorities: One must work in coalition with other groups to advance the common good. [He] often quoted from the Hebrew "Ethics of the Fathers," saying, "Ours is not to complete the task, but never to lay it down."
>
> *(Naegle, 2014)*

Rustin's cosmopolitan nature was aided by his pragmatic Quaker faith and his acquaintance with the Jewish *Pirkei Avot* (in Hebrew) or "The Ethics of our Fathers," the Mishnah tractate that is devoted to kindness, humility, piety, and ethics. His pragmatic Quaker faith (combining the Quaker "Inner Light" theology [Figueroa, 2012, p. 60], an occasional evangelical strand and reliance on traditional testimonies) helped Rustin navigate the worldwide problems. His tendency toward religious pluralism encouraged Rustin to venture into other traditions that also incorporated ethical teachings for the betterment of the human family – from Gandhian philosophy (*Truth is God* and nonviolence) to the rabbinical teachings of Jewish/Hebrew sages offering similar messages of love, peace, kindness, and ethical character. In the end, for Rustin, promoting peace, love, and freedom was not enough; serious and political action required *clear goals and objectives, explicit policy demands, broad mobilization,* and *efficient organization* to bring about true transformative structural and societal change with dignity but in community (D'Emilio, 2003, p. 56).[8]

Conclusion

Bayard T. Rustin was deeply committed to a radical gradualist politics resting on a deep sense of human community inextricably linked to an open and fluid Quaker sensibility that originated in West Chester, Pennsylvania, while living with his grandparents but which later developed with every social encounter within the labour movement, in and outside civil rights institutions, and across Western and Eastern traditions. Throughout his political and social activist life, Rustin grounded his discourses, strategic thinking, and organizing in various Quaker values; in particular, he relied on simplicity, peace, integrity, equality, and community as he understood them. Although he was not necessarily explicit or open about the role Quakerism played in his politics, his justifications in public statements, private correspondences, published works, and political actions show how he drew on his *pragmatic Quaker faith* during the various labour and civil rights struggles from the 1940s through the 1980s at home and abroad.

Until his death at age 75 on August 24, 1987, in New York City, Rustin understood quite well the importance of human community, family, interracial and across-class collaborations, and those involved in political struggles and social movements.[9] His aim was often to find common moral and practical ground to develop effective plans and strategies to bring about positive change. Nonetheless, Rustin was undervalued by many of his contemporaries, despite his long line of successes since the early 1940s and into the 1980s. These successes were based on Rustin's ability to organize and reach out to often disparate segments of society notwithstanding ideological and partisan differences. He did so through his *pragmatic Quaker faith* rooted in his "oneness of the human family" belief that in subtle ways provided Rustin with the internal strength to commit to alleviating the harsh and oppressive conditions faced by working and poor people, including blacks, whites, and others in cities and rural areas in the United States and abroad.

Notes

1 There is no clear evidence, however, of any official membership into the Religious Society of Friends for his grandmother Julia (Wilson).
2 The Brotherhood of Sleeping Car Porters and Maids was the first black labour workers union to obtain a charter under the American Federation of Labor in 1935.
3 According to James Farmer (1985), in his autobiography, Rustin had reported in *Fellowship* magazine (a FOR publication) that he had experienced "many individual encounters with discrimination in public places, which he resolved nonviolently – by talking with the manager and appealing to his conscience and reason, thus winning them over." Rustin's courageous actions led to *Fellowship* magazine editors to calling him "the FOR's one-man nonviolent army" (p. 110).
4 In addition to their shared membership in CORE and experienced activism, Farmer and Rustin collaborated on a musical project along with Margaret Davison that comprised Rustin singing, Davison on the harpsichord, and Farmer narrating. This was a project produced by the Bayard Rustin Fund for Global Equality with the help of the FOR in 1992.
5 Rustin wrote for *Harper's, Commentary, Newsweek,* the *Crisis,* the *New York Times,* and *New American,* among others.
6 Quoted in Barbara Lewis, "Civil Rights Leader Rustin Lauds Zionism," *New York Times,* December 2, 1975.
7 Walter Naegle upon accepting the Presidential Medal of Honor on Rustin's behalf in 2013.
8 Without seeming anachronistic, we might even consider Rustin an early "Convergent Friend" toward the end of his life based on his "holistic expression of faith" (Daniels, 2012, p. 87).
9 Rustin left the management of his estate to Walter Naegle, his last partner, who subsequently became executive director of the Bayard Rustin Fund for Global Equality in 2015.

Bibliography

Anderson, J. (1997) *Bayard Rustin: Troubles I've Seen, A Biography*. New York, NY: Harper Collins.

Austin, A. W. (2012) *Quaker Brotherhood: Interracial Activism and the American Friends Service Committee, 1917–1950*. Urbana, Chicago, and Springfield: University of Illinois Press.

Cazden, E. (2013) 'Quakers, Slavery, Anti-Slavery and Race', in Angell, S. W. and Dandelion, P. (eds.) *The Oxford Handbook of Quaker Studies*. Oxford, UK: Oxford University Press, pp. 347–362.

Daniels, C. W. (2012) 'Convergent Friends', in Abbott, M. P. et al. (eds.) *Historical Dictionary of the Friends (Quakers)*. Lanham, Toronto, and Plymouth: The Scarecrow Press, Inc., pp. 87–88.

D'Emilio, J. (2003) *Lost Prophet: The Life and Times of Bayard Rustin*. New York, NY: Free Press.

Farmer, J. (1985) *Lay Bare the Heart: An Autobiography of the Civil Rights Movement*. New York and Scarborough, Ontario: Plume Books.

Figueroa, C. (2011) 'Pragmatic Quakerism and American Political Development, 1898–1917', *Western Political Science Association,* Annual Meeting Paper, 9 April.

Figueroa, C. (2012) 'Quakerism and Racialism in Early Twentieth-Century U.S. Politics', in Jacobson, R. D. and Wadsworth, N. D. (eds.) *Faith and Race in American Political Life*. Charlottesville and London: University of Virginia Press, pp. 56–79.

Figueroa, C. (2022) 'Bayard T. Rustin: The Faith of a Conscientious Objector During the 1940s', Chapter 22, in Daniels, C. W. and Grant, R. (eds.) *The Quaker World*. London: Routledge Press.

Friends Historical Library, Bayard Rustin papers, Swarthmore College, Swarthmore, PA.

Garver, N. (2012) 'Bayard Rustin at Swarthmore College' *Friends Journal*, 16 March: https://www.friendsjournal.org/bayard-rustin-swarthmore-college/

Goldfield, D. R. (1990) *Black, White, and Southern: Race Relations and Southern Culture, 1940 to the Present*. New Orleans: LSU Press.

Hamilton, C. V. (1972) 'The Nationalist vs. the Integrationist: Ideological foes' *New York Times*, 1 October.

Hamm, T. D. (2003) *Quakers in America*. New York: Columbia University Press.

Hirschfelder, N. (2014) *Oppression as Process: The Case of Bayard Rustin*. American Studies. Heidelberg: Universitätsverlag Winter.

Houtman, J., Naegle, W., and Michael, G. L. (2014) *Bayard Rustin: The Invisible Activist*. Fitchburg, MA: Quaker Press of FGC.

Jones, W. P. (2013) *The March on Washington: Jobs, Freedom, and the Forgotten History of Civil Rights*. New York, NY: W. W. Norton & Company, Inc.

Lapsansky, E. J. (2013) 'Plainness and Simplicity', in Angell, S. W. and Dandelion, P. (eds.) *The Oxford Handbook of Quaker Studies*. Oxford, UK: Oxford University Press, pp. 335–346.

Levine, D. (1999) *Bayard Rustin and the Civil Rights Movement*. Newark: Rutgers University Press.

Lewis, B. (1975) 'Civil Rights Leader Rustin Lauds Zionism' *New York Times*, 2 December.

Long, M. G. (2012) *I Must Resist: Bayard Rustin's Life in Letters*. San Francisco, CA: City Lights Books.

Naegle, W. (2014) 'Human Rights Hero: Remembering Bayard Rustin' *Human Rights*, 40(1), American Bar Association, 1 January: https://www.americanbar.org/groups/crsj/publications/human_rights_magazine_home/2014_vol_40/vol_40_no_1_50_years_later/human_rights_hero_bayard_rustin/

Podair, J. (2009) *Bayard Rustin: American Dreamer*. Lanham, MD: Rowman & Littlefield.

Reed, T. F. (2020) *Toward Freedom: The Case against Race Reductionism*. New York: Verso Books.

Rustin, B. (1968) 'Topics: The Negro and the Unions' *New York Times*, 26 April.

Rustin, B. (1971) 'Blacks and the Unions' *Harper's Magazine*, May.

Rustin, B. (1972) 'Coming of Age Politically' *The Crisis*, November, pp. 296–298.

Rustin, B. (1973) 'The Washington March: A Ten-Year Perspective' *The Crisis*, September, pp. 224–227.

Rustin, B. (1976) *Strategies for Freedom: The Changing Patterns of Black Protest Politics*. New York: Columbia University Press.

Steinberg, S. (1997) 'Bayard Rustin and the Rise and Decline of the Black Protest Movement' *New Politics*, 6(3), whole no. 23, Summer: http://www.hartford-hwp.com/archives/45a/128.html

Toure, K., and Hamilton, C. V. (1967) *Black Power: A Politics of Liberation*. New York: Vintage Books.

Wiley, A. T. (2014) Angelic Troublemakers: Religion and Anarchism in America. New York, NY: Bloomsbury.

40

THE BODY IS ENOUGH

Towards a Liberal Quaker Theology of Disability

Benjamin J. Wood

Blessing: Being Visible, Being Present

Those possessing visible disabilities are frequently the object of unsolicited requests by street evangelists to 'pray over them'. The motive is always clear. Behind these gestures is Jesus' command to 'heal the sick, raise the dead, cleanse those who have leprosy, drive out demons' (Matthew 10:8, NIV). The experience can have many layers for the unwilling recipients of this command – a mix perhaps of anger, bemusement, or embarrassment. In my own case, these incidents always evoke a sense of sorrow. I am distressed that the person engaged in this ministry cannot understand that disablement is a complex facet of human experience and cannot be reduced to sickness, inability, or ailment. Disability can frequently be bound up with one's own sense of personal identity such that the fabled removal of the experience of disablement would itself remove part or all of the self. Disability is not just about diagnosis and intervention; it is about stories. Thus, when I speak of my cerebral palsy, it is impossible to disentangle my disability from my life course or indeed how I interpret the lives and struggles of others. I would not want to suggest that disability always teaches one affirmative lessons. Self-knowledge is not always uplifting or salutary. But I do want to suggest that one's way of interpreting the world is always framed by bodily sensations and capacities. We are not disembodied minds in vats but feeling, sensing, needful beings. We get tired, strained, hungry, delighted, and intoxicated *in our bodies*. Disability is one more interweaving aspect of the shifting sands of 'being human'. Those who seek to 'pray away' disability are often unaware of marring a deep source of self-knowing. Such a faith undoubtedly attempts to flatten human experience, but it also renders people mere objects for modification. In this insidious guise, prayer robs the disabled person of the possibilities of self-affirmation or agency. Under the paternal gaze of the Evangelist, one becomes something to be fixed, so that 'Jesus' name may be glorified'. One's life is reduced to a point of pitying apologetics. But blessing (as patronising as it is) is still a recognition of presence. Even in its pathologizing of the disabled body, any blessing seeks to know the object it claims to fix. It is impossible to bless without drawing bodies into relationship. At the very least, the spectre of disability must be acknowledged and given a spiritual response, even if the end goal of such recognition is its final negation.

This fact leads us to a strange acknowledgement concerning the erasure of the disabled self in some Quaker communities. True, my Liberal Meeting would never seek to heal me of

DOI: 10.4324/9780429030925-44

my disability, but neither is my disability acknowledged as a portal of knowledge, wisdom, or spiritual discernment. It is a fact about me that neither impinges upon nor illuminates my life or that of my Quaker community. But the problem of invisibility goes much deeper. Many Liberal Friends would be shocked at the impropriety of the street evangelist, but would not be able to say (in recognisably Quaker terms) from where their discomfort came. At least the one who seeks to pray away disability knows (or thinks he knows), what his primary religious language entails. In contrast, there is an omission in daily Liberal Quaker speak analogous to the evangelist who seeks to erase disability with prayer. Many Friends don't feel they can speak about disability in ways informed by our Spiritual Discipline. In this void, the gap is filled by the secular nostrums of accessibility and inclusion. There is nothing wrong with these commitments in themselves. When put into practice, they help us meet the diverse needs of others. But something is lacking in this purely practical approach, namely the deep meaning of disabled experience. What is lacking is any theological attempt to say what disablement means for our talk about God and community. We are left with the bare facts of human experience, unintegrated into our prayer and worship. What are the roots of this theological deletion? In the following discussion, I argue that disabled invisibility is rooted in the theological assumptions of Liberal Quakerism itself. Through some extended reflections on the Mysticism of Rufus Jones (1863–1948), I show how an exaggerated Liberal Quaker emphasis upon inwardness and universalism leaves embodiment a marginal concern among modernist Friends. Instead of being an independent source of knowing, the body is reduced to the haphazard instrument of a disembodied soul. This move leaves physicality at the edge of religious life. What is the proper remedy to this disembodied conception of the self? In the second part of this chapter, I consider the embodied theology of early Friends. By being attentive to the themes of Eucharistic feasting and epiphanic suffering, I suggest ways in which first-generation Quakers possessed a framework more hospitable to the affirmation of disabled bodies. In the final part of the discussion, I consider whether Liberal Quaker theology can indeed be saved from the charge of Ableism. I suggest, through a Friendly dialogue with the post-metaphysical philosopher Ludwig Wittgenstein (1889–1951), that Jones' focus upon mysticism can be redefined in ways that reject the dualism of body and soul and instead affirms the beauty and wholeness of embodied experience as a divine gift.

Rufus Jones: Romanticism, Mysticism, and the Problem of the Body

Rufus Jones remains one of the clearest articulators of liberal-modernist Quakerism to date. A guiding impulse of Jones' scholarly work was the elucidation of the concept of Mysticism and its relation to Quaker history and Worship. This project proved powerful in the social upheavals of the late nineteenth and early twentieth centuries. As William James had suggested in his 1902 study *The Varieties of Religious Experience*, one could now study religious belief in ways that cut across the peculiarities of culture and doctrine and instead encourage often jaded Western believers into an expansive psychological and non-literal appreciation of religious ideas and forms. In this mode of analysis, the feelings evoked by Notre Dame Cathedral or the Golden Temple at Amritsar were just as important as the finer points of ritual purification or theology. For James, this new lens was called 'mysticism'. The core of this label rested on the claim that the coherence of religion did not ultimately depend upon complex theologies but upon the direct experience of each believer of spiritual realities. When the Spirit, Divinity, or Absolute was felt by the worshipper as an immediate and tangible presence, then religious rites and symbols became active and operative. Such presence was often followed by feelings of certainty, harmony, and self-transcendence. As James reflected concerning the character of mystical experiences:

> It is as if the opposites of the world, whose contradictoriness and conflict make all our difficulties and troubles, were melted into unity. Not only do they, as contrasted species, belong to one and the same genus, but one of the species, the nobler and better one, is itself the genus, and so soaks up and absorbs its opposite into itself.
>
> *(James, 2012:272)*

But for psychological inquirers into these unitive states, it was possible to glance social implications far beyond the merely academic. As the theologian Peter Tyler notes concerning the potency of this Mystical turn, to postulate a personal and inward form of religious life was to imagine something 'liberal and universal without being dogmatic, ecclesiastical, sacramental, or sectarian' (Tyler, 2011:8). In an age after absolute authority and unquestioned religious belonging, Mysticism offered a new glue and a new programme for disparate religious communities seeking to make sense of the fragmentation and pluralism of the modern world. In this progressive spirit, Jones claimed a perennial core to Quakerism which transcended theological lexicons, geography, or particular practices. This secured for progressive British and American Friends potent new ways of thinking about their faith in a scientific and multireligious age. While externally the Religious Society of Friends constituted a peculiar outgrowth of sectarian Puritanism, at the level of abiding substance, Quakerism expressed for Jones the shared human stirring for divine immediacy. As Jones summarised the tone of this project in his 1923 *Studies in Mystical Religion*:

> There have been religious geniuses in all ages and in all countries who have had experiences of spiritual expansion. They have been made aware of a Realm of reality on a higher level than that revealed through their senses. They have sometimes felt invaded by the inrush of a larger Life; sometimes they have seemed to push a door inward into a larger range of being with a vastly heightened energy. The experience is . . . always one of joy and rapture; in fact it is probably the highest joy a mortal can feel.
>
> *(Jones 1923:xxx)*

In chronicling these exalted experiences, Jones saw Friends' distinctive mission as 'mystical and prophetic; a body of believers that should be judged not according to doctrines or habits but 'by the way it has been an organ of the Spirit' (Jones, 1921:5). Universal personal revelation, not particulars, animates what is most essential for Jones in the Quaker Way. In positing an inward religion of mystical experience as primary, Jones had two outstanding preoccupations. The first was to link the unity-seeking self of mystical excursion to the creative reflexive Romantic individualism of early modernity (Birkel, 2018:76). By extending the range of Mystical sources to include contemporary figures, Jones sought to show a basic sympathy between the striving contemplative and the restless souls of modern democratic civilization. In seeking to expand the category of 'mystical experience', Jones mined artists and poets for a keener expression of the Ultimate. One of Jones' guiding assets in this endeavour were the New England Transcendentalists. With their combined interests in individual self-expression and a Vedantic over-soul (Jones, 2001:68), writers such as Thoreau and Emerson offered a Quaker Liberal such as Jones a compelling conduit between archaic wisdom and contemporary conditions. For Jones the Transcendentalists illustrated that mysticism was not merely the passive receipt of Divine Wisdom but was creative and affective. This focus upon matters of artistic sensibility encouraged Jones to disregard orthodox ontological separations between human and divine action and instead stress the deep analogy between human and divine creativity. As Jones expresses this identification:

> We carry in the form and structure of our inner selves the mark and badge and lineage and kinship with a realm that can best be called the Eternal, since it is real in its own essential being and of the same nature as God who is the centre of its life and ours.
>
> *(Jones, 2001:77)*

This exaggerated subjectivism had considerable implications for Jones' understanding of both cultural production and aesthetics. If the inner domain of consciousness is part of the spiritual world, when human beings strive to create something from the recesses of their imaginations, they discover something of the divine within themselves (Birkel, 2018:67). The implication is that the human production of beauty is an extension of, and co-terminus with, divine creativity.

Conjoined with Jones' Romantic theology of co-creation was a second preoccupation, the de-secularisation of human life. Like his Romantic predecessors, Jones attempted to cultivate a deep appreciation of the natural world as a shield against the tendency to reduce everything to a mere object of calculation (Jones, 2001:141). If Jones shared the general healthy-mindedness and optimism of the Romantics, he also displays the Romantic appeal to individuality and radical inwardness, co-equal buttresses against the rigidities and conventions of the world. This manifests most markedly in Jones' anxieties concerning the sacrilegious effects of Enlighten-ment rationalism and Darwinian Naturalism on the spiritual description of human experience. Despite his sense of ordinary life's sacredness, in the face of profound irreligion, Jones seeks to separate human beings from the temporal world and into a realm of transcendence. In an effort to define the person against the grain of scientific materialism Jones seeks to demarcate the bodily nature of human beings from their essential non-material essence. This spiritual quality is defined by Jones as that which 'unifies, organizes and interprets everything presented to it' (Jones, 2001:75). It is identical with the words 'mind', 'consciousness', and 'soul', containing within itself the capacity to see the invisible structure of the world under the mundane order of things. While this inner self is affected by the character of outer experience, its essence is altogether different from the world it surveys. There is, says Jones, 'nothing outside itself which can explain it'; it is unique and 'belongs to a different order' (Jones, 2001: 75). While Jones is at pains to insist that this Deep Self 'is not a spectator mind' (Jones, 2001:49), his radical turn inward introduces us to the cardinal tension at the heart of Jones' conception of Liberal Quak-erism. Despite Jones' assertion of a world-engaged 'affirmative mysticism' (Jones, 2001:89), his attempts to preserve the spiritual self from the brutalising currently of secular modernity leaves the human person, in its deepest essence, radically separate from the world. The language of mysticism as contacting a 'higher' reality conceals this judgement within a spatial metaphor. Whatever divine qualities the physical world conveys, it must be regarded as quite secondary to the Spirit which is altogether other than the world of time and space. As Jones summarises this trajectory in a lecture of 1941:

> There can be no question that we as persons have biological traits and that the mark of the animal is on us, as the hairs on our arms indicate, and in us, as many of our instincts suggest. But something else, and something higher, is just as unmistakable in our structure. The divine likeness does not lie in external conformity. It consists in spirituality of being, in a moral and spiritual integrity of soul. He has made us for

immortal life and has set eternity in us. 'The spirit of man', as a great text of the Bible says, 'is a candle, a flame, of the Lord'.

(Jones, 2004:n.p.)

What are the consequences of Jones' mystical-romantic self for the lives of disabled persons within Quaker communities? Jones never addresses these matters directly, but several vital implications can be gleaned. Firstly, given the affective and introspective qualities of Jones' mystical self, this conception can be unmasked, not as the time-bound expression of a universal human core but as the uncritical adoption of the restless bourgeois self of the Romantics. By postulating a radical fusion of divine and human creativity, Jones elevates a particular kind of human identity, fluid, selective, and self-willed. What matters most to such a personality is the proper nurture of its distinctive private identity despite context. In our culture, teenage rebellion is the most paradigmatic example of this posture. But in Jones' case, this sense of opposition to unchosen circumstances is radicalised to include all that does not communicate sublime non-materiality. In this account the soul is not so much of fragment of divine light, connected to all creatures through its source, but a kind of Pure Individuality, which is quite other from its surroundings. While such mystic independence may have social, even altruistic consequences, such selfhood is always understood as an observer in its own world, never quite part of the ebb and flow of its myriad relations. It always conceives of itself as autonomous from the history that shapes it. Such a vision of identity unconsciously valorises willing and determined separateness while obscuring notions of care and reciprocity as inherent in personhood. Those whose sense of identity arises not from introspective creation but from the daily interflow of practical care will find little in Jones to affirm them. Any anthropology that is premised upon an absolute distinction between self and world cannot be anything other than inattentive to the kind of frailties and independencies involved in experiences of disablement. While Jones frequently waxes lyrical concerning the centrality of spiritual community and the reality of Church, his mysticism renders persons within that body so many isolated Monads.

Encoded in this implicitly solipsistic account of human identity is a further problem, namely the near divinising of the artistic personality to the exclusion of other ways of being human. The one swept up in wordless intuition of the transcendent is free to choose what meaning this ultimate experience will have for him. Like the beauty of a sunrise before the eyes of the intentional poet, the Mystic self of Jones feels tasked to extract from immediate experience what an event might mean for the growth of the inner self. Once extracted, this self-made meaning can be identified with divine creativity. Despite Jones' warning against 'the lonely track of egoism' (Jones, 2001:119), implicit in this notion of the artistic soul is a form of privatised self-making, one that regards external facts as unimportant contingencies that must be transcended in the name of higher purposes. As Jones summarises this impulse:

Where can God be found? Not in our world of sense anywhere, answers the mystic. Every possible object in our world is a mere finite appearance. It may be as huge as the sun or even the Milky Way, or as minute as the dust speck in the sunbeam; it makes no difference. It is a form of the finite. It is in contrast to the Absolute an illusion, a thing of unreality. It cannot show God or take you to him.

(Jones, 2001:88)

The flipside of this proposition is obvious. The inward self is the most real thing in the world, the most solid object, other than God Himself. We might call the terminus of this position, the Mysticism of infinite licence or to use Ben Pink Dandelion's concise term, 'sacro-egoism'

(Dandelion, 2014:47). Since the self in its depth is intrinsically bound to the divine, such a being can in theory become its own self-contained universe, guided solely by its own internal sense of divine co-relation. Such a being is free to reinvent itself in any way that its inner promptings incline. Here we see the embryonic underpinnings of the postmodern posture that Dandelion calls 'Liberal-Liberal Quakerism' (Dandelion, 2007:134). In this mode, the mystic/creative inner self is given complete free reign, as belief is largely 'pluralised, privatised, but also marginalised' (Dandelion, 2007:134). In this latter form, Quakerism increasingly resembles a subjective therapeutic project of self-discovery, spiritual autonomy, and personal authenticity. But what is personal freedom for one is exclusion and impoverishment for another. What of selves that cannot, for reasons of cognitive capacity, be the connoisseur of their own spiritual experience? What kind of mystical oneness is open to a child with profound learning disabilities? Jones' overinvestment in the notion of the *Imago Dei* as artistic imagination could place the child's status as a participant in Worship in doubt. What of the person experiencing late-stage dementia? Does their inability to order their inward experience in imaginative ways render them insensible to the divine immediacy promised by Quaker Worship? Jones' model cannot answer these questions because its conception of the Mystical is premised upon a narrow dualistic anthropology of subjective creativity. Such a description of humanness is too monotone and too brittle to encompass a larger range of human experiences. As Tyler summarises the problem:

> The notion of 'pure' experience, (religious or otherwise divorced of all categories of culture, prior experience, tradition, structures, institutions, and relationships is suspect. Lying behind the concept is a sense of experience, perhaps as 'conscious mental goings on' . . . which betrays a Cartesian metaphysic with a disembodied 'I' trying to relate to specific sensations and 'experiences'.
>
> *(Tyler, 2011:19)*

To put the matter more bluntly still, we are not abstract creatures that greet a world of abstracts, we are sensuous, interrelated beings. As Tyler expresses this corrective: 'Our words, our speech cannot be extracted from our life and our meaning in words comes from . . . the series of relationships in which we dwell' (Tyler, 2011:223). And lest we think of Tyler's 'relationships' too bloodlessly, to be in such relation is to care and be cared for, to touch and recoil, embrace, and part, mingle and shun. To relate in actuality is to be bodies in various degrees of togetherness or separation from other bodies. To obscure this fundamental reality by a theory of transcendent mysticism merely serves to lessen the world and the diverse persons in it. These observations vividly draw out, not merely the marginalisation of cognitive diversity in particular, but Liberal Mysticism's stunning indifference to the particularities of bodily life in general. The greatest of philosophical horrors for Jones, is the prospect of human beings becoming reduced to 'bits of the earth's crust' or 'biological exhibits' (Jones, 2001:77). As Jones notes somewhat disdainfully:

> Life in our times has been profoundly secularized by a thousand drives and influences. But one of the most subtle and insidious of all these influences has been the scientific implication that man is merely a complicated biological specimen, the later offspring of flat nosed baboons. . . . There has been a widespread loss of faith in immortality, which naturally goes with the acceptance of a biological estimate of man, and Friends greatly need to have the eternal aspect of life brought to light with power and authority.
>
> *(Jones, 2004:n.p.)*

But by using interiority as a counterweight to the secularising potentialities of contemporary science, Jones ends by secularising the very body he fears has been reduced to *mere animality*. Both the trajectory and terminus of Jones' thought encourages us to believe that only the inner world can save us from irreligion. Bodies are mere incidental obscurers of what is most essential about us, the inward spark of the divine. My own body, with its daily tensions and spasms, its heightened sensitivity to heat and cold, its fluctuations of weariness and energy, can never reach the heights of Jones' sublime inner self. Instead it must be left forlorn on the banks of the world, devoid of spiritual significance. In the pattern of Jones' mystic dualism, my body remains a mere burdensome contingency, an outer trapping that obscures the inner self. But how can we disentangle ourselves from our bodies? What meaning can the notion of immortal light have without the prior experience of sun on the skin? What can be said of the depths of divine love without the teaching of touching and embrace? Of what substance is Divine judgement without the acid convulsion at the pit of a nervous stomach? Indeed, what does it mean to say that the Spirit is like quenching water if we are inattentive to the sensation of cool liquid on cracked lips? The concepts of inner and outer, spirit and eternity, possess meaning precisely because we can ground these concepts in our immediate fleshly life. We must have a faith and a mysticism worthy of these guttural realities. To treat these deep facets of our humanity as impediments is to shrink our conception of God.

Worship and the Dynamics of Embodied Revelation

What alternative is there to the interiorised mysticism of Jones? To answer this question, we need to recover a lost emphasis within the story of Quakerism; that of *the body as a medium of mystical knowing*. In the Puritan milieu from which Quakerism sprang, it was commonly said that there were two sources of epistemic illumination: the indirect Light of nature, ordained by Providence and the Light of grace which emanated from God directly. As the preacher Jonathan Edwards summarised this doctrine in 1734:

> Mortal men are capable of imparting the knowledge of human arts and sciences and skill in temporary affairs. God is the author of such knowledge by those means; flesh and blood is made use of by God as the mediate or second cause of it; he conveys it by the power and influence of natural means. But . . . spiritual knowledge . . . is what God is the author of and none else; he reveals it, and flesh and blood reveals it not. He imparts this knowledge immediately, not making use of any intermediate natural causes as he does with other knowledge.
>
> *(Edwards, 2005:156)*

The intent of such a boundary between natural and divine knowledge was to emphasise the absolute sovereignty of divine decision. Just as Jones had sought to protect the coherence of religious claims by securing them in a 'mystic' inner core, Edwards' unfleshly immediate grace shielded God from the accusation that the Eternal was dependent upon physical constraints or historical contingency. In the intense, often sudden, conversion experiences of tearful congregants, the Puritan preacher observed the invisible hand of a power that was not dependent upon the vagaries of autobiography. Divine activity was conceived of as absolute and irresistible. While early Friends emulated the Puritan insistence on the absolute independence of divine knowledge, they envisioned revelation in ways that radically undercut distinctions between nature and spirit, empirical knowledge, and subjective sensation. Nowhere is such undercutting more in evidence than in early Quaker conceptions of the Eucharist. While the early Quaker movement expressed its distinctive theology in terms of the blanket rejection of all outward sacramental rites, the first Quaker preachers nonetheless insisted that their Meetings constituted a form of Eucharistic sharing. In an attempt to put this motif into words, one early Quaker used a striking image: 'Life flows from Vessel to Vessel, and here a Communion, indeed not a communion of Bread and Wine, as the World Receives which is carnal' (quoted in Graves, 2009:167). For the writer just quoted, the gathered Meeting is identical in substance to the Eucharist rite of ceremonial Christendom, capable of conveying both grace and forgiveness. Like the Real Presence of Catholic doctrine, first-generation Friends felt Christ among them, feeding them from his own bounty. But what should we make of the marked contrast between 'soul' and 'carnality' in the articulation just offered? A casual reader might assume that early Friends agreed with the radical interiority of Jones and his concerted deflation of the body in religious life. But when we look more closely at the contours of the Quaker tradition, we discover that such disembodiment is based on careless reading of Quaker texts. While early Friends' appeals to 'inward' religion seem world-denying and Gnostic (Gwyn, 1986:115) contemporary scholarship has drawn attention to the early Quaker doctrine of 'the celestial flesh', the direct indwelling of Christ in the body of each person gathered in Worship (Kopelson, 2014:134). As Sally Bruyneel summarises this commitment in the writings of Margaret Fell:

> In Fell's theology, the idea that those who are in the Light are the body of Christ has both a literal and metaphorical sense. As the Spirit of the Lord Jesus Christ is perfected, the prophetic promise of his coming in the flesh is fulfilled. In this sense we as a group (corpus) literally become the body of Christ incarnate, risen and rising. In this way Jesus Christ has come and is coming in the flesh. At the same time, the concept of the true church as a body with many parts serves as a guiding metaphor for a group of diverse persons who must work together through the leading of the Light.
>
> *(Bruyneel, 2010:108)*

This forceful organicism had radical implications for the way the first Quakers treated both the body and the senses in the context of Worship. Firstly, sensory experience was a vehicle of proclamation beside verbal ministry and the use of the written word of Scripture. When first-generation Friends spoke of partaking of Communion, they were not referring to a purely cognitive or out-of-body experience of encounter, but frequently understood their ordinary embodiment as the locus of divine/human interchange. In trembling, convulsions, the movements of the stomach, and copious tears, the bodies of early Quaker worshippers were seen giving precognitive assent to the activity of the Spirit (Philippians 2:10–11). Words spoken or heard were often quite secondary to the primary experience of being 'moved' (Mack, 1995:151). But if the visible prompts of the body signified the dying and rising of Christ in the heart, the acts of God, particularly the promise of redemption, also became a sensuous experience. Francis Howgill, in his highly poetic meditation on the theme of Communion of 1655, spoke of those Friends who 'have eaten at his [Christ's] Table, and drunken of the new Wine in the Kingdom of God, who are nourished . . . . who suck at the Breasts of everlasting Consolation' (Howgill, 1676:35). This picture of the body as a site of direct revelation and Eucharistic feast was given a highly literalistic tinge by James Nayler who after his arrest in 1656 insisted that he could go without food for long periods on account of being sustained by nothing, 'except the Word of God' (Bayly Howell, 1816:834). Beside feelings of life-giving satiation, early Friends would also turn to smell and taste to express this Eucharistic infolding of the Spirit. In moments of blissful lucidity, some worshippers would describe God's presence like costly ointment sweet in their nostrils (Mack, 1995:151).

Such a sumptuous religiosity points in a single direction. To be in the presence of Christ was to be invited into an inclusive dance of the senses. For early Friends, the flow and excitement of bodily sensation constituted the wordless corporeal immediacy of their primitive faith. While we should not dismiss the potent symbolism behind Friends' appeals to drinking, smelling and tasting, neither should we wholly allegorise their content. The doctrine of the 'celestial flesh' suggests a reality more direct, more primordial than the abstraction of symbol. We must move beyond the transcendent mysticism of Jones and attend instead to the particular sensations of our needful bodily selves. This extravagant affirmation of sense-experience as illuminative of the Spirit offers us a fresh way of conceptualising diverse bodily experiences within Quaker Worship, including those who know disablement. To take the testimony of early Friends seriously is to affirm that our encounters with God do not take place beyond bodies. The Spirit is with us not in some grand Beyond but in the pits of our stomachs, on the tips of our fingers, and in the soles of our feet. To know God does not depend upon a refined and cerebral inwardness but a sacramental relatedness. In this space of waiting and encounter, bodies with diverse abilities are held. No one needs see or hear in particular ways to know the presence of the Inward Christ. No one needs a reflective vocabulary to navigate the ocean of divine love. This is not because embodiment is irrelevant to the spiritual life. Rather, it is because God embraces manifold portals of presence, enticing and enfolding whatever capacities can best communicate the status of affirmation and grace-filled wholeness which sits behind the language of salvation. Human difference of capacity, in reasoning, hearing, speech, sight or mobility, does not change Worship's power to shift persons into states of deep knowing. Indeed, this is the act of trust that is nestled at the heart of our waiting, that all gathered can be expressions of divine presence. To return to the language of Edwards, God's decision to act does not take place despite our bodies but in them, with them, and beside them. To the street preacher, a Quaker should reply that ours is a God that crosses all boundaries. What we perceive as walls God defines as so many doors of perception. Disabled people are not theological problems to solve but centres of divine activity in their own right.

Healed and Unhealed: Justice Against Stigma

But does such an answer really deter the street preacher from his ministry, or help Liberal Quakers forgo their silence regarding the theological significance of disabled bodies? After all, is not the Christian grammar of early Quakerism clear concerning the healing and modification of disabled bodies? Did not Jesus heal 'many who had various diseases'? (Mark 1:34) Is it not the case that this author's cerebral palsy is precisely the kind of condition that Jesus' Messianic ministry sought to eliminate? These questions are troubling in all manner of ways, not least in illuminating the Scriptural roots of Ableism. If Jesus' ministry was about freedom from infirmity, sickness or disablement, then God wills a world in which no disabled persons should exist. If this is so, then disabled people embedded in Christian communities will always suffer from the stigma of being 'un-fixed'. How can the embodied Worship of early Friends respond to such charges? To reply convincingly, we must consider the nature of the bodies that felt themselves inhabited by the Spirit. As a movement that drew inspiration directly from the New Testament, early Quakers possessed a complicated relationship with the miraculous healing associated with Jesus and his Apostles. On the one hand, Friends sought to show their own prayer and Worship was marked by the same inexplicable events of the broken becoming whole. George Fox had closely imitated the Gospel accounts of bodily restoration in his own healing ministry, setting the power of prayer against fevers, paralysis, kidney stones, mental disturbance, even death (Shaw, 2006:53). But alongside this practice of faith healing was the incarnational theology of Friends in prison. This thought-world was deeply subversive, owing less to the healing stories of the Gospels and more to the personal agonies of the apostle Paul. Paul's profound sense of possessing a cruciform life allowed him to understand both hardship and bodily frailty as marks of God's redeeming presence. Bodies who experienced extremes of pain, cold, hunger or darkness were not lesser entities in the Pauline economy of Worship. Indeed, in the social hierarchy of bodes, Paul saw it as the risen Messiah's task to ensure that 'the last will be first, and the first will be last' (Matthew 20:16). Those lives regarded by the secure or powerful as lacking or feeble were to be brought into the very centre of God's Kingdom. Practically, this meant a radical revaluation of the social position of persons, so that marginal lives were to be elevated above the vigorous and mighty. As Paul expresses this reversal in his own life:

> Therefore, in order to keep me from becoming conceited, I was given a thorn in my flesh, a messenger of Satan, to torment me. Three times I pleaded with the Lord to take it away from me. But he said to me, 'My grace is sufficient for you, for my power is made perfect in weakness.' Therefore I will boast all the more gladly about my weaknesses, so that Christ's power may rest on me. That is why, for Christ's sake, I delight in weaknesses, in insults, in hardships, in persecutions, in difficulties. For when I am weak, then I am strong.
>
> *(2 Corinthians 12:7–10)*

For Paul, we are closest to Christ when we experience the same marginality as the one 'who made himself nothing by taking the very nature of a servant, being made in human likeness' (Philippians 2:7). In a comprehensive reaffirmation of Paul's notion of Jesus-shaped imitation, early Friends understood impediment and incapacity as expressions of a Christ-filled life. To be deprived (by sickness, hardship or stigma) was to be made a vessel of God's unfolding power. In Paul's theological vision, the object was not to be fixed but to observe the divine spirit working in bodies that others despised or disregarded. This had a profound impact on the early Quaker understanding of persecution. Margaret Fell, writing to Friends in Newgate prison in 1660, assured her recipients:

> I have not bene unmindful of you nor unsensible of your sufferinges but it is faith and patience that most [must] carry through. For whenever the Lord suffers his enemyes to exercise their Cruelty upon his Children and servents it is for the Accomplishing of his owne will and pleasure, which is for his owne service; And therefore dear harts be not weary.
>
> *(Fell, 2003:287)*

While there is always the risk that such exhortations encourage us to uncritically glorify suffering, when understood through the early Quaker notion of the indwelling Christ, we see a conception both more just and more profound. God's love always dwells in bodies that are placed on the fringe of the social world. Just as Christ was made invisible by his relative poverty and despised for his prophetic visibility, those who are framed by their marginality are cherished by a tender and affirming God. In a general epistle of 1665, Fell bids Friends:

> Beware of going from you Guide, which keepeth you low and tender, and prize the love of God that ever He should visit you; and beware that you do not requite Him

evil for good, for He is a jealous God, and will not clear the guilty; it is the low, and the meek, and the humble that the Lord God teacheth, it is the broken and contrite spirit, that God will not despise. And He, who is the high and lofty one, that inhabiteth eternity, dwelleth in the hearts of the humble.

(Fell, 1859:n.p.)

Fell's point is radical in its embodied implications. The God who early Friends worshipped particularly valued those pushed to the edge of the social world, persons whose lives refuted the underlying forces of power and self-assertion. These were the humble lives the early Quaker polemicist Francis Howgill bracketed under 'the outcasts of Israel', those particularly loved by God (Howgill, 1662:5). This radical elevation of frailty was not intended to transform the weak into the strong but rather to transform weakness into a site of dignity.

What implications does this orientation have for the construction of a Quaker disabled theology? The chief theological lesson of early Friends' suffering might be summarised as the moral significance of the *unhealed*. God works in the world, not by adjusting us according to some inflexible norm, but by calling into question structures and values that buttress our sense of normality. This focus is powerfully explored in the story of the wealthy tax collector Zacchaeus (Luke 19:3–5). In the context of first-century Judaism, Zacchaeus endures a double stigma. As a little person, Zacchaeus is deemed religiously impure by the Mosaic law and thus excluded from the cult of sacrifice (Leviticus 21:20). But as Amos Yong observes, this exclusion invited a more profound process of moral othering: 'In the case of Zacchaeus, his shortness of stature . . . would have been generally seen in physiognomic terms as reflecting "smallness of spirit", small-mindedness, greediness and other derogatory characteristics in the ancient world' (Yong, 2011:67). In the Lukan narrative, this low status is compounded by his occupation. As a tax collector, he would have been viewed as a collaborator with Roman rule, contributing towards general conditions of poverty and social misery. In this way, the story is surprising. Jesus does not transform Zacchaeus' body, nor does he tell the tax collector to leave his profession behind. He simply says: 'Zacchaeus, come down immediately. I must stay at your house today' (Luke 19:5). In the eyes of society, Zacchaeus' interlocking deviances remain intact. What Jesus offers is not adjustment but radical welcome that resists the logic of stigma. But Quaker history makes a still stronger claim, drawing as it does upon the distinctively Pauline experience of Jesus as co-sufferer. If the bodies of those deemed weak are places where the Spirit dwells, God's blessing is not imposed on disabled bodies from another body, somehow possessed of the right capacities. Blessing is born in and through what the world regards as limit or inability. God takes stigma and exclusion and renders them loci of restorative power. Such restoration does not require a fixed standard of physical or cognitive functioning. As the Disabled theologian Nancy Eiesland reminds us, using the striking image of the wounded Risen Jesus:

> In presenting his impaired hands and feet to his startled friends, the resurrected Jesus is revealed as the disabled God. Jesus the resurrected Saviour, calls for his frightened companions to recognise in the marks of impairment their own connection to God, their own salvation. In so doing, this disabled God is also the revealer of a new humanity. The disabled God is not only the One from heaven but the revelation of true personhood, underscoring the reality that true personhood is fully compatible with the experience of disability.

(Eiesland, 1994:100)

329

Eiesland's theological emphasis on the profound woundedness in the heart of God, draws us back into the deep meaning of our Worship as Friends. The God that rests in and through our own bodies in waiting together, dignifies and affirms our human boundedness in all its concrete truth. Here we are not merely living in bodies or living despite our bodies. Rather, we are bodies, signs of dependence upon a giving God, who delights in our embodiment, in its diverse fleshly and cognitive forms. We are more than minds or souls. We are totalities that must be taken as human wholes. To seek to bless disabled persons in the pursuit of an imagined wholeness divides persons between their selves and their possible selves. It renders individuals mere projects for the standards of others. It negates the capacity of disabled persons to be bearers of divine possibility in the world. The same painful fissure is introduced if we render the human being a mere spirit having a material experience. Any mysticism that hinges upon 'higher' and 'lower' in its exploration of the spiritual life risks degrading bodily life and thus the particular concreteness of disabled experience.

Touching an Embodied Quakerism: Some Final Reflections

God grant the philosopher insight into what lies in front of everyone's eyes.
(Wittgenstein, 1977:63e)

At this juncture, it might be supposed that the present project is chiefly concerned with a partial return to some embryonic Quakerism, bypassing some inauthentic Liberal aberration. Such an interpretation assumes that Jones' theological Liberalism has nothing within it that corresponds to the earliest Quaker imaginary. Such a reading of the present endeavour would be hasty, not least because it ignores an underlying faith experience that unites both Quaker tradition and Quaker modernity; namely, a commitment to divine imminence. Friends both primitive and progressive have assumed that the divine life greets us in the world if time in the body and biography of Jesus of Nazareth, and that this indwelling fundamentally transforms our relationship to God. As Jones observes:

> What Christ brought to light in the unfolding of the Eternal Gospel is the Face, the personal aspect, the revelation of the Heart, the Love, the Grace, the Character-Nature of God. We see Him at last. We know now what He is like. We are confined no-longer to abstract attributes such as 'infinite', 'omniscient', 'omnipotent' and 'absolute'.

> *(Jones, 2001:111)*

Much as early Friends experience Christ within themselves, Jones is able to say with conviction that 'God is nearer to us than we supposed; more truly an Emmanuel God than we have wont to believe' (Jones, 2001:125). Here we see one of those rarer moments where Jones abandons his dualistic mysticism and instead embraces the earth as an expression of Heaven. In the body of Jesus, Mysticism is seen renouncing appeals to what is 'above' and 'beyond' and instead sinks into the world *as it is*. The truth that Jesus brings in this vein is not a spiritual absolute, but 'something a person can be' (Jones, 2001:110). In this most concrete of moods, Jones is able to imagine Christian discipleship less as an intangible experience and more as 'a life that corresponds to an ideal, a pattern, an architectural plan' (Jones, 2001:111). To construct a Quaker disabled theology is not the abandonment of this terrain but its logical completion. To say that the Spirit abides in us is to say that the divine dwells in bodies, affirming our physicality and our capacities. At its most consistent, to affirm the mystical and immediate presence of God is to sink down into the realities of life. The moment we place a barrier of transcendent absolutes between ourselves and this immediate appreciation of existence as sense and sensing is the moment we water down the essence of mystic intuition. Either the Spirit is present, or it is not. If present, then it is enfolded in the stream of our sense experience, in the solidity of our bodies, and in the borders of our capacities.

Thus, a Quaker disabled theology requires not merely the inclusion of disabled voices in the task of reflecting about God but a considered re-orientation of the language of the Liberal Quaker story. We must move from a mysticism of sublime transcendence towards one of deep knowing in the bodily present. What might such an orientation look or feel like? A compelling guide to restoring this embodied mode of faith is the twentieth-century Austrian philosopher Ludwig Wittgenstein. Known primarily as the last century's great philosopher of language, Wittgenstein's work strode the disciplinary borders between philosophy, linguistics, anthropology, and religion. When placed alongside his contemporaries, Wittgenstein is remarkable for his commitment to the notion of the philosopher as a sensuous being, a creature whose intellectual purposes are aspects of a social world. In repudiation of both Platonic otherworldliness and Cartesian dualism, Wittgenstein wanted us to recover the sense that life in all its messiness and changeability possesses an abiding meaning and beauty. In contrast to Jones' fear of animality, Wittgenstein regarded our creatureliness as the root of spiritual and philosophical reflection. In a notebook entry of 1931 Wittgenstein remarks: 'It is humiliating to have to appear like an empty tube which is simply inflated by a mind' (quoted in Brenner, 1999:102). Given this resolutely non-dualistic trajectory, one of Wittgenstein's great preoccupations was understanding the ways in which talk about God and religious experience are embedded in networks of culture and webs of bodies. As a child of the post-metaphysical twentieth century, Wittgenstein could no longer find coherence in a God beyond time or in the idea of souls without bodies. He claimed that he wanted to 'report how I found the world. What others in the world have told me about the world is a very small and incidental part of my experience of the world' (quoted in Genova, 2016:146). When such empiricism was applied to the Spirit, religious language became for Wittgenstein not a transmission of information from an ethereal world but constructive social symbols concerned with the ordering of concrete relations. As Wittgenstein expressed it:

> [The words] you utter or what you think as you utter them are not what matters, so much as the difference they make at various points in your life. How do I know that these two people mean the same when each says he believes in God? And just the same goes for belief in the Trinity. A theology that insists on the use of *certain particular* words and phrases, and outlaws others, does not make anything clearer. . . . It gesticulates with words, as one might say, because it wants to say something but does not know how to express it. *Practice* gives the words their sense.
>
> (Wittgenstein, 1977:85e)

But these admissions of radical imminence did not translate into an irreligious materialism. Instead Wittgenstein sought a new path, one in which the Spirit was revered in the concrete ebb and flow of the ordinary world. This was defined at the conclusion of Wittgenstein's early text *Tractatus Logico-Philosophicus*: 'It is not *how* things are in the world that is mystical but *that* it exists' (Wittgenstein, 1961:73). Instead of looking outside life for the sense of affirmation, Wittgenstein wants us to view this world as the true expression of spiritual hope. In this muddy iteration of the mystical, we make sense of God not by questing for transcendence but by finding a sense of eternity in the present (Wittgenstein, 1961:72). This had profound philosophical implications. No longer could religiosity be grounded on talk of some disembodied afterworld but must arise from the gifts of ordinary life. To stress his opposition to abstract speculation Wittgenstein claimed that the divine could only be grasped through the still-mindedness offered by silence (Wittgenstein, 1961:73). While other philosophers stressed the continual progression of concepts and the general refinement of thought, Wittgenstein describes a different posture: 'Where others go on ahead, I stay in one place' (Wittgenstein, 1977:66e).

But if God cannot be known through the thinking of a noisy grasping mind, what routes are left for comprehension? In a stunning rejection of logocentrism, Wittgenstein suggests that 'the human body is the best picture of the human soul' (Wittgenstein, 19770:49a). This enigmatic observation draws out two insights already gestured at in this essay. Firstly, the things of the divine world are analogous to things of the body. To be *in* our bodies is something that lies beyond words. It is an immediate experience of aliveness and presence that defies our abstraction. In this way, embodiment is like the mystery of the divine world. It is known only by its direct unveiling. Words and concepts are but so many trails attesting to the silent fact of its existence. Secondly, we know the mysteries of God through the patterns of bodily life. We know God through the courses our bodies take, in prayer, in quaking, in the quickening heartbeat, in the still sense of accompaniment. Properly worked through, this orientation of religious life has profound effects on the language and practice of Liberal Quakerism. If Wittgenstein joined us in Worship, he would tell us that the Spirit is adequately expressed by our bodies, that they provide an image of all the substantive spiritual words we use ('God', 'Spirit', 'Christ', 'love'), and that our focus should be upon making them manifest in and through cultivated practice. Through this lens, our gathered silence can be understood as a particular way of perceiving and affirming the lives of others, saying a profound 'yes' to their unique presence. Translated into purely theological terms, this attentiveness is concerned with the affirmation of all that we are as creatures. If eternity is a quality of the present as Wittgenstein insists, we enter most surely into the orbit of God when we allow ourselves to be inspired by the immediacy of being alive. By tarrying in the immensity of 'just being', we can be taught more than words alone can teach. If we sit long enough with the frailty and beauty of the bare needful facts of being, we may find words capable of serving one another with Eucharistic intent. Instead of a narrow *Imago Dei* framed by private creativity and an exaggerated interiority, the Wittgensteinian turn restores to our horizon the human body as *Imago Christi* (the vulnerable body of Christ, in our own frail bodies). When Pilate asks Jesus the ultimate question, "What is truth?" (John 18:38), no answer is given in words or concepts. Pilate's answer is standing before him in the shape of a beaten and battered prisoner. The body of Jesus is able to speak the divine into reality beyond the constraints of theory or abstraction. The body is both a source of a knowledge and in instrument of teaching. Contained in this generous conception of embodied revelation is all that makes us human, not merely thinking, speaking, and imagining, but our capacities for pain and delight, hunger, and fullness; these too are portals to divine unveiling.

It is in the latter possibility that a deep theological deconstruction of Ableism can take place. Under the auspices of secularity, many Liberal Friends find themselves unable to fully connect the words they use in meditation and prayer to the bodily experiences of themselves or others. This leaves a deep gulf at the heart of a Meeting's spiritual life, one which may push many to the edge of consideration, especially those who will not or cannot conceive their lives in terms of liquid self-selection. Pain, disablement, deprivation, bliss, and sensual delight may provoke deep religious questions in individuals, but they sit uneasily with the presuppositions of Liberal Quaker Mysticism. By pursuing inward self-actualisation, Friends are encouraged to strip away the sacred significance of bodily demands, or else instrumentalise them as so many tools to better relate to the Spirit. But by waiting for the God who manifests in fingers and feet, breath and perspiration, we rediscover the Spirit as personal relation. Adopting such an embodied theology demands more than the secular language of inclusion since it presupposes disablement and interdependence as sites of epiphany. In theological Ableism, disabled bodies are half-visible objects, the passive recipients of care. In the reaffirmation of early Quaker body-talk we discern a powerful account of agency and value that surpasses the limits of inward subjectivity. Along with all others who wait in silence, disabled people are Icons, helping the community see, feel, and know God in the world. When we are at home in our own bodies or make a home for the body of another, God's justice is manifest. Such a vision, of lives in divinely manifest relation, is one without superiority or hierarchy. Disabled people do not need blessing since their bodies already convey the blessing of God who lives and loves in and through bodies. This status does not depend upon any apprehension of a terrain beyond the body, nor does it depend upon any theory that makes the world secondary to Spirit. If Mysticism has any substantive meaning, it begins here. For many, this shift of emphasis requires considerable trust, for it tells us that God does not need our intellect, our concepts, even our subjective creativity. For the God at the heart of our Worship, the body is enough.

Bibliography

Bayly Howell, Thomas, *A Complete Collection of State Trials and Proceedings for High Treason and Other Crimes and Misdemeanours* (Peterborough: T. C. Hansard, Vol. V, 1816)

Birkel, Michael, *Quakers Reading Mystics, Quaker Studies* (Leiden: Brill, 2018)

Brenner, William H., *Wittgenstein's Philosophical Investigations* (New York: New York State University Press, 1999)

Bruyneel, Sally, *Margret Fell and the End of Time,: The Theology of the Mother of Quakerism* (Waco: Baylor University Press, 2010)

Dandelion, Ben Pink, *Quakerism: An Introduction* (Cambridge: Cambridge University Press, 2007)

Dandelion, Ben Pink, *Open for Transformation: The 2014 Swarthmore Lecture* (London: Quaker Books, 2014)

Edwards, Jonathan, *Sinners in the Hands of an Angry God, and Other Puritan Sermons* (New York: Dover, 2005)

Eiesland, Nancy, L., *The Disabled God: Towards a Liberatory Theology of Disability* (Nashville: Abington Press, 1994)

Fell, Margret, *The Life of Margaret Fox, Wife of George Fox. Compiled from her Own Narrative, and other Sources; with a Selection from Her Epistles, etc* (Philadelphia, 1859): http://www.qhpress.org/texts/old qwhp/mf-e-2.htm (Accessed 1 November 2021)

Fell, Margret, *Undaunted Zeal: The Letters of Margret Fell*, ed. Elsa F. Glines (Richmond: Friends United Press, 2003)

Genova, Judith, *Wittgenstein: A Way of Seeing* (Routledge: London, 2016)

Graves, Michael P., *Preaching the Inward Light: Early Quaker Rhetoric* (Waco: Baylor University Press, 2009)

Gwyn, Douglas, *The Apocalypse of the Word: The Life and Message of George Fox* (Richmond: Friends United Press, 1986)

Howgill, Francis, *The Dawnings of the Gospel-day and Its Light and Glory Discovered (A Testimony Concerning the Life and Death, Trials, Travels and Labours of Edward Burroughs . . .)* (London: S.N., 1662)

James, William, *The Varieties of Religious Experience: A Study in Human Nature* (London: Routledge, 2012)

Jones, Rufus, *The Later Period of Quakerism, Volume I* (London: Macmillan, and Co, 1921)

Jones, Rufus, *Studies in Mystical Religion* (London: Macmillan and Co, 1923)

Jones, Rufus, *Essential Writings*, ed. Kerry Walters (New York: Orbis Books, 2001)

Jones, Rufus, *The Vital Cell* (Quaker Heron Press, 2004): https://quaker.org/legacy/pamphlets/wpl1941a.html (Accessed 1 November 2021)

Kopelson, Heather Miyano, *Faithful Bodies: Performing Religion and Race in the Puritan Atlantic* (New York: New York University Press, 2014)

Mack, Phyllis, *Visionary Women: Ecstatic Prophecy in Seventeenth Century England* (Berkley: University of California Press, 1995)

Shaw, Jane, *Miracles in Enlightenment England* (London: Yale University Press, 2006)

Tyler, Peter, *The Return of the Mystical: Ludwig Wittgenstein, Thresa of Avila, and the Christian Mystical Tradition* (London: Continuum, 2011)

Wittgenstein, Ludwig, *Tractatus Logico-Philosophicus* (London: Routledge & Kegan Paul, 1961)

Wittgenstein, Ludwig, *Culture and Value*, trans. Peter Winch (Oxford: Basil Blackwell, 1977)

Yong, Amos, *The Bible, Disability, and the Church* (Cambridge: William B. Eerdmans, 2011)

41

THEOLOGICAL FOUNDATIONS IN DISABILITY ISSUES

Evaluating the African Christian Quaker Experience

Oscar Lugusa Malande

Introduction

There are incidences I have encountered while serving in ministry concerning questionable disability issues. A particular one worth noting is that in which I visited and prayed with a family who had buried the deceased, who was a child born with disability. I noticed there was no grave and on inquiring where it was; I found out that it was behind the homestead in the banana plantation. Usually, in this part of the world, the grave is situated at the front of the homestead. According to the culture of the day, it meant casting away the bad omen to avoid anyone being born with disability. The bone of contention here was relating disability with bad omen.

Other questionable incidences concern most of the worship places that are not conscious of disability needs. At times, those living with disabilities find a very difficult time, as the Church seems to stand at the periphery. Church sponsored educational institutions speak for themselves, as there are separate special schools for the handicapped; for instance, Kaimosi Friends Special School. These are a few examples that can be mentioned from the many that could be in existence. In this case, there seem to be long-held worldviews that contribute to the differentiation of those living with disability. It means the practicing of Christian faith in the African context, especially in Quakerism, concerning disability issues has to be analysed. Therefore, in this chapter, I explore matters touching on hermeneutical principles, theological reflection, the role of the church, and ministerial formation as I evaluate the African Quaker experience concerning disability issues.

Hermeneutical Principles

The premise of hermeneutics is to interpret the Scripture correctly. One important thing to note here is that the centrality of Scripture among most African Quakers is inescapable. In the *Christian Faith and Practice* document in the Friends United Meeting in East Africa in Richmond declaration of faith, it is noted that "the Scriptures are the only divinely authorized record of the doctrines which we are bound, as Christians to accept, and of the moral principles which

DOI: 10.4324/9780429030925-45

are to regulate our actions."[1] Anything going wrong on the handling of disability issues may as well depend on the interpretation of Scripture.

In the community I come from, you will hear statements such as *fulfilling the law* in affirming certain practices that are otherwise questionable. A close look at this, you will notice that it emanates from the close relationship of cultural practices recorded in the Bible with that of Africans. One of the scriptural references usually used to defend this is that Jesus did not come to destroy the law but to fulfill it (Matt. 5:17, NRSV). It means practicing handed-down teachings and a way of life laid down in the traditions.

Such a view is misguided according to Jesus' words recorded in the Gospel of Mark:

> ' "in vain do they worship me, teaching precepts as doctrines". You abandon the commandment of God in order to keep your tradition!' Then he said to them, 'You have a fine way of rejecting the commandment of God in order to keep your tradition!'
>
> *(Mk. 7:7–9)*

Being a Christian requires following Jesus' way, which is not an easy task. Quakers hold to being friends with Jesus in obeying his commandment (Jn. 15:14). It requires hearkening to the promptings of the voice of God recorded in Scripture and acting upon it.

Fulfilling the law is relatively summarized in Jesus' answer to the question related to fulfilling the *greatest law*; " 'Love the Lord your God with all your heart, and with all your soul, and with all your mind.' This is the greatest and first commandment. And a second is like it: 'You shall love your neighbor as yourself'" (Matt. 22:37b–39). Cultural practices that are affirmed contrary to obeying these two great commandments are questionable. Seeing disability as a bad omen or even as evil or originating from sin has to be reanalysed. It is not just a matter of *fulfilling the law*.

A clear distinction in having Quaker hermeneutics is as asserted by Pyper that "the word is to be lived out. Again, this is to be found in Quaker writings on the Scriptures."[2] The fact that the right interpretation is necessary; *living out the word* is crucial to Quakers. It simply translates to letting your life speak. Otherwise, there is no way of birthing the embodiment of that which is recorded in Scripture as manifested in Jesus Christ.

Towards a Theological Reflection

The short hermeneutical reflection explored above is deliberate in transitioning towards the theological reflection that will follow. The role of the Bible in doing theology is vital in studying African Christian Quaker theology. The need for Christian theology, in general, is to allow Christ to speak to the lives of African Quakers and their theology. It is a replica of George Fox's great transformation in which Jesus Christ spoke to his condition. In the Journal of George Fox it is recorded,

> And when all my hopes in them and in all men were gone, so that I had nothing outwardly to help me, nor could tell what to do, then, Oh then, I heard a voice which said, 'There is one, even Christ Jesus, that can speak to thy condition', and when I heard it my heart did leap for joy.[3]

In this experience, a turnaround of events on the role of the Bible and doing theology developed. That is the primacy of the Spirit in revealing that which Christ was teaching through the Bible became vital. In every way, this has to be embraced in developing an authentic Christian Quaker doctrine in Africa.

Disability is part of life, and it is a reality to grapple with theologically, more so in an African Christian Quaker context. It is necessary to give space for this in every doctrine of Christian Quaker faith and practice to reveal God in Jesus Christ to humanity. In every perspective of doctrine, then it should be centered in understanding the role of Christ in them. At times, this can be a struggle, especially in changing worldviews or traditions that are destructively rooted in how Christianity is practiced in the African Quaker context founded in the Bible and the African religion.

Therefore, a living Christian faith must adequately address disability issues in propagating what is right. Oduyoye says, "A living Christian faith in Africa cannot but interact with African culture."[4] Allowing Christian faith to interact faithfully with African culture genuinely and truthfully is needful in changing assumptions about disability. In this sense, there is a need to revisit the real essence of Christian faith in practices that are both informed by African culture and Christianity influenced by Jewish culture and other inherent cultures in the history of the church. African Quakerism, then, needs to bridge the gap in doing theology that creates normalcy on the view about disability. Concerning this, what follows is just but a primer in briefly looking at theological discourse about God, human being, sin and evil.

God

Practices of the adherents of both African and Christian religions attest to setting aside of the disabled in society. For instance, in the African religion, the association of disabled with bad omen and the seclusion of the disabled in worship places unfolds a God who rejects a group of people with special needs.

Bringing into the scene a God who values and embraces the rejected is to analyse the revelation of God in Jesus Christ. Understanding God in this manner brings sense to those at the periphery of the society as inclusive in God's creation. The evidence that is shaped by Jesus' ministry here on earth changes the whole perception of the concept of God. A particular example is how Jesus responds to the leper who was set at the periphery of the society. The leper begs Jesus to make him clean, and he does, and the man is healed of leprosy (Mk. 1:40–45).

Seeing God through this act constructs a view that makes those who seem to be rejected to have a chance to be accepted both by God and human beings. The rituals enforced for the lepers conditioned a life that was not valuable in the eyes of God. It created a worldview that made the society reject the lepers. This was done in the name of religion. Seemingly this informed a deficient concept of God. It may apply to the developed worldviews that could be inherent in practicing Christian faith, especially in the African Quaker context that needs to be revisited in clarifying the concept of God.

A familiar reference used by Quakers is that God does not show partiality. It is recorded, "There is no longer Jew or Greek, there is no longer slave or free, there is no longer male and female; for all of you are one in Christ Jesus" (Gal. 3:28). To know that all are one in God who is revealed in Christ revitalizes the essence of valuing one another. In turn, the disability issue would get a new face in being included and integrated fully into society.

Human Being

From a Christian perspective, a human being is a creation of God. In the story of creation, the human being is the last creature to be created by God (Gen. 1:26–27). The uniqueness of humanity is the fact that we are created in the image of God. Migliore underscores this by noting that, "I would contend that the symbol "image of God" describes human life in relationship with God and with other creatures. . . . To be human is to live freely and gladly in relationships of mutual respect and love."[5]

Being human is relating to fellow human beings in mutual respect and love. It clearly defines what it means in being created in the image of God. As Quakers say, it is to see that of God in every human being. There is a famous saying that at times a human being is referred to as a beast. When this happens, the aspect of being human is relegated to being more of an animal that can even devour a fellow human being. This is the picture that is created when human beings do not respect and love each other.

In doing this, the mistreated person's life is affected. They are not allowed to live life to the fullest as intended by God. This happens a lot in day-to-day life. It has happened along in history, and there have been many questions raised about the 'other' human being considered to be different. This could be because of situations that might be deemed as unworthy. It may as well apply to where those living with disability are treated differently.

The intention of God's revelation in Jesus Christ about being human is reflected in how human beings relate to each other. This has to translate into experiencing the new life as intended by God through Jesus Christ. Copeland points to the Eucharist as the constructive proposal of the body, race, and being, which is not far from the disability issue, denoting human solidarity. Jesus calls for *communion with all, especially those who are stigmatized in society*.[6]

In the act of fellowship, where gathering or inward communion happens in the presence of God, as Quakers would put it, human solidarity can be the greatest gift to those living with disabilities. It is the beginning step in transforming defective worldviews. It requires us to be able to reach the essence of what a human being is as revealed in Jesus Christ.

As human beings gather in every aspect of life, Christ has to be experienced in how they view each other. This clearly defines what it means in being created in the image of God. As Quakers say, it is to see that of God in every human being. No one should feel different from the other. It translates to embodying the value of equality among Quakers. Therefore, there is a need for African Christian Quakers to continue discerning who we are as human beings, correcting misperceptions in repentance, and learning how to appreciate each other. Cooper notes:

> Everyone was believed to be precious in the sight of God because everyone was created in the image of God. In the twentieth century this same concept has been expressed in the phrase 'that of God in everyone', which we have indicated before was Fox's way of declaring the worth and dignity, as well as the divine capacity, present in all persons.[7]

Sin and Evil

The relationship of disability to sin and evil or bad omens has to be thought through carefully. Both Christian and African religions have some history of connecting disability with sin or evil. The Christian understanding of sin and evil emanates from the fall of Adam in the Garden of Eden. Kamitsuka and others explain that the story of Adam and Eve has two underlying points that are deeply embedded in Christian religious imagination. It includes human free will choice and our choices that violate God's law.[8]

In African religion, the concept of sin is not so clear, but evil is connected to unseen powers that are against the good. O'Donovan observes, "As many Africans know, evil spirits threaten men with sickness, tragedy and other punishments if they do not obey them."[9] In a tier to this, Pobee explains that "in other words, evil is the confluence of anger from the spirit-world and man's waywardness."[10] There is a feeling in both contexts that in a given situation in life, such as disability, it can easily be looked as determined by what kind of choice is made concerning obeying or disobeying God's will. In these views, therefore, it is assumed that if one obeys, then nothing bad should happen, or evil should not exist.

This creates difficulty in explaining the cause of some things in life in both the Christian and African contexts. What is to be drawn here is the obedience to power beyond human reach has a more significant part in given situations in life. As Christianity comes on stage, it seems Africans had already a way of figuring out the cause of evil. The act of personal choice and the demand of God's law heightens the assumption that disobeying God is the cause of evil. This becomes a dilemma, especially when thinking about disability, which is viewed as bad omen or evil to some extent.

Kabue explains:

> Throughout history, disabilities have been commonly seen as acts of a vengeful God. In a world in which real or imagined sin abound, the emergence of a child with a disability in a family was regarded as a punishment for sin.[11]

The problem with this kind of worldview is that it refrains from seeking further any other possible causes of some situations in life. This can be ruinous to the many precious lives of people struggling to understand their life circumstances. It is necessary to look deeper into the problem of sin and evil and its relation to disability.

A good example that is used by many is the one recorded in John 9:1–5, where the disciples ask Jesus whether blindness was caused by sin. Jesus, as the light of the world, unfolds a new way of looking at those living with disability in connection with sin and evil. Quakerism vehemently acclaims to embody this in the practice of faith as children of light. I mean this is as a bridge to use as an African Quaker in exemplifying this principle to the world.

There is a need to critically look into the concept of disability and sin with Jesus' teachings. While doing this, there is also a need to understand that living with informed assumptions can be ruinous. Working on pulling down cultural assumptions and rethinking on the long-held worldviews can be a great step of success. In a very simple way, being bound in the status quo can be one of the greatest sins so far. The disabled are not the sinners; those who differentiate them are sinning. It is necessary to go a step ahead in working on this deficiency that is explicit in the way most African Christian Quakers have lived.

Role of the Friends Church

As a move to push for the necessary changes, there should be reinforcement, especially within the Quaker Church in Africa and the whole world about disability issues. I once shared with one official of one of the yearly meetings in Kenya, and he told me they have in their vision a policy document advocating for the needs of the disabled. This is the way to go. Having the Church as the voice of the voiceless is what Christ intended.

Kabue's words are of significance to the church as observed in his presentation to a conference on World Mission and Evangelism:

> The church is, by definition, a place and a process of communion, open to and inviting all people without discrimination. It is a place of hospitality and a place of welcome, in the manner that Abraham and Sarah received God's messengers in the Old Testament (Gen. 18). . . . It is a community of people with different yet complementary gifts. St Paul reminds us: "For as in one body we have many members, and not all

members have the same function, so we, though we are many, are one body in Christ, and individually we are members one of another."[12]

Valuing and accepting each other as members of the church is as well as sharing the Gospel. It is about these actions that reveal God in Jesus Christ to the whole humanity and the creation. Rising to this occasion should be the regular call of the church.

Other important ways Friends churches can have an impact is through theological education and training of ministers. Theological colleges should lead by example in embracing in their curriculums the concerns about disability issues. An example of this is while serving at Friends Theological College, Kaimosi, Kenya, I had the opportunity to participate in a theology workshop on disability under the World Council of Churches organized by Ecumenical Disability Advocates Network (EDAN). As representatives of the Association of Theological Institutions in East Africa, we prepared a draft curriculum for disability studies that I hope someday will be implemented.

Another example is as part of ministerial formation; in their studies, Friends Theological College students get to serve in one of the Friends special schools. This is one way of including in the curriculum a means by which Church leadership formation embraces the concerns of disability issues. Disability issues discussion forum should also be formed among the Quakers to see how theological engagement can take place and see the way forward in Africa and the whole world.

Notes

1 Friends United Meeting in East Africa, *Christian Faith and Practice*, p. 30.
2 Pyper, 'A Quaker Hermeneutic', p. 66.
3 Fox, *The Journal of George Fox*, p. 11.
4 Oduyoye, 'African Religious Beliefs and Practices', p. 110.
5 Migliore, *Faith Seeking Understanding*, p. 122.
6 Copeland, 'Constructive Proposal: Body', p. 109.
7 Cooper, *A Living Faith,* p. 110.
8 Kamitsuka, 'Sin and Evil', p. 126.
9 O'Donovan, *Biblical Christianity*, p. 193.
10 Pobee, *Toward an African Theology*, p. 100.
11 Kabue, *Disability, Society, and Theology*, p. 11.
12 Kabue, 'Ecumenical Disability Advocates', p. 5.

Bibliography

Cooper, W. A., *A living faith: An historical study of Quaker beliefs* (Richmond, IN: Friends United Press, 1990).

Copeland, M. S., 'Constructive proposal: Body, race, and being', in *Constructive theology: A contemporary approach to classical themes,* ed. Serene Jones and Paul Lakeland (Minneapolis: Fortress Press, 2005).

Fox, G., *The journal of George Fox: A revised edition.* ed. John L. Nickalls. Cambridge Library Collection – Religion (Cambridge: Cambridge University Press, 2010, doi:10.1017/CBO9780511710971.).

Friends United Meeting in East Africa, *Christian faith and practice in the Friends church* (Kenya, Kisumu: National Printing Press, 2002).

Kabue S., 'Ecumenical disability advocates network, A programme of the World Council of Churches: Addressing Disability in a healing and Reconciling Community', in *Come holy spirit-heal and reconcile: Called in Christ to be reconciling and healing communities,* Plen 11 May Doc No 1 – Disability – Sam Kabue (Switzerland, Geneva: World Council of Churches, 11 May 2005), 5. Accessed December 11, 2019. https://www.oikoumene.org/en/resources/documents/other-meetings/mission-and-evangelism/plen-11-may-doc-no-1-disability-sam-kabue

Kabue, S., *Disability, society, and theology: Voices from Africa* (Limuru, Kenya: Zapf Chancery Publishers Africa Ltd, 2011), 11.

Kamitsuka, M. D. et al., 'Sin and evil', in *Constructive theology: A contemporary approach to classical themes,* ed. Serene Jones and Paul Lakeland (Minneapolis: Fortress Press, 2005).

Migliore, D. L., *Faith seeking understanding: An introduction to Christian theology* (Grand Rapids, MI: William B. Eerdmans, 1991).

O'Donovan, W., *Biblical Christianity in African perspective* (SIM-USA: Oasis International Limited, 1997).

Oduyoye, M. A., 'The value of African religious beliefs and practices for Christian theology', in *African theology enroute,* ed. Kofi Appiah-Kubi and Sergio Torres (New York: Orbis Books, 1979).

Pobee, J. S., *Toward an African theology* (Nashville: Abingdon Press, 1979).

Pyper, H. S., 'Can there be a Quaker hermeneutic', in *Quaker religious thought vol. 97, article 10* (2001). http digitalcommons.georgefox.edu/qrt/vol97/iss1/10://

42

REPRESENTATIONS OF QUAKERS IN TELEVISION AND FILM

An Overview

Stephen D. Brooks

At first glance it would appear that representations of Quakers in the mediums of film and television are sparingly few. Indeed during his conclusion to *Celluloid Friends: Cinematic Friends, Real and Imagined (1922–2012)*, film reviewer David N. Butterworth (2015) writes: "Rebuked, ridiculed and regularly misunderstood, Friends have seen limited screen time over the years" (Butterworth, 2015, p. 55).

In his study, Butterworth reviews twenty-two films that either have a significant Quaker character or some reflection on Quakerism. He also mentions a further twenty-seven motion pictures or television programmes that have secondary or walk-on characters who can be identified as Quaker. These include silent-era features and shorts, plus those that use Quakers to provide one-liners and jokes, such as Woody Allen's *Sleeper* (1973):

> Miles Monroe (played by Allen): "I'm telling you. You got the wrong man. I'm not the heroic type. Really. I was beaten up by Quakers".
>
> *(Monroe, 1973)*

This chapter is an overview that will build on the aforementioned work by Butterworth and also that of James Emmett Ryan's *Imaginary Friends, Representing Quakers in American Culture, 1650–1950* by discussing films and then consequently television programmes from 1900 to the present day.

To achieve this, I firstly cross-referenced Butterworths' forty-nine films with the web-based resource the Internet Movie Database (IMDb) and self-compiled lists put together by Quakers online. These were the "Friends Media Project", "Quakers on Film" from Pendlehill.org and the Michiganquaker.org entry of "Quakers in Popular Culture". By doing so, I identified at least 171 examples of Quakers either portrayed or mentioned in either a film or television programme.

By looking at the number of films or television programmes in which Quakers are represented by decade from the beginning of the twentieth century until the present day, five distinct periods can therefore be surmised found. These are 1900–1919 and the beginnings of cinema as a popular form of entertainment, with a peak of portrayals in the 1910s; a lull throughout the 1920s and '30s as cinemas moves from silent to sound; a continuing rise from the 1940s, '50s and

DOI: 10.4324/9780429030925-46

'60s as television becomes dominant over moviegoing; a further decline in the 1970s and '80s before a final rise in representations that has continued to increase over the past three decades.

It will be a discussion of these phases that will form the structure of this overview in order to answer the following questions. What kind of cinematic short hands are employed to denote that a character is in fact a Quaker? Do these portrayals conform to an overriding story arc or set pattern within each narrative? In which genres do depictions of Quakers appear? And finally, what has changed in these characterisations over the course of time?

The first instance I have found of a representation of Quakers was in a very short silent, *Topsy-Turvy Dance of Three Quaker Maidens* (1902), which was about a quarter reel in length. The terms "reel" and "reels" were used during the early formative years of cinema to denote a film's length rather than a given time, as is common today. This is due the fact that there was no uniformity in the size of the gauge of the physical film or the projection equipment, which meant the speed that films were played at could vary (Bowser, 1994, p. 139). The advent of sound, which needed to be played at 24 frames per second to function properly meant that consistency and standardization of both production of and the playback of the film reel was required. Thus the "talkies" began to be measured in minutes.

The British Film Institute (BFI) lists *Topsy-Turvy Dance of Three Quaker Maidens* (1902) as being made and directed in Brighton by George Albert Smith, along with the following synopsis:

> Three girls in Quaker costume dance before an American flag held by two male attendants. They retire behind the flag and apparently dance with their legs in the air; the dance is repeated, but this time the flag is dropped, and the girls are seen to be holding dummy legs. Two of the girls make their exit, leaving the leader holding a pair of legs. She then makes her exit.
>
> *(National Film Archive, 1966, p. 75)*

The visual signifier of definable Quaker dress is also apparent in the following description of another very early one-reel feature from the United States, *A Quaker Dance* (1903):

> A Quaker and his dame are seen in their own peculiar style. They are dressed in the usual Quaker garb. Broadbrim and wife appear to enjoy themselves. This is a subject you don't see every day.
>
> *(Internet Movie Database, 2021)*

In both these cases, which are comedies, characters are identifiable to the audience as Quakers because of their attire. This becomes by far the principal trope of depicting Quakers during not only the silent era but also well into the mid-twentieth century and beyond. Portrayals of Quaker women and girls routinely consist of plain, simple dresses accompanied with aprons and bonnets. Quaker men and boys are also depicted in plain clothes topped with black wide-brimmed hats, hence the slang expression "Broadbrim" in the film outline above. However, historically speaking, by the time cinema arrived plain-style dress was not the norm amongst real-life Quakers, yet it had become a recognisable stereotype. This is due in some part to the creation of the Quaker Oats company logo. Designed in 1877, it showed a full-length picture of a Quaker man based upon depictions of William Penn, sometimes holding a scroll with the word "Pure" written on it. Despite some alterations over the years, the artwork used by the Quaker Oats company, which has no connection to Quakers or Quakerism, has stuck in the public's imagination as epitomising how a member of The Religious Society of Friends should appear. Moreover, the popular use of stock Quaker characters in nineteenth-century American theatre would persevere, as James Emmett Ryan writes:

> Attention to Quaker theatricality persisted in the twentieth century. Much of this attention appeared in the observations of writers and illustrators who detailed – either for serious or comic effect – the "peculiarity" of a sect that dressed austerely and produced an aesthetic for domestic life reflecting the otherworldliness of their spiritual values.
>
> *(Ryan, 2009, pp. 202–203)*

During the 1910s there is a sharp rise in Quaker characters seen on screen. It is relatively straightforward therefore to suggest that this was partly because cinema itself was becoming more established as a form of entertainment, and that many of these features were reproductions of stage performances in which Quakers were already depicted, consequently continuing the visual shorthand of Quaker costume and mannerisms. Story arcs tended to evoke the otherworldliness, innocence and naivety of Quakers in the real world; this trope has persisted right up to the present day. Female Quakers also tended to fall into two main character types: either that of "severe Aunts" who adhere to the older traditions, as in *Beauty's Worth* (1922), or younger, more innocent girls who become the object of desire for non-Quaker worldly wise and often violent men. As with the plain-dress stereotype, these depictions once established continue into the sound era.

Almost all the thirty-three films made in the silent era (1900–1928) that had representations of Quakers in them are divided between two main genres: drama and comedy. According to the IMDb, exceptions to this were *The Little Quakeress* (1912) as a romance; *Down to the Sea in Ships* (1922) as an adventure and *When Uncle Sam Was Young* (1912), *The Quakeress* (1913) and *Abide With Me* (1914) as westerns. Using IMDb to identify film or television programmes into categories of genre brings with it a level of consistency; however, it should be noted that the IMDb definitions are by no means infallible; for example, until recently, *High Noon* (1952) was shown as an action drama thriller but not as a western, the label it is most often given. Nevertheless, for the purposes of this chapter, the IMDb definitions do show the range of material that Quakers have appeared in as characters, plot devices or reference points.

With the advent of sound, there appears to be a lull in the number of Quakers portrayed on film, with just five occurrences between 1929 and 1939. However, this period does see the first movie not created in either the United States or the United Kingdom. This is the Indian-produced comedy *Rajat Jayanti* (1939), in which the Quaker character is a swindler who deceives the lead character Rajat's guardian. Of course, sound does bring with it the other major trope or signifier to state that a character is a Quaker, that of plain speech. This indicator is used primarily to introduce the Quaker character both to another character that is not a Friend and to the audience. Usually by the non-Quaker asking about the use of "thee" and "thou" in a sentence, for example when John Wayne's outlaw Quirt Evans, who has been nursed back to health from gunshot wounds by a Quaker family, inquires just that of the family's adolescent daughter Penny Worth (Gail Russell) in *Angel and the Badman* (1947).

Quirt: Do all you people from Pennsylvania talk like that?
Penny: Like what?
Quirt: Thee?
Penny: Oh, we're Friends.
Quirt: Friends of who?
Penny: Of all. The Society of Friends. Many people call us Quakers.

(Evans and Worth, 1947)

The stereotypes of plain dress and/or plain speech continue to be prevalent in the increased presence of Quaker characters during the period 1940–1969. This rise in depictions can almost be certainly attributed to the number of westerns in which Quakers appeared. This is especially true in the 1950s and '60s, as television began to overtake cinema in the volume of representations of Quakers, with serials such as *Gunsmoke, Wagon Train* and *Bonanza* becoming ever more popular. The aural sign of someone being identified as a Quaker as illustrated above can also be found in an episode of the television western series *The Restless Gun*, called "Take Me Home". The audience discovers that saloon girl Lee Laney (Mala Powers) is actually the long-lost daughter of a Quaker couple by her reaction to lead character Vint Bonner (John Payne) discussing meeting "some folks" with a strange way of talking.

So far, we have seen Quakers identified by their austere clothing or somewhat antiquated speech. However, an interesting question arises if we consider why Quakers are repeatedly used around this time, especially in westerns. Quakers, particularly female Quakers, I would argue, are used in westerns as a pacifying or restraining counterpoint to the gun-wielding archetype of the Wild West cowboy. They are often shown as schoolteachers such as Annie Morgan (Loretta Young) in *The Lady From Cheyenne* (1941) or missionaries akin to Patience Miller (Rhoda Fleming) in *Wagon Train: The Patience Miller Story* (1961). In the two cases above, the men of violence, a con man in the former and an Arapaho warrior in the latter, eventually desist from their natural tendencies and bend to the peaceful will of the Quaker character. However, these are exceptions not the rule. Quakers' pacifism was acknowledged, that is true, but only in the sense that this leaves them ill-equipped to survive the harshness of life in the Old West. The best-known example of this is Fred Zinneman's *High Noon* (1952). Here, the Quaker character Amy Kane (Grace Kelly) tries to persuade her husband Will Kane (Gary Cooper) through her conviction to non-violence to depart from the town of Hadleyville, where he has just retired as sheriff and they have married, before his nemesis Frank Miller arrives upon the noonday train. Will Kane refuses, with Amy finally succumbing to violence herself to shoot one of Miller's men in the back to save Will.

Gary Cooper also starred in William Wyler's *Friendly Persuasion* (1956). Based on the novel of the same name by Jessamyn West, *Friendly Persuasion* depicts a Kansas Quaker community caught up in the American Civil War. Again the devices of plain dress and plain speaking are used to denote that Jess Birdwell (Cooper) and his family are Quakers, verbal confirmation coming from Jess when he is asked to explain his use of "thee" and "thou" by travelling organ salesman Professor Quigley (Walter Catlett). *Friendly Persuasion* is notable for its scene of silent worship in the Birdwells' local Quaker Meeting, and although a number of scenes use Quakers' austere nature for laughs, Butterworth does describe it as one interpretation that "*does* paint one of the better portraits of Quaker life" (Butterworth, 2015, p. 30).

The decline in popularity of the television western throughout the 1970s and '80s is also reflected in the drop in number of portrayals of Quakers over this period. During the past three decades, however, the use of Quaker characters has risen dramatically. While television is still the dominant medium, it is worth noting that technological developments have resulted in not only increased channels for watching but also the means to (e.g., digital formats and online streaming). This has led to a shift away from the traditional fictional genres with Quakers in them (comedy, drama, romance and the western) to not only non-fiction genres (biography, documentary and history) but also others including reality TV, musicals, thrillers, crime and even science fiction.

Common tropes continue to be employed as confirmation of Quakerism in more recent representations. For example, the TV movie *A Prayer in the Dark* (1997), which takes place in a Quaker community in modern-day upstate New York, opens with the juxtaposition of a frantic prison break with that of the calmness of a silent Quaker Meeting. Those at the meeting are dressed in plain but twentieth-century clothing. The matriarch of the group, Emily Hayworth (Linda Carter), often quotes biblical text but does not use plain language in her everyday speech.

Male plain dress, in particular the Broadbrim image, appears in Martin McDonagh's *Seven Psychopaths* (2012) in the episode of a silent Quaker father (Harry Dean Stanton) who pursues his daughter's killer not just through life but eventually into death. One noticeable change in depictions of Quakers is that modern Quakers are shown to be Quakers by convincement rather than by birth. In the previously discussed westerns *Angel and the Badman, Wagon Train, The Patience Miller Story* and *The Restless Gun*: "Take Me Home", the leading female Quaker characters are all birthright Quakers. Of course, the exception at that time was Amy Kane in *High Noon*, who was convinced to become a Quaker after experiencing the trauma of seeing her father and brother murdered. Amy's backstory foreshadows contemporary interpretations, such as that of Jennifer Neal (Jenny Bacon) in the *Law & Order Special Victims Unit* episode "Limitations" (2000) and Lucy Canonbury (Lesley Sharp) in the British television series *Paranoid* (2016), who both find solace in Quaker communities after being sexual assault victims. In both these depictions, the characters confirm themselves to be Quakers to law enforcement officers, in "Limitations", Jennifer's Quakerism is seen as an obstruction to the arrest of the main suspect, whereas Lucy in *Paranoid* becomes key to solving the crime through her developing friendship with police detective Bobby Day (Robert Glenister). By the end of the series, Detective Day has joined Lucy at her local Quaker Meeting.

Interestingly, the final two portrayals of Quaker of the 2010s bring us full circle back to comedy as with our first two examples from the 1900s. These are the British TV serials *Catastrophe* and *Fleabag*. Both use the Quaker Meeting for comic effect. In *Catastrophe*, the lead character Rob Norris (Rob Delaney) enjoys his first experience of a Quaker Meeting, in particular the silence, and so he continues to attend hoping that Friends will be able to help him in overcoming his alcoholism. Unfortunately, Rob becomes irritated at the Quakers placidity in response to his questions over whether they feel angry at the world situation. He then stands and leaves the Meeting with the line, "I'm quitting . . . and erm, I'm not saying that you guys should quit . . . but . . . you should have a plan . . . in case . . . you get into power" (Norris, 2019).

Similarly, *Fleabag* finds comedy in the silence of a Meeting which Fleabag finds "very, very erotic", leading her to minister with the first thought that comes into her head, "I sometimes worry that I wouldn't be such a feminist if I had bigger tits" (Fleabag, 2019).

Writing in the *i* newspaper, Holly Williams reflects on these episodes and finds that the producers treat Quakerism with a respect not necessarily shown when comedy targets faith groups. She writes, "crucially, they don't just sneer, and it feels significant that we're seeing people genuinely turning toward religion as they try to make sense of life" (Williams, 2019).

In conclusion, cinematic shorthands employed to denote that a character is in fact a Quaker tend to be imagery that the audience is familiar with, such as plain dress, vocalisation through plain speaking, or through locale such as a Quaker Meeting. In addition to these factors, a verbal confirmation from the Quaker character is applied, especially in those cases where plain dress or plain speech are not immediately obvious.

Although portrayals of Quakers no longer conform to an overriding story arc or set pattern within each narrative in the strictest sense, there is still an element that Quakers are seen as outside the mainstream world that the other characters, particularly the protagonist, inhabit. However, it can be said that the modern depictions of Quakers are based on a more realistic interpretation of contemporary liberal Quakerism. Whether this is due to wider knowledge of The Religious Society of Friends among writers, actors or the audience is certainly something which deserves greater examination.

Biography

Abide with Me. 1914 [Film] unknown dir. USA. St. Louis Motion Picture Company.

Angel and the Badman. 1947 [Film] James Edward Grant dir. Republic Pictures. John Wayne Productions.

A Prayer in the Dark. 1997 [TV Movie] Jerry Ciccoritti dir. Power Pictures. Dover Road Productions. Wilshire Court Productions.

A Quaker Dance. 1903 [Film] Seigmund Lubin dir. USA. The Lubin Manufacturing Company.

Beauty's Worth. 1922 [Film] Robert G. Vignola dir. USA. Cosmopolitan Productions.

Bowser, Eileen. 1994. *The Transformation of Cinema 1907–1915 History of the American Cinema Vol. 2* General Editor Charles Harpole. Berkeley, Los Angeles, London, University of California Press.

Butterworth, David N. 2015. *Celluloid Friends: Cinematic Quakers Real and Imagined (1922–2012)*. USA, Amazon Press LLC.

Catastrophe. 2019 [TV] Jim O'Hanlon dir. UK. Avalon Television. Merman. Birdbath Productions.

Down to the Sea in Ships. 1922 [Film] Elmer Clifton dir. USA. The Whaling Film Corporation.

Evans, Q. and Worth, P. 1947. *Angel and the Badman*. 1947 [Film] James Edward Grant dir. Republic Pictures. John Wayne Productions.

Fleabag. 2019. [TV] Harry Bradbeer dir. UK. Two Brothers Pictures.

Fleabag. *Fleabag*. 2019. [TV] BBCTV Series 2. Episode 4. Harry Bradbeer dir. UK. Two Brothers Pictures.

Friendly Persuasion. 1956 [Film] William Wyler dir. USA. Allied Artists Pictures. B-M Pictures.

High Noon. 1952 [Film] Fred Zimmerman dir. USA. Stanley Kramer Productions.

Internet Movie Database (IMDb). 2021. Website. https://www.imdb.com/title/tt0423018/?ref_=fn_al_tt_1 Accessed 29/05/2020

Lady From Cheyenne, The. 1941 [Film] Frank Lloyd dir. USA. Frank Lloyd Productions. Universal Pictures.

Law and Order: Special Victims Unit. Limitations. 2000 [TV] Constantine Makris dir. USA. Wolf Films. Studios USA Television. Universal Worldwide Television.

Little Quakeress, The. 1912 [Film] unknown dir. USA. Majestic.

Monroe, M. 1973. *Sleeper*. 1973 [Film] Woody Allen dir. USA. Jack Rollins & Charles H. Joffe Productions.

National Film Archive. 1966. National Film Archive catalogue. Pt.3, Silent fiction films, 1895–1930 / foreword by J.B. Priestley.

Norris, R. 2019. *Catastrophe*. 2019 [TV] Jim O'Hanlon dir. UK. Avalon Television. Merman. Birdbath Productions.

Paranoid. 2016. [TV] Bill Gallagher creator. UK. Red Production Company.

Quakeress, The. 1913 [Film] Raymond B. West dir. USA. Broncho Film Company.

Rajat Jayanti. 1939 [Film] P.C. Barua dir. India. New Theatres Limited.

Restless Gun, The: Take Me Home. December 1958. [TV] Edward Ludwig dir. USA. Window Glen Productions.

Ryan, James Emmett. 2009. *Imaginary Friends: Representing Quakers in American Culture 1650–1950. Studies in American Thought and Culture*. Series editor Paul S. Boyer. Madison, WI, The University of Wisconsin Press.

Seven Psychopaths. 2012 [Film] Martin McDonagh / Christopher Walken / Sam Rockwell / Woody Harrelson / Abbie Cornish dirs. UK/USA. Blueprint Films.

Sleeper. 1973 [Film] Woody Allen dir. USA. Jack Rollins & Charles H. Joffe Productions.

Topsy-Turvy Dance of Three Quaker Maidens. 1902 [Film] George Albert Smith dir. UK. George Albert Smith Films.

Wagon Train: The Patience Miller Story. January 1961 [TV] Mitch Leisen dir. USA. Revue Studios.

When Uncle Sam Was Young. 1912 [Film] Frank E. Montgomery dir. USA. Bison Motion Pictures.

Williams, Holly. 2019. *Catastrophe and Fleabag Have Caught on to the Comedic Potential of the Quaker Meeting*. Opinion 29.03.2019 The i Newspaper. website. Accessed 30/05/20

43

QUAKERS WILL SOON ENGROSS THE WHOLE TRADE OF THE KINGDOM

Michael Dutch

One may be surprised to learn that a 1681 warning that Quakers will "in short time engross the whole trade of the kingdom in their hands" (Thirsk & Cooper, 1972, p. 394) almost came true. At one time, members of the Society, consisting of perhaps 1% of the population of England, may have controlled 60% of that economy (King, 2014, p. 109).

History shows that Quaker beliefs and large-scale business are, or at least were, not only compatible but complementary and that the early Quaker psyche may have even enabled the emergence of modern capitalism (Ingle, 1994, p. 3). The Quaker application of capitalism, however, stands distinct from today's in that it was self-limited.

A Brief Review of the Early Quaker Thoughts on Trade

In the mid-1600s, those that would become known as Quakers rejected the State Church of England and the various other nonconformist religious movements of the day. The "genius" of Quakerism is said to be its simplicity, in the removal of potential substitutes for God, including sacraments, liturgy, creed, and the Bible (Yount, 2007, p. xxii). This simplicity produced an action-oriented Quaker business "code" that transcended the faith and is equally applicable in a secular setting.

George Fox on Business

George Fox, commonly taken as the founder of Quakerism, grew up with commerce. His father was a successful weaver, with two looms in the house. At the appropriate age, he was sent off to apprentice as a shoemaker and shepherd. Fox took pride in his business acumen, boasting that as an apprentice, he was able to make a substantial profit for his master without misleading or mistreating customers. He viewed his contribution as so impactful that he bragged that his master's business failed after his departure (Ingle, 1994). Fox saw the use of deceit as a common practice in the marketplace and addressed this behavior in a 1649 journal entry underscoring the absolute requirement for honesty (Grubb, 1929, p. 107). A version of the integrity phraseology, "let their yea be yea and their nay be nay," is found in virtually all early Quaker writings concerning commerce.

DOI: 10.4324/9780429030925-47

In 1658 Fox again called for absolute integrity in business but also chided merchants for their outward signs of wealth while the poor were left unattended (Barbour & Roberts, 1973, p. 431). This warning was as much about a call for plainness and community as integrity. While Fox presented a harsh rebuke to deceitful business practices, it is important to note that he does not condemn business in general. Fox did point to problems with wealth accumulation; however, he appears to focus more on the methods used to achieve the wealth and the temptations it produces. In 1656, he warned that, in effect, the need for success in business could become all-consuming, causing one to lose themselves and their relationship to God (Fox, 1698, p. 102).

Being an "outsider" group, Fox could have guided Quakers to create a closed and separate community, but he wanted the Society to remain in the world. Fox saw that evil was in the heart of every man and that it could not be escaped simply by separating from the world (Birkel, 2004, p. 100). William Penn expressed a similar sentiment in 1669 when he advocated that God is best served when one does not turn from the world but remains in it addressing its problems (Penn, 1853, p. 61). We will see later in this chapter that Fox's advice for high integrity in business not only served the Society of Friends but also English society as a whole.

Other Serious Warnings

The earliest remaining record of Quaker Advices and Queries dates back to 1656 (Birkel, 2004, p. 100). This work provided specific directions for, among other topics, tradesmen. For this group, it required absolute honesty, the honoring of all obligations, and ideally being free of financial debts (Elders at Balby, 1656). The latter was a practical matter. Quakers still suffering from systematic oppression were smart not to invite more avenues of coercion.

Rigge wrote his "Brief and Serious Warning" in 1678. He pointed out poor behaviors that must be avoided but also seemed to endorse capitalism. He expressed his desire that those that behave righteously have lives of comfort and joy.

Numerous Epistles from the "First Establishment of the (London) Meeting" were gathered and published in 1821 (Friends Society of London Yearly Meeting, 1821). In this collection, a 1692 Epistle cautioned against taking debt that cannot be repaid on time and presented the need for advice and oversight by elders. Those that were new to trade, or needed to debt to trade, were expected to consult with the more experienced members of the meeting before starting their ventures. We see in a 1693 Epistle the danger of a single-minded pursuit of wealth but not the pursuit of wealth itself. John Barclay echoed that point. While pointing out business is "absolutely necessary," he cautioned against "gaining a worldly spirit, and of losing that tenderness of conscience, that love of religion, which is the ground of all virtuous conduct" (Barclay & Barclay, 1881, p. 26).

"Features" of Quakerism Supporting Commercial Success

The early Quaker condition, even absent any specific religious underpinnings, promoted commercial success. Government restrictions on occupations forced members into areas ripe for innovation. Their outsider status encouraged personal independence and interdependence within the Society. Aversion to debt default made it easier for Quakers to borrow money, and a desire for plainness freed funds for investment. Perhaps most importantly, self-policing of commerce and community oversight promoted and protected a Quaker brand.

Concentration of Talent

Quakers were initially prohibited from pursuing many professions by the Corporation Act of 1661, effectively pushing them into business. Even within this narrow domain, the group applied further restrictions.

Fox was firmly against drinking to excess. In 1682 he admonished the producers and sellers of wine and liquor, as they profit from and encourage overindulgence (Fox, 1831, p. 143). Quakers tolerated the sale of liquor only when "one believes it (will be used) in moderation, or medically, or on proper occasions" (Clarkson, 1806, p. 61).

Pacifism dictated that their business not support war-making. While this generally referred to the production of arms, it was not limited to such. The Clarks were criticized for producing sheepskin coats to keep soldiers of the English army from dying of cold during the Crimean War (Emden, 1940, p. 177).

In 1806, Clarkson offered a general description of what Friends found to be permissible areas of commerce. He stated that Quaker practice is not to sell things that by their very nature are evil, things that are fundamentally evil, and items that have explicitly been discarded because they were anti-Christian (Clarkson, 1806, p. 61). These self-imposed constraints did bar Friends from profitable areas of commerce but also served to reinforce the Quaker brand and perceptions of integrity. Ultimately, the constraint may have enhanced their financial positions.

Honesty Principle

Honest dealing became the hallmark of the Quaker brand. Since Friends would not "cozen" or deceive customers, they were safe to do business with. Quakers may have been the first to introduce the fixed-price methodology. Fox directed shopkeepers specifically not to "ask for things more than you will take" (Fox, 1831, p. 161).

Honesty also influenced views on debt. Quakers were morally accountable for debt repayment. This obligation remained as long as one was able to work. Even a legal discharge of debts did not forgive a Quaker's obligation for repayment. Members that refused to honor their debts were removed from the Society (Tolles, 1963, p. 74).

Simplicity or Plainness

The constraint in the pursuit of worldly things is a central tenet of Quakerism. John Barclay describes living in a simple manner as a "duty" (Barclay & Barclay, 1881, p. 12). Rigge in 1678 points to how the desire for worldly things can lead to dishonesty in trade, causing the ruin of oneself and a stain on the reputation of the Society (1771, pp. 4–5). It is interesting that Rigge mentions that a movement away from simplicity could damage the image of Quakers. One hundred years later, in 1782, the Philadelphia Meeting was still recording the need to protect the image of the Society (1999, p. 121). While the central message in these passages is a caution against excess, the protection of the Quaker "brand" that is also communicated was essential to the continued success of Quaker firms.

Plainness was promoted, but limits on wealth accumulation were not. Having enough was not a reason to slow down one's efforts, as doing a job well was a benefit in itself (Nevaskar, 1971, p. 129). The potential for accumulation of wealth and the constraint on its use allowed for investments in business and egalitarian activities that may otherwise not have been funded.

The Perceived Evil of Idleness

William Penn, the founder of his namesake British colony, unquestionably could have lived a life of leisurely idleness. Penn; however, saw idleness as against the faith. He questioned, "What poets, romances, comedies, and the like, did the apostles and saints make, or use to pass away their time withal?" (Penn, 1853, p. 233). Penn was less forceful than a 1676 "command." This directive characterized as unlawful such activities as games, sports, plays, and even laughing, as they were not Christian (Emden, 1940, p. 9).

Although Quakers saw an obligation to care for those less fortunate, they expected all that were able to work to do so. The Elders of Balby, drawing on a biblical passage (Thessalonians 3:10), advised that, after warning, those that were able to work but did not need not be provided for (Hamm, 2010, p. 67).

The Supply of Capital

Business success supplemented with Quaker probations on frivolous spending produced ready cash for investment and lending. The Quaker commitment to repay debts made borrowing money easier. Internal financing also helped create Quaker business relationships and networks, prompting more business opportunities.

Community Oversite and Networking

Meetings were called to be "properly watchful" over business activities and provided oversight and direction (Rigge, 1771, p. 15). Elders visited and counseled those suspected of not fulfilling their financial obligations. Business leaders were directed to reflect upon "Queries," which captured the Society's restrictions on business activities. Meeting oversight may have also served to reinforce that profitability was not the only metric of importance in commerce. Quakers found to be continually violating the Society's expectations of behavior were removed from membership.

Meetings also provided for non-judicial settlement of disputes through mediation and, ultimately, arbitration. This action served the Quaker disdain for the legal system (Tolles, 1963, pp. 73–77) but may have also produced better future relations than would be had after a legal settlement.

The community of Friends also provided seed money and supervision to its young members. Atkin, in 1660, describing the practices of Quakers, observed that young Quakers were offered interest-free loans, for a period, with which they could start their businesses (Atkin, 1660). However, funding came with "strings." Young business people were to be frequently counseled by more experienced members so that their exuberance did not lead them to overextend themselves (Elders at Balby, 1656).

Quaker oversight addressed a broader societal problem identified in 1650. It was said that naiveté in how to conduct commerce impacted the well-being of England itself (Thirsk & Cooper, 1972, p. 59). The meeting helped overcome this issue for society members, and the eventual scale of Quaker economic control no doubt benefited the nation as a whole.

Quaker oversight was not coercive but consultive. Quakers were just expected to help each other and promote each other's success (Walvin, 1997, p. 56).

Semi-separation

While Quakers wanted to be part of the world, they simultaneously remained notably separate behind their "sectarian hedge" (Birkel, 2004, p. 26). This semi-separation served both the spiritual and business health of the Society. Quakers were criticized for their preference for trading among themselves (Tolles, 1963, p. 89). Extending the quote in the opening of this chapter, "they only buy from their own tribe. . . . in a short time (Quakers will) engross the whole trade of the kingdom in their hands" (Thirsk & Cooper, 1972, p. 394). This preference to trade with other Quakers is understandable, perhaps for the same reasons that non-Quakers wanted to do so. Quaker views on honesty made transactions less risky than others. They also benefited from the supervision and mediation of the meeting. Perhaps most important, Quakers, through marriage, apprenticeships, and availability of business funding, had pre-established business networks.

Quaker dominance in commerce may have been a key factor in the Society's survival. In 1649 it was observed:

> If we [the nation-state of England] desire to be long free from the yoke of foreign dominion, and to enjoy that liberty . . . [[we must] seriously to inquire into all the ways and means, whereby trade and may be increased and multiplied unto the utmost.
>
> *(Thirsk & Cooper, 1972, p. 53).*

Quakers were an outsider group, a sub-society within a generally hostile country. Excelling in trade was a means for them to gain an increased measure of self-determination within the larger British society.

Education

Education and apprenticeships were critical factors in Quaker business success. Friends schools were needed, as Quaker children may have been excluded from public schools (Walvin, 1997, p. 37), and when they were allowed to attend, the education was not sufficiently reflective of Quaker beliefs and was seen as corrupting (Philadelphia Yearly Meeting, 1999, p. 113). Almost at its founding, the Society established a priority to set up meetings for worship, care for the imprisoned, and create schools. While the precise curriculum of early Quaker schools is unknown, education was to be useful. Learning was not merely for learning's sake. Early writings advised that the children of poor Friends should learn trades and business so that they may make comfortable earnings, and freed slaves and their children were to be educated so that they could be "useful members of civil society" (Philadelphia Yearly Meeting, 1999, p. 92).

Quakers continued the practice of apprenticeships that were common in the day. Those apprenticed within the Quaker system had little time outside of work for mischief and followed a strict code of behavior. This supervision not only allowed for the semi-separation but also may have allowed for a broad career planning methodology within the larger Society.

Quakers as Employers

Quaker beliefs impacted their treatment of workers. Quaker success was had, at least in part, due to hard work and long hours. Quakers saw value in work with a "bonus" benefit, in that it limited time to pursue offending behaviors. Quaker employers may not have seen the need to pay workers to the extent that they could afford frivolous items but generally felt compelled to pay enough to address their essential living conditions. This approach seems consistent with the Quaker desire that employment allows for a comfortable living (Philadelphia Yearly Meeting, 1999, p. 92).

Noted Quaker John Bright, while discussing the establishment of a ten-hour workday, expressed that decisions regarding worker treatment should remain solely in the employer's domain. While Bright did not object to the concept of reducing the working, he was vehemently opposed to the government mandating such an act (Emden, 1940, p. 86). Quakers were generally wary of government intervention in business.

In a brief publication in defense of Quakers in 1660, it was noted that members of the Society "take care to pay the rent of poor widows. . . . [and] they provide for such fatherless children . . . by setting their families to work when work is scarce and by giving them better wages then shop-keepers [*sic*] will" (Atkin, 1660). This publication points out that while Quakers paid rent, they also provided work. This "gift" of work may be more central to Quaker philanthropic activity than the providing of rent.

Industrialization and the growing scale of operations created new social issues, which led to harsh conditions, even by the standards of the day. The Quaker sense of community led them to try to ameliorate these conditions, and they pursued private actions parallel to what has been termed welfare capitalism. The desired outcomes of state welfare are consistent with the Quaker application of capitalism. These outcomes are "promoting economic efficiency; reducing poverty; promoting social equality; promoting social integration and avoiding social exclusion; promoting social stability; and promoting autonomy" (Goodin, Headey, Muffels, & Driven, 1999, p. 22).

While the listed outcomes align with the efforts of early Quaker industrialists, we should again note that Quakers were historically against government intervention. In addition to a fear of government oppression, there may have been "doctrinal" reasons for this resistance. Just as Quakers did not believe in swearing oaths, as one should always tell the truth, Quakers may have resisted state social initiatives, as one should care for their community without the threat of government coercion.

The End of Quaker Commercial Dominance

The growing scale of operations and the shrinking size of the Society may have made the end of the Quaker business era inevitable. Quaker business mainly faded because members stopped leading them. The strict application of Puritan standards of behavior led many to flee the Society and others to be expelled. With the eventual removal of occupational restrictions and the relaxation of allowable areas of study, Quakers may have left commerce merely because they could.

Quaker success challenged their business model. Moving from small shops to industrial complexes outpaced the ability of meetings to provide meaningful oversight. Control of organizations also lessened as businesses converted to corporations. Non-Quaker shareholders (owners) may not have shared the community-oriented perspective of Quakers.

While early Quakers were quick to seize upon new technologies, others followed suit. We should note that Quakers, at times, did not patent their innovations, wanting others also to benefit. The early advantages they had through innovation were quickly equalized by their competition. This too may have forced more focus on efficiency than welfare.

As Quakers were able to pursue other interests and business became increasingly competitive and challenging to Quaker sensibilities, it is easy to see the roots of their departure from prominence in commerce. This departure lessens Quaker influence in the world. Clarkson, speaking to the "peculiar customs" of Quakers, may have provided the best summary of the benefit of Quaker leadership in business. "Trade seldom considered as a question of morals, But Quakers view it in this light!" (Clarkson, 1806, p. 46).

Bibliography

Atkin, T. (1660). *Some reasons why the people called Quakers ought to enjoy their meetings peaceably published for the information of those who are not acquainted with their way, and to prevent mistakes concerning them.* London: Robert Wilson.

Barbour, H., & Roberts, A. O. (1973). *Early Quaker writings, 1650–1700.* Grand Rapids: Eerdmans.

Barclay, J., & Barclay, A. R. (1881). *A selection from the letters and papers of the late John Barclay* (Stereotype ed.). Philadelphia: Philadelphia Friends' Book-Store.

Birkel, M. L. (2004). *Silence and witness: The Quaker tradition.* Maryknoll, NY: Orbis Books.

Clarkson, T. (1806). *A portraiture of Quakerism volume II* (Vol. II). New York: Samuel Stansbury.

Elders at Balby. (1656). The Epistle from the Elders at Balby 1656. Retrieved from http://www.qhpress.org/texts/balby.html

Emden, P. H. (1940). *Quakers in commerce; a record of business achievement.* London: S. Low, Marston & Co.

Fox, G. (1698). *A collection of many select and Christian epistles, letters and testimonies.* London: Printed and sold by T. Sowle.

Fox, G. (1831). *Gospel truth demonstrated in a collection of doctrinal books* (Vol. 1). Philadelphia: Gould.

Friends Society of London Yearly Meeting. (1821). *A collection of the epistles from the Yearly Meeting of Friends in London, to the Quarterly and Monthly Meetings in Great Britain, Ireland and Elsewhere from 1675 to 1820 being from the first establishment of that Meeting to the present time.* New York: Samuel Wood & Sons.

Goodin, R. E., Headey, B., Muffels, R., & Driven, H.-J. (1999). *The real worlds of welfare capitalism.* Cambridge, UK: Cambridge University Press.

Grubb, E. (1929). *What is Quakerism? An exposition of the leading principles and practices of the Society of Friends, as based on the experience of "The Inward Light".* London: Headley Bros. Publishers, LTD.

Hamm, T. D. (2010). *Quaker writings: An anthology, 1650–1920.* New York: Penguin Books.

Ingle, H. L. (1994). *First among friends: George Fox and the creation of Quakerism.* New York: Oxford University Press.

King, M. (2014). *Quakernomics: An ethical capitalism.* London, UK: Anthem Press.

Nevaskar, B. (1971). *Capitalists without capitalism; the Jains of India and the Quakers of the West.* Westport, CT: Greenwood Pub. Co.

Penn, W. (1853). *No cross, no crown.* Philadelphia: Collins.

Philadelphia Yearly Meeting. (1999). *The old discipline: Nineteenth-century Friends' disciplines in America.* Glenside, PA: Quaker Heritage Press.

Rigge, A. (1771). *A brief and serious warning to such as are concerned in commerce and trading, who go under the profession of truth, to keep within the bounds thereof, in righteousness, justice and honesty towards all men: And now re-printed, together with the Advices of several yearly-meetings of like tendency, by order of the last yearly-meeting in London.* London: M. Hinde.

Thirsk, J., & Cooper, J. P. (1972). *Seventeenth-century economic documents.* Oxford: Clarendon Press.

Tolles, F. (1963). *Meeting house and counting house: The Quaker merchants of colonial Philadelphia, 1682–1763.* New York: W. W. Norton.

Walvin, J. (1997). *The Quakers: Money and morals.* London: John Murray.

Yount, D. (2007). *How the Quakers invented America.* Lanham: Rowman & Littlefield Publishers.

44

JOHN WOOLMAN AND DELAWARE INDIANS

Envisioning Cross-Cultural Peace in a Time of Conflict

Jon R. Kershner

In 1764, the Quaker tailor, farmer, and abolitionist John Woolman (1720–1772) recorded a dream in which he had volunteered to go on a peace mission to an American Indian[1] tribe on the eve of open conflict (1971, p. 297). Woolman recruited a guide to take him to the "chief man" of the neighboring country and set out. In his recounting of the dream, Woolman emphasized that the two countries were not separated by a sea, but simply by a line and that the "chief man" lived within a "day's journey of where I was" (1971, p. 297). On the journey, Woolman encountered people from the presumed enemy country who at first took up weapons against him, but when he extended his hand in a gesture of peace, they laid down their weapons and took him to their chief's home. Woolman waited outside the chief's house, in "a green garden with green herbs before the door," while his guides took the news of the stranger's message to their leader (1971, p. 298).

The dream ends with the chief man coming out of his home and, having learned of Woolman's mission, approaching Woolman "with a friendly countenance." The two men returned to the chief man's house to share a meal together, "and as I was about to enter on the business I awoke" (1971, p. 298). This dream came after nearly a decade of bloody conflict between many Native American tribes and European colonists in the French and Indian War (1754–1763), which was followed closely by Pontiac's War (1763–1766), a rebellion of Great Lakes Region American Indians against British forces. Even as conflict between colonists and Indigenous people seemed to become entrenched, Woolman's dream upheld a vision that those who seek peace and are sincere in their motives will be able to bridge racial and cultural divisions and, through honest diplomacy, could live in peace. This emphasis was typical of other Quaker dreamers who, as Carla Gerona argues, "sought to disarm Indians" in their dreams and "hoped that Indians would recognize Christian truth and voluntarily join both their holy and secular polities" (2004, p. 43).

John Woolman's grandfather, also named John, was among one of the early waves of Quaker settlers to the Jerseys in 1679 (Proud, 2007, p. 11). Between those early waves of British immigrants and the later John's adult years, the situation of both Quakers and Native Americans had changed dramatically. Quakers had become a leading economic and political force in the colonial mid-Atlantic, while many Native American groups had been pushed farther west. Woolman lived near some Indian towns that remained closer to their traditional lands and had some

DOI: 10.4324/9780429030925-48

Native American neighbors, but he did not mention these in his journal. Rather, he was most concerned with those tribes that had moved farther west, beyond the ever-encroaching colonial frontier (Soderlund, 2003, pp. 150–51).

John Woolman was a minister, which meant that he would often go on religious trips throughout colonial America, preaching God's message and calling on colonists to love God in word and deed. As a young man, Woolman came to believe that loving God and loving all of creation were intertwined:

> That as the mind was moved on an inward principle to love God as an invisible, incomprehensible being, on the same principle it was moved to love him in all his manifestations in the visible world; that as by his breath the flame of life was kindled in all animal and sensitive creatures, to say we love God as unseen and at the same time exercise cruelty toward the least creature moving by his life, or by life derived from him, was a contradiction in itself.
>
> *(1971, p. 28)*

Woolman was a frequent critic of slavery, war, excessive consumerism, religious tribalism, and abusive labor practices (Kershner, 2018a, 2018b). He was also a frequent dreamer, recording more dreams – or night visions – than any of his Quaker peers (Marietta, 1984, p. 95; Sobel, 2000, p. 64).

For Woolman, and for other Quakers, dreams carried special meaning as revelations from beyond. In seventeenth- and eighteenth-century Quakerism, dreams were often places where new ways of thinking about others became possible. As Quaker immigrants to America came into contact with "alien others" (Sobel, 2000, p. 14), such as Native Americans and people of African descent, dreaming became a means of extending accepted social and spiritual ethics to new, unfamiliar, and strange people. For Woolman, dreaming pointed toward a future where Quakers would reclaim the principles of peace and care he believed they held in the past. Woolman was not the only one who dreamed of a better day ahead, a future that was also a reinvigoration of an idealized past. At the same time, Native American prophets, such as "the Delaware Prophet" Neolin, were dreaming of a world without European encroachment, a world that would be made possible by a return to traditional practices of hunting, warfare, and defined gender roles. Through purification from the corruptions of European society – corruptions like alcohol, fiddles, and Christianity – "Nativist" prophets rejected the emerging trade markets of encroaching colonial society, forged pan-Indian alliances, and proclaimed native independence (Richter, 2001, pp. 180–181; Dowd, 1992, p. 33). The dreams and prophecies of Neolin and other indigenous prophets inspired Pontiac to defy the British, wage a "cleansing war against 'the Whites,'" and, most importantly, to advocate a return to Indian ways as the best path forward if Native Americans would be able to resist assimilation (Richter, 2001, pp. 198–199).

Dreams and dreaming connected Quaker and American Indian visionaries. Both groups were also connected by the fact that neither Quakers nor American Indians had a single vision for the future. Just as Quakers in America held to many different views of what it meant to be a good Quaker and how they should interact with Native Americans, so, too, American Indians were not monolithic. Some American Indians held to the "nativist" views of Neolin and Pontiac, while other groups held to what Gregory Dowd has called an "accommodationist" view that sought to work with colonists and prosper together with them through trade and diplomacy (1992, p. xviii).

While this chapter is not specifically about eighteenth-century dream work, the history of John Woolman and Native Americans is incomplete without it, because dreaming enabled a future beyond the circumstances that were actually playing out. This chapter shows how Woolman, like all colonists, was entangled in a web of geopolitics and colonialism. Woolman was aware of the imperial forces at play and criticized the effects they were having on the Native American population. Having insufficient political power to recreate Pennsylvania in a way that would minimize, let alone undo, the damage to the Euro-Indian relationship, Woolman looked to spiritual visions and a revival of the Quaker myth in Pennsylvania, and asserted an image of Quakers as a plain-speaking, simple, honest, and faithful people who lived in equanimity and peaceableness with everyone. While the content of the visions and traditions differed, many Native Americans also looked to spiritual visions and a return to traditional practices as a way to revive Native American culture. For Woolman, an apophatic listening to God and Native Americans, coupled with abstention from unjust economic practices, were seen as the paths available to Quakers interested in establishing just relations with Native Americans. Ultimately, he was not optimistic that these efforts would have a substantial impact in his earthly life without divine intervention, but they were nonetheless requirements for those who would seek to live faithfully.

Reform-minded Quakers like Woolman believed the way Indigenous people were treated was a test of Quaker faithfulness. That is, the truth of Quaker claims and the vindication of Quaker hopes for America could only be realized if colonists treated American Indians with integrity. By the middle of the eighteenth century, war between European settlers and Indians on the frontier of Pennsylvania, and political compromises in Philadelphia, convinced Woolman that individual Quakers must act on their convictions apart from the policies of the British government and the Quaker-dominated Pennsylvania Assembly (Kenny, 2009; Tolles, 1948, pp. 3–4). Woolman's vision of a peace mission coincided with many Quakers' hope of reviving the peaceable ways that they believed had characterized Pennsylvania's European settlement in the early 1680s (Gerona, 2004, p. 57). That history of just relations between Native Americans and early Quaker settlers was inaccurate, but it formed many eighteenth-century Quakers' vision of an ideal future in their quest to establish a just co-existence with Indigenous people.[2] Woolman believed his own experience of interactions with Native Americans showed that a sincere trust in God, laying down weapons, and seeking to understand others would lead to the harmonious society that could transcend seemingly insurmountable differences.

Perhaps no event has been as touted by generations of Quakers as the early settling of America and William Penn's treaty with Lenape Indians in 1681. The events and their interpretation are historically suspect, but the myth that evolved out of these events became essential to Quaker self-understanding as a peaceable people who could embody their religious convictions in their political dealings with others (Newman, 2012, p. 113; Spady, 2004, pp. 37–38). It is true that William Penn took the unprecedented step of reaching out to Lenape sachems in the lands he had been given by the King of England with a conciliatory letter that proposed a mutually beneficial relationship between colonists and Indigenous people (Richter, 2013, p. 146). However, Penn's mission was one of colonization, and, ultimately, he believed that a charter from the King of England was the only authority he needed to establish settlements on the land that would take his name (Richter, 2013, p. 141). Moreover, Penn's Quaker principles were important tools in advancing his colonialist agenda. These principles were presented to the Lenape as a reason for them to trust him, so that land deals could be reached. In the early days of Pennsylvania, those principles were effective means of achieving a colonial beachhead in the midst of the superior power of the Lenape (Murphy, 2018, p. 145).

Seventy-five years later, the Pennsylvania government placed a bounty on the scalps of American Indians and dropped the peaceable hopes that had been, at least theoretically, present in many Pennsylvanian Quaker settlers' vision for the colony (Tolles, 1948, pp. 26–27). Strict, reform-minded Quakers, like Woolman and others, viewed the move to war as a religious and political compromise that indicated a spiritual declension, and they began a series of reforms they thought would return Quakers, if not the whole colony, to the original vision (Tolles, 1948, p. 242; Woolman, 1922). Those early encounters between Quakers and Lenape may have been sincere, but due to the economics of colonialism they were built on misunderstandings and quickly gave way to resentment. Unwritten in any of the early treaties was that the success of Penn, and that of his European neighbors and successors, would be built on the assumption of Lenape subordination and the incalculable disruption of their ways (Spady, 2004, pp. 19–20). The Lenape had many years of successful trading with Swede and Dutch colonial outposts prior to the English. Those European outposts were small, easily managed, and scattered, and it was the Lenape who were clearly in control. When the first few ships of English Quaker colonists landed on Jerseyan and Pennsylvanian shores in the late 1670s and early 1680s, the Lenape could not foresee the many waves of immigrants who would quickly populate the lands surrounding the Delaware River and their relentless push inland (Spady, 2004; Soderlund, 2018, pp. 20, 26, 29).

Two events in the eighteenth century were especially consequential for Native Americans and for Quaker views of their duty toward them. The first event was a fraudulent land purchase known as "The Walking Purchase" of 1737. Woolman was a teenager when this event happened, but Native Americans and some of Woolman's Quaker friends would recount the event as an example of colonial duplicitous dealings that were far short of William Penn's legacy. The Walking Purchase was orchestrated by William Penn's non-Quaker son, Thomas Penn, and James Logan, William Penn's Quaker secretary and, in 1737, governor of Pennsylvania. In the purchase, Logan and Penn found an unratified 1686 treaty with the Lenape that called for the sale of land between the Susquehanna and Delaware Rivers to the British – land that was sacred to the Lenape (Richter, 2011; Newman, 2012, pp. 138–147).

In all likelihood, the treaty was actually a 1700 agreement William Penn had made with a Lenape leader that regarded an already completed sale (Soderlund, 2018, p. 25), but since the treaty had not been fully ratified, it became something akin to a "blank check," a treaty that could be used to authorize a new land transfer that was never intended. Penn and Logan also secured a treaty with the Iroquois Six Nations in 1736 that released their claim to the Lenape land in question, land the Iroquois did not possess in the first place. The Iroquois treaty gave Penn and Logan the appearance of having a legitimate claim because an Indigenous group had signed off on it. The Lenape – who were often called the Delaware in the eighteenth century (Newman, 2012, pp. 10–11) – and the Iroquois had a running feud which only got worse after these events. The Lenape living on the lands in question did not recognize the right to make a treaty but felt compelled to honor the fraudulent treaty. The conduct of the surveyors was as fraudulent as the treaty itself. Instead of leisurely walking the boundary of the land to be purchased with time for lunch and breaks, according to Delaware practices, the Penns' representatives sprinted a path that claimed more land than the Lenape ever imagined, including many Delaware towns (Richter, 2011, pp. 374–376, 2013, p. 168).

The Walking Purchase enraged the Delaware, and when the hostilities of the French and Indian War broke out in 1754, the fraudulent treaty was given by them and their Quaker advocates as a primary reason for their violence against English settlers. The events of the French and Indian War are the second major event that shaped Quaker views of their responsibility toward Native Americans. During these war years, and perhaps in response to them, Woolman's concern for Native Americans developed into practical steps of cross-cultural peacemaking. In general, during and shortly after these war years Woolman's outspoken abolitionism intensified, his criticism of British imperial economics became more pronounced, and he became one of the first to use a boycott on consumer goods produced through enslaved labor as a form of moral protest (Holcomb, 2016, p. 4). He also curtailed his work as a shopkeeper so he could be more free to travel in the ministry and to nurture the apophatic spirituality that he believed would lead him in the path of God's will (Woolman, 1971, p. 35). In 1755, Woolman abruptly stopped retailing gunpowder and shot. According to Geoffrey Plank, during the war years "Woolman grew cautious about selling lethal equipment even to pacifist customers. He did not want to supply the military directly or indirectly," plus he may have been reconsidering whether hunting was an acceptable activity or only for vanity (2012, pp. 149–150).

Yet, despite the personal reforms and good intentions of many Quakers in the mid-Atlantic colonies, they could not stem the tide of European colonization and immigration to America, nor did they have the power to overrule British or French imperial policies. When the Delaware's diplomatic efforts failed to achieve redress, they resorted to the only means left to them. The imperial geopolitical pressures, land-hungry colonists, and Native American desires to stop colonial expansion exploded in the bloody French and Indian War, beginning in 1754. This conflict ended almost three-quarters of a century of peace in Pennsylvania (Marietta, 1984, p. 155; Richter, 2011, pp. 393–394).

When violence erupted in Pennsylvania in 1754 and 1755, it was not random or arbitrary. Delaware Indians allied with the French returned to the lands that had been fraudulently taken from them in the Walking Purchase of 1737. They attacked, burned, and destroyed European settlements that had sprung up in the disputed land (Harper, 2008, pp. 102–103). When American Indian violence erupted, European settlers felt unprotected and exposed on the colonial frontier. Since Pennsylvania had been controlled by antiwar Quaker legislators into the middle of the eighteenth century, no funds were set aside for defense. Without an army to defend them, frontier Pennsylvanians believed that urban, Philadelphia Quakers were unconcerned about their welfare (Kenny, 2009, pp. 80–81). In response, settlers formed their own unofficial militias to strike back in often brutal ways against American Indians (Richter, 2013, p. 172). However, during the conflicts of the French and Indian War a portentous change in colonial European views of Native Americans took place: instead of some American Indians being understood as "friendly" and others "hostile" based on their actions, some European settlers developed a racialized view of Native Americans in which all Indians were seen as a dangerous threat to be eradicated (Camenzind, 2004, pp. 215–216). Those Indian groups that had a long and successful alliance with the British were often believed to be spies working to protect hostile Native Americans. These two developments – the formation of ad hoc bands of settler militias and the development of racialized views of American Indians – all but precluded any hope of peaceful coexistence between Indigenous people and colonists. They also jeopardized and transformed the method of Quaker influence in the so-called Quaker colony.

When the conflicts of the French and Indian War erupted in earnest, Pennsylvania's non-Quaker majority was quick to point their fingers at Quaker legislators who had repeatedly prevented the colony from raising a militia for self-defense. Now that frontier settlers were dying, undefended, Quakers in the Pennsylvania Assembly became focal points for political attacks by their non-Quaker adversaries. They were portrayed as incapable of governing, uncaring of the plight of settlers, and sometimes as secret allies of Native American attackers. In truth, Quakers in Pennsylvania in the eighteenth century were politically and theologically diverse. While some Quakers did oppose raising an army to fight against the French and their Indian allies, many Quakers were not strict pacifists (Calvert, 2009, pp. 177–181). A minority of the Friends on the Assembly were in the group of reforming Quakers who wanted to expand the implications of Quaker pacifism and who believed the colony had declined in its Quaker zeal from the ideals of William Penn a generation before. In 1755 a bill came before the Assembly proposing using public funds for the purpose of raising a militia (Kenny, 2009, pp. 80–81). When it became clear that the bill would pass, a minority of Quaker legislators resigned their positions. In this moment, known as the Crisis of 1756, reforming Quakers gave up much of their voice as legislators rather than participate in an armed and militarized Pennsylvanian government. They did not completely give up their influence, though. Quakers were still a significant presence in the Assembly, and the Quaker reformers found new ways to exert influence (Bonomi, 2003, p. 169).

With the Assembly's move toward war, some Pennsylvanian Quakers formed a benevolent society known as the Friendly Association for Gaining and Preserving Peace with the Indians by Pacific Measures, taking subscriptions from area Quakers to support the Delaware Indians. The association operated from 1755 to 1764 and sought to restore the relationship with the Lenape that reforming Quakers believed Penn had intended and that now had been transgressed by non-Quaker aggressions against Indians, such as the Walking Purchase and the raising of a militia. Some important members of the Friendly Association, most especially Israel Pemberton Jr., had been among those assemblymen who resigned their seats in protest (Goode, 2012, p. 472; Thayer, 1943, pp. 103–104).

The Friendly Association's work terminated when Pontiac's War again pitted colonists and Native Americans against each other and effectively ended its ability to operate. Nonetheless, during its nine-year existence, it was a key advocate for Native Americans and it successfully made the case in the eyes of the general public that the cause of frontier violence was not Quaker pacifism, it was the injustices of the Proprietors as exemplified in the Walking Purchase (Thayer, 1943, p. 366). Like the more well-known Friendly Association in Pennsylvania, Quakers in New Jersey also wished to address injustices against Native Americans. In 1757 Woolman was a charter member of the New Jersey Association for Helping the Indians ("Articles of the New Jersey Assoc. for Helping the Indians," 1757, pp. 9–10). The New Jersey Association's articles state as their founding purpose the sentiments of many reform-minded Quakers: the Indians were the "original Proprietors of the Soil" and showed kindness to the European settlers at a time when they could have "crushed the growing Settlement" ("Articles of the New Jersey Assoc.," 1757, pp. 1–2). The Articles note that some Indigenous communities of the Jerseys were landless and that not only were their complaints just, but the continuance of the injustice could lead to future conflicts between these Indigenous communities and settlers. The Articles proposed the purchase of 2000 acres in New Jersey to give to these specific communities and their posterity for free, where they could eventually learn farming (Articles of the New Jersey Assoc.', 1757, p. 3). However, before the New Jersey Association could purchase the land, the colonial government purchased and set aside 3000 acres for the same purpose. Over 200 Lenape and Munsee Indians moved onto the land. Despite the fact that the government ultimately outdid the New Jersey Association and deprived it of its founding purpose, Plank notes that Woolman's involvement in the New Jersey Association shows his active engagement in contemporary political debates and his desire to ease the suffering of others, especially those in immediate danger (2012, p. 129). Woolman's involvement marks the first of several public actions taken during a time of war with Native Americans that recognized the inequity of their disenfranchisement and sought to find a peaceful future. Native Americans had been suffering from landlessness, dispossession, and poverty for some time, and there were Native American communities nearby where Woolman grew up, but the events of the French and Indian War marked a new chapter in Woolman's social consciousness (Soderlund, 2003, p. 155).

While Woolman's activity in the New Jersey Association marks his first public acts to ameliorate the suffering of landless American Indians, his conversation with the Lenape spiritual leader Papunehank and his followers would spark in Woolman a desire to learn from America's indigenous people firsthand (Woolman, 1971, p. 123). In 1761, four years after he helped start the New Jersey Association, Woolman was one member of a group of Quakers that gathered in Philadelphia to listen to Papunehank. A pacifist, Papunehank's delegation of Native Americans had travelled to Philadelphia to learn about Quaker religious beliefs and to share of his sense of religious matters (Benezet, 1761, pp. 4–5). Woolman heard much that impressed him in this conversation. Woolman's notes on the meeting portray Papunehank as a sensitive spiritual seeker who could sense the underlying sources of violence and who had a personal experience with the "spirit of Love" that inspired "Love and Affection to all men so that he might never slight nor under value the poor and weak" (Woolman, 1761, pp. 1–2). Beginning with this meeting, Woolman felt a "concern" grow in him that he must travel into the Pennsylvania frontier to visit Papunehank and his community at their town, Wyalusing. Two years later, Woolman set out for Wyalusing (Woolman, 1971, pp. 122–123).

In 1763, four days into his dangerous journey into the Pennsylvania frontier, at a time of war between colonists and American Indians, Woolman reflected on his motivations:

> Love was the first motion, and then a concern arose to spend some time with the Indians, that I might feel and understand their life and the spirit they live in, if haply I might receive some instruction from them, or they be in any degree helped forward by my following the leadings of Truth amongst them.
>
> *(Woolman, 1971, p. 127)*

Woolman's motivation for travelling to Wyalusing in 1763 echo Papunehank's motivation for travelling to Philadelphia in 1761. Both men were influenced by an apophatic spirituality in which they could listen to and be formed by God's presence with them in such a way as to understand the spiritual nature of socio-political events. For both Papunehank and Woolman, this spirituality encouraged them to make observations of the underlying causes and spirits of eighteenth-century events. These observations, spiritual revelations, and personal experiences with people who were suffering helped Woolman increase his cross-cultural compassion. He called this sensitivity being brought "into a nearer sympathy" with others, and it was one of the main reasons he decided to travel to Wyalusing at a time of war and when travel was dangerous and difficult due to stormy weather (Woolman, 1971, pp. 127–28), colonial encroachment, open conflict, and the assassination of Delaware leader Teedyuscung by colonists seeking to settle on Lenape land (Richter, 2013, p. 174; Soderlund, 2003). Woolman undertook this journey because he wanted to experience firsthand the hardships and consequences of the spreading colonial presence for Native Americans.

During his journey to Wyalusing with companion and guides, Woolman chronicled the history of displacement that had led to American Indians being pushed further off their lands and away from the markets they relied on to sell their goods. As a result, Indigenous peoples "have to pass over mountains, swamps, and barren deserts, where travelling is very troublesome, in bringing their skins and furs to trade with us" (1971, p. 127). As Plank contends, "Woolman saw the imperial economy as a machine" where the various parts supported each other so that all of its elements were interrelated (2012, p. 3). This "machine" functioned in a way that treated some humans as chaff to be discarded. Through English settlements on unpurchased land, through vanity hunting by English hunters that reduced Indian food sources, and through the excessive and targeted use of alcohol in trade negotiations, Woolman identified how colonial greed was destroying Indian communities (1971, pp. 125, 128). Soderlund has argued that Woolman "was almost certainly the first English writer" to connect the abuses of imperialism, colonialism, and transatlantic trade (2003, pp. 149–150). His journey to Wyalusing provided the space to make these connections, and to write them down, in pronounced ways.

It is common in Woolman's corpus for new social insights and critiques of British imperialism to be first written down while he was travelling. Practically, this feature relates to the fact that Woolman, like all Quaker ministers, had more time for reflection and writing while travelling than they did while maintaining their at-home lives. But more importantly, Woolman believed travel had a sensitizing spiritual effect. In line with his apophatic spirituality, each new location, meeting, and landscape posed an opportunity for new learning and revelatory breakthrough. Woolman's desire to travel to Wyalusing was, in part, a destabilizing event that he believed would lead him into new understandings of the consequences of British imperialism and colonialism and increase his empathy (Kershner, 2015, 2019). On the journey to Wyalusing, Woolman's critique of British colonialism deepened as he experienced and observed the extent to which Indigenous life and livelihoods had changed with British encroachment on their lands. These observations took place across many years as a travelling minister integrating his experiences with his apophatic spirituality.

Woolman stated that in the dangers of his trip to Wyalusing, his will was broken and "my heart with earnestness turned to the Lord" as he was made aware of the contrast between the condition of the English and American Indians. This led him to consider how he was implicated in the oppression of both African Americans and Native Americans:

> And a weighty and heavenly care came over my mind, and live filled my heart toward all mankind, in which I felt a strong engagement that we might be obedient to the Lord while in tender mercies he is yet calling to us. . . . And here I was led into a close, laborious inquiry whether I, as an individual, kept clear from all things which tended to stir up or were connected with wars, either in this land or African, and my heart was deeply concerned that in future I might in all things keep steadily to the pure Truth and live and walk in the plainness and simplicity of a sincere follower of Christ.
> *(1971, pp. 128–129)*

Colonial injustices and "numerous oppressions," Woolman believed, would lead to God's judgments and "desolation . . . on this continent" (1971, p. 129). A righteous God, he believed, would not be aggrieved forever.

On the way to Wyalusing, Woolman and his companions travelled through the Indian town of Wyoming, where Teedyuscung had been recently killed and where British settlers from Connecticut were actively trying to drive the Delaware out of the region so they could settle it (Soderlund, 2003, p. 159). The area of land around Wyoming was known as the Forks of the Delaware River and had sacred significance to the Delaware/Lenape people. It had been part of the land fraudulently taken in the Walking Purchase of 1737, and through much negotiation the colonial government of Pennsylvania had returned a portion of the land to the Delaware. The settlers who murdered Teedyuscung, and who wanted to drive the Delaware out of the Forks, cared little for such negotiations or the agreements reached between the colonial government and the Delaware (Harper, 2008, pp. 120–123).

When Woolman reached Wyoming, Indian war parties were active in the vicinity. At one point while at Wyoming, a Delaware warrior brandished a weapon against Woolman. Woolman responded by gesturing that he had no weapon and wanted only to shake the man's hand (1971, pp. 129–130). Woolman reflected on his time at Wyoming,

> here I expressed the care I had on my mind for [the people of Wyoming's] good and told them that true love had made me willing thus to leave my family to come and

see the Indians and speak with them in their houses. Some of them appeared kind and friendly.

(1971, p. 130)

Like his dream of a peace mission, these encounters with supposedly hostile Indians in a spirit of sincerity and love, trusting in God to teach both parties the way to live faithfully, vindicated the practices he believed had characterized the early Quaker relationships with America's Indigenous people and to which faithful people could return if they would put down their weapons, seek to live simply, and so "check the growth of [oppressive] seeds, that they may not ripen to the ruin of our posterity" (1971, p. 129).

For Woolman, the economic injustices he witnessed and the difficult and dangerous manner of living forced on Native Americans was indication of a spiritual depravity among colonists. But Woolman also had a positive goal for his journey: to learn of the spirit of love he witnessed in Papunehank in 1761. When he arrived at Wyalusing much of his time was spent listening to God in the presence of the residents. At one meeting, Woolman reflected that he was moved to speak to them without interpretation, "feeling the current of love run strong," and believing that the spirit of love he spoke out of would be communicated to those present, even "where all the words were not understood" (1971, p. 133). The purpose of his time in Wyalusing was to witness and learn from the apophatic spirituality he had already observed in Philadelphia. He also wanted to give voice to his leadings among the people there, forming a type of cross-cultural spiritual diplomacy.

At least from Woolman's perspective, this goal had been successfully met. After he had finished speaking to the community at Wyalusing, Papunehank reportedly said, "I love to hear where words come from" (1971, p. 133). Woolman records that phrase in his journal as an indication of the success of his apophatic mission of love and, no doubt, to encourage his future readers to be equally impressed with the merits of that spirituality. However, not everyone was as convinced the visit was successful. The Moravian missionary David Zeisberger was in Wyalusing while Woolman was there, and his journal characterized the communication between Woolman and the residents of Wyalusing as less adept than Woolman's journal lets on (Plank, 2012, p. 165). Woolman probably overstated the spiritual similarities between his brand of Quakerism and the spirituality of Papunehank, who became a Moravian (Plank, 2012, pp. 139–144, 166). Whether or not Papunehank and his followers ever became Quaker, Woolman approved of the sensitive and receptive spirit he encountered at Wyalusing and the earnest, peaceful conversations he had there.

Woolman's observations of British encroachments on American Indian lands made a lasting impact. Three months after returning from Wyalusing, Woolman and his fellow Quaker minister, John Pemberton, co-authored an Epistle to Long Island Yearly Meeting on behalf of Philadelphia Yearly Meeting that called on Quakers to refrain from being involved, directly or indirectly, from settling on "lands which have not been properly purchased of the natives" (2010). However, even if Woolman felt his view of the spiritual basis for peace with Indians to be vindicated, he would have also been aware, with increasing horror, of the social and political difficulties of the task. On Woolman's journey back home from Wyalusing, he passed through Wyoming again. This time, just eight days after the outward journey, Woolman and companions found that most of the Indian residents had abandoned the location. Woolman does not mention it, but the reason they had left Wyoming was the unabated encroachment of British settlers and the persistent threat that any who refused to leave would share the same fate as Teedyuscung. The Indian town at Wyoming was a symbol of things to come. Woolman still had hope for reconciliation between British colonists and American Indians, as illustrated in his dream of a peace mission in 1764, but the ongoing turmoil in Pennsylvania would convince him that any alteration in the current violent trajectory would require radical change, both spiritual and social.

Only six months after Woolman's trip to Wyalusing, a brutal massacre of twenty peaceful Conestoga Indians, including women and children, known as the Paxton Boys Affair of 1763–1764, shocked many of Pennsylvania's Quaker residents. The massacre was perpetrated by Scot-Irish settlers seeking revenge on any Indigenous person for the deaths their frontier community experienced in the French and Indian War and Pontiac's War (Camenzind, 2004, p. 206; Richter, 2001, pp. 203–204; Smith & Gibson, 1764, p. 3). Moreover, these settlers held to a conquest theory of land ownership whereby land taken through force, such as by murdering the Conestoga Indians that held a claim to the land, would constitute a legitimate land ownership transfer (Kenny, 2009, pp. 4–5). Not long after massacring the Conestoga, the Paxton Boys marched as a militia of no more than 300 men to Philadelphia with the intention of arresting high-profile Quakers who they believed were complicit in the violence their frontier communities had experienced. They also wished to murder remnants of Indian communities that had fled to Philadelphia in the aftermath of these events, including Papunehank and his community from Wyalusing.

These events are not mentioned by Woolman anywhere in his corpus, but he certainly would have been aware of them. The Paxton Boys' march on Philadelphia was averted because of a diplomatic delegation sent from Philadelphia to meet the militia en route and convince the Paxton Boys to submit their grievances in writing. None of the Paxton Boys was prosecuted for their involvement in the massacre or the insurrection (Kenny, 2009, p. 163; Smith & Gibson, 1764). Woolman's silence on the Paxton Boys' atrocities is hard to fathom, but he was well aware of racial tensions on the frontier prior to his visit to Wyalusing. Despite the Paxton Boys' murders, he remained confident that those who in faith and sincerity put aside the spirit of greed and violence could transcend racial divides and live in peace and justice. This message was reconfirmed for him in his dream of a peace mission, related above, five months after the Paxton Boys had marched on Philadelphia.

The next fall, Woolman hired a man to work on his farm who had fought in the French and Indian War and had been taken prisoner by Native American forces. The man told Woolman of the gruesome treatment of British men who had been captured and tortured to death, including one who had been stabbed with wood spikes and set on fire, in intervals, over two days, before he finally succumbed to his injuries (1971, p. 142). These stories upset Woolman, but the next morning he awoke with "a living sense of divine love . . . spread over my mind" (1971, p. 142). He reflected that by attending "to that wisdom from above," people would come to a sense of the "right use of all gifts both spiritual and temporal" (1971, p. 142). He mulled over the string of thought that could lead people to commit acts of gruesome violence: how pride led people to want more than they needed, which caused them to force others into inequitable relationship, how inequality then produced anger, hate, and a desire for revenge in those who were being oppressed. In other words, greed and violent revenge were related to each other. However, "those in whom Christ governs" seek to live in "perfect simplicity, [that they] may give no just cause of offense to any creature, but may walk as he walked" (1971, p. 143). The turmoil in Pennsylvania was part of what Woolman understood to be the mounting depravity of British imperialism. In the face of these geopolitical trends and the seeming intransigence of colonists' desire for a greater and greater share of resources and land, Woolman became more spiritually radical and adopted practices that posed a greater contradiction to the prevailing colonial mentality. For example, in 1763 he began to wear undyed clothing as a statement of spiritual transparency. At that time, he also started walking on many of his journeys, instead of riding a horse, to set an example of lowliness and humility amidst colonial avarice (Kershner, 2018a, pp. 67, 89, 110–111).

Woolman's journal account of torture on the frontier is the last specific reference to American Indians in his published writings. Soderlund argues that Woolman's silence on American Indians, and especially on the plight of the people from Wyalusing, suggest an "ambivalence toward Native Americans that he did not feel towards blacks" (Soderlund, 2003, p. 161). However, notes in Woolman's journal manuscripts from 1767 and 1771 indicate that Woolman continued to encourage Quakers to respond to Indian needs (1971, p. 134 n. 26). Most importantly, Woolman continued to further his anti-imperial theology and to proclaim the apophatic message that in listening to the voice of Christ with sincerity and letting go of excessive wants, all people could live in peace (Kershner, 2018a, p. 26). Rather than ambivalence toward the plight of American Indians, Woolman sought a holistic, global transformation powerful enough to turn back the tide of imperial greed at the center of British oppression.

In conclusion, Woolman's interactions with Indigenous peoples fits consistently with his larger agenda of empathy for those who suffer and his advocacy of a simpler, more humble, and reverent manner of living for British settlers. On one hand, Woolman was deeply implicated in the injustice of colonialism. His family's livelihood depended on the land deals made by the first European settlers a couple generations prior. On the other hand, at least from Woolman's perspective, if colonists lived in the spirit of the early Quaker myth in Pennsylvania, America could become a place of cross-cultural harmony where no one took more than they needed and everyone had enough to thrive, a veritable Peaceable Kingdom on Earth (Kershner, 2018a, pp. 107–109). The image of Woolman's 1764 dream of a peace mission – where sincere persons trusting in God and committed to peace would be shown the way to overcome differences – stands out as Woolman's hope for Native-colonial relationships. This vision was far from fulfilment in Woolman's day, and subsequent generations of Quakers largely abandoned it. At the end of the eighteenth century and through the nineteenth century, Quakers mostly took the dominance of White culture for granted and used their influence among Indians to urge them toward assimilation. These subsequent generations of Quakers after Woolman were resolute that they knew what was best for American Indians and had Indian interests at heart (Ross, 2018, pp. 133–35). Quaker benevolence notwithstanding, Quakers through the nineteenth century were at a loss as to how they might make substantial improvements to Indian conditions, and in some notable cases took jobs as agents of the federal government tasked with facilitating the assimilation process (Palmer, 2018, p. 306; Graber, 2018, pp. 11–13; Batchelor, 2018, 75–76; Daggar, 2018, p. 205). In this sense, Woolman's vision of a truly cross-cultural peace was abandoned for one that assumed the inevitability, if not the appropriateness, of the colonial enterprise.

Notes

1 The terms "American Indian" and "Native American" are common terms for America's Indigenous People. Both terms are problematic because they were coined by European colonizers and because they overlook the diversity of national identities that many of America's Indigenous Peoples find to be the most meaningful descriptor of cultural identity. "American Indian" or "Indian" is the racial or ethnic term preferred most by America's Indigenous people, followed by "Native American." Both terms are seen as having particular benefits and liabilities. This chapter uses the terms "Indigenous peoples," "American Indian," and "Native American" interchangeably when referring to pan-Indian experiences in the colonial mid-Atlantic region. Where possible, tribal identities are used. See Yellow Bird (1999, pp. 4–7, 17).

2   The romanticizing of William Penn and the myth of Quaker beginnings in Pennsylvania also influenced the antislavery reforms that developed into a movement among mid-eighteenth-century reform-
minded Quakers (Kershner, 2018b, pp. 16–17).

Bibliography

"Articles of the New Jersey Assoc. for Helping the Indians." Haverford College, Philadelphia, PA, April 16, 1757.975B. Haverford College Library.

Batchelor, Ray. "'Cast under Our Care': Elite Quaker Masculinity and Political Rhetoric about American Indians in the Age of Revolutions." In *Quakers and Native Americans*, edited by Ignacio Gallup-Diaz and Geoffrey Plank, 75–92. Leiden: Brill, 2018.

Benezet, Anthony. "Some Account of the Behaviour and Sentiments of a Number of Well-Disposed Indians Mostly of the Minusing-Tribe," 1761. Swarthmore College, Friends Historical Library.

Bonomi, Patricia. *Under the Cope of Heaven: Religion, Society and Politics in Colonial America*. Oxford: Oxford University Press, 2003.

Calvert, Jane. *Quaker Constitutionalism and the Political Thought of John Dickinson*. New York: Cambridge University Press, 2009.

Camenzind, Krista. "Violence, Race, and the Paxton Boys." In *Friends and Enemies in Penn's Woods: Indians, Colonists, and the Racial Construction of Pennsylvania*, edited by William Pencak and Daniel K Richter, 201–220. University Park, PA: Pennsylvania State University Press, 2004.

Daggar, Lori. "'A Damned Rebellious Race': The U.S. Civilization Plan and Native Authority." In *Quakers and Native Americans*, edited by Ignacio Gallup-Diaz and Geoffrey Plank, 197–217. Leiden: Brill, 2018.

Dowd, Gregory Evans. *A Spirited Resistance: The North American Indian Struggle for Unity, 1745–1815*. Baltimore, MD: Johns Hopkins University Press, 1992.

Gerona, Carla. "Imagining Peace in Quaker and Native American Dream Stories." In *Friends and Enemies in Penn's Woods: Indians, Colonists, and the Racial Construction of Pennsylvania*, edited by William Pencak and Daniel K. Richter, 41–62. University Park, PA: Pennsylvania State University Press, 2004.

Goode, Michael. "A Failed Peace: The Friendly Association and the Pennsylvania Backcountry during the Seven Years' War." *The Pennsylvania Magazine of History and Biography* 136, no. 4 (2012): 472–474. https://doi.org/10.5215/pennmaghistbio.136.4.0472.

Graber, Jennifer. *The Gods of Indian Country: Religion and the Struggle for the American West*. New York: Oxford University Press, 2018.

Harper, Steven Craig. *Promised Land: Penn's Holy Experiment, the Walking Purchase, and the Dispossession of Delawares, 1600–1763*. Bethlehem: Lehigh University Press, 2008.

Holcomb, Julie L. *Moral Commerce: Quakers and the Transatlantic Boycott of the Slave Labor Economy*. 1st edition. Ithaca: Cornell University Press, 2016.

Kenny, Kevin. *Peaceable Kingdom Lost: The Paxton Boys and the Destruction of William Penn's Holy Experiment*. New York: Oxford University Press, 2009.

Kershner, Jon R. "'A More Lively Feeling': The Correspondence and Integration of Mystical and Spatial Dynamics in John Woolman's Travels." *Quaker Studies* 20, no. 1 (December 1, 2015): 103–116. https://doi.org/10.3828/quaker.20.1.103.

Kershner, Jon R. *John Woolman and the Government of Christ: A Colonial Quaker's Vision for the British Atlantic World*. Oxford, New York: Oxford University Press, 2018a.

Kershner, Jon R. *"To Renew the Covenant": Religious Themes in Eighteenth-Century Quaker Abolitionism*. Leiden: Brill, 2018b.

Kershner, Jon R. "Woolman and Wilderness: A Quaker Sacramental Ecology." In *Quakers, Creation Care, and Sustainability*, edited by Cherice Bock and Stephen Potthoff, 115–131. Quakers and the Disciplines 6. Philadelphia, PA: Friends Association for Higher Education, 2019.

Marietta, Jack D. *The Reformation of American Quakerism, 1748–1783*. Philadelphia: University of Pennsylvania Press, 1984.

Moulton, Phillips P., ed. *The Journal and Major Essays of John Woolman*. 1st ed. Richmond, IN: Friends United Press, 1971.

Murphy, Andrew R. *William Penn: A Life*. Oxford, New York: Oxford University Press, 2018.

Newman, Andrew. *On Records: Delaware Indians, Colonists, and the Media of History and Memory*. Lincoln, NE: University of Nebraska Press, 2012.

Palmer, Paula. "The Quaker Indian Boarding Schools: Facing Our History and Ourselves." In *Quakers and Native Americans*, edited by Ignacio Gallup-Diaz and Geoffrey Plank, 293–311. Leiden: Brill, 2018.

Plank, Geoffrey. *John Woolman's Path to the Peaceable Kingdom: A Quaker in the British Empire.* Philadelphia: University of Pennsylvania Press, 2012.

Proud, James. "A Note on John Woolman's Paternal Ancestors: The Gloucestershire Roots; The West New Jersey Plantation." *Quaker History* 96, no. 2 (2007): 28–53.

Richter, Daniel K. *Facing East from Indian Country: A Native History of Early America.* Cambridge, MA.: Harvard University Press, 2001.

Richter, Daniel K. *Before the Revolution: America's Ancient Pasts.* Cambridge, MA: Belknap Press of Harvard University Press, 2011.

Richter, Daniel K. *Trade, Land, Power: The Struggle for Eastern North America.* Philadelphia: University of Pennsylvania Press, 2013.

Ross, Ellen. "'The Great Spirit Hears All We Now Say': Philadelphia Quakers and the Seneca, 1798–1850." In *Quakers and Native Americans*, edited by Ignacio Gallup-Diaz and Geoffrey Plank, 115–135. Leiden: Brill, 2018.

Smith, Matthew, and Gibson, James. *A Declaration and Remonstrance of the Distressed and Bleeding Frontier Inhabitants of the Province of Pennsylvania, Presented by Them to the Honourable the Governor and Assembly of the Province, Shewing the Causes of Their Late Discontent and Uneasiness and the Grievances Under Which They Have Laboured, and Which They Humbly Pray to Have Redress'd,* 1764. http://name.umdl.umich. edu/N07543.0001.001.

Sobel, Mechal. *Teach Me Dreams: The Search for Self in the Revolutionary Era.* Princeton, NJ: Princeton University Press, 2000.

Soderlund, Jean R. "African Americans and Native Americans in John Woolman's World." In *The Tendering Presence: Essays on John Woolman: In Honor of Sterling Olmsted & Phillips P. Moulton*, edited by Michael Heller, 148–66. Wallingford, PA: Pendle Hill Publications, 2003.

Soderlund, Jean R. "The Lenape Origins of Delaware Valley Peace and Freedom." In *Quakers and Native Americans*, edited by Ignacio Gallup-Diaz and Geoffrey Plank, 15–29. Leiden: Brill, 2018.

Spady, James O'Neil. "Colonialism and the Discursive Antecedents of Penn's Treaty with the Indians." In *Friends and Enemies in Penn's Woods: Indians, Colonists, and the Racial Construction of Pennsylvania*, edited by William Pencak and Daniel K. Richter, 18–40. University Park, PA: Pennsylvania State University Press, 2004.

Thayer, Theodore. "The Friendly Association." *The Pennsylvania Magazine of History and Biography* 67, no. 4 (1943): 356–376.

Tolles, Frederick. *Meeting House and Counting House: The Quaker Merchants of Colonial Philadelphia, 1682–1763.* Chapel Hill: University of North Carolina Press, 1948.

Woolman, John. "The Substance of Some Conversation with Paponahoal the Indian Chief at AB's in Presence of John Woolman," 1761. Pemberton Papers, vol. 13, p. 23. Historical Society of Pennsylvania.

Woolman, John. "An Epistle to the Quarterly and Monthly Meetings of Friends." In *The Journal and Essays of John Woolman*, edited by Amelia M. Gummere, 473–487. New York: Macmillan Company, 1922.

Woolman, John. "Journal." In *The Journal and Major Essays of John Woolman*, edited by Phillips P. Moulton, 23–192. Richmond, IN: Friends United Press, 1971.

Woolman, John, and John Pemberton. "The Epistle of 1763 from PYM to Long Island Yearly Meeting." In *John Woolman and the Affairs of Truth: The Journalist's Essays, Epistles, and Ephemera*, edited by James Proud, 262–263. San Francisco, CA: Inner Light Books, 2010.

Yellow Bird, Michael. "What We Want to Be Called: Indigenous Peoples' Perspectives on Racial and Ethnic Identity Labels." *American Indian Quarterly* 23, no. 2 (1999): 1–21. https://doi.org/10.2307/1185964.

45

A SHORT HISTORY OF QUAKER INCLUSION OF GAY AND LESBIAN PEOPLE

Brian T. Blackmore

In 2019, during a lip-sync performance of Taylor Swift's "You Need to Calm Down," a group of backup dancers removed Reid Arthur's shimmering hoodie to reveal a flourish of rainbow-colored streamers draping from his widespread arms. They did so immediately after the lyrics, "'cause shade never made anybody less gay," boomed through the auditorium. It was clear that Arthur, a senior at George Fox University (GFU) in Newberg, Oregon, was not only coming out as gay to the entire community at his Quaker college but he was publicly challenging the school's stance on homosexuality. In a Community Lifestyle Statement on their website, GFU declares: "In regard to sexual morality, we believe that only marriage between a man and a woman is God's intention for the joyful fulfillment of sexual intimacy . . . Sexual behaviors outside of this context are inconsistent with God's teaching."[1] Regardless, the audience gave Reid a standing ovation, and he won first place in the student-centered competition. A video recording of his performance went viral on social media, and it was celebrated as an act of courage in numerous magazines and news outlets throughout the United States.[2] Taylor Swift herself tweeted support by saying: "you did the brave thing and stood up for your truth."[3]

In the wake of national media attention, pressure from students to change the school's stance on gay and lesbian sexuality quickly intensified. The president of GFU, Robin Baker, responded by sending an internal email to all students saying that GFU is "a Christian community that holds that God intended sexual relations to be reserved for a marriage relationship between a man and a woman."[4] Unsatisfied by the school's resistance to change and reeling from years of controversy surrounding the school's refusal to recognize an LGBTQ student affinity group as an official club, Courtney Bither, a 2017 graduate of GFU, collected hundreds of signatures for an open letter she sent to President Baker, which said:

> Many Quakers (many former members of the NWYM [Northwest Yearly Meeting]) do not agree with GFU's statement on gender and sexuality. . . . It is disingenuous to appeal to the NWYM statement on sexuality as though it were universally accepted within the Quaker community.[5]

Bither is correct in pointing out that Quakerism, like most Christian traditions, has within itself a wide diversity of competing beliefs about gay and lesbian sexuality. This diversity has

DOI: 10.4324/9780429030925-49

resulted in some of the most heated debates and painful divisions within the Religious Society of Friends in recent history. Bither knows this experientially because while she was a student at GFU, she witnessed one of the most painful schisms among Friends over homosexuality. The controversy began when West Hill Friends Meeting minuted the spiritual gifts of lesbian and gay people in 2008 and later married a lesbian couple in 2015. In July 2015, only hours after the NWYM annual gathering had concluded, the leadership of NWYM informed West Hill Friends that their membership had been "released." After two years of rising mistrust between the NWYM and several other Monthly Meetings in the area with LGBT-affirming views, a group of about eighty Quakers organized themselves to form the Sierra-Cascades Yearly Meeting (SCYM) in 2017.[6] In their first Epistle, SCYM Friends declared: "We are led by the Spirit to commit ourselves to recognizing the full participation of LGBTQ+ people in all aspects of the life of the new yearly meeting."[7]

Similar splits have "shattered" or "disintegrated" many long-standing associations of American Quakerism. In the summer of 2018, Evangelical Quakers became increasingly offended by the inclusion of LGBT-affirming Meetings in the Wilmington Yearly Meeting and membership dramatically shrunk from twenty-eight to nineteen Meetings. A year earlier, 120 Friends at Quaker Lake Camp near Liberty, North Carolina, approved the dissolution of the North Carolina Friends Meeting (FUM) after tensions between Friends concerning homosexuality could not be reconciled. In a small number of cases, individual meetings have expressed dissent with the views of their tradition but sought to maintain unity. Notable examples include the Evangelical and gay-affirming Friends of Jesus Fellowship and the Swansea Monthly Meeting's disapproval of New England Yearly Meeting's support for same-sex marriage.

Sometimes Quakers are unable to stay in unity because of disagreements about non-discrimination policies towards LGBT people. When the Friends United Meeting (FUM) minuted a stance against homosexuality in 1988 and formalized this stance in a Personnel Policy in 1991, some Yearly Meetings with dual affiliations in the Friends General Conference (FGC) and FUM felt conflicted and morally compromised. In 2005, the Baltimore Yearly Meeting decided to maintain its dual affiliation but suspended its membership contributions to FUM, and in 2010 the Southeastern Yearly Meeting left FUM entirely.

According to historian Robert Frost, American Friends began to discuss homosexuality openly around 1970 at a Conference on Sexuality of the New Swarthmoor movement, in articles in the *Friends Journal* written by gay people using pseudonyms, and in young men declaring that they were gay during meeting for worship.[8] In the early 1970s, Quakers began to create coalitions of gay Friends and their first public action was to put pressure on the executive planning committee for the 1972 FGC annual gathering to allow same-sex couples to room together and to hold their own worship sharing groups. The committee granted their request by allowing same-sex couples to share bedrooms in a building designated for older conference attenders. The policy was later rescinded at the 1972 plenary sessions, and same-sex housing was not reinstated at FGC until 1975.

In 1973, while the housing policy for same-sex couples was temporarily suspended, the Religious Education Committee of FGC invited Mary Steinton Calderone, a Quaker, physician, and executive director of the Sex Information and Education Council of the United States (SIECUS), to give the honorable Rufus Jones Lecture. The committee recognized that,

> a searching look at our attitudes toward sexuality is going on within Quakerism today. . . . some Friends, yearly meetings and monthly meetings are asking: what can we say? How do we respond to these questions? What is appropriate behavior within the community of Friends?[9]

The committee selected Calderone as "the obvious choice to begin this dialogue [about sex] among Friends" specifically because her work at SIECUS was about "liberating human sexuality from the unhealthy atmosphere of suspicion, guilt, and fear that surrounded it." In her talk, Calderone did not explicitly state a positive or negative view of homosexuality, but she did ask her audience to consider that respect for sexual diversity and difference is an extension of Quaker beliefs and values:

> It is as simple as a [Quaker] syllogism . . . there is that of God in every human, and because sexuality is an innate part of the human being, then there must surely be that of God in human sexuality. . . . The great challenge of being a Friend has always been for me that only one of us may hear, each one for his or her own self, God speaking to us. No other human being can overhear these messages, nor our response to them, nor can any other human being respond to them on our behalf.[10]

Immediately after Calderone's lecture, FGC-based Friends began to mobilize their support for LGBT people with deliberate speed. San Francisco Monthly Meeting accepted the first same-sex Quaker marriage under its care, and New York Yearly Meeting was the first Quaker organization to endorse equal civil rights for gay and lesbian people. In the years that followed, Philadelphia, Baltimore, Illinois, and Pacific Yearly Meetings minuted their opposition to the criminalization of homosexuality. Philadelphia Yearly Meeting went so far as to commission an ad hoc Committee of Gay and Lesbian Concerns, which became a standing committee in 1976. In 1974, Young Friends of North America issued a declaration calling for the "equality of All persons before the Eternal in matters Spiritual regardless of their sexual orientation." In the fall of 1975 four American Friend Service Committee (AFSC) staffers publicly announced they were gay, and in 1978 eighteen more came out and received a letter of support from 250 people in the organization.[11]

Momentum for gay rights was intensifying in the 1970s, but one tumultuous event would prove that support for change was not widespread among all Quakers. In 1977, a few months prior to the Wichita Conference of Friends in the Americas, Gary Miller, a member of the San Francisco Monthly Meeting and lobbyist for the California Friends Committee on Legislation in Sacramento, wrote a letter to the conference's Oversight Committee on behalf of the Friends Committee on Gay Concerns (FCGC). He requested a table in the exhibition hall for FCGC to display literature about gay rights, a space for gay Friends to worship, and an event in the conference program open to all for discussion about gay concerns. Strong voices on the Oversight Committee opposed putting Miller's requests into action, and for a brief period it seemed as if his request had been laid down.

In days just prior to the start of the conference, it was revealed to many of the members of the Oversight Committee that its general chairman, Donald Moon, had received a second letter from the Committee on Civil Rights for Homosexuals of Philadelphia Yearly Meeting. At this time, the Philadelphia Yearly Meeting was the largest and most influential Yearly Meeting in America, and the letter was written on its official letterhead. The local newspaper received a tip and published the headline: "Gays Ask Spot in Quaker Meeting." Tensions mounted, and the Oversight Committee met the day before conference attendees were planned to arrive. As it became clear that most members of the committee were in support of the request from the Philadelphia Quakers, some members of the committee threatened to leave. In an effort to maintain unity, a subcommittee was formed of five Friends with various competing views on homosexuality. Soon after, the administration at the Friends University expressed disapproval about these discussions happening on their campus, and the decision was made to relocate to a large church nearby. Midway through the weeklong conference, 120 people arrived to watch the subcommittee debate and participate in an open discussion. The event was deemed a success by all sides. Evangelical Friends felt their interpretation of the Bible was respected and FGC-based Friends were able to openly express their concerns. The rest of the Wichita Conference proceeded without interruption, and the controversy did not seem to result in any immediate schisms within or between Quaker groups. Nonetheless, the Wichita Conference was the last instance during which all of the various traditions and major associations of American Quakerism congregated together in one place.[12]

Many Quakers and non-Quakers are unaware of this tumultuous history. Furthermore, a widespread admiration of Quaker leadership in social justice movements paired with a universalist interpretation of the doctrine of the Inner Light, a guiding principle within Quakerism that there is that of God in everyone, has shaped too many false assumptions that Quakers should and have stood in the vanguard of supporting freedom and equality for gay and lesbian people. This decontextualized view of Quakerism is disrupted when one examines the Quaker tradition on a global scale. In 2012, Friends Church Kenya – the umbrella organization that contains the largest population of Quakers in the world – released a press statement in the form of an epistle to the World Conference of Friends in Nairobi which stated that "God's attitude towards the vile behaviour of homosexuality is clear. . . . Homosexuals are those who have deliberately deviated from what is normal sexual practices as God intended it to be."[13] Indeed, the vast majority of Quakers in the world are affiliated with Yearly Meetings that have either communicated an ambivalence about supporting gay and lesbian people or condemned homosexuality as a sin that is fundamentally inconsistent with Christian teachings.

A more intellectually responsible understanding of Quakerism recognizes that Quakers express the entire spectrum of views and beliefs about gay and lesbian sexuality. While opposition to homosexuality among African Quakers is strong, and debates about LGBTQ inclusion have spurred many splits between and within Quaker institutions in the United States, in some parts of the Quaker World, there is unified and unrelenting support of gay and lesbian people. For example, in 2004 the FGC released an unequivocal statement recognizing the dignity and contributions made by LGBT Friends:

> Our experience has been that spiritual gifts are not distributed with regard to sexual orientation or gender identity. Our experience has been that our Gatherings and Central Committee work have been immeasurably enriched over the years by the full participation and Spirit-guided leadership of gay, lesbian, bisexual, transgender, and queer Friends. We will never go back to silencing those voices or suppressing those gifts.[14]

FGC's statement of support reflects a long history of hosting speakers, such as Calderone and George Lakey, to talk about gay and lesbian sexuality at annual gatherings. FGC has also had a long-standing tradition of providing affinity space for LGBTQ people at their annual summer gatherings. A group of FGC-based Quakers, now known as the Friends for Lesbian, Gay, Bisexual, Transgender, and Queer Concerns (FLGBTQC), has been meeting biannually since the 1970s.

Many Monthly Meetings affiliated with FGC have also updated their "Books of Discipline" to reflect a support for gay and lesbian people. There is a long history of Monthly Meetings in the United States, the United Kingdom, and Australia performing same-sex marriages long before marriage equality was written into civil law. In 1974, Illinois Yearly Meeting was one of the first Quaker organizations to denounce the criminalization of homosexuality.[15] While the Friends Council on National Legislation has historically avoided taking a stance on same-sex marriage in their effort to fairly represent the diverse views of many Quakers in the United States, the organization released a statement in 2004 that discredited the anti-gay Federal Marriage Amendment as a violation of civil and human rights.

The AFSC has done more for the LGBTQ community than any other Quaker organization, although its history is complicated and contains a few painful inconsistencies. AFSC staff in regional offices have been fighting for LGBT rights and recognition ever since the 1960s and the AFSC's national Community Relations Unit established its first Lesbian/Gay/Bisexual Rights Task Force in 1976. In the decade that followed, as the AFSC continued to develop the goals of their own task force, a new threat towards the lives of LGBT individuals emerged, with the first recorded diagnosis of AIDS in 1981. As cases of the still unnamed virus and death tolls rose, so did support of the community from AFSC, with a renewed understanding that support of LGBT individuals did not simply involve the pursuit of justice and equality but required an imperative to secure their survival.

Healthcare, in addition to familiar topics like marriage equality, the decriminalization of gay sex, the rights of gay parents, the fight against discrimination of LGBTQ people in the workplace, and support of LGBTQ youth would later become and remain cornerstones of the organization's goals.[16]

Before the AFSC began to fight for LGBT rights and equality, Bayard Rustin spoke openly about his Quaker faith, sexuality, and gay rights. When Rustin was arrested for "lewd" behavior in a parked car with two other men in San Francisco in 1953, his homosexuality was made public and his relationships with other civil rights leaders became strained. Two years later, Rustin would play a pivotal role in the creation of *Speak Truth to Power*, a 1955 AFSC report that urged nonviolent responses to international conflicts involving the United States. Out of fear that the visibility of his gay sexuality would hinder the success of the report, Rustin supported a decision to omit his name from the list of its authors. In 2010, the AFSC Board restored his name to the list and lamented the "regret[able] failure" of AFSC not to give Rustin the credit he was due.[17]

Even more Quaker support of sexual differences can be found in other parts of the world. While the Canadian Yearly Meeting allows local Monthly Meetings to make their own decisions about same-sex marriages, they stated in 2003 that they support civil marriage for same-sex couples and the right of gay parents to raise children.[18] Australian Quakers have spoken out against discrimination against lesbian and gay people since 1975, and the first Australian Quaker gay marriage was celebrated in 2007.

Quakers in Britain might rightfully claim the longest continuous history of any Christian group in demonstrating a public affirmation of gay and lesbian sexuality. Their public witness to LGBT people began in the 1950s when a group of Quaker youth began to express concerns about "homosexual difficulties" at Anna Bidel's home in Cambridge. Quakers have a long tradition of spiritual mentorship, however, when faced with the particular "problem" of homosexuality, Bidel and other Quakers felt

> The Society of Friends as such had little to say to people troubled sexually [sic], and that at the same time many Friends were in serious doubt whether the Church's traditional view spoke to this condition. The need was clear for research into sexual problems and morals, and for Friends to ask themselves where their responsibilities lay.[19]

Accordingly, they began to meet regularly for silent worship and conversation about homosexuality.

As the work of the group gradually deepened, they realized a need to re-examine human sexuality on a grander scale, Christian ethics, and Quaker consciousness. "Primarily the task of the group," they write,

> was to consider what Quakers could say to homosexuals and to others who found that society strongly condemned their sexual feelings and who found, too, that the expression of those feelings could lead to victimization, blackmail, and imprisonment, whereas "normal" heterosexual conduct, however irresponsible, went virtually unchallenged. The group soon found that the study of homosexuality and its moral problems could not be divorced from a survey of the whole field of sexual activity.[20]

They were teachers, headmasters, psychiatrists, psychologists, pediatric physicians, a lawyer, a zoologist from Cambridge University, and one anonymous member. They invited guests to speak with them, including representatives from the Friends' Marriage and Parenthood Committee, the Friends' Penal Reform Committee, the Temperance and Moral Welfare Union, and the Guild of Social Workers.

In 1963, they published *Towards a Quaker View of Sex* (VOS), and therein they amazed the world with a proclamation that homosexuality was entirely congruent with Christian morality:

> Homosexual affection can be as selfless as heterosexual affection, and therefore we cannot see that in some way it is morally worse. . . . An act which expresses true affection between two individuals and gives pleasure to them both, does not seem to us to be sinful by reason alone of the fact that it is homosexual.

VOS was first published by Friends Home Service Committee in London, and it immediately received considerable attention in the British press and the *London Friend*. In the United States, VOS was rarely mentioned in American Quaker literature, with the important exception of a review by Mitchell Lawrence in *Friends Journal*. At Pendle Hill, a Quaker study center in Wallingford, Pennsylvania, the pamphlet was not allowed to be displayed on the bookstore shelves, but copies were kept behind the counter at the register.[21]

According to Frost, American Friends in the 1960s were either avoiding discussion about homosexuality or preoccupied with other issues of sexual morality at this time, such as contraception and sex education in Quaker schools. Frost conducted a series of interviews with deans of Quaker schools, and he surmised from his research that in the 1950s and '60s "a pattern of silence and looking the other way remained the norm for Quaker institutions." For instance, a former dean at the historically Quaker Swarthmore college told Frost that an unofficial policy was in effect through the 1960s which meant automatic expulsion for any student reported or caught in a homosexual act, but this policy was never enforced.[22]

Today, VOS is celebrated among Liberal American Friends as a watershed moment for Quaker support of LGBT people. The March 2013 issue of *Friends Journal* noted the 50th anniversary of VOS. In a tribute to the authors of VOS, Mitchell Santine Gould writes:

> VOS's greatest value, therefore, came from its radical ability to reimagine – and to model for the rest of the world – Christian morality as a disciplined search rather than a draconian discipline. It declared that love is to be found in action more than in sentiment: it is a manifestation of the Spirit behind all Creation, found in the character of homosexual and heterosexual alike.[23]

Indeed, the publication of VOS in 1963 was groundbreaking. By some accounts, it represents the first public affirmation of gay and lesbian sexuality from an organized religious group.

British Quakers would continue their support for LGBT people for decades.[24] They led the way for a faith-based movement that put unprecedented pressure on the British Parliament to pass new legislation in support of same-sex marriage. Researchers at the University of Sussex were the first to study the spiritual lives of lesbian and gay Friends.[25] And in 2019, British Quakers further demonstrated their support of the LGBTQ community by supporting Hannah Brock Womack, a lesbian and active Quaker, to serve as their representative at Churches Together in England, an ecumenical organization aimed at coordinating the work of different Christian groups.

This overview chapter has illustrated the diversity of Quaker views about gay and lesbian sexuality. It has also outlined the recent history of discourses that have had the greatest influence on Quaker understandings of same-sex life partnerships. The historical scope of this chapter has been somewhat broad, but admittedly focused on significant events in the late twentieth and early twenty-first centuries. More research in the archives of Quaker writings and business minutes prior to the 1950s is needed in order to present a more vivid picture of Quaker views on gay and lesbian sexuality in earlier periods of Quaker history. This chapter has also implied an apparent correlation between contemporary Quaker beliefs in universalism and low degrees of biblical literalism with greater support of gay and lesbian sexuality in the 'Liberal' stream of Quakerism.

One can also surmise from this chapter a similar but contrasting correlation between contemporary Quaker beliefs in Christocentric salvation and high degrees of biblical literalism with opposition to gay and lesbian sexuality in the Evangelical stream of Quakerism. Another important finding is that Quakers in the unprogrammed tradition of worship tend to support gay rights, meanwhile most Yearly Meetings with congregations who worship in the pastoral tradition tend to oppose same-sex marriage legislation. Throughout this chapter, I have intentionally avoided asserting normative claims about what is essential to Quaker or Christian teachings about human sexuality. Furthermore, this chapter has offered a survey of the global tensions between Quakers on homosexuality with an attempt to fairly represent diverse and competing views, but most of it has focused on the development of Quaker thought about gay and lesbian sexuality in the United States and the United Kingdom. At the risk of contributing to the marginalization of Quaker voices from Africa in the academic literature about Quakerism, whom I recognize represent the majority of Quakers worldwide, this chapter presumes that its primary audience is readers in the United States and the United Kingdom who are seeking a greater depth of understanding about how Quakers in their most immediate context have related to homosexuality. Since the literature about African Quakers and other Quakers around the world is thin, more research involving interviews and participant observations is needed in order to produce a more complete study of Quaker views on homosexuality around the world.

Notes

1 George Fox University 2007, *Community Lifestyle Statement*, viewed February 2021, https://www.georgefox.edu/offices/hr/lifestyle-statement.html.
2 Engstrom, E. (2019), *Reid Arthur's Lip Sync 2019*, YouTube, viewed February 2021, https://www.youtube.com/watch?v=v445Nlpmbjc.
3 Swift, T. (2019), November 22, https://twitter.com/taylorswift13.
4 Jenkins, "Viral Video Reignites LGBTQ Debate at Quaker School."
5 Ibid.
6 Fager, "The Separation Generation."

7 Sierra-Cascades Yearly Meeting of Friends, "2017 Epistle."
8 Frost, *Three Twentieth-Century Revolutions*.
9 Calderone, *Human Sexuality and the Quaker Conscience*, preface.
10 Ibid., 1.
11 Brick, "Some Quaker Perspectives on Sexuality," *Friends Face the World*.
12 Fager, "'Quaking over Gay Rights'."
13 Friends Church Kenya, "Quakers and Homosexuality Press Statement."
14 Friends General Conference, "FGC Central Committee Minute Affirming LGBTQ Friends."
15 Illinois Yearly Meeting, Business Meeting Minutes, 1974.
16 Friends Journal, "Proclaiming Love and Justice."
17 Eason, "Gay, Black, and Quaker."
18 Canadian Yearly Meeting, *Faith and Practice*.
19 Friends Home Service Committee, *Towards a Quaker View of Sex*.
20 Ibid.
21 Frost, *Three Twentieth-Century Revolutions*.
22 Ibid.
23 Friends Journal, "From a Quaker View of Sex."
24 See Blamires, *Pushing at the Frontiers of Change*.
25 Munt, "Queer Quakers."

Bibliography

Blamires, David. *Pushing at the Frontiers of Change: A Memoir of Quaker Involvement with Homosexuality*. London, England: Quaker Books, 2012.

Brick, Peggy. "Some Quaker Perspectives on Sexuality." In *Friends Face the World: Some Continuing and Current Quaker Concerns*. Philadelphia, PA: Friends General Conference, 1987, 84–97.

Calderone, Mary Steichen. *Human Sexuality and the Quaker Conscience*. Philadelphia: Friends General Conference, 1973.

Canadian Yearly Meeting. *Faith and Practice*. Ottawa, ON: Canadian Yearly Meeting, 2011.

Eason, Leigh. "Gay, Black, and Quaker: History Catches Up with Bayard Rustin." *Religion Dispatches*, June 2012. https://religiondispatches.org/gay-black-and-quaker-history-catches-up-with-bayard-rustin/. Accessed September 2020.

Fager, Chuck. "The Separation Generation" In *Quaker Theology*. Belle Fonte, PA: QUEST, Quaker Ecumenical Seminars in Theology, Winter 2019.

Fager, Chuck. "'Quaking over Gay Rights' – Kicked in the Head in Wichita." Blog. https://afriendlyletter.com/quaking-over-gay-rights-kicked-in-the-head-in-wichita/. Accessed September 2020.

Friends Church Kenya. "Quakers and Homosexuality Press Statement." December 2012.

Friends General Conference. "FGC Central Committee Minute Affirming LGBTQ Friends." November 2004.

Friends Home Service Committee. *Towards a Quaker View of Sex: An Essay by a Group of Friends*. London: Friends Home Service Committee, 1963.

Frost, J. William. *Three Twentieth-Century Revolutions: Liberal Theology, Sexual Moralities, Peace Testimonies*. Swarthmore College Manuscript, July 2001.

Gould, Mitchell S. "From a Quaker View of Sex." *Friends Journal*, Vol. 59, No. 3, pp. 17–18, February 2013.

Jenkins, Jack. "Viral Video Reignites LGBTQ Debate at Quaker School." *AP NEWS*, Associated Press, 5 December 2019.

McNeil, Stephen. "Proclaiming Love and Justice: American Friends Service Committee and LGBT Rights." *Friends Journal*, Vol. 62, No. 5, pp. 23–27, 2016.

Munt, Sally. "Queer Quakers." In *Queer Spiritualities*. Falmer, UK: University of Sussex, March 2009.

Sierra-Cascades Yearly Meeting. "2017 Epistle." https://www.scymfriends.org/2017-epistle. Accessed September 2020.

46

YOUNG ADULT QUAKERS AND EPILOGUE

A Case Study of an 'Alternative' Worshipping Community

Matt Alton

Introduction

British Quaker worship is distinctive as a religious ritual by virtue of its plain nature. Worshippers enter a plainly decorated room lacking insignia or other religious symbolism and sit on uniform chairs placed in concentric circles around a table which holds flowers and copies of Quaker Faith and Practice and the Bible. Apart from when a participant stands to speak as moved by the Spirit, worshippers sit in silence for an hour until the worship is closed by an Elder who initiates a handshake which ripples around the room. Aside from the duration of worship decreasing by around half an hour per century, the form of Meeting for Worship for British Quakers has changed very little (Dandelion, 2008, p. 43). Dandelion cites the use of semi-programmed (as opposed to unprogrammed) worship, using music or other prepared offerings as the medium of worship, but suggests they exist as 'occasional experiments' (1996, p. 318); indeed, some Local Meetings now run regular all-age, child-inclusive semi-programmed worship, but this is still marginal.

Best's research at residential adolescent Quaker events (for those aged 11–18) found that their use of semi-programmed worship in the form of epilogue – twenty to thirty minutes of worship held in the evening, often after a whole day spent together – was 'normative rather than experimental' (2008, p. 52). He suggests that the setting, form and content of epilogue binds individuals to the group, transforming its participants into members of the collective (Best, 2010, p. 180). This chapter presents the findings of ethnographic research at Young Friends General Meeting (YFGM), Britain's national community for young adult Quakers, with particular consideration given to how the group's regular usage of epilogue cements community and communicates its unity. It details how these Friends remedy problems they perceive in mainstream Quakerism through their community formation and their practice of this 'alternative' form of worship. Aside from Best's (2008, 2010) research which touched upon epilogue, this is the first substantive sociological exploration of the practice; this chapter is also the first published analysis of contemporary British young adult Quakers, apart from my own (Alton, 2019) more journalistic investigation and an internally researched report published by Quakers in Britain in 2016 (Quakers in Britain, 2016).

DOI: 10.4324/9780429030925-50

Context

When Quakerism began in the mid-seventeenth century, 'leaders were typically in their twenties and thirties' (Carter and Best, 2013, p. 458). George Fox was twenty-eight in 1652 when he preached to a thousand people from Firbank Fell; Edward Burrough died while in prison for his Quakerism at the age of twenty-nine; and Robert Barclay published what is still considered 'the most significant work of Quaker systematic theology' at the age of twenty-eight (Carter and Best, 2013, p. 428). At the beginning of the twentieth century, a conference for young adult Friends drew over 400 participants, with the age group 'leading Quakers into the modern era and towards engagement with the world' (Carter and Best, 2013, p. 464). The establishment of Young Friends Central Committee in 1911 (which changed its name to Young Friends General Meeting in 1993) – a group responsible for coordinating the activities of young adult Quakers in Britain – was the beginning of 'increasing independence from the adult movement' and their 'consequent marginalisation' (Carter and Best, 2013, p. 465). In the 1980s, the group's tri-annual weekend gatherings 'regularly drew in excess of a hundred participants' (Carter and Best, 2013, p. 465). The early 2000s saw YFGM's attendance at between eighty and ninety,[1] dropping steadily to draw numbers in the fifties between 2008 and 2016, then rising again to draw numbers in the mid-seventies in the late 2010s[2] (Young Friends General Meeting, 2020).

Today, young adults are marginalised within a Quakerism with an average age of 'between 60 and 70' (Chadkirk, 2014, p. 259). In recent years the reasons for this marginalisation have been examined, with sources citing the membership system, which is found by young adults to be antiquated and exclusionary (YFGM, 1998, p. 166), older Friends not making young adults feel welcome and supported (Quakers in Britain, 2016), and inaccessibility of the structure of voluntary service, which expects role holders to commit to three-year terms (Alton, 2019).

To reflect the attendance of YFGM, young adulthood is defined here as between 18 and 30.[3] Edgell notes that when young adults take part in organised religion, they are often 'the driving force behind the development of new forms of worship and religious organization' (2010, p. 6). Indeed, Guest's research among young adults in the Protestant Evangelical tradition details their use of 'alternative' worship, which subverts tradition through the incorporation of popular culture via video imagery and sound technology and the involvement of the senses through the use of candles and incense (2002, p. 37). Additionally, the group's community formation employs a flatter hierarchy, rejecting the 'tradition of authority embodied in influential preachers' in favour of 'unofficial, shared and de-emphasized' (Guest, 2002, p. 46) leadership. While popular culture is not incorporated into epilogue, I suggest the differences in formation of the YFGM setting as opposed to the Local Meeting setting, the changes to the form of worship present in epilogue compared to that which is dominant in British Quakerism, and the engagement of the body through epilogue's content are sufficient to define epilogue as an 'alternative' worship practice.

Epilogue's Setting

Pilgrim (2008) argues that throughout Quakerism's history, the group has constituted an heterotopia, defined by Hetherington as

> spaces of alternate ordering [which] organize a bit of the social world in a way different to that which surrounds them. That alternate ordering marks them out as Other and allows them to be seen as an example of an alternative way of doing things.
>
> *(1997, p. viii)*

Heterotopia are spaces on the margins of society, geographically or socially, which 'offer opportunities for empowerment through practices of resistance, protest and transgression' (Pilgrim, 2008, p. 54); they are necessarily juxtaposed to a dominant order. Participants rehearse 'ideas and practices that represent the good life' (Hetherington, 1997, p. ix). Sites which uphold the dominant order are often chosen for performances of resistance in the hope members of the mainstream will observe, share and perhaps adopt the vision (Hetherington, 1997, p. 7). Meads' (2008) research with the marginal Quaker group Experiment with Light argues that in this group the 'heterotopic impulse operates only within [British Quakerism]' (p. 226), meaning for this group mainstream Quakerism becomes the dominant order to be transgressed. I argue that YFGM constitutes an heterotopia in opposition to mainstream Quakerism.

Where early Friends appropriated courtrooms and churches – 'orderly places' which 'were central to the upholding of social order' (Pilgrim, 2008, p. 56) – to make their truth visible, for three weekends a year YFGM takes over a Quaker meeting house. These are sites central to the dominant order of Quakerism, where YFGM's vision for the good life may be observed. After joining Sunday morning Meeting for Worship with local Friends, YFGM gives a notice of thanks for their inhabitation of the building, then joins these Friends for coffee where they converse about the weekend's activities, making their alternate ordering visible.

Young adults commonly arrive at Sunday morning Meeting for Worship in their localities to find a sea of grey and white hair. While young adults do often build nurturing intergenerational relationships with older Friends, YFGMers regularly feel patronised or are made to feel valued only because they reduce a Meeting's average age so dramatically. Fourteen local young adult groups exist (Quakers in Britain, 2020); however, many YFGMers do not live near enough to attend one. Accordingly, for many, YFGM is an escape from not only the difficulties of everyday life but also from less-than-perfect situations in their local Quaker communities, as well as a rare opportunity to connect with others whose faith, values *and* generational experiences are akin to their own. In addition, young adults, who are prone to geographical relocation, are frustrated by the system whereby becoming a member requires commitment to a locality (Young Friends General Meeting, 1998; Quakers in Britain, 2016); those who attend YFGM once are considered members and can thus access the spaces available to those in membership of the Religious Society of Friends.[4]

YFGMers regularly emphasise the 'understanding', 'compassion' and 'closeness' present at the event, comparing that to the 'distance and politeness' they experience at Local Meetings. One participant commented:

> I feel like our official name [of The Religious Society of Friends] is far more apt for YFGM, because you are amongst friends, you just are, even if it's your first time . . . people treat you like you're friends and there is just an implicit trust in that space.

Participants build strong relationships with each other, freely sharing intimate details of their lives. Meads' participants similarly 'exposed their vulnerabilities' and accordingly 'expressed greater trust' (2008, p. 219) in each other. This practice is 'uncommon in twenty first century British Quaker Meetings' (Meads, 2008, p. 216) and sets participants apart from other Quakers while binding them together as a group.

Epilogue is powerful for participants 'because of the whole space in which it happens', with one worshipper commenting:

> It comes from within, whereas when I go to Sunday worship that is me going into a space that's been organised by others.

Quaker nominations process, used to appoint to roles of spiritual, pastoral and practical support and organisation, ensures that all event organisers have been chosen by the community. The Spirit-led discernment process begins with a nomination from a community member, the name then being discerned upon by a nominations committee (also appointed by the community), who then return suggested names to the community for agreement and appointment. While a similar process is undertaken to appoint to roles in Local Meetings, young adults' relative disengagement from these communities leads to a lack of ownership over the Meeting's roles and the organisation of its space.

Throughout a YFGM day, Friends wake up having slept on floors or camping mattresses next to each other, worship together, participate in Spirit-led discernment on issues pertaining to the community, facilitate and attend workshops ranging from poetry to activism, cook, eat and clear up together, and attend entertainments such as a talent show or Cèilidh dancing. All of this contributes to the emotional openness and closeness described above. On attending epilogue, participants 'carry everything [they have] discussed and experienced as a community', which compares starkly with Sunday morning worship where 'all these different people come from their own weeks which are very different'. By Saturday evening's epilogue[5] participants are, to use a term coined by Best, in 'Quaker mode' (2010, p. 179). This 'Quaker mode' lasts a whole weekend, as opposed to the 'Quaker time' adopted by Sunday morning worshippers which lasts around two hours. Best suggests that 'adopting this "Quaker mode" represents a transformation' where 'ritual is instrumental in causing this transformation' (Best, 2010, p. 181).

Epilogue's Form and Content

Collins' ethnographic account of Meeting for Worship tells us that participants' physical arrangement signifies 'through 'ritual' embodiment, both equality between people and also the direct relationship each person has with God' (2005, p. 328). Worshippers sit on chairs in concentric circles facing the centre, no Friend sits higher than another, and nobody is marked as different by their clothing or other insignia (Collins, 2005, p. 328). Elsewhere, he argues that 'it is almost inconceivable that the spatial arrangement of worship should differ from that prescribed by convention' (Collins, 1998, p. 504). Dandelion writes that 'in the Quaker context, those who manage the space often define it' (2005, p. 107). It is powerful for YFGMers to choose the spatial arrangement of the room in which epilogue takes place, and they use this defining power to break the dominant spatial arrangement of Meeting for Worship, forming a new relationship with their embodiment during the ritual.

Rather than chairs arranged in concentric circles, Elders direct volunteers to lay chairs in one large circle around the border of the room. On entrance to the room which is lit by electric candles, some worshippers choose a chair, however just as many sit or lie on the floor, maintaining the singular circle. With many participants sleeping in the meeting house, they are legitimised in worshipping with bare feet, wearing nightclothes, or using cushions to make their chosen bodily orientation most comfortable – physical markers which I suggest indicate feelings of social comfort rather than any discrepancy in status. Participants feel supported in their decision to sit or lie comfortably because the rest of the community knows their 'situation':

> My bones make a lot of noises, I move around a lot and I have a lot of pain. In normal Meeting for Worship I'm trying not to disturb people, and I'm trying to sit in the way that's most appropriate, whereas in epilogue if my hip makes a really weird noise that's fine because I'm just lying here and people know my situation. Some people know my situation at my Local Meeting, but not very well.

This Friend describes and celebrates an outcome of the closeness experienced at YFGM, which is extended into epilogue. In addition, participants cite the relative darkness of the room as leading to social comfort, free from the surveillance of other worshippers, enabling them to make decisions which support their physical comfort.

The acceptance, or even embrace, of the body by epilogue's participants reaches further significance when we consider the comment:

> There's something about being able to be embodied and for spirituality to come into that as well. Often [in a Local Meeting setting] it's like it's all just in our heads and there isn't that space created for spirituality to be something that's in our bodies as well, and any way that we can fit more of that in is good.

Counter to the dualism experienced by this Friend, Tarter's (2004) research has shown how the earliest Quakers' theology affirmed the 'unity of the body and spirit in religious worship' (p. 89). As a result of this 'theory of the body' (Tarter, 2004, p. 94) early Friends were prone to unpredictable quaking during worship, as well as impulsive actions as led by the Spirit. Following a high profile and reputation-damaging occurrence known as the 'Nayler incident', where James Nayler re-enacted Jesus' Palm Sunday entry into Jerusalem, theology and practice was modified to separate the body and spirit, ensuring 'a conformity of spiritual practice' (Tarter, 2004, p. 91) and instructing Friends to 'test their leadings before giving them voice or movement' (Tarter, 2004, p. 90). According to Tarter, 'the theory of the body is most likely a foreign concept' (2004, p. 94) to contemporary Quaker experience, although she cites excitement and enthusiasm from many who at learning of this past 'suddenly have a history to which they can connect' (Tarter, 2004, p. 97) their physical experiences in worship. I suggest that the comment of the participant above, and the general attitude to the body in epilogue, represents an implicit (albeit inadvertent) step in returning to the theory (and experience) of body and spirit's unity.

One Saturday evening, I witnessed the Elders huddling in a quiet corner half an hour before the start of epilogue to decide what the prepared offering would be. At first I took this as poor organisation, but found out later:

> We never plan epilogues ahead of time, and that isn't just because we don't bother. Often, half an hour before, one of the Elders will suggest something and that just works. If we don't come up with anything maybe that's a sign that we just need to have an unplanned one.

Participants could see that epilogue's prepared contributions were chosen after participating in and reflecting upon the day, one commenting:

> Epilogue has the day stacked into it. It's full of the day in a way that the morning meeting isn't full of anything yet.

Here, they neatly summarise the previous section, that epilogue happens in the context of all the shared thoughts, feelings and actions that have preceded it. During my research period, Planning Weekend epilogues did not contain a prepared offering from Elders; I suggest the significantly smaller group needed less input to achieve group unity. At YFGM events, all four epilogues contained a prepared offering from Elders: in one, using 'gifts' to serve others was spoken about; one contained a message about the unity of the group and its potential to do good in the world; another contained a short meditation where participants were invited to focus their attention on their body, then consider the room's kindness at enabling their presence; and in one, participants were invited to 'get as comfortable as you can – lie down, put your head on someone's shoulder'. The last two prepared offerings cited link back to the engagement of the body present in YFGM epilogues.

Participants felt that Elders had a 'strong knack' for reading the events of the day (be them stressful, energetic or lacking unity) and choosing content which the community required. This role represents an extension of the power afforded to Elders, who in a Local Meeting setting occasionally choose readings from Quaker Faith and Practice or the Bible, but whose control of worship's content is otherwise limited to curbing transgressions of the rules worshippers should adhere to (Dandelion, 1996, pp. 193–236). Previous research with this age group found frustration at the suspicion of leadership present in British Quakerism, with young adults 'invok[ing] the Quaker theology of gifts to celebrate those who can lead' (Alton, 2019, p. 32). The extension of Elders' control over worship, and the community's trust in them to reflect back the day's fullness in their leadership of epilogue, shows the group to be practising what they hope to see in wider Quakerism. Guest (2002) found that 'alternative' worshippers in the Evangelical tradition de-emphasised the leadership roles which prevailed in mainstream Evangelicalism – here we see the inverse, where Quakerism's usual de-emphasis of leadership becomes more accentuated.

To return to the spatial orientation of worshippers, the singular circle enables epilogue's closing moment. After around half an hour, the whole group holds hands in a circle, with great effort being made to include each person. One YFGMer said:

> It does feel in epilogue more like we're together and connected, which is symbolised by what we do at the end. In Meeting for Worship we just shake hands with just the people around us and we don't get to everyone, but that seems OK, but then in epilogue we do all physically hold hands even with the person on the other side of the room. I think that it shows the connectedness more.

Table 46.1 Comparison of YFGM and Epilogue With Local Meetings and Sunday Morning Meeting for Worship

YFGM and Epilogue	Local Meeting and Sunday Morning Meeting for Worship
Shared generational experience	Intergenerational
Time spent together leading up to epilogue	No time spent together leading up to worship
Understanding and compassion	Politeness
Closeness	Distance
Space created by young adults	Space created by older Friends
Room is dark	Room is light
Social comfort	Social discomfort
Room laid out for people to sit and lie on the floor	Room laid out for people to sit on chairs (exceptions made if you know who to ask)
Physical comfort	Physical discomfort
Prepared offering responds to the day and can be anything Elders choose	Usually no prepared offering, occasional readings limited to Quaker Faith and Practice or the Bible
Elders' control over worship extended to discerning what the community requires	Elders' control over worship limited to curbing transgressions
Holding hands to close	Shaking hands to close

Best (2010, p. 179) suggests that this practice in the adolescent group is 'a symbol of community togetherness', and I apply this analysis to the young adult group.

I suggest that epilogue is a powerful ritual of community building, serving to bind participants to the collective. One participant commented:

> I would almost say that epilogue embodies the community that we feel at YFGM . . . the community is always there, but there's so many other things going on, but then in epilogue we're coming together and feeling that.

This echoes the experiences of adolescent Quaker accounts of epilogue, who speak of experiencing heightened connection and unity with other worshippers (Best, 2010, p. 75). Following Durkheim ([1912] 1995), Mellor and Shilling emphasise the capacity of embodied and emotional gatherings to 'surpass the individual characteristics' (2014, p. 50) of the self. Through participation in a totemic representation of the social group, the individual is 'swept up by a collectively generated effervescence' (Mellor and Shilling, 2014, p. 24) which transforms individuals into members of the group and attaches them to its moral norms, as represented by the ritual. I suggest that epilogue's intensity has this effect, acting as 'social glue' (Ramp, 1998, p. 137) between participants. The moral norms and 'rules of conduct' (Mellor and Shilling, 2014, p. 50) depicted by the ritual are communicated, emboldening worshippers to adopt them, which in this case consist not only of the ultimate equality of all (also communicated by mainstream Quaker worship), but trust in Elders to exercise some control over worship's content, and the promotion of the body as a place of comfort and spiritual integration.

Conclusion

Young adults are marginalised within British Quakerism, and through the formation of their national community and their use of an 'alternative' worship practice they model an ideal Quakerism, at odds with the mainstream in numerous ways (see Table 46.1). YFGM is held in a space central to the dominant order of Quakerism, where those they criticise may observe their alternative practices. A shared generational experience and extensive time spent together enables sharing and vulnerability, which leads to understanding, compassion and closeness between participants, as opposed to the patronisation and distance participants experience at Local Meetings. Young adults have ownership over the space, which they experience as heterotopic in juxtaposition to mainstream Quakerism. A speculative thesis would argue that YFGM also constitutes an heterotopia in relation to wider non-Quaker society; however, more research is required to explore this.

This ability to define the space comes to the fore during epilogue, where the spatial arrangement of the room is subtly but importantly different to that of a Local Meeting's Meeting for Worship. This arrangement, participants' intimate knowledge of each other, and the darkness of the room allows worshippers to position their bodies comfortably. YFGMers' acceptance, or even embrace of the body during epilogue represents an inadvertent move towards the founding theology of Quakerism. Having reflected upon the day and considered what the community would benefit from, Elders offer a prepared contribution, sometimes encouraging worshippers' engagement with their bodies through this. In contributing to the content of epilogue this way, Elders' power is extended beyond its usual limits, reflecting YFGMers' trust in their capacity to guide worship. Epilogue is understood by participants to 'embod[y] the community'; it is a powerful ritual that binds individuals to the group and communicates YFGM's moral norms.

The 'alternative' way of worshipping regularly used by YFGM supports Collins and Dande-lion's thesis that 'Quakers take the opportunity to adopt rituals and other modes of behaviour that are outside of . . . mainstream Quakerism' (2014, p. 298), demonstrating 'significant liquid-ity' (2014, p. 297). Through epilogue, and through the community in which it happens, these young adults transgress the norms of Quaker practice and demonstrate their ideal vision.

Notes

1 To find these figures, the mean average attendance of the three events each year has been calculated.
2 The significant increase from an average attendance of fifty-seven in 2016 to seventy-six in 2017 coin-cides with the beginning of the Engaging Young Adult Quakers Project and Britain Yearly Meeting minuting its commitment to 'remove barriers and actively seek wider participation' (Quakers in Britain, 2017) from young adults, both in 2017. An explanation of the correlation between these occurrences is beyond the scope of this chapter and would require further research.
3 There is some inconsistency with YFGM's (and British Quakerism's) categorisation of 'young adult', with some sources quoting eighteen to thirty-five years of age.
4 Members may attend local and national business sessions without pre-acquired permission, and can be appointed to a host of roles at local and national level which attenders cannot be considered for.
5 On attending Friday evening's epilogue, participants will have spent up to three hours engaging in YFGM activities.

Bibliography

Alton, M. (2019). Young Adults and the Future of Quakerism – Adding Voices to the Conversation. *Friends Quarterly.* 47(2), pp. 25–35.
Best, S. (2008). Adolescent Quakers: A Community of Intimacy. In Dandelion, P. and Collins, P. eds. *The Quaker Condition: The Sociology of a Liberal Religion.* Newcastle: Cambridge Scholars Publishing, pp. 192–215.
Best, S. (2010). *The Community of Intimacy: The Spiritual Beliefs and Religious Practices of Adolescent Quakers.* PhD thesis, University of Birmingham.
Carter, M.L. and Best, S. (2013). Quakers, Youth and Young Adults. In Angell, S. W. and Dandelion, P. eds. *The Oxford Handbook of Quaker Studies.* Oxford: Oxford University Press, pp. 458–473.
Chadkirk, J. W. C. (2014). *Patterns of Membership and Participation Among British Quakers, 1823–2012.* PhD thesis, University of Birmingham.
Collins, P. (1998). Quaker Worship: An Anthropological Perspective. *Worship.* 72(6), pp. 501–515.
Collins, P. (2005). Thirteen Ways of Looking at a 'Ritual'. *Journal of Contemporary Religion.* 20(3), pp. 323–342.
Collins, P. and Dandelion, P. (2014). Transition as Normative: British Quakerism as Liquid Religion. *Journal of Contemporary Religion.* 29(2), pp. 287–301.
Dandelion, P. (1996). *A Sociological Analysis of the Theology of Quakers: The Silent Revolution.* Lampeter: Edwin Mellen Press.
Dandelion, P. (2005). *The Liturgies of Quakerism.* Aldershot: Ashgate.
Dandelion, P. (2008). *The Quakers: A Very Short Introduction.* Oxford: Oxford University Press.
Durkheim, E. [1912] 1995. *The Elementary Forms of Religious Life.* New York: Free Press.
Edgell, P. (2010). Faith and Spirituality among Emerging Adults. *Lifelong Faith the Theory and Practice of Lifelong Faith Formation.* 4(2), pp. 3–8.
Guest, M. (2002). Alternative Worship: Challenging the Boundaries of the Christian Faith. In Arweck, E and Stringer, M.D. eds. *Theorizing Faith: The Insider/Outsider Problem in the Study of Ritual.* Birmingham: University of Birmingham Press, pp. 35–56.
Hetherington, K. (1997). *The Badlands of Modernity: Heterotopia and Social Ordering.* London: Routledge.
Meads, H. (2008). 'Experiment with Light': Radical Spiritual Wing of British Quakerism. In Dandelion, P. and Collins, P. eds. *The Quaker Condition: The Sociology of a Liberal Religion.* Newcastle: Cambridge Scholars Publishing, pp. 216–232.
Mellor, P. A. and Shilling, C. (2014). *Sociology of the Sacred: Religion, Embodiment and Social Change.* London: Sage.

Pilgrim, G. (2008). British Quakerism as Heterotopic. In Dandelion, P. and Collins, P. eds. *The Quaker Condition: The Sociology of a Liberal Religion*. Newcastle: Cambridge Scholars Publishing, pp. 53–67.

Quakers in Britain. (2016). *Engaging Young Adult Friends – What Do We Know So Far?* [Online]. [Accessed 25 July 2020]. Available from: https://quaker-prod.s3-eu-west-1.amazonaws.com/store/4ba899e84f3a ed8dee3f7968a0972fc63bc159c4c49b48d63d428a85896a.

Quakers in Britain. (2017). *Yearly Meeting Gathering 2017.* [Online]. [Accessed 25 July 2020]. Available from: https://www.quaker.org.uk/ym/all-meetings-1/yearly-meeting-gathering-2017-archive.

Quakers in Britain. (2020). *Young Adult Quaker Groups*. [Online]. [Accessed 25 July 2020]. Available from: https://www.quaker.org.uk/our-organisation/young-adult-quakers/yaf-groups.

Ramp, W. (1998). Effervescence, Differentiation and Representation in The Elementary Forms. In Allen, N.J., Pickering, W. S. F. and Watts Miller, W. eds. *On Durkheim's Elementary Forms of Religious Life*. London: Routledge, pp. 136–148.

Tarter, M.L. (2004). 'Go North!' The Journey towards First-generation Friends and Their Prophecy of Celestial Flesh. In Dandelion, P. ed. *The Creation of Quaker Theory: Insider Perspectives*. Abingdon: Routledge, pp. 83–98.

Young Friends General Meeting. (1998). *Who Do We Think We Are? Young Friends' Commitment and Belonging*. London: Quaker Home Service.

Young Friends General Meeting. (2020). *Documents Library*. [Online]. [Accessed 25 July 2020]. Available from: https://yfgm.quaker.org.uk/actions-forms/documents-library.

47

QUAKER ARCHIVES IN THE UNITED STATES

Mary Crauderueff

Introduction

William Penn once wrote that George Fox was "often where the records of the affairs of the church are kept and where the letters from the many meetings of God's people over all the world . . . come upon occasions" (Nickalls, *Journal of George Fox*, p. xlv). With this in mind, it's therefore easy to imagine, as historian Larry Ingle describes, Fox sitting down to write his now-famous *Journal*, sifting through "the movement's archives, kept by the diligent Margaret Fell" – the first Quaker repository of many, likely held at her Swarthmoor Hall home (Ingle, 'George Fox, Historian,' 28). Fox's interest in, and us of, archival materials is indicative of the importance of record-keeping and preservation as far back as the first generation of Friends.

Since the earliest days of the Quaker movement, Friends have recorded memoirs, testimonies, letters, vital records, minutes, and epistles: records of people, of faith, of land, of organizations, of family. While early Quakers were ministering around the English countryside in the 1650s, and continuing up to today around the world, Friends have been creating and saving these documents. All members of the Religious Society of Friends have histories that are important to collect, preserve, and give access to. Since the beginnings of Quakerism, individuals and groups have collected these materials, creating Quaker archives in their meeting houses and homes.

Around the world today, Quaker archives contain family papers, organizational records, books, photographs, and tracts. These archives exist in several ways, including formal and informal. Formal archives include those such as the National Library of Australia and the University of Tasmania (Australian Quakers), the Library of the Religious Society of Friends in Britain (British Quakers), and the new Africa Quaker Archives (African Quakers) – Quaker materials held in formal institutions with the understanding that these materials will be held in perpetuity. Informal archives include materials held in meetinghouses and organizations around the world – known to those who worship or work in those locations, but not connected with a formal institution.

A deep examination of all of these materials is worthy of book-length study, and this chapter will provide an overview of major, formal Quaker archives in the United States today, striving to detail where the stories of Quaker history have been preserved, to collect practices of those locations, and to explore whose stories have historically been represented within the archives

DOI: 10.4324/9780429030925-51

and the access provided to these records. The author researched policies on collection management and access primarily by gleaning information from library websites and available policy documentation. This examination occurred in early summer 2020.

History of Quaker Archives

The history of many Quaker archival collections in the United States is closely linked with the opening of the colleges that house them. For instance, the opening year of Haverford College in 1833–1834 included a manuscript donation by Henry Pemberton of "the Letters and Papers of William Penn" (Haverford College, 2020). Additional archival collections were donated over the next 89 years, and cared for by college librarians until 1922, when the first Curator of the Quaker Collection was hired: faculty member Rayner Kelsey. Today, the Haverford College Quaker and Special Collections are both programmatically and physically intertwined with the rest of the College Libraries. The Quaker and Special Collections includes college archives, Quaker family and organizational papers, and Quaker meeting records among its collections. These types of collections are paralleled at Haverford's sibling institutions.

Collecting Practices

In most areas of the United States, Quaker meeting records, including yearly, quarterly, monthly, and preparative meeting records, were originally held in yearly meeting archives before transfer to a Quaker college decades later. For instance, it was only in the 1970s when the Philadelphia Yearly Meeting records were divided from their home in the Arch Street Meeting House vault and brought to Haverford and Swarthmore Colleges. Each of the repositories detail in their collecting policies, not only genre, but geographic areas from which they collect. For example, the Quaker Archives at Guilford College "has a special responsibility for comprehensiveness in documenting and for nurturing research relating to the spiritual, intellectual and cultural heritage of Quakerism in the southeastern United States" (Guilford College, 2020). Many institutions, such as Earlham College, outline certain types of archival records they specialize in. Earlham College, for example, "collects . . . Records and other materials relating to Friends United Meeting" (Earlham College, 2020).

In addition to serving communities of Quakers and furthering the representation of Quakerism in the historical record, the location of these Quaker archives within academic institutions means there is a second, equally important goal of serving the campus community of faculty, staff, and students. This policy from the Haverford College Quaker and Special Collections (QSC) outlines these intersecting objectives:

> [QSC] collects, preserves, and makes available materials which serve the mission of Haverford College and the Haverford College Libraries. These materials, which are collected in a variety of formats, support teaching, research, and scholarship by Haverford students, faculty and staff, as well as researchers from around the world. As a major repository of materials by and about the Society of Friends, [QSC] serves as a resource for scholars engaged in critical work related to Quakers and Quakerism as well as for members of the Quaker community . . . [QSC] is committed to collecting materials which document hidden, undertold, or beyond the mainstream narratives.
>
> *(Haverford College, 2019)*

Access to Collections

Entering an archive to conduct research generally requires the researcher to register with the host institution, sometimes in advance. The majority of the Quaker archives do require some coordination before arrival on campus, including making appointments for visits. Many also require a photo ID for a visit. At Earlham, they state why they do not require IDs: "Consistent with Earlham's *Principles and Practices*, we put a high level of trust into our student workers and the Earlham community by not requiring researchers to show identification" (Earlham College, 2020). Fortunately, the Quaker repositories do not require any particular education level or academic recommendations in order to access collections, common practices in the field that can exacerbate disparities in archival access.

Quaker collections that have a larger staff are able to provide greater access to materials. For instance, the Haverford College Quaker and Special Collections are open 40 hours a week to all researchers, both on- and off-campus constituents, and do not require prior appointments. Others, such as Whittier College and George Fox University, do require researchers to make appointments. Once inside, curators, librarians and/or reference staff are available to assist researchers with their questions and retrieve materials for use. Collaboration with other institutions can expand capacity to serve patrons, as at Wilmington College, where responsibility for answering genealogy questions is shared with the Clinton County History Center (Wilmington College, 2020).

If researchers are unable to come to the archives, staff answer questions remotely, sending copies of materials as they are able (and as copyright allows), and usually referring long-distance researchers to local researchers for more involved questions. While the entirety of materials within these Quaker archives is not available online, many Quaker repositories have a selection of digital surrogates available in browsable and searchable collections. Materials are prioritized for digitization based on a variety of criteria, including funding, class support, and collaborations on projects with other archives and organizations. Digital collections such as the Earlham Digital Collections (Earlham College, unknown) bring together different projects into a digital asset management portal that can be searched. Materials from digital collections can then be pulled into online exhibitions, often with browsable materials, such as the "Beyond Penn's Treaty: Quaker and American Indian Relations" project co-hosted by Haverford College's Quaker and Special Collections and Friends Historical Library at Swarthmore College (Beyond Penn's Treaty, 2018). This project includes metadata spreadsheets and transcribed documents, which are freely available for visitors to download and reuse for their own projects. Another example of a collaboration is the Civil Rights Greensboro Collection, which includes materials like newspapers and faculty minutes contributed by Guilford College (University of North Carolina–Greensboro, unknown).

Shifts in Scholarship Over Time

For decades – over a century, for many of these repositories – the near totality of researchers in Quaker archives have been Quakers themselves. Pre-eminent Quaker scholar Dr. Emma Lapsansky-Werner has called this the "by Quakers, about Quakers, for Quakers" phenomenon (personal communication, February 1, 2016). Aimed at a specifically internal Quaker audience, this work tends to use Quaker jargon and exclusively center Quaker voices. In the twenty-first century, there has started to be a shift toward non-Quakers using Quaker records to explore topics like Quakers and women, Quakers and education, Quakers and abolition, or Quakers and philanthropy.[1] These researchers are publishing a larger breadth of scholarship than their predecessors, for more diverse audiences, in publications that are not only about Quakers.

The shift away from exclusively Quaker scholarship on Quaker topics has aligned with an increase in access to collections. Twenty-first-century technology advances have created opportunities for archives to promote their materials in online finding aids, digital repositories, social media, and more. Online access allows more people to interact with collection materials, and broader access in turn allows more critical lenses to be turned on the dominant narratives regarding Quaker social influence.

Conclusion

While these archives collectively strive to be representative of all Quakers in the United States, there is a perpetual need to grow collections to ensure representation of contemporary Quakers, including Quakers of diverse backgrounds. As there is no formal consortium to coordinate, this is done informally in intercollegiate conversations. Decisions about what materials, from and about which people, should be included in archival collections have a profound and ongoing impact on our understanding of who Quakers are and what Quakerism has been. What is chosen to be collected today – who is approached to donate personal papers, what topics and organizations we seek to represent in our collections – will have the same lasting impact on how recent and contemporary Quakerism is understood in the decades and centuries to come.

Notes

1 For example see:

Quakers and women: these references represent scholarship about Quaker women around the world, over different times of Quaker history:

Acosta, Ana M. (2019). "From Unnatural Fanatics to 'Fair Quakers': How English Mainstream Culture Transformed Women Friends between 1650 and 1740." *Eighteenth-Century Fiction* 31 (4): 705–725.

Bouldin, Elizabeth. (2015). *Women Prophets and Radical Protestantism in the British Atlantic World, 1640–1730.* New York: Cambridge University Press.

Othman, Enaya. (2016). *Negotiating Palestinian Womanhood: Encounters between Palestinian Women and American Missionaries, 1880s–1940s.* Lanham: Lexington Books.

Youngblood Ashmore, Susan, and Dorr Lisa Lindquist, eds. (2017). *Alabama Women: Their Lives and Times,* 129–144. Athens: University of Georgia Press.

Quakers and education: these materials represent how Quakerism can be brought into context with other subjects:

Hinitz, Blythe Simone Farb, and Susan A. Miller. (2013). *The Hidden History of Early Childhood Education.* New York: Routledge.

Jones-Branch, Cherisse. (2019). 'To Raise Standards among the Negroes': Jeanes Supervising Industrial Teachers in Rural Jim Crow Arkansas, 1909–1950. *Agricultural History* 93 (3): 412–436.

Rendell, Mike, and Daniel Defoe. (2018). *Trailblazing Women of the Georgian Era: The Eighteenth-Century Struggle for Female Success in a Man's World.* Barnsley, South Yorkshire: Pen & Sword History.

Who Writes for Black Children? African American Children's Literature before 1900. (2017). Edited by Katharine Capshaw and Anna Mae Duane, 117–144. Minneapolis: University of Minnesota Press.

Quakers and abolition: this scholarship portrays Quaker involvement in anti-slavery and abolition movements as a whole, and not centering their work as heroic:

Frost, Karolyn Smardz, and Veta Smith Tucker, eds. (2016). *A Fluid Frontier: Slavery, Resistance, and the Underground Railroad in the Detroit River Borderland.* Detroit: Wayne State University Press.

Gerbner, Katharine. (2019). *Christian Slavery.* Philadelphia: University of Pennsylvania Press.

Newman, Richard S. (2015). Freedom's Grand Lab: Abolition, Race, and Black Freedom Struggles in Recent Pennsylvania Historiography. *Pennsylvania History* 82 (3): 357–372.

Quakers and humanitarian aid and philanthropy: these articles are written by historians on work that occurred in the first half of the twentieth century:

Aiken, Guy. (2019). Feeding Germany: American Quakers in the Weimar Republic. *Diplomatic History* 43 (4): 597–617.

Garcia Ferrandis, Xavier, and Alvar Martinez-Vidal. (2019). Humanitarian Aid from the British Quakers During the Spanish Civil War (1936–1939): The Case of the Children's Hospital of Polop De La Marina (alicante). *Asclepio-Revista De Historia De La Medicina Y De La Ciencia* 71 (1): 253.

Reid, Fiona. (2019). The Friends Ambulance Unit. *Medicine, Conflict and Survival* 35 (2): 140–143.

References

Earlham College. (unknown). *Earlham College Digital Collections*. Retrieved June 20, 2020 from https://palni.contentdm.oclc.org/digital/collection/ec_archives/custom/earlham

Earlham College. (2020, July 1). *Reading Room Policies*. Retrieved June 10, 2020 from http://library.earlham.edu/c.php?g=82612&p=533219

Guilford College. (2020, March 25). *About*. Retrieved June 20, 2020, from http://library.guilford.edu/about

Haverford College. (2019, May 31). *Collection Description, Goals, and Policies, Quaker & Special Collections, Haverford College Libraries*. Retrieved June 20, 2020 from https://www.haverford.edu/sites/default/files/Office/Library/Quaker-Special-Collections-Collection-Goals-and-Policies.pdf

Haverford College. (2020, July 1). *About: Timeline*. Retrieved July 20, 2020, from https://www.haverford.edu/library/about

Haverford College and Swarthmore College. (2018, October 1). *Beyond Penn's Treaty*. Retrieved June 20, 2020 from https://pennstreaty.haverford.edu/

Ingle, Larry. (1993). "George Fox, Historian." *Quaker History* 82 (1): 28.

Nickalls, John L. (1995). *The Journal of George Fox*. Philadelphia: Religious Society of Friends, xlv.

University of North Carolina-Greensboro. (unknown). *Digital Collections, Civil Rights Greensboro*. Retrieved June 20, 2020 from http://libcdm1.uncg.edu/cdm/landingpage/collection/CivilRights

Wilmington College. (2020, June 18). *Quaker Special Collections*. Retrieved June 20, 2020 from http://libguides.wilmington.edu/c.php?g=238506&p=1585382

48

DISMANTLING WHITE SUPREMACY IN QUAKER ARCHIVES

A Case Study

Mary Crauderueff

Introduction

The work described here is the beginning of a long-term journey to dismantle the white supremacy and other forms of bias and oppression built into the Haverford College Quaker and Special Collections (QSC), as well as the library and archives fields more broadly. In this process, collections staff seek to uncover biased and oppressive practices, and to recognize and uplift voices and stories of those who have been marginalized by race, ethnicity, gender identity, sexual orientation, ability, education level, and more. This chapter will outline the steps the QSC department has taken in recent years to dismantle various elements of white supremacy and increase the diversity of staff, programs, and collections.

Haverford College was founded outside of Philadelphia, Pennsylvania, in 1833 as an Orthodox Quaker institution. Today the college identifies as nonsectarian and "historically Quaker," with roots in Quaker history and values. These values are reflected in the flat hierarchy among administration and the active role of faculty, staff, and students in decision-making. Within the college's curriculum, policies, and practices, there has historically been an emphasis on social justice (Haverford College, 2020).

The main library, where the Quaker and Special Collections (QSC) department is located, completed an 18-month renovation in fall 2019. During the renovation, the QSC department was closed to outside researchers. QSC and staff members took the opportunity to review all department policies to determine how to make them accessible and inclusive for all, while still protecting the collections, in perpetuity, for use by students, faculty, academic researchers, genealogists, and informal researchers.

Staff

The department staff includes 5.5 full-time equivalents, which represents six staff, including three curators, a full-time and part-time conservator, and a rotating two-year post-baccalaureate position. There are also several volunteers and student workers.

Two elements of the QSC staffing structure, in particular, reflect recent work supporting diversity within the department. First, in 2020 the department hired its inaugural Anne T. and

DOI: 10.4324/9780429030925-52

J. Morris Evans Post-baccalaureate Fellow. This Fellowship was developed with the intention of fostering a mentoring experience for members of groups who are dramatically underrepresented in the libraries and archives field, such as people of color (Rosa and Henke, 2017). A key element of the position is digitizing and promoting collections within the QSC. The hiring committee for the Fellowship has implemented a recurring implicit bias training, which occurs before any applications have been reviewed for the position. This training has been a useful tool for the committee and is beginning to be implemented as part of hiring processes throughout Haverford Libraries.

The second integral element is the role of student workers. The number of student workers varies year to year due to funding and availability, but the work they do is instrumental in the amount of work the department is able to complete. The library, and therefore QSC, prioritizes hiring students who are on work study, in particular from the John P. Chesick Scholars Program (Haverford College, unknown). This program provides employment and mentorship for students from backgrounds that are underrepresented in academia, often first-generation or low-income college students. Students are hired and treated as colleagues within the work of the department. Over time, increasingly complex projects build the students' knowledge and skills, allowing them to develop expertise in a particular type of project. Eventually, students rely on each other to learn, reserving high-level questions for their supervisors.

QSC has two tracks of students. Traditional student workers process collections to make them available for researchers. Liaisons work in the reading room, facilitating research for patrons. In addition, liaisons may be asked to complete projects that can be conducted in between assisting patrons. The liaison program is a peer-to-peer system implemented throughout the Haverford Libraries system. The goals of this program are to provide a welcoming presence in the libraries and to position students as experts able to answer patron questions or direct them to someone who can. Student liaisons are often the public face of the QSC and are usually the first people who researchers will interact with when they arrive in the QSC reading room. The department also welcomes student project interns during the summer.

Student workers also do critical work in digital scholarship collaborations. In recent years, digital scholarship projects like the Quakers and Mental Health portal, the Quaker Manumissions project, and the Quakers and Slavery and Penn's Treaty online exhibition and digitization projects have been part of the ongoing work to amplify marginalized voices in the collections.

Student worker projects are assigned with the intention of producing portfolio pieces or building skills that students will be able to use in their post-collegiate work. These have included building full and pop-up exhibitions, preparing social media posts, and capturing, editing, and sending images of materials for patrons, among other tasks. Teaching these students to be experts in their work, and then encouraging them to teach and support fellow student workers, helps to disrupt the traditional hierarchy of education in which knowledge only passes in one direction, from teacher to student. Instead, the student worker training model embraces the concept that knowledge can be passed seamlessly in all directions.

Programs

The renovation of Haverford College's main library presented an opportunity to intentionally create spaces in the physical plant that provide greater access to collections. One such space is a dedicated classroom for the Quaker and Special Collections and Digital Scholarship. New seminar rooms have been designed to include visible storage for manuscript and archives materials, breaking down barriers between students and the archives. Using these new storage spaces to democratize access necessitated changing the QSC's former policy, under which materials could only be stored within the department's vault. Now, faculty are entrusted with keeping materials secure, allowing their students continued access to relevant archival materials over several weeks or even the entire course of a semester. The visible storage is secured, but instructors are able to access it and provide access to their students within the confines of the seminar room.

Prior to the renovation, the department's policy was to collect images of researcher photo IDs. During the process of reevaluating this policy, the department concluded that requiring a photo ID may restrict access – due to implicit bias, or because of the patron's own concerns – for patrons whose ID might not match their gender identity or expression. Similar but distinct concerns and risks might make the ID requirement a barrier for users without US citizenship. Another shift that the QSC department implemented is that when material is pulled for a researcher, class, or exhibition of any kind, information is provided in oral and written form on whether materials can be touched or photographed. When possible, handling materials is encouraged. Staff engage in conversation with patrons around the materials, including why they are allowed to handle the materials or not. Open communication about how to interact with the materials, and the logic behind those expectations, make the archives more accessible to first-time users and others who might worry about not knowing the unspoken rules of the space.

To lessen the financial burden on anyone requesting reproductions, the department removed the cost of making and sending copies, while keeping a limit on the number of copies per year due to staff cost. This ensures that researchers who are unable to physically come to the QSC reading room are still able to complete research, balancing access needs with the limitations of staff time. Most of the QSC's collections have not been fully digitized due to the high costs associated with that work, so reproduction of requested materials is essential to accessibility.

As has been practice since the early 2000s, there is an open-door policy for the reading room. If the department is open, the door is open, and any researcher is able to come inside. The goal is minimum barriers, to make the research process less daunting.

Collections

Quaker archives in the United States have predominantly been built upon stories of white Quakers, often representing Quakers as saviors working with underrepresented groups such as enslaved people or indigenous peoples. When weighing possible changes to policies and practices, the QSC department considers how to collectively open space for Quakers of all genders, races, and sexual orientations to be recognized within the Quaker historical narrative. Two elements of Quaker collections work play a pivotal role in broadening this historical narrative: acquisition, and description.

The Quaker and Special Collections acquire new materials in three ways: through purchases, and through solicited and unsolicited donations. According to the goals of the department, Quaker and Special Collections is committed to "collecting materials which document hidden, undertold, or beyond the mainstream narratives" (Haverford College, 2019). The current Quaker collections are primarily from the early twentieth century and before, as the majority of the collections are donated from descendants of the creators of the materials. Over the past twenty years, the department has begun actively seeking out materials from Quakers during the entirety of the twentieth century and into the twenty-first – especially collections that reflect and add to full representation of the diversity of Quakerism. Collecting practices include maintaining a list of collecting foci, such as abolition and anti-slavery, public health, and relief work, which reflect the aspiration to acknowledge the recent history, past, and future of Quakers (Haverford College, 2019).

There is a growing interest among the archivists of Quaker repositories in collecting materials related to anti-racism, climate justice, and queerness within Quakerism, as well as materials by or connected to Friends of Color on other topics. This emerging trend in acquisitions results from both the need to represent the fullness of Quaker experience, and the imperative to collect materials that will interest researchers in both the near and distant future. The trajectory of increasing attention paid to these topics in the past two decades of historical research suggests that they are likely to be of interest well into the future.

The collections in QSC have had written inventories since the beginnings of the archives. Many of the original descriptions, including folder titles, biographical and historical notes, and content notes continue to be used today. Many are not simply out of date but also racist, sexist, and otherwise offensive. One example of this is a folder that was titled "Negro slavery." This was changed to "Manumissions," which not only removes harmful language but is overall more descriptive of the materials within the folder. Generally, archivists strive to keep original order and folder titles of collections. However, when retaining the original labelling may inflict harm on people doing research, the prevention of harm may override standard practice. Many within the archives profession have recognized that potentially harmful and biased language around race presents such a situation. In 2019, a group called Archives for Black Lives in Philadelphia produced a document called "Anti-Racist Description Resources" (Anti-Racist Description Working Group, 2019). This resource has been adapted and implemented by the QSC. In addition, members of the QSC staff are participants in the Archives for Black Lives in Philadelphia group, building a network of knowledge and connections to support long-term anti-racist transformation.

Part of the departmental strategic plan is to work through each existing finding aid to make sure it adheres to the Anti-racist Description Resources. Staff will also redescribe materials which only have a patriarch described in the biography, despite substantial representation of women in the materials themselves. Original descriptions that are not aligned with the department's standards are kept only when the collection would be impacted significantly if that was changed. For instance, the QSC houses the records of the Philadelphia Yearly Meeting Indian Committee. In 2022, the Committee's name was changed to the Quaker Fund for Indigenous Communities Granting Group. Adhering to current archival standards, any records from before the name change will retain the designation as being part of the Indian Committee, as the committee was working and was known under that name, so changing the name could impede researchers' discovery of the collection. However, in the collection descriptions, titles or descriptions that use the term "Indian" in any other capacity will be changed to best reflect the community, such as a tribal affiliation. As QSC receives records from 2022 and beyond from the Quaker Fund for Indigenous Communities Granting Group, that material will be described as such.

Conclusions

Just like all justice work, challenging and transforming white supremacy in archival practice work will take time, persistence, and resistance against the status quo. Where does the onus lie to do this work in Quaker repositories? Whose responsibility is it to take the next steps? How, as archivists and historians, can we lay the groundwork for a more complete, truthful, and just representation of Quakerism in the historical record? Quaker archives around the world need to partner together, and reorient themselves towards greater inclusivity, in order to gather stories that represent all Quakers. Archivists need to be open to continual learning and knowledge, adapt to new research, and respond proactively to criticism from those at the margins.

Until Black Quakers, queer Quakers, and every other group of Friends not currently represented in our archives have materials being preserved, Quaker repositories will not be representative of the whole of Quakerism. The work of the Haverford College Quaker and Special Collections is not perfect or complete, but it is an example of how one Quaker repository is working to align itself with the struggle for racial justice through its staffing, programs, and collection management.

References

Anti-Racist Description Working Group. *Anti-racist description resources* (Philadelphia: online, 2019).

Haverford College. (unknown). *John P. Chesick scholars program.* Retrieved June 22, 2020 from https://www.haverford.edu/chesick-scholars-program

Haverford College. (2019, May 31). *Collection description, goals, and policies, Quaker & Special Collections, Haverford College Libraries.* Retrieved June 20, 2020 from https://www.haverford.edu/sites/default/files/Office/Library/Quaker-Special-Collections-Collection-Goals-and-Policies.pdf

Haverford College. (2020, March 30). *The college.* Retrieved June 20, 2020 from https://catalog.haverford.edu/college/

Rosa, Kathy and Kelsey Henke. *ALA office of research and statistics demographic study report* (Chicago: American Libraries Association, 2017).

49

THE ECONOMIC AND POLITICAL THEOLOGY OF JAMES NAYLER

Stuart Masters

Introduction

James Nayler (1618–1660) was one of the most important early Quaker leaders. During the 1650s, he was a prolific writer and, arguably, the most proficient theologian of the first generation. Puritan minister Francis Higginson identified him as the principal spokesman of the Quakers (Moore 2000: 21). By 1655, as the Quaker leader in London, he was at the height of his powers and influence. However, in the context of growing conflict between Quaker leaders, Nayler and his followers reenacted Jesus' entry into Jerusalem as a prophetic sign at Glastonbury, Wells and Bristol on 23 and 24 October 1656. As a result, the group was arrested in Bristol, and Nayler was tried in a show trial before Parliament. He was convicted of 'horrid blasphemy' and suffered a brutal punishment before being imprisoned at Bridewell at Parliament's pleasure. He was disowned by many leading Friends, and tales about the fall of a false messiah spread across England and Europe. In 1659, Nayler was released from prison and returned to preaching in London. However, less than a year later, while walking back to Yorkshire to visit his family, he was violently attacked and died of his injuries on 21 October 1660, aged 42 years. Nayler's message was a challenging and uncompromising one, and this may help to explain his harsh treatment at the hands of those in power and his early demise. This chapter explores his economic and political theology and seeks to relate this vision to a range of radical religious ideas dating back to the late medieval period.[1]

Economics and Government in Adam

Nayler's economic and political theology is founded upon a fundamental distinction between a corrupted human will in the first birth in Adam, and a regenerated human will in the new birth in Christ.[2] It is this distinction that forms the spiritual basis of his economic and political radicalism. The corruption of the human will, that was associated with the fall, engendered a way of being in which "the spirit of pride, gluttony, drunkenness, pleasures, envy and strife, keep that in bondage which thou shouldst love by the command of God" (Nayler and Kuenning 2009: 16). Therefore, injustice and social divisions, far from being divinely ordained, are the inevitable consequences of life in the first birth. The insatiable desire to amass wealth and power at the expense of others is an essential outcome of human alienation from God. Opulence strengthens

DOI: 10.4324/9780429030925-53

the pride of the wealthy and inclines them to demand respect and deference from those they have exploited and impoverished. Hence, human society takes on a dysfunctional form, contrary to God's will, characterised by inequitable relationships, greed, violence and oppression. Nayler condemns such iniquity when he writes,

> God is against you, you covetous cruel oppressors who grind the faces of the poor and needy . . . getting great estates in the world, laying house to house and land to land till there be no place for the poor; and when they are become poor through your deceits then you despise them and exalt yourselves above them.
>
> *(Nayler and Kuenning 2003: 66–67)*

When the wealthy and powerful expect deference and honour from those they regard as their social inferiors, this is idolatrous, because only God is worthy of such worship: 'where men's persons and riches is respected . . . the law of God is perverted' (Nayler and Kuenning 2009: 101). This view may have brought Nayler into conflict with Friends of high birth, like Margaret Fell, who continued to behave and dress in a manner that signified their superior social position. Mabel Brailsford suggested that this issue may have prompted Nayler to express concern about 'presumption' in a letter to Margaret Fell and others in 1652 (Brailsford 1915: 48). In the letter, he writes that 'there is presumption got up amongst you, and boasting; but in the meantime, the pure seed lies under' (Nayler and Kuenning 2003: 310).

Nayler believed that earthly government had been created for positive purposes but was subsequently perverted. Because fallen humanity had become a chaotic and disorderly presence within the creation, the consequent evil and destructiveness needed to be controlled. God therefore established earthly government as a tool of benevolent constraint. The scope of this authority, however, was strictly limited. Government was established to restrain evil, protect the poor and weak, and encourage the good. It should not interfere in matters of conscience or enable some people to amass great wealth and power. Nayler asks, 'Is it not the principal end of magistrates to judge the cause of the strangers, poor, and helpless, to relieve the oppressed and set the prisoners free, etc?' (Nayler and Kuenning 2004: 236). Despite its benevolent origins, earthly government had become corrupted by human sinfulness. Proud and greedy men had misused their powers and abused their positions for selfish ends, leading to the oppression of the poor and powerless. These authorities also began to exceed their powers by seeking to control matters of conscience. As a result, God's people are unjustly condemned and persecuted, and seen as a threat to social order. Nayler notes that 'persons who should have set up that power which is of God have set up their wills instead of it, and so have turned the edge of the sword . . . against them that do well' (Nayler and Kuenning 2003: 527–528). He cautions those who lack compassion and exploit the poor. Their greed, hard-heartedness and oppression reveal their sinfulness. God is not unaware of this, and those whose actions create injustice and suffering will inevitably face divine judgement. Nayler assumes that God is deeply concerned for the well-being of the poor and oppressed. Hence, a person who does God's will acts justly to ensure that 'the poor may be delivered from him that is too mighty for him', and they 'hath an ear open to the cries of the poor and helpless who hath but little money and few friends' (Nayler and Kuenning 2003: 140). In December 1656, at the time of his trial and cruel punishment, Nayler links his own suffering with that of all oppressed people, and prays, 'let not the wicked have dominion over the poor and helpless; break the wills of the blood-thirsty man' (Nayler and Kuenning 2007: 597–598). Finally, at the end of his life, following the restoration of the monarchy in 1660, he warns Charles II to 'do justice and judgment in this thy day, relieve the helpless oppressed and break the yoke of bondage that lies upon the poor . . . lest the meek of the earth cry to God against thee' (Nayler and Kuenning 2009: 408–409).

Economics and Government in Christ

If life in Adam is associated with pride and greed, resulting in injustice and oppression, life in Christ leads to generosity and justice, establishing the peace and equity of God's kingdom. As men and women come to experience spiritual regeneration, as the first birth in Adam is crucified, and the new life in Christ is born, the evils of pride and greed are weakened, and the spirit of humility and love is raised up. The way of Christ becomes visible in the lives of his people. Nayler's vision of a better world is therefore predicated on Christ being revealed again in the bodies of men and women. A human society based on pride, greed, hatred, violence and injustice is overcome by the humility, generosity, love, peace and justice of God's kingdom. This was the way of the apostles, and since Christ's first disciples were poor and powerless, his true followers remain so today. The rich and powerful dismissed Christ because he appeared 'too poor, too plain, and of too mean a stock to be king of Israel' (Nayler and Kuenning 2003: 54). Nayler asks, 'was not he ever poor as to this world, and therefore rejected of the rich and learned? lowly, and rejected of princes and them that was high?' (Nayler and Kuenning 2009: 102). At this time, itinerant Quaker ministers tended to follow the way of poverty, humility and powerlessness, and fully expected the world to treat them with the same contempt and brutality the apostles faced. In 1655, an opponent questioned Nayler's economic views and challenged him to provide a biblical basis for them. In response, Nayler denied that Quakers supported the redistribution of private property by force. However, he defended the idea that the example of the Jerusalem church after Pentecost provided a powerful biblical model of economic sharing (Acts 2:42–45). He wrote, "But if the power of the gospel fall upon the rich or poor, and move them to distribute their own, thou that thinks the Scripture warrants not this art blind" (Nayler and Kuenning 2004: 93).

New life in Christ also had significant implications for politics and government. In the new covenant, Christ is 'an everlasting king and saviour in his people' (Nayler and Kuenning 2007: 249). The authority of all human rulers is therefore temporary and limited; 'none can deserve the name of Christian governors but who by him are governed and do receive his authority' (Nayler and Kuenning 2007: 83). Those ruled by Christ need no external constraint or encouragement, because they live under divine guidance. They are now 'guided and governed by the law of his Spirit in their consciences' (Nayler and Kuenning 2009: 275). Living in the new birth in Christ implies loyalty to God's kingdom over all earthly powers. Although God's people exist within a fallen world, they are spiritually and ethically separated from it. They are willing to be subject to the earthly authorities, who 'are to be owned and obeyed in all things, as they are appointed by God' (Nayler and Kuenning 2007: 84). However, should these powers act against the divine will, 'God is to be obeyed, and man denied for conscience sake' (Nayler and Kuenning 2007: 85). Like the holy people throughout history, God may call them as prophets to communicate divine judgement, and they are prepared to endure suffering and persecution for their testimony. Nayler lived in a time of feverish apocalyptic expectations and, like others, believed that the coming of the kingdom of Christ was imminent. He understood the Lamb's war to be a revolutionary dimension of this process, a fight to free people from bondage to the worldly powers, so that Christ might rule within them. Because the Lamb's war was about inward transformation, a spiritual struggle to determine which power ruled within the creature, it was not violent or coercive. The Lamb's warriors do not war 'against men's persons, so their weapons are not carnal, nor hurtful to any of the creation' (Nayler and Kuenning 2009: 3).

The Loss of This Radical Vision

During the Restoration period,[3] Quakers significantly moderated the economic and political radicalism we see in Nayler's writings. In the context of severe persecution, the revolutionary implications of the early Quaker witness were toned down and reinterpreted. By the mid-1670s, Robert Barclay[4] was denying any levelling tendencies among Friends, and arguing that social stratification was divinely ordained (Barclay 2002: 433). It may be, however, that while Nayler's radical economic and political ideas were neglected at this time, they influenced later Friends who had a passion for social justice, such as John Bellers (Clarke 1987) and John Woolman (Woolman 2001). Over time, like later Anabaptist[5] communities, Quakers 'struggled less against the social order and worked instead to open up spaces within which their unique religious practices could be tolerated' (Biesecker-Mast 2006: 196). Barclay's writings reflect this change. When he addresses the role of government, he does so exclusively in terms of freedom of conscience (Barclay 2002: 407–428). By the end of the seventeenth century, Friends had adopted a position similar to that expressed by the Dutch Mennonites in the Dordrecht Confession of Faith. They held firm to their peculiarities but recognised the value of civil government and appreciated its protection (Biesecker-Mast 2006: 200).

Conclusion

James Nayler's economic theology reflects a stream of radical religious thought rooted in the popular piety of late medieval and Reformation Europe and visible in English radical Puritanism. Gordon Leff has suggested that the importance of poverty as a route to holiness was a powerful aspect of all medieval reform movements (Leff 1967: 389). During this period, many ordinary people rejected the wealth and power of the Church and sought instead to follow the way of the apostles, by renouncing their worldly goods. This tendency, often called the *vita apostolica*,[6] was threatening to established authority and provoked persecution. During the Reformation, the Anabaptists made a direct link between inner regeneration and outer behaviour. They assumed that one's relationship to material possessions reflected one's spiritual condition (Snyder 2004: 142). Many followed Thomas Müntzer[7] in arguing that an obsession with private property resulted from the fall of Adam and Eve (Stayer 1991: 109). Like Nayler, the Dutch Anabaptist leader Menno Simons[8] expressed concern for the poor and oppressed and associated the desire for wealth with unjust practices and exploitative economic arrangements. He wrote that wicked merchants and retailers 'lie and swear; they use many vain words, falsify their wares to cheat the people, and strip them of possessions; they sell, lend, and secure the needy at large profit and usury' (Klaassen 1981: 242). In terms of salvation, therefore, Anabaptists refused to separate their spiritual well-being from their economic practices. God's people avoided riches and cared for those in need, both within the community and beyond (Snyder 1995: 247). A commitment to mutual aid was understood to be an expression of a commitment to Christ-like sacrificial giving (Klaassen 1981: 232). The Digger leader and radical Puritan, Gerrard Winstanley,[9] understood human sin primarily in terms of the private buying and selling of the earth's resources, which creates great wealth and real poverty (Bradstock 1997: 89). For him, it was greed, above all else, that had corrupted humanity (Gurney 2007: 100). Like Nayler, Winstanley believed that this problem would only be resolved when the covetous First Adam was overcome in each person by Christ, the Second Adam. Such an experience would restore 'right Reason' within people's hearts and gather them into a truly egalitarian community in which all things were held in common (Bradstock 1997: 115, 127).

Resonances of late medieval and Reformation radicalism can also be seen in Nayler's political theology. He shares the anticlericalism associated with the *vita apostolica*, along with their contempt for the earthly wealth and power of the Christendom Church. His position fits within the diversity of approaches adopted by sixteenth-century Anabaptist groups (Masters 2019: 26–40). Like most early Anabaptists, he assumed a dualistic and antagonistic relationship between the ways of the world and the way of Christ, and between the kingdoms of the world and the kingdom of God. However, although he takes a spiritually separatist stance, he adopts a more positive attitude to involvement in earthly government than many early Anabaptists. Because his faith in the transformative power of Christ is so strong, he is willing to accept that a Christian might hold office within temporal government: when people are genuinely ruled by Christ, they will conduct themselves in a Christ-like manner in whatever they do. Nayler's standpoint fits most closely with nonviolent and spiritualist expressions within German, Austrian and Dutch Anabaptism.[10] Like these Anabaptists, Nayler internalises and spiritualises Müntzer's conception of holy war, while sharing his mystical focus on the need to turn away from creaturely attachments in order to experience the birth of God within (Stayer 1972: 73–74). It might be argued that the early Quaker position, revealed in Nayler's writings, represents a re-emergence of spiritualist Anabaptist emphases that had largely disappeared within continental Europe.

James Nayler, like Gerrard Winstanley, never developed a strategy to achieve his economic and political vision. For such mystical and spiritualist radicals, transformation was God's work, and all humans could do was surrender their will to the divine will. When the anticipated renewal of all things did not take place, and when the kingdom of God was not realised, most found a way to survive, to get on with their lives and adapt to the way the world is rather than the way they wanted it to be. Some, like Nayler, didn't live long enough to do this. In a sense, like the martyrs throughout history, he had already become a citizen of God's kingdom, and so he could no longer exist within any earthly jurisdiction.

Notes

1 The contents of this chapter draws on material taken from Masters (2021).

2 This is a key theme in Nayler's first single-authored tract, *A Discovery of the First Wisdom from Below and the Second Wisdom from Above*, published in 1653 (Nayler 2003: 41–71).

3 The Restoration was the reintroduction of the monarchy following the fall of the English Commonwealth in 1660.

4 Robert Barclay (1648–1690) was a Scottish Friend with aristocratic connections. He is known primarily for his theological writings, especially *An Apology for the True Christian Divinity* (Abbott 2011: 38–39).

5 The Anabaptists were radical Christian groups that emerged during the European Reformation. They rejected the state-church alliance of Christendom, infant baptism and a territorial definition of the church, in favour of a voluntary association of believers. They suffered severe persecution at the hands of both Catholic and Protestant authorities. Modern Anabaptist groups include the Mennonites, Hutterites, Amish, the Church of the Brethren and the Bruderhof.

6 The *vita apostolica* was a medieval movement of popular piety influenced in particular by St. Francis of Assisi, which regarded the way of voluntary poverty, powerlessness and service associated with the life of Christ and the apostles as the norm for all authentic Christians.

7 Thomas Müntzer (1489–1525) was a German theologian, who became a rebel leader during the Peasants' War (1524–25). Initially a follower of Martin Luther, he preached a radical message of the coming of God's kingdom as an egalitarian society in which all things would be shared in common. In May 1525, he was captured after the Battle of Frankenhausen and executed.

8 Menno Simons (1496–1561) was perhaps the most important Anabaptist leader of the Low Countries during the sixteenth century. His followers became known as Mennonites.

9 The Diggers or "True Levellers" were a radical group during the English Revolution who believed that God was reversing the divisions of the fall, and again making the earth a 'common treasury for all'. In 1649, they began to cultivate the common land as a practical sign of this coming transformation. Gerrard Winstanley (1609–1676) was a Digger leader and the group's principal apologist.
10 Resonances can be seen especially with the mysticism of Hans Denck, the new covenant vision of Clements Adler, and the spiritualism of David Joris (Biesecker-Mast 2006: 109–125, 170–178).

Bibliography

Abbott, Margery Post. 2011. *Historical Dictionary of Friends*. Lanham, MD: Scarecrow Press.

Barclay, R. and Kuenning, L. 2002. *An Apology for the True Christian Divinity*. Glenside, PA: Quaker Heritage Press.

Biesecker-Mast, Gerald. 2006. *Separation and the Sword in Anabaptist Persuasion: Radical Confessional Rhetoric from Schleitheim to Dordrecht*. Telford, PA: Cascadia.

Bradstock, Andrew. 1997. *Faith in the Revolution: The Political Theologies of Müntzer and Winstanley*. London: SPCK.

Brailsford, Mabel R. 1915. *Quaker Women, 1650–1690*. London: Duckworth & Co.

Clarke, George. 1987. *John Bellers: His Life, Times and Writings*. London: Routledge & Kegan Paul.

Gurney, John. 2007. *Brave Community: The Digger Movement in the English Revolution*. Manchester: Manchester University Press.

Klaassen, Walter. 1981. *Anabaptism in Outline: Selected Primary Sources*. Waterloo, ON: Herald Press.

Leff, Gordon. 1967. *Heresy in the Late Middle Ages: The Relation of Heterodoxy to Dissent, 1250–1450*. Manchester: Manchester University Press.

Masters, Stuart. 2019. "The Sword, Separation and Nonviolence in Early Quakerism: The Testimony of James Nayler (1618–1660)" in *Anabaptism Today*, Volume 1, Number 2.

Masters, Stuart. 2021. *The Rule of Christ: Themes in the Theology of James Nayler*. Leiden: E.J. Brill, 2021.

Moore, Rosemary A. 2000. *The Light in Their Consciences: Early Quakers in Britain 1646–1666*. University Park, PA: Pennsylvania State University Press.

Nayler, J. and Kuenning, L. 2003. *The Works of James Nayler – Volume 1*. Glenside, PA: Quaker Heritage Press.

Nayler, J. and Kuenning, L. 2004. *The Works of James Nayler – Volume 2*. Glenside, PA: Quaker Heritage Press.

Nayler, J. and Kuenning, L. 2007. *The Works of James Nayler – Volume 3*. Glenside, PA: Quaker Heritage Press.

Nayler, J. and Kuenning, L. 2009. *The Works of James Nayler – Volume 4*. Glenside, PA: Quaker Heritage Press.

Snyder, C. Arnold. 1995. *Anabaptist History and Theology: An Introduction*. Kitchener, ON: Pandora Press.

Snyder, C. Arnold. 2004. *Following in the Footsteps of Christ: The Anabaptist Tradition*. London: Darton, Longman & Todd.

Stayer, James M. 1972. *Anabaptists and the Sword*. Lawrence, KS: Coronado Press.

Stayer, James M. 1991. *The German Peasants' War and the Anabaptist Community of Goods*. Montreal, QC: McGill-Queen's University Press.

Woolman, John. 2001. *A Plea for the Poor*. Wallingford, PA: Pendle Hill Publications.

50

GEORGE CADBURY

Faith in Practice

Andrew Fincham

Even a century after his death, George Cadbury has a justifiable claim to be the embodiment of practical Quaker Christianity. His success in the varied worlds of international commerce, social action and spiritual reform were acknowledged by contemporaries – whether they were employees, business associates or members of the wider community, and few individuals since, whether inside or outside of the Religious Society of Friends, have equalled his achievements.

The Quaker

George was born at Edgbaston (Birmingham, England) in 1839 with a legacy of sixteen Quaker great-grandparents and a family tradition of commercial success and public service. This had begun with his grandfather, Richard Tapper Cadbury, who set up as a silk merchant in the rapidly developing Birmingham of 1794 and went on to serve over three decades on the town's governing Board of Commissioners, earning the sobriquet 'King Richard' (Gardiner, 7). This blend of business and service was maintained by his son John, whom he set up as a tea merchant in 1824 and who would become prominent in both civic life, steering the bill through Parliament that turned expanding Birmingham into a corporation; and social action, successfully campaigning to prohibit the use of 'climbing boys' as chimney sweeps (Phillips, 33). John married Candida (the daughter of a wealthy Lancaster Quaker, George Barrow, who made a fortune in trade from the West Indies); it was Candida who brought the fight for total abstinence from alcohol into the family, and it would be their sons Richard and George who would go on to create the great chocolate firm (Davies and Clark). The youthful Cadbury was brought up to respect the Quaker 'Discipline' of London Yearly Meeting, a written code of values and behaviour which had been revised in 1832, just a few years before his birth. While sharing a general Christian morality, the critical Quaker tenet was that the Light of God shone for all humanity – including the enslaved and imprisoned – and an emphasis that all should take responsibility for bringing about 'God's kingdom'. Of particular interest considering the future development of George Cadbury is the Quaker advice on *Liberality and Benevolence*, which advised Friends to open "hearts and hands freely for the relief of the poor and needy of all denominations: . . . none are entrusted with riches that they may indulge themselves in pleasures, or for the gratification of luxury, ambition, or vain glory; but to do good' (LYM, 79).[1] George was educated first at home and then at Lean's Quaker day school, and he had only a short experience of

DOI: 10.4324/9780429030925-54

grocery work (with fellow-Quaker Rowntree in York, England) before taking over his father's business (Williams and Fitzgerald). This rather narrow experience may help explain his single-minded determination to live up to values which characterised a Quaker's personal life, and in the process developed his preference for practical action to change the world, above theological theorising.

The Man of Business

His father John had begun trading in tea and coffee, before adding 'drinking chocolate' in 1831. This was a mixture of one part cocoa to four parts potato starch and sago flour (to absorb the cocoa butter), sweetened with treacle – later acknowledged by George to be a 'comforting gruel' (Gardiner, 28).[2] The business expanded into larger premises in Bridge Street in 1847, and Richard joined in 1851. Within three years Cadbury & Son received royal warrant from Queen Victoria, yet it appears that frequent failures amongst those shopkeepers they supplied seriously impaired finances; faced with these pressures and mourning his wife, John finally decided in 1861 to leave the salvation of the business to his sons. It was then that George returned from York and, supported by an inheritance from their deceased mother of about £5000 apiece, the brothers rapidly introduced changes (Carrington, 17);[3] first halving the twenty-strong work-force and then dealing exclusively in chocolate and cocoa as losses continued (Dellheim, 17). Richard had married, so George in particular exercised extreme economy and self-denial, famously denying himself a newspaper containing his beloved cricket reports! (Gardiner, 24).[4] While success eluded them, there was a reluctance to borrow external capital, but a modest profit in 1864 supplemented by the remains of the legacy enabled George to acquire rights to an innovative Dutch invention – the Van Houten hydraulic press extraction machine – which not only produced cocoa fit for drinking but provided a pure, quality product which would give Cadbury's a competitive edge over all other domestic manufacturers (Cadbury, 56).

The brothers' new marketing slogan, 'Absolutely Pure, therefore best', has been noted as a happy echo of the Quaker pursuit of simplicity; however, it was designed to be both wider and more contemporary in its appeal. The adulteration of food had become a major popular concern following the widely reported Bradford Sweets Poisoning of 1858, when twenty-one people died after eating humbugs in which arsenic had been mistakenly used as a sugar substitute (Jones). The next two decades saw the first British legislative measures on food safety, with which the Cadbury brothers' production values aligned strongly (Hassall).[5] The business was now on a secure financial footing, and it seems Richard would have been satisfied with 'a few hundred a year for certain' with which to enjoy his family and the country (Alexander, 112). George, however, had larger ambitions – although not for himself – and began to drive forward expansion. That his will prevailed was perhaps the result of the death in 1868 of Richard's wife, which left him with four children under seven years of age; while he continued to engage in both commercial and philanthropic works – not least the founding of a creche for the care of the very young poor, with standards of cleanliness that rendered some youngsters unrecognisable to their parents (Alexander, 135). Yet perhaps his most notable final contribution was to paint the unique designs which adorned the brothers' chocolate boxes.

The Factory in a Garden

The increase in business led to the creation of what has become Cadbury's best-known legacy: the Bournville Village Trust. Yet this village originated as an adjunct to a greater work: the 'Factory in a Garden', created on a former country estate alongside the Bourn brook, a rural stream running four miles east of Birmingham.[6] Construction began in March 1879, with the production commencing in October. The layout was an example of the international trend for 'Industrial Betterment', with innovations designed to improve working conditions (and so efficiency), and the 300 staff who transferred would ultimately be joined by thousands more (Meakin). By 1905, both factory and supporting infrastructure were well established, and a contemporary evaluation of model factories held the complex to be the 'high watermark' of industrial betterment in England (Meakin, 68). Many of the ideas Cadbury implemented would gain wide acceptance, but the extent of their implementation made Cadbury's unique. Thus a healthy work environment was championed by other companies – Levers' Port Sunlight, Clark's at Street, and Chivers' in Cambridge, as well as many others abroad – but few went as far as Cadbury to address so many other detailed aspects of working life, considering gardens, architecture, ventilation, cleanliness and dress, provision of drinking water, and services for employees who fell sick (with on-site medical staff and facilities, and health education). Cadburys' staff welfare appears advanced even when compared with many global markets today: employees were given medical examinations monthly, with those not considered fit for work provided with sick pay. A Work's Medical Department housed a doctor, a dentist and nurses, while nutritional supplements were offered to those believed underfed, backed up by two free convalescent homes (Meakin, 72–152). Financial innovations went beyond sick pay to include paid holiday, and dedicated pension funds for men and women, a Women's Savings Trust, and Pensioners' Widows' Fund, and an early unemployment scheme. Even the formula used for calculating piecework was identified as particularly praiseworthy, since Cadbury excluded the fastest workers, basing rates on an average output while factoring in a complex set of supplementary payments to ensure staff earned more than a base 'living wage' (Meakin, 316).

The factory infrastructure included a new station, for which Cadbury personally negotiated dedicated Midland Railway trains, at Cadbury rates (Carrington, 31–34),[7] while a 200-place cycle shed (very advanced for the time) encouraged more environmental transport (Meakin, 234). On-site catering was considered a model of best practice in subsidy, efficiency and hygiene, as well as being unsurpassed in scale: the dining capacity of 2000 was also utilised by up to 100 retirees daily, who ate for free (Meakin, 172–189). The brothers' personal enjoyment of sports was reflected in recreation: sports clubs had coaches, swimming pool and gym, set in 12 acres of gardens. Space was made for allotments (annual rent 1 shilling, including instruction and free seeds) with annual prizes (Meakin, 246).

The Cadbury brothers' actions were grounded in a tradition of Quaker responsibility for all stakeholders formed in the eighteenth century (Raistrick, 49–51), although such practices were becoming the inspiration for many outside the Society, as evidenced by early nineteenth-century social utopians and the works of such as Robert Owen, Joseph Rowntree and Titus Salt. By the latter half of that century, such efforts were considered a necessary part of the Christian's pursuit of social reform. In all this, George Cadbury proved unique in the extent to which he took the lead in dedicating business profits into practical measures to ameliorate the negative effects of mass industrialisation.

Social Action

Bournville Village

Bournville Village arose from George Cadbury's fear that the scale of the factory operations would encourage the development of poor housing in the immediate neighbourhood; as such it was rather 'aligned to' than 'responsible for' the nascent Garden City movement (Bryson and

Lowe, 21). Cadbury purchased considerable land in the vicinity (some 300 acres) and later gifted this to the independent Bournville Village Trust (created in 1900; Williams and Fitzgerald).[8] The village was never intended for exclusive use of Cadbury employees, although examples abound of the founder's detailed interest in every aspect of the inhabitants' lives – including printed advice for each home on how to breathe correctly! (Bournville Village).[9] Functional and practical aspects were given close oversight, with each house built to a superior standard, including plumbing, while costing less than £150; importantly, each was originally sold with a mortgage which ensured that the owner, over 13 years, would actually pay less than the equivalent rental cost. When Cadbury found 'his' houses were being re-sold at inflated prices beyond the means of the 'skilled artisan, clerk, or shopkeeper', the policy became one of building for rent only (Cherry, 497), while following at the same time a substantially low-weighted distribution of property types (Gardiner, 147). Some additional almshouse property ('The Quadrangle' cottages built in 1897) were also built and financially secured as a trust endowed by rents from 35 houses. In such details, particularly financial, Bournville Village demonstrated that such projects served as 'an example which can be followed with advantage not only by the private investor satisfied with a reasonable interest, but by public bodies' (Meakin, 433).

Adult Education

Cadbury had served the adult school movement from his youth, and continued to teach until finally prevented by ill health in his seventy-fourth year (Gardiner, 289). Much has been made of his insights into working-class conditions gained from the classroom, yet it would be perhaps equally valid to acknowledge how much satisfaction and encouragement Cadbury gathered from seeing his efforts and those of his students bear fruit. Even when unable to teach, he greatly enjoyed associating with former attendees, then 'as grey-headed as himself', and would remark on the beneficial effects – as when noting '"one of the best workers" for the cripples in Birmingham is the son of one of my old scholars' (Gardiner, 271–288).[10] Constant association with the fruits of education was reflected in his creation of learning facilities both at the works and in Bournville village, with schools for men, girls and youths, a library and reading room (Meakin, 293). Fifty years as an Adult School teacher convinced him that 'real reform must begin with the individual' – albeit supported by progressive legislation (Gardiner, 236).

Newspapers

As a means to getting his message across, Cadbury invested in certain Birmingham newspapers in 1891. However, it was somewhat against his own wishes that he was subsequently persuaded by British politician David Lloyd George to invest (in 1901) in a national newspaper, the 'Daily News', to promote anti-war views – Cadbury would ultimately own this outright in order to prevent it supporting the bellicose 'Jingo Frenzy'. The initial reasoning was to ensure some publication of the opinions of the Liberal Party (not least the opposition to populist imperialism which was encouraging war with the Boers) while also spreading the views of non-conformist religion. George took no active part in the running of the paper, but it was used to support his campaign against sweated Labour (for which Cadbury personally bore the cost) and in so doing helped establish both the Trade Boards Act and a minimum wage (Gardiner, 234–235). His underlying motivation for his considerable investment is best observed in the memoranda which accompanied the deed with which he gave away ownership to a trust in 1911: namely, a desire 'that it may be of service in bringing the ethical teachings of Jesus Christ to bear upon National questions' (Gardiner, 234).

Cadbury was also engaged in more personal activism which may be overlooked. The saving and restoration of Selly Manor illustrates one important aspect of Cadbury's practicality – a stubborn ability to ignore those who claimed to know better. Once a fine medieval house, it had by the eighteenth century fallen to a set of poor dwellings known as 'The Rookery' before acquisition by a speculative developer, on whose death in 1907 Cadbury determined to restore the almost 500-year-old property. This involved moving and re-erecting what could be saved of the building in Bournville, a move vigorously opposed by the William Morris Society for the Protection of Ancient Buildings while offering no alternative to destruction. The ever-practical Cadbury acquired, removed and restored the derelict building as a museum. In a similar manner, when he and his wife determined there should be recreation and entertainment for the needy – whether a crippled child, an overworked teacher or an exhausted Salvation Army lady – they had built in the grounds of their home a vast dining hall of 700-seat capacity and staffed a commensurate catering facility capable of serving 20,000 people annually: Cadbury noted in 1921 that they had entertained, over a forty-year period, around 800,000 guests (Gardiner, 288).

Spirituality

As noted above, Cadbury's outward actions tended to raise awareness of the ethical teachings of Jesus in the minds of the nation. It is possible to see this desire manifest in all his practicality. His personal religion, while clearly steeped in Quakerism, is perhaps a little more complex. That this is so is indicated by his frustrations, expressed in his mature years, with what he perceived as 'the dead formality' of so many Quaker Meetings, responsibility for which he placed firmly at the door of Elders who needed to realise the importance of 'earnest, life-giving, educated Gospel ministry' (Kennedy, 171).[11] These frustrations with the Quakers may partially explain why he did not seek office within the Society of Friends, but there is much wider evidence that Cadbury was inspired less by the Society of Friends and more by the values he considered it embodied. But these values he could find echoed in other Christian denominations and even beyond. On building the Quaker Meeting House at Bournville (for which he made the unique inclusion of an organ), he wrote to the Clerk of Meeting for Elders, suggesting that the said meeting 'be entirely independent of the Society of Friends' until they had found their way. His biographer describes him as 'indifferent to controversies . . . never discussed questions of dogma, and content to judge every man's Christianity by its fruits rather than by its professions' (Gardiner, 167). He worked over decades with the clergy of Birmingham of all denominations, perhaps the most celebrated of which was Henry Newman, whom Cadbury encountered when the cardinal (whom Cadbury recalled as 'lovable old man') intervened to request separate prayers for Catholics at the Works (Gardiner, 168).[12] His practical solution to the stagnation of the Society of Friends was to donate his former family home, Woodbrooke, in 1903 as college to help 'qualify men and women more spiritually, intellectually and experimentally for the work to which they have felt called by the Holy spirit' (Gardiner, 200). Subsequently, Cadbury was instrumental in helping to realise four further institutions, co-located in the Selly Oak area of Birmingham. Kingsmead (founded 1905) was run by the Friends' Foreign Mission Association for the training of missionaries and, later, admitted Methodists. Westhill College (1907) trained Sunday school teachers and, later, many others who worked in the community; by 1912 this was one of the first teacher-training establishments, governed by the Free Churches. In 1909 Fircroft College offered a working men a residential base for further adult education, alongside the growing Workers Education Association. Finally, in 1912, the missionary activity of the Baptists, Congregationalists and Presbyterians was consolidated in a training establishment for female missionaries: Carey Hall. While differing in details, the Selly Oak Colleges serve best to illustrate the broad nature of the Christian spirit which characterised Cadbury's time – a spirit too easily obscured by the simplistic dualism of Evangelical versus Liberal which has character-ised some historic analysis of this period of Quakerism.

Conclusion

George Cadbury died at his home, the Manor House, Northfield, Birmingham, on 24 October 1922. Those who knew him closely mourned the loss of 'not a saint, but . . . someone very good' (Gardiner, 201).[13] Subsequently, Quaker historians have accentuated the achievements, while some revisionists have attempted to undermine the reputation – some going as far as to claim the Quakerism of Cadbury's was a fiction.[14] Obvious if perhaps anachronistic accusations are those of paternalism – as with the policy of forcibly retiring women who married. Yet George Cadbury would have argued that this measure was in fact designed to protect women and their nascent 'family concerns'. In this, as in everything, Cadbury followed his own understanding of what was the practical way forward, as when he bought the house in the Malvern Hills where he had enjoyed many holidays. Here he retained the former owner's Catholic décor, if not from sentiment then because change served no purpose; he did, however, have installed a device which automati-cally turned down the voltage such that no guest could read after ten at night – forcing repose in the cause of recuperation! (Gardiner, 256–8). Against such accusations of paternalism, others have suggested that his 'use of wealth was always carefully guarded against the taint of "charity" or paternalism, and his life is an enviable example of Quaker ideals put to practical purpose' (Sylvester Smith, 107). A balanced conclusion – that there was always more genuine concern for others than economic self-interest in the philanthropy – seems both appropriate and evidenced (Wagner).

Cadbury's social activism also attracted several hostile attacks during his lifetime, largely from those attempting to maintain the political status quo. His stance against war and for the rights of workers angered many in the establishment who responded less with counter-argument than with personal accusation. The wildest of these was to claim Cadbury supported (or at least con-nived at) slavery, buying cocoa from the Portuguese colony of São Tomé, where the plantation owners used indentured workers (Clarence-Smith, 152–172).[15] Cadbury, forced to defend at law, argued successfully that the continued trade had been conducted solely to leverage changes negotiated with the Portuguese government, and even Cadbury's political rivals at the *Morning Post* admitted that had these 'produced an amelioration of the lot of the San Thomé slaves, no question of the wisdom of the course adopted would have arisen' (Gardiner, 248). A similar accusation of hypocrisy occurred in the rather greyer moral area of gambling, after Cadbury concluded with reluctance that removing betting tips from his penny newspaper would result in losing the very readership he was trying to educate. Thus even *The Spectator*, the very publica-tion which had enthusiastically conducted this campaign against him, concluded in its obituary:

> He was a devout Quaker and followed the Inner Light as though a vision of spiritual things were always before him. Yet he was intensely practical in detail. He did not pour out money for other people to carry out charitable ideas. Having invented the ideas he himself attended to their fulfilment.
>
> *(The Spectator)*

If George Cadbury was not alone in his concern for industrial betterment, he was a leader, one in the tradition of the now largely forgotten archetypal Christian businessman Samuel Budgett, who some decades before practiced practical interventions to improve the lives of his community, busi-ness partners and employees in an approach to successful merchanting that reflects 'Quaker values'

(Arthur, Wardley). Cadbury operated in a wider context where others were trying to establish social change; figures almost as well known at the time, such as Minister Andrew Mearns (1837–1925) whose 1883 *The Bitter Cry of Outcast London* led to the Royal Commission on the housing of the working classes (1884–5) (Wohl), or Henry Solly (1813–1903), a clergyman who founded Working Men's Clubs and promoted the Society for the Promotion of Industrial Villages.

Cadbury represented the flowering of a profound Quaker heritage – a personal inheritance of financial rectitude, hard work and abstinence but a wider acknowledgement of the value in all (Dellheim, 14–15).

He learned to apply this, trusting his own judgement as a result of success in his family business, and he increasingly extended his activities to help address an ever-wider set of concerns identified as a result of engaging with the urban mass of Birmingham. His approach to business proved unique primarily because (unlike some other Christian magnates) he never sought to maximise profit: instead, rather than assess how an investment in stakeholders could translate into improved performance, his unique philosophy appears to have been characterized by a desire to see how far his business could sustain the improvements in the lot of his stakeholders – all in pursuit of bringing a little nearer that Kingdom of God on earth which the earliest Quakers had sought to establish.

In this, he remains the pre-eminent example of a commercial Quaker faith in action.

Notes

1 In this revised third edition of the LYM *Book of Discipline*, the chapter on 'Liberality' runs to six pages compared with two in the second, with twelve 'advices' rather than six.
2 Gardiner cites Cadbury's New Year's speech at Edgbaston Assembly Rooms, 1921.
3 The contemporary value of this amount, some £8000 to £10,000, is between £840,000 (real prices) to £6.5 million (labour value).
4 George noted (in 1914) that his brother, having married, had little to contribute to the economising.
5 Adulteration of Food Acts (1872 and 1875); the detailed volume of reports are in Hassall (1855), *Food and Its Adulterations*.
6 See *The Bournville Story: A Film of the Factory in a Garden* (Anglo-Scottish, 1953). Narrated by Richard Attenborough, this was, remarkably, awarded both the Industrial Documentary prize and the overall first prize at the Turin International Film Festival. Further west, the stream becomes known as Wood Brook; it flows into the Quaker study centre of the same name, for it is sited at George Cadbury's former family home.
7 Carrington, *Cadbury's Angels*, gives correspondence between Cadbury Bros and Pearson dated 12 Nov 1878 and 7mo.31 1879.
8 By 1931 the capital of the trust had increased from £170,000 to over £500,000, and it held more than 1000 acres of land.
9 The *Bournville Village Suggested Rules of Health* state: "Through the nostrils with the mouth closed, especially at night."
10 GC Letter June 27, 1921.
11 Kennedy, *British Quakerism*, 171, quoting GC at the 1895 Manchester Conference.
12 GC recalled the Saint's final words of blessing were 'Mr. Cadbury, God will find some means of saving you.'
13 Letter, Mrs. George Hodgkin to Dorothea Cadbury.
14 For a view on Rowlinson's and Hassard's 1993 discursion into 'invented tradition', see Fincham, 49.
15 Clarence-Smith's paper relies heavily on the detail of William Cadbury's report into the local practices.

Bibliography

Alexander, Helen Cadbury, *Richard Cadbury of Birmingham* (London: Hodder & Stoughton, 1906).
Arthur, William, *The Successful Merchant: Sketches of the Life of Mr. Samuel Budgett* (London: Hamilton, Adams, 1852).

Bournville Village, *Suggested Rules of Health* (s.l., 1897).

Bryson, John R., and A. Lowe Philippa, 'Story-telling and History Construction: Rereading George Cadbury's Bournville Model Village', *Journal of Historical Geography,* Vol. 28, No. 1 (2002), 21–41.

Cadbury, Deborah, *Chocolate Wars: The 150-year Rivalry between the World's Greatest Chocolate Makers* (New York: Public Affairs, 2010).

Carrington, Iris, *Cadbury's Angels* (Warsaw: IBiS, 2011).

Cherry, G. E., 'Bournville, England, 1895–1995', *Journal of Urban History*, Vol. 22 (1996), 493–508.

Clarence-Smith, W. G., 'The Hidden Costs of Labour on the Cocoa Plantations of São Tomé and Príncipe, 1875–1914', *Portuguese Studies*, Vol. 6 (1990), 152–172.

Davies, H. M., and Christine Clark, *Cadbury, John (1801–1889), Cocoa and Chocolate Manufacturer* (Oxford: Oxford Dictionary of National Biography, 2004).

Dellheim, Charles, 'The Creation of a Company Culture: Cadburys, 1861–1931', *The American Historical Review*, Vol. 92, No. 1 (Feb. 1987), 13–44.

Fincham, Andrew, 'Cadbury's Ethics and the Spirit of Corporate Social Responsibility', in *Quakers, Business and Corporate Responsibility*, eds. Nicholas Burton and Richard Turnbull (Cham, CH.: Springer, 2019), 40–60.

Gardiner, A. G., *Life of George Cadbury* (London: Cassell and Company, 1923).

Hassall, Arthur Hill, *Food and Its Adulterations* (London: Longman, Brown, Green and Longmans, 1855).

Jones, I. F., 'Arsenic and the Bradford Poisonings of 1858', *The Pharmaceutical Journal*, Vol. 265, No. 7128 (2000), 938–939.

Kennedy, T. C., *British Quakerism, 1860–1920: The Transformation of a Religious Community* (Oxford: OUP, 2001).

London Yearly Meeting, *Extracts from the Minutes and Advices of the Yearly Meeting of Friends Held in London from Its First Institution*. 3rd Revised edition (London: W. Phillips, 1832).

Meakin, James, *Model Factories and Villages: Ideal Conditions of Labor and Housing* (London: T. Fisher Unwin, 1905).

Phillips, George L., 'Quakers and Chimney Sweepers: A Supplement', *Bulletin of Friends Historical Association*, Vol. 39, No. 1 (1950), 32–36.

Raistrick, Arthur, *Quakers in Science and Industry* (London: The Bannisdale Press, 1950).

Rowlinson, Michael, and John Hassard, 'The Invention of Corporate Culture: A History of the Histories of Cadbury', *Human Relations*, Vol. 46, No. 3 (1993), 299–326.

Spectator Review, 'The Life of George Cadbury, A.G Gardiner', *The Spectator* (14 July 1923).

Sylvester Smith, W., 'London Quakers at the Turn of the Century', *Quaker History*, Vol. 53, No. 2 (Autumn 1964), 93–108.

Wagner, Gillian, *The Chocolate Conscience* (London: Chatto & Windus, 1987).

Wardley, Peter, 'Budgett, Samuel (1794–1851)', in *Oxford Dictionary of National Biography* (Oxford: OUP, 2004).

Williams, I. A., and Robert Fitzgerald, 'Cadbury, George (1839–1922)', in *Oxford Dictionary of National Biography* (Oxford: OUP, 2004).

Wohl, Anthony S., 'Mearns, Andrew (1837–1925)', in *Oxford Dictionary of National Biography* (Oxford: OUP, 2004).

51

QUAKER DRESS

Deb Fuller

Introduction

Unlike other 'plain people', such as the Mennonites or Amish, Quakers have never had strict rules on dress. Instead, typical to Quaker beliefs, they were admonished against frivolities, excess, and slavishly following fashion. These admonishments turned into a distinctive form of plain dress that became easily recognizable to themselves, as well as to people outside of their communities. The overall guiding principle was that while elegance, style, and quality of material were allowed, plainness and simplicity are most important. What constituted plain changed over time and was often a reaction to the latest fads and fashion. By the 1900s, plain dress had all but died out and transitioned to a testimony of simplicity, which is still practiced today.

Quaker clothing has national, regional, and personal variations; to attempt to cover the entire history of Quaker dress in one chapter would be impossible. Instead, this chapter is an attempt to summarize the general trends of Quaker dress over the course of Quaker history, outline the reasons for 'going plain' and/or wearing distinctive Quaker clothing, show what guidance existed for dress, give examples of Quaker dress for specific time periods, and give an overview of how Quakers make decisions on clothing in contemporary times. The focus will be on Britain and the United States, as that is where most of the academic research into Quaker clothing has been done.

What Is Plain?

Plainness was never specifically defined but was always understood by those who practiced it. At times, it seems like Quaker plain dress is a study in contradictions. On the one hand, Amelia Mott Gummere notes in *The Quakers: A Study in Costume* that drab colours were common from the eighteenth century on.[1]

On the other hand, Quaker women wore colourful or 'gay' aprons in the latter half of the same century because white aprons were in fashion.[2] Likewise, green was considered a plain colour[3] in the 1700s until it becomes fashionable later in the 1800s[4] and was dropped from being plain.

Quakers would adapt and react to fashion, redefining what was acceptable as plain and what was not until sects start to drop plain dress starting in the 1840s.[5] It had all but vanished by 1900.

DOI: 10.4324/9780429030925-55

Afterwards, plain dress and occasionally plain speech are seen and heard only among a small group of conservative American Quakers, mainly from Ohio Yearly Meeting (OYM), formerly OYM (Conservative).[6] Today, OYM still has a concentration of plain-dressing Quakers, but there are also individual plain Quakers, mainly in the United States and Canada.

Early Quakerism: Founding to c. 1700

The early Quakers spoke against 'vain fashions' and took to heart the biblical teachings against wearing clothing deliberately for show.[7] This stays central to the idea of plainness throughout Quaker history. However, the founders of Quakerism had different opinions on dress and were not unified.

George Fox said in *Some Principles of the Quakers*, published in 1661:[8]

> The Apostle saith, it is not for Women to wear Gold, Silver, Pearl, Costly Apparrel, nor Plated Hair . . . . And if Christendom had minded this, there had been more Vertue, more Sobriety, and less envy at one another about their Fashions.

Fox himself wore leather breeches, as they were sturdy and long-lasting.

Robert Barclay codified Fox's words in his *An Apology for the True Christian Divinity* by denouncing 'Vanity and Superfluity of Apparel'.[9] Combined, these two standards would continue to influence Quaker clothing choices for the next two centuries.

Vanity

The first part, vanity, considers both the status of the wearer and their location, and states that dressing alike does not suit all bodies and lifestyles. Barclay acknowledges that people in the country dress differently than their city counterparts, and masters dress better than their servants. Regardless, Quakers should be mindful to not stand out by dressing luxuriously or extravagantly compared to those around them.

Quakers were advised to wear what is commonly available and not use cost as the sole factor to determine luxury or extravagance. Silk was common in some areas, so it was acceptable there, whereas wool was the standard in other areas, so it would be vain to wear silk in those places. Gold and silver are even acceptable if they are widely available; otherwise, Quakers were to use iron and brass.

Superfluity

For the second standard, superfluity, such as unnecessary trims, fashionable patterns, jewellery, and other ornamentation, Barclay expanded upon the Scriptures Fox referenced and continued against 'use of *Ribbands* and *Lace*, and much more of that Kind of Stuff, as *painting the Face, and plaiting the Hair*, which are the Fruits of the *fallen, lustful*, and *corrupt Nature*'.[10] He specifically admonishes women against braiding their hair or wearing ornamentation, as he claims they are 'the sex more inclined to that vanity'.[11]

In 1682, *The Rules of Discipline* issued by the Philadelphia Yearly Meeting (PYM) censured specific items such as striped and floral textiles, long scarves, or non-functioning buttons.[12] Friends would update these guidelines periodically as they adapted to changing fashions. By 1711, women were admonished to avoid 'gaudy stomachers', the height of fashion at the time.

Dissent

In 1700, Margaret Fell, George Fox's wife, denounced plainness as a 'silly, poor gospel'.[13] She thought that concentrating on dress was creating false idols and taking away attention from the inward light, which was the true focus of Quakerism. Unfortunately, she was alone in this sentiment, and Quakers continued to pursue plainness in all aspects of their lives. By the end of the seventeenth century, it was easier to say what wasn't plain than what was.[14]

1700–1800

In the 1700s, Quakers continued to define plainness and to issue rules and guidance based on fashions. Testimonies advised Quakers to pursue simplicity and to be wary of fashionable goods and appearances. Observers of the time noted that Quakers wore contemporary dress without fashionable details.

On his travels to Philadelphia in the 1750s, Peter Kalm noted that Quaker women's dresses were just as fashionable as non-Quaker dresses and often made of the best materials except they didn't have cuffs. He also noted that Quaker women seemed to ignore plainness when it came to shoes as Quaker women wore 'just as gaudy shoes as other English women'.[15]

One of the key issues for Quakers during this century was how different classes expressed plainness. In England, Quakers in the rural north disdained London fashions. This caused tensions with the wealthier London Quakers.[16]

In America, wealthy Quaker families were merchants and involved in manufacturing.[17] Portraits of the time reflect the differences between wealthy and less wealthy Quakers. Portraits were frowned upon as pride by the first Quakers but not by subsequent generations of Quakers.[18]

Those portraits and silhouettes show that there was still a wide variety of interpretation on plainness and probably some stretching of the rules. For example, in 1704, PYM noted that Friends were to keep clear of unnecessary and extravagant wigs. Yet in Diane Johnson's study of Colonial American Quaker portraits, she notes that wealthy Quaker merchant Charles Norris wears a short, modest wig in his portrait painted in 1739.[19] While it could be argued that Norris' wig was unnecessary, by wearing a modest wig and not a fashionable one, he is technically making his wig more 'plain'.

Amelia Mott Gummere notes that American Quakers were always stricter than their British counterparts. She speculates that it is because the 'proximity to the continent familiarized the English man with more cosmopolitan ideas.'[20] By the mid-1700s, Americans were no longer limited to class and rank by birth. Quakers had access to increased social mobility and accumulation of wealth through hard work and good business sense. 'Being "high class" no longer meant "well-bred" but increasingly meant "well-moneyed."'[21] The relative affluence of Americans gave them access to high-quality imported goods from all over the world. It was harder for Quakers to apply the concept of plainness to Barclay's advice to wear what was commonly available. Pushing back against what they perceived as problems with 'luxury', Quaker reformers tightened the rules for plainness.[22]

By the end of the century, Quakers had a distinct style that would define them well into the next century. Plain or drab colours were nearly universal. For women, the first step in going plain was adopting a Quaker-style cap and pinning her neckerchief outside of her bodice as opposed to the fashionable way of tucking it inside.[23] Women also started wearing distinctive bonnets that would stand out among the more fashionable hats.

1800s

While the 1700s saw the rise and definition of Quaker plain dress, the 1800s would see it wane and eventually be relinquished. During this time, plainness shifted from signalling group identity to engaging in moderation in how they lived their life and practised good works.

Some items of plainness such as caps, bonnets, and neckerchiefs were fossilized fashions that Quakers continued to combine with simplified versions of contemporary fashions. These would slowly get replaced during this time until most Quakers completely transitioned to contemporary styles. In the United States, the Quakers split into distinct sects who each viewed plain dress differently. In England, Quakers started to give up plain dress in the 1860s. By the end of the century, all but a small handful of conservative Quakers in the United States had abandoned plain dress and wore contemporary fashions.

One example of how plainness changed can be seen in Quaker school uniform guidelines. At the Westtown School in Pennsylvania, students were given a list of clothing items and plain dress guidelines. In the early 1800s, green was considered a plain colour, but by 1820 it had become fashionable and was no longer plain. Students were advised to wear dark or drab colours, and small-print calicos were also acceptable. Matrons at the school inspected clothing to ensure plainness and required students to alter or cover clothing that did not meet guidelines.[24]

Around mid-century, Quakers started to abandon plain dress. Quakers in the Delaware Valley started to shed plainness as early as the 1840s. It would take another fifty years before they fully renounced the plainness testimony. By 1870, Hicksites loosened their plain dress testimony,[25] and by 1896, Hicksites in Philadelphia would end their plainness testimony completely.[26] Gurneyite Friends aligned themselves with the evangelical Christian movements in the mid-1800s. They saw plain dress as alienating themselves from other Christians and repudiated plain dress and speech.[27] At the turn of the century, it was only older Quakers and conservative Quakers who had aligned themselves with conservative Christians who kept the plainness testimony.

Twentieth and Twenty-First Centuries

In the twentieth century, Quakers shifted from plainness to a testimony of 'simplicity'. The guidelines of plainness had become too legalistic, and as Margaret Fell cautioned so many years ago, they shifted to focus on rules instead of spirituality. Liberal Quakers argued that it took them further away from George Fox's original message. The 1961 PYM statement on simplicity incorporated the older language of cautioning against undue luxury but added words about 'simple tastes'. 'Simplicity, when it removes encumbering details, makes for beauty in music, art, and living'.[28] Quakers were now free to dress, act, and live like their contemporary neighbours while keeping mindful of Quaker values.

Simplicity allowed Quakers to adapt to contemporary needs. They could live 'in the world but not of it'.[29] Quakers could also express modern concerns through simplicity, such as the need for a sustainable life. Because simplicity was defined by the individual, not the Meeting, it became a personal testimony as opposed to a show of dedication to a singular ideal.

As happened in the eighteenth century, many contemporary Quakers are part of the affluent middle class and wrestle with the same concerns about locally sourced goods versus cheap imports. Current criticism of the simplicity testimony focuses on talk about simple living, but that often turns out to be 'Volvo simple living'.[30] Volvos have long been associated with fashionable and upper-middle-class suburban lifestyles. Simplicity, like plainness, is refined according to current fashions, trends, and attitudes.

Today, it encompasses much more than just dress, speech, and furnishings. It expands to include matters such as use of technology, media consumption, and even diet.

Contemporary Plain Quakers

Today, most remaining plain Quakers are part of Ohio Yearly Meeting (OYM), formerly OYM (Conservative). They represent a strain of American Quakerism most resistant to change.[31] Susan and Jack Smith joined Rockingham Monthly Meeting, under OYM, in the 1960s. They remember going to yearly meeting in the 1960s and meeting elderly Quakers who had grown up plain. Most of the members of OYM back then were plain, even if they did not grow up that way.[32]

The Smiths are part of only a handful of plain Quakers left in OYM. Modern plain Quakers do not seek to revive the old traditions and style of plainness but to create their own version of plain.[33] The Smiths were led to dress plain when they moved to Rockingham County, Virginia, and Susan started teaching at a Mennonite School of mainly plain Mennonites.

Like many other plain Quakers, they wear garments worn by other contemporary plain people (such as cape dresses and collarless jackets), but with a distinct look indicating they are plain but not part of those groups. Jack mainly wears regular dress shirts, suspenders, trousers, and a collarless jacket. Susan used to take the collars off of his shirts but doesn't any more.

Susan started out wearing simple dresses without the cape that she made herself, but she later added the cape. She also wears a cap called a covering, which she copied off of a statue of Quaker martyr Mary Dyer.

Her wardrobe is much brighter than historical plain clothes, comprising lively blues, greens, and purples. She recalls once wearing a salmon-coloured dress to OYM and feeling very out of place. That led her to determine that God was telling her 'that colour is not for you'.

By contrast, the local Mennonite women wear calicos and small prints for everyday and darker, solid colours for Sunday best. Children tend to wear brighter colours than adults as well.

Why Be Plain?

Plainness as an Identifier

For some Quakers, adopting plain dress 'signified a deep commitment to the Quaker's basic testimonies: honesty, simplicity, equality, and peace'.[34] In the early days of the Quaker movement, Quakers were routinely persecuted and jailed for their faith. Later generations of Quakers viewed plainness as honouring the first Quakers' intentions, since they had endured this persecution and spoken against luxury and fashion. Adopting a similar style of dress helped preserve their identity in a hostile world. It was important to Quakers that a 'Friend should always be able to recognize a fellow Quaker'.[35]

Plainness as Rejecting Worldly Fashions

The first Quakers found an ideal middle ground for their plain dress between the austere Cromwellian Puritans and the lavish Cavaliers.[36] Their styles clearly signalled that they were rejecting worldly fashions without aligning themselves with even more reactionary religious movements that adopted strict codes of dress. Rejecting following established styles and opposing the idea of plainness can be considered 'antifashion', as defined by Fred Davis in *Fashion, Culture, and Identity*.[37]

For men, plainness was a backlash against radically changing fashion. Between 1660 and 1680, men's fashion changed more often than women's fashions, making it expensive and extravagant to keep a man's wardrobe current with laces and wigs.[38] Later in the seventeenth century, men were mainly advised against wigs, while women continued to be cautioned against wearing many other types of finery such as lace and jewellery. Men also refused 'hat honour', removing or doffing their hats in the presence of superiors, as they rejected artificial social orders.[39] Plain Quakers to this day still keep their hats on at all times except when someone is speaking in Meeting for Worship.

Plainness for Instilling Quaker Values

Wearing plain dress was a way to instil Quaker values, especially in children. A 1669 advice to Quaker women advised them to train up their children and dress them plainly.[40] This allowed the larger Quaker community to act as a large family to all of the Quaker children and to model proper behaviour and dress. Children who started to stray could be reminded of proper dress and deportment by any Quaker elder, which would help the entire community adhere to Quaker ideals.

When Susan and Jack Smith went through their journey to be plain, they also made their children dress plain as required at their Mennonite school. Even with plain dress, Susan noticed that her daughters still got caught up in 'plain fashion': differences in the width of the same-fabric belt on dresses or the style of sleeves. Susan saw dressing plain as an example of consistent, modest dress for her daughters to follow.[41]

While Quakers were not specifically evangelical after the 1700s, they did feel as if they were living a life more in line with biblical teachings. They saw that plain dress showed why Quaker values were better.[42] 'Gay' Quakers, who chose not to dress plain, were allowed to remain in plain communities with the hopes that they would eventually turn plain.

Contemporary plain Quakers Fred and Judy Ceppa see dressing plain as ministry as well as identifying them with God and a shared-faith community. It reminds them of the sacrifices of the early Quakers and makes them more conscious of their own actions.[43]

Plainness as Social Consciousness

Plainness has always contained an element of social consciousness. Dressing plain meant less money spent on worldly goods so more money could be put towards other causes. Quality and durability were important aspects of plainness. George Fox was known for wearing leather breeches for their durability.[44] At the Westtown School, students had to bring durable clothing that could withstand laundering. White undergarments were discouraged in favour of grey or natural coloured items, presumably because they hid stains and did not need to be bleached, which weakened fabric over time.[45]

Quakers were also mindful from where their clothing came as well as the labour that went into producing clothing. Traveling Quaker preacher John Woolman tirelessly preached against slavery and the slave trade. His former profession of tailor meant that he was very familiar with the slave labour in the clothing industry, both with fabric dyeing and production, especially cotton. His convictions led him to wear only undyed cloth as an outward testimony against these practices.[46]

British Quaker women were also concerned about clothing and ethics. First was using 'ethical cotton cloth' and sourcing clothing made from free labour as opposed to slave labour.[47] Secondly was concern over the use of endangered birds' feathers on fashionable hats in the late

1800s. Even after Quaker women started to relinquish plain dress in the 1860s, they didn't seem to adopt fashionable hats, especially feathered ones, as none exist in collections. At the time, Quaker women spoke out against hunting endangered birds for fashion. The lack of fashionable hats seems to indicate that they refused to wear such items as well.[48]

Modern Quakers link social justice work to Quaker dress. Quaker lawyer Scott Holmes was led to relinquish his tie in deference to male patriarchy and privilege. Giving up the tie made him feel free of the arbitrary rules of dress and also helped him understand the oppression of women from these rules. Judges pushed back on his decision, which he had to justify, similar to what he felt women and other people who encounter oppression have to navigate on a daily basis.[49]

Conclusion

For nearly 200 years, Quakers adhered to the testimony of plainness in dress. While plainness was always up to the individual, Quakers maintained a distinctive look, which made them recognizable to people in their own faith communities as well as those outside of it.

Key to the testimony of plainness was denouncing vanity, luxury, and slavish adherence to current fashions. Plainness became a hedge between Quakers and the outside world and a way to express their commitment to Quaker values.

This wasn't enough for Quakers to keep plain. By the end of the nineteenth century, all but a handful of conservative American Quakers had relinquished plain dress. Today, most of the plain-dressing Quakers are members of OYM.

Instead of trying to recreate historical Quaker fashions, they are guided by their own consciousness and Quaker testimonies to develop their own version of plain. Modern Quakerism evolved from plain to a testimony of simplicity, which centres more about making ethical decisions about lifestyle choices.

As we continue in the twenty-first century, Quaker dress will continue to evolve and change with or in reaction to current fashions and trends, just like it has since the beginning.

Notes

1 Gummere (1901, p. 31).
2 Gummere (1901, p. 136).
3 Kendall (1985, p. 62)
4 Caton (2003, p. 257).
5 Caton (2003, p. 269).
6 Hamm (2003, p. 3).
7 Frost (2003, p. 17).
8 Fox (1661, p. xxiii).
9 Barclay (2018, p. 468).
10 Barclay (2018, p. 468).
11 Barclay (2018, p. 470).
12 Philadelphia Yearly Meeting of the Religious Society of Friends (1797).
13 Barbour (1976, p. 32).
14 Frost (2003, p. 19).
15 Benson (1937, p. 651).
16 Johnson (2003, p. 134).
17 Hamm (2003, p. 19).
18 Johnson (2003, p. 123).
19 Johnson (2003, p. 129).
20 Gummere (1901, p. 71).

21 Eiler (2008, p. 13).
22 Hamm (2003, pp. 31–32).
23 Caton (2003, pp. 247–248).
24 Caton (2003, p. 257).
25 Caton (2003, p. 270).
26 Frost (2003, p. 36).
27 Hamm (2003, p. 53).
28 Philadelphia Yearly Meeting (1961, p. 24).
29 Hamm (2003, p. 102).
30 Earlham School of Religion (1999, p. 76).
31 Hamm (2003, p. 3).
32 Smith & Smith (2020).
33 *Why Do Some Quakers Dress Plain* (2020).
34 Caton (2003, p. 247).
35 Frost (2003, p. 29).
36 Gummere (1901, p. 14).
37 Rumball (2016, pp. 89–90).
38 Gummere (1901, p. 21).
39 Kesselring (2011, p. 300).
40 Rumball (2016, p. 113).
41 Smith & Smith (2020).
42 Hamm (2003, p. 102).
43 Ceppa & Ceppa (2000).
44 Fox (1911, p. 52).
45 Caton (2003, p. 257).
46 Woolman (2011, p. xv).
47 Rumball (2016, p. 83).
48 Rumball (2016, pp. 210, 212).
49 *Why I Don't Wear a Tie in Court* (2014).

Bibliography

Barbour, H., ed., 1976. *Margaret Fell Speaking*. Wallingford, PA: Pendle Hill.

Barclay, R., 2018. *An Apology for the True Christian Divinity*. [Online] Available at: http://www.gutenberg.org/files/56487/56487-h/56487-h.htm [Accessed 25 May 2020].

Benson, A. B., ed., 1937. *Peter Kalm's Travels in North America*. English Version of 1770 ed. New York: Wilson-Erickson.

Caton, M. A., 2003. The Aesthetics of Absence: Quaker Women's Plain Dress in the Delaware Valley, 1790–1900. In: E. J. Lapsansky & A. A. Verplanck, eds. *Quaker Aesthetics: Reflections on a Quaker Ethic in American Design and Consumption*. Philadelphia: University of Philadelphia Press, pp. 246–271.

Ceppa, F. & Ceppa, J., 2000. Why We Dress This Way. *Friend's Journal,* 1 December, pp. 24–31.

Earlham School of Religion, 1999. *Among Friends: A Consultation with Friends About the Conditions of Quakers in the U.S. Today*. Richmond, IN: s.n.

Eiler, R. E. M., 2008. Luxury, Capitalism, and the Quaker Reformation, 1737–1798. *Quaker History,* 97(1), pp. 11–31.

Fox, G., 1661. *Some Principles of the Quakers*. London: Robert Wilson.

Fox, G., 1911. *The Journal of George Fox*. 1858 ed. London: The Cambridge University Press.

Frost, J. W., 2003. From Plainness to Simplicity: Changing Quaker Ideals for Material Culture. In: E. Jones Lapsansky & A. A. Verplanck, eds. *Quaker Aesthetics: Reflections on Quaker Ethic in American Design and Consumption*. Philadelphia: University of Philadelphia Press, pp. 16–40.

Gummere, A. M., 1901. *The Quakers: A Study in Costume*. Philadelphia: Ferris and Leach.

Hamm, T. D., 2003. *The Quakers in America*. New York: Columbia University Press.

Johnson, D. C., 2003. Living in the Light: Quakerism and Colonial Portraiture. In: E. J. Lapsansky & A. A. Verplanck, eds. *Quaker Aesthetics: Reflections on a Quaker Ethic in American Design and Consumption*. Philadelphia: University of Philadelphia Press, pp. 122–146.

Kendall, J., 1985. The Development of a Distinctive Form of Quaker Dress. *Costume,* 19(1), pp. 58–74.

Kesselring, K.J., 2011. Gender, the Hat, and Quaker Universalism in the Wake of the English Revolution. *The Seventeenth Century,* 26(2), pp. 299–322.

Philadelphia Yearly Meeting, 1961. *Faith and Practice.* Philadelphia: s.n.

Philadelphia Yearly Meeting of the Religious Society of Friends, 1797. *Rules of discipline and Christian Advices of the Yearly Meeting of Friends for Pennsylvania and New Jersey, first held at Burlington in the year 1681, and from 1685 to 1760, inclusive, alternately in Burlington and Philadelphia: And since at Philadelphia.* Philadelphia: Samual Sansom.

Rumball, H.F., 2016. *The Relinquishment of Plain Dress: British Quaker Women's Abandonment of Plain Quaker Attire, 1860–1914.* Brighton: University of Brighton.

Smith, S. & Smith, J., 2020. *Interview with Jack and Susan Smith, Plain Quakers of OYM* [Interview] (8 May 2020).

Why Do Some Quakers Dress Plain, 2020. [Film] Directed by Rebecca Hamilton-Levi. Philadelphia, PA: Friends Journal.

Why I Don't Wear a Tie in Court, 2014. [Film] Directed by Rebecca Hamilton-Levi. Philadelphia, PA USA: QuakerSpeak.

Woolman, J., 2011. *John Woolman's Journal.* Project Gutenberg EBook ed. London: J.M. Dent and Sons.

52

MODERN UNDERSTANDINGS OF PLAIN DRESS

Mackenzie Morgan

Introduction

The relationship between plain dress and Quakers today is controversial. On the one hand, non-Quakers – particularly in the United States and Canada – sometimes expect Quakers to dress in ways similar to the Amish, conservative Mennonites, and Hutterites. On the other hand, Quakers sometimes respond to this idea by asserting that plain dress is no longer relevant.

Plain dress is still practiced among Friends, though its forms may differ from the Amish-like expectation. Isabel Penraeth categorized religiously observant styles of dress for women into three categories: plain, plain modern, and modest dress (Penraeth, 2007c). This paper focuses on the first two styles, herein called "traditional plain" and "modern plain." They are applied to men's observant dress as well.

Plain-dressing Quakers have connected online, such as on QuakerQuaker and Facebook. For the "Clothe Yourself in Righteousness" project, Quaker songwriter Jon Watts interviewed a number of Quakers about their relationship to clothing. Through these media, twenty-first-century Friends have written in their own words about how faith influences clothing choices, which in turn influence interactions with the world around them. These personal testimonies show that plain dress does continue to be a witness and to testify to the world.

Guidance

The Bible

Early Quaker theologian Robert Barclay lists a number of Biblical passages and arguments for plain dress. He argues that as clothing is the punishment for the fall, humanity ought not delight in it. He cites 1 Timothy 2:8–10 and 1 Peter 3:3–4, which give examples of a number of "immodest" ways of showing off wealth and status through personal adornment. In referencing Matthew 6:25, he reminds readers not to worry about what they will wear and what the fashions are (Barclay, 2002, pp. 447–449).

DOI: 10.4324/9780429030925-56

Unwritten Discipline

As stated in Fuller's chapter on historical plain dress, yearly meeting Books of Discipline or Faith and Practice no longer contain strict rules for plainness. Instead, they emphasize applying simplicity as a Quaker value to decisions about how to dress. For example, Baltimore Yearly Meetings[1] advises that "ostentation and extravagant expenditure should not be a part of Friends' lives" (Baltimore Yearly Meeting of the Religious Society of Friends, 2001).

This lack of distinct guidance has led Friends to seeking peer guidance online when feeling called to plainness.

The Internet

QuakerQuaker is a Quaker social network run by Martin Kelley (Anon., "About"). It has a number of interest groups available, including one for Conservative Friends and another for Plainness and Simplicity. At the time of this writing, those two groups have 178 and 239 members, respectively (Anon., "Beliefs/Groups"), showing the broader interest in plain dress beyond the Conservative tradition.

Social media website Facebook is home to many Quaker-related groups. The Facebook group Plain Quakers is considerably smaller than the QuakerQuaker equivalent group, at only 37 members (Anon, 2020). However, discussion of plain dress comes up from time to time in other Quaker groups on Facebook.

Features of Plain Dress

Gender

Attitudes toward clothing and gender are intimately related. One of the Biblical passages Barclay cites, 1 Timothy 2:8–10, specifically addresses women, and Barclay considers that the women in that context may have been particularly swayed by fashion (Barclay, 2002, p. 449). Clothing choice is one aspect of gender expression, and clothing choices have historically been restricted by gender. For example, trousers on women were a radical new fashion in the early twentieth century (Bill, 1993, p. 45). Traditional plain dress evolved within this highly binarily gendered context.

This chapter refers to only two genders, women and men, in the arrangement sometimes called the gender binary. This should be read as descriptive rather than prescriptive and as a simplification of the more complex reality of gender.

As modern ideas about gender shift, there are two ways this can interact with plain dress: conflict and remix.

Conflict

Some members of the LGBTQ+ community have expressed concerns about sex segregation (Eindride, 2020) and noted that it can give the appearance of being part of sect that does not accept LGBTQ+ people (Zubizarreta, 2020).

In *Friends Journal*'s March 2020 issue, "Unnamed Quaker Creeds," one featured article was titled "Thou Shalt Wear Comfy Shoes." It was written by a trans woman named Suzanne

W. Cole Sullivan. What Cole Sullivan found was that in the absence of written rules about dress, a "come as you are" attitude was projected, but a "come as we are" attitude manifested. Her preference for feminine shoes such as high heels made her the target of snide remarks. She writes, "for many trans and genderqueer people, dressing to our gender expression is unwelcome in Quaker meetinghouses because it is too formal, too fancy, or too feminine." This compounded society's oppressive stifling of her gender expression (Cole Sullivan, 2020).

Remix

Annalee Flower Horne, a member of Adelphi Friends Meeting in Baltimore Yearly Meeting, discovered they were non-binary after going plain. "Forms of plain dress traditionally associated with women made me feel gender incongruence," they say (Flower Horne, 2019a). Instead, they remixed the tradition.

> So I started wearing masculine plain dress – button-up collarless shirts, vests [waist-coats], jeans or trousers. I wear head coverings, which is a feminine thing, but because my hair is long and v. curly, covering it is in keeping with the simplicity testimony.
>
> *(Flower Horne, 2019b)*

"Simplicity testimony" here refers to how Quakers apply simplicity as a shared value to their lives.

In a conversation on 14 April 2018 among members of Ohio Yearly Meeting's Rockingham Quarterly Meeting, one Friend expressed scepticism that non-binary plain dress was possible. One by one, Friends at the table were shown a photo of Flower Horne with the question "if thee saw this person out in public, would thee recognize them as plain?" The unanimous answer was yes.

Traditional Plain

The description of women's traditional plain provided by Isabel Penraeth is that they

> wear long dresses, often with a cape or kerchief or other second layer to cover the bosom. Fabrics are usually solids or simple prints. Aprons are also common. Most distinctive is probably the headcovering, which falls into a fairly limited range of styles.

Penraeth refers here to a gallery of coifs and bonnets from a variety of plain traditions. The term "coif" is used by costume historians to describe a shaped fabric head covering worn directly against the head, possibly under a hat (Cumming et al., 2017, p. 51). It is used here because it is unambiguous in meaning regarding women's headwear. A bonnet is a hat with no brim in the back, often tied under the chin (Cumming et al., 2017, p. 26). Penraeth notes that "makeup and jewelry are avoided" in deference to 1 Timothy 2:9 (Penraeth, 2007**a**).

Martin Kelley published a list of items of clothing as a starting point for men interested in traditional plain dress. His list includes broad fall trousers (trousers which have a wide flap instead of a zipper fly), braces, and a broad-brimmed hat. He is careful to note this does not constitute a uniform and mentions "good-hearted ribbing" between Friends who prefer wide braces and those who prefer narrow (Kelley, 2004). As mentioned by Flower Horne above, waistcoats may also feature.

Penraeth provides a number of resources for women led to traditional plain dress, including links to Mennonite and Amish clothing retailers (Penraeth, 2007a). Similarly, Kelley refers the reader to a retailer of Amish clothing (Kelley, 2004).

Simply put, this is the category of plain dress more likely to be mistaken for Amish or Mennonite by outsiders.

Modern Plain

Penraeth writes that modern plain "is the most difficult to categorize." She says that "actual plainness (solid colors, simple print, limited-palette wardrobes) is a hallmark of the plain modern look." She says there are no symbolic items or anachronisms. For women, she says that this category is least likely to involve head covering and most likely to involve trousers (Penraeth, 2007b).

In Chapter 51 of this volume, Deb Fuller noted that eighteenth-century Quakers "wore contemporary dress without fashionable details." In this sense, modern plain dress follows closely in the spirit of the plain dress of the past. Julie Courtwright, a traditionally plain Friend and longtime attender of Alexandria Monthly Meeting in Baltimore Yearly Meeting, posted on Facebook on 2 December 2020 regarding her husband's modern plain dress: "The Amish lady I made friends with thought it was hilarious that Eli's Plain dress is grey sweatpants and t-shirts."

Kelley uses the term "Sears plain" to describe a plain wardrobe comprising garments commonly available "in any box store or mall" and describes it as having been the first step on his path to traditional plain dress. Kelley says of modern plain:

> Modern plainness can lessen the temptation to show off in clothes and it can reduce the overall wardrobe size and thus reduce our impact on the environment and with exploited labor. But all this is nothing new and it never really disappeared. If you looked around a room of modern Quakers you'll often see a trend of sartorial boringness; I was simply naming this and putting it in the context of our tradition.
>
> *(Kelley, 2014)*

This "sartorial boringness" may be the best summation of modern plain dress.

Head Covering

Women's head covering was mentioned earlier in the section on traditional plain dress. Yet, some women are called to head covering without changing their other clothing (Shryock, 2016).

Women's head covering is addressed in the Bible as a practice to be undertaken when a woman prays or prophesies, in 1 Corinthians 11:5. Since the early days of Quakerism, Quakers have traditionally identified vocal ministry and women's preaching with prophesy. Barclay defended women's preaching by appealing to that instruction regarding "how women should behave themselves in their public preaching and praying" (Barclay, 2002, p. 277). Within a Quaker framework, it therefore can be argued that women's head covering symbolizes women's authority to preach.

Some men, whether their clothing is plain or not, continue to wear hats at all times. Some give as their reason, that it is "just a reminder that God is with me always" (Smith, 2016). In keeping with the next verse of 1 Corinthians 11, which commands men uncover their heads when praying and prophesying, Penraeth has observed that men in Ohio Yearly Meeting remove their hats when vocal prayers are being offered in meeting for worship (Penraeth, 2012).

Reasons for "Going Plain"

Discipline and Testimony

Richard Foster says that "to move beyond surface living into the depths" is the purpose of the spiritual disciplines (Foster, 1998, p. 1). Yet he is firm that the inward reality must come first. He specifically cautions against allowing concerns for the environment or wealth redistribution to become central reasons for practicing simplicity (Foster, 1998, p. 87).

Testimony has a number of definitions. Pink Dandelion defines testimony as "the consequences of the spiritual life as expressed in daily life" (Dandelion, 2007, p. 221). Lloyd Lee Wilson says the essence of Quaker testimony is "an attempt to communicate by direct action what we have witnessed about the truth of God and God's creation" (Wilson, 2005, p. 141). Paul Buckley says the actions involved in testimony "were not things [Friends] chose to do in order to prove themselves righteous or to move themselves Godward" (Buckley, 2018, p. 94).

That difference of attitude toward movement provides a distinction between discipline and testimony.

Discipline

According to Foster, "if we ever expect to grow in grace, we must pay the price of a consciously chosen course of action which involves both individual and group life. Spiritual growth is the purpose of the Disciplines" (Foster, 1998, p. 8).

In response to a video about plain dress, *Friends Journal* published a letter to the editor from Rachel Kopel:

> I have found myself thinking "yes, I could do that, but would I want to be doing it while wearing my 'I am a Quaker' t-shirt? . . . When Quakers gave up plain dress and plain speech – their version of that t-shirt – they gave up the instant recognition of being a peculiar people. . . . [W]e have also lost a great deal in opportunities to witness, to minister, and to remind ourselves of the Light we carry.
>
> *(Kopel, 2020)*

This speaks to the discipline of plain dress. The self-conscious visibility of plain dress serves as a check on the impulses and behaviour of the wearer. This is a recurring theme among plain Friends online. Barbara Smith says:

> Every time I touch my cap, or see myself in the mirror it reminds me – though hopefully I remember more times a day than that. Friends have also mentioned to me multiple times the feeling of restraint it gives them – and the sense that they are representing a Christian to the public and are therefore mindful that how their behavior is viewed may affect attitudes toward other Christians.
>
> *(Smith, 2013)*

Regarding all disciplines, Foster writes of both inward state and outward practice. Particular to the discipline of simplicity, Foster writes that "the central point for the Discipline of simplicity is to seek the kingdom of God and the righteousness of his kingdom *first*" (Foster, 1998, p. 86). Like Barclay (Barclay, 2002, p. 448), he is referring to Matthew 6:25–33.

Testimony

Most testimony is found in word or deed. A Friend may verbally testify to how God has worked in their life. A Friend may break up a fight. A Friend may refuse to swear an oath. These actions are momentary. The plain dress testimony is uniquely physically embodied, visible on the bodies of Friends who practice it, essentially at all times. Flower Horne says, "it became extremely important to me to embody that faith to everyone I met" (Flower Horne, 2012).

The Sisters of Amigas del Señor in Honduras, affiliated with both Multnomah Monthly Meeting and the United Methodist Church, say of their clothing, "our physical habits represent our spiritual habits." They then examine their habitual clothing in light of simplicity, peace, equality, community, and integrity. They write, "Each person in the world lives her or his values. The lived values may not be the spoken values, but the life lived speaks the truth" (Blodgett & Cutting, 2017, pp. 207–208).

Testimony to Non-Quakers

In the same issue of *Friends Journal*, there was another letter to the editor responding to an article about being publicly Quaker. This one compares clothing with other ways Quakers communicate messages.

> Imagine a march or rally where all the Quakers dressed plainly: no colors, no accoutrements – just black, white, and Quaker gray bonnets and broad brimmed hats. This would say clearly who we are and what we stand for. That is, we are members of a historic peace church, bearing public testimony for peace.
>
> . . . Integrity requires that our simplicity not just be for public gatherings. An adoption of simple dress means putting on Quaker gray every day. This requires the courage to look peculiar all the time. But why not? We are ready to let the world know who we are with an abundance of bumper stickers.
>
> *(Thomas, 2020)*

Katie Wonsik responded to Jon Watts' *Clothe Yourself in Righteousness* project by pointing out the new avenues for evangelism opened by practicing plain dress:

> Dressing plain can be a method of evangelism – inviting conversation from your friends and neighbors and the guy selling kale at the farmer's market – providing you with an opportunity to share your faith.
>
> *(Wonsik, 2012)*

Testimony to Other Quakers

A long discussion of plain dress arose in the Young Adult Friends (Quakers) group on Facebook in 2020. In a comment, Jade Souza summed up well the common reaction to discussions of plain dress among Friends online today:

> Periodically, someone will post on the various Friends forums about a leading for plain dress. What is striking is how instant and how strong the backlash. Folks quakesplaining

all the reasons why this leading is "wrong", and giving their reasons for not liking or agreeing with plain dress, and giving (misinformed) historical arguments for why Friends should not dress plain . . . much stronger reaction than to other leading type posts generally.

(Souza, 2020)

In Souza's analysis, dressing to "conform to the wider culture" has become a "cultural idol" for Quakers. She observes that any style which is not "clearly religious" is acceptable among Friends, including "counter culture" styles. She says, "you will be harshly judged and all sorts of ill intents will be assumed about you" if your style is too religious. "When this rule is violated it makes Friends incredibly uncomfortable" (Souza, 2020).

Souza concludes that not only does plain dress testify to non-Quakers, but it has an important role to play in testifying to Quakers as well:

I now see its irrationality as the testimony. Plain dress reveals our irrational obsession with conformity through fashion, and how oppressive it is to us, like any idol.

I believe that it reveals our deep fear of the irrational . . . we are terrified that God might place a mystical calling on our hearts that we cannot defend with logic, and we will look silly, or will be cultural outcasts, or whatever other thing. I think the plain dress testimony is about wearing such a leading visibly and without fear, with total trust in who God is and that God's sense is sufficient.

(Souza, 2020)

Seen in this light, plain dress becomes a small – but uncomfortable – reminder to Quakers that God's leadings can be entirely irrational. In a pamphlet, Maggie Harrison explored the early Friends' practice of "going naked as a sign." She calls it "a radical exploit, enacted out of deepest faith and trust in God." She says:

I don't just want to tell myself that I would carry out a leading as ground shaking as our forebears; I want to *know* that I would, with all the certainty of a Friend that has been completely transformed by my relationship to the Divine.

(Harrison, 2011)

While of a different degree than a leading to go naked, a leading to plain dress represents what George Fox would call a "cross to the will" (Fox, 1831, p. 38).

Conclusion

The practice of dressing plainly is alive today among Quakers in both overt and subtle ways. Quakers practicing plain dress may be doing so as a form of spiritual discipline or as a testimony. To non-Quakers, this testimony may represent who Quakers are, while to other Quakers it may represent being made a fool for Christ.

Note

1 Affiliated with both Friends General Conference and Friends United Meeting.

Bibliography

Anon, 2020. *Facebook Search Results for Quakers*. [Online] Available at: https://www.facebook.com/search/groups/?q=quakers [Accessed 25 12 2020].

Anon, n.d. *About QuakerQuaker/FAQs*. [Online] Available at: http://www.quakerquaker.org/notes/Notes_Home [Accessed 21 12 2020].

Anon, n.d. *Quaker Beliefs/Groups*. [Online] Available at: http://www.quakerquaker.org/groups [Accessed 21 12 2020].

Baltimore Yearly Meeting of the Religious Society of Friends, 2001. *Faith and Practice*. Sandy Spring, MD: Baltimore Yearly Meeting.

Barclay, R., 2002. *Apology for the True Christian Divinity*. Farmington, ME: Quaker Heritage Press.

Bill, K., 1993. Attitudes Towards Women's Trousers: Britain in the 1930s. *Journal of Design History,* 6(1), p. 45.

Blodgett, B. & Cutting, P. N., 2017. *Giving Up Something Good for Something Better*. Cushing, WI: Amigas Press.

Buckley, P., 2018. *Primitive Quakerism Revived*. San Francisco: Inner Light Books.

Cole Sullivan, S. W., 2020. Thou Shalt Wear Comfy Shoes. *Friends Journal*, March, pp. 6–8.

Cumming, V., Cunnington, C. W. & Cunninton, P. E., 2017. *The Dictionary of Fashion History*. 2nd ed. London: Bloomsbury Academic.

Dandelion, P., 2007. *An Introduction to Quakerism*. Cambridge: Cambridge University Press.

Eindride, P. A., 2020. *Comment on Facebook*. [Online] Available at: https://www.facebook.com/groups/YAQNET/permalink/3087786407924889/?comment_id=3087858471251016 [Accessed 25 12 2020].

Flower Horne, A., 2012. *Annalee and Clothing*. [Online] Available at: https://web.archive.org/web/20150407043127/http://www.clotheyourselfinrighteousness.com/annalee-and-clothing/ [Accessed 07 04 2015].

Flower Horne, A., 2019a. *Twitter*. [Online] Available at: https://twitter.com/LeeFlower/status/117705792 5065519104 [Accessed 21 12 2020].

Flower Horne, A., 2019b. *Twitter*. [Online] Available at: https://twitter.com/LeeFlower/status/1177 058333951496192 [Accessed 21 12 2020].

Foster, R., 1998. *Celebration of Discipline*. New York: HarperOne.

Fox, G., 1831. *The Works of George Fox*. Philadelphia: J Harding, Printer.

Harrison, M., 2011. *Clothe Yourself in Righteousness*. West Philadelphia: s.n.

Kelley, M., 2004. *Gohn Brothers, Broadfalls, & Men's Plain Dress*. [Online] Available at: https://www.quakerranter.org/gohn_brothers_broadfalls_mens/ [Accessed 23 12 2020].

Kelley, M., 2014. *Normcore and the New-old Quaker Plain*. [Online] Available at: https://www.quakerranter.org/normcore-and-the-new-old-quaker-plain/ [Accessed 23 12 2020].

Kopel, R., 2020. Letter to the Editor. *Friends Journal*, 5, p. 46.

Penraeth, I., 2007a. *Plain Dress*. [Online] Available at: http://www.quakerjane.com/index.php?fuseaction=plain_dress.plain [Accessed 21 12 2020].

Penraeth, I., 2007b. *Plain Modern*. [Online] Available at: http://www.quakerjane.com/index.php?fuseaction=plain_dress.modern [Accessed 21 12 2020].

Penraeth, I., 2007c. *Women's Religiously Observant Plain Dress*. [Online] Available at: http://www.quakerjane.com/index.php?fuseaction=plain_dress.main

Penraeth, I., 2012. *Comment on QuakerQuaker*. [Online] Available at: http://www.quakerquaker.org/xn/detail/2360685:Comment:83178 [Accessed 25 15 2020].

Shryock, S., 2016. *Comment on Quakers Group on Facebook*. [Online] Available at: https://www.facebook.com/groups/2207263944/permalink/10154228635933945/?comment_id=10154238293623945 [Accessed 24 12 2020].

Smith, B., 2013. *Comment on QuakerQuaker*. [Online] Available at: http://www.quakerquaker.org/forum/topics/the-discipline-of-covering?commentId=2360685%3AComment%3A115003 [Accessed 23 12 2020].

Smith, S., 2016. [Online] Available at: http://www.quakerquaker.org/xn/detail/2360685:Comment:145929 [Accessed 25 12 2020].

Souza, J., 2020. *Young Adult Friends (Quakers)*. [Online] Available at: https://www.facebook.com/groups/YAQNET/permalink/3087786407924889/?comment_id=3089118711124992 [Accessed 21 12 2020].

Thomas, C., 2020. Letter to the Editor. *Friends Journal*, May, pp. 46–47.

Wilson, L. L., 2005. Friends Testimonies in the Marketplace. In: *Wrestling with Our Faith Tradition*. Philadelphia: Quaker Press, pp. 141–161.

Wonsik, K., 2012. *Katie Wonsik and Clothing*. [Online] Available at: http://www.clotheyourselfinrighteousness.com/katie-wonsik-and-clothing/ [Accessed 06 04 2015].

Zubizarreta, C., 2020. *Comment on Facebook*. [Online] Available at: https://www.facebook.com/groups/YAQNET/permalink/3087786407924889/?comment_id=3087858311251032 [Accessed 25 12 2020].

53

CAPTURING THE LIGHT

Materializing Past Quaker Lives

Christopher Allison

On December 20, 1719, John Whiting sat down in his London study to write a remembrance of a recently deceased Friend, John Gratton. Gratton had been one of the first generation of Quakers in England, a tireless itinerant preacher from Derbyshire. Gratton had the distinction of being convinced of the "light of the true way" independent of the preaching of the early leaders, such as George Fox and Margaret Fell. He heard the "Voice of the Lord" tell him that Quakers were the true path amid the religious cacophony of post-Restoration English north and midlands – Presbyterians, Baptists, Congregationalists, and the ever-roving – and much derided by Quakers – "Priests" of the Church of England.[1] Gratton's death led his friend John Whiting to reflect on the role of past Friends. This was a crucial moment in Quaker history; it represented a major transfer of generational authority, and Whiting knew it. The Society of Friends was no longer a new religious movement; it now had a history. The need for intergenerational transfer of memory, wisdom, and identity had become clear as the first generation of Friends passed away.

Founding moments are important in forging a religious community's memory and identity. When that founding moment is clearly passing, there is a felt need to articulate, indeed, materialize the identity it represents. It is about capturing the light, if you will, of that moment. Whiting knew this instinctually: "The removing of so many of the Lord's worthies from among us of late these years is a matter of weighty consideration, with which my heart has often been deeply affected." Whiting argued that the "LOVE to the precious truth," which he received when he was young, "has made me love the messengers and ministers of it, and their testimony for its sake." For Whiting, Gratton was a "true minister of the everlasting gospel of life and salvation to the sons and daughters of men in life and power." Memory is too often assumed to be a misty, cognitive act. But Whiting acted very tangibly with the remains of Gratton's life. Whiting had been given, he writes,

> in several manuscripts, of his life, labors, travels, and sufferings, which, being sent up to London since his decease, were put into my hands, with the desire that I would peruse and compare them. This I carefully did, and brought the substance of all into one, according to the order of time, as near as I could in his own words, not omitting anything that was material. May the Lord make it serviceable to all that read it,

DOI: 10.4324/9780429030925-57

that it may redound to his glory, the advancement of his truth, and the comfort of his people.[2]

In the face of the void of this life Whiting revered, Whiting brought order to the fragments of Gratton's life. He was not alone. Across Quaker history, Friends took great care to preserve and honor the Testimony and lives of deceased Friends. It was a series of countless material acts that honored sundry Friends' testimony to the Light, in word and life, and became a ritual of Quaker mortuary practice.[3] But it wasn't just physical journals that were cherished. This overview essay is about the material culture, or embodiment, of Quaker memory, how objects became agents in the historical imaginary of Quakers over time. Objects of past Friends helped focus their historical attention, and allowed them to materially cherish the Light within past Friends' lives. It was a crucial way in which Quakers created a community across generations, and they did so through tangible things.

In capturing and revering past Friends' lives, if in object, photograph, or in manuscript, there was a clear attempt to capture the Light that shone within these people, not in a primary way, but in a secondary one. There is little evidence that Quakers thought exceptional Friends *were* the Light, rather, that the Light shone especially bright within them. At stake here is the dialectic in Quaker thought, largely beyond the scope of this essay, between "outer" (material) and "inner" (spiritual) realities. This is a dialectic in play in all Christian traditions, but especially explicit in Quaker thought for its intense emphasis on interiority as the locus of divine encounter. Protestant traditions that have emphasized robust belief in divine indwelling or "heart religion" tend to have a robust material culture surrounding revered figures of their past; and their material efforts tend to focus keenly upon people and the body.[4] The reason for this in Quaker theological praxis is the person is the locus of religious feeling, revelation, and experience. Such traditions (like Quakers, Methodists, evangelical Baptists, etc.) have had, at times, a strong mystical strain to their religious experience, thus the way they revere historic individuals can often seem more Catholic than, say, Puritan. Quakers have traditionally emphasized that the Holy Spirit or Light dwells within people *and* that God "visits" individuals in a mystical way.[5] But Quakers also have singled out individuals from their past that have been particularly connected to the Light, or, from whom it shone especially brightly. Their absence, often in death, was the catalyst for the collection and creation of embodiments of their presence in material ways.

This desire to materialize the presence of past Friends manifested in a number of ways.

Indeed, preserving historic meeting houses, and visiting them, has been a major concern for Friends over the years. It is not simply preserving a building, but rather the vessel for the Friends who gathered there across time. History matters for Friends, and for history to be preserved, you have to snatch material out of the maw of forgetfulness. This desire to capture the material vestiges of past Friends may seem ironic, given Quakers' well-documented worry about idolatry and insistence on simplicity in all things. The focus on the "Christ within," "inward Light," or later, the "Inner Light" might suggest an interiority that is anti-material. But many theorists of visual and material culture have often pointed to the phenomenon that less visible realties are some of the most generative sources of visual and material culture. As art theorist Hans Belting has observed about images, absence is a potent precondition for the materialization of presence.[6] Furthermore, Alfred Gell noted in *Art and Agency* that objects that index an individual are a way of establishing "distributed personhood."[7] Whiting's attempt to preserve Gratton's journals was not simply a sentimental act, but one in which he attempted to distribute the personhood of this exceptional and absent Quaker friend. Much like taking pieces of wood from the tree under which George Fox preached his first sermon on Long Island, distributed not only the personhood of Fox as a significant Friend, but also asserted that his arrival and preaching in North

America was significant. Or like collecting a spoon from the cave home of Benjamin Lay in Abington, Pennsylvania, distributed, in its own way, the radical witness of Lay's activism around food, against slavery, and his late-life John-the-Baptist-style prophetic role as a voice calling out from the Pennsylvania wilderness.[8]

It need not be famous Friends. The collection of one Jemima White's "plain bonnet which was last worn in New Garden Meeting," in the historical collection of Guilford College in North Carolina, for example, was neither idolatrous nor overly ostentatious.[9] It, even as a singular object, distributed her personhood and witness. It revered Jemima as a faithful Friend, materialized the role of women in Quaker communities, but also her simplicity and humility, in covering her head with a bonnet. Quaker relics were not mere knickknacks but functioned in serious ways in Quaker communities to name and materialize exceptional Quakers, convey their witness and testimony, explain their lifeways over time, assert their theological and ethical values, and unite Friends across generations. Many Quaker archives have thankfully accepted not only the books and manuscript remains of eminent and ordinary Quakers, but also art and artifacts. This reflects a certain understanding by historically proximate Quakers that these things were of value. Archivists and historical society members have clearly agreed, for they have kept preserving them. Thus the ubiquity of these objects in Quaker collections, familial and institutional, suggests a wide phenomenon of Quaker collecting to embody the witness of past Friends.

For those familiar with the history of Quakerism, the opening anecdote will sound like a familiar process of commemorating the dead, especially revered ones. Quaker book history is full of these transformations, from handwritten manuscripts to galleys of metal type, pressed onto paper, assembled into books, bound, sold, gifted, and borrowed.[10] Books are objects, after all. Yet, in book form, the editor mediates the memory of the person. Elias Hicks, one of the most influential and controversial Quakers of early nineteenth-century America, had his journals published with extensive omissions of his sometimes intense mysticism; Paul Buckley estimates about a quarter of his journals are missing from the 1832 edition of his journals. Similarly, the committee formed out of the Philadelphia Yearly Meeting to publish John Woolman's journal after his death in 1772 made a similar move – the 1774 published *Journal* is missing all of his dreams.[11] It is important here to clarify that Quakers were not unique in this respect. Methodists, who also had often intense mystical religious experiences and a vibrant sense of dreams as revelation often downplayed these aspects of early Methodist life in their publication history. As Methodism became "respectable," its radical edge was something that was often omitted in their history writing.[12] Book objects come with interpretation; other things give a different sense of presence that is less about legibility and more about material presence.

A pamphlet published in 1873 in Philadelphia gives a view into the functions of these book and non-book collections. The Friends' Historical Association published their "Appeal" after their founding. They explained to living Friends that their aim was "to rescue from the hand of time the names and deeds of those Friends unknown to fame, whose memories are worthy of being perpetuated." So they asked for donations of "Books, Mss. Letters, Relics &c." The purpose of these materials, from books to relics, was to be the material sources that could be used to "illustrate the history of the Society" but also to "foster kindly feelings toward" all Quakers, or those "whose affiliations attract them towards us" – someone like this historian. It was not just fodder for history writing but built bonds of affection the Friends of old. The society tipped their generational hand by also stating that a major part of their mission was to foster "the cultivation of Historical tastes and pursuits" in Quakers writ large, but "particularly in the young."[13] Fostering historical connection with the Quaker past was a mission that would help connect young Quakers with their spiritual ancestors.

While the Friends Historical Association was a formal entity, the circulation of Quaker objects for historical and emotional connection occurred in informal ways as well. Take, for example, a turned wood banister topper (or architectural finial) in the collection of the Friends Historical Library at Swarthmore College; at the bottom we get a sense of how these objects circulated. The label, written in black paint or ink, reads: "Part of the Oak Tree on Long Island, New York under which George Fox preached. Presented by Sarah Hicks to Lydia W. Price. 1842." Here we have two women gifting a fragment of a tree from a place of sacred historical value marking the arrival of Quakerism in America. This simple wood fragment was aestheticized to easily be adapted to home décor, or, the desk.[14] For this to happen, someone had to mark the spot of Fox's sermon, take the material out of the place, hand it over to a woodworker, and then it somehow made it to Sarah Hicks' hands, who then gifts it to another Friend. The gift, as Marcel Mauss famously observed, is never free. It always invokes obligation – which at first sounds onerous, but Mauss showed that these are crucial for acts of binding people together and forging cultures of mutual dependence.[15] Quakers seemed to sense that gifting and collecting material things from their past was essential in this work. There are many artifacts that bear the mark of gifting. We don't know for sure what was dancing in Sarah Hicks' mind when she gave that wooden relic to Lydia Price, but we can probably assume that there was a mutual understanding of a connection being made, not only between each other but also to a shared Quaker past and identity.

Their act was not unique. For example, when Walt Whitman, who was born into the Quaker community on Long Island, New York, sat down to write a remembrance of Elias Hicks, whom he encountered in the flesh as a boy in Brooklyn in 1829, Friends began to send him Hicks' material, and not just the written kind. He begins his entry for June 1 in *Specimen Days* (1882) by noting that he had received a letter from "Mrs. E.S.L." of Detroit that included "a rare old engraved head of Elias Hicks" in addition to a remembrance of encountering him herself. She wrote Whitman, "I have listen'd to his preaching so often when a child and sat with my mother at social gatherings where he was the centre, and ever one so pleas'd and stirr'd by his conversation." Having heard that Whitman was contemplating "writing or speaking about him," she felt the need to not only write down her remembrance, but also send the "head": "I wonder'd whether you had a picture of him. As I am the owner of two, I send you one."[16]

This leads us into the realm of Quaker portraiture. Despite the common belief that the plainness testimony precluded portraiture, as it may signal vanity, Quakers were strong supporters of portrait artists. As Diane Johnson has shown, many Quakers had portraits made, and they worked out their simplicity in diverse and personal ways. Johnson has scanned the disciplines of the Delaware Valley in the eighteenth and early nineteenth centuries and concludes "there appear to have been no formal disciplines banning paintings or portraits."[17] Yet there was a memory that "primitive Quakers" had resisted portraiture. In 1760, Benjamin Franklin was offered a portrait by Lord Kames of William Penn, but he had his doubts about its provenance "because the primitive Quakers us'd to declare against Pictures as a vain Expence; a Man's suffering his Portrait to be taken was condemn'd as Pride; and I think to this day it is very little practis'd among them." But even more interestingly he told Kames that he knew "some eminent Quakers have had their Pictures privately drawn, and deposited with trusty Friends."[18] Indeed, Penn likely had multiple portraits.[19] Hidden below this comment was both his experience among urban Quakers in Philadelphia – most likely to embrace the material ambitions of early American merchants – but also the need by Friends to appear plain.[20] They wanted these visual embodiments but could only could trust those objects with people in whom they had confidence.

430

Thomas Clarkson related this same historical consciousness in his 1806 ethnography of Quakers, titled *A Portraiture of Quakerism*: "The first Quakers never had their portraits taken with their own knowledge or consent," wrote Clarkson. The reason being that they considered themselves "poor and helpless creatures, and little better than dust and ashes," but also that "pride and self-conceit would be likely to arise to men from the view, and ostentatious parade, of their own persons." Of course the reality was a bit less pure. Elias Hicks preached something very similar; he refused to have his portrait taken, and yet we have lots of portraits of Hicks, and lots of historical detail about the great lengths people went to get them (as extreme as digging up his corpse to cast his face).[21] Furthermore, when Quaker historical societies began collecting, the portraits flowed from Quaker homes and families. The most iconic subgenre is probably the silhouette, which satisfied Quaker desire to possess embodiments of fellow Friends while protecting their simplicity. As Ann Verplanck has shown, these small forms of portraiture, often collected into albums, became crucial ways of envisioning the Quaker community over, sometimes, great distance, and mediating the divide between the living and the dead.[22]

Quakers were deeply affected by the emergence of antiquarianism in the late eighteenth and nineteenth centuries, and were some of its most avid proponents. Quakers went out into their worlds – attics, fields, caves, forests, meetinghouses – to find the material remnants of their sacred history. In 1969, Dorothy Gilbert Thorne, curator of the Quaker Collection and professor of English at Guilford College, North Carolina, wrote a long description of their collection for *Quaker History*. In the essay, she gives us not only a sense of the library holdings of the collections, such as "the first Philadelphia copy of William Bartram's *Travels*" or the papers of "General Nathanael Greene, once a Quaker," but also how the collections were set up and the objects they had gathered. At every point Thorne draws the connections to Quaker history with each object. The "large map of North and South Carolina drawn by Henry Mouzon in 1775" is shown to have "Quaker significance," for it marks multiple regional meetinghouses and "graveyards" and is evidence of a time of considerable "Friends sufferings." Other pictures on the walls needed less explanation, such as the thirteen "Robert Spence etchings illustrating *The Journal of George Fox*." The collection was mostly defined by the books and manuscript records, but Thorne does give a sense of the objects in the collection and nudges her reader to appreciate their significance. For example, "there is a small black leather trunk once the property of Harriet Peck, teacher from 1837 to 1839," filled with abolitionist Joseph John Gurney's "elegant and opulent" "alpaca cape with velvet collar and silk lining," which he "seems to have left behind on his 1838 visit to New Garden" (a sly swipe at the opulence of evangelical British Quakers traveling the United States). There is also "Eliza Kirkbride Gurney's brown wool shawl, a recent gift" that joined the "bonnets and shawls, hats, and black broadcloth coats worn by outstanding Friends." At least for the objects, the defining collecting principle was that they be reliably "outstanding Friends."[23]

As we have seen, Quakers have often turned toward objects to capture the light of the testimony of past Friends' lives. In so doing, they helped shape what it meant to be Quaker across generations. Things brought them closer, lifted up exemplars great and small, and could be theological vessels of Quaker values. A far-flung, transatlantic religious community could find a common history in things; they helped embody their world.

Notes

1 John Gratton and John Whiting, *A Journal of the Life of That Ancient Servant of the Lord* (London: J. Sowle, 1720), iv–vi.

2 Gratton and Whiting, 120.

3 Patricia C. O'Donnell, "This Side of the Grave : Navigating the Quaker Plainness Testimony in London and Philadelphia in the Eighteenth Century," *Winterthur Portfolio* 49, no. 1 (2015): 29–54.

4 Phyllis Mack, *Heart Religion in the British Enlightenment: Gender and Emotion in Early Methodism* (Cambridge; New York: Cambridge University Press, 2008). I make this larger point in my forthcoming book, including Quakers, from the University of Chicago Press, *Protestant Relics: Capturing the Sacred Body in Early America*.

5 Particularly good here about sketching out these ideas over time across the many splits in Quaker history is Carole Dale Spencer, *Holiness: The Soul of Quakerism: An Historical Analysis of the Theology of Holiness in the Quaker Tradition* (Milton Keynes: Paternoster, 2007).

6 Hans Belting, *An Anthropology of Images: Picture, Medium, Body*, trans. Thomas Dunlap (Princeton: Princeton University Press, 2014): 84.

7 Alfred Gell, *Art and Agency: An Anthropological Theory* (Oxford; New York: Clarendon Press, 1998): 21.

8 Marcus Rediker, *The Fearless Benjamin Lay: The Quaker Dwarf Who Became the First Revolutionary Abolitionist* (Boston, MA: Beacon Press, 2017): 119–41.

9 Dorothy Gilbert Thorne, "The Guilford College Quaker Collection," *Quaker History* 58, no. 2 (1969): 109.

10 Pink Dandelion's work has been particularly attentive to the role of the printed journals in Quaker history. Pink Dandelion, *An Introduction to Quakerism* (Cambridge; New York: Cambridge University Press, 2007); Stephen Ward Angell and Pink Dandelion, eds., *The Oxford Handbook of Quaker Studies*, Oxford Handbooks (Oxford; New York: Oxford University Press, 2013).

11 Paul Buckley, *The Essential Elias Hicks* (San Francisco: Inner Light Books, 2013): 23; Jon R. Kershner, *John Woolman and the Government of Christ: A Colonial Quaker's Vision for the British Atlantic World* (Oxford: Oxford University Press, 2018): 48–49.

12 David Hempton, *Methodism: Empire of the Spirit* (New Haven: Yale University Press, 2005): 33–35 and passim.

13 "Friends' Historical Association: An Appeal" (Philadelphia, 1873), American Antiquarian Society.

14 Artifact # 71, Relic Collection, Friends Historical Library, Swarthmore College, Swarthmore, PA.

15 Marcel Mauss, *The Gift: Expanded Edition*, trans. Jane I. Guyer, Expanded ed. Edition (Chicago, IL: HAU, 2016): 73–76, 121–30.

16 Walt Whitman, *Complete Poetry and Collected Prose*, ed. Justin Kaplan, Library of America [3] (New York, NY: Literary Classics of the United States, 1982): 879–80.

17 Diane C. Johnson, "Living in the Light: Quakerism and Colonial Portraiture," in *Quaker Aesthetics: Reflections on a Quaker Ethic in American Design and Consumption*, ed. Emma J. Lapsansky-Werner and Anne A. Verplanck (Philadelphia: University of Pennsylvania Press, 2003): 123.

18 Benjamin Franklin, "To Lord Kames," January 3, 1760, Volume 9, Page 5, Benjamin Franklin Papers, Original at Scottish Record Office, http://franklinpapers.org/franklin/framedVolumes.jsp?vol=9&page=005a.

19 Daniel K. Richter, "Three Relics of Pennsylvania's Founding," *Pennsylvania Legacies* 4, no. 2 (2004): 6–9.

20 Johnson, "Living in the Light: Quakerism and Colonial Portraiture."

21 Sarah (Sarah Lea) Burns, *Painting the Dark Side: Art and the Gothic Imagination in Nineteenth-Century America* (Berkeley, CA: University of California Press, 2004): 104.

22 Anne Verplanck, "Facing Philadelphia: The Social Functions of Silhouettes, Miniatures, and Daguerreotypes, 1760–1860" (Williamsburg, VA: College of William and Mary, 1996).

23 Thorne, "The Guilford College Quaker Collection."

Bibliography

Angell, Stephen Ward, and Pink Dandelion, eds. *The Oxford Handbook of Quaker Studies*. 1st ed. Oxford Handbooks. Oxford; New York: Oxford University Press, 2013.

Belting, Hans. *An Anthropology of Images: Picture, Medium, Body*. Translated by Thomas Dunlap. Princeton: Princeton University Press, 2014.

Buckley, Paul. *The Essential Elias Hicks*. San Francisco: Inner Light Books, 2013.

Burns, Sarah (Sarah Lea). *Painting the Dark Side: Art and the Gothic Imagination in Nineteenth-Century America*. Berkeley, CA: University of California Press, 2004.

Dandelion, Pink. *An Introduction to Quakerism*. Cambridge, UK; New York: Cambridge University Press, 2007.

Franklin, Benjamin. "To Lord Kames," January 3, 1760. Volume 9, Page 5. Benjamin Franklin Papers, Original at Scottish Record Office. http://franklinpapers.org/franklin/framedVolumes.jsp?vol=9&page=005a.

"Friends' Historical Association: An Appeal." Philadelphia, 1873. American Antiquarian Society.

Gell, Alfred. *Art and Agency: An Anthropological Theory*. Oxford; New York: Clarendon Press, 1998.

Gratton, John, and John Whiting. *A Journal of the Life of That Ancient Servant of the Lord*. London: J. Sowle, 1720.

Hempton, David. *Methodism : Empire of the Spirit*. New Haven: Yale University Press, 2005.

Johnson, Diane C. "Living in the Light: Quakerism and Colonial Portraiture." In *Quaker Aesthetics: Reflections on a Quaker Ethic in American Design and Consumption*, edited by Emma J. Lapsansky-Werner and Anne A. Verplanck, 122–146. Philadelphia: University of Pennsylvania Press, 2003.

Kershner, Jon R. *John Woolman and the Government of Christ: A Colonial Quaker's Vision for the British Atlantic World*. Oxford: Oxford University Press, 2018.

Mack, Phyllis. *Heart Religion in the British Enlightenment: Gender and Emotion in Early Methodism*. Cambridge; New York: Cambridge University Press, 2008.

Mauss, Marcel. *The Gift: Expanded Edition*. Translated by Jane I. Guyer. Expanded ed. Edition. Chicago, IL: HAU, 2016.

O'Donnell, Patricia C. "This Side of the Grave : Navigating the Quaker Plainness Testimony in London and Philadelphia in the Eighteenth Century." *Winterthur Portfolio* 49, no. 1 (2015): 29–54.

Rediker, Marcus. *The Fearless Benjamin Lay: The Quaker Dwarf Who Became the First Revolutionary Abolitionist*. Boston, MA: Beacon Press, 2017.

Richter, Daniel K. "Three Relics of Pennsylvania's Founding." *Pennsylvania Legacies* 4, no. 2 (2004): 6–9.

Spencer, Carole Dale. *Holiness: The Soul of Quakerism: An Historical Analysis of the Theology of Holiness in the Quaker Tradition*. Milton Keynes: Paternoster, 2007.

Thorne, Dorothy Gilbert. "The Guilford College Quaker Collection." *Quaker History* 58, no. 2 (1969): 108–112.

Verplanck, Anne. "Facing Philadelphia: The Social Functions of Silhouettes, Miniatures, and Daguerreotypes, 1760–1860." Williamsburg, VA: College of William and Mary, 1996.

Whitman, Walt. *Complete Poetry and Collected Prose*. Edited by Justin Kaplan. Library of America [3]. New York, NY: Literary Classics of the United States, 1982.

54

QUAKERS AND OTHER ANIMALS

Chris Lord

Most people think they know two things about Quakers. One is that they worship in silence. The other, largely from Quakers' high visibility in the abolition of Atlantic slavery and in prison reform, their opposition to wars, and their probity and decency in business, is that they are 'good people' – with all that those inverted commas imply. This chapter examines the record of Quakerism in a different area of ethics: the treatment of other animals. Dealing mainly with Quakerism in Britain, it makes two main points. First, that, from its beginnings, Quakers directed their main ethical energies elsewhere, namely into the (then radical) view that all humans are equal. This led them, in the eighteenth century, into abolitionism, and, from the late seventeenth century, but more famously in the twentieth, towards pacifism and conscientious objection. Humanity has been the focus of Quaker ethical attention: historically, Friends have been explicit, articulate and successful in arguing that the 'common humanity' of all human beings entails fair and compassionate treatment for all. Concern for animals' wellbeing has not been insignificant, but, ultimately, peripheral – not part of an integrated Quaker ethic, but the territory of outliers – a few individuals sometimes ignored, sometimes patronised, sometimes even disowned by the Religious Society of Friends. The chapter's second point is the tracing of a shift in the reasons used by Quakers to motivate their ethical positions. In the seventeenth century the reason for not mistreating animals was that such behaviour displayed, and encouraged, human sinfulness, whereas in the eighteenth century the actual suffering of animals becomes itself a motivation. This pity for the suffering of others, expressed in the case of animals as 'anti-cruelty', then becomes the dominant ethical driver from the nineteenth century until the present day. Yet, mainly from the second half of the twentieth century onwards, there has been a gradual, and slow, move towards seeing other animals not just as objects of pity but as partners in life, deserving of respect and consideration in their own right. But, even among the 'good people' of the Religious Society of Friends, this remains incipient, mainly the choice of the young. The chapter ends with an example of the Quaker reluctance to confront the extension of compassion to other species: the mysterious Quaker ignorance of Ruth Harrison.

Historical Overview

In the first two centuries of Quakerism a few individuals took moral positions against the exploitation of other animals, but these were isolated cases, whose views didn't become

DOI: 10.4324/9780429030925-58

mainstream and who were viewed as eccentrics. The ethical focus of Friends as a whole didn't expand beyond humanity until the nineteenth century, when Quakers took prominent roles in wider societal moves opposing cruelty to other animals, particularly, as that century drew to a close, anti-vivisection, and then vegetarianism. The resultant formation of what became Quaker Concern for Animals, now a Quaker Recognised Body, has made the issue at least official, if not central, within contemporary Quakerism. And yet the inclusion of non-human animals into Quakers' ethical concern has come on its own special terms, different from those which deal with human animals. What is particularly striking about early Quaker abolitionists is their vehement opposition to the racist justification of slavery on the alleged grounds that black Africans were not fully human beings. Central to their position are concepts of an equality and respect due to fellow humans, and it is this emphasis on humanity which has driven, and continues to drive, Quakers' ethical activities against, for example, economic injustice and warfare. When Quakers turned to the suffering of other animals, however, they focused on humans' cruelty towards them: the core issue was the wickedness of humans' mistreatment of animals, and animals' suffering as sentient beings, rather than treating animals as, in themselves, deserving of equal and respectful treatment.

My experience is of British Quakers. These, today, are largely signed up to minimizing cruelty to other animals. The typical British Friend might well be vegetarian, and might well choose 'cruelty-free' food, cosmetics and cleaning products if available. With the recent and sudden prominence of veganism, and with the wide range of vegan convenience foods now available, many young Friends have become vegan. Older Quakers, however, are more reluctant to change their habits. Imagine Quakers queuing for coffee and biscuits and being given a choice between biscuits labelled 'Fairtrade' and 'not Fairtrade'. How many would actively choose the non-Fairtrade option? Now imagine a choice between animal milk and plant milk.[1] But Quakers are 'good people'. The Australian Quaker Les Mitchell asked, 'how can good, kind, caring people continue to support the mass institutionalised abuse of non-human animals in its many forms?' (Mitchell, 2019, cited in Layton, 2020, p. 34).

The Seventeenth Century

Early Quakerism, emerging from the anti-clerical and anti-aristocratic positions of the regicidal British Civil War, granted spiritual authority to ordinary people. George Fox's famous phrase 'that of God in everyone' (*passim*, e.g., Quaker Faith and Practice, 19.32; for caveats against taking the phrase out of context, see Benson, 1970) captured this inclusivity, embracing the whole of humanity. He didn't, however, go further but followed Christian orthodoxy in seeing humanity as metaphysically distinct from animals – between the angels above and the beasts below. Fox included hunting as (just) another frivolously sinful activity, preaching against 'the foolish pleasures of the world, as bowling, drinking, hunting, hawking, and the like' (Fox, 1827, p. 340). Even when he appears to complain of hunting's cruelty towards animals, he seems to be warning more against harming God's creation: 'Where did the christians in the apostles' days make and use matches at football, and wrestling, and appoint horse races, and hunting for pleasure, and such like, and so glory in their own strength, and *abuse the creatures*?' (Fox, 1666, Query VI; my italics). Another early Friend, Thomas Elwood (1639–1714), shared Fox's view of hunting as something in which the spiritual damage to the hunter was more important than any physical harm done to the hunted: 'Some in a tavern spend the longest day, / While others hawk and hunt the time away' (from the poem 'All is Vanity'; Ellwood, 1791, p. 199).

James Nayler (1618–1660) is more complicated. In line with orthodox Christianity, he and other Quakers saw the condition of the physical creation as dependent on the spiritual status of humanity. With Paul in Romans (8:21–22), he saw the physical world as first corrupted by Adam's Fall and then restored by Christ's redemptive sacrifice. More than Fox, however, Nayler reveals a concern and a focus on nature which looks forward to people like John Woolman in the next century. He places repeated emphasis, for example, on the fallen and redeemed states of the physical creation. In utterances such as 'God is the Life of every Creature, though few there be that know it' (Nayler, 1829, p. 272), he betrays a strand of panentheist thought (i.e., that God both pervades all of creation *and* transcends it; not, as the pantheist would say, that God and creation are *identical*) reminiscent of the Digger Gerrard Winstanley, who wrote of 'the spiritual Light that is in every creature' (Winstanley, 1649, p. 157, quoted in Masters, 2020, p. 33). This kind of writing opens up the possibility of a 'proto-ecological ethic within Nayler's theology' (Masters, 2018, p. 20), and indeed, while we can find in Nayler an unusually (for the time) strong sense of the natural world being infused with the divine, even in Nayler such insights are rare. Nayler's thought seems, in fact, to be fundamentally human-centric: there is little sense of the physical world as something in its own right, beyond and other than as a sign of human sinfulness or greed. An indication of this is his 1655 letter to the parish priest of Lichfield in protest at a bull-baiting. It is important to see the full text because, even though the inclusion of the word 'torment' (at the end of the first sentence) might encourage us to think that Nayler's concern was the suffering of the animals, the rest of the letter makes clear his real focus (Nayler, 1655):

> To thee who calls thyself a minister of Jesus Christ and pretends to be called to this town of Chesterfield this people to teach, but this day is the fruits of thy ministry manifest, in the open streets, a multitude gathered to sport themselves in setting one of the creatures of God against another to torment. And thy people thou teaches, hooting, yelling, swearing and cursing and blaspheming the dreadful name of God – is this thy ministry, and these thy brethren with whom thou joins to worship the living God? Oh how dare you take his name into your mouths? Did ever any minister of Christ lead a people thus or own such a people to maintain them? Oh shame that ever you should own the name of Christians, those that never heard of the name of Christ shall rise up in judgment against you. Is this the voice that this day is heard in your streets? or are these the people God accepts when you pray? Nay, your prayers is abomination to God, and you never knew him, that lives in these things or joins with them. Didst thou love God thou could not suffer these things and be silent; O thou man-pleaser! I declare to thee this day in the presence of the Lord that God hath a controversy with thee and the rest of thy generation, who hath suffered these wickedness to lie upon his people so that he cannot be reconciled to them, nor they know him, because of their sins; and you daub them and call them Christians; and thus they perish under you for want of knowledge of God, and yet you cry peace and tells them they cannot be free from sin, nor know God as the children of God have ever done; and thus you strengthen the hands of the wicked so that none turns from his wickedness, but God is risen to cut you off and to deliver his people out of your mouths upon whom you have made a prey; and woe unto you. It had been good for you that you had never been born; and in that day thou shalt witness that this is the word of God.

The Eighteenth Century

The later seventeenth century saw wider growth in concern for animals. Examples include the (non-Quaker) vegetarians John Robins, Roger Crab, and the prolific Thomas Tryon, whose writings influenced Benjamin Franklin and Benjamin Lay (see below) to stop eating meat. The first sign of Quaker involvement, after Nayler, is a handful of individuals active in America in the second half of the eighteenth century: the Englishman Benjamin Lay (1682–1759), the Frenchman Anthony Benezet (1713–1784) and the Americans John Woolman (1720–1772) and Joshua Evans (1731–1798). Known more for their campaigning against human slavery, they also extended their compassion to other animals. What is interesting is how this group was inspired as much by pity for the suffering of all sentient beings, both human and other animals, as by concerns of human sinfulness. They thus form a bridge between an orthodox Protestant model focused solely on the redemption of the individual human soul and the dominant 'anti-cruelty' ethic of later periods. We can also, in small measure, detect, in this tiny minority of special and unassimilated individual Quakers, the beginnings of the application to non-human animals of the respect-as-equals which Quakers were already giving to all human beings.

Of this group, the most prominent are Lay and Woolman. The remarkable Benjamin Lay's reputation, once eclipsed by those of Woolman and Benezet, has been rehabilitated by Jean Soderlund (1985) and Marcus Rediker (2017). Famous for his confrontational and theatrical campaigning against slavery, Lay

> made honey a staple of his diet, never killing the bees . . . He ate only fruits and veg-etables, drank only milk and water; he was a strict vegetarian and very nearly a vegan two centuries before the word was invented. Because of the divine pantheistic pres-ence of God he perceived in all living things, he refused to eat 'flesh.' Animals too were 'God's creatures'. He opposed the death penalty in all instances, including for animals.
>
> *(ibid., pp. 115–116)*

Rediker gives a series of reasons for Lay's singular ethical stance: in the passage just quoted he ascribes Lay's motivations to a kind of panentheism; elsewhere in his book he cites the youthful Lay's positive experience as a shepherd, his negative experiences working with animal skins as a glover, his reaction to his killing and dismembering a groundhog which had eaten his veg-etables, and his reading of the works of Thomas Tryon. These attempts to explain his concern for animals are not mutually exclusive, but cumulative: before he had even encountered slavery (which he did after travelling to the Caribbean and the US colonies) his ethical attitudes had begun to be formed through his work as shepherd and glover, and yet it was only after his sig-nificant engagement with the evils of slavery that he began living as an ethical vegetarian. Lay seems to be the first Quaker on record to arrange the whole of his life according to integrated ethical principles – a practice for which John Woolman is better known.

For, if there is a Quaker saint, it has to be John Woolman. Often described explicitly as such,[2] he is the subject of a stream of books (several major works in this century; see bibliography) and homages outside Quakerism; for example, his portrayal in the stained-glass window of San Francisco's Grace Cathedral (Sox, 1999, p. 1). Woolman had probably met Benjamin Lay (whose famous book-stabbing took place at Woolman's Burlington Meeting House in New Jersey; Rediker, 2017, p. 137), and followed the older Friend's lead in an uncompromising ethi-cal lifestyle and stance against both human slavery and the exploitation of animals: 'to say we love God as unseen and at the same time exercise cruelty toward the least creature moving by his life, or by life derived from him, was a contradiction in itself' (Moulton, 1971, p. 28; *Journal* 1720–1742). In a reversal of Lay's travels, the American Woolman visited, and died in, Britain. While there he remained consistent to his values, regardless of the cost to himself:

> Having made himself unpopular with the elders of London Yearly Meeting by his anti-slavery message, he set off for York on foot, rather than contribute to the burden

of enslaved coach-horses. No doubt weakened by the ordeal, he took ill with the smallpox and soon died.

(Brindle, 2011, pp. 66–67)

(Kershner [2018, p. 131] has an alternative explanation for Woolman's catching smallpox.) Woolman was upset by all kinds of cruelty towards animals, from his own childhood unthinking killing of a robin and her chicks (a parallel, in the guilt which the incident induced, to Lay's groundhog), to the over-working of domestic animals by farmers trying, sinfully, to extract too much from their land (see the quotation below from *A Plea for the Poor*, chap. 2). A vivid example of his pity is this detailed and clearly heartfelt reaction to the sufferings of chickens on the boat to England (also typical is his concluding practical suggestion on how to improve matters; *Journal*, 1772, in e.g., Moulton, 1971, pp. 178–179):

> Some dunghill fowls yet remained of those the passengers took for their eating. I believe about fourteen perished in the storms at sea by the waves breaking over the quarter deck, and a considerable number with sickness. . . . In observing . . . the pining sickness of some of them, I often remembered the Fountain of Goodness, who gave being to all creatures, and whose love extends to that of caring for the sparrows; and [I] believe where the love of God is verily perfected and the true spirit of government watchfully attended to, a tenderness toward all creatures made subject to us will be experienced, and a care felt in us that we do not lessen that sweetness of life in the animal creation which the great Creator intends for them under our government, and believe a less number carried off to eat at sea may be more agreeable to this pure wisdom.

Unlike Lay, Benezet and Evans, however, Woolman was not a vegetarian (publicly at least, despite some claims to the contrary (e.g., Helstosky, 2015, p. 180: ebook location 789.5/1538; her references don't mention vegetarianism). Plank (2012, p. 85) comments, 'Indeed Lay, Evans, and Benezet took a step Woolman never publicly took, and became vegetarian', and

> Although some in the twentieth century have claimed that he was a vegetarian, he never explicitly opposed the consumption of meat, and indeed his account books make it clear that he sold beef almost continuously, as a shopkeeper and then as a small farmer, from the early 1750s until the last year of his life.

(Plank, 2012, p. 90)

This is likely to be due to his particularly high regard for what he saw as divinely ordained proper husbandry – a concern shared by his younger brother Abner, who also wrote a journal (ibid., pp. 30–32). Plank adds (ibid., p. 27):

> Woolman's experience of farm life confirmed his reading of Genesis. He believed that the structure, appearance, and appeal of plants and animals provided evidence of God's original plan for creation. He was convinced that there was a 'superiority in men over the brute creatures'. He thought that some animals were 'so manifestly dependent on men for a living, that for them to serve us in moderation so far as relates to the right use of things looks consonant to the design of our Creator'. He observed that sheep in particular 'are pleasant company on a plantation, their looks are modest, their voice is soft and agreeable; their defenseless state exposeth them a prey to wild beasts, and they

appear to be intended by the great Creator, to live under our protection, and supply us with matter for warm and useful clothing'. The sheep's amiability, helplessness and good service proved that the animal deserved and needed humanity's attention.

In line with this, Jon Kershner warns against anachronistically seeing these Friends as early animal rights activists. Supportively discussing Plank, he writes (2018, p. 199 n. 132):

Plank notes that eighteenth-century Quakers were more likely to study animals than other religious groups. In fact, he contends that many Quaker journal writers of the eighteenth century gave an experience of finding God in creation. Elsewhere, Plank argues that the harmony of 'all animal and sensitive creatures', as Woolman put it, was a model for God's intention for the whole of the created world and inspired Woolman's social vision. Indeed, Plank is perceptive to argue that 'the key to understanding Woolman's perspective is not to associate him with later advocates of animal rights, but to see him as the product of a millenarian tradition within Quakerism, one that assigned the animals in every landscape cosmological significance.' Plank, 'The Flame of Life', 573–74; Plank, *John Woolman's Path to the Peaceable Kingdom*, 3.

In their opposition to the mistreatment of other animals, both Lay and Woolman, like Fox and Nayler, were primarily concerned with human sinfulness. The nature of the sinfulness, however, was greed more than frivolity, a failure of stewardship, of good husbandry – the protection of God's perfect natural creation from human greed. Lay: 'Mammon – cursed love of mammon – mammon surfeits and corrupts the mind, and darkens the understanding' (Vaux, 1815, p. 35, quoted in Rediker, 2017, p. 104). And Woolman: 'But he who with a view to self-exaltation causeth some with their domestic animals to labour immoderately, and with the moneys arising to him therefrom employs others in the luxuries of life, acts contrary to the gracious design of him who is the true owner of the earth' (*A Plea for the Poor*, chap. 2, in e.g., Moulton, 1971, pp. 239–240). As we have seen, however, it is not that simple: there are also indications of the two later ethical motivations which we have been tracing. We can certainly see in both some 'anti-cruelty' feeling: Woolman was certainly moved to pity at the suffering of both enslaved people (see in particular *Considerations on Keeping Negroes [Part Second]*, in e.g., Moulton, 1971, pp. 210–237) and the 'dunghill fowls' (see above). Similarly, the experiences in Lay's early life which encouraged him to become a vegetarian show what we can recognize as pity. And, again for both, their panentheism offers a perhaps surprisingly early, and Quaker, foundation for viewing sentient animals as beings with whom we share existence, rather than who exist for our benefit. Yet overall the imperative for human beings is one of stewardship: to govern the animal kingdom with kindness and skill.

Yet, while Lay and Woolman are undeniably of great significance, the very fact that modern Quakers constantly turn to just these two (indeed, until recently, to just Woolman) is indicative of the fact that they were exceptional. While their views on human slavery did gradually percolate through the Society of Friends, and beyond, their concerns for animals were not generally accepted, let alone assimilated into the mainstream of Quaker thought. Lay's aggressive campaigning – mainly against slavery – led to his being disowned by Quaker Meetings in both Britain (London's Hackney Quakers apologized for this in 2017; Hackney Citizen, 2017) and America. Woolman's gentler style, on the other hand, meant that he was listened to and tolerated but still treated rather patronizingly and disdainfully. His visit to England prompted behind-the-scenes letters, giving kindly yet patronizing warnings of how to treat this quaint eccentric. For example, '[Woolman] walks in a straiter path than some other good folks are led . . .

though he may appear singular, . . . he will be found to be a man of a sweet, clean spirit' (Letter to London Friends from John Pemberton, 28th of 4th month, 1772, quoted in Cadbury, 1971, p. 52). Woolman's reception in particular, among Quakers and beyond,[3] is a fascinating tension between hagiography and benevolent dismissal of his impractical idealism, a caution about his (to use a phrase from Kershner's excellent summary of this ambivalence) 'obsessive compulsive moralism' (2018, p. 170). Perhaps the best example of the second is the introduction to the 1910 Everyman edition of Woolman's *Journal*, written by the non-Quaker socialist (and now an Episcopalian saint) Vida Scudder. Her belief in the superiority of collective action over individual acts of sainthood is clear:

> For the conclusion is forced on us that Woolman was in an *impasse*: and while we love and reverence the heavenly sturdiness of soul possessed by this eighteenth-century saint, *we must recognize with amusement touched by tenderness the hopelessness of his efforts to attain personal purity, the ridiculous extremes of isolation into which such a conscientious effort, if logically carried out, would lead us.* The definite inference from Woolman's life and thought will be for most modern people the conviction of *the hopelessness of the attempt to achieve, by individual means and private effort, a satisfying social righteousness in an unchanged world.*
>
> *(Scudder, 1910, p. xiii; my italics)*

The Nineteenth Century

The spirit of Lay's groundhog and Woolman's robin can also be found in an entry in the Journal, for 1811–1813, of the American Quaker Elias Hicks. Here he describes, and meditates on, the slaughtering of a bull (Buckley 2009, pp. 169–170):

> Sixth Day: Spent part of this day and the evening in assisting my workmen in slaying a fat beef and laying it away for part of our winter's provision. After which, my mind was seriously impressed with the subject and led to take a view of the whole process and the extraordinary change that had taken place in so short a space with a strong, well-favored, living animal, that in the morning was in a state of health, vigor, and comely proportion, and at the close of the evening, all its parts were decomposed, and its flesh and bones cut into pieces and packed away in a cask with salt to be devoured by the animal-man – its entrails already devoured by the swine, and its skin deposited with the tanner to be converted into leather for man's use.
>
> What a wonderful wreck in nature, affected in so short a period by two or three individuals, but which cannot be restored to its former state by all the combined power and wisdom of all the men in the universe, through all the ages and generations of men.
>
> My meditation hereon produced this query: Is it right, and consistent with divine wisdom, that such cruel force should be employed and such a mighty sacrifice made necessary for the nourishment and support of these bodies of clay? Or is there not a more innocent and more consistent medium to be found, amply to effect the same end of man's support? And if so, will it not become a duty? If not for the present generation, for those in future to seek it and employ it.

As with Lay and Woolman, Hicks recounts the killing of an animal and his subsequent regrets. Hicks, however, draws stronger and more prophetic conclusions than the earlier pair:

his third paragraph in particular speaks to the twenty-first century. So this is an important piece of writing, but its significance should not be exaggerated: Hicks' sentiments seem to have been peripheral to Hicks himself, for unlike Lay and Woolman, he doesn't seem to have become vegetarian himself. Furthermore, the episode appears to have been unimportant, or unwelcome, to Quakers then and since: the incident was suppressed in earlier editions of the Journal, only surfacing in Buckley's edition (Angell 2012, p. 7). Lay, Woolman, Hicks and a few others are the exceptions which prove the rule, at least for the eighteenth and early nineteenth centuries.

But this was about to change, for the nineteenth century did see a shift, particularly in Britain, with the emergence of various attempts by individuals and Parliament to protect animals from abuse. The ideas of the eighteenth-century outliers were now becoming more accepted, at least within certain sections of the elite. And, while anti-cruelty dominates as a motivation, we can still see both the earlier concern with human sinfulness, and the later idea of respect for equals.

'Cruelty' is the key concept: Thomas Fowell Buxton, an early 'Quanglican' (Quaker Anglican), chaired the ('Royal' from 1840) Society for the Prevention of Cruelty to Animals (Baigent, *Dictionary of National Biography*, 2004, pp. 292–294). In 1856 the Tract Association of the Society of Friends published a four-page pamphlet titled 'On Cruelty to Animals'. This little work, while maintaining that 'the beasts of the field are properly the servants of man' (p. 2), also makes it clear that (p. 1)

> The proper treatment of animals highly deserves the consideration of all and every class, rich and poor, young and old. All have it in their power to be either merciful or cruel; and all will do well to remember that 'Blessed are the merciful.' Those of all ages, and of all descriptions, who are obeying the commands of Christ, will doubtless have their reward.
>
> It cannot be denied, that much and abominable cruelty is exercised and it is greatly to be regretted, that many who themselves abhor barbarity, are yet deficient in the duty of 'opening their mouths for the dumb.'

As for Quaker action, rather than words, the first half of the century offers two inspiring, and in some ways bizarre, grassroots Quaker protests, of a style we would now call non-violent direct action. In 1805 Quakers in Lewes, Sussex, England, disrupted a bull-baiting:

> the Brighton Quakers quietly stepped out of the crowd, joined hands and made a circle around the bull. The dogs were loose, and pandemonium broke out. . . . The constabulary came and arrested all the Quakers, put them into horse wagons and took them off to jail.
>
> *(Quaker Concern for Animals, Newsletter, Spring 2011)*

And later, in the 1830s or 1840s, a lone English Quaker burst into the Parisian vivisection laboratory of François Magendie:

> 'I have heard thee spoken of', said the Quaker . . . 'and I see I have not been misinformed; for I have been told thee does experiments on living animals. I have come to see thee to ask thee by what right thee does so, and to tell thee that thee must stop experiments of this kind because thee has no right to cause the death of animals or to make them suffer, and because thee sets a bad example and accustoms thy fellows to cruelty'.
>
> *(Olmsted, 1952, p. 31, cited in Glaholt, 2012, p. 168)*

Such incidents speak of surprisingly urgent, almost desperate, attempts by ordinary Friends to protect animals, decades, or centuries, before wider society, or even the wider Society, caught up.

Ordinary Quakers continued to create impact: Anna Sewell's 1877 novel *Black Beauty*, one of the first animal autobiographies, increased awareness of the plight of working horses and reduced usage of the cruel 'bearing reins' (Guest, 2011, p. vii). But it is the ideological shifts in this century which are of particular interest, especially Quakers' gradual recognition of animals as a hitherto unnoticed group of 'oppressed creatures' analogous with enslaved humans. Hayley Rose Glaholt shows that from the 1870s (particularly with the publication of Whittier's 1871 edition of the *Journals*) the writings of John Woolman became popular among Friends (Glaholt, 2012, p. 159). She argues that this encouraged Quakers to see their faith as having a 'humanitarian' ethic, centred on kindness towards the oppressed. This virtue-ethics approach combines the seventeenth-century motivational focus on human sinfulness (i.e., the importance of behaving ethically for *one's own* spiritual well-being) with a more clearly nineteenth-century, this-world, compassionate, anti-cruelty stance. Glaholt's authoritative work thoroughly explores the explicit connections which Quakers made between their campaigns against warfare and against the oppression of enslaved humans and non-human animals.[4] For example, S. E. Clark wrote, in a letter to *The Friend* in November 1886 (26[313], pp. 286–287), about the 'essential identity of this battle [against vivisection] with all the preceding ones [e.g., pacifism, abolitionism]', and the 'contagious spreading of defended cruelty from any one class of victims to others'; that is, from enslaved humans to enslaved animals (Glaholt, 2012, pp. 160 and 167).

Towards the end of the century the moves to prevent cruelty to animals, associated ever more closely in Quaker consciousness with their opposition to warfare, increasingly focused on the campaign against animal vivisection. In 1890 the Friends' Anti-Vivisection Association (FAVA) came into being (ibid., p. 157), led by (non-outlier) Friends from major Quaker families: Joseph Storrs Fry was its first president (ibid., p. 155; Quakers were big in chocolate: Cadbury, Fry and Rowntree remain household names). This was probably the world's first pro-animal organisation named after a religion.

The Twentieth and Twenty-First Centuries

Victorian themes of anti-vivisection and pacifism persisted into the twentieth century; for Glaholt the whole anti-vivisection push was for Friends an attempt to make 'the Quaker witness for peace more consistent, by forcing Friends and fellow Christians to rethink the species boundaries of their testimony' (ibid., p. 170). Yet as the century progressed there was a gradual shift towards a broader opposition to all human-caused animal suffering, which we can see in the changes in name of the main Quaker campaigning organisation. The Friends' Anti-Vivisection Association inserted 'Animal Welfare', to become the Friends' Animal Welfare and Anti-Vivisection Society; in 1978 it was renamed Quaker Concern for Animal Welfare, and in 1989 Quaker Concern for Animals (QCA). Now a Quaker Recognised Body, the group publishes a hefty newsletter, hosts popular presentations and discussions at Britain Yearly Meeting Gatherings, and supports individual Quaker in their actions and witness, yet it still seems to have limited reach among Quakers in general.

Quaker institutions followed a similar path. Woodbrooke Quaker College was founded in Birmingham in 1903. Its first director of studies, the biblical scholar James Rendel Harris, had in 1885 resigned from Johns Hopkins University in protest at the vivisection practised there, and Woodbrooke's first reader in Quakerism, Gerald K. Hibbert, wrote 'I cannot believe it is the Creator's will that the preservation of human health should involve the torture of other creatures' (*Journeys in Compassion*, p. 19). By this time vegetarianism was becoming fashionable in wider society: in 1915 the Theosophical Society founded the vegetarian St. Christopher's School in Letchworth, and in the late twenties the words of its co-principal Eleanor Harris, 'Let the law of kindness know no limit; show a loving consideration to all God's creatures', were added to the new edition of the epitome of Quaker wisdom, *Advices and Queries*.

These moves were 'not at the time, however, without some opposition; wider Quaker concern over animal issues tends to emerge prominently only after the Second World War, in particular in the context of factory farming and ecology' (Twigg, 1981, chap. 7, n. 195). Perhaps animal welfare was seen in times of war as a luxury amid so much human suffering – witness the huge pet cull at the start of World War II (Feeney-Hart, 2013). Yet even in the second half of the twentieth century, Quaker attention to animal issues seems limited, as evidenced by the Quaker response to Ruth Harrison which ends this chapter.

And still, in the present century Quakers' main concern remains for humanity. There are countless examples of this limitation right up to the present. Lloyd Lee Wilson's 2002 *Essays on the Quaker Vision of Gospel Order* sets out a modern, conservative, Quaker theology. He uses Nayler's vision of a pure people to trumpet Quakers' readiness to take ethical stances (p. 8):

> The experience of that joy [obeying God's laws even when this brings outward hardship] has kept Friends constantly at the edge of human understanding of right relationships, speaking and living prophetically for more than three centuries about what our common life on this planet could and should be. More than either the Catholic or Protestant faith traditions, Friends have claimed already to be living in the restored gospel order, and to be enabled by that restoration to live lives of witness and testimony to the power of Christ among us.

The particular example he returns to is Quaker opposition to enslavement. Yet nowhere in his book can I find (there is no index) reference to non-human animals as objects of ethical concern. Patricia A. Williams' 2008 *Quakerism: A Theology for Our Time* is a bold plea for Christianity as a whole to follow Quakers' ethical lead. For her, Quakerism is the form of Christianity most compatible with modern science. Again, although she has lots on evolutionary biology and humans' biological kinship with non-humans, her view is exclusively human-centred, shot through with the absolute, and tacit, assumption that everything theological relates solely to the relationship between humans and God, not between humans and non-humans, nor indeed non-humans and God. Her one concession is the admission that 'many Quakers are vegetarians' (p. 60). Generally, where contemporary Quakers express this kind of concern, it is either in the form of opposing cruelty to animals, or of stewardship: the idea that God has put humans 'in charge' of creation, so, like good stewards, they have a duty to look after what has been entrusted to them. Examples include *Quaker Faith and Practice* 25.07 ('As to our own planet which God has given us for a dwelling place, we must be mindful that it is given in stewardship'), as well as *Advices and Queries* 42:

> We do not own the world, and its riches are not ours to dispose of at will. Show a loving consideration for all creatures, and seek to maintain the beauty and variety of the world. Work to ensure that our increasing power over nature is used responsibly, with reverence for life. Rejoice in the splendour of God's continuing creation.

Indications of a more inclusive understanding are few, but can be found. Anne Adams' 1996 anthology of Quaker writings on 'Creation' includes many passages from the second half of the twentieth century. This, to her, is a period when 'it seems that at last, and very slowly, Friends may be finding their way back to the original Quaker conviction that to be fully in the spirit is to be fully and joyfully aware of oneself as part of the Universe' (Adams 1996, p. xiii). I'm not sure if the historical record justifies the implication that early Quakers would have fully agreed with her, but she is surely right in sensing a gradual, perhaps accelerating, shift to the view that the respect which Quakers have historically given to all human beings should be shown more widely. In addition, communities of Friends have 'Books of Discipline', collections of pieces of writing considered of spiritual and practical value. These collections present distillations of the collective thought of a generation of Quakers in a particular time and place. In current Books of Discipline there are some, but not many, indications of respect for other animals not as objects of stewardship but as beings equal with humans. In the current British one, Rex Ambler writes (*Quaker Faith and Practice*, 25.15):

> Our testimonies against war and inequality have been aimed at persuading people, and reminding ourselves, as to where their wealth lies: in the discovery of a common identity and a common cause with other human beings. Those testimonies apply in the same way to our treatment of our natural environment which, as Augustine said, is itself like a 'commonwealth', in which every creature in its own way serves the interests of the others. The difference now is that the commonwealth of people and the commonwealth of the earth have become inseparably interrelated and interdependent – have become in fact one new commonwealth of life. Our thinking about God and the world and the way we live in relation to them must now give recognition to that fact.

Here Ambler gives full expression to an idea whose time has perhaps now come: a fusion of the formerly opposed concepts of humanity and nature into a 'commonwealth of life'. The implications of this give rise, in the following anonymous contribution to the Australian Book of Discipline, to a pair of challenging questions (Australian *Advices and Queries*, p. 44, cited in Mitchell and Mitchell, 2011, p. 83):

> All life is interrelated. Each individual plant and animal has its own needs, and its importance to others. Many Australian species and other species worldwide are now extinct and countless more are endangered. Do you treat all life with respect, recognizing a particular obligation to those animals we breed and maintain for our own use and enjoyment? In order to secure the survival of all, including ourselves, are you prepared to change your ideas to your environment and every living thing in it?

I conclude, as promised, with the case of Ruth Harrison (1920–2000), and her 1964 book *Animal Machines*, the first exposure of the suffering of farm animals in post-war intensive agriculture. Harrison already had form in opposing violence against humans and other animals – she was a lifelong vegetarian and had served in the Friends' Ambulance Unit in the Second World War. *Animal Machines* had considerable impact in the wider: Rachel Carson, author of the 1962 environmental classic *Silent Spring*, wrote its foreword, *Animal Machines* changed UK and European farming policy, and in 1986 Harrison was awarded an OBE. *Animal Machines* also inspired Peter Singer to write in 1975 what became the seminal text of the animal-rights movement: *Animal Liberation*. Furthermore, Harrison's work led to the formation of Compassion in World Farming, whose director, Philip Lymbery, wrote in 2014, with Isabelle Oakeshott, *Farmageddon* (Lymbery and Oakeshott, 2014) – effectively an update to *Animal Machines*. In 2013 Oxford University held a conference to examine the legacy of Harrison and Carson (see https://www.

oxfordmartin.ox.ac.uk/events/conference-rachel-carson-ruth-harrison-50-years-on/). Ruth Harrison deserves to be as famous as other Quaker reformers like Elizabeth Fry and John Woolman – as another Quaker who, it seems, initiated an entire ethical movement. And yet Harrison is so little known among Quakers: in my experience, it is only Quakers actively involved in pro-animal work who have ever heard of her. Samantha Calvert (2012, p. 198) tells how Harrison 'was apparently unknown to the Friends' Animal Welfare Society' when she published *Animal Machines* – though she later became involved in the society's work. This is how Colin Spencer describes how she started (Spencer, 1993, p. 319):

> In 1960, Ruth Harrison, a Quaker, received through the post a leaflet on veal production; she had been a vegetarian all her life and her first reaction was to think that any facet of the meat trade was nothing to do with her so she put it aside. But 'in doing nothing I was allowing it to happen', so she sent the leaflet to every Friends meeting in the country; she received only twenty replies. All but two said there was enough suffering among humans without getting involved in animals.

Harrison herself can perhaps suggest part of the answer:

> If one person is unkind to an animal it is considered to be cruelty, but where a lot of people are unkind to a lot of animals, especially in the name of commerce, the cruelty is condoned and, once large sums of money are at stake, will be defended to the last by otherwise intelligent people.
>
> *(quoted in Thom Bonneville's profile of Harrison in the Quaker Concern for Animals Newsletter, Autumn 2015, pp. 14–16)*

Quakers may be 'good' (and 'intelligent'), but they are also still people. The Nantucket Quakers slaughtered whales with no compunction (Wetlaufer, 2020), and Jean Soderlund (1985) charts how Quakers only gradually rejected their economic interest in slave labour. In both these cases as well, 'cruelty [was] condoned', and 'large sums of money [were] at stake'. Soderlund shows that change was achieved piecemeal, in slow stages, and encouraged more by the gentleness of John Woolman rather than the confrontational theatre of Benjamin Lay. Quakers today who share the concerns of Lay, Woolman and Harrison face the challenge of how to present to the 'good people' of Quakerism Les Mitchell's direct question: 'how can [you] good, kind, caring people continue to support the mass institutionalized abuse of non-human animals in its many forms?' (Mitchell, 2019, cited in Layton, 2020).

Notes

1 My more recent experience is that this is changing: Quakers are drinking less dairy milk. But the motivation is climate related, not from opposition to the suffering of cows.

2 Examples include the anonymous review of the 1847 edition of Marsh's edition of Woolman's *Journal* in the 'Eclectic Review' (June 1861, pp. 559–578 in the collected edition [see https://books.google.co.uk/books?id=dW43AAAAYAAJ&printsec=frontcover&redir_esc=y&hl=en#v=onepage&q&f=false (accessed 3rd June 2021)]); and Edwin Harrison Cady's 1966 book *John Woolman: The Mind of the Quaker Saint* (New York, Washington Square Press).

3 A few examples, beyond those already cited: Reginald Reynolds' 1947 anthology *The Wisdom of John Woolman*, whose preface (by Stephen Hobhouse) compares him to St. Francis and Gandhi; and Birkel's devotional work (2003): 'John Woolman is my friend' (p. xiv).

4 For non-Quaker discussion of the relations between human and animal slavery, see Spiegel (1996) and – less groundbreaking but more up to date – Ko and Ko (2017).

Bibliography

Sources which deal extensively with Quaker approaches to animals are shown in bold.

Adams, A. (ed.), *The Creation Was Open to Me: An Anthology of Friends' Writings on That of God in All Creation*, Quaker Green Concern (now Living Witness), 1996.

Angell, S. W., 'New Light on Elias Hicks,' *Quaker Religious Thought*, Vol. 119, Article 3, pp. 7–13, 2012. At https://digitalcommons.georgefox.edu/qrt/vol119/iss1/3, accessed 22nd June 2021.

Anonymous, *On Cruelty to Animals*, Tract Association of the Society of Friends, London, Edward Couchman (printer), 1856.

Australian *Advices and Queries*, https://www.quakersaustralia.info/sites/aym-members/files/pages/files/Australian%20Advices%20and%20Queries.pdf, accessed 5th June 2021.

Baigent, E. *Buxton, Sir (Thomas) Fowell, Third Baronet. Oxford Dictionary of National Biography* (online ed.). Oxford University Press, 2004. https://doi.org/10.1093/ref:odnb/32225.

Benson, L., ' "That of God in Every Man" – What Did George Fox Mean by It?', *Quaker Religious Thought*, Vol. XII, No. 2, Spring 1970.

Birkel, M., *A Near Sympathy: The Timeless Quaker Wisdom of John Woolman*, Richmond, IN, Friends United Press and Earlham Press, 2003.

Brindle, S., *Answering That of God in Everyone*, in Mitchell and Mitchell 2011 (Chapter 6, pp. 61–79).

Brinton, A. C., 'Quakers and Animals'. In A. C. Brinton (Ed.), *Then and Now: Quaker Essays, Historical and Contemporary* (pp. 188–199), Philadelphia, University of Pennsylvania Press, 1960.

Buckley, P., *The Journal of Elias Hicks*, San Francisco, CA, Inner Light Books, 2009. I am grateful to Stephen Angell for this reference.

Cadbury, H., *John Woolman in England; a Documentary Supplement*, Supplement No. 31 to the Journal of the Friends Historical Society, 1971.

Calvert, S. J., 'Eden's Diet: Christianity and Vegetarianism 1809–2009', PhD thesis, University of Birmingham, 2012, pp. 163–201.

Carson, R., *Silent Spring*, Boston, MA, Houghton Mifflin, 1962.

Ellwood, T., *The History of the Life of Thomas Ellwood*, London, James Phillips, 1791. Found at https://books.google.co.uk/books?id=SURGAAAAYAAJ&source=gbs_navlinks_s, accessed 7th June 2021. Also https://www.hallvworthington.com/Ellwood/Ellwood-2.html, accessed 20th August 2020.

Feeney-Hart, A., 'The Little-told Story of the Massive WWII Pet Cull', *BBC News Magazine*, 2013, https://www.bbc.co.uk/news/magazine-24478532, accessed 7th June 2021.

Fox, G., *A Journal or Historical Account of the Life, Travels, Sufferings, Christian Experiences, and Labour of Love in the Work of the Ministry, of That Ancient, Eminent and Faithful Servant of Jesus Christ, George Fox*, 13th of the 6th month, 1656, London: W. Phillips, 1827. Also https://www.hallvworthington.com/wjournal/gfjournal4c.html, accessed 20th August 2020.

Fox, G., *Some Queries to All the Teachers and Professors of Christianity to Answer*, 1666. Also https://www.hallvworthington.com/FoxDoctrineBooks/Book4Part7.html, accessed 31st May 2021.

Glaholt, H. R., 'Vivisection as War: The "Moral Diseases" of Animal Experimentation and Slavery in British Victorian Quaker Pacifist Ethics', *Society and Animals*, Vol. 20, 2012, pp. 154–172.

Guest, K. (ed.), *Black Beauty: His Grooms and Companions. The Autobiography of a Horse*, Newcastle, Cambridge Scholars Publishing, 2011.

Hackney Citizen, 22nd November 2017, https://www.hackneycitizen.co.uk/2017/11/22/hackney-quakers-make-amends-disowning-radical-anti-slavery-dwarf-300-years-ago/, accessed 3rd June 2021.

Helstosky, C. (ed.), *The Routledge History of Food*, Abingdon, Routledge, 2015.

***Journeys in Compassion: 125 Years of Quaker Concern for Animals*, Quaker Concern for Animals, 2016**.

Kershner, J., *John Woolman and the Government of Christ: A Colonial Quaker's Vision for the British Atlantic World*, Oxford University Press, 2018. Also https://www-oxfordscholarship-com.ezproxyd.bham.ac.uk/view/10.1093/oso/9780190868079.001.0001/oso-9780190868079, accessed 3rd June 2021.

Ko and Ko, S. and A., *Aphro-ism*, Brooklyn, Lantern Books, 2017.

Layton, M., 'Review of Mitchell, Les Reading the Animal Text in the Landscape of the Damned', *Quaker Concern for Animals Journal*, Spring 2020, pp. 34–36.

Lee Wilson, L., *Essays on the Quaker Vision of Gospel Order*, Wallingford, PA, Pendle Hill Publications, 2002.

Lymbery, P., with Oakeshott, I., *Farmageddon: The True Cost of Cheap Meat*, London, Bloomsbury, 2014.

Masters, S., '"He Will Overturn You and Raise Up His Kingdom another Way": The Radical Political and Economic Vision of James Nayler', *Friends Quarterly*, Issue four 2018, pp. 18–33.

Masters, S., 'The Spirit of Christ and the Renewal of Creation: James Nayler's Eco-theology', *Friends Quarterly*, Issue one 2020, pp. 25–35.

Mitchell, L., *Reading the Animal Text in the Landscape of the Damned*, Makhanda, NISC (Pty) Ltd, 2019.

Mitchell, P. and L. (eds.), *Living by Voices We Shall Never Hear: Seeing Animals Differently*, NISC, 2011. Also https://australianfriend.org/wp-content/uploads/2011/12/Living-by-voices.pdf, accessed 3rd June 2021.

Moulton, P., *The Journal and Major Essays of John Woolman*, New York, Oxford University Press, 1971.

Nayler, J., *A Collection of Sundry Books, Epistles and Papers*, Cincinnati, Whetstone and Buxton, 1829.

Nayler, J., *A Dispute between James Nayler and the Parish Teachers of Chesterfield*, 1655. Also http://www.qhpress.org/texts/nayler/chestfld.html, accessed 2nd June 2021.

Olmsted, J.M.D., *Claude Bernard and the Experimental Method in Medicine,* New York, H. Shuman, 1952.

Plank, G., *John Woolman's Path to the Peaceable Kingdom: A Quaker in the British Empire*, Philadelphia, PA, University of Pennsylvania Press, 2012.

Quaker Concern for Animal Welfare, *Regarding Animals, statements from the conference: 'Non-Violence – Extending the Concept to Animals' held at Woodbrooke College in September (21–23) 1984* (Quaker Concern for Animal Welfare newsletter, Winter 1984)

Quaker Faith and Practice, London, Britain Yearly Meeting, 2013.

Rediker, M., *The Fearless Benjamin Lay: The Quaker Dwarf Who Became the First Revolutionary Abolitionist*, London, Verso, 2017.

Reynolds, R., *The Wisdom of John Woolman with a Selection from his Writings as a Guide to the Seekers of Today*, London, George Allen & Unwin Ltd., 1947.

Scudder, V., *The Journal with Other Writings of John Woolman*, London, Everyman (J. M. Dent & Sons Ltd.), 1910.

Singer, P., *Animal Liberation: Towards an End to Man's Inhumanity to Animals*, London, Granada Publishing Ltd., 1975.

Soderlund, J., *Quakers and Slavery: A Divided Spirit*, Princeton, NJ, Princeton University Press, 1985. Also https://www.jstor.org/stable/j.ctt7ztwkr, accessed 2nd June 2021.

Sox, D., *John Woolman: Quintessential Quaker*, York, Sessions Book Trust, in association with Friends Reunited Press, IN, USA, 1999.

Spencer, C., *The Heretic's Feast: A History of Vegetarianism*, Lebanon, New Hampshire, University Press of New England, 1993.

Spiegel, M., *The Dreaded Comparison: Human and Animal*, New York, Mirror Books/I D E A, 1996.

Twigg, J., *The Vegetarian Movement in England, 1847–1981: A Study in the Structure of its Ideology*, PhD thesis, LSE, 1981, https://ivu.org/history/thesis/quakers.html#7, accessed 18th September 2020.

Vaux, R., *Memoirs of the Lives of Benjamin Lay and Ralph Sandiford, Two of the Earliest Public Advocates for the Emancipation of the Enslaved Africans*, Philadelphia, Solomon W. Conrad, 1815.

Wetlaufer, E., 'Quakers With a Vengeance? A look Into the Pacifistic Religion That Waged War Against Whales', *Quaker Concern for Animals Journal*, Spring 2020, pp. 6–16.

Williams, P. A., *Quakerism: A Theology for Our Time*, West Conshohocken, PA, Infinity Hub, 2008.

Winstanley, G., *The New Law of Righteousness* (in Sabine, *The Works of Gerrard Winstanley*), 1649.

55

QUAKERS AND MARRIAGE

Kristianna Polder

As the Society of Friends movement took shape in England, seventeenth-century Quakers proclaimed the dawning of an apocalyptic age in which Christ was actively manifest in the conscience through what they called the inward light. Their religious fervor compelled them to separate themselves as a religious community from other religious groups they considered the "false church" – most immediately, the state church in England. In doing so, they urgently needed to create their own marriage practice that would deem their marriages and offspring legitimate in the eyes of the state, while perhaps more importantly reflecting their understanding of God's direct intervention – physically and spiritually – in their lives. They fundamentally dismissed the Church of England's ecclesiastical hierarchy, and asserted that God, not a human individual, including an educated priest or justice, joins people in matrimony. As they refused to be married by any one person in the marriage ceremony, they believed God alone directly brought two persons into marital union, of which fellow Quakers were witnesses.[1] Though the marriage practice has evolved amongst Quaker circles, across the world over the years, the central conceptual tenet that God joins two people in marriage while "we are but witnesses" remains.[2] This core principle, coupled with the need for a unified affirmation of that marriage from the Quaker community, has consistently shaped Quaker understanding of marriage throughout the generations.

Margaret Fell, George Fox, and other early Quakers believed marriage was a reflection of the first marriage, when God joined the first couple, Adam and Eve, in the Garden of Eden. They asserted the present apocalyptic age was witness to a restoration of the relationship between humanity and the divine as first enjoyed in the Garden of Eden, where Adam and Eve experienced direct communion with God before the Fall. Marriage was thus an important social symbol and catalyst of this divine communion, as God joined people in marriage by leading them to each other through the inward conscience.[3] This interpretation of the apocalyptic era's impact on marriage lay in stark contrast with other dissenter interpretations, notably the Ranters, who often advocated open sexual relations in the perceived last days of the apocalyptic age. Sexual promiscuity amongst the Ranters generated social derision and suspicion.[4] Rejecting Ranter free love, or polygamy, the Quaker understanding of the inward return of Christ in the perceived new age cast a somber and serious approach to the marriage union between two people. Early Quakers believed it was direct, divine activity that brought a couple together – only two people – whilst the proof of God's inward revelation was evinced in an outward, orderly process of marriage.

DOI: 10.4324/9780429030925-59

Eager to ensure the legality and moral legitimacy of Quaker marriages, Fox and Fell set out to implement an orderly process of marriage in the early years of the increasingly organized Quaker movement. Fox referred to the Quakers as the True Church – a separated community of believers who shunned radical dissenting attitudes on the one hand but who also stopped attending the Church of England and shunned its hierarchy of power. Quakers instead believed they were married by God within their own worship communities called Meetings. Without an attending magistrate or ordained minister, Quaker marriages were not at first recognized under English law. A clearly delineated process that could also be legally recognized would leave no room for accusations of adultery or bigamy and would also protect the legitimacy of children born of Quaker marriages. Fell was the first to instruct Quaker Meetings to draw up a marriage certificate and take a copy immediately to the local magistrate.[5] Fox instructed that marriages within Quaker meetings should be proclaimed publically, for instance in the market square. The marriage certificate, and its communal signing within a Meeting, was another crucial step towards Quaker marriages being made public and legally binding. In a Nottingham case regarding issues of the transfer of estate in widowhood, Quaker marriages were finally considered legally valid in 1661.[6]

Endogamy, or marrying another Quaker, was essential in creating a spiritually unified community, as both partners (man and woman equally) had to be awakened to the seed of God within the conscience in order to follow through with a marriage commitment. Likewise, the community of Quaker believers needed to be in agreement in a communal witness that the marriage was brought together by God, thus strengthening the unity of the spiritual body. This ensured that both members of the couple were led and joined by God, and this also solidified the unity of both the marriage, as well as the wider Quaker unity with the marriage in both agreement and support of the marriage. Marrying a non-Quaker could essentially weaken the unity and purity of the community. Because of the weighty spiritual significance of marriage, marrying outside the Quaker fold could lead to disownment from the meeting.[7] Parents also disowned children who married outside the Quaker faith.[8] When a new generation of Quakers emerged who were born to Quaker parents, brought up in Quaker households, and began to rebel and marry non-Quakers, endogamy was in danger. By the 1750s, there was a clamping down by Meetings on "marriage out of unity".[9] Over time, endogamy grew difficult to maintain, particularly in light of the rise of evangelicalism and declining membership. In the mid-nineteenth century, London Yearly Meeting discontinued disownment for marriage to non-Quakers, whilst in the United States after the Civil War, Hicksite and Gurneyite meetings also ended the practice.[10]

The process of moving towards marriage and the signing of the certificate was time-consuming in the early generations of Quakerism. Because the significance of marriage for early Quakers was so vital to the spiritual cohesion of their community, meeting approval occupied the majority of Quaker Meeting time in the seventeenth and eighteenth centuries.[11] Thorough-going evidence that Quakers were "clear" of any obstacles to marriage was crucial, and careful record keeping, including meeting minutes and certificates, were incorporated to keep track of the various steps towards marriage. Adequate time also allowed to verify no embarrassing entanglements existed, such as bigamy.[12] Anxious to be sure that God was prompting a possible union, it was not uncommon for a Quaker couple to wait months, even years before even proposing an intent of marriage to the Meeting.[13] After the couple brought their "sense" of being led together by God to the Meeting, a parental consent certificate was presented.[14] A clearness committee would then investigate to see if the couple was clear of any obstructions to marriage. The committee ensured that the couple was attending a Meeting, conducting themselves with an "upright carriage" or good character, and were secure financially. Earthly reasons for marriage, such as carnality or money, were shunned. There was also a strict condemnation of dynastic marriages, while marriage based on mutual affection, coupled with personal and communal assurance of God's bringing the couple together, was encouraged.[15]

Once a couple gained approbation, or approval from the Quaker Meeting, a date would be set for the Marriage Meeting. The marriage was not meant to be a ceremony per se but rather a time of sober reflection on the work of God joining two Quakers in marriage. Those in attendance were considered witnesses to God's work, and often shared testimonies of support for the couple. Rings were not exchanged, as these were seen as forms and symbols of vanity which were frequently rejected by Quakers. Simplicity and humility were hailed hallmarks of Quaker marriage meetings, though not all Quakers followed the practice of simplicity. Fox had suggested that money that would have been spent on marriages be given to the poor.[16] Women were not given away, nor ever coerced into marriage. While the notion of helpmeets between husband and wife was supported, in the seventeenth and eighteenth centuries, women were at times still expected to support and obey their husbands. Yet often, like for Fell, no vows of obedience were uttered by the bride.[17] Rather, "I take thee, my Friend . . ." was the frequent spoken commitment to one another, in place of any vows from either gender. Finally, those in attendance would sign the marriage certificate, an important symbol of the Quaker communal confirmation that God had joined the couple, as well as a public statement that the couple was now married.

Today, many of the core principles set out by Fell, Fox, and other early Quakers remain, whilst at times, and in various ways, there is some conformation to contemporary societal norms. Quaker meeting approval is still required, and clearness committees continue to provide counsel for couples intending to marry. The signing of the marriage certificate of the witnesses remains a celebrated and central part of the marriage meeting, stressing the continued communal aspect to the marriage celebration. As Fox and Fell instructed, Quaker marriage meetings today are usually silent and simple rather than extravagant occasions. There remains no giving away of the bride, and many Quakers still say "I take thee my Friend" rather than vows of obedience, both practices indicating a clearer commitment for some Quakers to gender equality, both in entering marriage as well as within marriage. However, perspectives on marriage amongst Quaker branches vary. There are those amongst evangelical Quaker branches, for example, who emphasize male authority in marriage.[18] While some Quakers today accept couples living together before marriage, as well as divorce, others do not.[19] Yet, Fox's words that "we marry none; but it is the Lord's work and we are but witnesses" is still the most enduring and central concept that Quakers universally accept.

The notion that "we are but witnesses" to God's work of joining a couple has lent to a shifting of attitudes amongst some Quakers towards same-sex marriage. For the first 300 of Quakerism, heterosexuality was seen as the norm, and homosexual behavior was seen as sin.[20] In 1963, a group of eleven Quakers in Britain published a text titled *Towards a Quaker View of Sex*, in which would include the first affirmation of homosexuality from a religious group in Britain. In 2009, the Britain Yearly Meeting in London affirmed support for same sex marriage, asserting that they were witnesses to God's leading couples together who happen to be of the same sex.[21] In doing so, they became the first religious organization in Britain to formally celebrate and recognize same-sex marriage. Not all Quakers agree, but this notion is important in defining their understanding of marriage as a public, spiritual, and legal commitment between two individuals regardless of gender. Many Quakers in Britain then worked for legislation. In 2013, the Marriage (Same Sex Couples) Act was passed, allowing same-sex marriage in England and Wales, whilst the Scotland Parliament approved a same-sex marriage law in 2014. Finally, in 2020 same-sex marriage became legal in Northern Ireland.[22]

As the Quaker community spread around the world, so has the Quaker marriage practice. There are variations, just as there are variations in the Quaker diaspora today. But the common thread of practice are appealing to many even outside the Quaker fold. The absence of an officiant is appealing to those who are not churchgoers. The self-uniting marriage license, available in various states in the United States including Pennsylvania, was directly inspired by the Quaker tradition. Many are likewise inspired to have Quaker-like marriages, being attracted to the characteristic silence and simplicity, even if they are not Quakers themselves. Finally, Quakers themselves, by and large, continue to see God's uniting of two individuals as a sacred expression of God's direct revelation and a profound moment of communal worship – just as the founding Quaker members intended.

Notes

1 Bruyneel, 68.
2 "We Are but Witnesses", 2009, 8; Fox, *A Collection of Select and Christian Epistles*, 281.
3 Fox, *Journal*, 5.
4 Hill, 229–230.
5 Fell, *To Friends, An Epistle on Marriage (1656)* in Glines (ed.), 195; Bruyneel, 69; Polder, 48; Brinton, 7.
6 Braithwaite, 145; Polder, 45–47.
7 Abbott, 213.
8 Sugar, 46.
9 Dandelion, 53; Abbott, 128.
10 Abbott, 128. Historian Thomas Hamm explains the Hicksites, who split from Orthodox Quakes in the Philadelphia meeting, had by the 1880's "openly described themselves as liberals, in sympathy with Unitarians and liberal movements in other Protestant denominations . . . [and] a commitment to toleration of dissent and freedom of thought" (Hamm, 46). Guerneyites, a later schism from the remaining Orthodox Quakers, was led by John Gurney (1788–1847), who advocated work with other evangelical Protestants in good causes (Hamm, 47). The openness of these groups to other Protestants helped relax attitudes towards marrying outside Quaker circles.
11 Due to the lengthy time devoted to ensuring a couple's preparedness for marriage, the responsibility of marriage approbation was eventually shifted to the Women's Meetings in the eighteenth century.
12 Such cases did emerge where unfortunate suspicions of a living spouse were proven, thus ending the matrimony process.
13 Dandelion, 49–50.
14 Polder, 62. If parents of a Quaker were not Quaker themselves, the Meeting would overrule the need for parental approval.
15 Sugar, 47. Margaret Fell and her eldest daughter, Margaret, stood in defiance against Judge Fell, denying the proposal of Colonel West to the young Margaret (Polder, 155–161).
16 George Fox, *Epistle CCCCXIX to London, Written the 4th Day of the 4th Month, 1690* (Polder, 93).
17 Hamm, 195.
18 Abbott, 129.
19 Abbott, 215. Until the twentieth century, Quakers generally accepted that sex outside of marriage was sin (Hamm, 137).
20 Hamm, 137.
21 "We Are but Witnesses," 2009.
22 Booth.

Bibliography

Abbott, Margery Post, Mary Ellen Chijioke, Pink Dandelion, and John William Oliver, Jr. *The Historical Dictionary of the Friends (Quakers)*, Second Edition. Lanham, Toronto, and Plymouth, UK: The Scarecrow Press, Inc., 2012.
Booth, Michael. "A Testimony of Divine Grace: Quakers and Same-sex Marriage." 21 February 2018. https://www.quaker.org.uk/blog/quakers-and-same-sex-marriage

Braithwaite, William. *The Beginnings of Quakerism to 1660*. Cambridge: Cambridge University Press, 1955.

Dandelion, Pink. *The Liturgies of Quakerism*. London and New York: Routledge, 2017.

Fell, Margaret. *To Friends, an Epistle on Marriage*. 1656.

Fox, George. *Epistle CCCCXIX to London, Written the 4th Day of the 4th Month*. 1690.

Fox, George. *A Collection of Select and Christian Epistles*. London: T. Sowle, 1698.

Fox, George. *A Journal or Historical Account of the Life, Travels, Sufferings, Christian Experiences, and Labour of Love in the Work of the Ministry, of That Ancient, Eminent, and Faithful Servant of Jesus Christ*. 2 volumes. Leeds: Anthony Pickard, Sixth Edition, 1836.

Hamm, Thomas D. *Quakers in America*. New York: Columbia University Press, 2003.

Hill, Christopher. *The World Turned Upside Down: Radical Ideas During the English Revolution*. London: Penguin Books, 1991.

Polder, Kristianna. *Matrimony in the True Church: Seventeenth-century Quaker Marriage Approbation Process*. London: Routledge, 2015.

Sugar, Max. *Religious Identity and Behavior*. New York: Plenum Publishers, 2002.

"We Are but Witnesses." 2009 London pamphlet.

56

PAUL CUFFE'S ECONOMIC RELIGION

Cuffe's Quaker Identity Beyond the Race Hero Archetype

Timothy Rainey II

The Westport Monthly Meeting admitted Captain Paul Cuffe to their assembly just three years before he landed on Africa's shores in 1811. He began preparing for the journey months after his admittance in April of 1808 and gained the Meeting's blessing the same year.[1] Cuffe, along with members of the London African Institution, hoped to restore the promise of the Atlantic world's first post-slavery society in Freetown, Sierra Leone, initially planted there in 1792 with Black Loyalists from Nova Scotia.[2] When American abolitionists sought a principal from their new union to support efforts to end the transatlantic slave trade, members of the Philadelphia African Institution identified Paul Cuffe in 1807 as a likely choice.[3] His election to the Westport Meeting in 1808 solidified his access to a commercial network of Quakers peppering the Atlantic world that would facilitate his role in a bold new experiment in black freedom.

Born in 1759 to an ex-enslaved Asante man and Wampanoag woman from the Gay Head Aquinnah people living in Martha's Vineyard, Cuffe rose to fame in Westport, Massachusetts, following the American Revolution. His success as a merchant, his immense wealth, and his Quaker business connections contributed to his celebrity. Philadelphia's *Claypoole's American Daily Advertiser* and Wilmington's *Delaware and Eastern-Shore Advertiser* began publishing news of the black shipping captain's journeys as early as 1799.[4] With 200 acres of land, ships, a store, and employees by 1800, Paul Cuffe was unlike most free blacks in New England. A wealthy black merchant and philanthropist, Cuffe notably transported thirty-eight free black Americans to Freetown, Sierra Leone, in 1815 to promote abolitionism and commerce in West Africa. During his inaugural journey to the colony four years earlier, the New Englander helped establish the Friendly Society of Sierra Leone, a collective centered on promoting economic cooperation and black-run trade in the colony. For Cuffe, it would become the first step in God's Providential plan for political and economic freedom for members of the black diaspora.

While Cuffe's unique achievements primed him for absorption within American dream ideology, his unprecedented rise is more than a narrative of American remaking and overcoming. Like most heroic portrayals, popular representations of this figure in histories, biographies, and local histories belie deeper truths. Scholars often overlook the more complicated narrative of religion and economy regarding Cuffe. Such readings affirm the myth of America without attempting to grapple with the failures the myth elides. A close reading of Cuffe might also lead to ways of probing his America and its tradition of religio-political mythmaking. As a

DOI: 10.4324/9780429030925-60

rags-to-riches phenomenon alone, scholarly and popular narrations of this figure largely ignore the possibility of the "race hero" as a historical and political problem.

In addition to his classical liberal persona, Cuffe's Quaker Protestantism participated in the literary production of Cuffe's Americanness. Cuffe's unique story has the potential to enrich African, American, and Quaker Studies. By elevating Africana readings within studies of black Quakerism, figures like Cuffe might offer a path toward understanding how religion, race, and economy intersect. Interpreting Cuffe's spiritual identity demands that researchers give attention to his Quaker business ethics along with his emerging *black economic internationalism*. This chapter aims to show how viewing Cuffe's Quakerism from the angle of his mercantile career in the black Atlantic world has the potential to expand how historians read and contextualize his spiritual identity.

Race Hero Readings

Research agendas focused on Paul Cuffe have often been preoccupied with his New England context. The privileging of his American influences has facilitated the relative silencing of possible competing theoretical approaches, including analyzing his multiple Atlantic identities. Looking at how Cuffe viewed African repatriation through his black Atlantic identity and mercantilist attitude might show that broadening the narrative frame, which more aggressively includes his Atlantic identity, effectively pauses currents of scholarship and popular productions and consumption of Cuffe. Such narrow readings lead to the uncritical absorption of figures like him within American consensus.[5] Rather than making his values commensurable with early Protestant America, I propose clarifying how those values are discussed.[6] Like Horatio Alger's *Ragged Dick* and Stephen Thernstrom's poor industrious hero, the notion of the race hero also reflects the myth of American progress.[7] The race hero manifests through an ethnicized version of 'progress' disseminated through classical liberal rhetoric. The race hero, I argue, in its simplest form is the one who is transformed, who tips the scale of their racial baggage, and emerges as an example to unconverted kinsmen. In the way Phyllis Wheatley (1753–1784) or Olaudah Equiano (1745–1797) are changed from West African enslaved people to literary celebrities, Cuffe is used to simultaneously vindicate black humanity and affirm the idea of America's democratic exceptionalism.[8]

The dual work of Cuffe's narrative – both resistive to bad America and affirmative of good America – is observable in nineteenth-century romantic literature that valorized his Protestant morality. Wilson Armistead (1819–c. 1868), a British businessman, abolitionist, and Quaker, in his 1848 book *A Tribute for the Negro*,[9] portrays Cuffe with what I refer to as moral aesthetics, describing him as "tall, well formed, and athletic [. . .] his countenance," he writes, "blending gravity with modesty and sweetness, and firmness with gentleness and humanity."[10] British and American newspapers similarly celebrated Cuffe's racial exceptionalism, with the *Federal Gazette and Baltimore Daily Advertiser* describing him as a "pious and humane citizen."[11] When the great-grandson of Paul Cuffe, Horatio P. Howard, produced a pamphlet detailing his famous forebear's life, he viewed the work as a contribution to black uplift. Titling the short biography "A Self-Made Man: Capt. Paul Cuffe," he published it in 1913, believing the story of an early black American icon – his relative – would be an "inspiration," he writes, "to Negro youth all over the United States."[12] Howard's memorial joined a bevy of literature celebrating the black merchant and shipping captain over the past century and was illustrative of a narrative trend focused on Paul Cuffe's heroic symbolism that would persist for another century.

Sheldon Harris most notably attempted to contextualize Cuffe's Atlantic identity in his 1972 book, *Paul Cuffe: Black America and the African Return*, but affirms his participation in the tradition of Benjamin Franklin and the Protestant ethic without sustained critique and analysis.[13] From scholarly works to a twelve and up book series with an introduction written by Coretta Scott King, moral heroism discourse has historically dominated the literature on Cuffe.[14] To varying degrees, four texts have participated in narrativizing Cuffe's heroics and are also the four preeminent studies cataloging Cuffe's life and papers. These texts include Sheldon H. Harris's 1972 edited volume *Paul Cuffe: Black America and the African Return*; George A. Salvador's 1969 biography *Paul Cuffe, The Black Yankee, 1759–1817*; Lamont D. Thomas's 1988 biography *Paul Cuffe: Black Entrepreneur and Pan-Africanist*; and Rosalind Cobb Wiggins's 1996 edited volume, *Captain Paul Cuffe's Logs and Letters, 1808–1817*.

The twentieth-century accounts by Thomas, Wiggins, Harris, and Salvador are each significant works of history and historical preservation but demonstrate a need for studies that decenter America. While Salvador produced the earlier of the twentieth-century books, Lamont Thomas is regularly credited with bringing Cuffe's story to a broader audience. In her edited work, Rosalind Cobb Wiggins credits Salvador, Harris, and Thomas, noting that she pulled essential material for her volume from their respective biographies, with Thomas's work being a "constant resource." Wiggins's work is impressive, and she importantly publishes unedited versions of Cuffe's writings. Cuffe's crude grammar has been used to unfairly deem him a bad speller at least and illiterate at worst. However, Wiggins's contextualization of Cuffe's compositional imperfections does more to emphasize the educational limitations he defeated rather than the ones that remained. Still, the introductory chapter, written by Rhett S. Jones, and chapter 1 by Wiggins, "Introducing Captain Paul Cuffe, Friend," problematically engineer what I see as a New England encounter with Cuffe by imposing curatorial privilege in a way that potentially predetermines how readers experience the contextual scope of Cuffe's world.

Cuffe's biographers often launch Americentric interpretations without an extensive investigation into the varieties of value systems the Cuffe family embraced. Cuffe's Quakerism instrumentally influenced the formation of his pragmatic religious attitude, but this influence must be viewed and analyzed in light of Cuffe's multiple worldviews. By emphasizing Cuffe's New England sensibilities through his archetypical image, recent biographers displayed Cuffe's Americanness at the expense of identifying unexamined elements of his Africanness that become intelligible, I contend, by centering the black Atlantic world. How Cuffe viewed repatriation as an ideological partnership between Pan-African thought and Western mercantilism might show that rather than making his values commensurable with Protestant American values, clarifying how the black Atlantic world became central to his spiritual orientation opens new analytical doors.

Slavery, Quakerism, and the Cuffes

Highlighting the life of Kofi Slocum, Paul's Ghanaian father shows how his son's American story must be framed as an African story, too. Quaker abolitionism was well underway by the 1740s, and Kofi's manumission had undoubtedly been a subject of interest among the Quaker families who owned him. While George Fox failed to condemn the practice of slavery, he did preach humane treatment, education for the enslaved, and the system of indenturing over making human chattel.[15] Though Fox did not decisively condemn slavery, Quakers discussed the ethics of slavery and debated how their Protestant tradition might best respond. Following the radical 1688 Germantown Petition in Pennsylvania – the first known piece of abolitionist literature[16] – Keith George offered his 1693 "An exhortation & caution to friends concerning buying or keeping of Negroes." George's exhortation protested slave ownership as an immoral practice and encouraged Friends to only buy bondsmen and women for the purpose of setting them free.[17] Quaker prophet, John Woolman, was beginning to make his rounds at Quaker monthly meetings, urging friends to free their slaves by the mid-eighteenth century.[18] By the 1740s, several papers had been released regarding the immorality and the detrimental impact of slavery on the life of the owner. However, Quakers did not come close to a firm stand on abolition until 1776, when they affirmed their position against slavery at an annual meeting of Friends.[19]

John Slocum, the last owner of Kofi, likely saw himself acting within Quaker principles when he allowed Kofi to "work off" his freedom – probably around two or three years after he purchased Paul's father.[20] Perhaps he saw it as good industry and imagined himself as resisting the ills Quaker abolitionists believed attended the life of the southern enslaver (i.e., idleness, cruelty, violence). Quakerism and Quaker abolitionism surely influenced the life of Kofi and likely played a role in shaping how he imagined religion in his freedom. There is no evidence of African religious forms animating the life of Kofi. Still, it should not be assumed that Quakerism was the only spiritual practice at play in Kofi's imagination of the sacred. Slavery and Quakerism studies have primarily focused on white abolitionists, but the ways Quakerism may have combined with the contemplation of Africa as homeland demands more attention. The manners in which "work" can be related to Asante principles and values may provide deeper insights into how we discuss Kofi's agency in his emancipation, which his granddaughter Ruth Cuffe contends he purchased through his labor.[21]

In addition to Paul Cuffe's Asante roots, it is also imperative to account for his Wampanoag heritage. The Cuffe family culture is incomplete without deepening both identities. Kofi's narrative, emancipation, and new beginnings in New England are incomplete without a conversation on the love story he shared with Ruth Moses.[22] Born into the Wampanoag people of Martha's Vineyard, under the laws of inheritance, Ruth's children were born free people.[23] It was not uncommon for black men and Wampanoag women to develop romantic relationships and settle down on reservations. Due to a shortage of Wampanoag men, women often married outsiders.[24] However, such instances of exogamy produced tensions. Records between the 1780s and 1820s show problems among the Mashpee people who denounced Wampanoag women marrying "Negro men." Lawsuits and legal proceedings demonstrate this hostility. One instance even records Paul's son-in-law, who stood trial in 1823 for the murder of his daughter Mary Cuffe.[25]

The Wampanoag people were heavily missionized but many kept the old spiritual traditions even as they practiced Christianity, with converts recognized as praying Indians. The religious worship of Wampanoags in that region included traditional religious worship, most prevalent before colonization, and it centered on the pursuit of spiritual force, which they called *manit*. Manit is the power that moved through the world. Physical entities could conduct and contain this power, including "human artifice, certain animals, and especially spirits, all of which Indians called *manitou*."[26] Similarities between the Wampanoag and Asante belief systems offer some perspective on the potential unaccounted features of the family culture. Kofi's people, the Asante, honored a supreme being, Nyame, or the "Great God of the Sky." This name relates to the widely used root throughout West Africa, *nyama* or "supernatural force." It is a potency that fills all living creatures, and *abosom* are spirits, like orisha, that take power from the supreme god to the natural world.[27] While distinct, the foundational beliefs in the closeness of nature to a pervading supernatural force that enters entities in human environments might have been an orientation that Kofi and Ruth shared, engaged individually, or integrated into their Quaker beliefs. In the ways that African diaspora religions have filled the gaps created by epistemic and cultural violence abetted by Christian missionaries in the New World, the potential for reading indigenous orientations as a mediating force for families like the Cuffe's is substantial.

Cuffe's early contact with Quaker business practices and Quaker ideology[28] provides further context for his religion. In addition to traditional spiritual practices, his imagination of black Providential destiny in Africa also invites scholarly interpretations focused on religion and economy. As an international black figure, Cuffe's economic imagination was as much a creation of his liberalism as it was his religion. His moral thought, informed by Quakerism, a sense of black collectivism, and a mercantile way of pursuing liberty and freedom, would eventually be combined with a concept for black-run trade.

Black Mercantilism as Religion

The new economy Paul Cuffe imagined, an alternative to the slave trade and race-based monopolistic commerce, proceeds from two adjacent but distinctive ideological locations: the economic expression of his liberalism and the economic expression of his black internationalism. Within his agenda, he attempted to combat the legal institutions bolstering the slave trade and the hierarchical mercantile systems that prejudicially obstructed black commerce in Sierra Leone. Cuffe's liberalism operated with a sense of salvific purpose. He combined Christianity and commerce as others had done in New England, but instead of imagining westward expansion, Cuffe looked East. The most explicit articulation of his commercial agenda took shape within a short petition crafted by him in 1811 along with members of the black Nova Scotian community in Sierra Leone.

Following his attendance at the Baptist Meeting in Freetown on April 7, 1811, he met privately aboard his ship, the *Traveller*, with John Kizell, Thomas Wainer, Sarha Francis, James Reed, and others and drafted a short petition. The Friendly Society's central objective focused on decentering the monopoly on trade held by English merchants in Freetown so that an independent black industry could emerge. In a letter to William Allen, Quaker and founding member of the London African Institution, Cuffe stated, quite plainly, that their objective was to achieve the "Liberty to trade."[29] Established with twelve total signatories drawn from Sierra Leonian civic leaders and entrepreneurs, the Friendly Society presented three demands within their petition:

> 1stly that Encouragement May be given unto all our Breatheren who may Come from the British Colonies or from America and Become farmers in order to help us Cultivate the Land
>
> 2dly our foreign Breatheren who may have Vessels that Encouragement may be given to Establish Commerce in Sierra Leone
>
> 3dly Would Encouragement be given unto all those who may Establish whalefishery in the Colony of Sierra Leone[30]

This petition stands prominently within Cuffe's narrative. It points to the potential for black commercial energies in Freetown, which they hoped would spark more extensive Atlantic intercourse and an economic revolution. Five months after the meeting on the *Traveller*, the three demands sketched in the petition were approved by the African Institution in London. Yet, the hope for progress communicated by the petitioners was unfulfilled.[31]

While Cuffe remained hopeful about the potential for Freetown to emerge as a nucleus of black business, he was also troubled by the ways large European firms in the settlement suppressed the expansion of black trade by controlling credit, debt, currency, banking, and the transference of property.[32] William Allen summarized the troubles inhibiting black progress in Freetown in a letter to Cuffe dated October 29, 1812. In this letter, he explained how the dire conditions of black people in Sierra Leone related to the fact that white people in the region simply wanted to seek greater profits and do so in the shortest way. The only intervention Allen believed to be feasible within the colony was to supplement black capital on his own account and ensure settlers received the "whole of the profits." Nearly a year later, Allen confirmed in a letter to Cuffe that their provision of "a little capital to trade with" had been received by settlers giving him confidence that the black people in the colony would soon be on "good footing."[33]

The letters shared between Cuffe and Allen reveal that abolitionist hope in Freetown extended beyond political and social liberties. The moral goal of freedom also centered on ensuring black economic upbuilding. In addition to ending the slave trade, Cuffe envisioned a path toward industrializing Sierra Leone with black people placed at the center of their plan. Cuffe's vision included setting up a sawmill in Freetown and perhaps founding black banks with the primary aim of funding industry in Africa.[34] He shrewdly, though not unproblematically, discussed with his brother John the attractiveness of Sierra Leone to potential American producers who might find cheaper labor in the colony.[35]

In the fall of 1810, when Paul Cuffe prepared for his first journey to Sierra Leone, the US Quaker Friends began laying the foundation for a partnership between British and American abolitionists interested in Freetown. Benjamin Rush, MD, wrote a letter supporting Cuffe's travels in 1810 and spoke to the friends of liberty, humanity, and religion in every part of the world, affirming the virtues of Cuffe and that of his mission.[36] Cuffe also carried letters from his own New England Yearly Meeting, the Philadelphia Yearly Meeting, and had received other individual letters of support from John James and William Dillwyn.[37] In addition to the letters that Paul carried to West Africa, he took his infectious belief and conviction that black Americans were destined to thrive in the land of their ancestors. He wanted to open the door to expand a black economy throughout the Atlantic world that coalesced ideas of benevolence, power, and democracy.

Cuffe died in 1817 nearly broke, having invested deeply in Freetown, facing resistance from black people not in favor of emigration, and finally lying on his death bed regretting that he could not do more.[38] I am not sure if it ever occurred to Cuffe that he failed or that living in an anti-black world perhaps doomed the project from the beginning. On February 28, 1817, in one of the last letters he would ever pen, Cuffe wrote:

> Dear friend the African Cause Still Lives in the View of my mind Although it is out of my power to Do much for Two Special Reasons first is that the Government do not furnish with the Aid that is much Needed in order to enable one to Step forward in Safty. Second my funds being Small wich bespeaks that not Great things can be Looked for. I have many Applications, and enquiries from Different quarters. [. . .] The African Institution in Philadelphia Seems to be Alarmed at the movements of the times. By [sic] my Desire to them are to be quiet and trust God. If we the African race are faithful I believe that God will not be Wanting on his part.[39]

Cuffe's sense that God would respond to faithful human action, even those carried out in the domain of commerce and trade, shows how the study of black religious life can be expanded to include previously unexamined primary sources like the shipping logs of a merchant or the archives of black businesses. Cuffe's writings, read as a spiritual way of striving through economic life, can become a site of black intellectual interruption that responds to a world of gratuitous violence, anti-blackness, and deep uncertainty. As an international black figure, Cuffe's economic imagination was as much a creation of his liberalism as it was his religion. His moral economic thought, informed by Quakerism, a sense of black collectivism, and mercantile way of pursuing liberty and freedom, combined with a belief in black-run trade that illuminates why a study of his biography must be an interdisciplinary endeavor. Paul Cuffe's unique identity has the potential to do more than show why race matters within Quaker Studies. His commitment to African uplift through pragmatic experimentation within the marketplace invites research agendas focused on the ways black Protestants saw economic activism as religion and a divine path toward experiences of democratic freedoms.

Notes

1 "Copy of Certificates of Membership in the Monthly Meeting, Westport," Paul Cuffe Personal and Family Papers, New Bedford Free Public Library, no. 698 in Town of Westport Massachusetts Digital Archive (https://www.westport-ma.com/historical-documents/pages/cuffe-paul-personal-and-family-papers) (hereinafter Cuffe MSS). Also see Westport Monthly Meeting, Men's Minutes, Special Collections Section of the W.E.B. Du Bois Library, University of Massachusetts, Amherst, Massachusetts.

2 Sierra Leone Company. *Substance of the report delivered by the Court of Directors of the Sierra Leone Company, to the general court of proprietors, on Thursday the 27th of March, 1794* London, 1794. Slavery and Anti-Slavery. Gale. Emory University Robert W. Woodruff Library, accessed June 9, 2018 (hereinafter SLC 1794). The 1794 Report notes that the number was 1196, 7; also see James Sidbury, who numbers the group at 1192, James Sidbury, "'African' Settlers in the Founding of Freetown," in *Slavery, Abolition and the Transition to Colonialism in Sierra Leone* (Trenton, NJ: Africa World Press, 2015), 132.

3 William Allen, *Life of William Allen: With Selection from His Correspondence,* vol. 1 (London: Charles Gilpin, Bishopgate Street Without, 1846), 133–138. Also see Lamont D. Thomas, *Paul Cuffe: Black Entrepreneur and Pan-Africanist* (Champaign: University of Illinois Press, 1988), 34–36. In August of 1807, New Jerseyan William Dillwyn, the principal mediator between English and American abolitionist, wrote from England to Friend James Pemberton, president of the Pennsylvania Abolition Society, to inquire about his possible assistance with the new settlement in Freetown. Knowing the good reputation of Paul Cuffe, Pemberton – who succeeded Benjamin Rush as the head of the Pennsylvania Abolitionist Society – and his niece Ann Emlen Mifflin met with him after he had recently disembarked in Philadelphia and asked if he was willing to transport free blacks to Sierra Leone. By this time, Cuffe had already considered the possibility of participating in the African trade in goods to support West African communities. He was also in favor of the mission's objective to use trade as a method of ending the illegal trade continuing after the 1807 British abolition.

4 Thomas, 18.

5 See Judith Butler, *Frames of War: When Is Life Grievable?* (London: Verso, 2016); also see Sacvan Bercovitch, *The American Jeremiad* (Madison, WI: The University of Wisconsin Press, 1978).

6 In *Wittgenstein's Antiphilosophy,* Alain Badiou considers points of similarity and dissonance between Nietzsche's and Wittgenstein's antiphilosophy and remarks on philosophical failings in being clear about thought. He writes: "Philosophy is a sick and regressive non-thought, because it pretends to present the nonsense that is proper to it within a propositional and theoretical register. The philosophical sickness appears when nonsense exhibits itself as sense, when non-thought imagines itself to be a thought. Hence, philosophy must not be refuted, as if it were a false thought; it must be judged and condemned as a fault of non-thought, the gravest of faults: to inscribe itself nonsensically into the protocols (propositions and theories) reserved for thought alone. Philosophy, with regard to the eminent final dignity of affirmative non-thought (that of an act that crosses the barrier of sense), is guilty." Clarification becomes the philosophers art. At the beginning of his essay, Badiou uses Wittgenstein's military experience to illuminate one of his philosophical claims, that what matters is the "clarification" of propositions. Imagining Wittgenstein activity as a soldier, Badiou states, "the point is not to shoot but to clarify the shot." But in traditional philosophy what is being clarified are eternally impotent propositions. Clarification itself comes to have meaning to the degree the chaos of life becomes intelligible through heroic expression; Alain Badiou, *Wittgenstein's Antiphilosophy*, translated by Bruno Bosteels (London: Verso Books, 2011), 77–8.

7 Horatio Alger Jr., *Ragged Dick and Struggling Upward*, Carl Bode ed. (New York: Viking Penguin Inc., 1985). When Alger published *Ragged Dick* in 1867, he participated in a tradition of constructing America's myth of progress. Dick's rags-to-riches rise was a fictional spin on what Alger felt were the real fruits of moral maturation and industrious energy; and Stephen Thernstrom, *Poverty and Progress: Social Mobility in a Nineteenth Century City* (Cambridge: Harvard University Press, 1980). In 1964

Stephen Thernstrom asked in *Poverty and Progress* if the myth was or could be more than just that. and The book was important in several ways and interestingly identifies a cultural archetype Thernstrom deemed the "poor industrious hero" – fittingly set within the geographic backdrop of the nation's Puritan beginnings (68).

8 Anders Stephanson, *Manifest Destiny: American Expansionism and the Empire of Right* (New York: Hill and Wang, 1995), xii.
9 Wilson Armistad, *A Tribute for the Negro* (New York: W. Harned, 1848). http://hdl.handle.net/2027/nc01.ark:/13960/t42r4z659.
10 Armistad, 464.
11 When he arrived in London for the first time after surveying Sierra Leone, people lined wharves and the *Edinburgh Review* noted the spectacle; Rosalind Cobb Wiggins, *Captain Paul Cuffe's Logs and Letters, 1808–1817: A Black Quaker's "Voice from within the Veil"* (Washington, DC: Howard University Press, 1996), 128; Thomas, 76.
12 This pamphlet was written by the great grandson of Paul Cuffe to commemorate Cuffe on the occasion of the erection of a monument to him on June 15, 1913, at a Quaker Meeting House in Westport, MA. "A Self Made Man, Captain Paul Cuffe, Cuffe MSS 1123–1139.
13 Sheldon Harris, *Paul Cuffe: Black America and the African Return* (New York: Simon and Schuster, 1972), 20.
14 Arthur Diamond, *Paul Cuffe: Merchant and Abolitionist,* Black Americans of Achievement Series (New York: Chelsea House Publishers, 1989).
15 Donna McDaniel and Vanessa Julye, *Fit for Freedom Not for Friendship: Quakers, African Americans, and the Myth of Racial Justice* (Philadelphia: Quaker Press, 2009), 11.
16 Gerret Hendricks, Derick op de Graeff, Francis Daniell Pastorius, and Abraham op den Graef, "Resolution of Germantown Mennonites," in *American Antislavery Writings: Colonial Beginnings to Emancipation,* James G. Basker, ed. (New York: The Library of America, 2012).
17 George Keith, "An Exhortation & Caution to Friends Concerning Buying or Keeping of Negroes," in *American Antislavery Writings: Colonial Beginnings to Emancipation,* James G. Basker, ed. (New York: The Library of America, 2012).
18 Wiggins, 46–47.
19 McDaniel and Julye, 33–34.
20 Ruth Cuffe to James P. Congdon, February 12, 1851, Cuffe MSS 679.
21 With some exceptions, including Maurice Jackson, *Let This Voice Be Heard: Anthony Benezet, Father of Atlantic Abolitionism* (Philadelphia: University of Pennsylvania Press, 2009). For studies on the development of an Afro-American consciousness in New England broadly, see William Dillon Pierson, *Black Yankees: The Development of an Afro-American Subculture in Eighteenth-Century New England* (Amherst: The University of Massachusetts Press, 1988).
22 For a critical study of black love stories during slavery and beyond, see Dianne M. Stewart, *Black Women, Black Love: America's War on African American Marriage* (New York: Hachette Book Group, Inc., 2020) and Tera Hunter, *Bound in Wedlock: Slave and Free Black Marriage in the Nineteenth Century* (Cambridge: The Belknap Press of Harvard University Press, 2017).
23 Wiggins, 47. Ruth Moses came from the Gay Head Aquinnah Wampanoag people living in Martha's Vineyard. They were likely counted among the Cape Cod Mashpee people when they lived in the Cuttyhunk Elizabethan Islands between 1750 and 1766. In 2007, these were the two federally recognized tribes of the Wampanoag people in Massachusetts. Harris, *Paul Cuffe*, 15, and David J. Silverman, *Faith and Boundaries: Colonists, Christianity, and Community among the Wampanoag Indians of Martha's Vineyard, 1600–1871* (Cambridge: Cambridge University Press, 2005), 253.
24 David J. Silverman, *This Land Is Their Land: The Wampanoag Indians, Plymouth Colony, and the Troubled History of Thanksgiving* (New York: Bloomsbury Publishing, 2019), 392.
25 Ibid., 248.
26 Ibid., 27.
27 Geoffrey Parrinder, *West African Religion: A Study of the Beliefs and Practices of Akan, Ewe, Yoruba, Ibo, and Kindred Peoples* Rpt. 1961 (Eugene, OR: Wipf and Stock Publishers, 2014). 12, 14–17, 48. Also see R. S. Rattray, *Ashanti* (Oxford: The Clarendon Press, 1923), 86–90.
28 See William Fox, *An Address to the People of Great Britain, on the Propriety of Abstaining from West India Sugar and Rum*, 10th ed. (London, 1792).
29 Paul Cuffe to William Allen, April 24, 1811, Sierra Leone, Cuffe MSS.

30 The Friendly Society of Sierra Leone to Governor Columbine, "his Excellency gov Columbine [. . .] governor of His Majesty Colony Sierra Leone, MSS 215. Cuffe also included a copy of this petition in his April 24th letter to William Allen intended for Parliament and the African Institution of London; also see Wiggins, 114–116; Thomas, 53–55.

31 "At a Committee of Directors of the African Institution held on the 27th of August 1811; His Royal Highness the Duke of Gloucester in the Chair," Cuffe MSS 268–271.

32 Padraic X. Scanlan, *Freedom's Debtors: British Antislavery in Sierra Leone in the Age of Revolution* (New Haven: Yale University Press, 2017), 110–11.

33 William Allen to Paul Cuffe, August 10, 1813, London, Cuffe MSS 309–310.

34 "I this Day Rote a Letter to William Allen and Stated nesary of Establishing Commerce in Africa and building a Vessell in Africa and if there could be any owner found in London," Wiggins 150; 2 Day 9th mo 1811 Remarks; for notes regarding the establishment of a sawmill, see Cuffe MSS 279–280. Also see Paul Cuffe to Freelove Slocum and Peter Williams, December 1, 1816, Cuffe MSS, 135. In January of 1812 Cuffe surveyed the land in Freetown for building a "sawmill, a gristmill, a saltworks, and a rice-processing factory." Thomas, 70; Paul Cuffe to Peter Williams, Westport [n.d.]; also see Wiggins, 437–438.

35 Paul Cuffe to John Cuffe, August 8, 1811, Liverpool, England, Cuffe MSS 55. Cuffe, speaking of the business prospects in Africa, notes that in Sierra Leone that there is "labor so cheap there is no need to labor oneself"; also see Thomas, 60.

36 "Recommendation of Paul Cuffe to the Friends of Liberty, Humanity, and Religion in Every part of the World," signed Benjamin Rush, MD, president of the Society for Abolishing the Commerce in Slave and for Extending Liberty to them, established in Philadelphia, December 27, 1810, Cuffe MSS, 203.

37 William Dillwyn to John James and Alexander Wilson August 30, 1810; and John James to Paul Cuffe October 29, 1810. Wiggins, 88–90.

38 Thomas, 108–111.

39 Paul Cuffe (perhaps to John James), February 28, 1817, Cuffe MSS; also see Wiggins, 507.

57

DISTINCTIVE AND HARMLESS? QUAKER NONVIOLENCE AS A RESOURCE FOR FUTURE RELIGIOSITY

Stewart David Yarlett

In *The Cultivation of Conformity* (2019), Quaker sociologist Pink Dandelion presents a 'perpetual conundrum' faced by religious organizations. That conundrum is between gaining adherents via 'distinctive appeal' (with 'unique' and/or 'universal' claims) and 'securing rights' by appearing equivalently 'harmless' to 'state-sanctioned religious expression'. Following this, Dandelion argues for a process of 'internal secularisation', seen particularly in the Liberal Quaker case with the group's beliefs shifting to conform with 'societal norms'; becoming more benign and secular (2019:i). Contrary to this, this chapter examines the extent to which the Quaker historical commitment to nonviolence is being drawn upon as a resource of response to the group's 'internal secularisation'. Thus, becoming a potential new marker of the Liberal Quaker identity and/or religiosity; a marker which is ostensibly both distinctive and harmless.

Subsequently, the chapter considers (1) the uniformity of such responses within the group; (2) the extent to which such a response can remain distinctive; and (3) the extent to which radical nonviolence and its manifestations may properly be considered equivalently harmless to 'state-sanctioned religious expression'. Whilst sensitive to potential complications in these areas, the chapter argues that if the success of Liberal Quakerism in attracting adherents and securing rights depends on the appearance of distinctiveness and harmlessness, then strategic presentation is a key factor. Consequently, the chapter considers the way Quakerism's historic and public association with nonviolence aids Liberal Quakers in presenting their commitment to nonviolence as distinctive and harmless, as compared to secular expressions of nonviolence and peace activism. In this sense nonviolence is a resource for a presentation and construction of the Liberal Quaker identity as both distinctive and harmless. A line of response that the chapter looks to demonstrate is being developed by components within Liberal Quakerism and its potential implications for the future identity and/or religiosity of the group.

Internal Secularisation

In developing his theory of 'internal secularisation', Dandelion begins with the 'perpetual conundrum' outlined above. Initially this is set up as a tension between a religious organization's

DOI: 10.4324/9780429030925-61

desire to win state approval and secure rights, by presenting as harmless citizens, and the desire to have popular appeal and gain new adherents. Prevailing secularisation theory maintains that the latter requires the group to make strong, distinctive and universal belief claims. However, such claims are liable to conflict with the fostering of an image of conformity and harmlessness that makes a religion likely to be sanctioned by a secular state (2019:i).

Examining Liberal Quakers as a case study, Dandelion argues that the group is on a course of development with 'an end point of extreme assimilation' (2019:117). He justifies this by pointing to the current state of belief amongst Quakers as diverse and post-Christian, to the point of accommodating 'secular and atheist viewpoints' (2019:117, 146). The 2013 British Quaker Survey saw 14.3% of respondents claiming no belief in God (Hampton 2014:7–43). Indeed, current internal discussions around expressions of Quaker nontheism[1] indicate general aspirations to accommodate them (as a valid form) on an institutional level (Yarlett 2020:196–204). Dandelion reflects upon how such a pluralistic framework, where multiple views (both religious and secular) are placed as equally valid options, can lead to 'the *raison d'être* of organised religion becom[ing] . . . less obvious' and secularity potentially becoming the dominant default presumption (2019:146, 138).[2]

Regarding the aforementioned conundrum, all this seems to suggest that by presenting as harmless and highly assimilatory to a pluralistic and secular civic framework, Quakers are opting for state approval (over distinctiveness and popular appeal). However, Dandelion argues that the interactive dynamics between religious groups and wider society are more complex. He delineates a four-way model of continual negotiation between state authorities, wider (popular) culture, organizational religion and popular religious belief. The relationships between these four components are usefully displayed in Figure 57.1.

Thus, Dandelion emphasizes that both institutional *and popular* elements (both internally and externally) play a role in informing Quakerism's societal expression. It is this formulation that

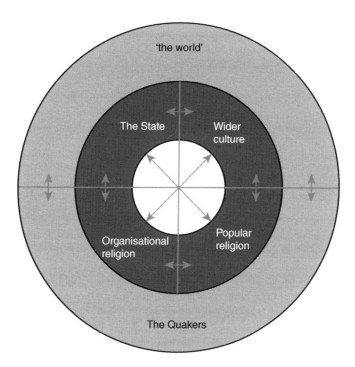

Figure 57.1   The elements of Quaker religion and non–religion (Dandelion 2019:94)

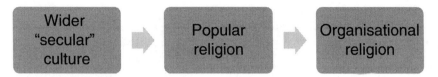

Figure 57.2   The major trajectory of Quakerism's 'internal secularisation'

informs Dandelion's more nuanced understanding of an internal process of secularisation. He contends that Quakerism's assimilation should not simply be understood as a top-down process; where the religion's organizational components accede to pressure from a secular State; but that the primary mechanism of Quakerism's secularisation occurs at a popular level. Individual believers are influenced by the wider secular culture and choose to moderate and align their expressions of their beliefs and values to fit with the wider population. This preceding popular secularisation then both 'undermines' and 'drives' organizational expressions of Quakerism (2019:149–161). In relation to the previous diagram the trajectory of influence emphasized by Dandelion's theory can be displayed as in Figure 57.2.

Concurrently, however, the quaternary framework he establishes implies alternative possibilities for Liberal Quakers in the construction and presentation of their identity. Significantly, drawing attention to the role of popular cultural dynamics raises questions concerning how Quakers influence wider culture and how they can potentially leverage this influence to develop 'softer' forms of power in responding to societal pressures (Pennington 2020) alongside the reflexive impact such manoeuvrings may have upon internal Quaker views. The remainder of this chapter looks to elucidate these lines of inquiry, along with some complexities implicit in Dandelion's model, via an exploration of the Quaker commitment to nonviolence and how its expressions might play out, primarily in the context of Dandelion's four-part nexus.

Quaker Nonviolence

Quaker nonviolence is a suitable candidate for exploring both further complexities in the dynamics demarcated by Dandelion, and potential future directions in the construction of Quaker identity for a number of reasons. Nonviolence has historically been used both to present Quakers as assimilatory, and as the basis for challenges towards societal norms. Quakerism's initial adoption of an *absolute* testimony against war in 1661 was motivated by a desire to reassure king Charles II of their harmlessness in the wake of uprisings by other religious radicals (Ceadel 2002:12; Dandelion 2019:3; Healey 2018:32). Conversely, the group's pacifism later informed one of British Quakerism's most prominent stances against both state policy and public opinion in its affirmation of a pacifist position during World War 1 (Dandelion 2019:89, 110). At times it has factored in motivating extremely radical actions, such as the self-immolations of the American Liberal Quakers Alice Herz and Norman Morrison in protest of the Vietnam War (Welsh 2008:48). In more recent years it can be seen in motivating the actions of Quakers Ellen Moxely and Sam Walton, who sabotaged a nuclear submarine in 1999 and a military plane in 2016, respectively (Dandelion 2019:92). These striking counter-cultural/counter-state actions seem to fill the requirements of cultivating 'distinctive appeal',[3] in the sense that they are not state sanctioned. The fact that the commitment to nonviolence may be framed as either a mark of harmlessness or distinction means its potential activity is worth examining in light of the more multifaceted, 'fluid' and 'turbulent' dynamics Dandelion invokes (2019:100–102).

Additionally, Quaker nonviolence is worth exploring because it is widely recognized, both internally and externally, as a key feature of the Quaker identity. This is noted in the opening sentence of *Quaker Faith and Practice*'s[4] chapter on the peace testimony,[5] which relates that it: 'is probably the best known and best loved of the Quaker testimonies' (1995:24.01). Similar acknowledgements, that in the wider culture Quakers are likely known for their pacifism above anything else, appear throughout the group's literature (Bishop and Jung 2018:174; Ceadel 2002:22; Dale *et al.* 1980:6). The awarding of the Nobel Peace Prize to the peacebuilding wings of the Quaker movement in 1947 also reflects and informs the prominent association of Quakers with peace held by wider society.

Quakers' engagement and association with peace-work also generates some popular appeal; attracting new adherents. Caroline Plüss has identified an interest in Quakerism's peace-work as one of four typical, primary motivations for new adherents joining the group (2007:268). This certainly applies to one of the participants of Francesca Montemaggi's more recent study on the spirituality of new Quakers, who relates that she became a Quaker after 'she realised that there were many Quakers in the peace and justice organisations she joined' (2018:13). This demonstrates a way Quakerism influences wider culture to its advantage: the relationship not being unidirectional.

Concerning internal Quaker dynamics, Montemaggi argues that Quaker social activism, particularly peace activism, is a major component of what is distinctive and defining about Quakerism:

> Prominent in Quakerism is the combination of contemplative practice . . . with activism in the public sphere. . . . Quaker activism . . . is not peripheral to Quaker experience; rather, it is a defining characteristic. The association of Quakers with peace, in particular, has a long-standing history and is still prevalent today.
>
> *(2018:21)*

She goes on to maintain that in valuing the testimonies and engaging in social activism 'Quakers show a high degree of uniformity in ethical-political identity'[6] (2018:31) and even that 'the ethical training' informed by a seemingly 'common basis of shared values, encapsulated in the testimonies' is 'perhaps *the most* defining characteristic of being a Quaker' (2018:25, emphasis mine). To an extent, this parallels Thomas Kennedy's claim that since the 1920s pacifism has been Liberal (British) Quakerism's defining ideal:

> Although not every Briton who claimed to be a Friend adhered absolutely to this fundamental basis, the world at large defines Quakerism chiefly in pacifist terms, and the Society of Friends in Britain could scarcely survive as a separate religious body if it were to disavow or seriously weaken its peace testimony.
>
> *(2001:413–414)*

Interestingly, Montemaggi's and Kennedy's invocations of wider perceptions of Quakerism are suggestive of a reflexivity, where Quakers start to see the peace testimony as more central because that accords with external cultural perceptions. The influences of wider culture are more varied than a simple drive towards secularism.

Significantly for internal matters, however, the emerging nontheistic elements within Liberal Quakerism often similarly declare a maintained esteem for the ethics and practices of the movement, including those around peace. The entry on nontheism in *The Cambridge Companion to Quakerism* entertains arguments that 'Liberal Quakerism should be mainly focused on practice and ethical concerns . . . [or that] Quakerism is a way of life based on ethics and peacemak-ing' (Randazzo 2018:275, 277). Additionally, the opening of *Godless for God's Sake* (a key book released by the nontheist movement) declares that 'the Society is defined by its values and "testimonies" rather than by dogma' (Boulton 2006:2).

Liberal Quakerism, therefore, apparently has a prominent distinctive characteristic with popular recognition and appeal for both potential adherents and the movement's disparate sub-groups. It appears tempting to posit that nonviolence presents alternative possibilities for the group's development to that of a simple assimilation to a wider secular culture. This hypothesis however, encounters a number of complications.

Uniformity

A key reason Dandelion dismisses nonviolence as a credible basis for sustaining a distinct Quaker identity is that, despite the peace testimony being presented as collectively adopted on an organizational level, the manner in which it is interpreted or adhered to on a popular level is not uniform, or reliably consistent with the organizational line (Dandelion 2019:90–91, 1996:121–122). This is supported by a 2013 survey which found that a significant minority of British Quakers did not identify as pacifists (Hampton 2014:29). Additionally, publications resulting from internal Quaker discussions around their "theological" divisions indicate that Liberal Quakers from various sub-alignments recognise that there is extensive variation in the way individual Quakers interpret the peace testimony, and that pacifism is not universal (Boulton 2016:60–61; Rowlands 2017:72). Quakers' own lack of consistent commitment to pacifism makes the claim, that it may be used a resource for constructing a sustainable and attractive sense of religiosity, suspect.

Such a dismissal may, however, be based on too crude a conception of how the commitment to nonviolence functions within the Liberal Quaker milieu. In his ethnographic research, Zachary Dutton found that amongst the group, 'nonviolence still influences subjects who do not explicitly call themselves pacifists' (2013:111). He argues that the Quaker history of nonviolence acts as a cultural resource for Liberal Quakers. He defines a cultural resource as 'a linguistically constituted notion used in turn to constitute existential meaning' (2013:96). He frames Liberal Quakerism as 'a collection of associated cultural resources' (2013:112) and claims that 'subjects use cultural resources understood as "loose" toolkits or "loose" frames' (2013:97). He notes how individuals will subjectively employ cultural resources to construct senses of 'social position' and accordingly 'existential meaning' and/or 'solidarity' (2013:99). Even though a subject's constructions may be idiosyncratic, common resources are employed and communal negotiation is necessary for establishing a credible social position. This need for a degree of communal negotiation potentially acts to limit the factious tendencies amongst Liberal Quakers. Dutton demonstrates that individuals with less commitment to one cultural resource, such as nonviolence, will compensate by emphasizing another, such as 'spirituality' or 'the Quaker community' (2013:105, 108–109, 110).

Considered in light of Dandelion's framework, Dutton's insights have significant implications for the role of nonviolence in Liberal Quakerism's future development. Whilst Dutton focuses on individuals subjectively negotiating their identity, I have previously suggested that the dynamics he outlines are now being played out on a more collective (quasi-organizational) level. In that, as Quakers increasingly recognize, engage and embrace their diversity of belief, *including* nontheistic elements, other cultural resources (notably nonviolence) are being increasingly deployed and emphasized within the broader internal discourse on Quaker identity (Yarlett 2020:235, 270–300).

Moreover, Dutton notes that Quakers also draw upon external cultural resources from wider society (2013:99). Given the strong public association of Quakerism with nonviolence, it again seems reasonable to propose that wider culture may influence Quakers on a popular level by buttressing nonviolence's position as a Quaker resource, incentivizing them to further associate with it. This resonates with how Kennedy refers to the wider world's definition of Quakerism in arguing for the fundamentality of the peace testimony despite the lack of universal adherence.

Within the fluid context Dandelion sets out, there is reason to believe that nonviolence may remain, and perhaps grow more, influential as a marker of Quaker identity despite the discrepancies in its varied implementations.

Distinctiveness and Religiosity

However, another major reason why a shift to nonviolence and peace-work may be discounted as a resource for Quakerism's positive future development is that such a move may be seen as entwined with internal secularisation. The move perceivably being liable to result in something so superficial and content-less that it will be unable to sustain distinctive appeal. Montemaggi does note that 'Quaker activism takes place within external organisations' (2018:22). Moreover, if Quaker activists view their Quakerism as 'atheological', they seemingly no longer have recourse to legitimate or motivate their politics by appealing to the sacred or the 'extra-rational' (Dandelion 2019:92; Smith 1996:9). Their social work/activism risks becoming indistinguishable from other secular popular forms, in line with internal secularisation. Indeed, elements of Quakerism have previously raised concerns that their peace-service bodies were drifting 'towards left-wing secularism' (Fager 1988; Healey 2018:35).

Such a possibility strongly mirrors historian Alec Ryrie's cautionary tale of the Student Christian Movement (SCM; 2016:5). Ryrie relates that in 1968, inspired by Martin Luther King, the civil rights movement, and Bonhoeffer's concept of 'religionless Christianity', the SCM leadership moved the group's primary purpose towards one of 'political struggle' and working 'to promote justice and world peace'. They began viewing 'Marxist Revolution' and 'the Kingdom of God' as synonymous, supported secular campaigns and adopted an 'openness policy', refusing to distinguish between Christians and non-Christians. Christian identity was curbed by the SCM in favour of radical politics. Their raison d'être became unclear, and by the following decade the membership of what was once Britain's principal Christian student organization had dropped by 90% (ibid.). Ryrie also characterizes the typical hesitancy of left-leaning religious groups to 'assert their religious identity' or 'put their faith at the centre of their politics' (due to a valuing of 'inclusion') as a 'self-sacrificial' 'systematic problem' (2016:5, 7). These considerations closely parallel Dandelion's picture of Liberal Quakerism's internal secularisation. The fact that they relate to religious groups that have explicitly shifted to a focus on peace, justice and politics seriously queries whether a similar shift can generate a distinct and/or effective response for Liberal Quakers.

The question is whether or not there is anything particular about Liberal Quakerism's relationship with nonviolence and social activism which would make them more robust and resilient identity markers than they were for groups like the SCM. One response is that, unlike the SCM, Quakerism's own associations with peace and social activism are historically and publically well established; for Quakers such a move is not *as clearly* as dramatic a shift motivated by external contemporary forces. Indeed, the Quaker activist Bayard Rustin was one of Martin Luther King's first advisors and a key influence on the adoption of nonviolent direct action by King and the civil rights movement (Carbado and Weise 2015:ix, xxii–xxiii). The American Friends Service Committee also encouraged King's nonviolent protests. The Committee organised for King to tour India, visiting locations associated with Mahatma Gandhi in 1959, and nominated King for the Nobel Peace Prize in 1963 (Bruce 2003:135–136). Quakers were generally very active in the civil rights movement, and there is an argument that Quaker values influenced the civil rights movement rather than vice versa.

Quaker theologian Ben Wood (2016) has suggested that whilst Quakers may disagree on theological matters (including the existence of God), they should ensure that they maintain a coherent identity by delving into their distinct historical narratives. He associates such particular stories with the movement's connection to peace and social witness as he relates:

> How do we know when we are speaking and acting coherently as Quakers? We know because our speech and consequent action are consistent with our story of 'peace', 'truth' and 'love'.

He also posts a photograph alongside the discussion, showing three figures holding a banner with the words 'Quakers oppose all war'.

However, even if historic-cultural resources (including popular opinion) allow Quakers to centralize ethical-political concerns in a manner that appears more authentic than the SCM, their religious authenticity may still come under scrutiny. In following this course of development, Quakers may still be said to be secularizing in the sense that they can no longer make definitive appeals to the divine or sacred when asserting their religiosity. History may not provide enough content; their religiosity may still ring hollow and unappealing.

Here, issues may be raised around what (actually) constitutes religiosity. Erin Wilson has cautioned scholars against viewing religion in 'fixed' and limited ways as 'what "religion" is and what it is perceived to be are the products of complex social, political, economic, cultural and historical dynamics' (2014:348). She contends that religion and politics are especially 'entangled', as both are 'concerned with casting a vision for what society should be' (2014:358). Nevertheless, following Jürgen Habermas, Wilson holds that religious language and symbology can powerfully communicate ethical-political messages in a way that secular efforts cannot (Wilson 2014:352–353; May et al. 2014:343). But is this distinct power exhausted if a religious group can no longer categorically appeal to the sacred? Does religion then become, not entwined with politics, but subsumed by it? Or, being that religions are products of complex forces, can alternative cultural resources, such as historical ones, be employed and potentially linked with others, such as ethical-political ones, to construct a distinct Quaker "religiosity"? This "Dutton-esque" account seems to be a reasonable way of understanding what Wood was attempting.

However, other internal attempts at constructing a reconciled sense of Quaker identity do (perceivably) attempt to consider what might be called "extra-rational" aspects of being Quaker. They, therefore, may be better candidates for considering the potential development of what might be publicly and tangibly perceived as a distinct and appealing Quaker religiosity (particularly in a Western/British context).[7] Significantly, these constructions also typically make substantial reference to ethics and nonviolence, thus they add credence to the contention that nonviolence could potentially play a key role in Quakerism's future development.

In her book *Testimony* (2015), Rachel Muers holds 'that Quaker approaches to theological ethics . . . are . . . distinctive . . . in their own right' (2015:3). She details that, related to Quakerism's initial focus on experiential religion, their method of theological ethics is not driven by linguistically codified, systematized beliefs but is practice led, whereby Quakers look to follow a process of 'knowing experimentally' (2015:1–4). She elaborates on this by delineating a typical structure for Quaker testimonies/testimony. Notably, she employs nonviolence as one of the clearest lenses for illuminating this structure (2015:21, 58, 68). Muers' claim is that Quaker testimonies are structured as 'double negatives', or denials of negatives; lies or destructiveness (2015:21). Nonviolence is a denial of the negative of violence (2015:58). Muers maintains these Quaker denials of negatives 'open up space for a "positive" future that they do not predict or control' (2015:21). She connects this willingness to be open to an uncertain positive, for the sake of denying a destructive negative, to eschatological[8] notions that this is the 'world-before-God'; awaiting God (2015:63). However, it is significant that Muers suggests that an openness and uncertainty operate around this eschatological endpoint (Yarlett 2020:143–146). Furthermore, Muers contends that a distinct contribution Quakers can make to political-ethical movements in wider society is this motivation to pursue a course despite the uncertainty of success. She explicitly frames this, not with reference to God-language but via a commitment to pursuing positives like 'truth' and 'love':

> The best reason for persisting in the face of a very limited chance of success is . . . not . . . 'We should just give it a try' or 'We can't just do nothing'. Nor . . . 'We must, in any case, live in accordance with the commands of God'. It is more like 'We must, in each case, live truthfully', or 'We must, in each case, do what love requires'.
>
> *(2015:190)*

This suggests that the ethical-orientation Muers demarcates can potentially make distinct and motivating, perhaps rhetorically "extra-rational", appeals without explicit recourse to the divine. The distinctiveness instead being derived from the method and structure of Quaker ethics, with close associations to their history of nonviolence. This might give one reason to think that Quakerism has the potential to be more creatively resilient than groups like the SCM.

Additionally, other Quakers have expressed comparable viewpoints to Muers, some of which overtly centralize the role of nonviolence. Liberal Quaker philosopher Laura Rediehs has similarly suggested that Quaker nonviolence can inform a distinctive Quaker approach to truth, which she associates closely with justice (2015:164170). She directly indicates that 'higher strivings' 'beyond mere survival' such as a desire to 'bring forth justice' are sufficient to be called 'spiritual' (or perhaps "extra-rational"; 2015:172). This claim of Rediehs' may be tied to the assimilatory secularisation outlined by Dandelion. However, Rediehs puts a limit on Quaker fluidity in that she holds that Quakers should maintain the practice of nonviolence as the only way to build and reveal truth and justice:

> The only path to true justice is the path of nonviolence . . . it is only the constraint of nonviolence that can ensure that the end be true justice, because the process of enacting nonviolence itself builds justice.
>
> *(2015:169)*

Through a commitment to nonviolence, Rediehs advocates that Quakers can enact in the world a 'dynamic kind of truth powered ultimately by love' (2015:168).

Another example comes from Hugh Rock. This example may be taken as particularly significant when considering the potential creative reconciliation of Quakerism's secular and non-secular elements, as Rock is directly associated with the Nontheist Friends Network (Boulton 2017). Nevertheless, his thoughts on the Quaker religion bear some striking resemblances to Muers'. He explicitly connects nonviolence with what he considers a basic principle of Quakerism:

> The principle of respect for the autonomy of others is the beginning of the architecture of the Quaker religion . . . absolute refusal to reciprocate violence, to the extent that one is prepared to be killed rather than retaliate, represents absolute respect for the autonomy of others.
>
> *(2014a:22–23)*

He also endeavours to outline a way that a sense of "extra-rational" religiosity can emerge out of the internal structure, and perhaps the powerful symbolism, of radical nonviolence. He argues that it is the likelihood that non-reciprocal nonviolence is impossible to fully enact in real life that gives it the 'energising' character of religiosity:

> It is impossible that human society could be organised on the basis of non-violence. . . . It only takes one person to destroy that basis. But it is right here in the tension between the visionary and the rational that we encounter the energising principle essential to religion. Non-violence is both a fabulous ideal . . . and . . . fabulously irrational.
>
> *(2014b:302)*

Notably, similar to Muers, Rock connects the striving for such a radical ideal with eschatological notions concerning the desire for a coming 'kingdom' or 'ideal society', which is uncontrollable, and likely un-accomplishable:

> Humans are immersed in a bipartite social structure consisting of a political and religious dimension, we . . . do not control it. Humans are condemned by the twin levels of human existence perpetually to work for an ideal society that will never be accomplished. The social reality of the kingdom is the contrast between the human nature that is and the human nature that can be imagined.
>
> *(2014b:395)*

He nonetheless maintains that this imagined ideal can and should motivate action.

Rock's "eschatological talk" and his connecting of nonviolence with a 'respect for the autonomy of others' also resonates with theologian Stanley Hauerwas' claim that the 'love that is characteristic of God's kingdom . . . is the nonviolent apprehension of the other as other' (1983:89). Hauerwas however, holds that such "nonviolent love" is only properly accomplishable in the community of 'forgiven people' (i.e., Christians) 'who have learned not to fear one another' (ibid.). Liberal Quakerism, in encountering its diversity, may be understood to have provoked in itself questions of how far this 'nonviolent apprehension of the other' can be pushed? Does not apprehending 'the other as other' precisely include a hospitable stance to those with contradictory views? Can Quakers become a group 'who have learned not to fear each other' based on this principle of "nonviolent love" itself? Again similar to Rock, the popular Quaker writings of Harvey Gillman (2012, 2014, 2018) push at such boundaries and grapple with the resultant tensions; at points placing such openness as constitutive of a Quaker spirituality and a potential solution to the group's fractiousness:

> The fear . . . of being without boundaries may lead us backwards to a time . . . when we were not confronted by otherness. This is the root of fundamentalism, which is

the theology of exclusion. The form of spirituality which speaks to my condition is one of hospitality.

(2012:33)

As indicated by Hauerwas' and Rock's formulations such an understanding of spirituality as involving an openness towards otherness can easily synergize with ideals of nonviolence.[9]

One might question the strength of these attempts to construct reconciled accounts of a distinctive and "authentically religious" Liberal Quaker identity. They may be framed as per-mutations of secularisation, signified by their hesitancy around the use of unequivocal religious language (Dandelion 2019:143–147; Bruce 2011:112–119, 2006). However, the manner in which these accounts draw upon nonviolence and the powerful symbolism its practice enacts (concerning a resoluteness to principles and ideals) may give one pause about easily categorizing such a manoeuvre as benign or assimilatory. Furthermore, the power and effectiveness of this symbolism may again be strengthened by wider cultural associations that already exist between Quakers and nonviolence.

Indeed, both the symbolic power of nonviolence and overall popular familiarity with Quak-erism's historical connection to nonviolence, may be considered factors in why it features in a number of the internal attempts to demarcate a common and distinctive sense of Liberal Quaker identity (Wood's, Montemaggi's and Kennedy's included). They are additional (and external) forces that enhance nonviolence as a prominent and appealing resource within the internal Quaker culture. Quaker interpretations of their religion may be varied and disparate. How-ever, due in part to the dynamics Dandelion outlines, nonviolence has the potential to emerge as a fulcrum around which these interpretations can revolve, even if complete coalescence is unlikely. It may thereby afford Quakers some sense of distinctiveness and hence resilience to assimilatory secularisation.

Harmlessness, Culture Wars, Strategy and Soft Power

Contrariwise to the concerns that nonviolence may not provide a distinctive enough basis for a Quaker identity, a shift to an emphasis on ethical-political positions and radical nonviolence may risk damaging Quakerism's perception as benign and equivalently harmless to state-sanctioned religious expression. The contravening of social norms via nonviolent action, for example, may be disincentivized because it risks less goodwill from civil authorities.

It may seem unusual to suggest that in highly developed democratic countries like the United Kingdom or the United States (where most Liberal Quakers are based) that state pres-sure could be a major concern (Smith 1996:21–22). However, it is notable that in January 2020 a number of nonviolent and 'Left-Wing and Associated Single Issue Groups' appeared on the 'UK's counter-terror watch list' and documents distributed to anti-terrorism police (Dodd and Grierson 2020; Drake and Wood 2020; Martin 2020; Ullah 2020). A number of these groups are ones with which Quakers are often involved (Montemaggi 2018:22–23). This intimated clampdown appears to only pressure the Quakers by proxy; however, it is pertinent to consider in light of possible ramifications concerning the group's future development.

This future development must be placed in the wider context of the polarization and culture wars that have intensified in Western society over the past decade (Koch 2017; McCrudden 2015). Wider society, like Quakerism, is also open to 'fluidity', 'turbulence' and change. The polarization also speaks to a weakness in Dandelion's model in the sense that wider culture (much like Quaker popular culture) is not homogenous. As the phrase "culture wars" implies, this period may be taken as one of intense negotiation of societal norms, carried out primarily via wider cultural and softer forms of power, and involving various subgroups within the wider culture.

Within such a polarized context, public perceptions of what is "mainstream" and what is "counter-culture" also become further complicated. Representatives of both "sides" of the cultural divide are able to position themselves as either representing the mainstream, in relation to their in-group's perceived cultural prominence, or as counter-cultural, in relation to the out-group's perceived cultural prominence. The potential for this blurring of the lines between "mainstream" and "counter-cultural" has been exacerbated by social media with its propensity to develop echo chambers (Yardi and Boyd 2010). This all further complicates the dynamics of how groups in society may present themselves as having distinctive popular appeal. Groups may increasingly position themselves as making bold claims not only in opposition to that which is state-sanctioned but also other perceived power bases within the cultural sphere.

Nevertheless, the upsurge in more "populist" politics concurrent with this cultural conflict does in some ways reflect the relationship between institutional and/or state actors and the wider culture, as outlined within Dandelion's model. Indeed, the political scientist Elizabeth Oldmixon has made the point that 'latent cultural factions can be ginned up by elites, activists and extremists', going as far to say that 'cultural conflict . . . really is a style of argumentation that mobilizes latent cultural differences for strategic or ideological reasons' (2005:13). Thus she highlights the possibility that, whilst the negotiations of societal norms may take place within the cultural sphere, the impetus for the conflict may come from more organized or institutional bodies, including the state. However, Oldmixon also underscores that

> what matters is that when cultural groups are mobilized, they apply countervailing pressures on political institutions to enact policies that are consistent with their vision of society.
>
> *(ibid.)*

This brings Oldmixon's view of cultural conflict closer to the dynamics set out by Dandelion regarding the relationship between wider popular culture and institutional bodies being complex, fluid and multilateral. Indeed, one can be ambivalent about the initial direction of causality, but it is true that institutional state actors have engaged in the current cultural conflict, as indicated by the aforementioned intimated clampdown. Furthermore, whilst the turbulence of a culture war may shake up and blur public perceptions of power bases and distinctive appeal, this does not necessarily mean that all cultural groups are equal when it comes to the question of being state sanctioned. Some groups may in fact become more liable to experience pressured from both the state and oppositional elements within the wider culture. Suffice to say, in the current climate of cultural conflict the impetus to conform and present as harmless in relation to state-sanctioned religious (or political) expression still very much exists in countries like the United Kingdom and the United States. Indeed, the question of how a group balances presenting itself as distinctive and harmless to the ideal degree is in some ways more complex during such a period of polarization. Moreover, the potential to be pressured by the state is still a concern for individuals and groups who are at least connected with Quakers.

However, here it should be noted that Quakers also have the potential to be strategic (as both institutional and cultural actors) within this culture war. Given the dynamics set out by Dandelion, both the state and Quakers have the potential to influence and be influenced by cultural negotiations, especially in the context of a polarized culture. Essentially, the elements of Dandelion's model under consideration here are expressed in Figure 57.3.

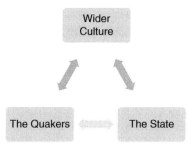

Figure 57.3   Wider culture's wider influence network

This set of relationships are essential to consider for potential caveats to the trajectory empha-sized in Figure 57.2; however, they become particularly significant when there is societal volatil-ity. It is my contention that the strategic possibilities open to Quakerism within this polarized context further incentivize the movement to emphasize its public and historic associations with nonviolence in order to maintain its presentation of both harmlessness and distinctiveness, alongside accruing popular appeal.

This notion of Quakerism acting strategically can be illuminated by considering Jeremy Car-rette's work on Quakers at the UN (2013). Carrette advocates that in their engagement with the UN, Quakers face a paradox, which has structural similarities to the conundrum outlined by Dandelion. Carrette describes this paradox as

> the paradox of all-powerful institutions allowing greater representation or what I will call the paradox of hegemony and plurality . . . [the] paradox of inclusion and the centralized systems that structure the inclusion.
>
> *(2013:46, 52)*

Carrette holds that as centralized political institutions expand to include a greater plurality of civil, non-governmental groups within their system, the price is that the groups – both religious and secular – are pressured towards 'a tendency to nondifferentiation', as they become equiva-lent parts of a whole with a dominant centre (2013:49). This strikes me as basically the same type of dynamic as Dandelion is concerned with when he discusses the state pressure on diverse religious groups to present as equivalently harmless. The key difference being that Dandelion is discussing the centralized power of the state rather than that of a global political institution like the UN. Notably, Carrette argues that such a dynamic causes religious groups to respond by being strategic.

> Part of this inclusion rests on the ability of groups, including religious groups, to be strategic; and in this sense we are witnessing a new phenomenon in the study of reli-gion: *religion as a strategic category inside the paradox of global politics.*
>
> *(2013:52)*

Carrette understands 'religion as a strategic category' in reference to a Foucauldian understand-ing of 'strategic power' (ibid.). That is power that is 'never completely stable' and 'exercised from innumerable points'; some of which are outside of the institutional power of a judiciary or sovereign state (Foucault cited in Carrette 2013:52). Again this has resonances with Dandelion and his picture of 'fluid', 'turbulent', multilateral social dynamics, involving interplays between institutional bodies and popular culture. However, in drawing attention to the concept of 'religion as . . . strategic' and the notion that there are 'innumerable points' from which strategic power can be drawn, Carrette's work raises questions concerning how easy it is to say Quakers are heading towards 'extreme assimilation'. Furthermore, in examining how Quakers strategically negotiate their position in the UN Carrette does seem to look to softer historic cultural sources of power: 'Quakers . . . still hold a unique historical reputation as a valuable currency within the system of exchanges' (2013:50). Carrette's focus is on considering how Quakers attempt to coherently work within the dynamics of the UN. However, the concept of unstable and multifaceted strategic power seems even more relevant and significant in the context of a polarized culture, along with the question of how Quakers may employ softer forms of strategic power within that context.

The obvious point to make concerning Liberal Quakers potentially leveraging soft power to abate state pressure is that wider cultural perceptions of Quakers as harmless and nonviolent elevate the group's legitimacy (Smith 1996:20–21). It is thereby more difficult for state authorities to convincingly portray and treat Quakers as societal deviants, affording them some privilege in civic and political domains. Sociologist Steve Bruce has made the point that while 'the FBI tried to prove that Martin Luther King was a communist . . . [they] would have found a more receptive audience for such demonization if . . . King had been a secular trade unionist' rather than a nonviolent Baptist minister (2003:13). The political landscape Liberal Quakers now inhabit is different from 1960s America, but the point still stands that their institution's reputation within the wider culture may act to insulate them from some forms of state pressure.

However, if the wider culture is particularly turbulent and polarized in its political-ethical leanings, one may question whether this privileged position is likely to be sustained by such soft power. Moreover, one may question whether Quakerism's association with nonviolence affords it anymore privilege than other nonviolent secular groups; media responses were generally critical of nonviolent groups' inclusion on the counter-terror watch list (Dodd and Grierson 2020; Drake and Wood 2020; Martin 2020; Ullah 2020).

Here again it is worth considering the implications of Quakerism's associations with nonviolence being historically well established. Indeed, controversial Quaker decisions made in the public domain often include references to their history of ethical-political stances and peace-work. Quakers in Britain's statement on their decision not to invest 'in companies profiting from the occupation of Palestine' is prefaced with the claim that the decision

> fits into a long Quaker history of pursuing ethical investments. It follows decisions not to invest funds in, among others, the fossil fuel industry, arms companies, Apartheid South Africa, and – going even further back – the transatlantic slave trade.
>
> *(Quakers in Britain 2018)*

The statement itself begins by referencing Quakers' 'long history of working for a just peace' before going on to note that 'We know this decision will be hard for some to hear' (ibid.). It seems Quakers do deploy their longstanding historical reputation concerning ethical peace activism, as a resource for offsetting potential public scorn. It is also notable that Ellen Moxley and Sam Walton were both acquitted of criminal charges; being associated with Quakerism may offer one some protection in judicial courts as well as the court of public opinion. Historical factors and the longevity of Quakers' 'accumulated' cultural associations may afford them a more resilient legitimacy in their presentation of not only distinctiveness but also harmlessness (Parc and Moon 2019).

This remnant legitimacy may, in turn, make Quakerism more attractive to potential adherents who, within a polarized society, are able to view it as both appropriately nonconformist, and offering a strategic or tactical way to maintain some civic legitimacy. Indeed, having both historical and NGO structures, alongside being sensitive to popular dynamics, may make Quakerism ideally placed to harbour elements of the wider culture who may experience both cultural and state pressure in a polarized social context.

Questions might arise concerning the extent to which adherents with such motivations ultimately lead to a type of internal secularisation, with Quakerism (primarily) becoming a political advocacy group; this would return one to the issues considered in the previous section. However, it is significant that within a more polarized society the dynamics and trajectory of Liberal Quakerism, in light of Dandelion's own model, become further complicated. It is not clear what would count as assimilation to a secular culture when that culture is itself divided. Indeed, within this context, Quakerism's association with nonviolent and social activism may become more attractive for its ability to present as both distinctive and harmless. This may further explain and incentivize interest in nonviolence as a resource for future Quaker religiosity. Whether its potential to be used as such will be creatively fulfilled remains to be seen.

Conclusion

This chapter has explored Quaker nonviolence as a potential resource for future developments in the construction of Liberal Quaker identity/religiosity in light of Dandelion's theory of internal secularisation alongside his four-part framework that he developed between both the organizational and popular forms of both the Quaker religion and wider society.

Dandelion's internal secularisation theory focuses on the trajectory of wider culture influencing Quakers on a popular level. Subsequently, this then impacts upon the religion's organizational form, feeding into an assimilation towards secularity. However, this chapter has argued that the four-part framework he delineates suggests far more complex dynamics within, and via which, the Quaker identity is negotiated. Accordingly, the chapter considered Quaker nonviolence as a potential marker of identity/religiosity. Nonviolence was taken as a suitable candidate as the wider cultural association between Quakerism and nonviolence is well established, and nonviolence can lend itself to Quakers presenting themselves as harmless citizens to better accrue favour from a secular state, or as distinctive and/or counter-cultural to better accrue popular appeal.

The chapter considered caveats to nonviolence taking such a role, questions around whether Quakers approach nonviolence with any kind of uniformity and whether Quaker nonviolence was actually distinctive or harmless in the relevant ways. The chapter argued that under Dandelion's model what matters is strategic presentation, and that the established nature of the historical and wider cultural association may allow Quakers to both sustain these presentations whilst being publically perceived as authentic, a dynamic that may also offer some protection from state pressure in the form of soft (and/or strategic) power. Concurrently, the wider cultural perceptions may reflexively encourage Quakers to draw upon nonviolence as a marker of their identity, particularly as other aspects of Quaker identity become weaker.

The chapter has additionally contemplated a number of ways Quaker commentators may be seen to employ nonviolence in their attempts to speak to a sense of the extra-rational in Quaker religiosity whilst also reconciling with Quakerism's internal secular elements. The suggestion was reiterated that wider cultural influences may play a role in promoting the use of nonviolence in these reconciliatory accounts, encouraging its role as a potential fulcrum.

The final section also reflected upon how wider culture itself is not static or homogenous, and how societal polarization complicates Dandelion's nexus yet further. The chapter considered how such polarization may jeopardize the soft protection public perceptions may offer Quakerism from state pressure. However alternatively, given the long-established nature of Quakerism's association with nonviolence, the religion may have more protection from state pressure than similarly ethico-politically aligned secular groups. This in turn may offer Quakerism another route to accruing popular appeal within a polarized social context.

In any case, overall, the conclusion that Quakers are heading towards an endpoint of extreme assimilation towards secular society may be premature.

Notes

1 An umbrella term which relates the diverse subgroup of Quakers who explicitly identify as not having a belief in a deity. The group includes atheists, agnostics, those who believe in a mystical experience but have an aversion to theistic language, and those who more radically question the mystical basis of the Quaker religious experience. I explore further the internal dynamics of nontheism and the Quaker nontheism-theism debate in Chapter 33 in this volume.
2 Here Dandelion draws upon insights from the work of Charles Taylor (2007) and José Casanova (2010), which I discuss further in Chapter 33 in this volume.
3 Here critics may raise the point that Sam Walton was accompanied in his action by a Methodist minister (Daniel Woodhouse) and Ellen Moxley by two non-Quaker peace activists (Angela Zelter and Bodil Ulla Roder), which queries the extent to which such peace-work really is distinctive for Quakers. In response to this I would make two points: (1) There are different forms and degrees of distinctiveness, as indicated in the main text, such acts of nonviolent direct action are at least distinctive to the degree that they are not falling in line with that which is state-sanctioned. (2) Even if there are other religious groups are equally (if not more) committed to enacting nonviolence, in the public imagination, for the most part, nonviolence is still a notable and particular Quaker trait, and regarding questions of popular appeal public perceptions are instrumental.
4 The latest and current iteration of the Quaker Book of Discipline, 'the closest thing Quakers in Britain have to an authoritative text', which is 'revised . . . approximately once in each generation'. Grant, *Wittgensteinian Investigations*, pp. 28–29.
5 Quaker 'Testimonies are adopted collectively' and relate to values and 'that which the group has to say on . . . [certain issues] the importance of which goes beyond individual concern' (Dandelion 1996:121). They also typically relate to how Quakers engage with the wider world. British Quakerism currently recognises testimonies to peace, equality and justice; truth and integrity; and simplicity and sustainability (Quakers in Britain n.d.).
6 Typically left-leaning. Montemaggi, *The Changing Face of Britain*, p. 23.
7 Albeit ones where the manner of appeal to the "extra-rational" may break down the boundaries between theism and atheism, and between the sacred and the profane.
8 The term *eschatology* refers to a branch of "theology" that is concerned with the end times, the final destiny of the world, and, in traditional terms, the coming (and nature) of God's kingdom.
9 I have previously made comparisons between these developments in Quaker thought and ones seen in that of deconstructionist Jacques Derrida (primarily via his engagement with Emmanuel Levinas). Derrida employs the call of a radical openness towards the other in attempts both to break down the distinction between theism and atheism and to defend the deconstructive proliferation of meaning from accusations of 'nihilism'. See Derrida, *The Gift of Death*, p. 84; Kearney, *Debates in Continental Philosophy*, pp. 154–155; and Sherwood and Hart, *Derrida and Religion*. I intimated that as Liberal Quakers encountered analogous challenges, it seemed they were (mostly unknowingly) developing parallel lines of response. Yarlett, *The Accommodation of Diversity*. This is relevant to questions around the potential role of non-violence in the future construction of Liberal Quakerism's religiosity/identity. However, the demands of brevity (long footnote notwithstanding) prevent a deeper examination. Additionally, this chapter has primarily framed its examination of Quaker developments in the context of Dandelion's four-part nexus, which better facilitates an understanding of Quaker developments with a consideration for the group's relational dynamics with external societal elements. My other chapter in this volume

(Chapter 33) focuses more on internal Quaker dynamics, with the later sections touching on similar themes to this footnote, albeit approached from a different angle. It may therefore, be particularly edifying if the two chapters were read in tandem.

References

Bishop, E. and Jung, J. (2018). 'Seeking Peace: Quakers Respond to War'. In Angell, S. W. and Dandelion, P. (eds), *The Cambridge Companion to Quakerism*. Cambridge: Cambridge University Press, 106–128.

Boulton, D. (2016). *Through a Glass Darkly: A Defence of Quaker Nontheism*. Dent, Cumbria: Dales Historical Monographs.

Boulton, D. (2017). 'Regional Conference in Bristol' [online]. *Non-theist Friends Network*. 9 November [Viewed April 5 2020]. Available from: https://nontheist-quakers.org.uk/2017/11/09/383/

Boulton, D. (ed) (2006). *Godless for God's Sake: Nontheism in Contemporary Quakerism*. Dent, Cumbria: Dales Historical Monographs.

Bruce, S. (2003). *Politics & Religion*. Cambridge: Cambridge University Press.

Bruce, S. (2006). 'Secularization and the Impotence of Individualized Religion'. *Hedgehog Review*. Spring and Summer, 35–45.

Bruce, S. (2011). *Secularization: In Defence of an Unfashionable Theory*. 1st edition. Oxford: Oxford University Press.

Carbado, D. W. and Weise, D. (eds) (2015). *Time on Two Crosses: The Collected Writings of Bayard Rustin*. 2nd ed. New York, NY: Cleis Press. [2003]

Carrette, J. R. (2013). 'The Paradox of Globalization: Quakers, Religious NGOs and the United Nations'. In Hefner, R., Hutchinson, J., Mels, S. and Timmerman, C. (eds), *Religions in Movement: The Local and the Global in Contemporary Faith Traditions*. London: Routledge.

Casanova, J. (2010). 'A Secular Age: Dawn or Twilight?'. In Warner, M., Vanantwerpen, J. and Calhoun, C. (eds), *Varieties of Secularism in a Secular Age*. Cambridge, MA: Harvard University Press, 265–281.

Ceadel, M. (2002). 'The Quaker Peace Testimony and its Contribution to the British Peace Movement: An Overview'. *Quaker Studies*. **7**(1), 9–29.

Dale, R., McCarthy, J., Moorhouse, F. and South, A. (1980). *Quaker Peace Testimony Today: Some Present Day Interpretations*. 2nd edition. Leeds: Northern Friends Peace Board.

Dandelion, P. (1996). *A Sociological Analysis of the Theology of Quakers: The Silent Revolution*. Lampeter: Edwin Mellen Press.

Dandelion, P. (2019). *The Cultivation of Conformity: Towards a General Theory of Internal Secularisation*. Oxford and New York, NY: Routledge.

Derrida, J. (2008). *The Gift of Death*. 2nd revised edition. Chicago, IL: University of Chicago Press. [1999].

Dodd, V. and Grierson, J. (2020). 'Greenpeace Included with Neo-Nazis on UK Counter-terror List'. *The Guardian* [online]. 17 January [Viewed 5 April 2020]. Available from: https://www.theguardian.com/uk-news/2020/jan/17/greenpeace-included-with-neo-nazis-on-uk-counter-terror-list

Drake, M. and Wood, V. (2020). 'Cycling advocacy group listed alongside extremist groups on counter-terror watch list'. *Independent* [online]. 25 January [Viewed 5 April 2020]. Available from: https://www.independent.co.uk/news/uk/home-news/critical-mass-cycling-group-terror-watch-list-home-office-a9301516.html

Dutton, Z. (2013). 'The Meaning of Nonviolence: Exploring Nonviolence as a Cultural Resource for Liberal Quaker Subjects'. *Quaker Studies*. **18**(1), 96–114.

Fager, C. (1988). *Quaker Service at a Crossroads: American Friends, the American Friends Service Committee and Peace and Revolution*. Falls Church, VA: Kimo Press.

Gillman, H. (2012). 'Wrestling with the Stranger: Dilemmas of the Spiritual Life'. *Friends Quarterly*. (2), 29–40.

Gillman, H. (2014). 'Everyday Mysticism'. *Friends Quarterly*. (4), 28–39.

Gillman, H. (2018). 'Why Should the Religious Society of Friends Have a Future?'. Presentation presented at The Nontheist Friends Network Annual Conference. 10 March [Viewed 5 May 2020]. Transcript available from: https://nontheist-quakers.org.uk/2018/04/01/2018-conference-reports/

Grant, R. (2014). *Wittgensteinian Investigations of Contemporary Quaker Religious Language*. PhD thesis. University of Leeds.

Hampton, J. (2014). 'British Quaker Survey: Examining Religious Belief and Practices in the Twenty-first Century'. *Quaker Studies*. **19**(1), 7–136.

Hauerwas, S. (2011). *The Peaceable Kingdom: A Primer in Christian Ethics*. Notre Dame, IN: of Notre Dame University Press, 1983.

Healey, R. R. (2018). 'Diversity and Complexity in Quaker History'. In Daniels, C. W., Healey, R. R. and Kershner, J. (eds), *Quaker Studies: An Overview – The Current State of the Field*. Leiden: Brill, 13–50.

Kearney, R. (2004). *Debates in Continental Philosophy: Conversations with Contemporary Thinkers*. New York, NY: Fordham University Press [1985].

Kennedy, T. C. (2001). *British Quakerism 1860–1920: The Transformation of a Religious Community*. Oxford: Oxford University Press.

Koch, I. (2017). 'What's in a Vote? Brexit beyond Culture Wars'. *American Ethnologist*. **44**(2), 225–230.

Martin, G. (2020). 'Peace Groups and NGOs on Anti-terror List'. *Third Force News* [online]. 24 January [Viewed 5 April 2020]. Available from: https://thirdforcenews.org.uk/tfn-news/peace-groups-and-ngos-on-anti-terror-list

May, S., Wilson, E. K., Baumgart-Ochse, C. and Sheikh, F. (2014). 'The Religious as Political and the Political as Religious: Globalisation, Post-Secularism and the Shifting Boundaries of the Sacred'. *Politics, Religion & Ideology*. **15**(3), 331–346.

McCrudden, C. (2015). 'Transnational Culture Wars'. *International Journal of Constitutional Law*. **13**(2), 434–462.

Montemaggi, F. E. S. (2018). *The Changing Face of Britain: How Should Quakers Respond? Part 2: The Spirituality of New Quakers*. London: Quaker Committee on Christian and Interfaith Relations.

Muers, R. (2015). *Testimony: Quakerism and Theological Ethics*. London: SCM Press.

Oldmixon, E. A. (2005). *Uncompromising Positions: God, Sex, and the U.S. House of Representatives*. Washington, DC: Georgetown University Press.

Parc, J. and Moon, H-C. (2019). 'Accumulated and Accumulable Cultures: The Case of Public and Private Initiatives toward K-Pop'. *Kritika Kultura*. **32**, 429–452.

Pennington, M. (2020). 'The Cultivation of Conformity Review' [online]. *Theos Think Tank*. 24 February [Viewed 5 April 2020]. Available from: https://www.theosthinktank.co.uk/comment/2020/02/18/the-cultivation-of-conformity

Plüss, C. (2007). 'Analysing Non-doctrinal Socialization: Re-assessing the Role of Cognition to Account for Social Cohesion in the Religious Society of Friends'. *British Journal of Sociology*. **58**(2), 253–278.

Quaker Faith and Practice: The Book of Christian Discipline. (1995). London: The Yearly Meeting of the Religious Society of Friends (Quakers) in Britain.

Quakers in Britain (2018). 'Quakers Will Not Profit from the Occupation of Palestine' [online]. *Quakers in Britain*. 19 November [Viewed 5 April 2020]. Available from: https://www.quaker.org.uk/news-and-events/news/quakers-will-not-profit-from-the-occupation-of-palestine

Quakers in Britain (n.d.). 'Our Values' [online]. *Quakers in Britain*. n.d. [Viewed 31 May 2020]. Available from: https://www.quaker.org.uk/about-quakers/our-values

Randazzo, D. C. (2018). 'Quakers and Non-theism'. In Angell, S. W. and Dandelion, P. (eds), *The Cambridge Companion to Quakerism*. Cambridge: Cambridge University Press, 274–289.

Rediehs, L. (2015). 'Truth and Nonviolence: Living Experimentally in Relation to the Truth'. In Dudiak, J. (ed), *Befriending Truth: Quaker Perspectives*. Quakers and the Disciplines (2). No location given: Friends Association for Higher Education, 164–181.

Rock, H. (2014a). 'Do Quakers Possess a Theology?'. *Friends Quarterly*. (2), 17–27.

Rock, H. (2014b). *God Needs Salvation: A New Vision of God for the Twenty First Century*. No location given: Christian Alternative.

Rowlands, H. (ed) (2017). *God, Words and Us: Quakers in Conversation about Religious Difference*. No location given: Quaker Books.

Ryrie, A. (2016). 'What Would Jesus Do? Christian Culture Wars in The Modern West'. Lecture presented at Gresham College. 14 April [Viewed 5 April 2020]. Transcript available from: https://www.gresham.ac.uk/lecture/transcript/download/what-would-jesus-do-christian-culture-wars-in-the-modern-west/

Sherwood, Y. and Hart, K. (eds) (2004). *Derrida and Religion: Other Testaments*. London and New York, NY: Routledge.

Smith, C. (1996). 'Correcting a Curious Neglect, or Bringing Religion Back In'. In Smith, C. (ed), *Disruptive Religion: The Force of Faith in Social Movement Activism*. London and New York, NY: Routledge.

Taylor, C. (2007). *A Secular Age*. Cambridge, MA: Harvard University Press.

Ullah, A. (2020). '"We Are Not Neo-Nazis": Anti-arms Group Placed on UK's Counter-terror Watch List'. *Middle East Eye* [online]. 17 January [Viewed 5 April 2020]. Available from: https://www.middleeasteye.net/news/we-are-not-neo-nazis-why-anti-arms-group-uks-extremism-watch-list

Welsh, A. M. with Holiday, J. (2008). *Held in the Light: Norman Morrison's Sacrifice for Peace and His Family's Journey of Healing.* Maryknoll, NY: Orbis.

Wilson, E. K. (2014). 'Theorizing Religion as Politics in Postsecular International Relations'. *Politics, Religion & Ideology.* **15**(3), 347–365.

Wood, B. (2016). 'Boulton, Lindbeck and Rorty: Imagining Quakerism without Metaphysics (part 2)' [online]. *Armchair Theologian.* 30 May [Viewed 5 April 2020]. Available from: https://summeroflove85.wordpress.com/2016/05/30/boulton-lindbeck-and-rorty-imagining-a-quakerism-without-metaphysics-part-2/

Yardi, S. and Boyd, D. (2010). 'Dynamic Debates: An Analysis of Group Polarization over Time on Twitter'. *Bulletin of Science, Technology and Society.* **30**(5), 316–327.

Yarlett, S. D. (2020). *The Accommodation of Diversity: Liberal Quakerism and Nontheism.* PhD thesis. University of Birmingham.

58

BRITISH QUAKERS AND THE BOER WAR 1899–1902

Penelope Cummins

Some 440,000 British soldiers, the biggest British military force ever until the First World War, were imported to southern Africa to take part in the Second Boer War of 1899–1902.[1] They fought against a local militia of barely 35,000, supported by about 10,000 international volunteers from Ireland, France and elsewhere.[2] Thanks to the British scorched-earth policy and 'endemic' looting by British soldiers,[3] women and children were forced off their farms, having lost their farmhouses and also their livestock. Between June 1901 and May 1902, some 116,500 Boer (Afrikaans) women and children were confined to concentration camps, where conditions were so poor that almost a quarter of the prisoners died, including some 22,000 children under 16.[4] More than 115,700 African people were similarly confined, in different camps, under even worse conditions.[5]

The Quaker decision to contest the war, the causes of war and its outcomes was neither simple nor easy. In the years leading up to the war, British Friends, like the rest of British society, had been exposed to the rhetoric of the government and also of the Cape government, the prime minister of which was Cecil Rhodes, the head of the British South Africa Company, whose expansionist ambition – possibly even in the absence of gold and diamonds – was to extend his company's remit (and that of the British Empire) from the Cape to Cairo. Rhodes had sponsored the Jameson Raid in 1895, an attempted coup, which had prompted the Transvaal government to arm itself in expectation of war.

It is easy enough nowadays to identify the Second Boer War (1899–1902) in Southern Africa as one in which the forces of British imperialism and capitalism were deployed against the farming communities of the two Boer republics near the tip of Africa, the Transvaal and the Orange Free State, where gold and diamonds happened to have been found. The whole situation was, of course, clouded by the fact that both Boers and British were incomers, and their very presence – and also their attitudes to land tenure and to the availability of potential labour – dispossessed the local African population.

But in the 1890s, when London Yearly Meeting came to this perception, it was utterly at variance from the national mood. The Society of Friends allied itself on the part of the Boer republics, not because they thought them particularly admirable but because they perceived British policies and actions to be aggressive, greedy and unjust. British Friends aligned themselves with groups such as the Women's Peace and Arbitration Society and the Anti-Slavery Society, both of which had Quakers among their members.

DOI: 10.4324/9780429030925-62

At the time, in Britain, the war was depicted as a struggle for justice; the mine owners and their associates were required by the Transvaal Republic to pay taxes, but unless they were citizens they might not vote.[6] One of the slogans of the war was 'no taxation without representation'.[7] There were, of course, individual Friends who took the popular view of the conflict; and there were some, such as Thomas Hodgkin, who explained in a letter to the *Friend*[8] that he found it impossible to support the Boer cause due to their history of slaveholding and of their displacement of the local African population. (Subsequent correspondents pointed out that the British colonists were no more innocent than the Boers in these respects.)[9]

British Friends were exercised by the bellicose attitude of the British imperialists and their unwillingness to seek a negotiated solution to its differences with the Boer republics. The Quaker journal, the *Friend,* covered events in some detail, with many articles and thirteen editorials between June 1899 and the start of the war in October.[10]

In September 1899 both sides were mobilising in preparation for war, and the governor of the Cape Colony, Lord Milner, was publicly making inflammatory demands for concessions by the Transvaal Republic. A British Quaker, Guy Arthur Enock, a mechanical engineer working in Pretoria, felt moved to approach President Kruger 'as one who also loved the Lord', with a list of proposals which might lead to an honourable settlement.[11] With the concurrence of the Boers, the clerk of London Yearly Meeting communicated with the prime minister, Lord Salisbury, with a view to achieving an arbitrated settlement, which the British government chose not to pursue.

Some Friends, such as John Stephenson Rowntree, were active in the South African Conciliation Committee, set up in early 1900 by individuals such as Lloyd George and C. P. Scott of the *Manchester Guardian,* who had reservations about the British stance. Individual Friends helped arrange public meetings and lobbying of MPs. This was not always harmonious; Josiah Rowntree and other members of his family had their homes attacked by a mob when they hosted a South African speaker, Samuel Cronwright-Schreiner, husband of the author Olive Schreiner.[12]

In December 1899, Friends had set up their own committee to discern whether they should re-establish a 'War Victims Relief Committee', which had been active in the Crimean war; they dithered for a year, by which time other, effective, channels for relief had been set up for the people in the camps, though their efforts were appreciated later, in the post-war reconstruction.[13]

While, at the beginning of the conflict, the Society of Friends was opposed to war on principle, many individual Quakers were sympathetic to the British cause. John Bellows, for instance, had been active in Quaker peace-work since the 1860s: he had taken part in relief work during the Franco-Prussian War; he was a Quaker delegate to the Peace Conference at The Hague in 1899; he was a friend of Tolstoy; and he was an advocate for the Dukhobors, who were persecuted in Russia for their faith. He had negotiated with the Swedish government on behalf of Norwegian conscientious objectors. But when it came to the Boer War, Bellows was vituperative about President Paul Kruger of the Transvaal, and he published a booklet suggesting that while war was abhorrent, for this war, the British had no alternative.[14] This support from a well-known Quaker was, of course, welcomed by the press and other advocates of the war.

By the time of the 1900 Yearly Meeting, seven months after the conflict began, many Friends had found themselves caught up in patriotic fervour; some had even joined their neighbours in creating triumphant window displays to celebrate the lifting of the siege of Mafikeng in May 1900. A Quaker chocolate manufacturer, George Cadbury, was so exasperated by the jingoistic coverage of the war by most of the press that he was persuaded by a Liberal MP, Lloyd George, to buy the *Daily News* to dilute the national message of war fervour.[15]

Elizabeth Isichei finds that Boer war 'laid bare the potential divisions among Friends on the peace issue';[16] and the deliberations at the 1900 and the 1901 Yearly Meetings, held during the course of the war, certainly exposed widely differing points of view, though eventually helping to clarify the Society of Friends' attitude not just to the Boer War but to war in general. Richard Rempel points out that 'the Boer war came at a time when the Quakers were in the throes of significant internal strain and transition',[17] citing the Manchester Conference of 1895, with the concomitant transition from the Evangelical period of nineteenth-century Quakerism to a more liberal Christianity. He finds that 'the Boer War was an important stage in the process whereby Quakerism ceased to be almost wholly a middle-class sect looking upon philanthropy as the best means of remedying social evils',[18] and that Friends' engagement with the issues associated with the war led to a new attitude towards social relief, closer engagement with the parliamentary liberal party and, among some Friends, also with socialism and the rights of labour.

In the end, the Yearly Meeting's statement in 1900 went beyond general pacifist aversion to conflict; it took seriously the Quaker insight that not merely war but also the causes of war should be averted, and recognised that it was all too easy for demure, hard-working Friends to implicate themselves:

> We shall not condemn increase in the army and condone the lust of dominion which causes the increase, or denounce war while we worship dividends. . . . We shall endeavour to be free from all that would deface manhood and womanhood in industrial conflict, or the keen warfare of relentless competition.[19]

In 1900 Joshua Rowntree, with his wife and nephew, visited the Cape and Natal with a view to seeing the situation for themselves and to liaise constructively with the British officers managing the camps. These were not the worst-afflicted places, and the Rowntrees sent home reassuring reports. Their experience was very different to that of Emily Hobhouse, the secretary of the women's section of the South African Conciliation Committee, who visited the camps in the Transvaal and the Orange Free State, where living conditions were squalid, people were cold and hungry, and dysentery was rife. When Hobhouse returned to England, her reports and speeches were vitriolic. Two Quaker women who later distributed clothing and relief parcels to the camps, Anna Hogg and Francis Annie Taylor, confirmed Hobhouse's accounts, though not publicly, on the grounds that that would have compromised their access to the camps. Greenwood comments that this encapsulates a recurring Quaker dilemma in conflict relief: Friends have often found that speaking out too loudly against the injustices observed compromises access to the people whose experiences they hope to help ameliorate.[20] However, two other visitors associated with Friends, Helen Balkwill Harris[21] and Georgina King-Lewis, were more sympathetic to their British hosts.

By the time that Quaker aid on a large scale had begun to arrive at the end of 1901, the reports by Hobhouse and a committee of women appointed to investigate her allegations had together led to the removal of the camps from military control. With better hygiene and better rations, the death rate fell dramatically and the food relief was no longer needed. Instead, several Quaker women went to South Africa as nurses, teachers and matrons of orphanages. These included Margaret Clark, later Gillet, who established a long-standing friendship between the Quaker Clarks of Street and the family of the Boer General Jan Smuts.[22]

A British Quaker, Francis Fox, persuaded the Dutch prime minister, Abraham Kuypers, to offer himself as a mediator for the peace negotiations which finally ended the war.[23] The Treaty of Vereeniging was signed in May 1902.

Once the war was over, British Quaker assistance was directed towards reconstruction. Friends supported Emily Hobhouse's efforts to equip women returning from the camps with opportunities for earning money from home industries such as weaving, sewing and lace-making. They also helped missionaries and ministers of religion to replace books lost or destroyed during the conflict. Looting had been endemic on the part of the British soldiers engaged in farm-destruction,[24] and one much-appreciated, though mainly symbolic, initiative was the Quaker attempt to trace and return family Bibles appropriated by soldiers. A total of 123 Bibles, some of them more than 200 years old, were returned to their owners over a period of twenty years. Friends also distributed new copies of the Bible, in Dutch, to Boer families.

British Friends' deliberations during the 1900 and 1901 Yearly Meetings, and their anxieties about the scale of military recruitment and the possibility of national conscription all helped the Society of Friends to become more explicit in its understanding about the ways in which the peace testimony might be relevant in the twentieth century. The discernment undertaken in relation to the Boer War helped prepare for the discernment needed during World War I, especially in relation to conscription, which was eventually introduced under the Military Services Act of 1916.

One of the first big issues in South Africa after the Boer War was another one over which British Friends were initially divided: the importation of what eventually became more than 50,000 indentured Chinese labourers to work on the mines.[25] When the issue came to Meeting for Sufferings in March 1904, Joseph Bevan Braithwaite suggested that 'the matter should be deferred, it was unfair to call it slavery'.[26] However, the Society of Friends eventually took the view, already held by many churches, the Aborigines Protection Society, members of adult schools and members of the Liberal party, that it was indeed a situation allied to slavery, and that they should petition the Colonial Office and other government departments to that effect. (The Chinese were eventually repatriated in 1910).

London Yearly Meeting's engagement with political and social conditions in South Africa, and with British policies in relation to that country, continued through most of the twentieth century, and these issues figured repeatedly in the Yearly Meeting agenda until the end of apartheid, particularly in the 1970s and 1980s. The Yearly Meeting maintained a South Africa committee until the early 1990s, and continued to provide volunteers to Quaker and other non-governmental organizations into the present century.

Notes

1 Hendrik W. van der Merwe, *Reconciling Opposites, Reflections on Peace-Making in South Africa*, James Backhouse Lecture, 2001, Armadale North, Backhouse Lecture Committee, p. 11.

2 Ibid.

3 Stephen M. Miller, 'Duty or Crime? Defining Acceptable Behaviour in the British Army in South Africa 1899–1902' *Journal of British Studies* 49:2, 2010, pp. 311–331, p. 331.

4 Betty Tonsing, *The Quakers in South Africa, a Social Witness* (Lewiston, Queenstown, Lampeter, Edwin Mellen Press, 2002), p. 69.

5 Ibid., refers on p. 69 to Peter Warwick, *Black People and the South African War* (Johannesburg, Raven Press, 1983), p. 145. Warwick cites a death rate of 380 per thousand in some of the camps incarcerating African people.

6 The Transvaal president, Paul Kruger, assumed that most members of the mining communities were birds of passage, only there so long as the mines – which he presumed to be a finite resource – survived. Kruger perceived that the Uitlanders were not interested in the long-term future of the country, only in their immediate self-interest, which was at variance with that of the farming community.

7 A somewhat ironic slogan within the context of the subsequent history of South Africa: the Union of South Africa was constituted on the basis that, except for a small remnant of non-white voters who met

the conditions for a qualified franchise in the Cape (scrapped in 1952), the majority of the population – all African and Coloured people – would not have the vote.

8 *Friend*, vol. 39, November 1899, p. 760.

9 Ibid., pp. 771–772.

10 Hope Hay Hewison, *Hedge of Wild Almonds; South Africa, the 'Pro-Boers' & the Quaker Conscience* (Portsmouth NH, Cape Town, London, Heinemann, David Philip, James Currey, 1989), p. 73.

11 Ibid., p. 76.

12 Hewison, *Hedge*, p. 117.

13 John Ormerod Greenwood, *Quaker Encounters, Vol 1: Friends and Relief* (York: William Sessions Ltd, 1975), p. 152.

14 John Bellows, *The Truth about the Transvaal War and the Truth about War* (Gloucester, John Bellows, 1900).

15 Hewison, *Hedge*, p. 181.

16 Elizabeth Isichei, *Victorian Quakers* (London: Oxford University Press, 1970), p. 151.

17 Richard A. Rempel, 'British Quakers and the South African War' *Quaker History* 64:2, 1974, pp. 75–95, p. 76.

18 Ibid., p. 78.

19 London Yearly Meeting, Statement on the Peace Testimony, 1900. Quoted by Edward Grubb, 'Third Period, 1825–1918' *London Yearly Meeting during 250 Years* (London: Society of Friends, 1919), pp. 69–92, 86–87.

20 Greenwood, *Quaker Encounters*, p. 155.

21 Wife of the Quaker biblical scholar, later the first director of studies at Woodbrooke, J. Rendall Harris.

22 Smuts later became prime minister of South Africa, a Commonwealth statesman, and the only person who was signatory to both the Treaty of Versailles and the United Nations Charter. As prime minister, he perpetuated and extended the race-based stratification of South Africa, which advantaged the 'European' population over African, Indian and 'Coloured' people. Through his friendship with the Clark and Gillet families, Smuts, when in Britain, began attending Quaker meetings. He later described sitting in meeting, and recognising that it was spiritually important, and necessary, to forgive one's enemies (Natal Monthly Meeting Statement on the Present Situation in South Africa, 1957, in Central and Southern Africa Yearly Meeting, *Handbook of Practice and Procedure*, [Johannesburg, C&SAYM, 2009]), p. 57. One of Smuts' political antagonists was Mohandas Gandhi, who had arrived in South Africa in 1893 as a young lawyer, hired by the local Indian community to defend their labour and citizenship rights, initially in the British colony of Natal. During the Boer War, Gandhi recruited a unit of Indian stretcher-bearers to help care for the wounded. He too became acquainted with Friends and their principles during the war and its aftermath, though did not succumb to the efforts of a British Quaker in South Africa, Michael Coates, to convert him to Christianity (M. S. Deshpande, ed., *The Way to God; Selected Writings by Mahatma Gandhi* [Berkeley, North Atlantic Books, 2009]).

23 Hewison, *Hedge*, p. 241 refers to the *Friend*, 5 June 1902, p. 395; also to the Chamberlain papers (letters 11 April and 12 December 1901).

24 Stephen M. Miller, 'Duty or Crime? Defining Acceptable Behaviour in the British Army in South Africa 1899–1902' *Journal of British Studies* 49:2, 2010, pp. 311–331, p. 331.

25 Peter Richardson, 'The Recruiting of Chinese Indentured Labour for the South African Gold-Mines, 1903–1908' *The Journal of African History* 18:1, 1977, pp. 85–108. *JSTOR*, www.jstor.org/stable/180418.

26 Hewison, *Hedge*, p. 272.

References

Bellows, John, *The Truth about the Transvaal War and the Truth about War*, Gloucester, John Bellows, 1900

Central and Southern Africa Yearly Meeting, *Handbook of Practice and Procedure*, Johannesburg, C&SAYM, 2009

Deshpande, M. S. (ed), *The Way to God; Selected Writings by Mahatma Gandhi*, Berkeley, North Atlantic Books, 2009

Greenwood, Ormerod, *Quaker Encounters, Vol. 1, Friends and Relief*, York, William Sessions Ltd, 1975

Grubb, Edward, 'Third Period, 1825–1918' *London Yearly Meeting during 250 Years*, London, Society of Friends, 1919

Hewison, Hope Hay, *Hedge of Wild Almonds; South Africa, the 'Pro-Boers' & the Quaker Conscience*, Portsmouth, NH, Cape Town, London, Heinemann, David Philip, James Currey, 1989

Isichei, Elizabeth, *Victorian Quakers*, London, Oxford University Press, 1970

Kennedy, Thomas C., *British Quakerism 1860–1920: The Transformation of a Religious Community*, Oxford, Oxford University Press, 2001

Miller, Stephen M., 'Duty or Crime? Defining Acceptable Behaviour in the British Army in South Africa 1899–1902' *Journal of British Studies* 49:2, 2010, pp. 311–331

Rempel, Richard A., 'British Quakers and the South African War' *Quaker History* 64:2, 1974, pp. 75–95

Richardson, Peter, 'The Recruiting of Chinese Indentured Labour for the South African Gold-Mines, 1903–1908' *The Journal of African History* 18:1, 1977, pp. 85–108. *JSTOR*, www.jstor.org/stable/180418. Accessed 11 January 2021

The Friend, vol. 39, November 1899

Van der Merwe, Hendrik W., *Reconciling Opposites, Reflections on Peace-making in South Africa*, James Backhouse Lecture, 2001, Armadale North, Backhouse Lecture Committee

59

QUAKER WORKCAMPS

Greg Woods

Beginning of the Workcamp Movement

One of the major forms of Quaker service for a large portion of the twentieth century was the workcamp movement. The idea behind the workcamp movement began when Swiss Pierre Cérésole and British Quaker Hubert Parris held a camp in a village of Esnes near Verdun, France, in 1920 which was damaged during a battle in World War I.[1] They saw this work as a way to build international peace and reconciliation after the brutal war that divided the European continent.[2] The first participants of this workcamp were Austrian, Dutch, English, German,[3] and Swiss.[4] This workcamp lasted for five months, and the participants built temporary housing for the farmers. The workcamps were not without controversy because of the inclusion of German participants due to lasting hostilities after World War I.[5]

After this first workcamp, Cérésole worked on setting up a Swiss organization to continue this kind of service. This work led to the founding of the Service Civil International (SCI) in 1924.[6] This organization continues to operate until this day and has affiliates all over the world. As of 2010, SCI reported that they were running 1000 workcamps per year for 4000 volunteers and continuing Cérésole's work for peace.[7]

British Friends began having workcamps in 1931 with inspiration and help from the SCI. The first workcamp was held in Brynmawr in Wales, a coal mining town which had been hit hard by the Great Depression and had 80% unemployment at the time. By the time of this workcamp, Quakers had already been involved with the community for several years. This involvement was called the Brynmawr Experiment.[8] During this first workcamp, Quakers built a pool and park for the community.[9]

Out of this workcamp, the British branch of SCI, International Voluntary Service was formed and helped to provide workcamp and alternative service opportunities for conscientious objectors during World War II. In the 1940s, British Friends felt that there was a need for workcamps for younger Quakers (ages 16–19) and started to organize workcamps for them. In 1947, with representatives from the Friends Peace Committee and Friends Service Committee, British Yearly Meeting formed the Friends Workcamp Committee to oversee workcamp opportunities for Friends.[10]

The workcamp movement began in the United States a couple of years later when the American Friends Service Committee (AFSC) started their workcamp program in 1934. Their

DOI: 10.4324/9780429030925-63

first workcamp was a summer-long program for young men held in the government homestead[11] community of Norvelt in Westmoreland County, Pennsylvania. This program attracted
55 young people where they worked on digging a mile and half long ditch, laying pipes, and
constructing a 260,000-gallon reservoir. The women at the workcamp also helped the women
from the community with household arts, canning, health, and playground projects.[12]

One of the participants of the Norvelt workcamp, David Richie, wrote this about the purpose of the first workcamp from his perspective:

> Intended primarily for convinced pacifists who wished to demonstrate their devotion
> to constructive work which was as rigorous as the destructive work demanded of sol-
> diers. The American Friends Service Committee, in 1934, sought to provide an edu-
> cational opportunity for both pacifist and non-pacifist students to better understand
> the economic and social injustices which causes violence, and to feel deeply through
> involvement the plight of human beings trapped in unemployment and desperate
> poverty.[13]

Also, the first workcamp was interracial and this commitment to having workcamps be
interracial was a high priority for AFSC.[14] After this first successful workcamp, AFSC continued
to expand the workcamp programs across the United States. According to Clarence Pickett,
former executive secretary, these workcamps happened

> in coal-mining communities, in overcrowded and underprivileged industrial areas, in
> sharecropper regions of the South, on TVA and other progressive social and techni-
> cal experiments, on American Indian reservations, in migrant camps, in burned-over
> parts of New England after forest fires, in the Ozarks and other Southern hill coun-
> try, in areas of special racial tension, especially among Japanese-Americans, Chinese,
> Mexicans, and Negros, and notably in spots where Negro-white tensions are acute.[15]

Then, after World War II, AFSC started the Quaker International Voluntary Service program to promote international workcamps. In the memoir of his time working for AFSC, *For
More Than Bread*, Clarence Pickett cited his inspiration for this idea to be from what Cérésole
did after World War I: using workcamps to help rebuild Europe and "start on the delicate task
of reknitting the social and spiritual fabric torn apart by bitterness and violence of war."[16]

The first workcamps organised by AFSC happened in the summer of 1947 in Austria, Finland, Italy, and Poland. Friends Relief Committee of London Yearly Meeting also operated a
workcamp that summer in Berlin, Germany. These camps helped to rebuild communities rav-
aged by the war. At the project in Italy, the campers helped to construct a cable car to replace
a destroyed bridge. The cable car carried the stone to help rebuild the village on a new site.[17]
AFSC continued expanding its international workcamps until 1970 across Africa, Asia, and
Europe. Stephen Cary, former associate executive secretary, reported that there were 400 to 600
people involved in the workcamps, both domestic and international, each summer.[18]

One of the participants of the first AFSC workcamp in Norvelt, Pennsylvania, David Richie
had his whole life changed by the workcamp movement. There at the workcamp, he met his
wife, Mary, another participant, and he proposed to her on the last day of the workcamp. David
and Mary both served as workcamp leaders for AFSC in the 1930s. Then, in 1939, he quit his
teaching job at Moorestown Friends School in New Jersey and became the executive secretary
of the Social Order Committee at the Philadelphia Yearly Meeting, which included providing
workcamp programs for the yearly meeting.

Richie recounts in his Pendle Hill pamphlet, *Memories and Meditations of a Workcamper*, that he thought up the idea of weekend workcamps, a short-term version of the workcamps he had attended and led. He wanted a way to reach other young people who were not attracted to summer-long programs. He thought that "what was needed were short-term workcamps capable of attracting many less socially conscious young people and helping them to grow in awareness and commitment to social justice and brotherhood through work that is 'love made visible.'"[19]

The Social Order Committee agreed to try this new idea, and Richie organized the first workcamp to assist the Wharton Settlement House's nursery facilities. This first weekend work-camp was a success, and Richie continued these weekend workcamps, primarily working in the Mantua and West Philadelphia neighbourhoods. These weekend workcamps reached hundreds of students each year from Quaker meetings, Quaker schools, and non-Quakers as well. Richie retired from being the executive secretary in 1973 after 34 years of service for the yearly meeting.[20]

Workcamps benefited Quakerism in two important ways. First, it provided opportunities to keep young people involved in service that was based on the Quaker process. Many Friends cite their workcamp experience as a pivotal point in their life.[21] Second, workcamps served as a good outreach tool for people to learn about Quakerism. It is hard to quantify how many people were drawn into Quakerism because of the workcamps. One example is Paul Lacey, professor emeritus of English at Earlham College and longtime supporter of AFSC, who first encountered Quakerism through a weekend workcamp when he was in high school.[22]

Decline of AFSC Workcamps

One of the pivotal points in the Quaker workcamp movement in the United States came in the late 1960s when AFSC started to pull back from the workcamp movement. Paul Lacey, a pivotal member of the AFSC governance for over six decades, once attributed two reasons to this decline. First, Harvey Cox's *The Secular City* was published in 1965; in this book, Cox criticized programs like the workcamp movement that came into inner cities from the outside without making real change. Second, the culture of young adults in the late 1960s focused on questioning authority, which made it difficult for workcamps to function due to people not wanting to listen to leadership and to find the staff to lead the workcamps.[23]

Also, by 1970 AFSC began to direct its youth work away from the workcamp/service model and towards working with youth and young adults on knowing and understanding their rights. This shift occurred with the dissolution of their entire Youth Services Department.[24] This shift also led AFSC to refocus on which youth population they serve. According to a board minute from 1983, "The Executive Committee affirmed that youth work is integral to AFSC, but that it is primarily the job of Friends General Conference and individual Yearly and Quarterly Meetings to respond to the needs of Quaker youth."[25]

Despite this decline in workcamps, AFSC still continued its Mexican Summer Project through the rest of the century and into the next.[26] Also, AFSC entered into two new work-camp partnerships in the 1990s, one with Intermountain Yearly Meeting (IMYM) in 1990 and the other with Southern California Quarterly Meeting of Pacific Yearly Meeting in 1993. These partnerships provided short-term workcamp opportunities in the western United States and northern Mexico for almost two decades.[27]

These programs continued the same kind of peace work that early workcamps did. Mike Gray, the former coordinator of the AFSC/IMYM Joint Service Project, put a quote by Danish-American photojournalist Jacob Riis ("One half of the world does not know how the other half lives") on his workcamp registration forms. In the mission statement of the workcamp program, the purpose was "to exponential understand the Quaker testimonies of the Religious Society of Friends."[28]

Recent History

The Friends Workcamp Committee of Britain Yearly Meeting continued offering workcamp opportunities for Friends within Britain Yearly Meeting and beyond. Over time the nature of the workcamps changed from manual labour to more of a social nature. To reflect this change, in 1987, the name of the workcamp program was renamed Quaker International Service Project (QISP).[29]

An example of this new kind of programming was a three-year youth summer program that QISP would run in housing estates. The first year, the participants would lead a short-term youth program in the estate; the next year, the participants would lead a short-term youth program and invite the parents/guardians to be engaged too; and in the third year, the participants would lead the youth program with parents/guardians from the estate. The ultimate objective of the three-year programs was to have the community take over the youth programming by the end of the three years.[30]

QISP ended in 1994, and in 1999 British Friends founded another group focused on Quaker service, the Quaker Voluntary Action. This new group continues in British Friends' legacy of Quaker workcamps through using the term *working retreats*. Currently, they hold these retreats five or six times a year – usually ranging from three to ten days – around the United Kingdom, France, Ireland, and Israel/Palestine.

The Philadelphia Yearly Meeting Workcamp Program expanded over the years to include weeklong opportunities and international workcamps. In 1983, the workcamp program brought a house within the West Philadelphia neighbourhood to be within the community where they were working. They would run programs from this house, and participants would sleep and eat meals there. The yearly meeting continued to run the workcamp program until 2006, when the yearly meeting laid the program down.[31]

As mentioned earlier, AFSC had a major decline in their workcamp programs starting in 1970. After 75 years, AFSC ended its last workcamp program, the AFSC/IMYM Joint Service Program in 2009 after 19 years of operation.[32] The program continued as Western Quaker Workcamps as a program solely under the care of IMYM and later through a relationship with William Penn House, a Quaker hostel/retreat centre in Washington, DC, and their workcamp program until 2017.[33]

Smaller more localized workcamps began in the 1980s with the creation of Washington Quaker Workcamps (WQW) in Washington DC in 1985 and the Youth Opportunities Service Project (YSOP) in New York City in 1983. These programs primarily worked in Washington, DC, and New York City, respectively. After 145 African American churches were burned in the South in 1995 and 1996, Harold Confer, then coordinator of WQW, organized an effort to rebuild a number of the churches, starting up the Ministry to Burned Churches.[34]

There were efforts within the United States to keep up the workcamp movement. Illinois Yearly Meeting's Quaker Voluntary Service and Training Committee initiated a conference that was held in April 1997, titled National Conference on Quaker Volunteer Service, Training, and Witness. Part of the purpose of the conference was to "discern ways to strengthen and support opportunities for volunteer service and witness throughout the Religious Society of Friends." This included short-term opportunities, such as workcamps.[35]

Also, short-term service projects in the last few decades have started to look in different ways due to theological differences. Starting after World War II, moderate and evangelical Friends disengaged from involvement with AFSC due to policies that these Quakers deemed "militant" and "extreme leftist".[36] More evangelical Friends, within both parts of Friends United Meeting and Evangelical Friends Church International, have adopted a more mainstream Christian concept of short-term mission trips with an emphasis on evangelicalism, like bible studies and vacation bible schools.[37] Evangelical Friends also tend to use the term "mission" rather than "workcamp."

As of 2021, although there are fewer Quaker workcamps than there were during the mid-twentieth century, there are still workcamp programs running in one way or another. Here are some of the examples around the world.

- Starting in 1978, Evangelical Friends in Ohio responded to help tornado victims in Xenia, Ohio, thus starting the first Friends Disaster Service.[38] Friends Disaster Service currently independently operates out of three yearly meetings to help with repairs after disasters: Evangelical Friends Church–Eastern Region, Mid-America Yearly Meeting, and North Carolina Friends Church. They offer short-term (usually a week) work projects across the United States in areas that suffer disasters, such as fires, floods, hurricanes, and tornados.
- Friends United Meeting (FUM) currently runs Living Letters programs. These programs promote cross-cultural connections, and some have work components like fixing up Friends centres, meetinghouses, and schools. In recent years, these trips have run to Belize, Cuba, Israel/Palestine, Jamaica, and Kenya.[39]
- Quaker Voluntary Action offers working retreats. During the COVID-19 pandemic, they have been holding virtual retreats on different topics, such as reflecting on service, ecological practices, and learning about the Israel/Palestine conflict through talking to peacemakers from the area.[40]
- African Great Lakes Initiative (AGLI) used to run five-week-long workcamps each summer from 1999 to 2007 with an equal number of African and non-African volunteers (5–7 participants each). Now, Quakers in the Great Lakes Region of Africa hold workcamps and help each other with needed repairs in the region's Friends churches, schools, and centres. Usually, these workcamps are either held as weeklong opportunities or over four weekends.[41]
- Youth Service Opportunities Project (YSOP) currently offers short-term workcamp experiences (both weekend and weeklong opportunities) in both New York City and Washington, DC.[42]

Notes

1 Cérésole later became a Quaker himself and joined the Geneva, Switzerland, Friends Meeting in 1936 after first encountering Quakers at inaugural meeting of the International Federation of Reconciliation in 1919 (Rodriguez and Béguelin, 'Pierre Cérésole: A Lifetime Serving Peace', 17).
2 Rodriguez and Béguelin, 'Pierre Cérésole: A Lifetime Serving Peace', 15.
3 Clarence Pickett includes this story about the first workcamp led by Cérésole and Parris in his book, *For More than Bread,* "'For a long time,' wrote one of the German volunteers, 'I have hoped for a chance to go and repair in France a little of what my brother (killed at Verdun) and his comrades were forced under military orders to destroy'" (339).
4 Pierre Cérésole, *Service Civil International – International Archives* [website], https://archives.sci.ngo/volunteers/ceresole-pierre.html.
5 Rodriguez and Béguelin, 'Pierre Cérésole: A Lifetime Serving Peace', 16.
6 Ibid., 18.
7 Ibid., 34.
8 Brynmawr Experiment, https://en.wikipedia.org/wiki/Brynmawr_Experiment.

9   Brynmawr Welfare Park, *Hidden Stories BBC Two*, https://www.bbc.co.uk/programmes/p00dtqf8.

10 Work Camps Committee, *Library of the Society of Friends Catalogue*, http://quaker.adlibhosting.com/Details/archive/110010854.

11 In the 1930s, the US government set up 36 homestead communities across the country as part of the New Deal program that helps factory workers and farmers in areas hardest hit by the Great Depression.

12 Pickett, *For More Than Bread*, 341.

13 Richie, *Memories and Meditations of a Workcamper*, 4–5.

14 Pickett, *For More Than Bread*, 344.

15 Ibid.

16 Ibid., 356.

17 Ibid., 357.

18 *National Conference on Quaker Volunteer Service, Training, and Witness*, 16.

19 Richie, *Memories and Meditations of a Workcamper*, 9.

20 David S. and Mary W. Richie Papers, *TriCollege Libraries: Archives & Manuscripts*, http://archives.tricolib.brynmawr.edu/resources/5264dari.

21 Some resources for reading about workcampers' memories are the AFSC website (www.afsc.org) and the pamphlet *Reflections & Memories – Fifty Years of Workcamps* published by the Weekend Workcamp Committee of Philadelphia Yearly Meeting in 1991.

22 Leading and Being Led, *Pendle Hill*, https://pendlehill.org/product/leading-led/.

23 Repoley, 'Prophetic Service: Roots of and New Directions for a Quaker Religious Practice', 37.

24 D. Davis, 'Re: Workcamps in the 70s and 80s' [email to G. Woods], 28 January 2021.

25 Repoley. 'Prophetic Service: Roots of and New Directions for a Quaker Religious Practice', 37.

26 No records could be found detailing workcamps sponsored by AFSC in the 1970s and 1980s besides the Mexican Summer Workcamps.

27 A. Manosous, Facebook message to G. Woods, 5 February 2021; M. Gray, Zoom interview with G. Woods, 14 January 2021.

28 M. Gray, Facebook message to G. Woods, 15 February 2021.

29 Work Camps Committee, *Library of the Society of Friends Catalogue*, http://quaker.adlibhosting.com/Details/archive/110010854.

30 B. Chadkirk, Zoom interview with G. Woods, 22 January 2021.

31 J. and M. Van Hoy, Facebook message to G. Woods, 3 April 2014.

32 'News', *Friends Journal* (March 2009), 22.

33 M. Gray, Zoom interview with G. Woods, 14 January 2021.

34 Washington Quaker Workcamps later became a part of William Penn House and ceased to operate when William Penn House was reorganized by Friends Committee on National Legislation and William Penn House officially became Friends Place on Capitol Hill in 2022.

35 *National Conference on Quaker Volunteer Service, Training, and Witness*, iii.

36 Burdick and Dandelion, 'Global Quakerism 1920–2015', 61.

37 Friend's Center (AL), *Friends Church of North Carolina*, https://www.friendschurchnc.org/mowa.

38 Friends Disaster Service, *Quakers in the World*, https://www.quakersintheworld.org/quakers-in-action/323/Friends-Disaster-Service.

39 FUM Living Letters, *Friends United Meeting*, https://www.friendsunitedmeeting.org/connect/living-letters/living-letters; C. Saxton, Zoom interview with G. Woods, 19 February 2021.

40 S. Watkins, Zoom interview with G. Woods, 14 January 2021.

41 D. Zarembka, Zoom interview with G. Woods, 12 January 2021.

42 History, *YSOP Youth Service Opportunities Project*, http://www.ysop.org/history.

Bibliography

Brynmawr Experiment, *Wikipedia* [website], https://en.wikipedia.org/wiki/Brynmawr_Experiment (accessed 16 February 2021).

Brynmawr Welfare Park, *Hidden Stories BBC Two* [website], https://www.bbc.co.uk/programmes/p00dtqf8 (accessed 16 February 2021).

Burdick, Timothy and Pink Dandelion, 'Global Quakerism 1920–2015', *Cambridge Companion to Quakerism*, Stephen Angell and Pink Dandelion (eds.) (Cambridge: Cambridge University Press, 2018).

David S. and Mary W. Richie Papers, *TriCollege Libraries: Archives & Manuscripts* [website], http://archives. tricolib.brynmawr.edu/resources/5264dari (accessed 10 February 2021).

Friend's Center (AL), *Friends Church of North Carolina* [website], https://www.friendschurchnc.org/mowa (accessed 15 February 2021).

Friends Disaster Service, *Quakers in the World* [website], https://www.quakersintheworld.org/quakers-in-action/323/Friends-Disaster-Service (accessed 14 January 2021).

FUM Living Letters, *Friends United Meeting* [website], https://www.friendsunitedmeeting.org/connect/living-letters/living-letters (accessed 12 February 2021).

History, *YSOP Youth Service Opportunities Project* [website], http://www.ysop.org/history (accessed 12 January 2021).

Leading and Being Led, *Pendle Hill* [website], https://pendlehill.org/product/leading-led/ (accessed 15 February 2021).

National Conference on Quaker Volunteer Service, Training, and Witness (Burlington, NJ, 1997).

'News' *Friends Journal*, Robert Marks & George Rubin (eds.) (Philadelphia, PA: Friends Journal Corporation, 2009), 22.

Pickett, Clarence, *For More Than Bread: An Autobiographical Account of Twenty-two Years' Work with American Friends Service Committee* (Boston: Little Brown and Company, 1953).

Pierre Cérésole, *Service Civil International – International Archives* [website], https://archives.sci.ngo/volunteers/ceresole-pierre.html (accessed 14 January 2021).

Repoley, Christina, 'Prophetic Service: Roots of and New Directions for a Quaker Religious Practice', unpublished M. Div. thesis, Chandler School of Theology, 2011.

Richie, David S., *Memories and Meditations of a Workcamper* (Wallingford, PA: Pendle Hill Publications, 1973).

Rodriguez, Philipp and Sylvie Béguelin, 'Pierre Cérésole: A Lifetime Serving Peace' (Bern: SCI Swiss Branch, 2010), https://archives.sci.ngo/uploads/documents/pierre-ceresole_a-lifetime-service-peace_2010_en.pdf.

Work Camps Committee, *Library of the Society of Friends Catalogue* [website], http://quaker.adlibhosting.com/Details/archive/110010854 (accessed 16 January 2021).

60

THE RAMALLAH FRIENDS MEETING

Examining 100 Years of Peace and Justice Work[1]

Maia Carter Hallward

History of the Ramallah Friends Meeting

The Quaker presence in Ramallah, Palestine, began after an 1868 visit to the area by Eli and Sybil Jones of New England Yearly Meeting and Alfred Lloyd Fox and Ellen Clare Miller of Britain Yearly Meeting. When stopping over in Ramallah, a small Christian town, they met fifteen-year-old Miriam Karam, who asked them to start a school for girls and volunteered to be the first teacher. The Quakers went home, raised funds, and returned in 1869 to set up classes for girls. In 1889 classes became institutionalised as a boarding school, called the Girls Domestic Training Center. The school was highly successful, and the community requested that Friends establish a school for boys, which they did in 1901 (Edwards-Konic, 2008; Leonard, 1989).

The American Friends Mission Board, which was responsible for running the schools, was concerned that Friends lacked a meeting house in Ramallah. A house was rented for ten years as the place of worship for those connected with the schools. A monthly meeting was established in 1890 for five years and was later revived in 1901 by Elihu and Almy Grant (Brinson et al., 2010; C.H. Jones, 1944). In 1906 members of the Ramallah community purchased land to construct a meeting house halfway between the Girls Training Home and the land that had been purchased for the Friends Boys School. While today this site is in the centre of downtown Ramallah, in 1910, when the meeting house was completed, it stood alone, with no buildings nearby. Foreign Quakers from Haverford College helped raise the money to construct the actual meeting house, but local Friends furnished the benches and other internal furnishings. A local Ramallah Friend said, 'I'll start with myself. I'll offer two benches. And then his friends were embarrassed that he offered and they didn't. And so in one sitting, they managed to get twenty benches for the meeting' (Author Interview, 2010). Unlike the schools, the meeting remained under the ownership of local Friends, not the American Friends Mission Board, and the property was registered as Kiniset Arabia le Friends (the "Arab Friends Church").

The meeting prospered in its early years, with attendance as many as 154 when school was in session and up to 400 children attending Sunday School in some years in the 1920s (Brinson et al., 2010). The Sunday School was one of the Meeting's most successful outreach programs, with some non-Christians and many Christians from other denominations attending. At both the re-dedication of the Ramallah Friends Meeting in March 2005 and the Centennial

DOI: 10.4324/9780429030925-64

Celebration in March 2010, local dignitaries including the governor and the mayor (neither of whom is Quaker) shared their memories of attending Sunday School at the Quaker meeting. Although a number of Friends assisted with the Sunday School over the years, it was the particular ministry of Ellen Audeh Mansour, who had a special gift of storytelling. As one local Friend shared,

> We still talk about our days at Sunday School today. Just like [my class at] school bonded, that was also a special group that went to Sunday School. We were bonded in that special way. Our clerk of the board of trustees at the [Friends Boys] School, Samir Shehadeh, he was a regular attender of the Sunday School, for example, so I think his relationship with the meeting in that respect made him more aware of Quakerism and maybe that has something to do with the fact that he's . . . the clerk.
>
> *(Author Interview, 2010g)*

Another local Friend noted that as late as the 1970s, 'Sunday school was the thing in town so everybody just joined in', regardless of whether they were Quakers, Greek Orthodox, or Catholic. In fact, the majority of the twenty to twenty-five children who attended each week were non-Quaker (Author Interview, 2010i).

The 1940s were a period of heightened nationalism, and many in the local community saw the Ramallah Friends Schools as an institution aimed at helping Palestinians build their expected state (the 1937 Peel Commission had recommended dividing the British Mandate into an Arab and a Jewish state). The meeting prospered, with approximately 170 members. Khalil Totah was a major figure in the meeting: he was the principal of the Friends Boys School and a leader in the Ramallah community, connected to Quakers around the world as a result of his speaking tours, and to Jewish leaders and Jordanian officials as well. However, a series of differences of opinion over the leadership and direction of the Ramallah Friends Mission between Totah and the Friends Mission Board led to Ramallah Quakers meeting separately from American Quakers. This conflict stemmed in part from

> different social, political and cultural traditions, practices and expectations of Palestinians engulfed in decades of violent struggles for their independence, and the American Quakers who were, in part, insensitive to the implications of the Palestinian war against Zionism and British colonialism, and, in part, to missionary hubris in bringing 'democracy' to Palestine and in 'creating' American Quaker Christians in the Middle East.
>
> *(Ricks, 2009, p. 34)*

Struggles over how to best manage and run the schools involved questions not only of nationality and personality but also questions of patriarchy, leadership style, and control over Mission property (Ricks, 2009, pp. 36–37). After several years of disagreements and debates within the Ramallah community as well as between local and foreign Quakers, in March 1944 Dr. Totah sent an ultimatum to the Friends Mission Board that unless all Friends work and property were turned over to the Ramallah Friends Meeting (where he played a leading role), he would resign. Willard Jones, whose wife Christina was education secretary for Friends United Meeting in Richmond, Indiana, was sent immediately to Ramallah to accept Totah's resignation. Practically overnight, the meeting lost over 120 members, as everyone except for those employed by the schools and a few other families resigned along with Totah (Leonard, 1989, 2010).[2] This break is best understood in the context of the ongoing political conflict between

Arabs, Jews, and British and Palestinian desires for independence and self-determination in all aspects of life. While theological issues may have played a role, particularly American Quakers' focus on democracy over Totah's more dictatorial style, other factors included the broader colonial struggles in which Quaker testimonies of democracy and equality were applied differently in different contexts (Author Interview, 2010).[3]

In addition to the at times strained relations between local and foreign Quakers over leadership and autonomy issues, the meeting has been greatly impacted by the Israeli-Palestinian conflict. In 1967, with the Israeli occupation of the West Bank, the meeting house was hit during the fighting, leaving two big holes in the roof, and it lost many weekly attenders when the Ramallah Friends Schools had to stop boarding students. Until this time, about forty girls and the boarding boys attended meeting each Sunday, sitting on either side of the meeting house with twenty to fifty meeting members and attenders sitting in the middle (Brinson et al., 2010; Leonard, 2010). As the occupation became more entrenched, Christians, including Ramallah Quakers, increasingly emigrated to the United States and elsewhere. By the 1970s there were usually about thirty to thirty-five people attending meeting on an average Sunday; in the 1980s this decreased to about twenty to twenty-five on average. During the First Intifada (1987–1993), Friends stopped using the meeting house. It was not safe to meet there since the main street of town was the site of frequent clashes between Israeli soldiers and local youth. Instead, the meeting began to meet in a small room at the Friends Girls School. In 1995 the meeting house was leaking so badly that it was no longer useable; experts from An-Najah University declared the building unsafe (Author Interview, 2010).

Given the cost of repairing the roof and the size of the meeting, local Quakers debated the future of the meeting house. However, after the First Intifada, Palestinians had an increased concern for preserving their cultural heritage and using it as a form of national resistance. The meeting house was declared to be a historical site by the Ramallah Municipality, ending the possibility of moving it (Nassar 2006; Author Interview 2010c, 2010i). In 2002, when presiding clerk Jean Zaru spoke at Philadelphia Yearly Meeting (affiliated with Friends General Conference), Philadelphia Quakers were so moved by the situation in Ramallah that even though Jean did not ask for funds for the roof, they raised $50,000 almost on the spot for the renovation. As the renovations occurred, first for the meeting house and then for the annex, local Quakers, in consultation with Friends from Philadelphia Yearly Meeting and Baltimore Yearly Meeting, which also contributed funds to the project, began to discuss how to best make use of this newly renovated space. In 2005, when the meeting house was re-dedicated, a group of Quakers gathered together in a consultation out of which emerged the vision of the Friends International Center in Ramallah (FICR), now Friends of the Ramallah Friends Meeting.

Ministry of Hospitality: Nurturing Peace and Justice Work

As evidenced by the interviews, a major service of the Ramallah Friends Meeting is providing hospitality in the practical and theological sense. This ministry stems in part from the small size of the meeting and its strong connection to foreign Quakers, although Palestinians also pride themselves on their culture of hospitality. This hospitality is a vital contribution to peace and justice work in the region as the meeting has nurtured and enriched Quakers and like-minded people visiting or working in Israel and the Palestinian Territories, often in connection with stressful humanitarian and peacebuilding efforts. At the same time, the visitors strengthen the meeting through their presence and solidarity. Due to the meeting's connections with FGC and Friends United Meeting (FUM), as well as its membership in the European and Middle Eastern Section of Friends World Committee for Consultation, this hospitality also connects Friends across differences and reflects (unintentionally) the Convergent Friends' emphasis on building relationships through hospitality, participation, public witness, and shared worship rather than narrow doctrinal agreement (Daniels, 2010, pp. 244–245). Unsurprisingly, given that the meeting was created to support the foreign Quakers working at the Ramallah Friends Schools, every respondent recalled that foreign visitors have always been a part of Sunday worship. As one foreign Quaker long connected to the meeting commented:

> What has keep a vibrant community has been the long-term and short-term visitors. Mostly foreign, occasionally a Palestinian. The nature of the meeting [in 2010] is very similar to what it was twenty or thirty years ago. Jean [Zaru, clerk of the meeting] in her person makes a difference, she is a Quaker internationally known and she is large part of the meeting and she remains a large part of the meeting, but for many years there haven't been very many Palestinians besides Jean to keep the meeting going.
> *(Author Interview, 2010e)*

The meeting's connection with FUM, while not of a direct or material nature, is one reason for the regular presence of foreign Quakers. FUM has supported the meeting through its sponsorship of foreign Quaker teachers at the Friends schools, because

> anybody that came to the schools has a commitment to participate in the life of the meeting because it's basic for their activity. I mean, if they do not function out of a faith base and a commitment to these values . . . they will be burnt out.

As one foreign Quaker affirmed, 'the meeting served as a good refuge and support for the Quaker volunteers'. Another, who taught at the schools in the 1970s, shared, 'the meeting and meeting community was really an anchor for me during the years as a teacher and a respite from the craziness of teaching at the schools'. The meeting has supported foreign Quaker teachers over the decades, serving as their 'support system' and 'community for the people who came' (Author Interview, 2010c, 2010e, 2010f, 2010g). One foreign Quaker who joined the meeting in the 1970s while working in Jerusalem said that the meeting provided 'hospitality with all of the theological implications of hospitality', noting that while this might be easy to take for granted, 'as soon as you think about it, you think about how important those relationships were, how much you felt empowered by them, embraced by them' (Author Interview, 2010h). He explained how knowing 'that there were Palestinians open to a just and equitable relationship with Israelis' made his peace and justice work easier (Author Interview, 2010h).

The support function of the meeting extends beyond Quaker teachers at the Ramallah Friends School to include other foreigners, such as the Mennonites or volunteers with Christian Peacemaker Teams in Hebron, who engage in peace and social justice work and come to the meeting for 'respite' and for 'a moment of quiet reflection and trying to hush their spirits' from their difficult work (Author Interview, 2010e). The meeting house has provided this same 'respite' function for local Ramallah Quakers as well. Although the bustling commercial centre of Ramallah has grown up around the meeting house, Friends shared that the meeting house continues to serve as a refuge from the chaos of everyday life.[4] As a local Quaker said, 'We go to the meeting house with all the noise around you, and I don't know how, but you stop listening to the outside world. A lot of people were pushing to move the meeting somewhere else. I think it's great that it is still where it is in the middle of town' (Author Interview, 2010i).

The meeting also served as a place of restoration for Quakers travelling in the region for a variety of reasons, including peace and justice efforts. Such visits also strengthened the worship experience and connected worshippers to other ideas, experiences, and communities. One foreign Quaker recalled a moving message

> from Landrum Bolling, probably in 1971. He had been engaged in secret shuttle diplomacy between Egypt, Israel and Syria, and probably the PLO in exile. He spoke of how the situation was more hopeless than he had seen over his many years of engaging in this activity but that it was important to maintain hope anyway, that you can't give up hope. In fact, that tension led to the 1973 October War, but later those same parties found a way to make peace in the late 1970s and again later talk to each other in the Oslo Accords.
>
> *(Author Interview, 2010c)*

While not all Quaker visitors have engaged in that level of diplomatic peacemaking, over the years the meeting has helped network individuals and groups involved in peace and justice work. As a result of meeting at the Ramallah Friends Meeting, people 'were able to coordinate activities and exchange information, form friendships' (Author Interview, 2010e). Quakers have supported the World Council of Churches' Ecumenical Accompaniment Program in Palestine and Israel and Quakers working for a host of different non-governmental organisations in Ramallah and Jerusalem. In this way, the Ramallah meeting has, in the manner of convergent Friends, supported the public presence of Friends' testimonies in society.

Outreach Projects: Speaking to That of God in Everyone

Collins asserts that 'Quaker identity is sustained primarily through the generation and regeneration of stories, primarily in and around the Meeting House' and that Quakerism tends to be a behavioural creed rather than a theological one (Collins, 2009, pp. 215, 217). Indeed, Ramallah Friends have demonstrated their commitment to peace and justice work, as well as their Quaker identity, through behaviour in the community and through the presence of the meeting house itself. In a very fundamental way, the Ramallah meeting opened its doors to refugees during the Nakba of 1948, with nine families (a total of fifty-eight people) making their home in the small meeting house until the end of 1949. The Quakers ran a refugee school from 1948 to 1952 and eventually opened a series of play centres for the refugee children, both in the Annex of the meeting house and also in the Am'ari refugee camp on the outskirts of Ramallah/El Bireh (Brinson et al., 2010; Zaru, 2008).

In addition to providing physical space and schooling to refugee families, the meeting women organised a sewing cooperative to make clothes for refugee women and children. Ellen Mansour, Azizi Mikhail, Violet Zaru, and Bahia Salah were particularly concerned with social outreach projects, including the sewing circle, a cross-stitch cooperative started by Mansour so refugee and village women could sell their handicraft work, and the Am'ari playcentre, which was the special ministry of Violet Zaru until her death in 2006. The Quaker testimony of equality and the particular concern that Quakers have always had for gender equality in particular may be a contributing factor to the continued presence of these strong women in the Ramallah meeting, even while the early Quaker stance against smoking kept their husbands from attending. The actions and beliefs of two of the strong, independent Quaker missionaries, Mildred White and Annice Carter, seem to have influenced local Quakers as well.

The ecumenical Sunday School run by Mansour, which occurred for an hour each Sunday before meeting, was perhaps the most cited ministry of the meeting. 'Everyone' went to Sunday School, from the current mayor of Ramallah to the Christian and Muslim friends of meeting attendees. There were more than ninety children on the roll in 1950, approximately one-third of them refugee children, and only eleven of these from Quaker homes. Several local Quakers reflected positively on their Sunday School experience, saying, 'I remember a very vibrant team of friends from my school who were non-Quakers who came to Sunday school . . . we still talk about our days at Sunday School today . . . that was a special group' (Author Interview, 2010g). Beyond personal friendships, the Sunday School experience instilled Quaker values in the local community. One local Friend noted that many of his friends reflect positively on how accepting the Quaker meeting was and how supportive of the issues they faced. 'How people treat each other and accept each other regardless of background or colour or religion is still a major impact locally' (Author Interview, 2010i). This Friend continued, saying:

> Sometimes we take these things for granted, but when I sit back and evaluate how I'm dealing with my friends how I'm dealing with others in the community or even with my family and daughters and stop to think about why I am doing these things, I think that is a major impact of the way I was raised as a Quaker within my family, within the community in the Quaker way of beliefs and teaching. And if this affected me, it affected the hundreds who attended over the years.

The impact on individual behaviour and openness to others is difficult to measure or demonstrate beyond anecdotal evidence, although the large number of Ramallah residents attending the re-dedication of the meeting house in March 2005 and the Centennial in March 2010 speaks to the import of the Quaker community. The Sunday School continued up until the First Intifada, when the location of the meeting house rendered it no longer safe. The loss of the meeting house as a central space for meeting resulted in the loss of the Sunday School, and a major sphere of Quaker influence on the community. Many of these graduated were grateful to see a renewed Quaker presence when the building was renovated; despite the Quaker belief that worship can occur in any space, the presence of Quakers openly worshipping in the centre of Ramallah sent a symbolic message to those historically connected to the ministry of the meeting.

Many of the peace and justice efforts of Ramallah Friends have been 'outside the corporate meeting framework' largely 'because the Palestinian Friends are so few in number. [Yet the meeting] projects an attitude of nonviolence and commitment to justice. It's not terribly visible and public, but I think nonetheless these have been important contributions' (Author Interview, 2010h). Another interview subject noted:

> And I think Quakers at their best, with this quiet diplomacy, are sort of like a chemical agent that disappears when it all comes together. So that's in some ways, you know, that's what makes it hard for you to do this particular project about the meeting. Because some of the best Quaker work is not known. And people don't claim ownership. . . . they are quiet, the kind of presence, and the modesty, the genuine humility of Quakers.
>
> *(Author Interview, 2010e)*

Several examples of this type of quiet peacemaking work include a story of foreign Quaker teachers providing space for their high school students to sleep during the Tawjihi exams because of the Israeli practice of rounding up kids right before the exams and holding them for two weeks so that they missed the exams and had to wait until the following year, or the impact of the Quaker workcamps run by AFSC, FUM, Friends Center and other Quaker organizations

over the years that have impacted the lives of Israelis, Palestinians, and the international participants (Author Interview, 2010e).

One of the more visible forms of peace and justice outreach done by a meeting member,
again, outside of the 'corporate meeting framework' but nevertheless connected to the Quaker
presence in Ramallah, is the ministry of Jean Zaru, who has become internationally known as
a representative of Palestinian Quakers. Jean has been active in international women's activism
and in interfaith dialogue efforts over the decades. In addition to her role as clerk of the Ramallah Friends Meeting, Jean has served on the Board of Sabeel Ecumenical Liberation Theology
Center in Jerusalem, was honoured with the Anna Lindh Memorial Prize in 2010 for her commitment to nonviolence and to challenging systems of structural violence and injustice, serves
on the Council of the Charter for Compassion, and is the author of *Occupied With Nonviolence:
A Palestinian Woman Speaks*. As one Friend noted:

> Jean is a public Friend and one of the best known Friends of her generation. She is
> well known in Europe and Australia and the United States. She has been a principle
> spokesperson for Palestinian Friends in Europe and the United States. I think that is
> a very important and the most far-reaching contribution the meeting has made. Yes,
> it's personal, but Jean's faith and involvement grows out of her involvement in the
> meeting.

Jean has travelled around the world giving talks on nonviolence, the role of justice, and the
equality of women, and providing a Palestinian Quaker perspective on the Israeli-Palestinian
conflict; she has helped many understand the Quaker testimonies of peace, justice, and equality in the context of conflict and oppression (Author Interview, 2010c, 2010d, 2010e, 2010h).

Conclusion

Although a very small meeting, the Ramallah Friends Meeting has continued to play a critical
role in supporting those working for peace and justice in the region, expanding the conception
of peace and justice work to one that includes a ministry of presence and a space for nurturing
and connecting visitors engaged in short- or long-term peace and justice activities. Through
its ministry of hospitality for Quakers and fellow travellers working in the region, as well as
through providing meeting space for groups working for a better future, the meeting has secondary and tertiary impacts beyond the individuals who physically walk through its doors.

It has been challenging for the meeting to conduct peace and justice work in the way
Western Quakers conventionally think of peace and social outreach committees that engage
in demonstrations or awareness campaigns or fundraisers in part due to the size of the meeting
(although the meeting engaged in that type of work with refugees in the wake of the Nakba)
and in part because of the location of the meeting a conflict zone. The meeting house has literally been on the front lines over the past century because of its location on the main street of
Ramallah. This has had negative repercussions on the meeting's physical structure and spiritual
life. Because of conflict during the 1967 War and again in the First and Second Intifadas, meeting members often could not worship in the meeting house itself but gathered quietly in rooms
at the Ramallah Friends Schools or in private homes. This lack of a public gathering space
meant that it was more difficult for Friends to attract visitors or new members, and it made
it more difficult to organise activities like the Sunday School. Despite the physical, sociological, psychological, and economic challenges of working within a zone of protracted conflict,
including many restrictions placed on Palestinian freedom and movement by the Israeli military,

and the fact that the core membership of the meeting was women with domestic responsibilities, the meeting engaged in local peace and justice efforts focused on educational activities (the play centre, the refugee school, the Sunday School) and handiwork (sewing circle, cross-stitch cooperative), building on their individual strengths.

At the same time, precisely because of the ongoing conflict, the meeting has served as a focal point for Quakers and fellow travellers who come to the region to engage in peace and justice work. By supporting these individuals and helping connect them with other individuals with similar concerns, the meeting has served a vital peace and justice function through both its spiritual and physical hospitality. Thus, the meeting in many ways is an international one, with weekly attendance comprising primarily foreigners living and working in Ramallah along with visitors passing through. In many ways this demographic parallels those found in the United States, where many visitors enter the doors of Quaker meeting houses, but membership continues to age and numbers decline.[5] Although the future of the local Quaker community remains unclear, the meeting will endure in some manner due to the ongoing commitment of the International Friends of the Ramallah Meeting community and the importance of Ramallah Meeting to so many Quakers around the world, who continue to foster relations with the Ramallah Meeting and local people working for peace and justice.

Notes

1 This piece is drawn from a longer article originally published in *Quaker Studies*, vol. 18.
2 More on Khalil Totah and his relationship with the Friends Mission Board can be found in Ricks (2009). Unfortunately the diary is missing entries from the time period surrounding the departure of Totah from the meeting.
3 Palestinians, particularly women, embraced Quaker principles of equality and peace as well as the manner of worship (Author Interview 2010; Jordan, 1995).
4 Although Ramallah is historically Christian, it is now majority Muslim, and Sunday is a working day for most.
5 At the July 2011 New York Yearly Meeting Summer Sessions, General Secretary Christopher Sammond noted that in the past fifty-six years, the Yearly Meeting lost 50% of its members, and that the lack of outreach programs means visitors do not stay.

References

Manuscript and Interview Sources

Author Interviews (2010, March), [Interview with Quaker connected to Ramallah Friends Meeting], labeled a–k.
Leonard, G. (1989), *Friends in Ramallah (1867–1989)*, Draft Book Manuscript.

Published Sources

Brinson, B., Kanaana, P., Rought-Brooks, H., Campuzano, P., and Bergen, K., 'Stories from the Ramallah Friends Meeting', in *F.I. C. i. R. (FICR)* (Ed.) (Ramallah: FICR [Friends International Center Ramallah], 2010).
Collins, P., 'The Problem of Quaker Identity', *Quaker Studies* 13 (2009), pp. 205–219.
Daniels, C. W., 'Convergent Friends: The Emergence of Postmodern Quakerism', *Quaker Studies* 14 (2010), pp. 236–250.
Edwards-Konic, P., *Enduring Hope: The Impact of the Ramallah Friends Schools* (Richmond, IN: Friends United Press, 2008).

Jones, C. H., *Friends in Palestine* (Richmond, IN: American Friends Board of Missions, 1944).

Jones, C. H., *American Friends in World Missions* (Elgin, IL: Brethren Publishing House, 1946).

Leonard, G. (2010), [Interview by Author].

Nassar, H. K., 'Stories from under Occupation: Performing the Palestinian Experience', *Theatre Journal* 58 (2006), pp. 15–37.

Ricks, T. M., *Turbulent Times in Palestine: The Diaries of Khalil Totah 1886–1955* (Jerusalem and Ramallah: Institute of Palestine Studies and PASSIA, 2009).

Tessler, M., 'The Political Right in Israel: Its Origins, Growth, and Prospects', *Journal of Palestine Studies* 15 (1986), pp. 12–55.

Zaru, J., *Occupied with Nonviolence: A Palestinian Woman Speaks* (Minneapolis, MN: Fortress Press, 2008).

61

'GO ANYWHERE, DO ANYTHING'

The Friends Ambulance Unit, 1914–1959

Rebecca Wynter

Decision making and shifting practices between the 1914 UK establishment of the Friends Ambulance Unit (FAU) and its final laying down in 1959 were often dramatic and rarely uncontroversial, from working with the armed forces to incorporating women members; and from operating in war-affected Britain to warzones in Europe, Africa, Asia, and the Middle East. Organised around two main themes, 'Faith' and 'Action', this chapter will argue that for all its faults, the FAU was successful. The comparative freedom it experienced, which sprang from its First World War status as an unofficial Quaker body, enabled it to react quickly to any need it encountered. The mix of Friends and non-Quaker members, whilst sometimes creating tensions, also created new connections, friendships, and even Friends. Moreover, the FAU was a potent interloper in the theatres of war, flattening divisions and creating a space for working together, for healing people from all sides, and for accommodating conscientious objectors and a spectrum of pacifist-informed consciences in the very midst of violent conflict. These remarkable qualities changed and even saved the lives of members, civilians, and combatants – and yet it is these elements that mean the true impact of the FAU is unquantifiable.

Introduction

The FAU (or the Anglo-Belgian Ambulance Unit, as it was initially called) grew out of discussions at the Meeting for Sufferings,[1] called in London in response to Britain declaring war on Germany on 4 August 1914. The convergence of Quakers three days later saw urgent conversations about what to do, not only amongst official meetings, but also between small huddles. It was from one such group, including Geoffrey Winthrop Young (1876–1958), Philip Baker (after marriage, Philip Noel Baker; 1889–1982) and Arnold S. Rowntree (1872–1951), that the notion of a frontline ambulance unit emerged. Within days, a letter from Baker was published in *The Friend*, soliciting volunteers for an 'Ambulance corps . . . under the auspices' of the British Red Cross (BRC) – a neutral organisation but linked to the military. The corps' activities would possibly 'involve some personal risk' though also 'result in the saving of a great many lives, and in the alleviation of a great deal of suffering among the primary victims of the war' (Baker, 1914). The voluntary body (for members never received wages *per se*, and, indeed, initially even needed to supply their own equipment) was envisaged as an embodiment, not only of Quaker belief, pacifism, and faith in action, but also of the prevailing patriotism and

DOI: 10.4324/9780429030925-65

muscular Christianity that abounded in Imperial Britain. Baker was inundated with volunteers. Even though the FAU was never an official body of The Religious Society of Friends, 1914 saw the birth of an organisation that dominated Quaker responses to conflict and conscription in the twentieth century.

Whilst over the next decades the FAU's character shifted across its various iterations and splinters, the 'middle course' it charted and the space it created, though 'ideologically difficult at times, ensured that the Unit was able to accommodate' a spectrum of pacifist-informed con-sciences and faiths (Wynter, 2016). Until the centenary of the First World War, with a handful of exceptions (Boulton, 2014/1967; Greenwood, 1975; Kennedy, 2001; Robson, 1997), the FAU had been largely overlooked by historical and corporate attention alike. That is now beginning to change (Aksamit, 2019; Armstrong-Reid, 2015; Armstrong-Reid, 2018; Baumann, 2020; Butterfield, 2017; Meyer, 2015; Palfreeman, 2017a, 2018; Reid, 2017, 2019; Wynter, 2016). This short chapter is the first scholarly attempt to provide an integrated overview of the Unit across its whole active history: the Friends' and later Friends Ambulance Unit of 1914–1919 and 1939–1946, and the FAU Post-War Service (FAUPWS) and FAU International Service (FAUIS) of 1946–1959, when National Service in Britain ceased. Finding the balance in this chapter between these phases is difficult, with each iteration recommended in importance by different qualities. The first was all-male body, which shaped the organisation throughout its existence through its maxim: 'find work that wants doing; take it; regularise it later if you can'. The Unit trained over 1800 men and boys (members of the Scouts), and worked closely with 103 women, the overwhelming majority of whom were nurses (Palfreeman, 2018: 8). The second iteration saw 1314 men and women members (the latter representing around 8% of the total member-ship) serving on four continents under the more vigorous motto (Tegla Davies, 1947: 481), 'Go anywhere, do anything'. The third and fourth phases involved a fraction of the earlier mem-bership numbers – 52 FAU members transferred, and 354 new people joined the FAUPWS or FAUIS (Bush, 1998: 131–136) – and were exclusively male. FAUIS existed for the longest continuous period of time (13 years) and has garnered the least academic interest. An overview of the ebb and flow of the FAU as a twentieth-century organisation, turning first to the contro-versy around the Unit, and then to its activities, broadens and deepens historical discussions of modern Quaker responses to war and conscience. This consideration will also reveal alterations in the long-term manifestation of peacemaking and peacebuilding, international brotherhood, and faith in action on a global stage.

Faith

Despite its bedrock of pacifism, the FAU was controversial throughout its active existence. From the very outset, what was a pacifist-rooted organisation caused disagreement within and with-out Quaker circles. Whilst this has been the crux of much of the recent scholarly work on the first iteration of the Unit (Meyer, 2015; Palfreeman, 2018; Reid, 2019; Wynter, 2016), diversity of conscience was a very real issue for the ability to work together and amongst people most at need throughout the twentieth century. Emotions were most heightened during two key points of the First World War and, though dissatisfaction continued, much of the heat was taken out of later disagreements because the issues had already been faced.

The guidance of individual conscience, the impact of the Quaker Renaissance and the recentring of peace, especially amongst Young Friends (see elsewhere in this volume), meant that when war came, the Society struggled to generate a unified response. The very establish-ment of an ambulance unit and its operating so closely with the BRC and under the aegis of the Joint War Committee of the BRC and St John drew the most ire, as letters in *The Friend* clearly demonstrate. A 'Quaker Ambulance Corps [going] to the seat of war and [forming] an essential and necessary part of the fighting force' was 'scarcely consistent with the views and principles of Friends', wrote one correspondent (*The Friend*, 28 August 1914). 'The primary aim of the Army Medical Corps and Field Hospitals, of which the Red Cross work forms a part', argued another, was 'to "patch up" the [military] unit and get it back into the firing line. Was this to be the contribution of the "eager and ardent" young Friend?' (*The Friend*, 25 September 1914). An attempt to establish a clear corporate line was made in September 1914, when Meeting for Sufferings pronounced: 'We see danger to principle in undertaking any service auxiliary to warfare which involves becoming part of the military machine' (Graham, 1922: 156). Whilst John W. Graham, weighty Friend and author of the 1922 official history of the radical No-Conscription Fellowship, argued that 'in time this cautious official attitude . . . was abandoned' (Graham, 1922: 157), that was certainly not so.

The introduction of conscription, under the Military Service Act 1916, caused dramatic ructions around the FAU. Two of the six MPs on the Unit's London steering committee, Arnold S. Rowntree and T. Edmund Harvey, were especially prominent in ensuring that the Act included a 'conscience clause' so that conscientious objectors (COs) could claim exemption from military service (Wynter, 2016). But they had also established the General Service Section (GSS) to work in Britain for those who did not feel able to conduct ambulance work, and manoeuvred, with government representatives, for the FAU to be recognised as '"indispensable" [and therefore exempted] the whole unit from the recruiting scheme' (TEMP MSS 881/C, 'Meeting of the Committee, 9 December 1915'). This centralised seizure of individual conscience was rejected by some, such as birthright Quaker T. Corder Catchpool, who left to face the consequences back home, but not before their protests threatened to destabilise the work of the whole Unit; after all, a significant amount of the FAU's existing and hoped-for activities involved the ambulance trains operating under the British military. Yet what conscription also meant was the arrival of more radical pacifists, 'with a C.O. Tribunal flavour about them, into rather aristocratic convoys of men of a different class' (MS327/A/1/40, 1917; for a more thorough treatment of this episode, see Wynter, 2016).

Whilst the diversity of conscience and class were areas of tension, there is little evidence that different faiths themselves caused widespread and significant issues for the inner harmony of the FAU. Never was the Unit an exclusively Quaker body, but rather embraced anyone who shared its values. So here, for instance, were Methodists, Anglicans, Congregationalists, those with no recorded religion whatsoever;[2] with the inclusion of overseas members, especially during 1939–1946, 'non-Western' faiths were represented too (Tegla Davies, 1947: 467–481). Whilst Quakers were often the largest single group associated with the Unit, they did not always make up the majority. Indeed, from its inception the Anglo-Italian Ambulance Unit, the splinter organisation of the First World War FAU, headed by Noel Baker, Young, and historian G. M. Trevelyan, held only 16 Friends out of 66 volunteers (Tatham and Miles, 1920: 197). As time wore on through each of the FAU's iterations, the diversity was clear: in 1943, for instance, only 40% of members were Quakers (*Central Somerset Gazette*, 1943: 4). Yet early in the formation of its distinct periods, most new joiners were Friends. For example, the first overseas deployment of the 1939–46 Unit, to the frontline in the Finland-Russia War, was 90% Quaker (*Midland Daily Telegraph*, 1940: 1).

As Europe had again tilted towards war, in May 1939, the Military Training Act was introduced, under which men aged between 20 and 22 had to undertake six months of service. As soon as Britain declared war in September, Parliament passed the National Service (Armed Forces) Act for men between 18 and 41; in December another, for unmarried women and child-free widows aged 20–30, and men under 51, became law. This meant not only that the FAU had begun to re-form in April 1939, but also that women were officially welcomed into the Unit for the first time – although this too became a tussle as to whether women should be allowed to serve overseas, and even then whether it was temperament or talent that should permit their dispatch (see Armstrong-Reid, 2018: especially 89–91). According to Rachel Cadbury, whose husband, Paul, reanimated the FAU, it was she who pressed for greater inclusion in the FAU as a whole:

> I said 'It's alright for Quakers, they can get by, but it's the pacifists who *aren't* Quakers I'm concerned about. . . . So I told Paul that's what the FAU's for; that's one of its missions.' Paul agreed. . . . [A]lthough I wouldn't say that the work of the FAU in the Great War was well known, it was sufficiently known for the authorities in the second war to realise what young COs *could* do. You could say the way was paved for them by the COs of the Great War.
>
> *(Smith, 1998: 3–4)*

As was the case in 1914/19, animosity existed outside and inside the Society of Friends:

> We had links with Yearly Meeting and were allowed to report to it about what we were up to but an arms-length relationship. . . . A lot of Friends felt hurt that this group of young Bolshie conchies were going to join the war. They gave support to those who went on the land or into prison – that was the Quaker stance. Ours wasn't.
>
> *(Smith, 1998: 8–9)*

Beyond Friends, the press in particular aided the stir against COs as the May and September conscription legislation was enacted. This ranged from a media sting, entrapping B. Cecil Davies and loudly denouncing him on its front page as 'Conchie No. 1' (*Daily Express*, 1939: 1), to the reporting of Judge Longson conjuring shadowy figures preying on youth and coaching them with 'the contemptible trickery of a mock tribunal' to avoid the military (*Birmingham Mail*, 1939: 7). Though immediately after, Longson recognised FAU service and granted seven men conditional exemption on this basis, ill feeling towards the Unit for its stance was real. Whilst their five years' work with the British Army especially was often fraught, though punctuated by significant success, their presence at Gloucester Hospital was a source of major dissatisfaction locally (Tegla Davies, 1947: 332–333). Nevertheless, FAU member A. Tegla Davies wrote, in the official history of the Second World War Unit, 'I like to think that we are better pacifists now than we were in 1939 or even in 1943, even if only that we have a greater respect for the soldier' (Tegla Davies, 1947: 176).

Indeed, the impact of witnessing the service of the FAU overseas and in forward areas led Tory MP, Lieutenant-Colonel Basil Nield, to argue passionately in Parliament against the framing of the 1945 National Service Bill for releasing conscientious objectors: it 'failed to acknowledge' the position of the FAU.

> They have served with quiet, self-effacing efficiency and with high courage. I do not think that any fighting soldier would hesitate to pay a tribute to these men who, prevented from bearing arms, have nonetheless willingly suffered the full dangers and rigours of war while pursuing their humane calling.
>
> *(Chester Chronicle, 1945: 6)*

With the end of hostilities and diminishing emergency need, the Unit turned more consciously than before to what it might now become, for it was certainly needed by COs at a time of National Service, especially those leaving school at 18. The FAUPWS and later the FAUIS were considerably smaller than their wartime precursors. Less publicly visible, with the latter especially having no links to the Military or British warzones, controversy largely abated, in Quaker circles too, as the Unit was devoted entirely to civilian aid. From 1950, the Unit was emphatically:

> trying to do a kind of social first aid and we think that practical experience should be the basis of our religious and idealistic approach to the problems of internationalism. We want young people to learn, not just intellectually, what is involved in the building of world peace. We want to give to the potential young peacebuilders an experience just as effective for their purposes as military training is for the fighting man.
>
> *(Bush, 1998: 28–29)*

In fact, the wider world was more accustomed to conscientious objection, and the exploits of the previous two wars ensured that the FAU name curried favour, enabling the overseas service FAUIS so desperately wanted.

Even so, low level and localised ill-feeling lasted for as long as did National Service for 18–30-year-old men; something which generally took eighteen months of their lives (two years during the 1950–1953 Korean War). Against the backdrop of Korea, a change of direction to a body engaged in more fervent peace-making and peacebuilding garnered complex responses. FAUIS headquarters naturally became the locus for conscientious objectors. In 1950, for example, *Portsmouth Evening News* reported that two men, prominently identified as FAUIS members from its location at Petersfield, Hampshire, rejected National Service, somewhat to the consternation of the presiding magistrates. 'We have to enforce the Act', it was said; 'I hope you will see the error of your ways' (*Portsmouth Evening News*, 1950: 16). In 1952, when the headquarters was at Melksham, Wiltshire, a 23-year-old literally 'Got What He Asked For. Six Months Sentence for Conscientious Objector' (*Wiltshire Times*, 1952: 8).

Action

The emphasis and seduction of the FAU field aid and civilian relief fluctuated throughout the twentieth century – and, indeed, created another strain within the Unit. Of the early Second World-War relief work, Tegla Davies argued that it 'had introduced a new tradition, not superseding the old', of activities associated with medicine and hospitals, 'but growing in parallel with it.' Hospital workers

> tended to be more at home in organised and routine work . . . The relief worker was more of an individualist, more restless, perhaps more versatile, anxious to make his own job, to manage people and to achieve results by agitation . . . Between them the two strands produced a curious brand of persons whom we liked to describe as "the unit type" – men and women who reckoned that with a mixture of knowledge and adaptability they could rise to most jobs, and very often did.
>
> *(Tegla Davies, 1947: 66–67)*

However, this duality was not entirely accurate. There was a third strand, one removed from both medical and aid work and engaged in Britain, tending the land, undertaking forestry and other manual labour, and occasionally youth work. The spirit of the General Service Section ran through 1939–45 and became the central focus of the FAUIS.

The FAU of the 1914/18 conflict therefore already had deep roots in all three strands and their administration, which contributed to the splintering of the group in 1916. Corder Catchpool's conscientious decision to leave was also due to Unit work settling into a boring routine, 'mending motor cars instead of men' (Catchpool, 1971/1918: 88–90). Laurence Cadbury, a more c/Conservative birthright Quaker, also struggled. Disillusioned by administration and the saving of 'ancient undeserving and ungrateful old [civilians]' ahead of injured soldiers (MS327/A/1/14, 1915: 20), he considered leaving to join the Army at various points (MS327/B/2, 1915; MS327/B/3/16, 1918). But whereas Corder felt bound to imprisoned COs, Laurence's duty was to the Unit. It was this loyalty – founded on pacifist-informed consciences, inculcated by living and learning together at training camps (at Jordans in Buckinghamshire, and Manor Farm in Birmingham) between 1914 and 1959, and the sense of actively doing good in co-dependent small deployments – which ensured overall cohesion. This continued sporadically to be tested, perhaps most acrimoniously in the 1941–1946 China Convoy due to the sometimes absent, often chaotic, leadership of American non-Quaker Bill McClure. Yet for all that, there was 'no section which attained so much character and coherence, so much sympathy and integration with the life of the country in which it served' (Tegla Davies, 1947: 235. For a detailed exploration, see Armstrong-Reid, 2018).

International fellowship was for the FAU a multi-layered activity, amongst and between its membership, with other relief agencies in the field, and amidst the people in the nations where it served. First and foremost, throughout the twentieth century, the organisation aided anyone in need, irrespective of soldier or civilian, 'ally' or 'enemy'; it created the space in the midst of war where this could happen.

The Unit of the First World War included members who resided in America, Canada, Australia and New Zealand.[3] Whilst much of the hospital work, as well as the GSS, operated in England, overseas the body worked with people from Belgium, France and beyond. These included Father Delaere and the Sisters of Lamotte in Ypres during the typhoid epidemic and decimation 1914/15 (Palfreeman, 2017b; see also Tatham and Miles, 1920). Not only did the Unit, under non-Quaker Geoffrey Winthrop Young, here help save religious artefacts and the town's archives from the utter destruction, it also evacuated bombed-out civilians, and their public health work all-but eradicated typhoid for everyone in the warzone (Winthrop Young, 1953). Birthright Quaker Henry Basil Darby's report from FAU's perspective to the American Red Cross informed their humanitarian response (Private Papers). With Countesses Louise D'Ursel (Lady in Waiting to the Belgian Queen) and van den Steen de Jehay (director of a nursing school in Brussels), the FAU formed the Aide Civile Belges (ACB). The ACB dealt with civilians, working with local people to help organise orphanages, schools and paid work (Tatham and Miles, 1920: Chapter II). This activity was partly enabled by the trust placed in the FAU by the British military, with whom it ran ambulance trains and ships, evacuating troops to hospitals. Yet the corps was more deeply embedded with the French Army, with the Sections Sanitaire Anglaise forming ambulance columns moving with the troops.

During the Second World War, official membership included 50 Americans, 24 Canadians, 10 New Zealanders, 4 Irish, 2 Chinese, and one each from South Africa, India, and Czechoslovakia (Tegla Davies, 1947: 461–481). Yet these numbers are profoundly misleading. In Ethiopia, Syria, India, Burma (Myanmar), the Netherlands, Belgium, France, Yugoslavia, Austria, Germany, Italy and Greece, the FAU worked with and trained local people. In China it is abundantly clear that the aid work was entirely dependent on Chinese men and women, in nursing and communicating with both the Imperial and Communist Chinese Armies and with civilians (Armstrong-Reid, 2018: *passim*). By the beginning of 1946, the Convoy numbered 139 members – 18 Americans, 26 Chinese, 71 British, 18 Canadians, and 6 New Zealanders (Tegla Davies, 1947: 289). This was not always harmonious, and many FAU members had a British colonial mindset, with local workers in Syria and Ethiopia particularly judged through the lens of race rather than poverty (Tegla Davies, 1947: 177). Racial prejudice existed amongst locals too: Ronald Joynes recalled 'I saw one of the best left hooks ever delivered by one of our number', a white Bristol Quaker, 'to an Egyptian orderly who had roughly picked up a wounded Libyan by his broken arm' (Smith, 1998: 108). Indeed, aid work and emergency relief were laced with tension and moral danger. ' "With no distinction of class, colour or creed" may be easier to state than to achieve; but only by its achievement can material relief become a possible instrument of reconciliation. When relief becomes a tool of politics and it can be the most potent of political weapons its virtue is gone' (Tegla Davies, 1947: 296).

Yet push on the FAU did. In the UK, from 1939, it operated in 83 hospitals and provided integral relief and rest centres to Blitzed cities such as London and Birmingham (Tegla Davies, 1947: 327), with one of the most valuable activities aiding in the formation of the Citizens Advice Bureau. From the 1940 work with Finnish civilians and soldiers and throughout the conflict, the Unit found itself constantly in precarious situations. In the confusion encountered in Finland, the group was split up, with some fleeing to Norway and Sweden, some making it back to Britain, and others having to subsist until a route out to Egypt was secured. It was there that the organisation first worked closely with the British Army, looking after troops in the drive to vanquish Italian forces. Much of the work in North Africa, including the vital contribution of the Blood Transfusion Units, aided soldiers wounded in the Western Desert, and from there work diversified, with groups moving into Syria and Ethiopia. The capture of over 20 FAU members by Nazi forces in Greece in 1941 and 1943, and the French/German border regions in 1944, resulted in these aid workers being detained as prisoners of war, despite the directives of the Geneva Convention (Smith, 1998: 347–356). Indeed, in working with the French Army, it was reported that some members of the Unit were the first Englishmen in liberated Paris (*Central Somerset Gazette*, 1944: 4; Tegla Davies, 1947: 156). Aside from the military medical work, the organisation also mobilised for disasters, wrapped inside public-health emergencies, wrapped inside war. Whereas in much of the civilian work, 'only' the latter two needed attention, in India the FAU responded to the 1942 cyclone and subsequent Bengal Famine (for more, see Baumann, 2020). Nevertheless, here and elsewhere, the corps worked with a welter of other local, nation, and inter- and transnational aid organisations, including the Indian Red Cross, Entr'Aide Française, the Council of British Societies for Relief Abroad (of which it was a founder member), and the United Nations Relief and Rehabilitation Administration.

Later iterations of the FAU also actively responded to emergencies. In 1953 alone, FAUIS men were deployed to the flood disaster areas of East Anglia and the Netherlands and to earthquake-hit areas of Greece, where Noel Baker smoothed the way to work with the Greek Red Cross. From 1956, the Hungarian Uprising saw the Unit working with Vienna's Quakerhaus and The British Council for Aid to Refugees to assist those fleeing the violence (Bush, 1998). Whilst the FAUPWS had also included different nationalities, FAUIS actively sought out people from overseas to join as associate members. The ideal of founding an internationalist educational facility rested on different nationalities coming together in common and peaceful purpose. German men were especially solicited; a 'small' and 'selected' group of '6–10 at first' (Bush, 1998: 27). At first, FAUPWS activities were a continuation of the conflict work, with the transferral of FAU projects, in Finnmark, Norway, and Haute-Loire, France. 'The first purely PWS overseas work' was at a French orphanage near Caen (Bush, 1998: 15). Gradually, FAUIS individuals and groups were in France, East and West Germany, Switzerland, India, and

'Go Anywhere, Do Anything'

elsewhere. Many of the placements, both in the UK and overseas, were as manual and maintenance labourers for sites dedicated to assisting displaced persons and refugees. At one point, in 1956, a FAUIS party found themselves close to a new warzone in Algeria, building a school with the International Voluntary Service and the Service Civil International.

Concluding Thoughts

Between 1914 and 1959, the three iterations of the FAU trained over 3500 men and women, Quakers and non-Quakers. The impact that the Unit had on their lives was often of great significance, shaping faith and practice, finding f/Friends, partners, and creating and shaping children and later generations. Indeed, for some, such as Noel Baker, Arnold Rowntree, and Paul Cadbury, associated in one way or another with every active stage of the FAU in the twentieth century, it was a constant. But the impact that it had had on the wider world is more difficult to quantify. Certainly, in recognition of Quaker peace and aid activities in the twentieth century, which included the FAU, the Friends Service Council and American Friends received the Nobel Peace Prize in 1947.

Such official markers, including the laying down of FAUIS in 1959, did not end the impact of the FAU. Its legacies continued throughout the twentieth century and into the twenty-first century. The funds of the Unit – donated by Quakers and non-Quakers, in numerous nations, via bring-and-buys and BBC appeals – have meant that the kindness which met wartime needs, has continued as a flowing currency across the globe. The money ensured the existence of The Penn Club, established as a London meeting place for former members of the First World War Unit, became a guesthouse with Quaker qualities, which unfortunately in its centenary year in 2020 had to contend with a new public health emergency; whilst it was then closed permanently, a small, dedicated space has been carved out at The Royal Foundation of St. Katherine, London. Thousands of pounds were also given over to the Friends' War Victims' Relief Committee and towards aid work in Austria and Germany (TEMP MSS 881/EC/M3, 'Meeting held on Thursday November 14th 1920'). This assistance would go on to help Quakers to have a presence in Germany in the 1930s, providing relief for people persecuted by the Nazis (von Borries, 2000). The cascade continued, working to liberate and help concentration camp victims and survivors from Sandbostel (see Barnard, 1999), de-programming Nazi children, and working with refugees over the decades. At the end of the first Gulf War in 1994, the FAUIS 'Committee decided to give nearly all its accumulated assets (£45,000) to the Quaker Peace Service . . . for use in relief and rehabilitation work in the former warzone' (Bush, 1998: 128).

Of course, we have the numbers, stories from Scotland to China, from 'David the Cave Baby', born to a China Convoy couple (*Daily Mirror*, 1948: 5), to the FAU and Flanders and Swann's Donald Swann leaving Tyneside its very own Blitz-nostalgia song (*Newcastle Journal*, 1962: 10). Yet the influence of fleeting and deep relationships forged in extremis, or a brush with kindness – personal or material – for countless people the world over can only be imagined.

Acknowledgements

This chapter is dedicated to Dudley Barlow (1927–2020), a Quaker member of the FAU between 1945 and 1948. He, like others who served with the FAU in the twentieth century, found that it changed his outlook and life, refining his faith and giving him a deep affinity with the nations in which he provided support.

Thank you to the archival assistance of the staff at The Library of the Society of Friends in London, especially Tabitha Driver, as well as the editors of this volume, Dr Siân Roberts, and Dr Rosemary Cresswell, who was kind enough to read an earlier draft. This chapter was written in 2020–2021, during the COVID-19 pandemic, so thanks should also go to the British Newspaper Archive for having digitised so much material that is accessible from home.

Notes

1 Meeting for Sufferings was originally a body, established in the seventeenth century, which recorded the persecution of Quakers. It evolved to provide an executive function at other points in the year outside of London (now Britain) Yearly Meeting, which itself discusses key points of and for the membership, as well as providing corporate discipline and guidance.
2 See the website which holds the record cards of the 1914–19 Unit, digitised by The Library of the Religious Society of Friends: https://fau.quaker.org.uk/ (last accessed 7 July 2022).
3 It is yet to be discovered precisely how many of those nationalities were members during the war, but afterwards, in 1919, the List of Members included eight in Australia; seven in the United States; three each in Canada, in New Zealand, and South Africa; and one each in the Netherlands, Rhodesia, Syria, Ceylon, Brazil, India, Malta, and France. *Friends Ambulance Unit. List of Names and Addresses* (London: FAU, 1919). There are issues here with indeterminate nationalities, and other nationalities living in Britain and Ireland, but research has demonstrated that various countries were represented amongst the membership. For instance, out of a core group of around 50 working on Ambulance Train 16, there was at least four Americans and one Australian (Papers of Alexander Pope-Russell, uncatalogued, Woodbrooke Library, Birmingham).

References

Documents

Laurence Cadbury Papers, Cadbury Research Library, University of Birmingham (UK).
  MS327/A/1/14, 'Letter from Laurence Cadbury to his parents Letter dated 25 May 1915, Parc St. Joris'.
  MS327/A/1/40, 'Letter, 25 January 1917'.
  MS327/B/2, 'Letters and papers relating to a proposed application by Laurence Cadbury for a temporary commission in the Royal Field Artillery' (dated March/April 1915).
  MS327/B/3/16, 'Letter from George Newman, 25 March 1918'.
Library of the Religious Society of Friends, London (UK).
  TEMP MSS 881/C, Friends Ambulance Unit Committee Minutes (October 1914 – July 1920).
  TEMP MSS 881/EC/M3, Friends Ambulance Unit Executive Committee Minute Book, Volume 3 (July 1918 – May 1921).
Private papers of Basil Darby, consulted by kind permission of Michael Darby.
  'Letter from John Van Schaick, Jr. (Acting Director, Department for Belgium, American Red Cross), no date'.
  'Letter from Paul Kellogg, *The Survey*, 21 June 1918'.
  'Report to Mr E. P. Bicknell (American Red Cross), 14 November 1917'.
Papers of Alexander Pope-Russell, uncatalogued, Woodbrooke Library, Birmingham (UK).

Press

Philip J. Baker, 'To the Editor of The Friend: A Suggested Ambulance Corps', *The Friend*, 21 August 1914, p. 626.
'Conchie' No. 1', *Daily Express*, 3 May 1939, p. 1.
Herbert Corder, 'Letter to the Editor', *The Friend*, 25 September 1914, p. 713.
'David the Cave Baby Comes Home from the Wars', *Daily Mirror*, Monday 6 December 1948, p. 5.
'Friends' Ambulance Unit', *The Midland Daily Telegraph*, Thursday 15 February 1940, p. 1.
'Friends' Ambulance Unit. Work in Many Lands Under War Conditions', *Central Somerset Gazette*, Friday 27 August 1944, p. 4.

'He Got What He Asked For. Six Months Sentence for Conscientious Objector', *Wiltshire Times*, Saturday 26 July 1952, p. 8.

Henry T. Mennell, 'The Suggested Ambulance Corps. Letter to the Editor', *The Friend*, 28 August 1914, p. 640.

'Release of C.O.s. Lt.-Col. Nield's Tribute to Friends Ambulance Unit', *Chester Chronicle*, Saturday 17 November 1945, p. 6.

'Self-Styled C.O.s Before Court Twice', *Portsmouth Evening News*, Wednesday 15 March 1950, p. 16.

'Tyneside Swann Song', *Newcastle Journal*, Friday 26 October 1962, p. 10.

'War Objectors. Strong Comment by Tribunal Judge', *Birmingham Mail*, Monday 18 December 1939, p. 7.

Other Published Sources

T. Corder Catchpool, *On Two Fronts*. Edited by his sister with a foreword by J. Rendel Harris (London: Friends Book Centre, 1971; 1918).

Friends' Ambulance Unit. List of Names and Addresses (London: FAU, 1919).

John W. Graham, *Conscription and Conscience: A History 1916–1919* (London: G. Allen Unwin, 1922).

M. Tatham and J. E. Miles (eds.), *The Friends' Ambulance Unit 1914–1919: A Record* (London: Swarthmore Press, 1920).

A. Tegla Davies, *Friends Ambulance Unit: The Story of the FAU in the Second World War 1939–1946* (London: George Allen and Unwin Limited, 1947).

Geoffrey Winthrop Young, *The Grace of Forgetting* (London: Country Life Ltd., 1953).

Secondary Sources

Nerissa K. Aksamit, 'Training Friends and Overseas Relief: The Friends Ambulance Unit and the Friends Relief Service, 1939 to 1948' (West Virginia University: Unpublished PhD Thesis, 2019)

Susan Armstrong-Reid, 'Two China Gadabouts: Guerrilla Nursing with the Friends' Ambulance Unit, 1946–8', in Helen Sweet and Sue Hawkins (eds), *Colonial Caring: A History of Colonial and Post-Colonial Nursing* (Manchester: University of Manchester Press, 2015), pp. 208–231.

Susan Armstrong-Reid, *China Gadabouts: New Frontiers of Humanitarian Nursing, 1941–1951* (Vancouver and Toronto: UBC Press, 2018).

Clifford Barnard, *Two Weeks in May 1945: Sandbostel Concentration Camp and the Friends Ambulance Unit* (London: Quaker Home Service, 1999).

Steven Patrick Baumann, 'Quaker Relief and Rehabilitation: The Bengal Famine, 1942–45', *Quaker Studies*, 25 (1), 2020, pp. 95–112.

Achim von Borries, *Quiet Helpers: Quaker Service in Postwar Germany* (London and Philadelphia: Quaker Home Service and American Friends Service Committee, 2000).

David Boulton, *Objection Overruled: Conscription and Conscience in the First World War* (Dent, Cumbria: Dales Historical Monographs, 2014 revised; original 1967).

Roger Bush, *FAU: The Third Generation. Friends Ambulance Unit Post-War Service and International Service 1946–1959* (York: William Sessions Ltd., 1998).

Mark Butterfield, 'Traumascapes of the First World War: Ambulance Trains, Public Perceptions and the Experiences of Staff and Casualties Aboard Them' (Leeds Beckett University: Unpublished MA Thesis, 2017).

John Ormerod Greenwood, *Quaker Encounters: Volume 1 Friends and Relief* (York: William Sessions, 1975).

Thomas C. Kennedy, *British Quakerism, 1860–1920: The Transformation of a Religious Community* (Oxford: Oxford University Press, 2001).

Jessica Meyer, 'Neutral Caregivers or Military Support? The British Red Cross, the Friends' Ambulance Unit, and the Problems of Voluntary Medical Aid in Wartime', *War & Society*, 34 (2), 2015, pp. 105–120.

Linda Palfreeman, *Friends in Flanders: Humanitarian Aid Administered by the Friends' Ambulance Unit during the First World War* (Eastbourne: Sussex Academic Press, 2017a).

Linda Palfreeman (ed.), *Diary of a Ypres Nun, October 1914 – May 1915. The Diary of Soeur Marguerite of the Sisters of Lamotte Suffering and Sacrifice in the First World War* (Brighton: Sussex Academic Press, 2017b).

Linda Palfreeman, 'The Friends' Ambulance Unit in the First World War', *Religions*, 9 (5), 2018, 165, p. 14.

Fiona Reid, *Medicine in First World War Europe: Soldiers, Medics, Pacifists* (London: Bloomsbury, 2017).

Fiona Reid, 'The Friends' Ambulance Unit', *Medicine, Conflict and Survival*, 35 (2), 2019, pp. 140–143.

Richard H. Robson, 'Work in Progress. Quakers in the Carnage of the First World War: An Individual Story from the Friends' Ambulance Unit', *Quaker Studies*, 2 (1), 1997, pp. 69–67.

Lyn Smith, *Pacifists in Action. The Experience of the Friends Ambulance Unit in the Second World War* (York: William Sessions Ltd., 1998).

Rebecca Wynter, 'Conscription, Conscience and Controversy: The Friends' Ambulance Unit and the 'Middle Course' in the First World War', *Quaker Studies*, 21 (2), 2016, pp. 213–233.

INDEX

Note: Page numbers in *italic* indicate a figure and page numbers in **bold** indicate a table on the corresponding page.

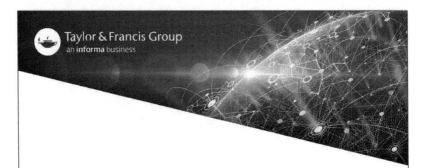